BTEC NATIONAL

Book 1

Children's Care, Learning + Development

Sandy Green

Published in 2007 by:
Nelson Thornes Ltd
Delta Place
27 Bath Road
CHELTENHAM
GL53 7TH
United Kingdom

07 08 09 10 11 / 10 9 8 7 6 5 4 3 2 1

A catalogue record for this book is available from the British Library

ISBN 978 0 7487 8197 3

Cover photo by image100/Corbis

Illustrations include artwork drawn by Jane Bottomley, Angela Lumley, and Pantek Arts Ltd

Page make-up by Pantek Arts Ltd, Maidstone, Kent

Printed and bound in Slovenia by Delo tiskarna by arrangement with Korotan - Ljubljana

Contents

Introduction

Early years practitioners work with children in a variety of care and education settings: schools, nurseries, preschools, crèches, hospitals, after-school clubs and playschemes, and in the home as childminders and nannies. Now is an exciting time to be an early years practitioner because there is more interest than ever before in supporting children in the earliest years. As more parents are working full-time and inclusion is the accepted preference for many children with an additional need, there are more opportunities. It is an interesting and challenging career, and career progression is improving with qualifications at levels 3, 4 and 5, including Foundation-level degrees. If you enjoy being with young children and are enthusiastic about training and development, then this course will provide you with opportunities to learn about the key areas and will support you in gaining practical experience within a range of settings. You may also be able to use your qualification to help you enter university or further your vocational studies.

How do you use this book?

Covering nine units of the new 2007 specification, this book has everything you need if you are studying BTEC National Certificate or Diploma in Children's Care, Learning and Development. Simple to use and understand, it is designed to provide you with the knowledge and understanding you need to gain your qualification. We guide you step by step towards your qualification, through a range of features that are fully explained over the page.

Which units do you need to complete?

There are 38 units available for BTEC National Children's Care, Learning and Development. For the BTEC National Diploma in Children's Care, Learning and Development you are required to complete 7 core units **plus** specialist units that provide for a combined total of 1080 guided learning hours (GLH). *BTEC National CCLD Book 1* provides you with the following:

Core Units	GLH	Specialist Units	GLH
Unit 1 Positive Relationships for Children's Care, Learning and Development	60	Unit 8 Research Methodology for Children's Care, Learning and Development	90
Unit 2 Positive Environments for Children's Care, Learning and Development	60	Unit 9 Promoting Healthy Development and Living for Children and their Families	30
Unit 3 Promoting Children's Development	120		
Unit 4 Reflecting on and Developing Practice for Children aged 0–8 years	120		
Unit 5 Protecting Children	60		
Unit 6 Promoting Children's Rights	60		
Unit 7 Children's Learning Activities and Play	90		

Is there anything else you need to do?

1 Talk to other childcarers about their work and listen to their guidance and advice on practice, qualifications and personal development.

2 Take time to observe others working with children, noting how they approach and respond to them. These observations will help you understand how to respond yourself.

3 Take whatever opportunities you can to gain experience working in different settings with children of different ages. This will broaden your understanding and practical skills and help you to identify where to start your career once qualified.

4 Keep yourself up to date with current thinking and ideas by reading the many magazines and journals especially for the early years.

5 Never be afraid to ask for help or advice when you need it.

We hope you enjoy your BTEC course – Good Luck!

Features of this book

Positive Relationships for Children's Care, Learning and Development

This unit covers the following objectives:

- Be able to develop relationships with children
- Be able to communicate with children
- Be able to support children in developing relationships
- Be able to communicate with adults

Being able to communicate and get on with others is extremely important in most people's personal and professional lives. Communication and interpersonal interactions, both verbal and non-verbal, are the means of giving and receiving information, and letting others know how you are feeling.

This unit will introduce you to different types of communication and look at the different factors that affect communication. You will learn how to develop and maintain good relationships with people, how to overcome the barriers that make communication difficult and how to communicate with and support someone who is distressed.

You will also reflect on your own interpersonal and communication skills and identify areas for improvement.

Learning Objectives

At the beginning of each Unit there will be a bulleted list letting you know what material is going to be covered. They specifically relate to the learning objectives within the specification.

grading criteria

To achieve a **Pass** grade the evidence must show that the learner is able to:	To achieve a **Merit** grade the evidence must show that the learner is able to:	To achieve a **Distinction** grade the evidence must show that the learner is able to:
P1 use examples from placement to describe how relationships can be developed with children	**M1** explain why communication skills are important in developing relationships with children in placement settings	**D1** evaluate own communication skills in terms of developing relationships with children in placement settings
P2 use examples from placement to describe how to communicate with children	**M2** use examples from placement to explain how children can be supported in developing relationships	**D2** evaluate own communication skills in terms of developing relationships with adults in placement settings
P3 use examples from placement to describe how children can be supported in developing relationships	**M3** explain the importance of effective communication with adults in the children's care, learning and development sector	
P4 use examples from placement to describe how to communicate with children		

Grading Criteria

The table of Grading Criteria at the beginning of each unit identifies achievement levels of pass, merit and distinction, as stated in the specification.

To achieve a **pass**, you must be able to match each of the 'P' criteria in turn.

To achieve **merit** or **distinction**, you must increase the level of evidence that you use in your work, using the 'M' and 'D' columns as reference. For example, to achieve a distinction you must fulfil all the criteria in the pass, merit and distinction columns. Each of the criteria provides a specific page number for easy reference.

Positive Relationships for CCLD **UNIT 1**

activity
INDIVIDUAL WORK

Think of an incident at your placement where children were learning by example.

1 Was this important, do you think?
2 Was it in response to a positive or negative situation?
3 What might have been the outcome had there been no example for them to follow?

case study 1.1 **Caleb**

Mr Collins takes Caleb to the supermarket to do some shopping. He usually buys Caleb some sweets in the supermarket when they shop on Saturdays, but not when they shop midweek. It is Tuesday and Caleb decides he wants some sweets and he wants them now! He shouts and stamps his feet and Mr Collins is so embarrassed that he buys Caleb what he wants and quickly leaves the shop.

activity

1 What has Caleb learned?
2 What should Mr Collins have done (ideally)?
3 What might be the long-term implications of this incident?
4 What does this tell you about boundaries?

Effective **communication** is central to the good working practice of all early years professionals, and relationships with children and families may be impaired without it, reducing the effectiveness of your working in partnership with parents. The way you communicate sends a message about you as a person – your attitude, the way you talk, how well you listen and your approach to various situations.

Professional Practice

- Children will test boundaries if the boundaries are not seen to be both clearly set and consistent, which is why a few really important boundaries are better than a whole range of desirable ones.

remember
When managing unacceptable behaviour, it is important to make it clear that it is the behaviour that is unwanted and not the child.

Refer to Unit 0, page 00, for information on sociograms.

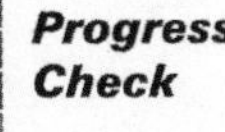

For examples and discussion of behaviour (and other) policies, refer to Good Practice in Nursery Management by Sadek and Sadek (1996).

Progress Check

1. Explain the communication cycle.
2. Name three aspects of verbal communication.
3. What is the difference between an open and a closed question?
4. What examples can you give of non-verbal communication?
5. What does the term 'barrier to communication' mean? Give an example.
6. List at least five different sorts of information you will listen to as an early years worker.
7. What is paraphrasing?
8. Give an example of reflective listening.
9. When is visual information particularly important?
10. What does the role of an advocate involve?

Activities

are designed to help you understand the topics through answering questions or undertaking research, and are either *Group* or *Individual* work. They are linked to the Grading Criteria by application of the D, P, and M categories.

Case Studies

provide real life examples that relate to what is being discussed within the text. It provides an opportunity to demonstrate theory in practice.

An **Activity** that is linked to a Case Study helps you to apply your knowledge of the subject to real life situations.

Keywords

of specific importance are highlighted within the text and then defined in a glossary at the end of the book.

Professional Practice

boxes highlight any professional practice points relevant to the topic being covered.

Remember boxes

contain helpful hints, tips or advice.

Links

direct you to other parts of the book that relate to the subject currently being covered.

Information bars

point you towards resources for further reading and research (e.g. websites).

Progress Checks

provide a list of quick questions at the end of each Unit, designed to ensure that you have understood the most important aspects of each subject area.

Acknowledgements

A big thank you to John for his love, support and encouragement. Also, to Hannah and Alan for their continued agreement for me to include photos of their children, my lovely grandchildren.

The interest and professionalism of Nelson Thornes staff is also acknowledged with grateful thanks.

The author and publishers would like to thank the following for permission to reproduce photographs and other material:

Stages of visual development bullet list on p.120-1 based on M. Sheridan, From Birth to Five Years: Children's Developmental Progress, 7th impression, nferNelson, 1997; Child's temperament bullet list on p.136 from T. Bruce and C. Meggit, Childcare and Education, Hodder & Stoughton, 1996, reproduced by permission of Hodder & Stoughton Ltd; Table 3.6 on p.128 from H. Bee, The Developing Child, Allyn & Bacon, 1992; self protection strategy bullet list, and illustrations on p.267–8 from C. Karp and T. Butler, Treatment Strategies for Abused Children, Sage Publications, 1996; definition of play therapy on p.279 from the British Association of Play Therapists Code of Ethics and Practice, 1996, see www.bapt.uk.com/aboutbapt.htm; 12 features of free-flow play bullet list from T Bruce, time to Play in Early Childhood Education, Hodder & Stoughton, 1991, reproduced by permission of Hodder & Stoughton Ltd

Photo credits:
Digital Vision (NT), p.77; ASCO Educational Supplies Ltd, p.229; Medipics, p.245; Milet Publishing and Andersen Press, p.306; Billy Ridgers/Team Video, p.313; Bob Watkins/Photovision, p.418.

Positive Relationships for Children's Care, Learning and Development

This unit covers the following objectives:

- Be able to develop relationships with children
- Be able to communicate with children
- Be able to support children in developing relationships
- Be able to communicate with adults

Being able to communicate and get on with others is extremely important in most people's personal and professional lives. Communication and interpersonal interactions, both verbal and non-verbal, are the means of giving and receiving information and of letting others know how you are feeling.

This unit will introduce you to different types of communication and look at the different factors that affect communication. You will learn how to develop and maintain good relationships with people, how to overcome the barriers that make communication difficult and how to communicate with and support someone who is distressed.

You will also reflect on your own interpersonal and communication skills and identify areas for improvement.

grading criteria

To achieve a **Pass** grade the evidence must show that the learner is able to:	To achieve a **Merit** grade the evidence must show that, in addition to the pass criteria, the learner is able to:	To achieve a **Distinction** grade the evidence must show that, in addition to the pass and merit criteria, the learner is able to:
P1 use examples from placement to describe how relationships can be developed with children page 3	**M1** explain why communication skills are important in developing relationships with children in placement settings page 16	**D1** evaluate own communication skills in terms of developing relationships with children in placement settings page 13
P2 use examples from placement to describe how to communicate with children page 16	**M2** use examples from placement to explain how children can be supported in developing relationships page 28	**D2** evaluate own communication skills in terms of developing relationships with adults in placement settings. page 29
P3 use examples from placement to describe how children can be supported in developing relationships page 10	**M3** explain the importance of effective communication with adults in the children's care, learning and development sector. page 27	

To achieve a **Pass** grade the evidence must show that the learner is able to:	To achieve a Merit grade the evidence must show that, in addition to the pass criteria, the learner is able to:	To achieve a Distinction grade the evidence must show that, in addition to the pass and merit criteria, the learner is able to:
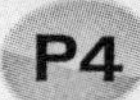 P4 use examples from placement to describe how to communicate with adults. page 12		

Be able to develop relationships with children

Developing relationships by encouraging appropriate behaviour

An important aspect of developing relationships with others is to understand and respond to boundaries, requests and guidance. Without this understanding and willingness to conform, relationships can become strained and impact on happiness, learning and well-being. Adult expectations of children need to be adapted to:

- age
- needs
- ability
- situation.

The adult's approach should:

- be welcoming
- help children feel valued
- be flexible
- involve children in decision-making and allow choice whenever practical
- take into account known factors that might have an impact, for example a specific fear or anxiety.

Setting boundaries

Setting boundaries involves making it clear to children which behaviours are acceptable and which are not.

Children need adult guidance and example to help them learn the social rules of the society into which they are born. In every family, the **routines** and boundaries vary but, whatever these may be, they are a crucial aspect of family life, enabling a household to run smoothly and the children to feel secure.

The boundaries set by parents should be reasonable without being too rigid and, once agreed, it is important to keep to them; otherwise, children will continually test them. Boundaries allow children to explore ever-increasing elements of their world, safe in the knowledge that the adults in their life are in overall control of the situation and are taking care of them.

The individual personality of each child will also have an impact on their behaviour.

Link

Refer to Unit 3, page 134, for more about personality.

case study 1.1

Caleb

Mr Collins takes Caleb to the supermarket to do some shopping. He usually buys Caleb some sweets in the supermarket when they shop on Saturdays but not when they shop midweek. It is Tuesday, and Caleb decides that he wants some sweets and he wants them now! He shouts and stamps his feet, and Mr Collins is so embarrassed that he buys Caleb what he wants and quickly leaves the shop.

activity
INDIVIDUAL WORK

1 What has Caleb learned?
2 What should Mr Collins have done (ideally)?
3 What might be the long-term implications of this incident?
4 What does this tell you about boundaries?

remember Children need clear, consistent and fair boundaries.

Early years **professionals** also need to set boundaries and make clear their expectations of children when they are in the school or preschool setting. These boundaries should be reasonable, consistent and fair and will reflect the **ethos** of the setting. This will contribute to the social and emotional stability of the children within the setting and to their **development** in general. Children need to learn the social rules of their own **culture** (their **primary socialisation**) in order to be fully accepted by others within that culture. Each culture places its own emphasis on certain social skills, and children will be encouraged to comply.

Reinforcement and learning by example

An approving look, a smile or a word of praise encourages a child to repeat an action, gesture or response, whereas a disapproving look or negative verbal comment is more likely to deter a child from repetition. Parents and early years professionals should lead by example, as children learn social behaviour by observing others.

Albert Bandura's social learning theory is relevant here; see Unit 3, page 140, for information on this theory.

activity
INDIVIDUAL WORK 1.1

P1

Think of an incident at your placement where children were learning by example.
1 Was this important, do you think?
2 Was it in response to a positive or negative situation?
3 What might have been the outcome had there been no example for them to follow?

When setting boundaries for children, it is important to think carefully about each 'rule' or boundary and consider how important it actually is. In a busy early years setting, you do not want to be constantly reminding children of boundaries; it will have a very negative effect if you are regularly repeating 'Don't do that, please', 'Off there, please', and so on.

Professional Practice

- Sometimes, we need to take a firm stand on issues for the long-term good of the child. Getting the balance right often comes with experience.
- Children will test boundaries if the boundaries are not seen to be both clearly set and consistent, which is why a few really important boundaries are better than a whole range of desirable ones.
- Newly qualified early years staff will benefit from observing the approaches taken by more experienced staff in setting and maintaining boundaries.

Fig 1.1 Only the child holding the teddy at circle time is allowed to speak

case study 1.2 Orange Blossom and Hillview Nurseries

Orange Blossom Nursery has recently opened and can accommodate 24 children aged two to five years. It currently has 14 children each day, mostly aged three. The managers of Orange Blossom have decided to run the nursery as a free-play nursery and have interpreted this as allowing the children to play with whatever they like, whenever they want to, with no restrictions on how many children can play with any one resource.

You are visiting Orange Blossom as part of your professional practice experience; the visit is also linked to an assignment in which you have been asked to make a comparison between different types of early years provision. You have already written notes on Hillview Nursery, which tries to ensure a balanced approach between **free play** and structured activities. At Hillview, the free-play activities are restricted to a range of resources predetermined by the staff, and there are guidelines for the children as to how many can play in any one place, whereas at Orange Blossom the children select or ask for whatever resources they want and play within small or large groups as they choose.

activity GROUP WORK

1 What are your first thoughts about the ethos of Orange Blossom Nursery?
2 What are your first thoughts about the ethos of Hillview Nursery?
3 Draw up a list of benefits and drawbacks for each nursery.
4 How might the children's developing understanding of boundaries be affected at Orange Blossom?
5 How might this free-play approach affect the working practices of the staff?
6 What might the children miss out on at Orange Blossom?
7 Would you have any other concerns? What are they?

Children feel secure with boundaries, and their understanding of them is made clear when they are heard trying to enforce them on others in the setting, for example 'You're not allowed to do that'.

It helps children to understand the need for boundaries if you can reinforce them by giving explanations whenever opportunities arise.

For example, imagine that, following an incident on the climbing frame, the nursery manager of Hillview Nursery talked to the children, saying, 'Jenny has had a nasty fall from the climbing frame, which is a shame, but too many children were trying to use it at the same time and were not listening to Monica who was asking Jenny and Sarah to get off and wait their turn. Hopefully, everyone will remember this; it is why we only allow five children on the frame at the same time.'

This is a clear explanation that would have meaning for the children. Such an explanation is more likely to be remembered by them for the future.

Managing behaviour

When **managing unacceptable behaviour**, it is important to make it clear that it is the behaviour that is unwanted and not the child. Children can at times display a range of unacceptable behaviours; if adults respond to them in a positive and consistent manner, it will help them learn what is and what is not acceptable. Certain behaviours may need to be eliminated because they:

- breach the boundaries of the setting
- affect the enjoyment and/or learning of others in the setting
- affect the enjoyment and/or learning of the child themselves
- are dangerous for the child or for others.

When challenging a child's behaviour, you should be aware of what expectations there are of the child at home, and how your views of the child's behaviour will be interpreted. It is important that a child's home life is not seen to be criticised or devalued, but the boundaries of the setting should still be maintained.

case study 1.3 Desmond

Desmond is six years old and is an only child, born to his mother, Denise, when she was just 14. Desmond and Denise lived with her parents for four years until she felt able to cope with him on her own. Desmond is a very lively little boy who is awake by 6.00 a.m. every morning and does not go to bed until Denise does – usually at around 11.30 p.m. Desmond's grandparents doted on him when he lived with them, giving him all that he asked for. They still come and see him most evenings, usually at around 9.00 p.m. This allows Denise time to tidy up a bit as she gets nothing done with Desmond there. In school, Desmond is difficult to manage, being irritable and unwilling to share. He clamours for the attention of the class teacher throughout the day.

activity INDIVIDUAL WORK

1 What is going wrong for Desmond?
2 What is Desmond learning from the adults around him?
3 What would be the first issue you would want to tackle for Desmond?
4 How could Denise help Desmond?
5 How could the grandparents help Desmond?
6 How could the class teacher help Desmond?

It is common in many primary schools for each class to display a list of the school 'rules'. These include statements such as 'We will not run in school', 'We will be nice to everyone', and so on. These statements make it clear what is acceptable or not acceptable within the setting and make no judgements about any one child's upbringing.

Examples

Kieron loves to jump on and off the tables. This is a game that he plays at home with his brothers who are both older than him. It would be far better for you to explain to Kieron that he cannot jump on and off the tables in nursery because he might hurt himself on the nursery floor, or that the younger children may try to copy him and hurt themselves, rather than simply telling him that it is wrong to jump off furniture. In Kieron's home, it may not be considered wrong and this could cause him confusion.

Similarly, it is better to explain to Maisie that shrieking at the top of her voice in the village hall (where she attends your preschool group) cannot be allowed, because the noise echoes around and disturbs everyone, but it is much more acceptable in the farmyard of the farm house where she lives, because that is an open space and the cows probably love to hear her coming to see them.

Professional Practice

- Children need to be given reasons and explanations which have meaning for them.
- On issues of health or safety, there is no room for negotiation. No must mean no.

ABC strategy

Behaviour, whether acceptable or not acceptable, is affected by the responses that it receives whether positive or negative. This is acknowledged in the **ABC behaviour strategy** for **behaviour management**, which is based partly on **social learning theory**.

Refer to Unit 3, page 140, for an explanation of social learning theory.

remember

Sometimes, children need to be taught how to respond to others. A child with a naturally 'neutral' facial expression may need help in learning to make eye contact and giving a welcoming look to others.

ABC stands for:

- Antecedent – what occurs immediately before the behaviour
- Behaviour – the nature of the behaviour being referred to, whether acceptable or not acceptable
- Consequence – the outcome of the behaviour, which will be either positive or negative.

Think of it this way:

- Positive antecedent + Positive behaviour = Positive consequence
- Negative antecedent + Negative behaviour = Negative consequence.

Strategies for exploring and managing behaviour

Set out below are some examples of strategies that you could take when exploring and managing behaviour.

The child without friends

1. You could produce a **sociogram** of friendships within the child's class or group, looking at:
   (a) who the child indicates as their friends
   (b) which children indicate that the child is a friend.
2. You could then consider the interests and personalities of the children identified in the **observation** above, thinking about who most closely relates to the interests and personality of the **target child**.
3. The next step would be to initiate activities to bring the children together (one or two at a time). It may be helpful at first for an adult to work alongside them.
4. The progress of the 'friendship' should be monitored; if it does not last, you should note what went wrong.
5. Information gained (from step 4) would inform you in helping the child to develop another friendship.

Refer to Unit 8, page 391, for information on sociograms.

The destructive child

1. A good starting point would be making a note as to whose belongings the child destroys: anybody's/their own/the belongings of children of a particular social group or culture.
2. It would be useful to see if the child seems to want to 'get back at' anyone in particular? If this is the case, the antecedent behaviour needs to be identified.
3. Observing to see if the child seems angry or frustrated would enable adults to offer opportunities for releasing anger and frustration, as these may help.
4. If the behaviour has started suddenly, it may be appropriate to consider what is happening at home.

Professional Practice

- Children may be taking out their confusion or unhappiness in the setting because they are unable to express it at home; giving opportunities to be creative and making time to talk may help.
- Whenever possible, ignore destructive behaviour (but comfort any child affected by the destruction), as sometimes the child's aim is to get your attention!
- Reward good behaviour with praise as this positively reinforces desirable behaviour.
- Whenever possible, work in partnership with parents to improve behaviour both at home and in the setting.

remember Use your understanding of child development to help you approach the child concerned appropriately.

The withdrawn child

1 Observing the extent of the problem should include seeing:
   (a) how easy it is to involve the child in everyday activities – easy/sometimes difficult/always difficult
   (b) how regularly the child seems withdrawn – occasionally/regularly/all the time
   (c) how much the child's learning or activity seems to be affected – a little/quite a lot/almost totally.

2 It is important to establish whether the child is withdrawn in all situations, or just in the early years setting. If it is just in the setting, you would need to observe closely to identify where the problem lies, for example:
   (a) Is it linked to separation anxiety?
   (b) Is the child being bullied?
   (c) Is there a problem at home?
   (d) Is the ABC strategy relevant?

3 Observation will guide you as to the best approach to take. Approaches might include:
   (a) encouraging greater parental involvement to help the child feel more secure
   (b) identifying children you need to keep separated from the withdrawn child, hoping to break the cycle and restore the child's confidence
   (c) involving an adult in activities to help the child to develop 'joining-in' skills.

Refer back to page 6 to remind yourself about the ABC strategy.

Professional Practice

- To help to gain the confidence of a shy or anxious child, you can set up a favourite activity and take part in it alongside the child. This is often called 'modelling'. The adult is demonstrating a method of doing something, but without actually directing the child in any way.

The attention-seeking child

1 You would need to consider whether the attention-seeking behaviour is due to:
   (a) not being accepted by others in the class or group
   (b) problems at home (feeling rejected, lack of interest shown in the child)
   (c) anxiety in new situations
   (d) the child's boredom with the activities offered or the work set
   (e) the child finding the activities or work too challenging and therefore lacking a sense of achievement.

2 Using your observational skills would enable you to identify when attention-seeking behaviour occurs.

3 Adult involvement in group situations may help alleviate any 'social' problems.

Professional Practice

- Giving plenty of praise and attention where appropriate can be beneficial. This will indicate to children that you are willing to give them your attention, but only at appropriate times.
- Providing more differentiation in the activities offered or the work set may help the child find the appropriate balance of stimulation and achievement.

remember

What is acceptable at two is not always acceptable at four or older.

Development and behaviour

The age or stage of development that a child has reached will of course have a bearing on the expectation of how a child should behave and how best to manage their behaviour if it becomes unacceptable.

A two-year-old who crayons on another child's drawing has not yet learned that this is not 'fun'. A four-year-old who does the same (usually) knows that it is not appropriate, but could be doing it for a number of reasons, such as:

- to try to gain your attention
- because they are jealous of the other child
- in retaliation for a previous act.

Before jumping to any conclusion, it is important to establish the facts, ensuring that the act itself is clearly acknowledged as unacceptable but exploring any other issues and helping the children to reach a resolution between themselves, if one is required.

Professional Practice

- Explanations will only work if the child concerned has the ability to understand.
- Children's behaviour often regresses during illness or at times of stress.

Refer to Unit 2, page 63, and Unit 9, page 418, for further information about children who are ill. Refer also to the strategies below.

Applying sector values in relationships with children

During your career as a childcare practitioner, you will work with children from a variety of family situations and structures, for example:

- nuclear families
- extended families
- lone-parent families
- stepfamilies
- economically challenged families
- children with gay and lesbian parents
- children from other cultures.

It is your responsibility as a professional early years worker to communicate with, and respond appropriately and equally to, all families. You should be aware of any personal **bias** or preconceived ideas that you may have about any social groups. Your responsibility is to welcome all families and respect their **rights**, ensuring that both your attitude and your language are appropriate.

Refer to Unit 6, page 281, for more on this.

Within the early years care sector there are certain values that all staff and students must work to. These include:

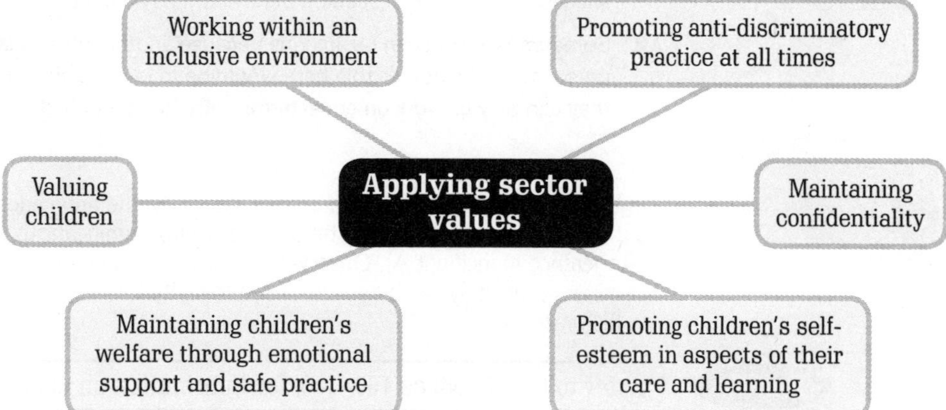

Fig 1.2 Applying sector values

remember A diverse community is a rich community, and the opportunities to share and explore elements of each other's lives will enhance the learning of all.

More on these values can also be found in Unit 4, pages 197–205, and Unit 6, page 281. You may find it helpful to refer to these sections now.

Any strategy used by early years staff will work best if supported by the parents and carers of the children who attend the setting. This is why **behaviour policies** are important; they set out what is acceptable to the setting and how unacceptable behaviour will be handled.

For examples and discussion of behaviour (and other) policies, refer to *Good Practice in Nursery Management* by Sadek and Sadek (1996).

Coping with unacceptable behaviour

Strategies for coping with unacceptable behaviour include:

- the ABC strategy
- time out
- **containment**
- setting goals
- helping children cope with change.

The ABC strategy

Refer back to page 6 to remind yourself about the ABC strategy.

case study 1.4

Cleo

Incident A: Cleo had been happily making a model using junk boxes for almost 20 minutes when Samuel came along and started telling her what to do next and interfering with her model. Cleo lost interest and went to play elsewhere.

Incident B: Cleo and Ginny were playing in the sand tray, driving cars through the sand. When Samuel joined them, Cleo left immediately and went to play in the water.

Incident C: The whole group was playing circle games, and you became aware that Cleo was avoiding being next to Samuel, specifically changing places to avoid him. Clearly something is not right here.

activity
INDIVIDUAL WORK

1 How do you think using observational skills will help you get to the bottom of this situation?
2 What strategies could you take to help build a better relationship between Cleo and Samuel?

Professional Practice

- Noting and responding to antecedent behaviour is a good way of starting to manage children's behaviour. As an early years professional, your role would be to intervene in a situation before the antecedent behaviour has an effect.
- Sometimes a child can be anxious because another child is larger or has a louder personality. The adult's role here would be to join in and help show the wary child that they can play or work on equal terms with the other child.

In the three incidents described in the case study, the antecedent was clearly Samuel, although he did not appear to be doing anything significant to upset Cleo (apart from some interference in incident A). Observational skills could be of importance here: observing Samuel, particularly when he is in close proximity to Cleo, could indicate why Cleo is anxious in his presence.

Refer to Unit 3, pages 168–180, for information on useful observational techniques.

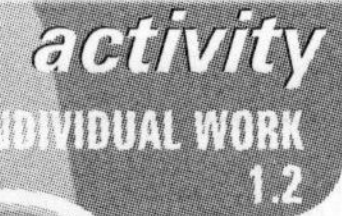

activity INDIVIDUAL WORK 1.2

1 With advice (and permission) from your placement supervisor, observe a child over a period of time and note any situations where the antecedent affects subsequent behaviour.

2 If these were negative effects, think through what could be done by the adults responsible to alter the situation and avoid it being repeated.

Time-out

This is the term given to removing a child from a certain situation. It should be seen as a strategy rather than as a punishment, allowing the child to calm down if distressed, and enabling others to continue with what they were doing. A child given time-out should still be within sight and hearing of the carer, and where the child is taken should be both safe and secure. Children should only be given time-out for very short periods of time. Many people use the estimate of one minute per year of age as a guide, but common sense should always prevail. Less will often be sufficient for most children.

Always explain to a child why they have been given time-out and make a point of giving the child your attention when there is no behaviour issue. This will reinforce the benefit of playing well and being rewarded with the adult's time, which is often the root of many unacceptable behaviour situations.

Containment

Sometimes children's frustration or anger overwhelms them and they are unable to deal with it themselves. At this point, a sensitive adult can step in and 'contain' their emotions for them, holding the child calmly and preventing the child losing control, gradually easing the child back into a relaxed state.

It is important for you as the adult to remain unflustered, offering children examples of how to behave another time by outlining, where appropriate, alternative measures that they could have taken.

Professional Practice

- Different cultures place different values on possessions and this can at times be a cause of conflict.
- Clear explanations must always be given to children as to why their behaviour is not acceptable.
- Some children will benefit from taking time out from the activity, to calm down, relax and compose themselves.
- Sanctions should be used only as a last resort, and, if sanctions are indicated to a child, they need to be carried through (this is part of setting boundaries).
- Sometimes children need opportunities to express anger. Providing them with clay, woodworking or a similar activity can be helpful.
- Distracting a child away from whatever is the problem can work well. This strategy can be particularly useful with younger children.
- If children continually have negative interactions with others, it may be helpful for an adult to join them in their work or play and help to direct their interactions, demonstrating a more positive way to play or work with others.

Helping children cope with planned and unplanned change

Behaviour can be affected by insecurity and anxiety about the unknown. When practitioners know that there is likely to be a new experience that could cause anxiety, such as going into hospital, moving home, etc., it can be helpful to read related stories with the children. Giving children the opportunity to discuss their feelings about past or forthcoming events can alleviate many of the issues for them.

The flexibility built into the daily routine of a school or day-care setting offers security for children, enabling them to face changes in other situations, whether planned or spontaneous. Sometimes the routine of a child's day in school or nursery is the only constant in their lives. Occasional changes to that routine help them realise that they can accept and cope with change. This is another good reason why the routine in any setting should never be too rigid.

Promoting self-esteem

Self-esteem plays a large part in children's behaviour. If they are secure and feel confident, they are less likely to display unwanted behaviour. There are many ways of encouraging good behaviour, and using reward stickers and star charts has become a popular approach. Some of these methods are aimed specifically at building self-esteem, for example stickers with the following messages:

- 'I have good thinking skills'
- 'I am a kind person'
- 'I have done really well today'.

At other times, rewards will be directed at a specific action, such as:

- 'Good work'
- 'Well done'
- 'A kind act'.

remember

There are no substitutes for praise given for effort and the giving of your time. These are usually the rewards that a child wants most of all.

Whole-class rewards are given in some schools by using golden time or something similar. Golden time is often on a Friday afternoon, and children are given greater autonomy in what they do. In some schools, children can even change to another class for the golden time session.

Setting targets for children can be successful, particularly if the children can see a tangible outcome in the form of a reward. Many primary school classes use charts to indicate which books have been read, or how often good behaviour has been noted, and so on. These give **positive reinforcement** to the children and encouragement to continue.

Be able to communicate with children

Effective **communication** is central to the good working practice of all early years professionals, and relationships with children and families may be impaired without it, reducing the effectiveness of your working in partnership with parents. The way you communicate sends a message about you as a person – your attitude, the way you talk, how well you listen and your approach to various situations.

Communication involves a successful exchange between two people. Sometimes, your work as an early years practitioner and team member will be judged on your ability to communicate appropriately, using suitable **body language** as well as words. It is important to remember that individuals with good **interpersonal skills** identify when communication has not been effective, by noting the responses of others, and are both willing and able to adjust their approach accordingly. As you read through this unit, there will be opportunities for you to reflect on your personal ability to communicate and interact, enabling you to review your current practice and build on it for the future.

Refer to page 13 for an explanation of the communication process, known as the **communication cycle**.

Interpersonal skills

If asked about good interpersonal skills, most people's responses would include the importance of communicating well and taking the other person's needs into consideration; but how many of them would actually put this into action on a day-to-day basis? What about you? How well would you do?

activity
INDIVIDUAL WORK 1.3
P4

Think of groups that you communicate with in a range of different settings, including college, home, your placement, social situations, in shops, and so on, and the ways that you communicate.

1 Identify ways in which your communication differs according to the age of the people in those groups and the type of group. Include babies, young and older children, your peer group, your parents and your grandparents' generations in your thinking, and consider how your communication differs when interacting with each of the groups you have identified.
2 Consider how you use your voice and what you say. Think about:
   - volume
   - tone
   - speed
   - the language used
   - the emphasis that you place on words.
3 What about your body language? Consider:
   - posture
   - gestures
   - **eye contact**
   - physical contact
   - spatial awareness.
4 Think of a conversation you have had where the communication felt unsuccessful to you. Why was this, do you think? What could you have done to have improved it?
5 How well do you consider the space between yourself and the person to whom you are speaking? Do you take into consideration issues of proximity, orientation and cultural differences with regard to contact?
6 When has communication felt particularly successful? What made it so?

1. Think about the range of communication and interpersonal interactions you have had during your placement experiences. Which have been most successful? Which, on **reflection**, could have been improved upon?
2. Copy the table below and add at least five examples of interactions with children from your placement practice. An example of a communication (with a parent) has been given to get you started.
3. Reflect on the examples you have given. How good is your relationship with the children you work with?

Types of communication	With whom?	Any potential barriers identified in advanced?	Evaluation of the success of the communication process
Informing parent about head lice in the nursery	Father of a child	Father speaks very little English	Information was successfully passed on through the use of a leaflet and gestures showing how head lice jump from head to head

Communicating successfully

Communication can be verbal (written or oral), visual, textual or aural, involving the written word, music, drama or creativity. When you begin a communication, you need to consider how the other individual involved communicates best and whether there are any barriers to their communicating successfully with you.

The communication cycle

For communication to be successful it has to meet the needs of both speakers. Any breakdown will result in a lack of communication. The same principles apply to communication with adults and communication with children.

The diagram below shows how communication can be explained as a cycle, in which we each in turn take the part of the 'encoder' (the person who sends the message) and the 'decoder' (the person who deciphers and tries to understand the message). During conversation, we continually swap roles from encoder to decoder and, as the diagram demonstrates, the common field of experience is where the message is initially decoded. Without a common field, the message is likely to get lost or distorted; this can be likened to conversing with another person when there is no shared language between you.

Fig 1.3 The communication cycle

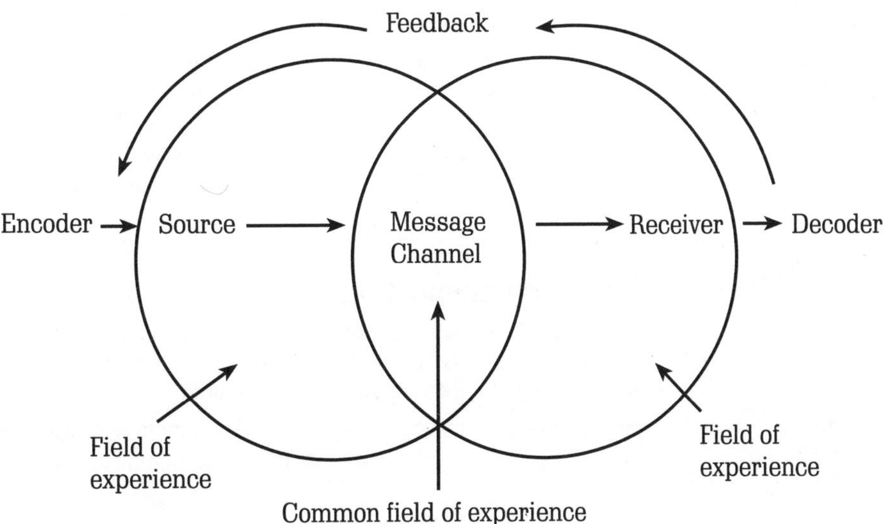

For communication to work successfully, the message channel needs to be a common field of experience for both the encoder (the speaker) and the decoder (the listener).

Communication can fail because of:

- lack of vocabulary
- inability to speak, see or hear
- lack of listening skills
- inability to concentrate
- lack of knowledge
- lack of interest
- misinterpretation
- wrong (or confusing) body language/facial expressions
- surrounding noises
- wrong timing/place/person.

Failing to communicate may make us feel:

- frustrated
- hurt
- angry
- misunderstood
- inadequate.

The importance of a common field of experience

A 'language' which is understood by early years workers and children, and early years workers and parents, is important to the building and maintaining of relationships. Without it, communication will break down quickly and hinder the sharing of information about the child's progress or needs and the setting's ability to work in partnership with parents.

Fig 1.4 A common field of experience is needed for successful communication

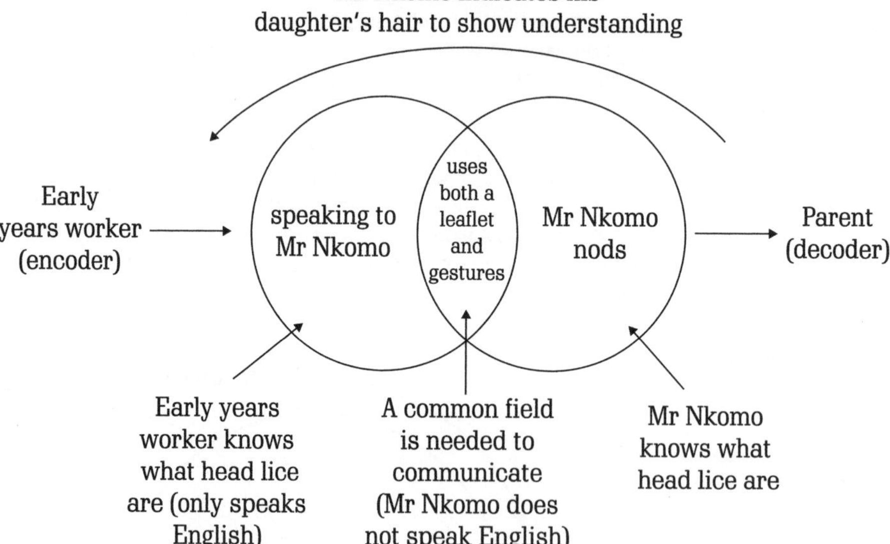

remember
Communication can be both verbal and non-verbal; it includes speech, looks and gestures. In children it is developed initially through the use of symbols.

Verbal communication

Verbal communication relies on mutual understanding of the spoken word. It can fail if a common language is not used, or if there is no common field of experience linking the person who is speaking to the person who is listening.

For example, a course tutor of early years students who discusses the development of motor skills with the group will achieve successful communication, as the topic of conversation is both familiar and of interest to all concerned. If, however, the tutor had decided to introduce the finer details of the structure of DNA (deoxyribose nucleic acid) prior to a discussion of gene inheritance, for some students in the group (the decoders) the scientific detail may be too great. The tutor (the encoder) would therefore only be partially successful in communicating the message.

In the example above, think how the tutor could have more successfully introduced the details of DNA.

Open and closed questions

Conversation often involves asking questions. The way in which the questions are phrased makes a difference to the answers (feedback) you receive. Questions can be useful to clarify something you are unsure of and, by extending the conversation further, can indicate to the other person that you are interested in what they have to say. **Open questions** offer the opportunity for a wide-ranging answer, whereas **closed questions** restrict the answer to one word, such as 'yes' or 'no', or a brief statement. You need to think carefully about the type of question you are asking and the message the question is giving.

> *remember*
> When encouraging a child to converse with you, you will only receive the information you are looking for if you ask the right questions in the appropriate way.

For example, 'Did you enjoy your lunch?' is a closed question; 'yes' or 'no' are the likely answers. Whereas 'What did you have for your lunch?' or 'What do you prefer to eat at lunch time?' offer the opportunity for a range of answers and therefore extend the conversation.

It is important to remember that many children do not have the opportunity for regular conversations with an adult who is interested in really listening to them. Your role as a professional is to listen to the children in your care and encourage them to converse; by making suggestions, re-telling, estimating and evaluating, they are building up their vocabulary and improving their verbal skills.

Non-verbal communication

Non-verbal communication can tell us a great deal about how people are feeling. At times we need to interpret what children are trying to say to us through their actions and body language (their non-verbal communication), which can be displayed either consciously or subconsciously. This can be particularly important if they have been hurt or abused, and the observational skills and level of understanding that you develop will enable you to be alert to such non-verbal signs.

> *remember*
> A smile gives encouragement and a gesture can indicate how to approach an activity.

However, it is important to remember that people have different requirements regarding personal space, and different cultures have differing cultural practices. As an early years worker, you should, whenever possible, research the cultural customs and practices of the children in your care, recognising that a cultural 'norm' will not be followed by all families of that particular culture. This will help you to avoid causing offence or embarrassment.

Fig 1.5 Non-verbal communication

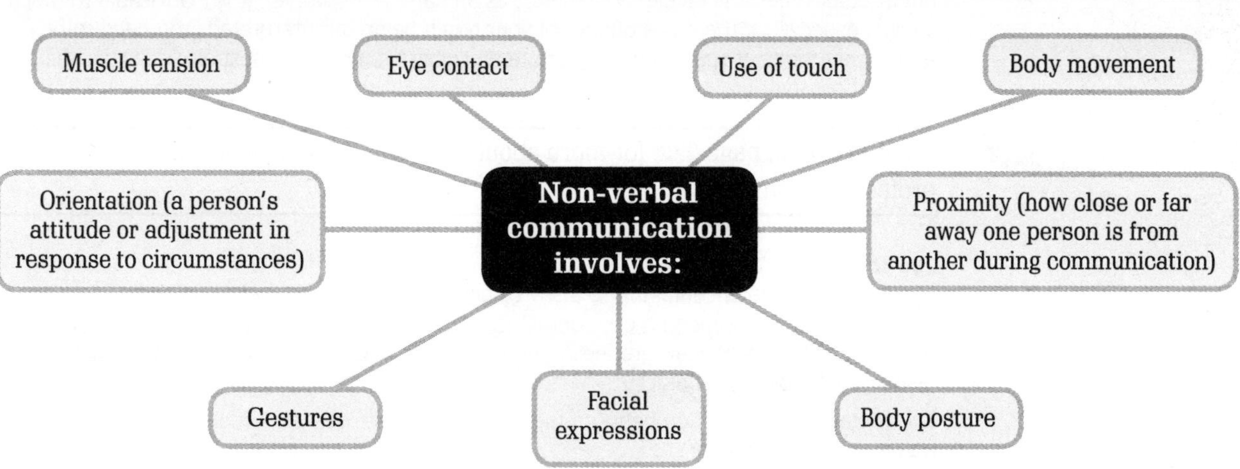

activity
INDIVIDUAL WORK 1.5

P2

M1

1 Using a copy of the table below, consider the non-verbal forms of communication listed and make notes about the messages you have observed for each of the emotions listed whilst at placement.

2 Think about your responses to the children whose non-verbal communications have been listed. Explain how they are being supported in their development through communication with the adults caring for them.

Non-verbal forms of communication	Sad	Anxious	Scared	Happy	Shy
Eye contact					
Tone of voice					
Body posture					
Voice level					
Facial expressions					
Level of activity					
Gestures					

Refer to Unit 5, pages 244–249, to remind yourself of indicators of abuse that may be identified through non-verbal communication.

Personal space

People differ in how close they prefer to be someone when in conversation. You need to ask yourself whether you ever 'invade the space' of anyone, and what signs they have given you to indicate this.

It is important to consider whether communication is taking place in an environment that allows for sufficient personal space. Each individual should feel comfortable within the personal space available to them.

Touch

Each of us has contact with other people everyday; at times this contact may just be verbal, but at other times it is tactile. Sometimes, as an early years worker, it is inadvisable to touch a child, especially if there is a danger of your touch being misinterpreted. You need to be aware what forms of touch are appropriate and what are not. You must also consider the issues of consent.

Refer to Unit 5, page 272, for more about this important area of your professionalism.

Eye contact

Eye contact can be encouraging to a shy or nervous person, and can help keep a conversation going. When no eye contact is made, it is likely that the conversation will trail away. When individuals are feeling nervous, embarrassed, shy or guilty, it is a natural response to avoid eye contact.

Eye contact is a connection between the speaker and the listener. It makes them feel accepted by one another.

Use of eye contact and other forms of body language can depend on personality.

Gestures

Some people are more physically demonstrative than others. Gestures and positioning of the body can suggest a range of feelings, including submission, aggression, defensiveness and assertiveness. They can also demonstrate welcome, humour, warmth and openness.

Refer to page 29 for information on assertiveness and aggression and the links to body language.

Other factors affecting communication

Location and size of group

Ask yourself if the environmental situation really is appropriate. Are all those involved likely to feel relaxed? Can you hear each other? Background noise can be an important contributory factor in poor communication.

Children are likely to communicate best in small groups, or one to one. If you want them to concentrate carefully on something, then an area with few distractions will be best. A parent who needs to convey information is likely to want to speak somewhere where they receive the full attention of the staff member. If a person is feeling anxious, they are likely to want space around them and not want to feel hemmed in.

These issues need to be taken seriously.

Listening skills

Listening skills, such as focusing and concentrating, are important. When communicating with others, we each need to give our time and attention to the communication for it to work well, and for each person to feel valued and worthy of the other's time. Listening involves taking in a range of different sorts of information. It is not the same as hearing (as when listening to music), because often you need to act on the information that you have taken in.

remember It can be useful to study the communication processes in a range of early years settings, noting the effects of the staff's responses on the children.

In an early years setting you will listen to:

- children telling you their news
- children asking for your help
- children sharing their experiences of activities with you
- children explaining their problems
- parents giving you important information about feeds, diet, **health**, and so on
- parents confiding in you about family issues that may affect their child
- colleagues explaining changes to the daily routine
- colleagues passing on useful hints and ideas
- colleagues updating you through the cascading of information
- outside professionals (for example, a **Portage** worker) giving you guidance.

Each of these speakers requires your attention so that you can meet the needs of the children in your care adequately. Listening carefully is a skill which is well worth practising.

It is important to:

- show that you are listening by focusing on the speaker
- make eye contact and use encouraging smiles and gestures
- try not to interrupt; let the other person's speech flow, particularly if they are upset or agitated.

case study 1.5

Hopes and Dreams Day Nursery

Hopes and Dreams Day Nursery is your new placement; your supervisor has suggested that you take a couple of days to observe how the nursery day is structured and how the staff work with the children. You settle with a notebook and observe the following:

Observation 1

Tom is crying as someone has scribbled on his picture. Sarah (nursery nurse) stops what she is doing (clearing a table for snack time) and sits down with Tom to listen to what he is saying. At first, he is very distressed, but he begins to calm down with her full attention and is able to explain to her what happened more clearly. Eventually, when Tom is completely calm and ready to go back to the activities, Sarah finds a special piece of paper for him to draw another picture.

Observation 2

Sophie runs to Stella (nursery nurse) telling her that her model has been knocked down again by James. Stella is more focused on a conversation between two members of staff about the changes to the rota. Stella tells Sophie, 'Never mind. Make another one.' Stella returns to the construction area and kicks the construction materials and then sits down in a corner and does nothing.

activity
INDIVIDUAL WORK

1 What was the main difference between the behaviours observed in these two observations?
2 How should Stella have responded to Sophie?
3 What does this tell you about the importance of listening?

Active listening

Active listening ensures that you are focused on what the speaker is saying; there are various ways of listening actively.

Paraphrasing

Paraphrasing involves summarising what has been said and is an easy means of checking that you have understood what you have heard. Your response would start with statements such as:

- 'So what you are telling me is ...?'
- 'Would I be right in thinking that ...?'

This checks that you have understood what has been said to you and also shows other speakers that you value them and were listening carefully to them.

Fig 1.6 Reflective listening at any age involves understanding the feelings of others

Reflective listening
The aim of **reflective listening** is to show that you understand what people are feeling, rather than the details of what they are saying. Your responses should focus firstly on the speaker's feelings and emotions, whether positive, such as excitement or elation, or less positive, such as anger, worry or sadness.

Identifying communication difficulties

Barriers to effective communication

Anything that interferes with the production and decoding of the message is a **barrier to communication**.

Fig 1.7 Barriers to effective communication

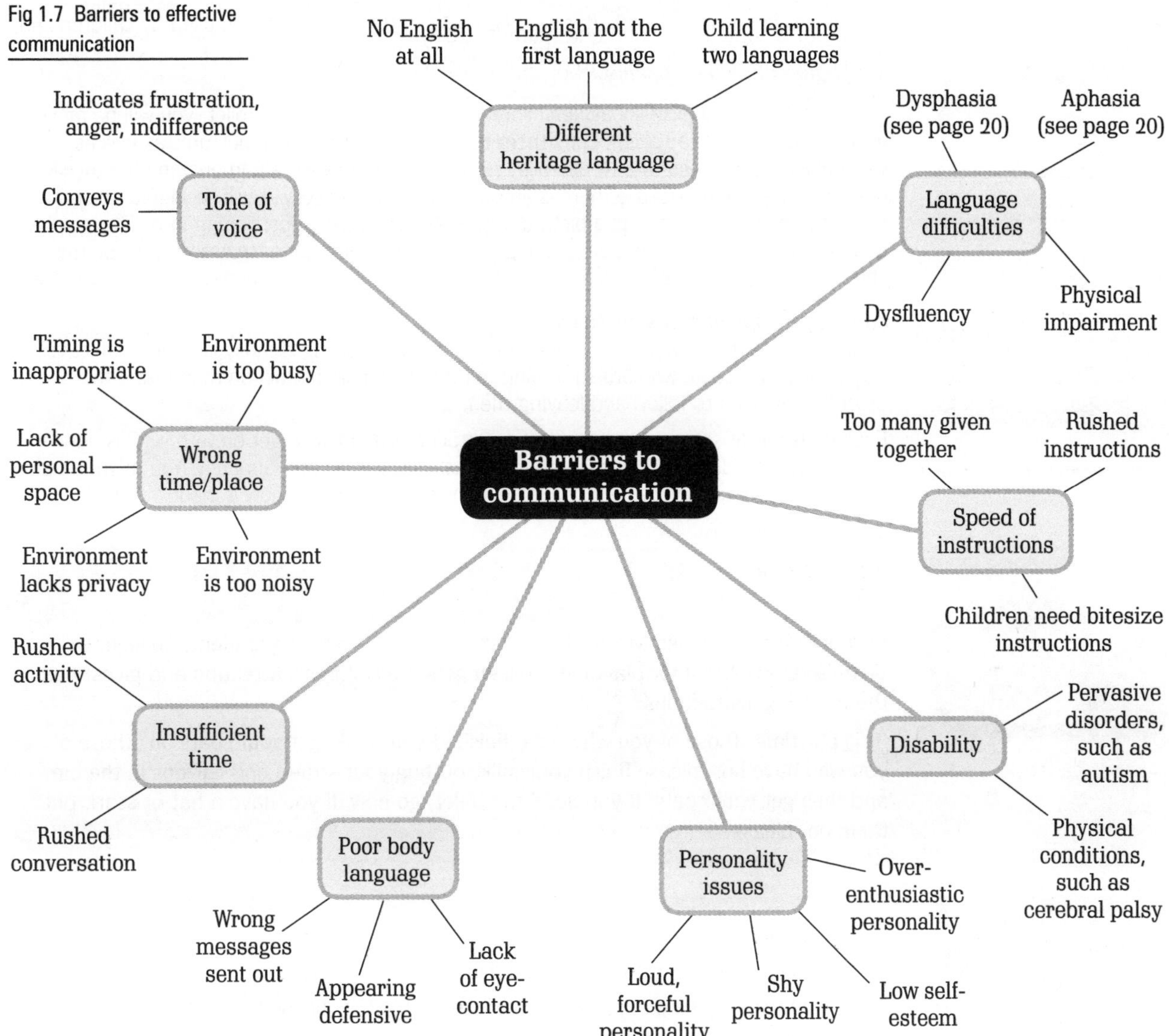

remember The use of language that is inappropriate for the stage of development or the child's depth of knowledge can prevent communication taking place successfully.

Let's look at some of these in more detail.

Tone of voice
The tone of your voice can convey many things: frustration, anger and irritation as well as pleasure, encouragement and praise. At times, the message conveyed by the speaker's tone of voice may differ from the one that is contained in the words. We all respond better to positive tones and are hurt or confused by negative ones. Young children may find it difficult to understand what is being said to them because of the tone in which the message is expressed. For example, the question 'What are you doing?' can be interpreted negatively by a child if the emphasis is placed wrongly. For example, '*What are* you doing?' suggests to the child that the speaker is annoyed, which may make the child feel anxious and hamper further communication.

Refer again to page 13 for the communication cycle diagram.

Language – different culture

The language usually spoken in the child's home is referred to as the first or heritage language, and it is passed on from generation to generation. An understanding of cultural practices, child-rearing, religious beliefs and elements of a child's heritage language will help you build appropriate communication pathways with the child and the family. It is important that you communicate within context (i.e. using words relevant to what is happening at a particular moment) and show that you value the heritage language by using it whenever you can, perhaps with a welcoming greeting at the door as a starting point.

Children will often quickly absorb a small amount of the main language used by children and staff in their school or nursery, but their parents may not yet have done so. It is, therefore, important to explore other ways of communicating.

When asking non-English speaking children if they need to use the toilet, you will be more easily understood if you accompany them to the bathroom and use gestures as well as vocabulary, emphasising the word 'toilet'. Similarly, if you need to find out whether a child has had chickenpox, because there is an outbreak in the nursery, it will be helpful to show non-English-speaking parents a picture of the rash and give a questioning look. If a member of staff speaks a child's heritage language, it is usually sensible for that person to be the child's key worker. However, all staff should be encouraged to communicate with all families.

Language – speed of instructions

Giving instructions or guidance in bite-sized pieces and talking steadily is a more effective way of helping people who are struggling to understand an instruction than listing the process they need to follow and leaving them to it.

Each of us has at some point been given instructions and left to get on with it. This neither fills us with confidence nor ensures that the task is achieved appropriately. You might be able to think of an occasion when you have been in this position and how it made you feel.

case study 1.6

Colleen

Reception class teacher, Mrs Jackson, asks her nursery nursing student, Colleen, to organise the children for playtime. Colleen gets the children's attention and gives them the following instructions:

'It is playtime. Those of you who have finished your milk, get your coats on. Those of you who have not, please finish your milk, putting your straws and cartons in the bin, and then get your coats. If you need the toilet, go now. If you have a hat or scarf, put them on, please.'

activity
INDIVIDUAL WORK

1 How did Colleen do?
2 How many different instructions were there?
3 Do you think all the children will have done all that they needed to? If not, why not?
4 How could you have improved upon this?

Children will focus on whatever grabs their attention most – playtime! It is unlikely that they will have taken in all of the student's instructions. Colleen ought to have broken down her instructions and given them one at a time, for example 'Who has not yet finished their milk? Please finish it before doing anything else.'

Language – difficulties

Problems with speech can hold back the flow of communication and interaction. Such difficulties include:

- **aphasia** (the child is unable to express thoughts in words)
- **dysphasia** (the child has difficulty in expressing thoughts in words)

Fig 1.8 It is important to give clear, 'bite-size' instructions

- stammering (**dysfluency**)
- language impairment (this can be part of a condition, such as cerebral palsy, or an impairment in its own right).

Refer to Unit 3, page 154, where dysfluency is discussed.

remember There may be cultural reasons why there is lack of eye contact.

When talking to children, it is often the adult who initiates the development of conversation. School or nursery provides some children with their only opportunity to have the full attention of an interested adult. It is particularly important for these children that you enrich their language as much as possible by extending and encouraging their use of new terms.

Personality issues
Some people tend to be loud and forceful in their approach to others, which can be off-putting to many individuals, particularly young children. Imagine you are two years old and sitting quietly in your pushchair, when suddenly a large face appears beaming at you, exclaiming loudly and poking at your cheeks. Think how might you feel and what response might be expected from a child in this situation.

Shyness
Sometimes, people are simply too shy to communicate easily; they need to feel comfortable and relaxed. Being given encouraging smiles and gestures and the time to speak at their own pace would help. Trying to hurry them along, or pre-guess what they are going to say is not productive.

Self-esteem
Self-esteem can be affected by poor communication skills.

For example, think how it might make you feel if you only had part of another person's attention when you were having a conversation. This situation is likely to affect how valued you feel. (Think about the impact of the tone of voice used, the other person's body language and whether eye contact is made with you.)

Now consider how you might feel if you were given a tatty piece of paper by your tutor with your assignment feedback scribbled on it hurriedly. You would probably be quite annoyed that the tutor had not taken more care when you had spent hours preparing the work. A person's sense of their own value can be impaired when others do not take time to prepare written material carefully. Think how children might feel if the paper you give them for drawing is a piece torn roughly from a larger sheet.

Responding to communication difficulties

Other forms of communication – signed languages

For children and adults with limited or no verbal skills, a variety of signed techniques can offer a helpful communication route. Techniques include:

- **signed language**
- Bliss symbols
- Makaton
- Braille
- cued speech.

Each can be used successfully and is favoured for different reasons.

Signing is used by deaf people, those with impaired hearing, people with certain forms of disability and by many people who communicate with them. Signed language does not only involve hand signs, but uses the whole face and body to communicate. Signed languages are languages in their own right; they are not simply a direct interpretation of a spoken language.

On page 152 of *Understanding Children's Language and Literacy*, Mukherji and O'Dea (2000), describe a range of non-vocal communication forms (see below).

Mukherji and O'Dea (2000) define signed language as 'the manual and gestural system of communication used by people who are deaf; the sign languages used in different countries are languages in their own right, and not manual means of communicating the spoken languages of those countries.'

Fig 1.9 The standard manual alphabet: each of the letters is represented by different hand positions

A B C D E

F G H I J K

L M N O P

Q R S T U

V W X Y Z

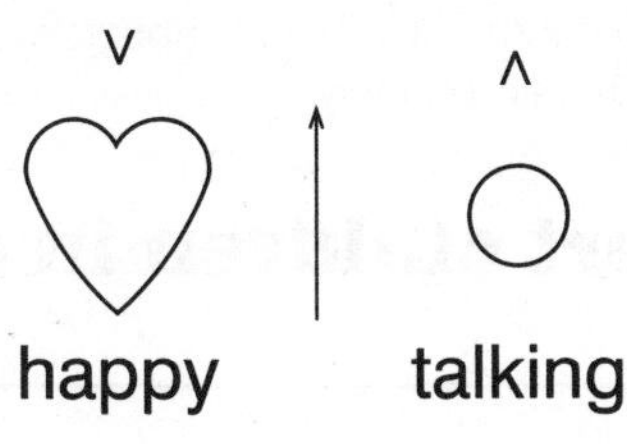

Fig 1.10 Bliss symbols: 'A universal language of pictographic symbols which is used by people with reading and writing disabilities' (Mukherji and O'Dea, 2000).

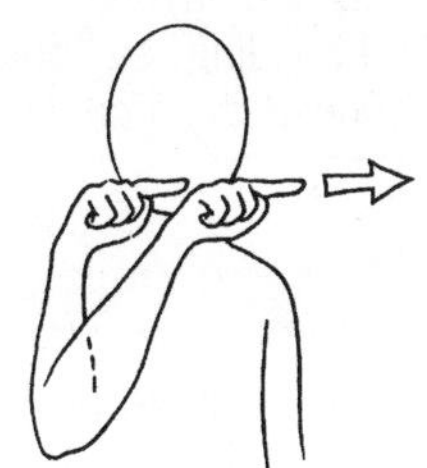
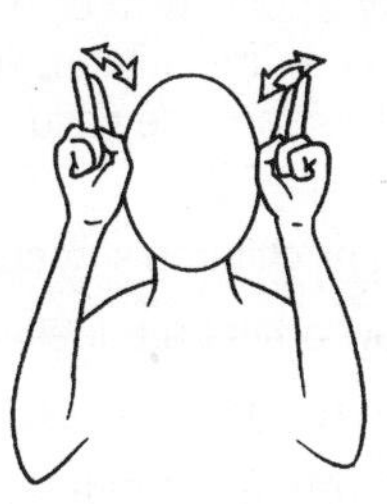

boy
Brush right index pointing left across chin

rabbit
Palm forward 'N' hands, held at either side of head, bend several times to indicate ears

fish
Right flat hand waggles forward like a fish swimming

bird
Index finger and thumb open and close in front of mouth like a beak

Fig 1.11 Makaton: 'A basic signing system using signs borrowed from British sign language, used by people who have severe learning difficulties' (Mukherji and O'Dea, 2000).

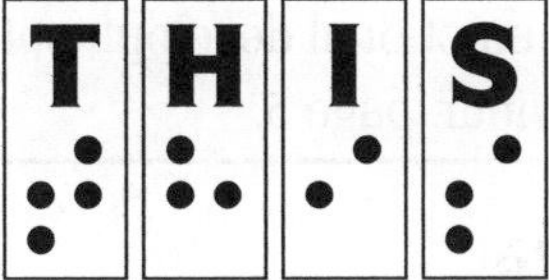

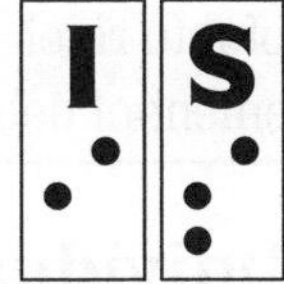

Fig 1.12 Braille: 'A touch-based reading and writing system used by people who are blind' (Mukherji and O'Dea, 2000). Braille is a system of letters made from raised dots.

Cued speech is a 'system of eight handshapes made in four locations near the face to assist children (or adults) who are deaf, in lip-reading' (Mukherji and O'Dea, 2000).

The support of advocates, interpreters and translators

Overcoming communication barriers can involve more than simply providing the right environment and using the appropriate skills. At times, the help of other professionals will be needed; such a person may be known as an advocate, an interpreter and/or a translator.

Advocacy means speaking on behalf of another individual and representing that individual's interests; the person doing so is referred to as an advocate. The role of the advocate is to listen and interpret for the parent or child, following this with liaison and negotiation regarding the outcomes of any meeting or consultation. Advocates are involved if parents are unable to gain access to the services they need because of a lack of sufficient spoken English. Their role is to ensure that the parents are understood, or to support them if they are unfamiliar with which services may be available to them and their children.

An advocate may also be brought in if parents feel that a child's needs are not being recognised by the professionals currently involved. Whenever possible, children are encouraged to contribute to the decision made about their future. Advocates are often involved here too, particularly if a child is looked after by the local authority through one of its care systems.

Advocates are usually known to the family through their role as health visitor, social worker or representative from an organisation to which they belong. They can be particularly useful to parents with a child who has a specific need, ensuring that the child's rights to suitable educational provision are met.

A non-specialist translator/interpreter helps translate between languages. A specialist translator/interpreter is able to translate between languages and also understands the nature of the discussion, for example in legal situations or when trying to reach an agreement regarding how to best meet a child's needs.

It is likely to be less beneficial to use a non-specialist interpreter, as a family's needs will be better served by someone who is able not only to translate between the languages being used but also understands the education, health and support systems currently in place and is able to identify and advise parents accordingly.

Be able to support children in developing relationships

Encouragement

Some children get on easily with everyone. They appear cheerful, smile readily, eagerly make friends and are happy to play with or work alongside anyone within their group or class. On the other hand, there are children who find building relationships and communicating extremely difficult. These are the children who need extra guidance and encouragement. They may:

- be unaware of other children's needs
- be unaware of how others are feeling
- be unaware of the need to take other people's feelings into account
- have difficulty in sorting out differences and conflict.

Each of the above are usual in the very youngest children, as they are at the stage of **cognitive development** when they are egocentric, i.e. they have not as yet reached the stage of being able to put themselves in another person's situation. With slightly older children, however, adults sometimes need to guide them in their interactions, modelling behaviour for them, and identifying and helping them understand when their behaviour has an impact on others.

You may find it helpful to refer to emotional development in Unit 3, page 129, and back to the management of behaviour, page 5.

Distressed individuals

This section looks at how communication and interpersonal skills can help to support others in a range of situations. Professionally, this can involve children, their parents and the colleagues you work with, but socially and at home the same skills apply. At times, we understand how others are feeling (we have empathy), perhaps due to previous experiences of our own, but at other times we cannot really imagine how an individual feels, or why they are so distressed about something. This is where your interpersonal skills will really help you to succeed. You will use these skills in respecting the views, feelings and needs of others and in finding appropriate means of supporting them.

Distressed behaviour

Distressed behaviour can include:

- anger
- aggression
- being withdrawn.

Anger and aggression

Verbal aggression can include shouting, swearing, pointed remarks and generalised unpleasant comments. Non-verbal responses would include stamping, negative gestures, throwing objects, slamming doors and negative facial expressions.

Withdrawn behaviour

When someone is withdrawn, there is likely to be lack of eye contact, disinterest in what is going on, and limited verbal communication.

Reasons for distressed behaviour

The main reasons for distressed behaviour are shown in Figure 1.13.

Threats to self-esteem

Self-esteem can be threatened by reduced confidence, following negative comments, or by bullying and abuse. Children need to be praised regularly to remind them that they are valued and appreciated. Bullying and any suspicion of abuse should be investigated.

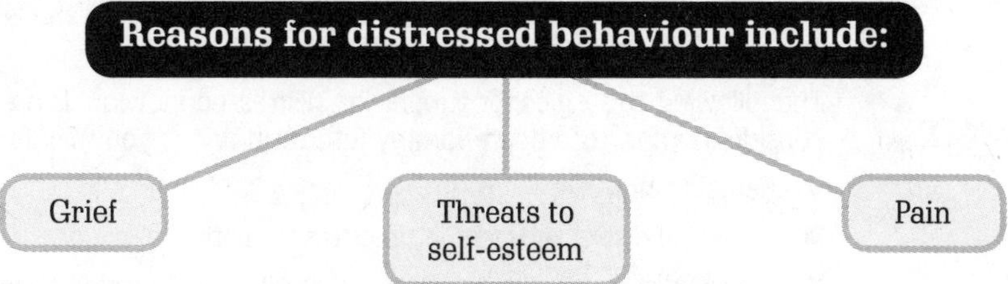

Fig 1.13 Reasons for distressed behaviour

Refer to Unit 5, page 244, for guidance.

Grief

Possible causes of grief are being parted from the main carer, losing a special object, and bereavement at the loss of a person or a loved pet. Understanding and your time will be helpful here.

Pain

Illness or injury can both result in pain. Adults and children have differing levels of pain tolerance and express feelings of pain in different ways. Young children can find it particularly difficult to explain pain to their carers. They often generalise their pain to a site that they can name or describe, for example 'tummy ache'.

Refer to Unit 2, page 51, for guidance on how to check for signs of injury and to pages 63– 76 for signs of childhood illness.

Communication difficulties

An inability to make oneself understood can cause practical difficulties as well as emotional frustration. Both can be equally distressing.

Refer back to the communication cycle on page 13.

Frustration

Being unable to achieve an objective can be hard to accept and may lead the individual to feel that they are not fully in control of a situation. Both adults and children can become frustrated.

Perceived loss of rights

Feeling disadvantaged by a lack of care or attention and missing out in some way can be seen by some as loss of rights. **Equity** of care should be considered and maintained at all times.

Skills for working with distressed individuals

Any feelings of distress are difficult for an individual to cope with, but imagine how much harder it might be if you did not have the skills or the language to express yourself and to ask for the help that you need. Who would you turn to in these circumstances? It is worth exploring who you would turn to and why – what makes them approachable? Is it their calm nature, their practical approach, or what? How do you think you might feel if someone confided in you or sought your advice on a serious matter?

It is useful to consider how you might feel if a distressed person turned to you. Perhaps you might feel:

- scared that you might 'get it wrong'
- pleased that they felt able to turn to you
- out of your depth
- unready for this level of responsibility.

Dealing with distress sometimes necessitates the helper (you) also being helped. This is the same for trained counsellors who are counselling clients regularly and have considerable experience. They have a mentor, to whom they can turn when necessary, and regular 'supervision' sessions, as taking on the stresses of another person can be stressful and, as the helper is bound by **confidentiality** much of the time, the lack of opportunity to 'offload' stressful issues can be hard to cope with.

The following strategies for supporting distressed individuals are a useful starting point when considering how to prepare for any future situations you may find yourself in:

- Remain calm.
- Allow the distressed person time to sit quietly.
- Let the distressed person release their emotions through crying if that seems to be needed.
- Offer practical support: drink, tissues, and so on.
- Use reflective listening.
- Paraphrase, when appropriate.
- Be aware that often you will only be able to start the helping process, not complete it.

Refer to pages 18–19 to remind yourself about reflective listening and how to paraphrase.

Professional Practice

- It is important to remember that there are cultural differences in the mourning process following death; developing your knowledge of these differences will ensure that you respond appropriately to the children and families within your care.
- Dealing with **disclosure** of abuse needs particularly careful handling.

Refer to Unit 5, page 262, for important guidelines on dealing with disclosure.

Fig 1.14 Your interpersonal skills will help you to support distressed individuals

Be able to communicate with adults

Showing respect, responding, and recognising communication difficulties

Much of the guidance on communicating with children applies when you communicate with adults. As with children (refer back to earlier sections of this unit) there are several issues for you to consider:

- Your own interpersonal skills. Are they good enough?
- Do you always show respect?
- Are you polite and courteous at all times?
- Do you treat each person as an individual, not just as 'a parent'?
- How well do you communicate verbally and non-verbally?
- What type of questions do you use? Do you use mostly open or closed questions? Do you use the right sort of questions at the right times?
- How spatially aware are you regarding where you stand in relation to the person you are talking to – i.e. your proximity to them.
- How much do you use eye contact?
- How much do you use touch? Is it always welcome? Appropriate? Culturally acceptable?
- How good are your listening skills?
- Do you understand when and how to use active and reflective listening?
- How quickly do you identify communication difficulties, and what do you do about them?
- Do you understand the range of strategies that you can take?

Refer back to 'Barriers to communication' on page 19.

activity
GROUP WORK 1.6
M3

A child's key worker, Sue, spoke to his mother when she came to collect him. Sue asked her if she had noticed an increase in Henry's spatial awareness. Henry's mother looked slightly embarrassed and shrugged her shoulders. Sue went on to say that a great improvement has been noticed by the staff in the nursery and Henry is pleased with his newly acquired skills.

Sue was assuming Henry's mother's shared knowledge of the developmental term 'spatial awareness'. Henry's mother went away without understanding what skill he was developing.

1 How else could Sue have phrased the question?
2 What effect might the embarrassment have had on Henry's mum?
3 Should Sue have noticed Henry's mother's discomfort?
4 What does this tell you about communication skills and parent–staff relationships?

It would have been far better for Sue to ask Henry's mother if she had noticed how Henry can now steer round obstacles or find a suitable space in which to carry out his roly-polies without knocking others over. This would have maintained a more positive form of communication, and Henry's mother would have understood what he had achieved.

You might find it helpful to put this example into a communication cycle like the one below.

Fig 1.15

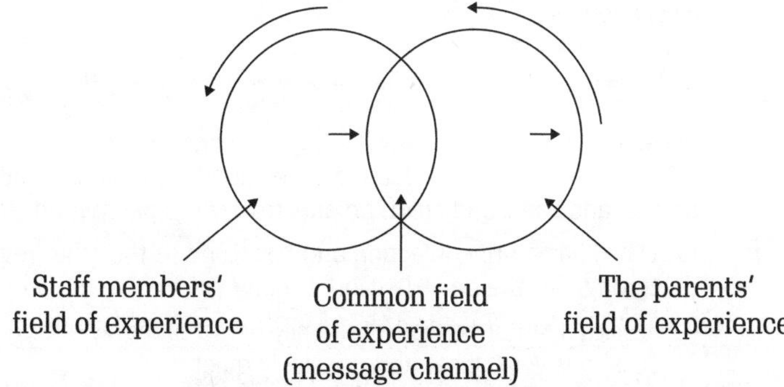

Professional Practice

- When conversing with children or adults, always focus your attention on them fully unless the safety of other children could be compromised.
- Think how you are communicating or presenting information to others. Would your own methods make you feel valued if you were the recipient?

remember

Good interpersonal skills enable you to support others.

Developing your listening skills, having good written skills and being able to present information clearly in a visual format will all help you to support others. Support involves understanding the need for individuals to feel valued, building up their self-esteem, knowing when help is required from additional sources and what form that help might take. As a good listener, you will develop a better understanding not only of the children in your care but also their families.

Refer back to page 17 for guidance on developing listening skills.

remember

It is very important to speak clearly and use plain language, particularly if communication difficulties have already been identified.

Managing conflicting beliefs

Early years practitioners will not always agree with the actions and practices of parents, nor will they share their belief systems. However, practitioners should be working with parents to provide the best for the child concerned, within that family's cultural practices and belief system. Once again, this is where the quality of a practitioner's interpersonal skills will be revealed.

Support for adults and issues of confidentiality

Sources of support

Once you have gained experience as an early years worker in day-care settings and have been made a key worker or room supervisor, it is likely that parents will turn to you for advice. Again, this is all part of successful communicating. It can be helpful to have previously researched and drawn up a list of useful contact addresses that can be passed on if appropriate. These might include local support groups for people learning English as a second language, helplines such as Cry-sis (for parents when an infant's crying becomes difficult to deal with), or Cruise, the bereavement support group. You can probably think of many more.

Confidentiality

Confidentiality is directly linked to communication and will be a vital aspect of your professional role in the early years sector. Confidentiality can be particularly important if parents talk to you specifically about their child, or about other matters that are worrying them. As your relationship builds up, you may be trusted with personal or family problems that are private to the individual or family. You should feel complimented that someone has trusted you sufficiently to speak to you in confidence and that your ability to listen is clearly valued – that trust should never be abused.

At other times, you may have information passed on to you that causes you concern. You will need to decide when it is appropriate to pass information on and when it is not.

Throughout this book you will find reference to the term 'need to know'. This means exactly what it says: the information that you are given should only be shared with those who need to know about it.

activity
GROUP WORK 1.7

M2

1 In each of the following cases, who, if anyone, do you consider should be told this information? How much detail do they need? How could relationships between carer and parent, and carer and child, be affected by the passing on (or not) of the information?

(a) David has a urine infection and has to go to the toilet regularly (and urgently) throughout the day. He cannot 'hang on' for five minutes until break time.

(b) Jessica's father has left the family home suddenly after a violent row with his wife. Jessica is very upset and unusually quiet.

(c) Selina's mother is depressed and takes anti-depressants regularly.

(d) Paula's mother leaves her alone for three hours each evening to work at the local store. There is a coal fire in the sitting room, which does not always have a fireguard.

cont'd

(e) Jerome's dad (who helps out regularly in your preschool) was placed on List 99 when he left his teaching post.

(f) Earl's mother is a stripper in a night club and he is cared for by his older sister much of the time. How have children been supported? What has been the impact on relationships.

2 Now share examples from your placement experiences. How have children been supported? What has been the impact on relationships?

Refer to Unit 5, page 274, for an explanation of List 99.

Professional Practice

- Information should only be passed on to people to enable them to care for a child more appropriately, or to maintain safety of the child or of the setting.
- Prejudging a situation based on 'hearsay' or 'gossip' can be dangerous.
- At times, you will have to break a confidence for the safety and well-being of a child. Whenever possible, the person who has initially given you information should be told if you have felt the need to pass it on. As a student always refer to and be guided by your tutor or placement supervisor.

Refer to Unit 3, pages 162 and 163, for further discussion of confidentiality.

Legislation

Confidentiality is protected through various Acts of Parliament, including:

- Access to Personal Files Act 1987
- Access to Medical Reports Act 1988
- Access to Health Records Act 1990
- Data Protection Act 1998.

This legislation is important because it helps to ensure that personal details are recorded appropriately and that unauthorised access to them is prevented. It directs what may and what may not be kept on record and what information can be kept manually and by using technology. Legislation states the rights of individuals to see their personal records; although in certain cases there are exceptions to this, for example if having access to medical records would be detrimental to a person's well-being. Legislation sets out that each person should know who has access to their files and that records held in respect of any enquiry should hold only facts and not personal opinions.

It would be useful to familiarise yourself with each of the Acts listed above.

The Acts are available from HMSO publishers and are also on the Internet.

D2

Think about the interactions you have had with adults in your placement settings. This can include parents, staff and other students.

1 How well do you get on with people in general?

2 How well do you get your point across? Give three examples where you have needed to communicate something to another person.

3 What impact do your communication methods have on your relationships with others?

Managing disagreements

At some point, you will no doubt have to use your interpersonal skills to deal with confrontation. You may be faced with an angry parent or an awkward member of staff, and the approach you take will make a difference to whether or not you achieve a successful outcome. Being constructive and showing respect for the views of others is what you should be aiming for. At times you will need to be **assertive**.

As some people confuse the word 'assertive' with '**aggressive**', it is worth exploring the difference between the two terms.

- An assertive person is one who can remain calm during an incident of confrontation or disagreement, clearly outlining what they wish to say, and repeating the point if necessary without becoming over-excited or angry. Assertive people remain in control of themselves and stay within appropriate boundaries.
- An aggressive person is one who often talks loudly and excitedly, displaying agitated and angry body language; such a person may make personal comments unrelated to the conflict or disagreement. Aggressive people are not, therefore, fully in control of themselves or the situation.

Assertiveness skills are useful when you need to stand up for something, for example when:

- justifying a course of action you have taken
- challenging a request to increase your workload when you are already overstretched
- declining to change your plans when you know that doing so will cause considerable stress at home, and others are available
- asking for an individual's views to be listened to by your manager
- requesting an increased level of support to enable you to achieve something specific.

In *Communicate! A Communication Skills Guide for Health Care Workers*, Burnard (1992) describes three approaches to coping with confrontation, which are summarised below.

Three possible approaches to confrontation

- **Submissive** approach (pussyfooting) – the person avoids conflict and confrontation by avoiding the topic in hand.
- Assertive approach – the person is clear, calm and prepared to repeat what they have to say.
- Aggressive approach (sledgehammering) – the person is heavy-handed and makes a personal attack of the issue.

Burnard clarifies this further by describing the body language of each approach as follows:

- Submissive approach
  - hunched or rounded shoulders
  - failure to face the other person directly
  - eye contact averted
  - nervous smile
  - fiddling with hands
  - nervous gestures
  - voice – low pitched and apologetic
- Assertive approach
  - face to face with the other person
  - 'comfortable' eye contact
  - facial expression that is 'congruent' with what is being said
  - voice – clear and calm
- Aggressive approach
  - hands on hips or arms folded
  - very direct eye contact
  - angry expression
  - loud voice
  - voice – threatening or angry
  - threatening or provocative hand gestures.

In reflecting on your own practice, think about:

- where you see yourself in the above three descriptions
- who you can identify as using each type of approach
- what you are learning about your responsibilities as an early years professional
- how well you are currently able to deal with aggression in a situation of conflict.

case study 1.7

Shabana

Shabana has just started work as a nursery nurse. Her working day is shared between two reception classes of a primary school. She is unhappy with her list of duties for the coming term, as the majority of her time will be taken up with preparing materials for the class teachers and supervising domestic tasks, such as the children undressing for PE, and toilet duties. Shabana understands that her role is to support the teaching staff, but she feels that the knowledge, understanding and practical experience that she has of young children, through her qualification and the two years of study taken to achieve it, is being underused and undervalued.

Shabana wishes to have her duties reviewed.

activity
INDIVIDUAL WORK

1 How would you put your case across to the teaching staff if you were Shabana?
2 Share your ideas with another student.
3 Where would your planned approach fit in with the thinking of Burnard?
4 What changes would you need to consider?

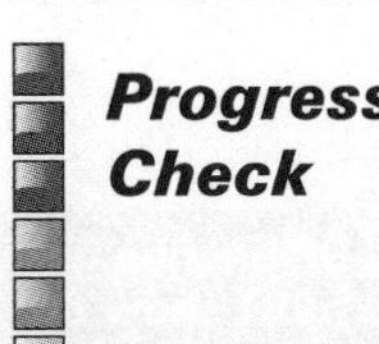

Progress Check

1 What is a boundary and why do children need boundaries?
2 What effect can a lack of consistent boundaries have on children?
3 Why is structure and routine important in early years settings?
4 What does the ABC stand for in the ABC behaviour management strategy?
5 What is meant by positive reinforcement?
6 Explain the communication cycle.
7 Name three aspects of verbal communication.
8 What is the difference between an open and a closed question?
9 What examples can you give of non-verbal communication?
10 What does the term 'barrier to communication' mean? Give an example.
11 List at least five different sorts of information you will listen to as an early years worker.
12 What is paraphrasing?
13 Give an example of reflective listening.
14 When is visual information particularly important?
15 What does the role of an advocate involve?

Positive Environments for Children's Care, Learning and Development

This unit covers the following objectives:

- Know how to establish and maintain a healthy, safe and secure environment for children
- Know how to supervise procedures for accidents, injuries, illness and other emergencies
- Understand and be able to demonstrate the skills required to care for babies and children aged 0–8 years

Children of different ages need differing types and degrees of care. This unit provides some of the main foundations of professional practice for your course, as it looks at the specific needs of babies and children.

All young children should be carefully supervised, but independence should be encouraged at a level appropriate to both the child's age and stage of development. Through studying this unit you will learn how to maintain a safe and secure environment and how to cope with emergencies. Information on diet and nutrition is provided, enabling you to plan, prepare and support the feeding of babies and young children.

grading criteria

To achieve a **Pass** grade the evidence must show that the learner is able to:	To achieve a **Merit** grade the evidence must show that, in addition to the pass criteria, the learner is able to:	To achieve a **Distinction** grade the evidence must show that, in addition to the pass and merit criteria, the learner is able to:
P1 describe legislation and policies relating to the health, safety and security of children in a care setting page 45	**M1** explain how legislation, policies, and procedures for risk assessment and hygiene control establish and maintain a healthy, safe and secure environment for children page 47	**D1** evaluate how legislation, policies and procedures in a childcare setting establish and maintain a healthy, safe and secure environment for children page 47
P2 describe procedures for risk assessment and hygiene control in a childcare setting page 50	**M2** explain how to ensure that procedures for dealing with accidents, injuries, illnesses and other emergencies are followed effectively page 61	**D2** evaluate own skills in caring for babies and children aged 0–8 years. page 98
P3 describe procedures for risk assessment and hygiene control in a childcare setting page 61	**M3** explain how to care for and develop the skills required for babies and children aged 0–8 years. page 94	

To achieve a Pass grade the evidence must show that the learner is able to:	To achieve a Merit grade the evidence must show that, in addition to the pass criteria, the learner is able to:	To achieve a Distinction grade the evidence must show that, in addition to the pass and merit criteria, the learner is able to:
P4 undertake a recognised first aid qualification page 51		
P5 describe how to care for babies and children aged 0–8 years page 90		
P6 demonstrate the skills required to care for babies and children aged 0–8 years. page 93		

Know how to establish and maintain a healthy, safe and secure environment for children

Issues of safety and the security of early years environments are covered in this first section, together with a discussion of personal hygiene, **cross-infection**, accident prevention and risk **assessments** (including health and safety legislation) both in early years settings and on outings. Reference is also made to the safe care of equipment and resources.

Guiding safe practice

It is the responsibility of the manager of any early years setting to ensure that they and their staff are up to date with all health and safety guidelines and information. There should be a range of health and safety **policies** to help ensure consistent safe working practice. These would usually include:

- adult:child ratios
- the control of access to the setting
- the collection of children from the setting
- the handling and disposing of body fluids and waste
- the administration of medicines
- risk assessment
- child protection.

For information about child protection, see Unit 5, page 237.

However, policies are only effective if they are put into practice. The actions and commitment to the maintenance of a safe and secure environment by the adults of a setting are what counts most.

Maintaining a safe and secure environment

Each early years setting must be registered with its local authority and has to meet certain criteria in order to retain its registration. This involves adhering to a range of regulations, Acts, guidelines and care standards regarding the setting up and maintenance of safe and healthy practice in all provisions, including those shown in Figure 2.1. The regulations are overseen by statutory authorities such as Ofsted and the Social Services Inspection and Registration Units (which joined forces in September 2001), environmental health officers, local education authorities and the Health and Safety Executive.

Fig 2.1 Maintaining a safe and secure environment

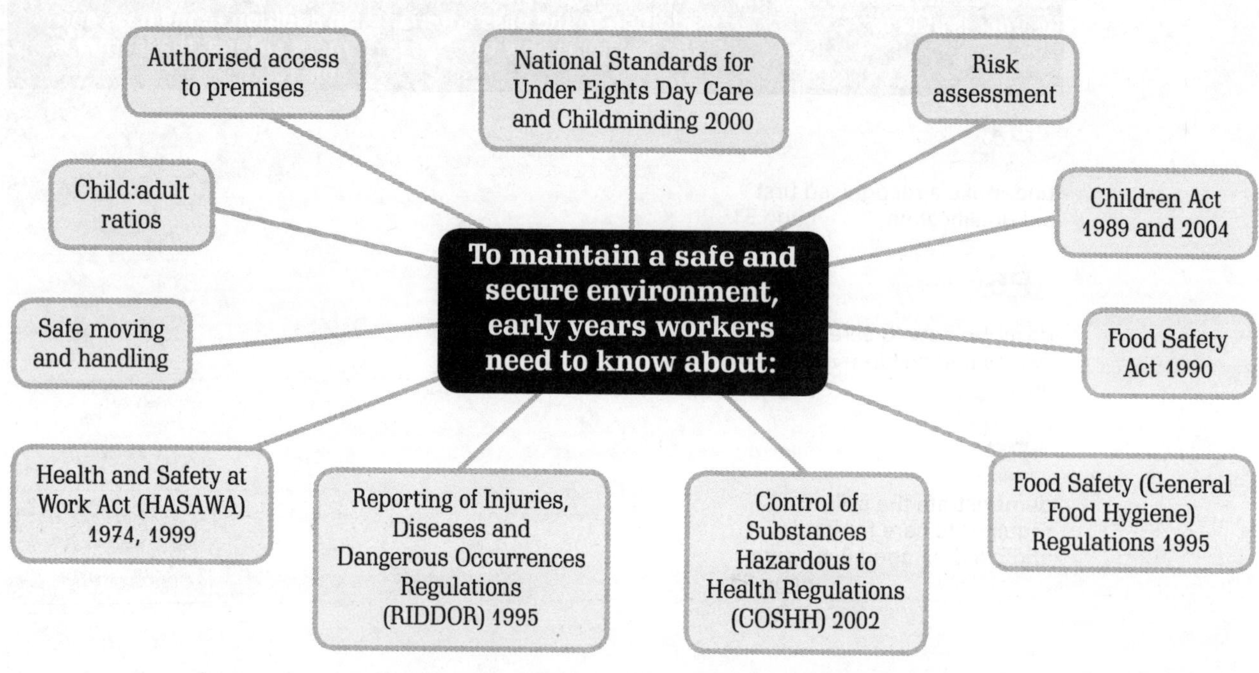

The Children Act 1989 includes statements on the safety of premises. To read these in detail, see *Family Support, Day Care and Educational Provision for Young Children*, Volume 2, Annex D.

The publication *Guidance to the National Standards For Under Eights Care* (2001, updated 2003; Addendum, October 2005) also sets out guidelines for safety, including fire safety (reference criteria 6.9–6.11). The guidelines can be downloaded from the Ofsted website (www.ofsted.gov.uk).

The guidelines referred to above cover the following five types of setting:

- full day care
- sessional day care
- childminding
- crèches
- out of school care.

Settings should refer to the most appropriate guidance document for the provision they are registered as. The main standards from the guidance linked to safety are Standards 4, 5, 6, 7 and 8. It will be useful to compare the types of provision, looking for differences. Each follows the same order for subject referencing.

Fire safety

Under the Fire Precautions Act 1971, some, but not all, premises require a fire certificate. This does not as yet apply automatically to day-care provision. However, advice from the fire services is available to a local authority or an individual provider on request, particularly when setting up a new facility, and fire safety information is usually available. In general, the main points of concern regarding fire safety in day-care settings, including childminders' homes, are:

- accessibility of the register
- the presence of smoke alarms in suitable places
- the means of escape from the building
- the heating and any fire/heating guards used
- safety of electrical systems and electrical equipment

- storage of any flammable materials
- the means of preventing unsupervised access to the kitchen
- ensuring that fire exits remain unobstructed
- who is responsible for checking fire exits regularly.

Children Act 2004 and National Standards

Guidance and regulations under the Children Act and the National Standards also cover:

- adult:child ratios
- minimum space requirements
- maximum number of places in a setting
- toilets and hand basins.

Adult:child ratios

There are standard recommended staff:child ratios for the under-fives in day-care and education settings.

Table 2.1 Recommended staff: child ratios

Type of setting/Age range	Ratio	Comments
Under 5 years' full day care 0 to 2 years 2 to 3 years 3 to 5 years	 1:3 1:4 1:8	Because of management and administration duties, managers or officers-in-charge should not be included in these ratios where more than 20 children are being cared for
Nursery schools and nursery classes	2:20 (minimum)	One adult should be a qualified teacher and one a qualified nursery assistant
Reception classes in primary schools		Where 4-year-olds are attending Reception classes in primary schools, the staffing levels should be determined by the schools and local education authorities
Childminding Under 5 years 5 to 7 years Under 8 (no more than three being under 5) years	1:3 1:6 1:6	All these ratios include the childminder's own children and apply to nannies employed by more than two sets of parents to look after their children
Day care services for school age children Where 5- and 7-year-olds are cared for on a daily or sessional basis (i.e. care at the end of the school day and full care in school holidays)	1:8	A higher ratio may be necessary if children with special needs are being cared for. A lower ratio may be appropriate for some short sessional facilities not lasting the full day
Where facilities are used by children aged over 8 years as well as under 8 years		Providers should ensure that there are sufficient staff in total to maintain the 1:8 ratio for the under eights

Source: reproduced by kind permission of The Stationary Office, from © The Children Act 1989, *Guidance and Regulations Volume* 2, Seventh Impression, 1998.

A higher ratio of staff to children will be required if staff are not all qualified or trained to the required level. The inclusion of children with a special need may also necessitate a higher staff ratio, depending on the children's level of individual need.

Minimum space requirements

Minimum space requirements vary according to the age of the children.

Table 2.2 Minimum space requirements

Age of child	Square feet	Square metres
0–2 years	37.7	3.5
2 years	26.9	2.5
3–7 years	24.8	2.3

Maximum number of places
No setting is allowed to place more than 26 children in one room except for special occasions. This is regardless of the size of the room. A separate room is always needed for babies and toddlers; it should be adjacent to changing and food preparation facilities.

Toilets and hand basins
- Hot and cold running water should be available.
- Water temperatures in children's hand basins should not exceed 39°C (102°F).
- There should be a minimum of one toilet and one hand basin for every 10 children in the setting.
- Staff should have separate toilet and hand-washing facilities.

See also page 39, for more on the physical environment, and page 42, for potential hazards.

Fig 2.2 Children's hand basins

Control of access

In any childcare setting, staff should be given clear guidance on who can enter the setting, and when. Clear procedures should be in place, and consideration should be given to:

- locks on doors
- control of visitors
- dealing with unwanted visitors
- raising the alarm.

Locks on doors
No child should be able to open doors and leave the setting. However, as complex locks can hinder **evacuation procedures**, simple child-proof locks should always be used. Some settings have coded entry and this works well, but it should be remembered that the code should be changed regularly and all appropriate staff notified. This will be of particular importance if there is any possibility of codes being used by unauthorised persons.

Control of visitors
Most early years settings have a variety of visitors; these can enrich the learning of the children and are mostly to be welcomed. It is important, however, that visitors are restricted in their movements around the setting, are not privy to personal details of children and staff, and are not left alone with children or asked to be involved in the personal care of children, unless under the supervision of a member of staff.

Dealing with unwanted visitors

Most settings ask potential visitors to make an appointment in advance. This enables staff to ensure that the setting maintains a suitable adult:child ratio at all times. In settings with lower numbers of children at any one session and where the supervisor is not supernumerary, this is extremely important. Visitors should also be discouraged from arriving at inconvenient times, such as mealtimes or main rest times, although this will not always be possible.

Raising the alarm

In the event that the behaviour of any visitor causes concern to staff, there should be a clear procedure for them to raise the alarm with other staff, bringing in outside help if necessary. Staff should know what to do if they identify anyone loitering outside or peering through the windows. Ask your placement supervisor about the setting's procedure if it has not been explained to you.

Policy for child collection

A policy for monitoring the collection of children should be held by all settings. It is likely to include the following or similar:

- A specific routine for handing over a child – this should be the same for all children to avoid confusion and maintain security for all. Many settings exchange a brief word with the parent/carer about the child at the time of the handover. Sufficient staff numbers would need to be maintained for this to take place safely and maintain legal ratios.
- A procedure where parents/carers sign their child out of the setting – this is quite common.
- A procedure for clarifying the named adult who should be collecting each child – this would usually be set out in the registration document for each child. Any permanent change would usually be required in writing.
- A procedure for checking validity if a different adult collects a child – this could occur if, for example, there has been an accident or delay or the named adult is ill. The procedure could involve the use of a code word or phrase; alternatively, a clear description of the person would need to be given in advance.
- A procedure for dealing with a parent unfit to take responsibility for a child due to alcohol, drug use, etc. – this would often involve social services, as the safety of the child must always come first.

Most settings will have included a statement in their registration document for each child regarding non-collection, or regular late collection, of a child. The potential for causing distress to the child will be pointed out; a fine may be issued by the setting and parents warned that social services may be contacted if the child is not collected.

Handling and disposing of body fluids and waste materials

Body fluids include urine, faeces, blood and vomit. To minimise the potential for cross-infection, staff should wear protective aprons and gloves when dealing with body fluids or waste materials.

Hands should be washed carefully and thoroughly, before and after dealing with personal care, and all parts of the hand, fingers and thumb should be well massaged with soap and hot water. Paper towels or hot air dryers should be used for drying; communal towels should never be used.

Clearing up body fluids

- All resources should be gathered before cleaning up begins.
- Protective apron and gloves must be worn.
- Absorb fluids with paper towels or kitchen paper.
- Use the towels to mop the main waste into a disposal bag.
- Clean the floor etc. with hot water and detergent. Disinfect if infection is suspected.
- Dispose of all waste, including apron and gloves.
- Always wash hands thoroughly.

Administering and recording of medication

Although children who are ill will not normally be attending school or an early years setting, there are occasions when a child has a chronic (ongoing) condition, which allows them to attend as usual but may need medication to be administered at certain times during the day. When this occurs, it is important that strict guidelines are adhered to.

Parents are responsible for keeping early years staff up to date with the health needs of their children. This includes any medication that has to be administered during the child's time at the setting. They should provide all relevant details.

Guidelines for administering medication in early years settings

- Parents' consent to give the medication should be in writing, and signed by them.
- Parents should give exact doses, timings and any other information for administering the medication, again in writing. Any potential side effects of the medication should be noted.
- Any possible contraindications should be explained to staff by the parents.
- If more than one medication is to be given, check with a pharmacist that the proposed items are safe to be given together.
- A trained member of staff must take responsibility for administering the child's medication.
- A second member of staff should check that the dose given is correct and is administered to the correct child.
- Medication should be administered quietly and without drawing undue attention to the child.
- The time and the dose of medication administered should be recorded immediately afterwards, and written records of when medication has been given must be kept by the setting.
- As a child becomes able to administer their own medication, they should be supported to do this.

remember

Each time medication is administered, staff should check details before hand and record the time and dose afterwards.

Health care plans

Each child with a specific health problem or care routine needs to have a regularly updated health care plan drawn up by the setting with input from all relevant parties: parents, staff, health visitor, GP, and/or any other health professional who supports the child.

Storing medication

All medication should be clearly labelled with the child's name, the frequency with which the medication is to be given, and the correct dosage. Storage should be in a locked cabinet. Staff administering the medication should always check that the medication is within its use-by dates.

In case children may need quick access to an inhaler, these should be kept easily to hand and all staff should be able to gain access to them immediately. They should, however, be kept out of children's reach.

Disposing of medication

Parents are responsible for the safe disposal of their child's medication. Large quantities of medication should not be kept at the early years setting.

Professional Practice

- It is good practice for a member of staff to witness the administering of any medication by another member of staff.
- Children should never be given medication that is not their own.
- Hands should be thoroughly washed before handling medicines and after the medicine has been given.
- An explanation should be given to the child as to what will take place, for example, that you will lay them back to administer eye drops, or lay them to one side to administer ear drops, and so on.
- Rewarding the child with a small treat if they have been reluctant or very 'brave' can be appropriate.
- Medicines should not be dissolved into food or drinks.
- Parents should be informed of any reluctance or failure to administer the medication, and the incident should be recorded.

Physical environment

Ensuring that the **physical environment** of an early years setting is safe and secure includes giving consideration to the:

- layout of the setting
- space available
- furniture and fixtures and their positioning
- mobility of the children, taking into account any specific physical needs
- supervision levels
- safety of all toys, activities and equipment.

It also means considering the heating, lighting, ventilation and ease of cleaning of the equipment and the setting itself.

Layout of the setting and space available

The design of every setting is different, determined by practicalities and the personal choice of the staff and management. The shape of rooms, types of equipment and furnishings, and whether the setting has sole use of the building will all have an impact on how it is arranged and how flexible the arrangements can be.

The layout of the setting should allow sufficient space for:

- children to play in groups
- children to use the floor
- differentiated use of the rooms for quiet activities, messy activities, active play, and so on
- displaying children's creativity, both two-dimensional and three-dimensional
- storing equipment and activities, allowing access to some items by the children
- moving safely between activities
- safe evacuation of the building in an emergency
- rearranging activities and equipment without undue disruption to the setting
- staff to oversee activities in general whilst involved in other areas of the room.

Furniture and fixtures and their positioning

- All cupboards, shelving and any other permanent storage must be securely held in place, and any doors should close firmly and remain closed when not in use.
- Access to storage should not interrupt play or be hazardous to children playing.
- Mobile storage should be stocked carefully, avoiding overloading or the risk of items falling.
- Furniture should be child sized.
- Ideally, tables that can combine to extend or alter shape should be used.
- Furniture should be sturdy and be kept in good condition.
- Wooden chairs should be checked regularly for splinters, and plastic moulded chairs should be examined for cracks.
- All surfaces used by the children should be hygienic and in good condition.

Adaptations needed for an inclusive environment

Mobility of children

- The layout of a setting should take into account the mobility needs of the children whom it caters for. For example, baby rooms require a significant area of floor space to encourage mobility and floor play with staff.
- A child with a physical disability may benefit from a more spacious layout, enabling easier access between activities, particularly if they use a wheelchair or walking frame, or need support from an adult.
- It may be appropriate to provide ramps. These will increase a child's sense of independence and range of access. A lift would normally be installed if the setting is on more than one floor.
- If a setting is supporting a child who is blind or has significant visual impairment, keeping a familiar layout will allow the child a degree of autonomy and independence.
- The use of textured edges to specific play areas can help a visually impaired child to find their way around more easily, and provide warnings of a change to the floor surface.

Other considerations

When a child has a hearing impairment, an environment which is tactile and visually stimulating will help compensate for the loss of aural stimulation. The use of vibration-based resources can be particularly helpful.

Keeping noise levels down throughout the setting will benefit a child with partial hearing loss, as what they can hear will be less likely to become lost in the overall hubbub of the day. Noise reduction can be helped enormously by careful use of carpets and table coverings.

Supervision levels

Not only must the correct adult:child ratios for the ages of the children within a setting always be maintained, but the additional requirements of a child with a specific need must always be taken into account. For example, some children will need one-to-one support at all times.

remember As in the home, kitchens and bathrooms are obvious places of potential hazard.

Consistency of care is important, both for the emotional security of children and for the smooth running of the day. However, at times staff may need to adjust their position within the setting in order to ensure that supervision levels remain safe and meet legal requirements.

Potential hazards in early years settings

Hazards can occur through accidents and thoughtlessness but also through poor planning. Early years staff must consider a range of **potential hazards**, for example:

- the effect of a dirty environment
- safety of toys, resources and equipment
- the importance of checking for **safety marks**
- the impact of messy play
- safety of outdoor surfaces
- poor heating, lighting and ventilation.

Consideration needs to be given to:

- potential hazards in the home
- potential hazards in early years settings
- safety issues on outings.

The effect of a dirty environment

Cross-contamination and the spread of infection can easily occur within the close-contact environment of a classroom or early years setting. This leads to illness and poor attendance, which can in turn have an effect on a child's learning.

Refer to pages 63–76, for a summary of common childhood illnesses and to page 47 for information on cross-infection.

Cleaning the environment

This includes both the setting itself and the equipment and furnishings within it.

- Cleaning should take place at the end of each session, or day, and as necessary throughout the day.
- Carpeted floor surfaces should be easily cleaned with a vacuum cleaner, and washable non-slip surfaces should be cleaned with a mop, which is disinfected daily.
- Suitable anti-bacterial products should be used regularly to clean all surfaces.
- Toys and activities should be regularly cleaned with anti-bacterial products.

Professional Practice

- It is particularly important to clean surfaces before any food preparation, cooking activities and before snack time.
- If early years staff are responsible for the general cleaning of the setting, there should be a rota to ensure that it is kept clean and hygienic at all times.
- Staff should not carry out cleaning duties while still responsible for supervising children. They should be supernumerary to the adult:child ratio at this point.

Safety of toys, resources and equipment

All equipment used in early years settings should be made to a recognised safety standard. A range of safety marks are used by manufacturers as required by legislation; these are set out in the table below. The marks are changed and updated from time to time, and it is worth checking for the most recent recommendations.

Table 2.3 Safety marks

Mark	Name	Meaning
	BSI Kitemark	Indicates a product has met a British safety standard and has been independently tested
	Lion Mark	Indicates adherence to the British Toy and Hobby Association Code of Practice and ensures a product is safe and conforms to all relevant safety information
0-3	Age Warning	Indicates: 'Warning – do not give the toy to children less than 3 years, nor allow them to play with it' Details of the hazard, e.g. small parts, will be near the symbol or with the instructions
BEAB Approved	BEAB Mark of the British Electrotechnical Approvals Board	Indicates that electrical appliances carrying this mark meet a national safety standard
	BSI Safety Mark on gas appliances, light fittings and power tool	Indicates the product has been made and tested to a specific safety standard in accordance with the British Standards Institute
RESISTANT	Safety Mark on upholstered furniture	Indicates upholstery materials and fillings have passed the furniture cigarette and match tests – a lighted cigarette or match applied to the material will not cause the article to burst into flames
LOW FLAMMABILITY TO BS 5722 KEEP AWAY FROM FIRE LOW FLAMMABILITY TO BS 5722	Low Flammability labels	Children's pyjamas, bathrobes made from 100% Terry towelling and clothes for babies up to 3 months old must carry a label showing whether or not the garment has passed the Low Flammability Test. Either of these two labels is acceptable. Always look for these labels when choosing such garments.
KEEP AWAY FROM FIRE	Keep Away From Fire label	Indicates the garment is not slow burning and has probably not passed the Low Flammability Test. Great care must be taken anywhere near a fire or flame

The impact of messy play

Messy play offers wonderful learning opportunities for young children. However, the fact that children are engaging with these materials at first hand means that the materials are potential routes of cross-contamination. Also, there is the potential for accidents if use of the materials is not controlled and they are not cleared up appropriately. For example:

- Sand should be sieved daily to remove any bits and cleaned regularly. Any sand that has been spilt on the floor should be sieved and cleaned before it is returned to the sand tray or should be discarded.
- Outdoor sandpits should be kept securely covered when not in use to prevent fouling by animals and to prevent rubbish and garden debris settling there.
- Water should be replenished daily, and water trays cleaned and disinfected regularly.
- Any pets should be kept scrupulously clean, following normal pet-care routines.
- Dough should be renewed regularly and stored in a refrigerator.
- Dough should be discarded and replaced following any infectious illness in the setting to avoid cross-infection.

Safety of outdoor surfaces

Concrete, gravel and similar surfaces are not suitable for use in areas where young children play because they do not absorb impact and a fall can result in serious injury. A more suitable surface for general outdoor play is grass but in dry summer months this will also become hard and unyielding.

It is particularly important that surfaces under and around play equipment from which a child may fall a distance of 60 cm (2 feet) or more should be able to absorb some of the impact of the fall, reducing the risk of serious injury.

Impact-absorbing playground surfaces (**IAPS**) include:

- loose-fill substances such as tree bark or sand (at least 30 cm (1 foot) deep)
- 'wet pour' rubber which sets to form a spongy surface
- thick rubber tiles.

Surfaces should meet the BSEN 1177 safety standard. They should be kept in good condition: any damage should be repaired, and tree bark and sand should be raked regularly to remove debris and animal excrement.

Poor heating, lighting and ventilation

If the working or living environment is wrong, it can lead to poor health and lethargy; individuals may be more prone to accidents and infection. The following guidelines should be considered:

Heating

- Room temperatures must be 18–20°C (65–68°F).
- A wall thermometer should be on display and checked regularly. The temperature of a room should be adjusted accordingly to reduce the risk of children overheating.
- Whenever possible, radiators should be controlled by individual thermostats.
- Fire guards or heater guards should be fitted where necessary.

Lighting

- Natural light is important to avoid headaches and eye strain.
- Lighting must be adequate for safe working practice.
- Accidents are more likely to occur in poorly lit settings.

remember

Potential hazards are everywhere.

Ventilation

- Children and staff work best within a well-ventilated environment.
- Good ventilation reduces the risk of cross-infection.
- Ventilation points should be kept clean, as they can easily attract dirt and a build-up of bacteria.

Potential hazards in the home

There are many potential hazards for young children in the average home, and you will need to think about these carefully. (As a student, you are likely to spend some placement time in a family setting, and you may choose to work as a nanny or a childminder when you have qualified.)

Kitchens, bathrooms and gardens are the obvious places of concern when considering dangers, but think also about the hazards posed by glass front doors; sofas beneath windowsills (ideal for climbing on and reaching window catches); electric leads from televisions, DVD recorders and computers, and so on.

Professional Practice

- **Children must be registered on arrival.**
- **Good adult supervision is needed at all times.**
- **Emergency evacuation procedures must be on display.**
- **Emergency exits should be clearly identified.**
- **Equipment must be stored safely.**
- **Safety glass should be used in any low-level windows, dividing panels or glazed doors.**
- **Window locks must be fitted to any windows accessible to children.**
- **Fire or heating guards must be fitted.**

Professional Practice

- Electrical sockets must be covered, and ideally should not be within children's reach.
- Electrical appliances must be checked regularly.
- Small parts should not be accessible to babies and toddlers.
- A safe area should be available for storing the personal belongings of staff, students and visitors, as these may contain hazards such as personal medications etc.

remember

It is important that your personal belongings are kept safely away from children. Try checking through the bag you usually take to placement. How safe would it be if a child gained access to it?

Safety issues on outings

Children gain a great deal from visiting other places, and for many of them it can be their only opportunity for such visits. There should be careful planning and a full check of details prior to the actual visit. The overall supervisor for the outing should:

- Ensure that the destination is suitable, for example that there is no open water that will completely restrict the children's freedom.
- Ensure that appropriate adult:child ratios for outings are adhered to:
  - 0–2 years 1:1
  - 2–5 years 1:2
  - 5–8 years 1:5.
- Ensure that an accurate register is with the party at all times.
- Ensure that the register is checked regularly throughout the day.
- Check that parental consent forms have been signed and returned before the outing takes place.
- Check that all adults know which children they are responsible for.
- Check that all adults understand their role and responsibilities for the day.
- Provide identification badges for children as a useful 'extra' precaution but ensure that these do not include their name or personal details, just the name of the school, nursery or group.
- Ensure that staff take a small emergency **first aid** kit with them.
- Identify in advance how they will call for emergency services if needed.
- Check that any transport used meets safety requirements regarding seat belts.

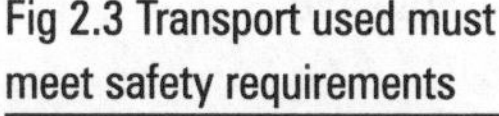

Fig 2.3 Transport used must meet safety requirements

remember

Always check that the coach meets the required safety standards.

Legislation and guidelines

Important legislation to be aware of includes:

- Control of Substances Hazardous to Health Regulations (**COSHH**) 2002
- Reporting of Injuries, Diseases and Dangerous Occurrences Regulations (**RIDDOR**) 1995
- Health and Safety at Work etc. Act (**HASAWA**) 1974, 1999

- Food Safety Act 1990
- (General Food Hygiene) Regulations 1995.

Control of Substances Hazardous to Health Regulations (COSHH) 2002

Health problems such as skin irritation and asthma can occur owing to the presence of certain chemicals in some substances. The symbols drawn up by COSHH have been devised to warn people in advance of potential hazards. Most of the substances covered by the regulations will not be used in early years settings. However, bleach and some other common cleaning products are used and can cause irritation and respiratory reactions.

In schools, chemicals may be used within the context of design technology or art. Although many products are now 'safe', potentially harmful substances include some marbling inks and spirits for cleaning, and some spray paints and glues. These would usually only be handled by adults, but children may be present during their use.

Fig 2.4 Hazard symbols

Corrosive

Oxidising

Toxic

Harmful irritant

Highly flammable

Explosive

Reporting of Injuries, Diseases and Dangerous Occurrences Regulations (RIDDOR) 1995

The RIDDOR regulations require a setting to report by telephone to the local authority all deaths and any serious injuries that result in a child, a parent, a visitor or a member of staff being taken to hospital from the setting.

If a member of staff is injured (but not seriously) or becomes ill due to their work, the local authority should be informed in writing, using a specified form.

Professional Practice

- **Always read instructions for the use and dilution of any product and for the importance of ventilation when using them.**
- **A risk assessment is a systematic check of any potential 'risks' in a setting. An assessment should be carried out by all settings and any potentially hazardous products identified. Relevant information on storage, use and treatment following spills should be noted.**
- **Cleaning products should not at any time be left where they can be reached by children.**
- **All settings should have an accident book in which they report all accidents and incidents, both large and small.**

Health and Safety at Work etc. Act (HASAWA) 1974, 1999

This Act protects employees and anyone else who could be affected by the procedures of a setting. HASAWA requires settings to have a safety policy and to assess, and reduce accordingly, the risk of accident or injury.

There should be a written health and safety policy and a named person with responsibility for health and safety in any setting which employs more than five people. Local authorities can (under the Children Act 2004) ask early years settings to produce health and safety policies irrespective of how many people are employed by the setting.

Refer to pages 49–50 for material relating to the Food Safety Act 1990 and (General Food Hygiene) Regulations 1995.

activity GROUP WORK 2.1

P1

1 What would you include in a health and safety policy? Draw up a list of ideas, explaining the reason for including each point, i.e. how will it help maintain health and safety?

2 Explain the main health and safety legislation to each other. How well do you each understand the requirements?

Professional Practice

- It is good practice to have a health and safety policy, whether or not it is required.
- All staff and students should be asked to read the health and safety policy.
- The policy should be available for parents to read if they so wish.
- Ask to read the policy at your work placement if you have not seen it already.
- Make a note of all areas of safety and health that it covers. How does it compare with your group's ideas?

Examples of health and safety policies can be found in *Good Practice in Child Safety* by Dare and O'Donovan (2000) and in *Good Practice in Nursery Management* by Sadek and Sadek (1996).

Risks

remember Risk assessments are needed throughout all aspects of early years settings.

Think what the term 'risk' actually means. It can be broadly defined as the potential for something to happen that could cause injury, harm or damage to persons or property, or could leave people open to infection through poor infection control. Any person entering the premises of a setting can be affected by hazards that have not been properly dealt with. Such people include staff, children, parents, visiting professionals, and all delivery and maintenance personnel. As an early years practitioner, it is of utmost importance that you strive to avoid injury, harm, damage or infection, and there should be risk assessment strategies in place to help you.

Risk assessment and relevant procedures

There are four main stages in a successful risk assessment procedure:

1 identifying hazards
2 assessing the level of risk
3 implementing appropriate controls
4 ongoing monitoring of procedures.

Fig 2.5a Risk assessments

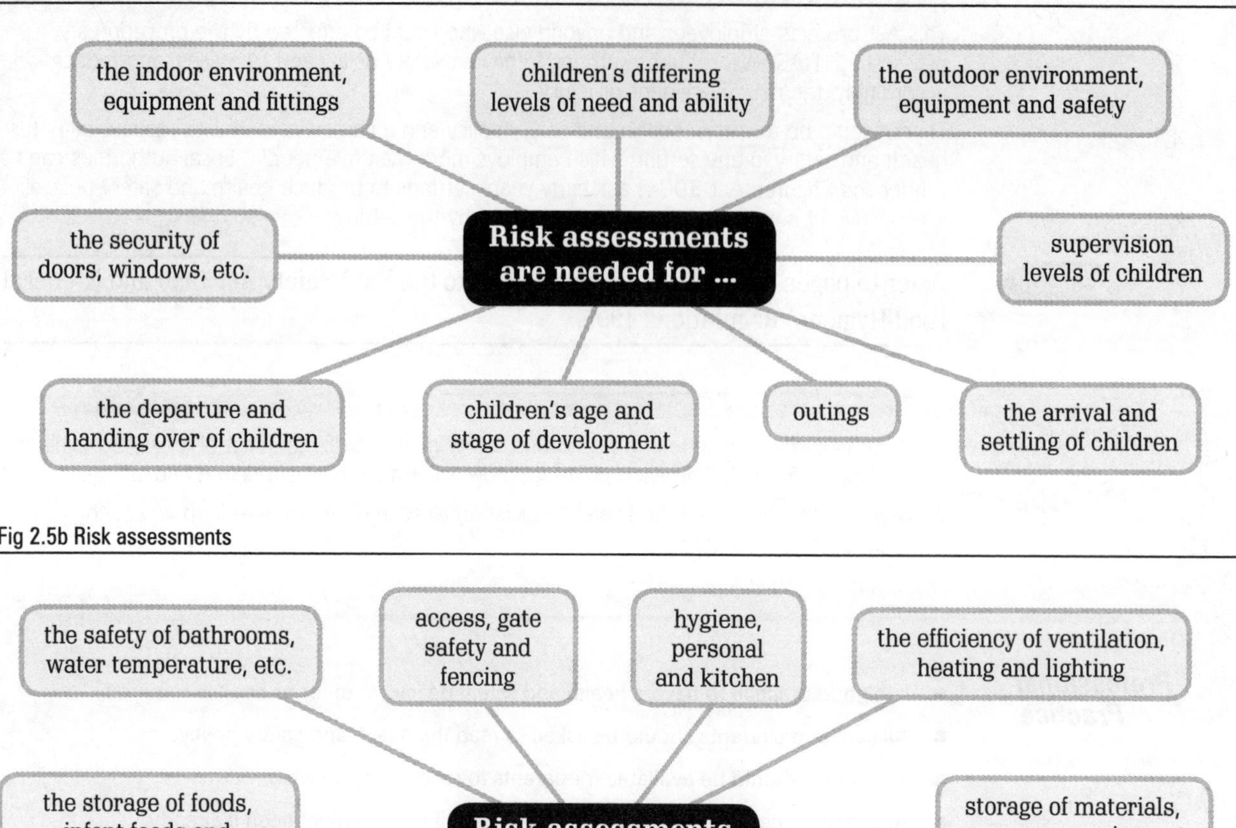

Fig 2.5b Risk assessments

the safety of bathrooms, water temperature, etc.
access, gate safety and fencing
hygiene, personal and kitchen
the efficiency of ventilation, heating and lighting
the storage of foods, infant feeds and individual baby/child equipment
Risk assessments are needed for ...
storage of materials, resources, equipment, foods and cleaning materials
any dealings with animals within the setting or on outings
feeding processes
the safe storage and administration of medication

Examples:

In a baby room, you might:

1 Identify that individual infant's feeds are not always labelled clearly.
2 Assess that this could cause cross-infection between infants and also result in individual infants receiving the wrong amount and/or strength of feeds.
3 Ensure that appropriate labelling facilities are available and that all staff understand the importance of this being carried out rigorously.
4 Check regularly for correct labelling and set up a recording system for this purpose.

Whereas, in the nursery garden you might:

1 Identify a worn safety surface underneath the climbing frame.
2 Assess that children could incur serious injury if they fall, and that the setting could be liable for this as the surface is unlikely to meet safety standards.
3 Take the climbing frame out of use until the safety surface is replaced or repaired satisfactorily.
4 Monitor the wear and tear on all equipment as part of a regular recorded checking process.

activity
INDIVIDUAL WORK 2.2

M1

D1

1 Using five examples of potential hazards that you can identify at your current placement, explain how any of the following support strategies can help maintain a safe environment for young children:
- legislation
- policies
- procedures
- risk assessment.

2 Using one of your examples, consider the likely outcome if the support strategies were ignored.

remember

A risk assessment should be made whenever there is a change to the use of the environment, or part of the environment, when there is new equipment, resources are used for new purposes, or children of a different age or stage of development are likely to be present.

It would be useful to identify and consider other examples.

Every setting should have a person responsible for risk assessment, although it is the collective responsibility of all staff to identify and report any concerns about safety as soon as they arise.

The person responsible for carrying out the risk assessment should:

1 Identify any hazards.
2 Consider who might be at risk.
3 Evaluate the level of risk.
4 Identify actions to be taken.

The aim is to check that:

- all legal requirements have been taken into account
- all staff work to a code of safe practice
- all risks are reduced to a minimum.

Procedures for hygiene control

remember

Without good hygiene, illness and infection can easily spread.

Hygiene includes personal care and food handling, as well as the care and cleanliness of floors and feeding equipment. Settings must abide by a number of practice guidelines, regulations and Acts that help maintain good hygiene.

Cross-infection

Cross-infection is the passing of infection from one person to another. It can happen very quickly and can be an ongoing problem for early years settings, as parents do not always put their child's needs first if there are pressures from work. It is not unknown for an obviously ill child to arrive for the day with a parent who reassures the staff that the child is just 'a bit off-colour' but still wanted to come. Other parents will claim that their child was 'sick in the night but is fine now'. Clearly, this is unacceptable as infections would spread around the classroom or preschool setting.

Policies to deal with this are necessary, and most settings refuse to take a child who has been sick or had diarrhoea, asking for them to be clear from their symptoms for 48 hours before attending again.

The most common infectious conditions that affect early years settings on a regular basis are:

- diarrhoea and/or vomiting – children should be kept away from the setting for at least 48 hours after suffering these symptoms
- conjunctivitis – this condition is highly infectious and parents should be asked to get appropriate treatment and keep their child away until the infection has passed
- threadworm, scabies and head lice.

Staff, students and parents should all be informed about the occurrence of these infections in the setting, so that they can be alert to signs or symptoms in themselves, their child or other children and get appropriate treatment. Most settings exclude children with these conditions.

Refer to page 432 for information about conjunctivitis, threadworm, scabies and head lice and to Unit 9, page 431, for information on communicable diseases in general.

Preventing cross-infection

In order to prevent cross-infection, every setting should plan how its staff would deal with any potentially infective material, including all body fluids (urine, faeces, blood and vomit) and associated waste materials. This is important when caring for children with any infectious condition, particularly HIV, AIDS or hepatitis.

Professional Practice

- You will not always know whether a child is potentially infectious, so sensible precautions at all times will protect both yourself and others.
- Having a standard policy for potential infection will prevent the labelling of any one child, where a known potential hazard such as HIV has been disclosed to the setting.
- Ask to see the policy for your setting if you have not already been shown it. If anything is unclear, ask for clarification.

General points for dealing with body fluids

- Disposable latex gloves and aprons should be worn during nappy changing and when clearing up any body fluids.
- Gloves and aprons should only ever be used once.
- For staff with an allergy to latex, alternative disposable gloves must be provided.
- After use, gloves and aprons should be placed in sealed disposal bags along with the disposable nappy or other waste material, and disposed of safely.
- Blood-soaked items should be immersed in cold water to release the staining before washing in the normal way.
- Sluice facilities should be used to rinse off vomit or solid matter from towelling nappies. The items should be securely bagged (two layers) and labelled with the child's name if not being washed in the setting.
- Wet or soiled nappies should never be left around the setting.
- Following accidents or vomiting, the affected area should be cleaned thoroughly with disinfectant or bleach (diluted according to the directions on the container).
- Soft furnishings should be cleaned with hot soapy water (bleach will discolour them).

Sharing health and safety information with parents

Parents and staff need to work together to support the healthy and safe care of children. Consider the following case study.

case study 2.1

Learn Through Play Nursery

When a parent takes up a place for their child at the Learn Through Play Nursery, they are given a contract setting out all the general aspects of nursery administration and nursery–parent agreements, together with a range of health and safety points. These points are as follows.

- An emergency telephone contact number is required for all parents.
- Parents have a responsibility to notify staff of alternative telephone numbers in advance.
- A health record and details of GP are needed for each child.
- A list should be given to parents of exclusion periods following communicable or common illnesses.
- Details regarding the administering of medicines, including consent forms, should be given.
- A statement regarding the handling of body fluids and washing responsibilities should be made.
- Notification of the whereabouts of evacuation procedure details and the assembly point should be given.
- Attention should be drawn to the nursery noticeboard where general health and safety information is placed.

activity
INDIVIDUAL WORK

1 How comprehensive do you consider these points to be?
2 How else could the nursery keep parents up to date on relevant health issues?
3 Consider the following scenario: a child at the Learn Through Play Nursery has contracted meningitis; the nursery staff have been contacted and have informed all other parents in writing of the incident. What else could they do to dispel the fears of parents?

Professional Practice

- Staff should deal with any incident calmly and in an informed manner.
- It is important to refer only to facts, and not to speculation or hearsay.
- At all times staff should ensure that a family's confidentiality is not breached.

Food Safety Act 1990 and Food Safety (General Food Hygiene) Regulations 1995

This legislation includes guidelines on both personal and general kitchen hygiene. It can be summarised as follows.

Personal hygiene

This involves:

- regular hand washing throughout the day
- washing hands before all food preparation
- washing hands after any activity where bacteria could be present:
  - nappy changing
  - using the toilet
  - coughing
  - sneezing
  - nose blowing
- using antibacterial soaps
- keeping nails clean and short
- covering cuts and sores
- using disposable gloves.

Also:

- Hair should be kept tied back to reduce the risk of infestation, cross-infection and general untidiness.
- Clean clothing and overalls should be worn at all times, changing as necessary for food preparation and cooking activities.
- Covering the nose and mouth when coughing and sneezing should be automatic and needs to be encouraged in all children too.

Kitchen hygiene

This involves:

- keeping surfaces cleaned and free from bacteria
- ensuring that all surfaces used are unblemished and unchipped
- using separate boards for cooked and uncooked foods
- using separate knives for cooked and uncooked foods
- keeping floors thoroughly clean
- washing up as dirty utensils occur to eliminate additional bacteria growth (where possible use a dishwasher as this is the most effective method)
- wrapping all waste securely and emptying bins regularly
- regular cleaning and defrosting of refrigerators and freezers

- ensuring that the temperature of a refrigerator is kept at 4–5°C (39–41°F)
- storing cooked foods at the top of the refrigerator, raw foods below
- minimal handling of all foods
- keeping food well covered
- adhering to use-by dates and not using out-of-date food
- serving any reheated food piping hot
- not keeping food warm for more than a few minutes.

activity
INDIVIDUAL WORK 2.3
P2

1. Check the temperature of the refrigerator at your home (if it has a thermometer).
2. Is the food in the refrigerator stored properly? Are all raw meats stored at the bottom?
3. Is there anything 'lurking' at the back? If yes, check its use-by date and discard if necessary.
4. Ask at your placement how often the refrigerator and freezer are defrosted and who is responsible. These procedures should be recorded.
5. How often is the temperature of the refrigerator at your placement checked and who checks it?
6. Is the food in the refrigerator at your placement stored properly? If not, talk to your supervisor about this.

Food hygiene course

Some colleges include a certificated food hygiene course in their training for early years students. Taking the opportunity to obtain this additional certificate will enable you to consolidate – and provide **evidence** of – your knowledge and understanding of food hygiene issues.

Obtaining the certificate during your training may help you in gaining future employment.

Floors

Floors should be cleaned at the end of every session and at the end of the day, and regularly throughout the day to clear up spills, to control the spread of dust and dirt, and to prevent general clutter accumulating. Cleaning would usually be by vacuuming, followed by washing thoroughly with soapy water. Any accidents involving body fluids should be immediately cleaned up, using an appropriate disinfectant, and all cloths disposed of safely.

Feeding equipment

Strict hygiene practices are paramount in the kitchen and appropriate sterilisation procedures should be carried out for all baby-feeding equipment.

Refer to page 88 for details on a range of sterilisation techniques.

Know how to supervise procedures for accidents, injuries, illness and other emergencies

First aid

Knowledge of first aid is essential in early years settings – the initial actions carried out following an accident or incident, before the arrival of the emergency services, can have a significant impact on the eventual outcome. First aid is about limiting the effects of an accident or incident and taking action to aid the recovery of the person concerned.

Many people will (thankfully) never have to use most of the techniques they learned during their first aid training. Nevertheless, every early years setting is required to have at least one person on duty at all times who is qualified in emergency first aid procedures. This person should be named and all staff should know who they are and where they can be found. All first aiders need to be regularly updated and assessed externally, and they are required to renew their qualification every three years to ensure that they remain up to date with current thinking and show that they can still remember and carry out basic procedures. Nannies and childminders must take responsibility themselves for updating their first aid qualification.

As an early years worker, you will need to know how to:

- check for signs and symptoms
- prioritise treatment
- deal with an unconscious casualty
- use the **ABC procedure**
- deal with allergies and anaphylaxis
- treat minor and major injuries:
  - bleeding
  - fractures
  - poisoning
  - burns and scalds
  - choking and breathing difficulties
  - seizures.

Information about some of the above is given below. You will learn more on your first aid course.

remember

Young children are often unable to describe the symptoms (and often the site) of their injury accurately.

Prioritising and checking for signs and symptoms

A potentially life-threatening injury must always take priority. Often (but not always), the silent, unconscious casualty will be in greater need of immediate assistance than the casualty who is making a lot of noise, even though they may still have serious injuries. Training in first aid enables practitioners to make informed decisions in these situations based on the knowledge gained of assessing patients and checking for signs and symptoms of various injuries, and of prioritising the urgency of each injury.

In prioritising you need to:

- Keep calm and in control.
- Ensure that other children are being cared for and kept away from any continuing danger.
- Ensure that the area is safe for you to be in: i.e. assess if you need to turn off the electricity; be vigilant (e.g. look out for broken glass etc.).
- Check if the casualty is conscious and breathing. Start resuscitation if necessary. Call emergency services (if possible get someone else to do this for you) if the casualty is unconscious or has other obvious signs of serious injury.
- Assess the casualty's symptoms (e.g. bleeding, burns, breathing difficulties, temperature, changes to skin colour). Note any description of feelings voiced by the casualty.
- Following initial first aid treatment, place casualty into the **recovery position** and stay with them until medical assistance arrives.

activity
GROUP WORK
2.4

P4

Refer to your notes and any material given to you during your first aid training to help remind you of the procedures covered in the following sections. In pairs, take turns to explain and/or demonstrate the procedures you have learned. Evaluate each other honestly.

Injuries – the unconscious casualty

Children's bodies are still developing and, to avoid injuring the child unnecessarily, it is not always appropriate to use the same techniques for emergency first aid as you would use on an adult. In some cases, techniques designed for adults can be extremely dangerous to a young child. For example, tilting the head of a young infant back too far may actually occlude (block) the airway, rather than open it. Similarly, if too much pressure is placed on the soft tissue under the jaw when opening the airway, this may block it.

> **remember**
> You should not put yourself in unnecessary danger.

Emergency procedures for babies and young children: a summary

Stage 1

- Review the situation, assessing as far as is possible what has happened.
- Decide your immediate priorities.
- Stay calm.
- Consider if there is anyone else who could help you.
- Professional help should be sought unless only a minor injury has occurred (if on your own, shout for help!).
- Whenever possible, any other children present should be reassured and led away.

Stage 2

Remove any dangers. You will be of little use to the casualty if you become injured yourself. Ask yourself if it is safe to proceed with first aid. For example:

- Is the fire out?
- Is the electricity turned off?

Stage 3

- Assess the casualty for any response. Remember that during the pre-verbal stage, inability to speak will not automatically mean that the child is unconscious. Consider:
  - Is the child moving?
  - Have they opened their eyes?
  - Have they given an audible response – a cry, moan or any other vocalisation?
- If no response is obtained, it is likely that they are unconscious.
- You will need to begin the ABC procedure.

The ABC of resuscitation

A stands for airway

The airway needs to be kept clear. If it becomes blocked, and the child stops breathing, they will soon become unconscious. This will eventually lead to the heart slowing down and stopping due to the lack of oxygen.

Remove any obvious obstructions from the child's mouth but be aware that a 'blind sweep' may block the child's airway further!

Ask yourself:

- Is the child's chest rising and falling?
- Is the tongue well forward?
- Can you hear breathing sounds when your ear is close to the mouth?
- Can you feel the child's breath on your cheek?

If not you will need to open the airway for the child.

To open a baby's airway:

- Place the baby on their back, tilting with the head back slightly.
- Use one finger under the chin to move it forwards (imagine the baby is sniffing a flower and position them accordingly).
- Look, listen and feel again for breathing.
- If there is no change, you will need to try **artificial ventilation** (see B below).

Fig 2.6 Opening a baby's airway

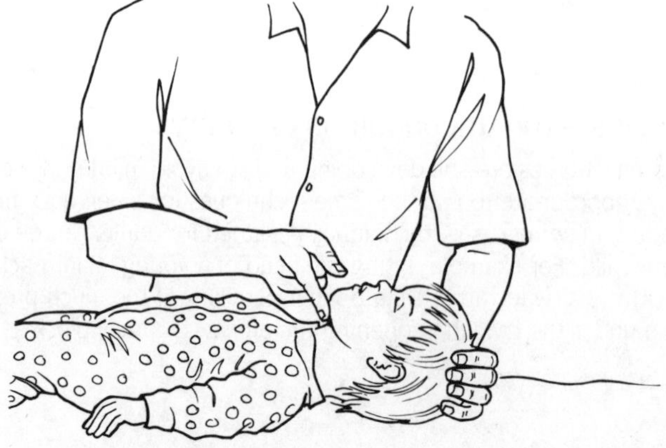

To open an older child's airway:

- Place the child on their back.
- Place two fingers under the chin.
- Place a hand on the forehead and tilt the head backwards, again ensuring not to tip it too far!
- Look, listen and feel again for breathing.
- If there is no change, you will need to try artificial ventilation (see B below).

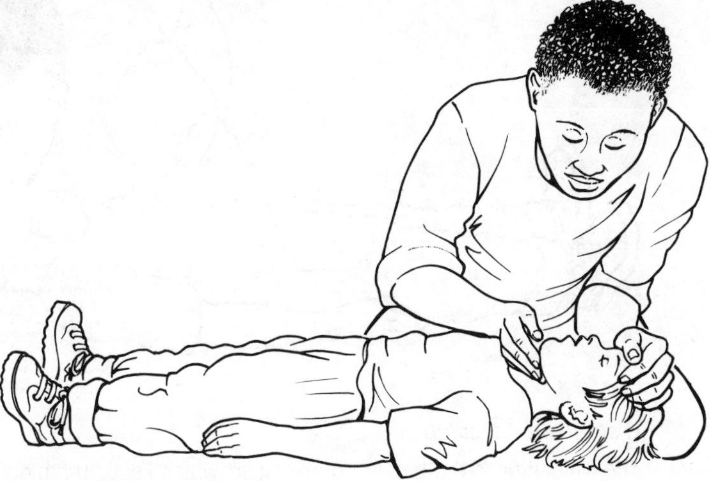

Fig 2.7 Opening a child's airway

B stands for breathing

Have a look at the casualty's tummy. Can you see it moving? If breathing has stopped, you may need to do this for them. Whenever possible, send someone to call for an ambulance. If you are on your own, perform the following procedure for one minute and then go and call an ambulance yourself. If the casualty is a young baby, you may be able to take them with you and continue the breathing procedure for them.

To carry out artificial ventilation for a baby:

- Open the airway as in A.
- Place your lips around the baby's mouth and nose.
- Give five 'rescue' breaths (breaths which are hard enough to make the chest move as though the casualty had taken a deep breath for themselves).
- Continue to blow, very gently at a rate of 20 breaths per minute.
- After each breath, remove your mouth and watch for the chest to fall as the air expires.
- If, after five rescue breaths, you have not been able to establish effective breathing, recheck the baby's mouth and head position and try again.

Fig 2.8 Artificial ventilation for a baby

To carry out artificial ventilation for an older child:

- Open the airway as in A.
- Pinch the child's nostrils together.

- Place your lips firmly over the child's mouth.
- As with a baby, give five rescue breaths, then
- Blow gently into the mouth at a rate of 20 breaths per minute.
- Again, as with a baby, remove your mouth after each breath and watch the chest fall as the air expires.

Fig 2.9 Artificial ventilation for a child

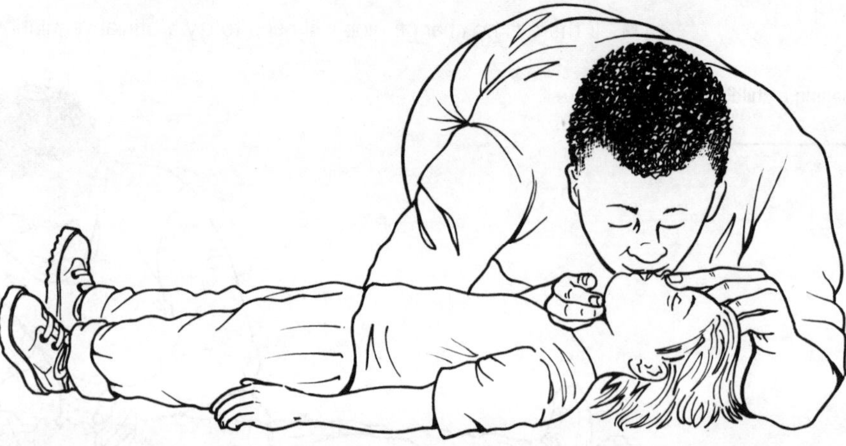

C stands for circulation

The circulation is the beating of the heart which keeps the blood flowing through the body. The usual signs of circulation are breathing, coughing or movement. If you cannot see signs of circulation, you will need to start the procedure known as **chest compression**.

Chest compression

Chest compression for a baby:

- Place the tips of your fingers one finger's width below the baby's nipple line.
- Press down sharply to between one-third and one-half of the depth of the chest.
- Give five compressions per one breath, 100 compressions per minute if working alone.

Fig 2.10 Chest compression for a baby

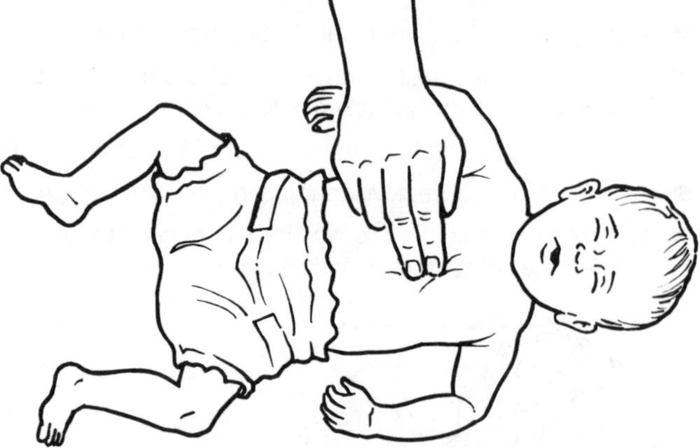

Press on lower breastbone with two fingers

Chest compression for a child:

- Use the heel of your hand rather than your fingers.
- Press down sharply to between one-third and one-half of the depth of the child's chest.
- Work in cycles of 15 compressions per two breaths, 100 compressions per minute if working alone.

Fig 2.11 Chest compression for a child

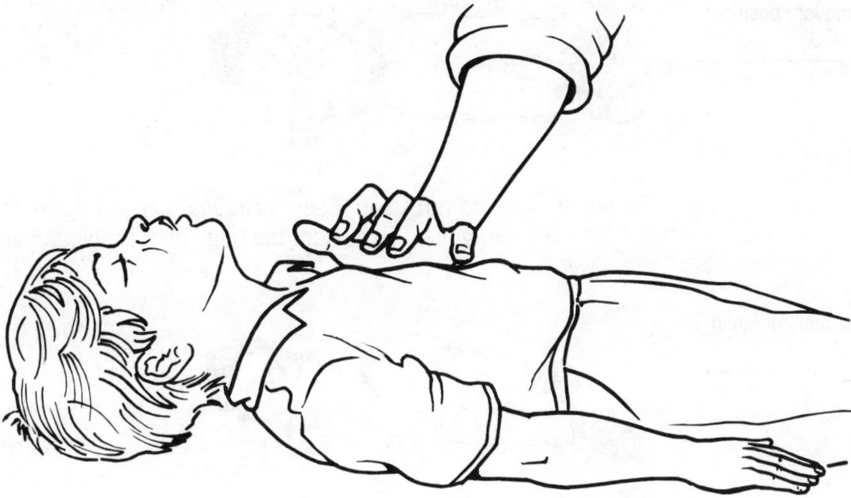

Professional Practice

- Remembering the ABC procedure will enable you to carry out procedures in the right order.
- The ABC procedure needs to be continued until either the child begins to recover or professional help arrives.
- The updated UK Resuscitation Council guidelines state that only professionally trained health workers should check the pulse during resuscitation attempts.
- It can be dangerous to continue with chest compressions once the casualty has started to recover.

The recovery position

Once a child has begun to breathe for themselves, they need to be placed in the recovery position.

The recovery position for a baby

Hold the baby in your arms with their head tilted downwards to help keep the airway open.

Fig 2.12 The recovery position for a baby

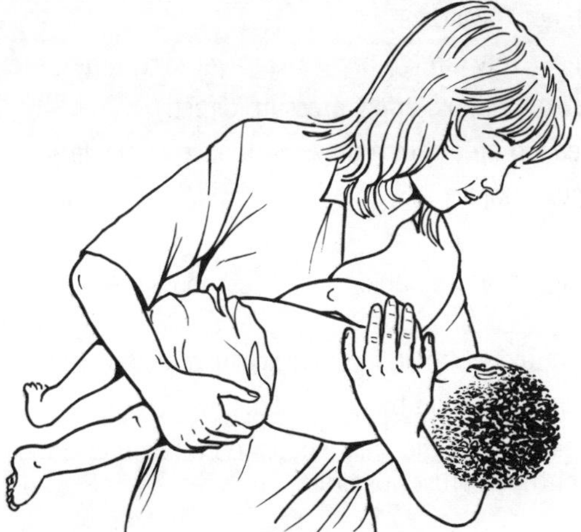

The recovery position for a child

1 Ensure that the airway is open.
2 Bend the arm nearest to you at a right angle. Bring the child's furthest arm across their chest and cushion their cheek with the back of their hand.

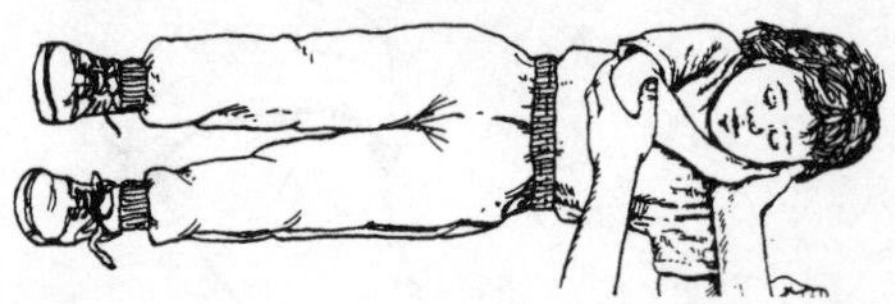

Fig 2.13 Recovery position stage 1

3 Roll the child towards you. Keep their hand pressed against their cheek. Bend their outside knee, grasp them under the thigh and, keeping their near leg straight, pull them towards you.

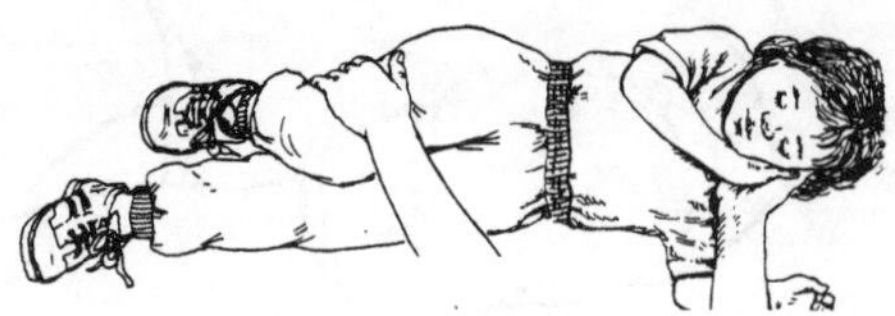

Fig 2.14 Recovery position stage 2

4 Bend the child's top leg at a right angle to their body to keep them on their side and to prevent them from rolling onto their front. Tilt their head back to ensure that their airway remains open. Check that their head is still cushioned by their hand.

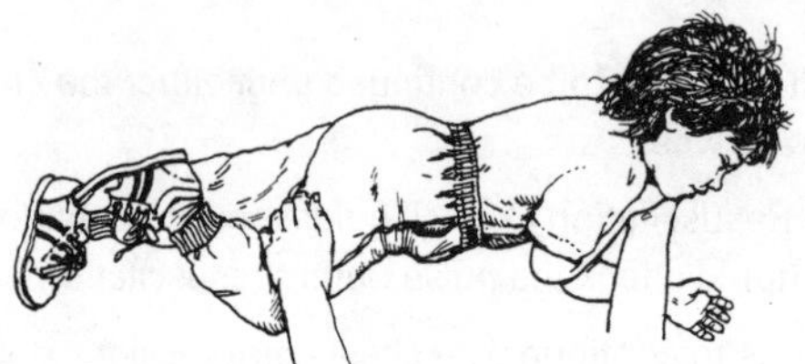

Fig 2.15 Recovery position stage 3

Once the child has been made comfortable in the recovery position, they should be closely monitored and reassured as necessary until professional help arrives.

Treatment of minor and major injuries

Bleeding

For cuts and grazes:

- Sit the child down somewhere suitable.
- Wash the cut with water and cotton wool or similar. Always wipe blood away from the open wound, not towards it.
- Carefully remove any foreign bodies – gravel, dirt, grass, etc.
- If bleeding is continuous, apply pressure directly.
- Cover the cleaned area with a dressing (gauze or similar).
- Inform parents of injury.

Fractures

When the injured person is unable to walk, stand or use a limb, or there is tenderness, swelling and pain:

- A qualified first aider should immobilise the affected limb.
- The child's parents should be contacted.
- If fracture is suspected, the child needs to be taken to the accident and emergency department of the nearest hospital.

Poisoning

If, for example, the child swallows berries, fungi or leaves, bleach, alcohol or drugs:

- Reassure the child.
- Call emergency services.
- Do not try to make the child vomit.
- Do not give the child anything to eat or drink.
- If the child becomes unconscious, place them in the recovery position.
- If at all possible, keep a sample of what has poisoned them, to show medical staff.

Burns and scalds

If, for example, there is blistering, pain and reddened skin:

- Cool the affected area under cool running water for at least 10 minutes to help reduce pain.
- Do not remove anything stuck to the affected area.
- Remove any tight clothing as the area is likely to swell.
- Cover the affected area with a clean cloth (avoid the use of fuzzy or fluffy surfaces).
- Do not apply creams or lotions.
- Any affected area measuring more than the size of a 10-pence piece needs professional medical attention.

Choking and breathing difficulties

These may, for example, be caused by foreign bodies and 'cloying' foods:

- If you can see the obstruction, try and hook it out with your little finger, but DO NOT RISK pushing it down further.
- Lay a baby along your forearm, face downwards and give brisk slaps between their shoulder blades.
- Lean a child forward, and again, apply five brisk slaps between the shoulder blades.
- It is not appropriate to hold a child upside down. This can cause them further injury.
- Seek medical help if unsuccessful.

Seizures

Seizures (convulsions) can occur following a sudden surge of electrical activity in the brain. This can be due to high temperature, infection, injury or epilepsy. Seizures can vary in severity and may present as major or minor symptoms. In all cases, parents should be told and medical help sought in line with an agreed written plan for the child if they have a history of seizures. Always seek help if it is the first seizure that a child has had.

Minor symptoms include:

- a blank expression or staring for a period of time
- seeming very vague and unfocused
- fluttering of eyelids or a slight twitching.

Major symptoms usually occur in stages, initially:

- a rapid rise in temperature
- pallor
- a sudden loss of consciousness
- blue lips
- involuntary urination.

This is likely to be followed by:

- body twitching, often involving the whole body.

The child then:

- sleeps or is dazed;
- often has no memory of the seizure.

Professional Practice

- Always sponge a child to cool them down if they show signs of a raised temperature.
- Clear any obstructions away, to minimise the risk of a convulsing child self-hurting.
- Supervise a child throughout a seizure.
- Once the child is asleep, place the child in the recovery position.
- Record the time, duration and any other relevant details of the seizure.
- DO NOT EVER place anything between the child's teeth. This can cause further injury and choking.

Training

To be both valid and relevant within the workplace, officially recognised programmes – such as the level 2 paediatric first aid course, a vocationally recognised qualification on the national training framework – should be successfully completed.

First aid training is carried out by a number of recognised providers: for example, St John Ambulance, St Andrews, the Red Cross, or independent fully qualified first aid trainers.

Each college offering the BTEC National in Children's Care, Learning and Development will arrange first aid training for its students, but the timing of this will vary from college to college, as there is different thinking on where it is best placed within a programme of study.

In some colleges, it will take place near to the beginning of the course, the thinking being to maximise your understanding of emergency procedures whilst you are on placement experience (although a student should never be considered to be the qualified first aider for the setting).

In other colleges, it will be placed near to the end of the course, the thinking here being that you will have gained in confidence and that first aid training at this point will build on your all-round knowledge and understanding of children. It also enables you to qualify with three years of first aid 'currency' ahead of you.

Some colleges will focus purely on first aid for young children, whereas others will incorporate the full first aid at work training into their programme, usually with a specific section on first aid for young children alongside it.

Refer back to pages 44 and 45 for an overview of safety legislation and guidance on reporting incidents and injuries.

remember

First aid manuals, like all other written first aid instructions, should never be used as an alternative to attending a recognised training course in first aid.

First aid manuals

Relevant training manuals are usually provided by the training provider. It is important that only current first aid manuals are referred to, as guidance on procedures changes from time to time, based on new understanding. Outdated materials should always be discarded.

First aid boxes

Every setting should have a first aid box. It is legally required of all employers under the Health and Safety (First Aid) Regulations 1981.

The container should be both airtight and waterproof and should be easily recognised – the most usual design is green with a white cross. The box should always include a guidance sheet on emergency first aid. Every setting will have different requirements according to the numbers and needs of its children and staff. The first aid box should be checked regularly and kept in good order by a specified person.

Contents of a first aid box

An employer with 10 or more staff is required by law to include the following in the first aid box:

- 20 individually wrapped sterile adhesive dressings (various sizes)
- two sterile pads
- four triangular bandages (ideally sterile)
- six safety pins
- individually wrapped, unmedicated wound dressings, six 12 x 12 cm; two 18 x 18 cm
- one pair of disposable gloves
- one first aid guidance leaflet
- additional items.

An early years setting will also need to include additional items such as:

- scissors (kept only for first aid use)
- tweezers
- several pairs of disposable gloves
- non-allergic tape
- non-allergic plasters (if used)

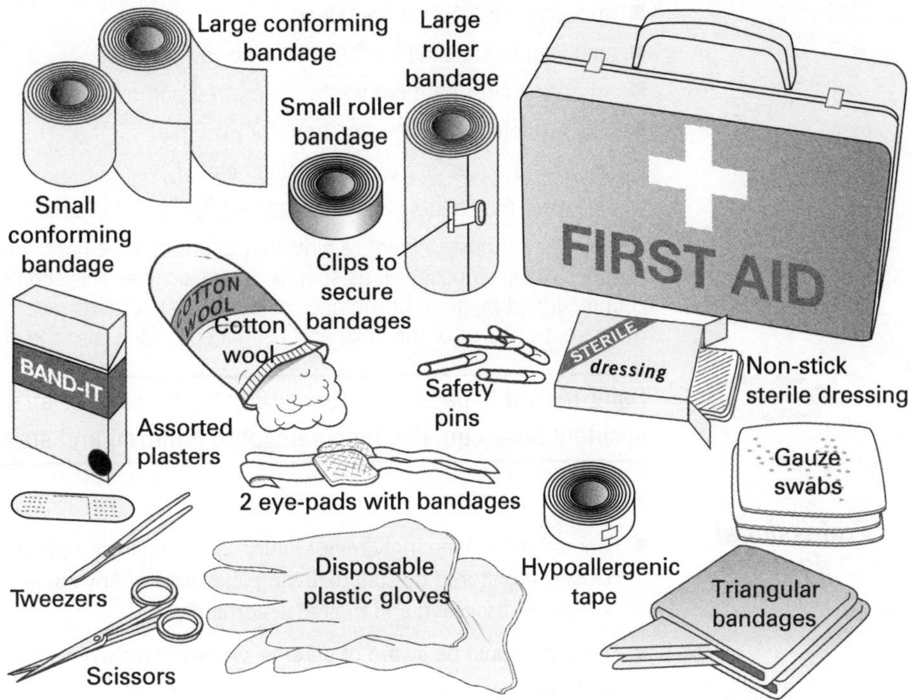

Fig 2.16 Some of the contents of a first aid box

- bandages in various sizes
- sterile gauze
- digital thermometer (never a glass or mercury thermometer)
- a checklist of the contents.

Local policy

Each setting should ensure that its first aid box is drawn up in accordance with local policy. Some local authorities recommend settings not to use certain items, such as plasters and lotions, because of the risk that some children may have an allergic reaction.

Professional Practice

- **A checklist of the minimum requirements should be kept in the first aid box.**
- **A specified person (or persons) should be responsible for checking and replenishing the first aid box regularly, and after every use.**
- **A form should be kept in the box and be signed and dated after every check and each time the box has been cleaned.**

Accidents and emergencies

Parental consent forms

Parents must give written consent for their child to have emergency treatment. Owing to their cultural or religious beliefs, some parents withhold permission for some forms of treatment.

Whenever possible, parents should be informed immediately that their child has had an accident, although in emergency situations you will dial 999 for an ambulance in the first instance. The parental consent form for emergency treatment should always go with the child to hospital to ensure that the wishes of the parents are acknowledged.

Recording accidents

Every setting must have an accident book, in which the details of all accidents and incidents, however large or small, must be recorded. It is never sufficient simply to tell a parent or carer what has happened. A written account must be made, which must include:

- the child's name
- the date and time the accident occurred
- where the accident occurred

- a description of what happened
- any injuries sustained by the child (however slight)
- what first aid treatment was administered and by whom
- any further relevant information, for example:
  - Was it necessary to get outside help?
  - Were the child's parents contacted, and at what time?

Following a serious accident, a written account of what happened should be drawn up, giving as much detail as possible, as soon as is practicable. This should then be signed and then countersigned by another member of staff. Most settings give copies of accident records to the parent or carer of the child and keep a copy filed with the child's records.

Refer to Unit 5, page 259, Case study 5.2 Kieron, for an example of how the accident book can also help safeguard children and staff in a setting.

Professional Practice

- Sometimes a seemingly minor injury can result in complications, so a child should be closely monitored by staff following an accident. Any change in a child's well-being should be assessed and treated accordingly.
- All staff should be aware of parents' wishes in the event of emergency treatment for their child.

Emergencies requiring evacuation

There are many emergencies, other than accidents, that early years workers must know how to react to; these include fire, suspected or actual gas leaks, flooding and bomb scares. Each setting should have a clear procedure for evacuating the building: all staff should know who and what they are responsible for and where they are to congregate following the evacuation. An agreed procedure for ensuring that the emergency services have been called must be established. This is likely to be the responsibility of the manager, but settings should consider what happens if it is the manager who has had the accident!

As a student, you should not be given any responsibility for evacuating children from the setting during an emergency procedure, but it is important that you are fully aware of what the procedure involves and where you should go, and that you remain calm and help to reassure the children.

Emergency exits

Emergency exits should be signposted with appropriate symbols, like these below.

Fig 2.17 Emergency exit signs

Emergency exits should be kept clear at all times and not obstructed by tables, cupboards, activities and temporary displays, etc. Each exit should be unlocked (though childproof) and be easily opened from inside.

Evacuation procedures

Clear instructions setting out the emergency evacuation procedure should be on display in the setting at all times. Copies should be placed near the main entrance and in all the rooms that are used. All staff, students and parents should be referred to these and asked to familiarise themselves with the instructions. Where more than one language is spoken in the setting, copies of the procedure should be translated accordingly.

activity
INDIVIDUAL WORK 2.5

P3

M2

Find out the emergency procedures for your current work placement.

1 Ask to see the relevant policies.
2 Read the evacuation procedure carefully. It should be on display.
3 Note which members of staff have particular responsibilities during an emergency.
4 Look at where the assembly point is situated and consider why this site has been chosen.
5 Following a practice evacuation, evaluate the success of the setting's procedure, considering timing, reactions of the children and staff, and the taking of the register at the assembly point.

Fire alarms and evacuation practice

An obvious fire alarm of some kind is needed, together with smoke detectors in suitable places. (The kitchen itself is not suitable, unless it is spacious, as steam from cooking may set the alarm off regularly, causing unnecessary anguish; by the kitchen doorway is more usual.) Alarms that automatically trigger lights when they are activated are ideal as these allow better vision in a smoky atmosphere.

Practising an evacuation (often called fire practice) should be a regular activity, and all new staff should be trained to fulfil their particular responsibility. During some practices, a different route should be taken out of the building, on the pretence that the straightforward route is impassable. This will help staff think through the procedure more thoroughly.

case study 2.2

Top of the World Nursery

Top of the World Nursery is based in the centre of a small town. Its sessions are held in the first-floor hall of a large community centre on a triangular 'island' of buildings. The emergency exit, which is approved by the registering authority for the nursery, involves taking the children down an outside staircase onto a narrow pavement below, which is the assembly point. The nursery staff are keen to have regular practices at evacuating the children, as some children are reluctant to walk down the outside staircase and staff worry about having to cajole them down it in a real emergency. The nursery currently has a fire practice every two weeks.

A new parent has questioned the wisdom of this, pointing out that the children are potentially in greater danger from being led onto a narrow pavement on such a regular basis. This has worried the staff further.

activity
GROUP WORK

1 Consider each argument in turn and identify its positive points.
2 Consider each argument in turn and identify its negative points.
3 How could the nursery reach a compromise on this, while still practising regularly?

Professional Practice

- A member of staff should have responsibility for taking the register with them to the assembly site.
- The times and days of practice evacuations should be varied so all children who attend the setting experience the procedure.
- Children need to be taught to respond to emergencies, which is why practising is important. They need to be familiar with holding hands, grouping together and standing still when required (for a head count).
- Early years staff should promote the importance of fire practices without raising undue alarm in the children.

case study 2.3

Safe as Houses Nursery

Safe as Houses Nursery looks after 20 children each day, predominantly for full day care owing to its proximity to a large local business.

Most of the children arrive between 8.00 and 8.30 a.m. each morning, with only three arriving later, usually just after 9.15. All the children gather together in one large group for news, weather and the register at 9.30, having played freely in the largest room until this point. The children then divide into their key-worker groups and move to pre-planned activity areas.

activity
INDIVIDUAL WORK

1 Is there any problem with this practice?
2 Would you change anything, if you were able?
3 What might be the problem if a fire broke out at around 9.00 a.m.?
4 How could Safe as Houses Nursery be made safer without altering its daily structure?

Rehearsing, reviewing and modifying procedures

It is important that practitioners continue to assess the effectiveness of the procedures they carry out. This applies particularly to all planned responses to emergency situations. Following any procedure, practitioners should be asking themselves:

- Was the most effective procedure used?
- Was the procedure successful?
- Were there any concerns regarding the outcome of a procedure?
- What could have been done to improve the situation and/or outcome?

Coping with children's emotional reactions

In an emergency, children may be scared to move or frightened by what they see. This is understandable as they will be feeling insecure. It is essential that you:

- remain calm
- give them clear instructions
- remove them from the scene if possible
- comfort them and offer reassurance
- be as honest with them as you can without adding to their fears.

After the event, children may refer back constantly to the incident. It is important to recognise that children sometimes need to talk about incidents in order to 'sort events out' in their minds. Reassuring books and stories, and plenty of active play, will eventually move most children on. On occasions, however, some children may need professional help to see them through the aftermath of a crisis or emergency.

remember

Early years staff need to consider the feelings and views of the parents as well as the children. As an early years worker, you have responsibility for what a parent holds most dear to them – their child.

Information for parents following an emergency

If an early years setting has had to relocate mid-session due to an emergency, there needs to be clear, informative and reassuring information left for parents in a central and obvious place. To leave a message reading:

Fig 2.18 Inappropriate sign

... will no doubt cause panic among parents and carers and much undue distress, with the parents thinking that children have been injured. Whereas to leave one reading:

Fig 2.19 Appropriate sign

... will help to dispel any initial panic in parents and carers concerning their children's well-being.

Signs and symptoms of common childhood illnesses and allergies

Chickenpox

What is chickenpox?

Chickenpox is an itchy and highly contagious condition. It causes spots which blister, weep and subsequently crust over.

What causes chickenpox and how is it spread?

It is a viral infection called herpes zoster, spread by **droplet infection**. The same virus can cause shingles in adults who have previously had chickenpox, if exposed to the virus a second time.

Recognising chickenpox

- Spots appear in groups, initially on the torso; these are followed by more groups of spots, which appear anywhere on the body over several days.
- The spots turn into fluid-filled blisters which weep and then dry after about three days.
- The spots appear in successive groups and dry up in successive groups.

See *Child Health: Care of the Child in Health and Illness* by Keene (1999), Plate 1.

Initial actions

- Comfort and reassurance are needed.
- If the initial spots appear in a day-care setting, parents should be contacted. Paracetamol is usually given to reduce the discomfort.
- Antihistamines can be useful to reduce the irritation.
- Calamine lotion (or similar) can be applied to the spots to soothe them.
- Bicarbonate of soda in a cool bath can also help to reduce the itching.

Ongoing care

- Paracetamol is usually given as needed.
- Use calamine and bicarbonate of soda over a few days.
- Ensure that the child has plenty of fluids and is kept comfortable.

- Cut the child's fingernails short to avoid scratching.
- In young babies, cotton mittens can be useful.

Possible complications
- Some children have internal spots (in the nostrils, throat, vagina and anus).
- Secondary infections can occur through scratching.
- Encephalitis (inflammation of the brain) may occur.
- Pneumonia (inflammation of the lungs) may occur.

Immunisation?
- None is available at present.
- It is important that pregnant women and immuno-compromised children and adults are not exposed to the chickenpox virus.

Incubation period and potential to infect others?
- The incubation period for chickenpox can be up to 21 days.
- Children are infectious for about three days prior to the first spots appearing and remain infectious until all the scabs have dried over.

Mumps

What is mumps?
It is an infection that results in painful swelling and inflammation of the salivary glands near the ear. Other salivary glands may also be involved.

What causes mumps and how is it spread?
It is caused by the parotitis virus. The infection is spread by droplets.

Recognising mumps
- The child appears to be generally unwell for several days before mumps is suspected or diagnosed.
- A raised temperature is usual with swelling on one or both sides of the face. This swelling can be very uncomfortable and may last for five to seven days.
- Children with mumps may not want to eat, as moving the jaws is painful; because the salivary glands are not producing as much saliva as usual, a dry mouth is common.

Initial actions
- Give paracetamol or ibuprofen syrup to reduce fever and pain.
- Offer child frequent non-acidic fluids with a straw to reduce painful movement of the jaw.
- Ensure that the child is seen by a doctor to confirm the diagnosis as mumps is a notifiable disease.
- Be aware of possible deterioration and seek medical assistance if the child complains of a severe headache or develops pain in the abdomen.

Ongoing care
- Make sure that the child has been given analgesia half an hour before eating as this helps with the pain that eating produces.
- Try to avoid hard or crunchy foods; offer soft foods and nutritious fluids such as soups. Food can also be liquidised.

Possible complications
- Mumps can result in inflammation of the meninges (the covering of the brain), and meningitis can develop within 10 days of the onset of the first symptoms of mumps. A full recovery from this type of meningitis is usual.
- Orchitis or an inflammation of the testes can occur up to five to seven days after the start of mumps, although this is usually rare before the onset of puberty.
- Deafness is sometimes noticed in children who have had mumps. A child who has had mumps and who appears to have impaired hearing in one or both ears will need investigating and a hearing test.
- Pancreatitis (inflammation of the pancreas) can cause severe abdominal pain that is acute in onset. Permanent damage is rare, but occasional cases can develop diabetes.

Immunisation?

- Immunisation is available as part of the triple vaccine for measles, mumps and rubella (MMR), given at 15 months and at 4 years.

Incubation period and potential to infect others?

- The incubation period for mumps is 14 to 21 days.
- Children will still be infectious for several days after the first symptoms of mumps appear.
- They usually recover within 7 to 10 days and can go back to nursery or school when they are no longer infectious and feel well.

Rubella (German measles)

What is rubella?

Rubella is usually only a mild condition in children. It involves a high temperature and an all-over rash.

What causes rubella and how is it spread?

Rubella is a virus. It is spread by droplet infection.

Recognising rubella

- The appearance of the rash is usually preceded by a raised temperature.
- The all-over pale rash, which usually starts on the face, does not itch.
- Glands are often swollen behind the ears and in the neck.

See *Child Health: Care of the Child in Health and Illness* by Keene (1999), Plate 1.

Initial actions

- Give paracetamol to reduce the temperature.
- Drinking plenty of fluids should be encouraged.

Ongoing care

- Avoid contact with women who are, or could be, pregnant as contact during the first 12 weeks can affect the foetus.
- No other special care is needed, and children usually recover quickly.

Possible complications

If the foetus is affected, there may be:

- loss of hearing or vision
- impaired hearing or vision
- heart deformities
- learning difficulties.

Immunisation?

- Rubella vaccine is given as part of the MMR triple vaccine, given at 15 months and at 4 years.

Incubation period and potential to infect others?

- The incubation period for rubella is 14 to 21 days.
- Children are infectious from about seven days prior to the rash appearing and until four or five days afterwards.

Measles

What is measles?

Measles is a highly contagious virus with a distinctive rash. It can be a very serious condition.

What causes measles and how is it spread?

It is caused by RNA-containing paramyxovirus and is spread by droplet infection.

Recognising measles

- Children usually appear unwell for three or four days before the rash appears.
- Runny nose and general cold symptoms are common.
- The rash is dense, blotchy and red, usually starting on the neck and face before spreading down over the whole body.

- White spots form inside the mouth and on the cheeks (Koplik's spots).
- Eyes become sore and avoidance of bright lights is common.

See *Child Health: Care of the Child in Health and Illness* by Keene (1999), Plate 1.

Initial actions
- Paracetamol should be given to reduce the raised temperature.
- Plenty of fluids should be encouraged.
- Children would only be visited by a GP in exceptional circumstances but will usually be seen by a health visitor who will confirm diagnosis and, if necessary, refer the child to the GP.
- Children will normally be most comfortable resting with the curtains closed to reduce the light.

Ongoing care
- Give paracetamol as necessary.
- Continue with a high fluid intake.

Possible complications
- Eye infections may need antibiotics.
- Ear infections may need antibiotics.
- Hearing should be checked within a few weeks of illness if ears were affected.
- Inflammation of the brain (encephalitis) can occur.

Immunisation?
- The measles vaccine is given as part of the MMR triple vaccine, given at 15 months and at 4 years.

Incubation period and potential to infect others?
- The incubation period for measles is 8 to 14 days.
- Children are infectious from the day before the symptoms appear until four or five days afterwards.

Hand, foot and mouth disease

What is hand, foot and mouth disease?
This is a mild, but highly infectious condition which is common in children of preschool age. It is in no way connected to foot and mouth disease found in cattle and other hoofed animals.

What causes hand, foot and mouth disease and how is it spread?
It is caused by a virus called Coxsackie and is spread by droplet infection.

Recognising hand, foot and mouth disease
- The child's temperature may be raised slightly.
- Very small blisters are often found inside the cheeks and may ulcerate.
- About two days after the mouth blisters, blistery spots with a red surrounding edge appear on the hands and fingers, and the tops of the feet.

Initial actions
- Give paracetamol to reduce the raised temperature.
- Provide plenty of fluids – avoid anything that might irritate the sore mouth.
- Foods suitable for a slightly sore mouth should be offered (e.g. porridge, jelly, custard, rice).

Ongoing care
- Prolonged mouth blisters may require treatment by the GP.

Possible complications
- No real complications have been noted.

Immunisation?
- There is no immunisation available for hand, foot and mouth disease.

Incubation period and potential to infect others?
- There is no known incubation period.

Coughs and colds

What are coughs and colds?
Coughs and colds can vary from the very mild to quite severe. They can be highly contagious.

What causes coughs and colds and how are they spread?
Coughs and colds are caused by viral infections and are spread by droplet infection. Coughs can also be part of another condition, such as bronchitis or pneumonia.

Recognising coughs and colds
- Colds usually start with a raised temperature and runny nose and eyes.
- Accompanying coughs can be dry and ticklish, or deep and chesty.

Initial actions
- Give paracetamol to reduce the raised temperature.
- Plenty of fluids should be offered.

Ongoing care
- Continue giving paracetamol as necessary.

Possible complications
- Ear infections may require antibiotics.
- Chest infections may require antibiotics.

Immunisation?
- There is no immunisation for the common cold.

Incubation period and potential to infect others?
- Each cold virus is unique and so there is no known incubation period.

Gastroenteritis

What is gastroenteritis?
Gastroenteritis is the most common irritant of the stomach and intestinal lining.

What causes gastroenteritis and how is it spread?
It is caused by bacteria and viruses. It can be spread in food due to poor hygiene during food handling. Spread is by **direct** or **indirect contact**.

Recognising gastroenteritis
Children appear unwell, lethargic and miserable before the onset of the main symptoms, which include:
- vomiting
- diarrhoea
- raised temperature
- loss of appetite.

Initial actions
- Only clear fluids (**cooled boiled water**) should be given for 24 hours.
- Dehydration drinks may be used for children over the age of one year, particularly if symptoms are severe.

Ongoing care
- Breastfed babies should continue to breastfeed as usual.
- If there is no improvement after 24 hours, medical advice should be sought, particularly for very young children.
- Continue with clear fluids, together with 'ice pops' to give the child some sugar.
- Light foods should be offered when the child's appetite returns.
- Diet drinks are not considered to be suitable.

Possible complications
- Dehydration can easily occur in very young children and babies.
- If the child ceases to pass urine frequently, medical advice should be sought.
- Intravenous fluids may need to be given in severe cases.

Immunisation?

- There is no immunisation available.

Incubation period and potential to infect others?

- There is no known incubation period.
- Strict hygiene is needed to try and minimise the spread of infection.
- Gastroenteritis often sweeps through families, nurseries and schools.

Fig 2.20 Minimising the spread of infection

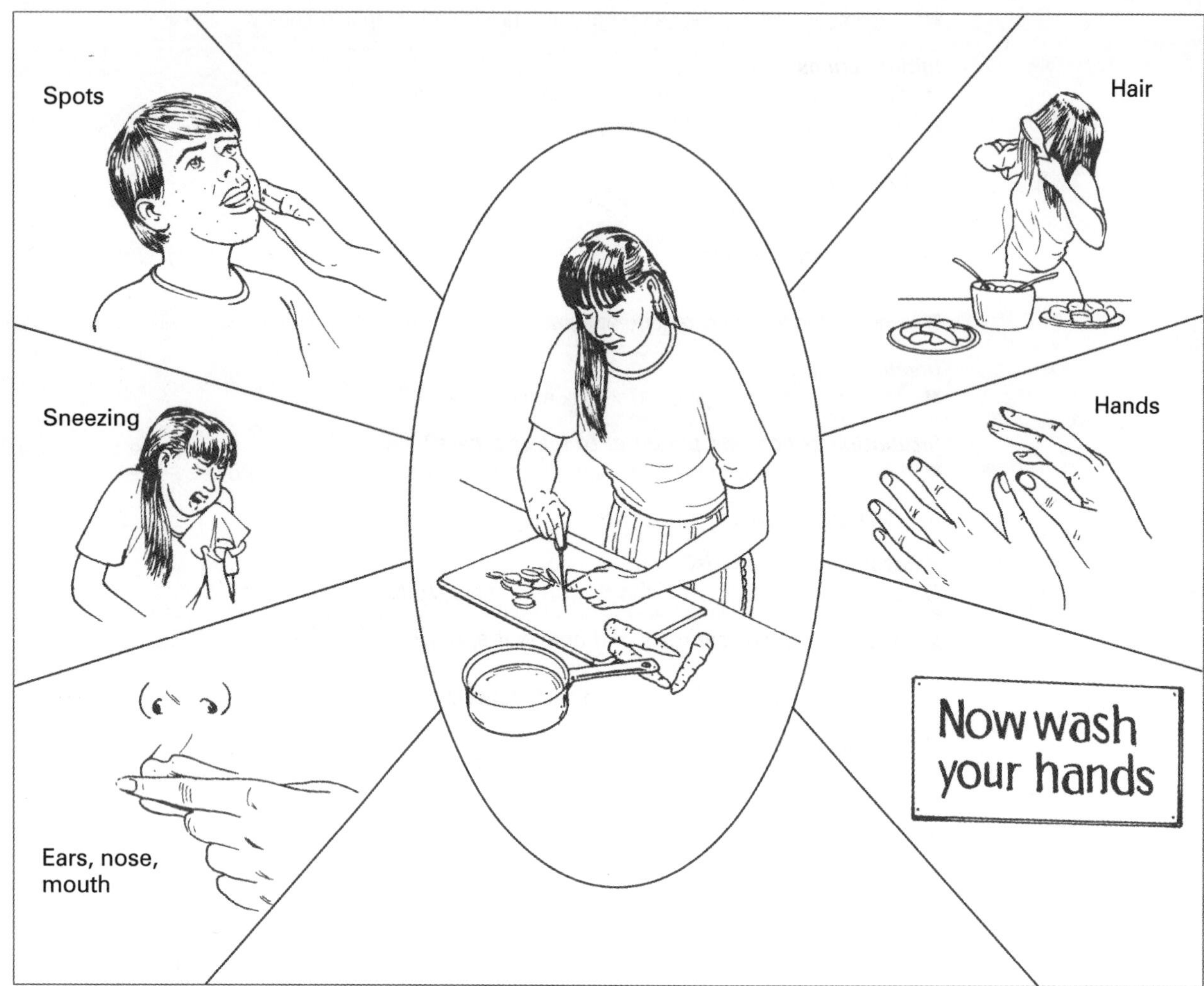

Eczema

What is eczema?

Eczema is due to an allergic reaction and is common amongst young children. It dries the skin, forming itchy inflamed areas which crack open and often weep. It is extremely unpleasant and causes great misery to many children. Fortunately, the majority of children cease to be affected by eczema by the time they reach puberty. Some, however, continue to suffer from eczema, along with asthma (another allergic reaction).

What causes eczema?

Eczema is a reaction to a 'trigger factor'. These triggers vary between individuals, with common causes being dairy produce, washing powders and soaps. It can also be triggered or exacerbated by stress or excitement.

Recognising eczema

The initial signs of eczema usually appear between 3 and 18 months. It occurs initially on the face and scalp, the shins and forearms, and later it affects the backs of the knees, the inside of the elbow joints, and the ankles. Symptoms include:

- dry scaly skin, which cracks and itches
- itchy rash, which often weeps
- crusts over the sore areas.

In the long term, the skin becomes thickened and leathery. Young children find it difficult to sleep due to the itching.

Initial actions

- If a child develops itchy or sore areas of skin, they should be seen by a health professional to confirm or discount a diagnosis of eczema.
- Childcare staff need to be aware that a child's condition may become more acute in extremes of weather. A child with eczema becomes very sensitive to changes in temperature.

Ongoing care

- It is important to keep the skin softened, using an emollient cream.
- Emollients should be applied regularly throughout the day, and this is particularly important after a bath. It can often be helpful to cover the affected area with cotton tubular sleeves (bandages).
- Special bath oils can be used to help remoisten the skin, which naturally loses its oils through bathing.
- Affected children should not use normal soaps; special preparations are available.
- Children should be taught to avoid any known trigger factors.
- Keeping fingernails cut short helps minimise scratching.
- Very young children may benefit from wearing cotton mittens at night.
- Loose cotton clothing helps the skin breathe and reduces chaffing of the skin.
- Some children need prescribed products to help control the effects of eczema.
  - Corticosteroids can be prescribed as creams or ointments for very intense phases.
  - Antihistamines are also used to reduce the itching, helping children to sleep better.
  - For some children, forms of Chinese medicine have been helpful in treating both eczema and psoriasis (under the guidance of a recognised and qualified practitioner).

remember

Any referral to an 'alternative' practitioner should always be with the full knowledge of the child's GP, as there could be contraindicative effects if treatment is used in conjunction with their current medication.

Possible complications

- Antibiotics, taken orally or as creams, may become necessary to counter the effects of secondary infections caused by excessive scratching.
- Children with severe eczema can become the victims of teasing. Early years staff should be ready to deal with this.

Familial?

- Many children with eczema are born into families where there are others with a range of allergic conditions.
- Many will have parents or older siblings who have had eczema as a child.

Professional Practice

- Consideration is needed to ensure that children with eczema are not excluded from activities because of their condition.
- Applying creams to the affected areas during the day should be done without fuss and with some privacy.
- It is important to wear disposable gloves when applying the creams, to avoid any risk of introducing infection to the child and to prevent the absorption of corticosteroids into your own skin.

case study 2.4

Christopher

Christopher is four years old and is severely affected by eczema. His hands are leathery and regularly encrusted with scabs from the weeping sores. He is pale and lethargic most of the time due to lack of sleep and constant discomfort.

activity
INDIVIDUAL WORK

1 The other children in the nursery are reluctant to hold Christopher's hands, which feel strange and rather unpleasant. How will you deal with this during circle games such as 'Farmer's in the den', without making Christopher feel isolated or different?
2 Christopher loves finger painting and playing in the sand and water. How will you ensure that his skin is protected while he plays? What precautions should you take?

Psoriasis

What is psoriasis?
Psoriasis is a severe skin condition which most commonly appears from the age of 10 onwards, but is occasionally seen in younger children where there is a strong family history of the condition.

What causes psoriasis?
- It is considered to be an inherited condition, but its cause is unknown. The first incidence of psoriasis often follows a period of stress or an infection involving damage to the skin. The most common form of psoriasis in young children is guttate psoriasis which causes small patches of the skin rash, often as a result of a severe sore throat. The skin cells form at a rate 10 times faster than the body discards cells, resulting in the thickened patches that appear on the skin.

Recognising psoriasis
- A thickened red rash appears on the scalp, arms, legs and body, often covered with silvery scales.
- The rash is not usually itchy but may irritate as the skin tightens, and there is a general feeling of discomfort.

Initial actions
- The child is likely to be referred to a dermatologist (skin specialist) who will consider the severity of the condition and treat as appropriate, usually with similar medications to eczema.

Ongoing care
- Treatment is with emollient creams, coal tar products and corticosteroids, both through direct application and as bath oil.
- As with eczema, some people will benefit from Chinese medicines in the treatment of psoriasis.

Possible complications
- Secondary infections can occur.
- Social isolation is possible if the condition is very noticeable.

Familial?
- Psoriasis is considered to be an inherited condition.
- It is also a condition for life, although for many people it can be managed quite well with medication.

remember Any referral to an 'alternative' practitioner should always be with the full knowledge of the child's GP, as there could be contraindicative effects if treatment is used in conjunction with their current medication.

Asthma

What is asthma?
Asthma is a condition of the lungs. It is a narrowing of the airways, which is reversible with the right treatment. The narrowing of the airways reduces the child's ability to breathe freely. The walls of the airways (bronchioles) swell and become inflamed. The inflamed airways secrete a sticky mass.

What causes asthma?

An asthma attack can be caused by a variety of triggers:

- infections
- going out into the cold air
- cigarette smoke
- exercise
- excitement or stress
- fumes (e.g. from cars)
- allergies to animals
- allergies to pollen or dust
- food allergies.

Many children with asthma belong to families where allergies are common.

Fig 2.21 Triggers for asthma

Recognising an asthma attack

Likely symptoms are:

- coughing
- shortness of breath
- wheezing
- a tightness in the chest area.

Initial actions

- You will need to keep calm in order to encourage calm in the child.
- If this is a child's first attack, seek medical help.

Managing an attack

Keene (1999) sets out a 10-point plan for managing an asthma attack:

1. Reassure the child.
2. Encourage relaxed breathing – slowly and deeply.
3. Loosen tight clothing around the neck.
4. Sit the child so that they are upright and leaning forward, supporting themselves with their hands in any comfortable position.
5. Stay with the child.
6. Give the child their bronchodilator to inhale if they are known asthmatics – dosage according to the GP's instructions.

remember Each setting should have a written plan for each known asthmatic child, issued by the asthma nurse at the child's GP practice.

7 Offer a warm drink to relieve dryness of the mouth.
8 Continue to comfort and reassure. Do not panic as this will increase the child's anxiety which will impair their breathing.
9 When the child has recovered from a minor attack, they can resume quiet activities.
10 Report the attack to the parents when the child is collected. If the child is upset by the episode, the parents should be contacted immediately.

An ambulance should be called if:

- It is the child's first known attack.
- After 5 to 10 minutes there is no improvement in the child.
- The child becomes increasingly distressed and exhausted.
- Blueness of lips, mouth or face begins to occur.

Ongoing care

There are two different types of inhalers:

- Preventers contain medicines to reduce the swelling and mucus in the airways; they are usually in brown/orange inhalers and are used on a regular basis to prevent asthma attacks.
- Relievers contain medication that dilates the airways; they are usually in blue inhalers and are used to relieve symptoms of wheezing and coughing when an attack occurs or are used prior to exercise to prevent an attack.

Possible complications

- Each year a small number of children die during an asthma attack.

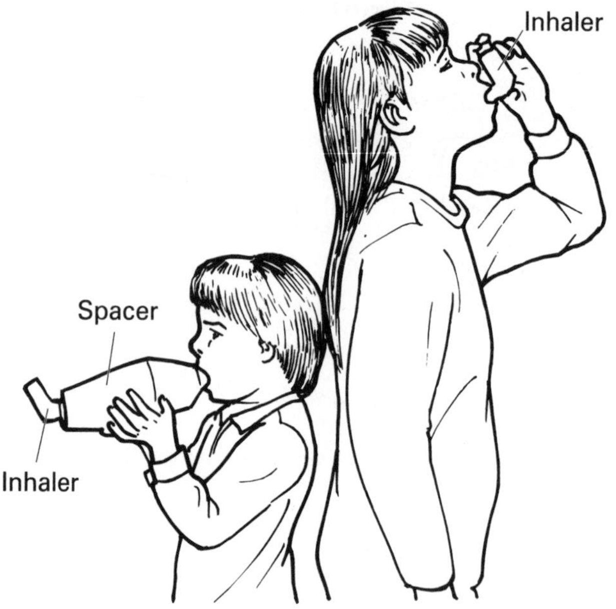

Fig 2.22 Spacers are used to enable very young children to inhale their medication more easily

Cystic fibrosis

What is cystic fibrosis?

Cystic fibrosis (CF) is a serious genetic condition of the respiratory and digestive systems. It is a life-limiting condition in which the secretions produced by the lungs are not able to flow away in the normal way. The secretions build up in the airways, and this subsequently restricts breathing. Risk of infection of the airways is high.

The digestive tract is affected as the pancreas is not able to produce the appropriate enzymes needed to break down the food and absorb it into the body's system.

What causes cystic fibrosis?

CF is inherited as an autosomal recessive condition. Approximately one in 1500 children has CF. It is more prevalent in some ethnic groups than others. The highest incidence is seen in Caucasians (light-skinned people of European, North African, SW Asian and Indian origin).

It is rare in families of African-Caribbean origin and almost non-existent in people of Far Eastern origin.

Recognising cystic fibrosis

- CF is present in some infants from birth. It is detected by the presence of a blockage (called meconium ileus) at the opening of the intestine.
- The Guthrie test at seven days after birth includes a test for CF.
- Infants not diagnosed at birth may fail to thrive during the first few months of life due to malabsorption of food.
- Chest infections and coughs may indicate CF chest problems.
- Diarrhoea and fatty offensive stools may indicate CF digestive problems.

Initial actions

- Any suspicion of CF must be referred immediately to the GP.
- A 'sweat' test is occasionally the initial action, if parents have noticed a salty taste to their child's skin, but this form of testing can be quite distressing for a child.
- Genetic testing will confirm whether the suspected diagnosis is correct.

Ongoing care

The ongoing care of a child with CF involves:

- physiotherapy of the chest at regular intervals throughout the day to loosen secretions (known as percussion physiotherapy)
- regular exercise to help expand the lungs regularly
- antibiotics to prevent chest infections
- pancreatic enzyme supplements, taken at each mealtime to help absorb food
- a diet that is low in fat, but high in protein and carbohydrates.

Children with CF will have continuous care and support from a dietician, a community children's nurse and/or a CF specialist.

Possible complications

- During periods of exacerbation or infection the physiotherapy sessions may need to be more intensive.
- Infections will sometimes result in admission to hospital.
- Some children also develop diabetes (the only type in which a high-carbohydrate/sugar intake is given).
- There is no cure for CF.
- A high-carbohydrate diet usually allows a longer and better quality of life.
- Some children benefit from heart-lung transplants.
- Currently, individuals with CF do not usually live into old age.

Diabetes mellitus (type 1 diabetes)

What is diabetes mellitus?

Diabetes mellitus is an endocrine disorder in which the pancreas does not make enough insulin. Insulin helps the body to use and store sugar; when it is not used efficiently, the sugar overflows into the urine.

What causes diabetes mellitus?

It is often triggered following a severe viral infection. Although it is not an inherited condition, there is a familial trait to diabetes.

Recognising diabetes mellitus

Most children are diagnosed following a sudden onset of the two most common symptoms:

- extreme thirst
- frequently passing urine.

Also the breath may smell of pear drops.

Less obvious onset includes:

- tiredness
- constant lethargy

- weight loss
- loss of appetite
- urinary tract infection due to excessive sugar in the urine.

Initial actions

- Medical diagnosis involves the testing of urine and blood for excessive sugar levels.
- A short stay in hospital is usual in order for the child's blood sugar levels to be stabilised and their dietary needs agreed and understood by parents.

Ongoing care

- Insulin injections and a carefully controlled diet will be necessary for life.
- Checks on blood sugar levels are taken (at least) daily.
- Diet will be monitored by a dietician.
- A 'healthy heart' diet is needed (high fibre, low sugar, low fat). Good long-term dietary care will help prevent other ill health, such as heart, liver and vascular disease, and eye disease.
- A return to hospital is unlikely, unless illness causes dehydration.

Possible complications

- Dehydration is likely.
- An imbalance of blood sugar levels can lead to either hypoglycaemia (sugar levels are too low) or hyperglycaemia (sugar levels are too high, so extra insulin is needed).
- Signs of a hypoglycaemic attack include clammy skin, sweating, dizziness, confusion and rapid breathing. A snack or a glucose drink or similar should be given to the child as extra sugar or a boost of sugar is needed. It is important that someone remains with the child until they have stabilised.
- Illness, underdosing on insulin and sudden **growth** spurts can both affect the blood sugar level balance.

See *Child Health: Care of the Child in Health and Illness* by Keene (1999), page 259.

Fig 2.23 Blood glucose is kept steady by a balance between exercise and insulin on one side and carbohydrates, excitement and infection on the other

Common reasons for hypoglycaemia are:

- unusual exercise (e.g. extra games)
- not enough carbohydrate (e.g. missed snack)
- too much insulin (mistaken dose).

Common reasons for hyperglycaemia are:

- less exercise than usual (e.g. missed games)
- not enough insulin (e.g. growing out of dose)
- too much carbohydrate (e.g. extra snacks)

- sudden excitement or strain (e.g. exams)
- infection (e.g. cold).

Professional Practice

- Supplies of glucose tablets should be readily available in the school or early years setting and should be taken with you when you accompany a child with diabetes on any outing.
- Staff working with a child with diabetes should be taught how to cope with their needs and with attacks.
- Children with diabetes should be closely observed during exercise, particularly if they are trying something new.
- Privacy should be allowed when children need to test their blood sugar levels during the day.
- Catering staff should be informed and be able to deal with special dietary requirements.
- Contact numbers for parents should always be readily available.

case study 2.5

William

William is five years old and is diabetic. He is on his first school trip to the zoo. He is very excited and has rushed around from enclosure to enclosure during the morning. At lunch time, William was so busy talking to his friends about their favourite animals that he did not eat very much of his packed lunch. As the afternoon wore on, William became lethargic and by the time he got onto the coach he was sweating a great deal and stumbled getting into his seat. Other children were also tired and stumbling.

activity
INDIVIDUAL WORK

1 Would you be concerned about William?
2 What signs of hypoglycaemia is William possibly displaying?
3 What would you do initially?
4 With hindsight, what else should staff have done?
5 What have you learned from this case study?

Coeliac disease

Fig 2.24 The gluten-free symbol

What is coeliac disease?
Coeliac disease is a condition affecting the lining of the small intestine. It is an immunological reaction to gluten, a protein found in wheat, rye and barley; some people also have the reaction to oats. Children are usually diagnosed when they start to have solid food from about six months onwards. In adults, coeliac disease can occur at any time, often triggered by an unknown cause.

What causes coeliac disease?
The reaction to gluten causes the villi protrusions along the intestine to become flattened, reducing the surface available for absorption of food.

Recognising coeliac disease

- Babies fail to thrive in the usual way; they do not put on weight and are low on the **centile charts**.
- Young children become very unwell, lethargic and miserable, with abdominal bloating.
- Stools are pale, fatty, smell unpleasant and are difficult to flush away.

Initial actions

- There has usually been some concern shown for the child (or adult) prior to diagnosis.
- Blood tests and faecal samples are taken initially.
- A biopsy of the jejunum usually follows if concerns are raised from the results of tests on blood and faeces.
- A dietary 'challenge' would be carried out in early puberty.

Ongoing care

- A gluten-free diet is necessary throughout life. Gluten is found in many everyday foods, and it takes time to identify all foods that should be avoided.
- Guidance is given from a dietician to help establish a balanced diet.
- Coeliac UK gives helpful advice and provides a regularly updated food list.
- Many supermarkets now display a gluten-free symbol on suitable foods.
- Since November 2005, it is a legal requirement that all forms of gluten are indicated on packaging.

Possible complications

- Iron deficiency anaemia is a possibility due to malabsorption of food.
- Calcium deficiency can also be present, again due to malabsorption.
- In the long term, there is a higher incidence of intestinal cancer in people with untreated coeliac disease.
- For individuals diagnosed at later ages, further problems can occur:
    - osteoporosis, which is a calcium-deficient condition resulting in repeated fractures
    - osteopaenia, which indicates borderline osteoporosis and is often picked up during bone density scanning for osteoporosis.

Bone density scans are offered for individuals where either condition is suspected or calcium supplements (with vitamin D) are then recommended for life.

Familial?

There is a familial tendency, but coeliac disease is not considered hereditary. Babies born into a family where coeliac disease has previously been diagnosed should be observed closely for early signs and some health practitioners recommend that gluten should ideally be withheld from the diet until the first birthday. In some cases, early exposure to gluten has been thought to have triggered the condition.

Understand and be able to demonstrate the skills required to care for babies and children aged 0–8 years

Human infants are totally dependent on their carers for all their health, care and developmental needs. Caring for babies takes a great deal of time, patience and energy. It is, however, extremely rewarding. Babies are usually very responsive to the adults who care for them, showing enjoyment of cuddles and close contact and rewarding the adult with smiles and by vocalising. The needs of young babies are simple: to be kept warm, clean, fed, happy and stimulated. Their care should be viewed holistically (looking at the baby as a whole person), rather than by compartmentalising their care into feeds, physical care and stimulation, as each of these areas is interrelated. Caring for babies includes caring for their environment, their diet, establishing a daily routine, providing stimulation and managing their times of distress. Caring for their physical needs includes their skin, hair and tooth care, bathing and nappy changing, rest, sleep and play routines.

Continuity of care is important as it is central to making babies feel secure. Care can involve a range of carers, but each must be familiar to the individual baby, and in a day-care setting it is particularly important that the baby has one main carer (their key worker). Assessing the needs of a baby involves knowledge of their stage of development, their current state of health, usual feeding patterns and any specific requirements or parental choices. Each baby should have a routine that suits them; they should not all be included in a routine care 'regime'.

Refer to pages 84–85 for discussion and activities on rest, sleep and play routines in day-care settings.

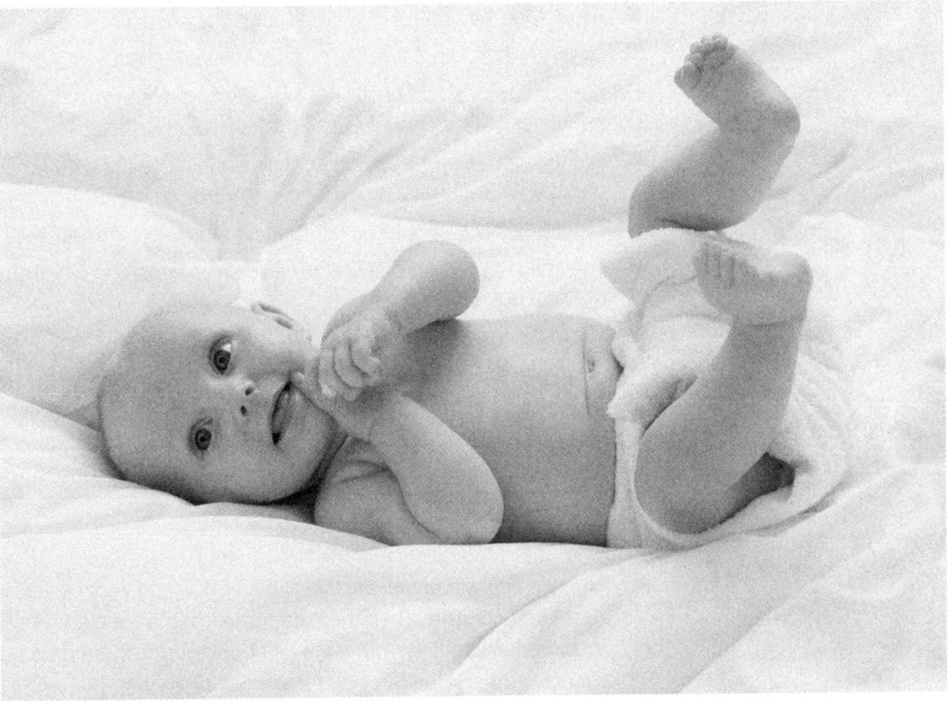

Fig 2.25 Human infants are totally dependent on their carers for all their health, care and development needs

Care needs – temperature

The environment

remember The infant's own temperature control is ineffective.

Babies

Care of the environment involves consideration of the safety aspects of the setting. One of the first points that you will need to understand is how to prepare an environment suitable for a baby. Room temperature and levels of ventilation are important, and any room where a baby spends much of their time should be a constant 20°C (68°F), day and night. A room thermometer should be placed on the wall in the baby room of any early years setting and be checked regularly, and the heating should be adjusted accordingly when necessary. Overheating of babies is thought to be a contributory factor in sudden infant death syndrome (cot death), and recommendations are that babies should not be piled high with blankets – a sheet and two layers of blankets are normally sufficient. Duvets and baby nests are no longer recommended, as they do not allow for temperature regulation. Cot bumpers are also advised against as these add extra warmth to a baby's cot, as well as putting the baby at increased risk of suffocation. Having a well-ventilated room will help to prevent cross-infection and make the working or living environment a more pleasant place to be, for babies and carers.

remember A blanket folded in half counts as two layers.

Children

Like babies, children require a suitable temperature in which to play, work and sleep, and in an early years setting the room temperature should not drop below 18.5°C/65°F. A wall thermometer should be displayed and regularly monitored.

Dealing with high temperature in a baby or child

Normal body temperature is between 36 and 37°C. A temperature above 37.5°C indicates **pyrexia** (fever). Young children's temperatures are often a sensitive indicator of the onset of illness, and pyrexia or any rise in temperature should never be ignored.

Deal with overheating in the first instance by:

- removing clothing or a layer of bedding
- reducing the temperature of the room
- sponging the child with a cool flannel.

If fever is suspected:

- take the child's temperature and record the outcome
- remove clothing or a layer of bedding
- sponge with a cool flannel
- offer plenty of fluids

- use a fan to circulate cool air around the child
- observe the child carefully, particularly very young babies.

Febrile convulsions can occur in some children when their temperature rises, involving loss of consciousness, flickering of eyes and general jitteriness.

- A child who has one febrile convulsion is more likely to have another. It does not, however, mean that they have developed epilepsy.
- Medical advice should be sought if a febrile convulsion occurs.
- The child should be placed in the recovery position when the convulsion is over, whilst medical advice is sought.
- The child needs reassurance and rest following a febrile convulsion.

Ask your placement supervisor about the setting's policy on dealing with a child with a raised temperature.

Refer to pages 50–58, for information regarding emergency first aid.

Professional Practice

- You can check if a well baby is too warm or too cool by feeling their abdomen. If it feels warm and clammy, then they are hotter than necessary. A slightly cool-to-the-touch abdomen is usual. Removing a layer of clothing should be sufficient to keep the baby at a more comfortable temperature.
- Cool hands and feet do not automatically indicate a 'cold' baby. Young babies are not able to regulate and control their temperature as well as adults and older children, and many babies have cool extremities, especially before they become mobile.
- If you are concerned that a baby is unwell or has a raised temperature, always check, using a thermometer, and seek medical advice as necessary.

Types of thermometers

Mercury thermometer

Mercury thermometers should never be used in childcare settings, but are sometimes still used in the family home. They are made of glass and should never be placed in the mouth: mercury is a poison and any breakage would mean a high risk of mercury poisoning. This type of thermometer is normally placed under the armpit. It takes a few minutes to get an accurate reading, which is not practical with very young children. It is less frequently used nowadays, being replaced by the digital thermometer.

Digital thermometer

A digital thermometer is a popular alternative to the mercury thermometer and gives a quick and accurate reading. It is usually placed in the armpit and offers no chemical risk. It should be cleaned after each use.

Fig 2.26 The four types of thermometer

Mercury thermometer

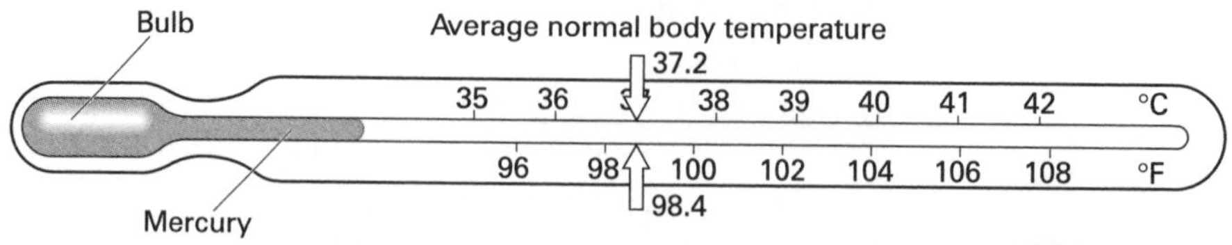

Digital thermometer

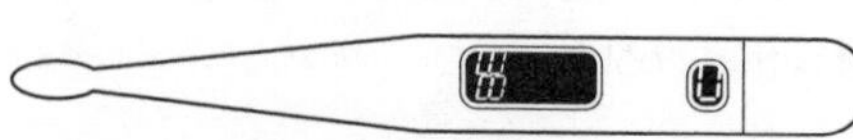

Temperature strip thermometer

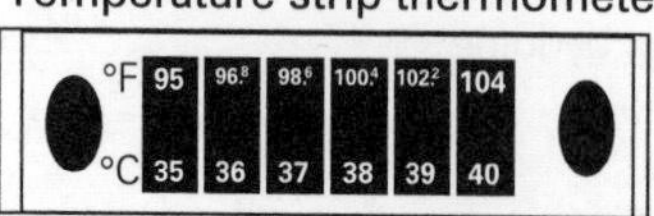

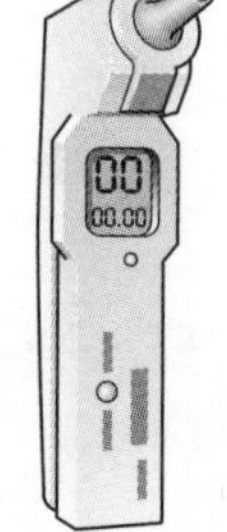

A tympanic thermometer

remember Parents should always be informed if a child has become unwell at an early years setting, even if the child appears well again by the time that they are collected.

Temperature strip thermometer

The temperature strip thermometer is placed on the forehead. It is easy to use but less accurate than digital or mercury thermometers.

Tympanic thermometer

The tympanic thermometer is favoured in hospitals. It is funnel shaped and is placed in the outer ear. It gives a quick and accurate reading. A disposable ear-piece is used each time and then discarded.

Child Health: Care of the Child in Health and Illness by Keene (1999) is a useful source of further information on febrile convulsions and managing ill health in young children.

remember Any oil used on babies and young children should be free of nut traces (almond oil used to be popular but is no longer used), as there is concern about links with the increase in nut allergies in young children. Many specialists recommend the use of organic sunflower oil.

Routines and care needs of babies and young children – skin, hair and tooth care

Skin care – babies

Skin care is important as it is one of the body's front-line defences against infection. Protecting the skin against damage has short-term benefits (protection from discomfort and infection) and long-term benefits (protection from sun damage and scarring). Babies have sensitive skin and many of our everyday products are far too harsh for them. It is therefore important, during all care routines, to use specially prepared baby products suitable for sensitive skins.

Skin types vary, as do cultural practices, and it is essential that the preferences of parents are taken into account. For example, many parents of black babies prefer their baby to have cocoa butter rubbed into the skin after bathing, as black skin often has a tendency to be dry. Some babies will also require a daily massage with an oil to alleviate the dryness. Most day-care settings ask parents to provide their own products, which are clearly labelled and kept solely for the use of their baby.

Refer back to page 68 for details of how to care for a child with eczema, which is a common skin complaint in young children.

Hair care – babies

Hair care is necessary to prevent infestation from head lice and to encourage good grooming for the future. Cultural practices differ: for example, Muslim babies will have their heads shaved within 40 days of birth as part of the cultural tradition, and many Caribbean parents traditionally weave and plait their babies' hair at a very early age.

Washing babies' hair can at times be traumatic, as not all babies are happy to have water in their eyes. Hair rings are available; these prevent water from reaching the eyes and can make for a happier bath time. Hair-washing products should be 'non-stinging' for the eyes and specially formulated for babies.

Refer to page 82 for advice on how to wash a baby's hair.

Skin and hair care – children

Skin and hair care applies to children in the same ways as it does to babies. Regular washing, bathing and also teeth cleaning should be encouraged. Children may now, however, be able to tolerate some of the bath products that are unsuitable for the more sensitive skin of younger babies. Whenever a new product is used, it is sensible to watch for any reaction such as a slight rash or irritation. If a reaction occurs, refrain from using the product.

Skin care includes using sunblock whenever the child is exposed to the sun. Early years settings need a clear policy regarding outdoor activity and sun-screening, and in hot weather parents should be responsible for putting sunblock on their child before leaving them at school or the day-care setting. With parents' written permission, early years staff must take on this responsibility, following parents' instructions.

Professional Practice

- Children who suffer any chronic skin problems, such as eczema, should not use perfumed bath-time products, unless use is sanctioned by their doctor, as these products are likely to irritate the skin further.
- Total sunblock should be used on babies and young children.
- Children and babies should not be exposed to the sun for more than a short period of time. Babies should be kept in the shade whenever possible (watch out for the sun moving round), and outdoor play should be restricted, particularly around midday when the sun is at its highest point.

A range of skin problems is described in *Child Health: Care of the Child in Health and Illness* by Keene (1999).

Tooth care – babies

Brushing of teeth should commence as soon as the first ones arrive and definitely when a baby has corresponding teeth top and bottom. Soft, baby toothbrushes are specially designed for delicate gums and first teeth, and regular use will encourage the baby into a habit of good oral health care. In day-care settings, each baby should have their own toothbrush, which should be labelled and kept separately.

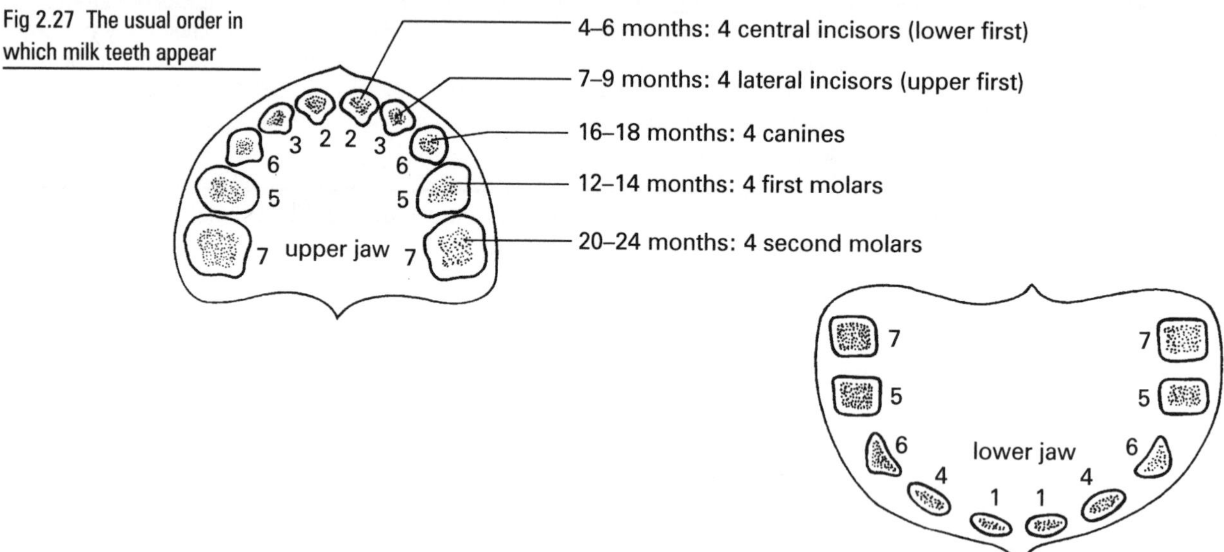

Fig 2.27 The usual order in which milk teeth appear

Tooth care – children

All children should be encouraged to clean their teeth after each meal and before bedtime, to prevent the build up of tartar and tooth decay. Separate toothbrushes should be available for each child. These should never be shared.

Routines and care needs of babies and young children – bathing and nappy changing

Hygiene is top priority when dealing with body fluids of any kind, and in day-care settings the use of disposable gloves is now the norm. In the home, good personal hygiene practice should be sufficient.

Refer to page 49, for information on health, safety and personal hygiene practice.

Babies are usually topped and tailed in the mornings and bathed at night before being put to bed.

Topping and tailing

Topping and tailing involves washing the face and refreshing the top half of the body, and changing the nappy.

Preparation

Get everything ready in advance. You will need:

- towel
- changing mat
- bowl of cooled boiled water
- bowl of warm water
- cotton wool
- barrier cream (if using)
- clean nappy
- fresh set of clothes
- access to nappy bucket (for towelling nappies) or a nappy sack (if using disposables)
- access to laundry basket for clothes.

Method

1. Place baby on changing mat and undress to their vest and nappy.
2. Using the cooled boiled water and cotton wool, wipe each eye from the nose corner outwards, using each piece of cotton wool only once.
3. Repeat two or three times for each eye.
4. Dry gently with the corner of a clean towel.
5. Gently clean ears and around the face using moistened cotton wool, ensuring that you reach all the creases, particularly under the chin and behind the ears. Dry gently.
6. Using a larger piece of moistened cotton wool, freshen up the baby's armpits and hands, removing all fibres collected between the fingers. Dry gently.
7. For newborn babies, check that the umbilical stump is clean but do not clean unnecessarily. Whenever possible, the stump should be left alone. (It tends to shrivel up and drop off 7 to 10 days after birth.)
8. Remove soiled nappy and place in bucket or nappy sack.
9. Clean the nappy area thoroughly, with warm water (or baby wipes if used), ensuring that you clean all creases, wiping from the front to the back.
10. Put on clean nappy (applying barrier cream if used); dress the baby and have a cuddle!

Professional Practice

- **When changing a baby girl's nappy, always wipe from the front to the back to avoid any infection from the bowels passing into the vaginal area.**
- **When changing a baby boy's nappy, do not pull back the foreskin. Excessive cleaning can cause irritation and infection, rather than prevent it.**

Bathing young babies

Bathing babies can be carried out by the traditional method or the modern method. Early years professionals need to be proficient at both, to meet with parental preferences.

Prepare everything in advance, ensuring that the temperature of the room is suitable (at least 20°C/68°F) with no draughts, and that all windows and doors are closed. All that you will need must be to hand, and the bath should be in a safe and secure place. A special bath stand or a firm surface is ideal, but many people choose to place the baby bath in their own bath or on the floor. Any of these options is acceptable.

You will need:

- bath, with water at 37°C – always check this (preferably with a bath thermometer or using your elbow) before putting the baby in
- changing mat

remember Cold water should always be added to the bath first, topping up with hot to the required temperature. This reduces the possibility of accidental scalding.

- towels
- cotton wool
- bowl of cooled boiled water (for the eyes)
- baby shampoo (if using)
- soap
- barrier cream (if using)
- clean nappy
- fresh set of clothes
- access to nappy bucket (for towelling nappies) or a nappy sack (if using disposables)
- access to laundry basket for clothing.

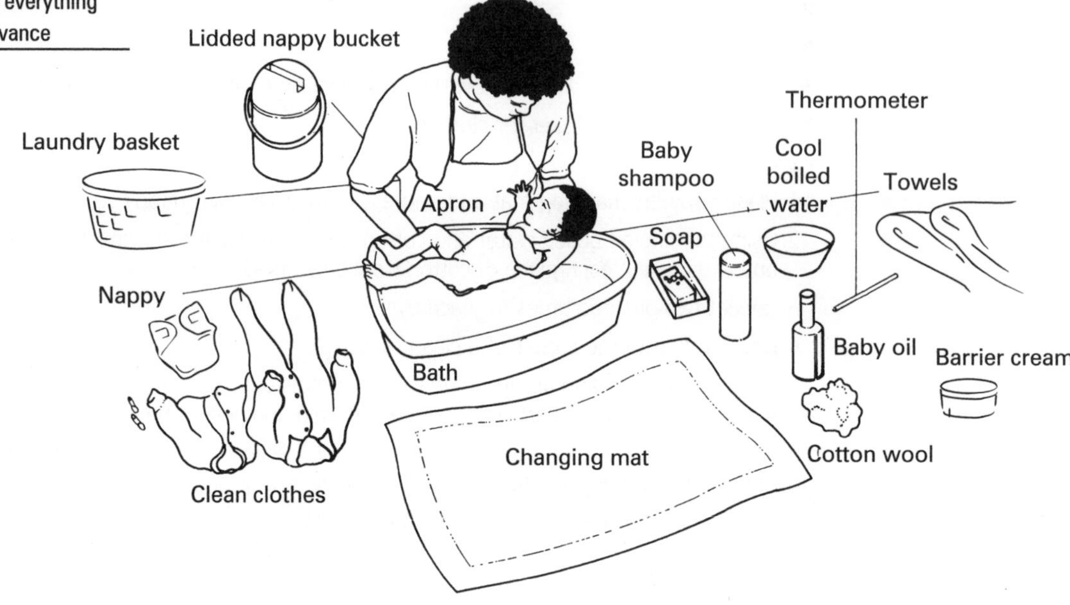

Fig 2.28 Have everything prepared in advance

Traditional method

1 Undress the baby to just the nappy and wrap in a towel with the top corner folded away from you.

2 Wash the baby's eyes and face as in topping and tailing.

3 Hold the baby (still wrapped in the towel) under your arm with the head over the bath, resting on your hip.

4 Gently wet the hair all over.

5 Add shampoo or soap and rub in gently but firmly.

6 Rinse the baby's hair by leaning the baby backwards over the bath. Towel the hair dry with the folded-over corner of the towel.

7 Lay the baby across your lap and remove the nappy, cleansing away excess faeces.

8 With your spare hand, gently wet and soap the baby all over, turning them onto their tummy by pulling them over towards you, holding the shoulder and thigh. When their back and bottom are also soaped, turn again in the same way (always towards you).

9 Supporting the baby's head and neck with one hand, and their bottom with the other, lower the baby into the bath.

10 Gently rinse the baby all over, continually supporting the head and neck, and holding their shoulder and arm.

11 When the baby is ready to be dried, lift the baby onto your lap, wrap in a towel and cuddle dry!

12 Apply nappy and clothing as before.

13 Brush or groom hair as appropriate.

14 Trim nails as necessary using blunt baby scissors (with parent's permission).

remember Always keep hold of the baby, by firmly holding the arm and shoulder furthest away from you. Even very young babies can move suddenly.

Professional Practice

- Babies usually have a feed after a bath and are then put down to sleep.
- Only use talcum powder if parents insist. It has been suggested that its use may be linked to the development of asthma in early childhood.
- Cultural practice regarding hair care and use of oils and creams should be adhered to.
- Never poke cotton buds into ears, noses, and so on.
- Babies need total supervision by a responsible adult at all times when being bathed.

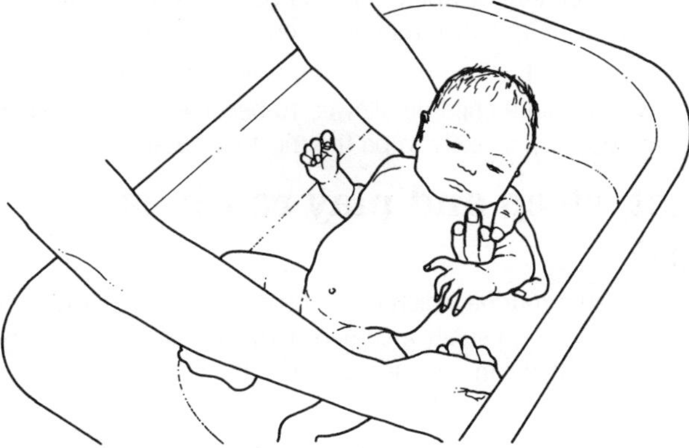

Fig 2.29 Support the baby's head and neck while holding their shoulder and arm

remember If a bathing preparation causes irritation of the baby's skin, do not continue to use it. Some preparations irritate a baby's skin in the early weeks but can be used later on.

Modern method

1. Prepare bath water, clothing, and so on in the same way as for the traditional method.
2. Add a bathing preparation to the water.
3. Lower the baby into the water after the eyes and face have been washed.
4. Soap the baby using the 'bubble bath'.
5. Continue as in the traditional method.

Using a bathing preparation can make the water (and the baby) quite slippery, so particular care is needed to hold the baby securely.

Bathing older babies

From seven or eight months onwards, babies can be bathed in the family bath, although some babies will prefer the security of the baby bath for far longer. Babies are usually much more active by this time and appreciate the additional room for splashing. Babies are often able to sit alone quite well by this stage, but remember that the water will make them buoyant and that you will need to be ready to support them if they slip.

Professional Practice

- The same precautions are needed regarding temperature, preparation and supervision as for younger babies.
- Ensure that the baby cannot touch the hot tap, which remains hot for some time after use.
- Do not have the water too deep, or the baby will 'float'.
- Sitting the baby on a rubber mat can help them feel more secure.
- Provide a range of containers and bath toys for the baby to play with.
- Never leave a baby under the supervision of an older child.
- No child under eight years of age should be left alone in the bathroom at any time.

remember Children should never be left unsupervised in the bath, and on no account should a child ever be left responsible for a younger sibling.

Bathing children

Starting when they are babies just playing in the bath, children can gradually be taught how to ensure that their bodies are properly cleaned. Regular bathing also engenders good habits for the future with regard to cleanliness and good grooming. A child may seem very sensible whilst in the bath, and competent at washing themselves, but it should be remembered that they are still very vulnerable. The fun of being in water and the desire to reach for different resources can easily lead to accidents.

Routines and care needs of young children – toilet training

By around 18 months, many toddlers are ready to start potty training, but others will not be ready to start until quite a few months later. Bladder and bowel control cannot be achieved until the nervous system is mature enough for the child to register that they want to use the potty and their muscles are able to control the process. Many people recommend having a potty around the house so that it becomes familiar to the child. After a while, they will feel ready to sit on it and, when doing so coincides with a successful 'outcome', much praise should be given (positive reinforcement for the behaviour).

The parents' wishes as regards potty training should be respected in early years settings, but in no way should a child be allowed to become anxious or upset about the process. A calm, patient approach is likely to be the most successful.

Rest, sleep and play routines

Babies

Babies need a routine which is not rigid but which provides them with continuity and security – a secure baby is usually a settled baby. Babies have periods of wakefulness and periods of deep sleep. They can appear very alert and content at times and restless and irritable at others.

Fig 2.30 A baby's day

Toddlers and older children

As a child develops, less sleep is needed: a couple of sleep periods during the day is gradually reduced to just one period, and then to occasional naps. Up until around three years, children often still need these daytime rests to help re-boost their energy after active play.

In nursery settings, it should be remembered that:

- many children would be resting if they were at home
- quiet times are important for all children
- specific rest times should be provided for those that need it.

remember As much as possible, practitioners should take their lead from the baby in their care. A baby who is mostly content, feeds as usual, and settles to sleep without uncustomary distress is usually receiving a care routine suitable to their needs.

Planning, implementing and evaluating routines

Careful thought needs to be given to the planning of a suitable routine for a baby or child. Practitioners should allow time for verbal interaction and play within care routines.

You will find it useful to see some examples of your current setting's plans for babies and children of different ages. When you look at a plan, think carefully about:

- its relevance to the age of the children concerned
- how well the plan meets the children's needs
- how much opportunity for flexibility there is in the planning.

case study 2.6

Jefferson, Chloe and Ainsley

Jefferson is 6 weeks old, Chloe is 5 months old and Ainsley is 10 months old. Each is the first child in their family. Imagine that they all have a non-working parent at home to look after them each day.

activity
GROUP WORK

1 What similarities and differences will there be in their daily needs?
2 Plan a suitable day for each baby.
3 Imagine that all three babies now attend the Lilac Tree Nursery, where the following routine is set out for the baby room, and that Jefferson, Chloe and Ainsley are cared for each day in this baby room. How well do you think the routine will meet the needs of these children?

8.30 a.m.	Arrival, settling in and play with key worker
10.00 a.m.	Feed or snack; nappy change
10.30 a.m.	Walk around the nursery grounds in prams/buggies
11.15 a.m.	Play with key worker and other staff
12.15 p.m.	Feed and/or lunch; nappy change and sleep
1.45 p.m.	Play with key worker and other staff
3.00 p.m.	Feed or snack; nappy change
3.30 p.m.	Play or fresh air
4.00 p.m.	Play until collected

4 What might indicate to you that the needs of a baby are not being met by the routine?
5 What changes would you make if you could?

Feeding

Principles of nutritional requirements – babies

The decision whether to breast- or bottle-feed is a personal one, and a mother's choice should be respected. However, all health professionals agree that the best start for any baby is to be breastfed, as breast milk is the most natural and well-prepared food they can be given. For the first few months of life, most babies will need only milk feeds – either breast or bottle – to give them all the nutrients they need for their development.

Breastfeeding

Breast milk offers a degree of **natural immunity** to the infant through the mother's own immunity, and it is considered to be nature's 'designer food' because, as the infant grows, the mother's breast milk changes to meet her child's developing needs. The colostrum-rich early milk (a thick, yellowish substance with a high protein content, secreted prior to the mother's full milk production) offers some protection against common infections and is particularly important to newborn infants. Even when mothers are not intending to breastfeed long term, they are encouraged to do so for the first few days to allow their babies to benefit from this.

For breastfeeding to be successful, the mother needs to eat well and drink plenty of fluids. The more the baby feeds, the more milk is produced, on a supply-and-demand basis. Once the initial stages of breastfeeding are passed, and any soreness or discomfort has been overcome, breastfeeding is usually considered a pleasurable part of mothering.

Babies suckle for different lengths of time – some will take all they need in just a few minutes, while others will suck for far longer. Letting the baby decide the length of a feed maintains a balance and helps to prevent engorgement of the breasts. At each feed, the baby initially receives the 'fore' milk, which offers satisfaction in the short term, but the richer 'hind' milk which follows often gives satisfaction for a longer period. It is usual for babies to feed from alternate breasts at alternate feeds.

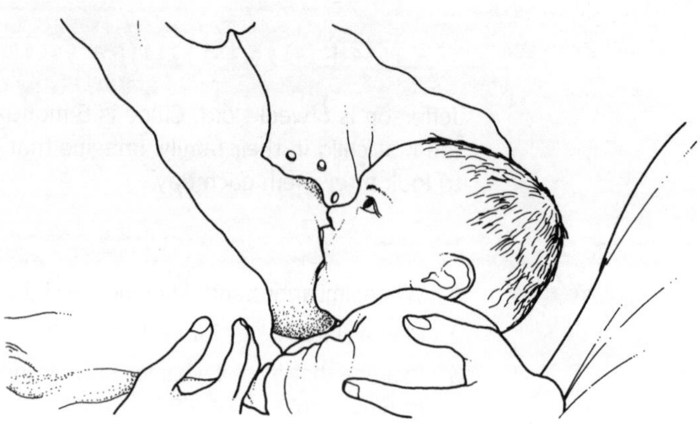

Fig 2.31 Breast milk offers the baby natural immunity

Expressing breast milk

Many mothers choose to express some of their breast milk, which can be given in a bottle or cup, and this can be a useful solution to the question of how to continue breastfeeding when returning to work. Breast pumps, which can be either manual or mechanical, produce a vacuum which draws out the milk in much the same way as the baby's sucking. Battery- or mains-operated pumps are far quicker to use than expressing by hand and are suitable for expressing significant quantities.

remember

Alcohol, spicy food, medication and nicotine are all passed on.

Expressed milk can allow other family members to enjoy feeding the baby too. It can give the mother some time for herself and is also useful if, for personal or cultural reasons, the mother is embarrassed to breastfeed in front of other people. Expressed milk must be kept in sterile containers and refrigerated until needed. Breast milk can be frozen (ice-cube trays are useful for this) and used in preparing solid food when the baby is ready for mixed feeding. The usual sterilising procedures should be followed.

Refer to pages 87–88 for information on sterilising and making up a formula feed.

remember

Breastfeeding is always the best choice for a baby, although, as an early years professional, you should respect the choices made by others and offer support accordingly. A mother has the right to choose the feeding method that suits her needs and you should simply inform and not judge or advise.

The diet of a breastfeeding mother

A lactating mother needs a healthy diet. She should also be aware that whatever she eats will be passed on to her baby. Medication should never be taken without checking that it is safe for the breastfeeding child; this applies to cough and cold remedies as well as to prescribed items.

Breastfeeding mothers need plenty of support, especially in the early days and weeks. It can be very tiring as the mother is usually needed at each feed time and may have few uninterrupted rest periods. At times, breastfeeding can be hard to establish, and the sensitive support and encouragement of health professionals and early years workers can be crucial to whether a mother feels able to continue. Support can be given in the form of:

- encouragement
- help with positioning of the infant
- advice on length of suckling
- advice regarding 'latching' the infant on to the breast
- advice regarding removing the infant from the breast.

Each of these is necessary to establish a feeding process which is free from soreness and discomfort.

Professional Practice

- **Feeding on demand allows babies to satisfy their hunger. If a baby sleeps well between feeds, it usually means that they are getting sufficient nutrients.**
- **Regular weighing of babies allows mothers to monitor the sufficiency of their milk production and gives them peace of mind.**
- **Green, slimy stools may indicate that a baby is not getting enough feeds – longer or more frequent feeds may need to be encouraged.**
- **The breastfeeding mother needs to sit comfortably, with her back supported. The baby sucks with lips curled back and takes the whole of the areola (the pigmented area around the nipple) into the mouth. Eye contact is made between mother and child, and as the baby develops they pat the breast contentedly.**

Fig 2.32 The baby should be held securely, with good eye contact

remember Each baby's feeds must be labelled clearly and stored separately to avoid confusion or cross-infection.

Formula feeding

Formula milk is an alternative to breast milk, but no artificial milk can be as ideal for a baby's stomach as breast milk. As the baby's nutritional needs change, linked to growth rate and levels of hunger, parents should make changes to the formula that they use. (Breastfeeding copes with such changes naturally.)

In early years settings, babies' feeds will usually be supplied ready prepared by the parents and should be stored in a refrigerator until required.

Making a formula feed – preparation

You will need:

- formula feed
- bottle
- teats
- knife
- kettle of water, pre-boiled and allowed to cool
- sterilising equipment.

Making a formula feed – method

remember Wash your hands thoroughly before feeding a baby or handling any feeding equipment. Prepare feeds on a cleaned surface. Have spare teats handy in case you drop one!

remember If suitable refrigeration is available, it is easier to make up enough feeds for the day in one go. This is particularly useful for families with twins or other multiples.

1 Boil the kettle in advance and allow the water to cool.
2 Remove the bottle from the steriliser unit and rinse with boiled water.
3 Pour sufficient cooled boiled water into the bottle for the feed required, following the manufacturer's guidelines.
4 Check that the level is accurate.
5 Open the tin of formula.
6 Using the scoop enclosed in the tin, add the correct number of scoops to the bottle. Level each scoop off with a flat knife.
7 If using straight away, put on the teat, ring and lid, and shake the bottle gently to dissolve the formula.
8 The feed is ready for use after checking that the temperature is OK (see page 88).
9 If storing the feed for later, put a disc and ring on the bottle and shake gently to mix.
10 Remove the disc and replace with an upside-down teat (do not allow formula to touch the teat, as bacteria could begin to form).
11 Cover with disc and lid and refrigerate until needed.

It is important that the scoops of formula are level. Heaped scoops or packed-down scoops lead to overfeeding, and overfeeding can result in excessive weight gain, high levels of salt intake and possible kidney strain. Using insufficient scoops of formula for the number of ounces of water leads to underfeeding, which can result in poor weight gain and a hungry baby.

A baby needs 75 ml of formula per 500 g of body weight ($2\frac{1}{2}$ fl oz per pound) in each 24-hour period.

Giving a formula feed

It is important to be prepared in advance, with everything that you might need easily to hand. You should be seated comfortably and be able to give the baby your full attention. Often a baby will be more comfortable having their nappy changed prior to feeding, but individual routines will vary.

remember Always throw away left over milk and never use the same bottle twice without sterilising.

1 Have all equipment together and suitably covered. The bottle can be kept warm in a jug of hot water whilst you settle with the baby.
2 Hold the baby close to you, offering a sense of security and pleasure.
3 Test the temperature of the formula against the inside of your wrist. It should feel warm, not hot.
4 Check that the milk is flowing at the appropriate rate for the baby you are feeding. The usual is several drops per second, but rates do vary from baby to baby.
5 Encourage the onset of feeding by touching the teat against the baby's lips before placing the teat into the mouth. The milk should always cover the whole teat to stop the baby taking in excess air and becoming frustrated at not receiving enough milk at a time. If the baby is reluctant to suck, pull the teat gently, as the tension will often give them the impetus to suck harder.
6 About half-way through the feed, stop and wind the baby (see next section).
7 Wind again when the feed is over and settle the baby down. They may need another nappy change.
8 When a baby has finished feeding, discard any remaining formula and wash the bottle thoroughly before placing it in a steriliser.

remember It is always useful to have a cloth handy as many babies posset (regurgitate) some milk during the winding process. Also, a young baby's head and neck should be well supported.

Winding

Winding a baby is the process of helping them release any trapped air taken in during the feeding process. The baby is best held in an upright position to allow the air to rise. Useful positions for this include:

- sitting the baby forward, resting against your hand, which allows you to rub or gently pat their back with your other hand
- placing the baby on your shoulder and rubbing or gently patting their back
- resting the baby along your forearm (very young babies only) and rubbing their back
- with some babies, laying them prone across your lap and rubbing their back works well.

Sterilising techniques

Bottles and all other feeding utensils need sterilising to prevent illness caused by the growth of bacteria. There are various **sterilising techniques** to choose from.

Cold-water sterilisers

This method of sterilising uses chemicals either in solution or tablet form. The steriliser should be filled to the required capacity and the solution added (or sterilising tablet allowed to dissolve) before adding the bottles, teats and other feeding equipment. Each item must be fully submerged and held under water by a float. Sterilising takes 30 minutes from the time the last piece of equipment has been added. The solution must be replaced every 24 hours. Most tanks hold a large amount of feeding equipment.

remember Fully submerging items such as bottles means ensuring that all air bubbles are released; an air bubble leaves an area unsterilised (a potential site for bacteria growth).

Steam sterilisers

The steam-sterilising method is quick and efficient but is expensive and, once opened, the bottles need to be prepared within a short period of time, as opening the steriliser allows the potential growth of bacteria. There is a risk of scalding from the release of steam if the unit is opened whilst still very hot, so care must be taken. Steam sterilisers usually hold six or eight bottles at a time; they are ready for use within approximately 12 to 15 minutes from switching the unit on.

Microwave sterilisers

This method works on the same principle as the steam steriliser. The units usually only hold four bottles, but the method is quick. Metal objects cannot be placed in the microwave steriliser.

Boiling method

Boiling an infant's feeding equipment is cheap but no longer a popular choice. There is considerable potential for accidents owing to the large quantities of boiling water used. However, if another form of sterilising is not possible, the method can offer reassurance that equipment is clean and free from germs. It is quick; only 10 minutes of boiling time is required. All equipment must be fully submerged, as with the cold water method.

case study 2.7

Janice

Janice is shortly due to give birth to her first baby and is unsure which sterilising method to use. She is currently on maternity leave and is planning to return to work when her baby is about three months old. Janice intends to breast-feed for the first few weeks, moving her baby onto formula feeds by about two months, as she will be working full-time and this will be a more practical option for her. Janice has asked for your advice.

activity
INDIVIDUAL WORK

1 What advice would you give Janice?

2 What are the advantages and disadvantages of the various sterilising methods?

remember There will always be some infants who need to start the weaning process earlier than others; no infant should be kept hungry simply to fit in with new thinking.

Principles of nutritional requirements – weaning and feeding older babies

Weaning is the process of introducing a baby to 'solid' food alongside their usual milk feeds. During the earliest months the baby's digestive system is not usually mature enough to cope with the components of solid food. The recent thinking by health professionals, based on research into children's development recommends that babies are not introduced to solid foods until they are around six months old. Up until quite recently most infants were given their first food experiences at around four months. However, the onset of the process should be led by the individual baby's needs; it is a good indicator that the infant is ready when they begin to seem less satisfied with just breast or formula milk and are hungry for their next feed more quickly.

Another important factor is that breast and formula milk do not contain sufficient iron for continued healthy development, so prolonged (exclusive) milk feeding will not provide enough of this important mineral. (Initially, an infant has sufficient stocks of iron taken from the mother during pregnancy.)

Weaning should be a pleasurable experience for both carer and child, and the infant should be encouraged to explore new tastes over a period of time. Weaning should not be a cause of stress or tension. At times, it can be difficult to get a baby interested in trying to take solids from a spoon, but it is important to keep on trying, without worrying about regular refusals. The baby will get there in time, and in the early stages of weaning they will still be having all of their milk feeds and so will not be losing out nutritionally.

Suitable foods for babies

Most babies start with baby rice, which is bland in taste and very smooth. They usually progress quite quickly to other puréed foods once they are used to taking food from a spoon. Whenever possible, freshly prepared foods should be given, rather than food from packets, jars or tins, as this will enable the carer (you) to control what the baby is eating more fully, particularly with regard to additives such as sugar, salt, colourings and preservatives. Preparing fresh food helps to integrate the baby into family mealtimes. Convenience foods are ideal as emergency options or when travelling, and many commercially prepared foods now have symbols showing whether they are sugar free, salt free, gluten free, and so on.

One of the main reasons for waiting until the child is six months is to try and reduce the level of food allergies; such allergies have increased considerably among young children in recent years (e.g. nut allergy, lactose intolerance). Nuts and products containing nuts should be avoided completely, as early introduction to these has been linked to later development of nut allergy.

remember The aim of weaning is to introduce babies to a variety of textures, tastes and experiences to integrate them fully into family mealtimes.

Carers should avoid giving babies foods containing wheat or gluten (a protein found in wheat, barley and rye) before six months of age, with oats (which also contain the protein gluten) only being allowed if there is no family history of coeliac disease – there is a suspected link between early introduction of these products and the development of coeliac disease later in life.

As the level of solid food intake increases, the milk feeds will decrease until the baby is having sufficient solid food at a mealtime to be satisfied with a drink of water to accompany it. The table on the Nelson Thornes website at www.nelsonthornes.com/btec sets out a sample programme for weaning a baby.

A Bristol University research project into children's development has shown that babies who are not introduced to mashed (rather than puréed) food by 10 months of age are likely to be fussier eaters later on in their life.

Refer back to pages 75–76 for an outline of coeliac disease.

Professional Practice

- **Milk remains an important part of the baby's diet and will remain so until they are at least a year old. Offering half of the milk feed before the solids and half afterwards works well for most babies, but each baby is different and they will soon indicate their preference!**
- **Do not introduce weaning (or a new food) when the baby is unwell or tired.**
- **Health visitors are always happy to advise parents and carers, and anyone with concerns should not hesitate to ask for their advice.**
- **Avoiding foods containing gluten etc. is a sensible precaution for all infants under six months old.**

activity
GROUP WORK
2.6

P5

Research weaning plans by reading parenting and child health magazines and books or through the Internet.

1 Plan a week's menu for a baby aged either:
   - six to seven months
   - eight to nine months.

   A blank table is available to download from the Nelson Thornes website.
2 How much of your menu could easily be prepared fresh?
3 How much of your menu could be taken from the family meals?

Look on the Nelson Thornes website for the blank table, 'Planning a menu 1', which you can use as a guide.
www.nelsonthornes.com/btec

Principles of nutritional requirements – children

A good balanced diet is one which includes all the nutritional requirements for the growth, maintenance and development of the body. The food we eat helps us maintain and repair our body tissues, keeping muscles and organs functioning. It also helps to prevent infection and supplies us with our energy needs. A balanced diet should abide by the **principles of diet and nutrition** and include elements from the four main food groups:

- proteins, which help growth, development and tissue repair
- carbohydrates, which provide energy
- vitamins, minerals and fibre, for general good health and the prevention of illness
- dairy products, which are high in calcium, help develop and maintain bones and teeth.

A fifth food group – fats and oils – contains higher-level energy-giving foods which should be consumed sparingly by adults.

Many foods contribute to more than one food group; for example, meat is a good source of iron, and pulses are a good source of fibre, but Figure 2.33 indicates where the main benefits of each food lie.

Tables 2.4 and 2.5 show the benefits of a range of vitamins and minerals and the possible problems that can occur if there is a deficiency.

Fig 2.33 The food groups

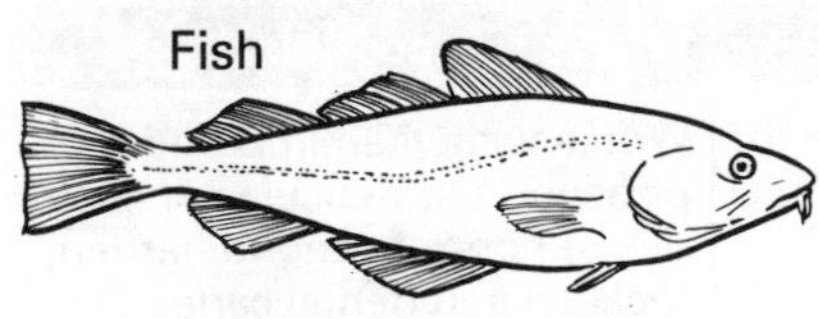

Proteins: meat, fish, poultry, offal, eggs, pulses, nuts (avoid giving to young children), textured vegetable protein (TVP, mostly made from soya)

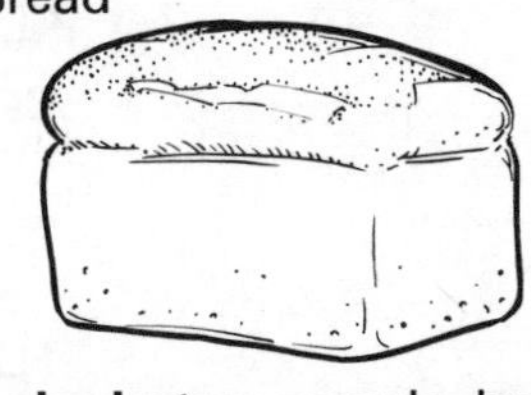

Carbohydrates: cereals, breads, pasta, rice, starchy vegetables (e.g. potato, yam, plantain)

Vitamins, minerals and fibre: all vegetables, all fruits, fresh and dried

Dairy products: milk, cheese, yoghurt, fromage frais

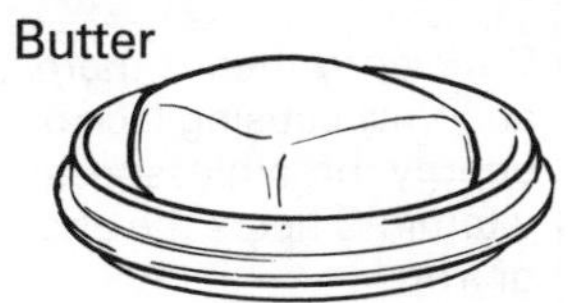

Fats and oils: butter, margarine, vegetable spreads, oils (cooking and dressing)

Table 2.4 The main vitamins

Vitamin	Food source	Function	Why is this possible?
A	Butter, cheese, eggs, carrots, tomatoes	Promotes healthy skin, good vision	Fat-soluble, can be stored in the liver; deficiency causes skin infections, problems with vision
B group	Liver, meat, fish, green vegetables, beans, eggs	Healthy working of muscles and nerves; forming haemoglobin	Water-soluble, not stored in the body, so regular supply needed; deficiency results in muscle wasting, anaemia
C	Fruits and fruit juices, especially orange, blackcurrant, pineapple; green vegetables	For healthy tissue, promotes healing	Water-soluble, daily supply needed; deficiency means less resistance to infection; extreme deficiency results in scurvy
D	Oily fish, cod liver oil, egg yolk; added to margarine, milk	Growth and maintenance of bones and teeth	Fat-soluble, can be stored by the body; can be produced by the body as a result of sunlight on the skin; deficiency results in bones failing to harden and dental decay
E	Vegetable oils, cereals, egg yolk	Protects cells from damage	Fat-soluble, can be stored by the body
K	Green vegetables, liver	Needed for normal blood clotting	Fat-soluble, can be stored in the body

Source: Beaver *et al*. (2001, p. 354)

Table 2.5 The mian minerals

Mineral	Food source	Function	Why is this possible?
Calcium	Cheese, eggs, fish, milk, yoghurt	Essential for growth of bones and teeth	Works with vitamin D and phosphorus; deficiency means risk of bones failing to harden (rickets) and dental caries
Fluoride	Occurs naturally in water, or may be added artificially to water supply	Combines with calcium to make tooth enamel more resistant to decay	There are different points of view about adding fluoride to the water supply
Iodine	Water, sea foods, added to salt, vegetables	Needed for proper working of the thyroid gland	Deficiency results in enlarged thyroid gland in adults, cretinism in babies
Iron	Meat, green vegetables, eggs, liver, red meat	Needed for formation of haemoglobin in red blood cells	Deficiency means there is anaemia causing lack of energy, breathlessness; vitamin C helps the absorption of iron
Sodium chloride	Table salt, bread, meat, fish	Needed for formation of cell fluids, blood plasma, sweat, tears	Salt should not be added to any food prepared for babies: their kidneys cannot eliminate excess salt as adult kidneys do; excess salt is harmful in an infant diet
Other essential trace minerals include: potassium, phosphorus, magnesium, sulphur, manganese and zinc.			

Source: Beaver *et al*. (2001, p. 354)

A healthy diet offers a range of foods from each food group, ensuring that the diet is well balanced, and is not deficient in any area. Encouraging children to try foods from a range of cultures and from amongst seasonal fruits and vegetables will promote a healthy and diverse approach to diet throughout life.

Fig 2.34 How a balanced diet promotes health and development

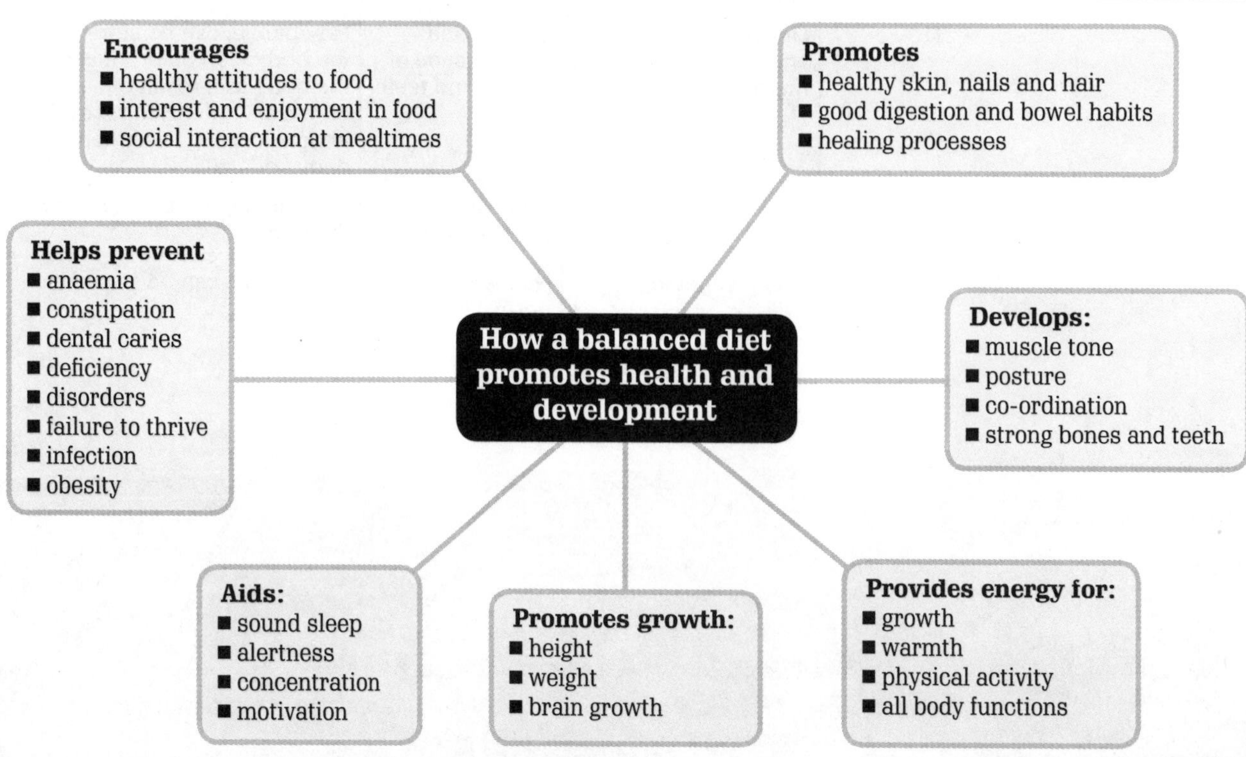

remember Children have preferences too.

Planning a diet for children

- Children need a diet that is high in protein and carbohydrates to meet their high energy needs. Ideally, the carbohydrates should come from starchy foods, such as potatoes, breads and cereals.
- Think about both colour and texture when planning meals, as an attractive meal will be more appealing, especially to a fussy or reluctant eater.
- Vary the meals that are offered to children, but do not offer more than one new food at a time.
- Large portions can be off-putting. It is better for a child to eat all of a small meal than half of a larger one, as it encourages good habits.

Daily portions for children

As a guideline for planning the dietary needs of young children, a good daily balance would include:

- five portions of fruit or vegetables
- two portions of protein foods
- two portions of dairy foods plus one pint of milk
- four portions of carbohydrates.

remember Snacks need to be nutritional to be of benefit to a child; this should set them a healthy example for the future.

Snacks

Most children will also need to be offered snacks. It is important that these are mostly nutritional and healthy.

Snacks are an important part of a child's nutritional intake. Children use a lot of energy in their play and often need an energy boost in the middle of the morning or afternoon. This is particularly important if they are at a stage when they are developing particularly quickly physically, or they are more active than usual.

case study 2.8

Redhouse Nursery School

Redhouse Nursery School has a fruit-only policy for snack time. Many children bring an apple or a carrot but still seem to be flagging at the end of the morning.

activity
INDIVIDUAL WORK

1 Why is this do you think?
2 What fruit would offer them a greater energy boost?
3 Is a fruit-only policy a good idea?
4 What other healthy options could be included?

activity
INDIVIDUAL WORK 2.7

P6

1 Plan a midday meal for a group of four-year-olds, ensuring that there are three colours and three textures within the meal. You can plan a meal from any culture you wish.
   (a) What have you included for colour?
   (b) What textures have you provided?
   (c) What food groups have you incorporated into your meal?
   (d) Are any food groups not represented? Is this a problem, do you think?
2 Collect labels from a range of frequently used processed products that are enjoyed by children.
   (a) What proportions are the ingredients in?
   (b) How near to the top of the list are sugar and salt?
   (c) What does this tell you about processed foods?
   (d) What alternatives could you offer in their place?
   (e) Look at the table on page 94. How much of the estimated average requirements (EARs) would the processed foods you looked at meet?

remember There are many hidden extras in processed foods, particularly sugar and salt. Whenever possible, offer fresh foods to children and do not provide salt or sugar on the table for them to add to their foods.

Table 2.6 Ideas for healthy snacks

Good as regular snacks	Occasional snacks, not regular
Fresh fruit: banana, orange, pear kiwi, melon Raw vegetables (washed thoroughly): celery, carrot, tomato, cabbage leaves, Chinese leaves Dried fruits: raisins, sultanas, banana, dates and figs, apple rings, apricots Small cubes of cheese Sandwiches (savoury fillings) Pitta breads (savoury fillings)	Sweet biscuits Chocolate biscuits Chocolate and sweets Cakes
Healthy drinks	**Less healthy drinks**
Milk Water Milkshakes (fresh fruit) Fruit juices	Milkshakes (powdered) Squashes Carbonated drinks (Coke, Cola, etc.)

Source: Beaver *et al*. (2001, p. 354)

Table 2.7 Estimated average requirements (EARs) for energy in the UK (per day)

Age	Males		Females	
	MJ	kcal	MJ	kcal
0–3 months (formula fed)	2.28	545	2.16	515
4–6 months	2.89	690	2.69	645
7–9 months	3.44	825	3.20	765
10–12 months	3.85	920	2.61	865
1–3 years	5.15	1230	4.86	1165
4–6 years	7.16	1715	6.46	1545
7–10 years	8.24	1970	7.28	1740

Source: Dare and O'Donovan (1996, p. 7)

Further information on nutritional sources can be found in *A Practical Guide to Child Nutrition* by Dare and O'Donovan (1996) and *Feeding the Under-5s* by Dyson and Meredith (2006). *Eating Well for the Under-5s in Child Care* by Walker (1998) includes a CD-ROM, the CHOMP menu planner, to help with menu planning, and provides nutritional advice for young children in all early years settings.

1 Using a chart like the one available to download from the Nelson Thornes website, plan a range of meals and snacks for a group of similarly aged children in a day nursery. Take into account their age, level of activity and the appropriate guidelines regarding EARs. National guidelines state that children in full day care (over eight hours) should be provided with 70 per cent of the EARs by the setting. Assume that all the children in your chosen group are in this category.

2 Explain the nutritional content of at least three meals and the ways in which they support an overall healthy diet for young children.

Look on the Nelson Thornes website for the blank chart, 'Planning a menu 2'. www.nelsonthornes.com/btec

remember

Mealtimes should be a time of pleasure and socialising.

Cultural and dietary needs

Children have their own preferences regarding food, which should be accommodated up to a point. A balance is needed between allowing a child to select what they eat, or do not eat, and encouraging them to try a range of new and familiar foods. When preparing meals for children, a range of dietary needs may have to be considered: children may have food intolerance or allergy; there may be family requirements, for example for vegetarian or vegan diets; and there may be cultural requirements. The table below sets out the **food-related customs** of several cultures.

Table 2.8 Food-related customs

	Jewish	Hindu[1]	Sikh[1]	Muslim	Buddhist	Rastafarian[2]
Eggs	No blood spots	Some	Yes	Yes	Some	Some
Milk/yoghurt	Not with meat	Yes	Yes	Yes	Yes	Some
Cheese	Not with meat	Some	Some	Possibly	Yes	Some
Chicken	Kosher	Some	Some	Halal	No	Some
Mutton/lamb	Kosher	Some	Yes	Halal	No	Some
Beef and beef products	Kosher	No	No	Halal	No	Some
Pork and pork products	No	No	Rarely	No	No	No
Fish	With fins and scales	With fins and scales	Some	Some	Some	Yes
Shellfish	No	Some	Some	Some	No	No
Butter/ghee	Kosher	Some	Some	Some	No	Some
Lard	No	No	No	No	No	No
Cereal foods	Yes	Yes	Yes	Yes	Yes	Yes
Nuts/pulses	Yes	Yes	Yes	Yes	Yes	Yes
Fruits/vegetables	Yes	Yes[3]	Yes	Yes	Yes	Yes
Fasting[4]	Yes	Yes	Yes	Yes	Yes	Yes

Source: Walker (1998, p. 68)

'Some' means that some people within a religious group would find these foods acceptable.
1 Strict Hindus and Sikhs will not eat eggs, meat, fish, and some fats.
2 Some Rastafarians are vegan.
3 Jains have restrictions on some vegetable foods. Check with the individuals.
4 Fasting is unlikely to apply to young children.

Ways of making foods more interesting

To help children take an interest in food and also simply for fun, try making meals and snacks visually appealing. For example:

- Sandwiches can be cut into interesting shapes: boats can be made from an oblong with two triangle sails (from one round of sandwiches), or use large pastry cutters: trees, stars, moons, and so on.
- Arrange food on plates into pictures (e.g. faces, clowns, cat with whiskers).
- Give meals exciting names (e.g. magic mash, nursery noodles, rocket of rice, planet of pasta).

Professional Practice

- Forcing a child to eat more than they want may make them resent food, or even vomit.
- The pudding should be an integral part of the meal, not a prize for those who eat their dinner.
- Some children have far greater appetites than others, so will need larger portions.
- Making meals exciting can entice children to eat foods that they may usually refuse.

Refer to *Food and Cooking* (Green, 2004) for further ideas.

Clothing and footwear

Babies' clothing

remember It is better for babies to be dressed in several layers of clothes that can be removed or replaced according to temperature, rather than one warmer layer which offers no opportunity for adjustment, as babies are not able to control their body temperature and could therefore become overheated.

Clothing for babies needs to:

- be easy to put on and take off
- allow room for the baby to grow
- allow unrestricted movement
- be suitable for the time of year and temperature of the environment they are in
- avoid cramping of toes (e.g. all-in-one suits)
- be free from long ties or ribbons (to avoid choking)
- be free from loose buttons or poppers (another choking hazard)
- be free from looped edgings on seams (may catch small fingers)
- avoid lacy designs (may catch small fingers)
- be easy to wash and dry
- be made of natural materials to allow skin to breathe
- not be made of fluffy materials or wools such as mohair
- be of a suitable length so that it does not get caught when the child is toddling or crawling.

Care of babies' feet

remember When babies are ready for their first pair of proper shoes, it is important to have their feet measured and the shoes fitted by a foot-care specialist.

Babies' feet are very delicate and their bones are still forming; therefore, they should not be given shoes before they are able to walk. Wearing shoes too early will hinder the natural growth of the feet, causing deformity. Socks, all-in-one suits and bootees should all have sufficient room for natural movement and growth.

Children's clothing

Adults need to be responsible for what the children in their care wear, as young children are not able to make an informed choice but will state preferences with little regard to temperature, weather or planned activity.

Clothing for children needs to:

- be easy to put on and take off, to encourage independence
- allow for growth, as children's growth rate is so rapid
- allow unrestricted movement, particularly for outdoor and any physically active play
- be suitable for the time of year and temperature of the environment they are in
- be free from long or loose ties or ribbons that could get caught during play
- be kept in good repair and washed regularly, setting a good example with regard to cleanliness
- be easy to wash and dry
- be made of natural materials to allow skin to breathe
- be of a suitable length to avoid the possibility of tripping.

remember Children's clothing should be suitable for the activities being undertaken.

Children should be able to play happily without worrying about getting their clothes messy. Aprons for painting and water play are of course appropriate precautions to take in school or day care.

Care of children's feet

Children's feet develop quickly, and it is not uncommon for a child to need four new pairs of shoes during the course of one year. Foot-care specialists recommend that children should have their feet measured every 12 weeks and sooner if there is any concern about cramping of toes or if soreness occurs.

As shoes made of leather allow children's feet to breathe, leather is therefore the ideal choice of material. It is unhealthy for children to wear trainers or similar footwear for long periods of time.

remember

It is better for children to wear several layers of clothes that can be taken off or replaced according to temperature, rather that one warmer layer which offers no opportunity for adjustment.

Sock sizes should also be monitored – socks that are too tight can cause damage to the structure of a child's foot.

Care of clothing and footwear

It is important that clothes are kept clean and in good repair. Not only does this help maintain a hygienic and safe environment, but it also supports the development of a child's pride in their appearance and their understanding of personal care. Soiled clothes should be sluiced clean and bagged up securely to send home with a child, or, if the setting has washing facilities, the items should be washed according to material type etc. and then sent home. Soiled nappies should be double bagged and sent home with the child.

Dressing and undressing

Children and babies are entitled to privacy. It is not appropriate in a care setting for children to be stripped off in front of others. Dressing and undressing should be undertaken in the bathroom or in a quiet area.

When handling young babies, it is important to be aware of delicate fingers and toes, ensuring that they do not get caught in materials, cuffs, etc. Often, the simplest and most comfortable way of dressing a young baby is to position your fingers down a sleeve and carefully draw the infant's arm into the garment by holding onto their hand and wrist. When applying an all-in-one outfit, it is always easier to position the baby's arms into the sleeves before positioning the legs.

remember

Support dressing skills through the provision of role-play clothes, dolls to dress and undress, and activities involving buttons, zips, etc. as this will help young children develop the fine motor dexterity they need for successful independent dressing.

As children grow older, they become interested in helping to dress themselves. This involves much trial and error and can take much longer to achieve. Whenever possible, allow additional time to encourage independence. This is how they will learn.

Choosing own clothes

Having choice helps build self-esteem. It makes a child feel that they have some control over a situation and that their opinion matters. Also, as children develop they often like to choose their own clothes. It is a natural part of growing up.

However, toddlers and very young children do not have the understanding of weather, temperature or situational needs to enable them to make suitable choices, and older children will often have favourite clothes which they would choose at any time, disregarding suitability

case study 2.9

Jasmine

Jasmine, aged two, was told that she could choose which socks she would like to wear that day. From the drawer in her bedroom she chose the pink ones, then changed her mind and chose the purple ones, then the flowery ones, then the pink ones again, then the white ones with hearts on, and so on and so on. This continued for a considerable time. Jasmine was unable to make a choice.

activity
INDIVIDUAL WORK

1 How could this opportunity to choose have been made easier for Jasmine?
2 What may have happened if time was limited that morning?

It can work well if the adult offers a limited choice of just two or three items, for example the pink socks or the purple socks, the blue jogging suit or the jeans and sweater, the pink dress or the brown skirt and top. This enables even a very young child to make a choice and with an older child can help to minimise the potential for battles, especially when time is limited.

Communicating with babies and children

Take time to observe an adult with a young baby; this will give you an example of preverbal communication. Notice how the adult encourages the baby to take a share in the conversation, asking them questions and supplying them with answers or making reaffirming comments following the baby's vocalisations. Welcoming the vocal sounds of babies encourages them to vocalise further, and responding to babies and watching them respond to you will enhance their communication skills and desire to communicate with you.

Fig 2.35 Methods of communication with babies

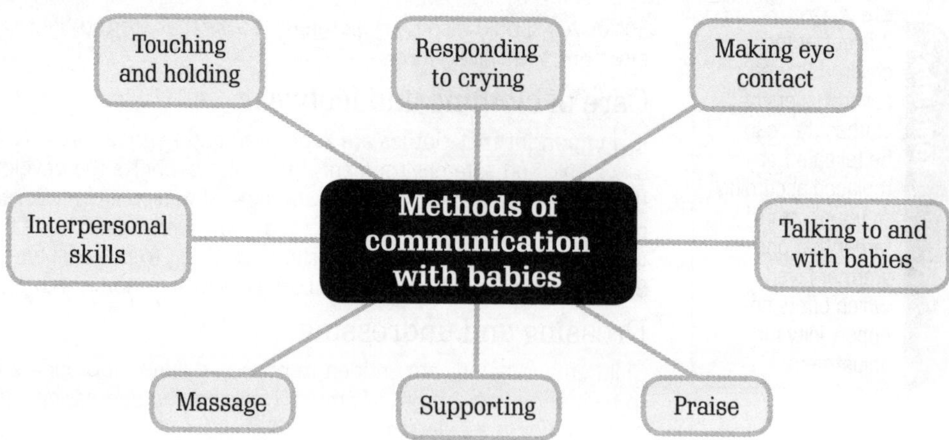

Adults communicate with babies in many ways. This can be through:

- eye contact during breast or formula feeds
- **turn-taking** vocally or visually
- initiating 'conversations' with babies during play
- observing their needs through their body language or facial expression
- responding to their cries (e.g. by giving them a cuddle)
- encouraging them to vocalise (e.g. by clapping and smiling)
- showing appreciation of their vocalising (e.g. by clapping and smiling)
- giving praise (e.g. by clapping and smiling)
- calling to them when out of their visual range
- **aural stimulation** (e.g. singing to the baby)
- **visual stimulation** (e.g. holding a mirror in front of the baby).

remember Like communicating with older children and adults, communicating with babies involves interpersonal skills.

Link You may find it helpful to refer to Unit 1, pages 11–24, to consolidate your understanding of communication and interpersonal skills.

activity INDIVIDUAL WORK 2.9

D2

1 Take time to observe an early years worker working with young babies in a baby-room setting.
   (a) Which of the forms of communications listed above did you see?
   (b) Were there opportunities for any other form of communication to have taken place?
   (c) Do you think the adult you observed missed any opportunities for communication? If yes, what were they?
   (d) What might be the outcome for a baby who does not have opportunities for communication?
2 Reflect on your own practice.
   (a) Identify some occasions when you have communicated well.
   (b) When could you have improved on your communication with babies or children, and how?

Baby massage

Baby massage can improve communication between a parent and their baby, as it enhances the parent's understanding of their baby's needs. Baby massage involves eye contact, touch, smiling and other facial expressions denoting pleasure. As it involves such close contact, interaction between parent and baby is heightened. Because baby massage strengthens the contact between the mother and her baby, it is used by therapists to help mothers who are suffering from postnatal depression.

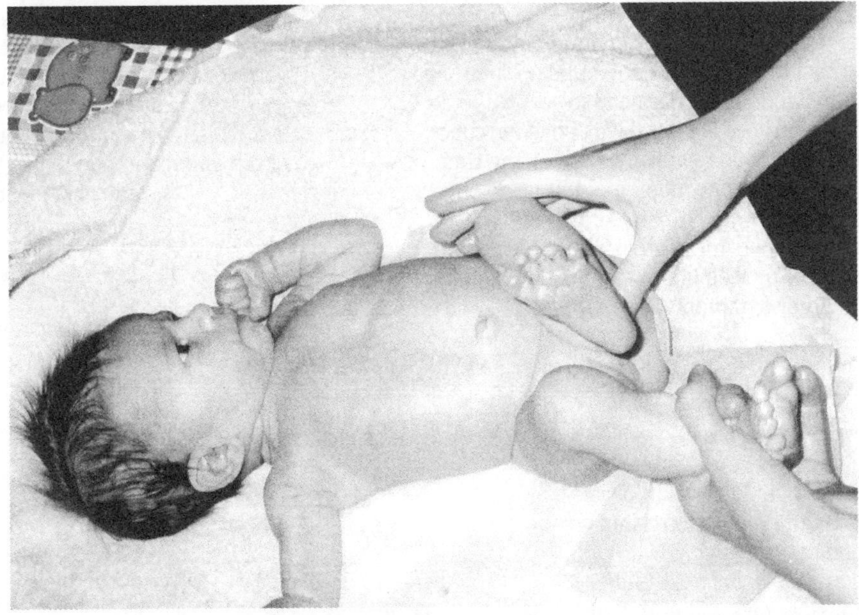

Fig 2.36 Baby massage can improve communication between parent and baby

Baby signing

Baby signing has been developed as a means of additional communication for hearing babies. The range of simple signs can be introduced very early on, and babies of just over a year old have been seen to communicate in this way, alleviating some of the frustration they experience when not making their needs clear. This approach to communicating is not something that early years staff should introduce to the infants in their care unless parents express a wish for them to do so.

Sign With Your Baby by Garcia (2000) is a useful reference on baby signing.

Refer to Unit 3, page 149, for a table showing how babies' language usually develops.

Management of a distressed baby

remember Babies sometimes want a drink in the same way as adults and older children do. Small amounts of cooled boiled water can be introduced to even very young babies, especially in hot weather.

Babies become distressed for lots of reasons. It may be because they are tired, wet, hungry, uncomfortable, unwell, teething or simply bored. Working out the cause of their distress is not always easy and not all babies like to be comforted in the same way. Every baby is different and has their own individual personality; for example, some babies cry much more than others. It is possible to overstimulate a baby, tiring them and causing irritability.

It is important to respond to an infant's distress in a way that is best for them as an individual. This is why continuity of care through key-worker systems is so important.

Illness must never be ruled out when a baby is distressed but will usually be considered when other causes have been eliminated unless additional symptoms are present.

Offer support to the parents of a constantly crying baby as constant crying can be very draining.

For information on illness in babies (and children), refer back to pages 63–76.

Fig 2.37 Why is the baby crying?

Why is the baby crying?

My tummy hurts
If a baby is distressed at the same time of day every day, it can often be attributed to **colic**. Colic is a painful condition, common in the first four months, in which the baby pulls up their legs indicating abdominal pain and is very difficult to console. There is no known cause for colic and it tends to disappear by itself by the time the baby reaches four months old. It is, however, distressing for both baby and carer and advice from a health visitor is advisable. The baby is usually thriving well in spite of the colic and no other symptoms are displayed.

My gums hurt
If a baby is unwell or teething, they may simply want to be cuddled. For a teething baby, a refrigerated teething ring will help cool down their gums and firm flexible teething toys will give them something appropriate to chew hard on. Preparations are available to rub onto the gums to alleviate discomfort of the gums and paediatric paracetamol can be given in times of extreme discomfort.

I'm tired
Babies become over-tired if they do not have sufficient periods of restful sleep, and a baby who is constantly disturbed may become irritable. It is important to allow babies an extended period of sleep whenever possible.

I'm so bored
Sometimes, however, babies are simply bored, and so it is important to offer them stimulation. Mobiles over the cot or hanging from the ceiling are ideal visual stimulants and musical toys will stimulate them aurally. Babies also enjoy the company of their carers and will respond with pleasure and recognition from a very early age.

I want my nappy changed
A wet or soiled nappy is uncomfortable, and most babies prefer to be clean and dry. Regular changing of babies helps prevent the development of nappy rash, as does allowing fresh air to their bottoms by leaving them to kick freely at some point each day.

I want my bottle
A hungry or thirsty baby is often the easiest to identify as they tend to root for the breast or bottle when picked up or suck on whatever passes their mouth. In a day-care setting, making a note of the time and amount of feed taken by the baby helps you to anticipate their next feed time and is a general requirement of those caring for babies.

I'm too hot
A baby who is too hot or too cool may also cry in discomfort. Adjusting the temperature of the room or their clothing will usually help.

Please leave me alone
Sometimes babies become distressed when being handled, but this is usually a stage that passes quickly. Handling should be gentle and kept to a minimum until they find it more pleasurable.

case study 2.10 Rosie

Rosie is seven months old and is teething. She has been unsettled for the past week, during the day, and has hardly slept for the past two nights. Her mother is exhausted as she is a single parent with sole responsibility for Rosie and her three older brothers aged two to seven. You live next door to Rosie's family and want to help.

activity
INDIVIDUAL WORK

1 What could you do to help?
2 What advice could you give Rosie's mother?
3 You have heard of a phone line called Cry-sis for parents with fretful babies. Where could you find out more about the help they offer?

Stimulation and stimulating play

Stimulating play is an essential part of a child's daily experience. As an early years professional, you will be responsible for providing the children in your care with a range of stimulating opportunities, both indoors and outside. Communication is significant here, with the adult describing, explaining, encouraging, etc. as they offer toys and provide experiences.

Ideas for providing stimulating play can be found in a number of excellent publications. See Bibliography and suggested further reading, pages 457–460.

Stimulating play for very young babies

Very young babies initially obtain most of their stimulation from the interactions with their mother or main carers, through feeding, care routines, gentle rocking and soothing, and the calming tone of their voice. By about six weeks, babies demonstrate that they have become much more visually alert and are usually smiling and focusing on the faces of their carers and familiar objects. By this time they will enjoy stimuli which hold their attention, such as mobiles, which should be brightly coloured and three dimensional. Many mobiles have a musical element which adds to the stimulation.

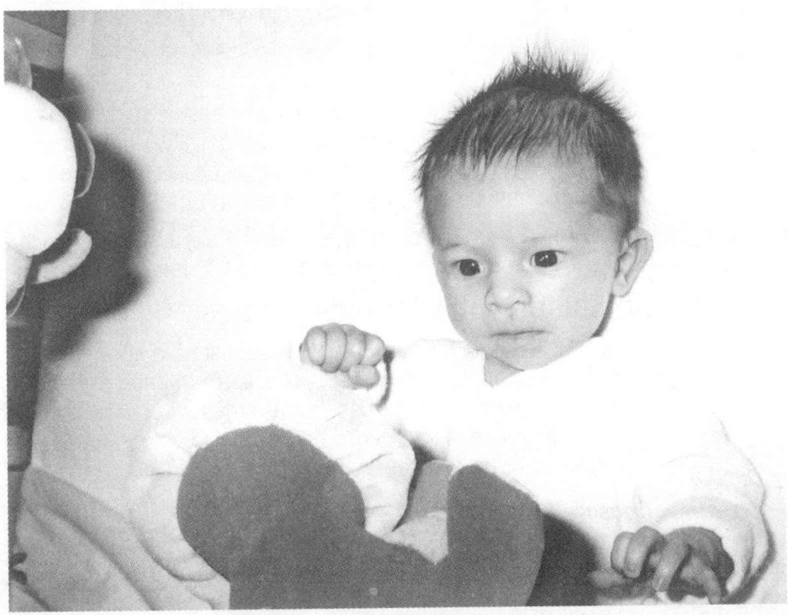

Fig 2.38 By about six weeks, babies enjoy stimuli which hold their attention

remember Babies absorb information from all around them and benefit from as many experiences as it is possible to give them. It is, however, important not to overstimulate them at any one time, as this can cause them to become tired and irritable.

From here, babies benefit from progressing to an activity frame or something similar which can be placed above them. Not only does this encourage them to focus visually and aurally on the items hanging in front of them but they also enjoy tactile experiences as they come into contact with the items during their natural body movements. Eventually, these movements become more intentional, and repeated actions will be observed, often in response to the 'reward' of a noise or visual 'experience' (movement, reflection or fluttering of material). Bath time and nappy changing provide opportunities to play free from the restriction of clothes and with full leg mobility; such play should be encouraged whenever possible.

Babies love music, and many will respond well to music familiar to them from the womb. They listen carefully to all that goes on around them and can often be seen to respond to gentle music (which has a soothing effect) and to lively music (which can agitate or excite).

Babies also enjoy books and pictures from a very early age, and there is now a scheme specifically designed for them: Books for Babies (published by Friends of Libraries USA – FOLUSA) is a literacy programme that helps parents understand the importance of books in a baby's development.

Reading with a baby involves close and pleasurable contact. It also encourages an early interest in literature as a medium of pleasure.

Babies outside

Babies enjoy being outside, watching the leaves on trees flickering and taking in the sounds and smells of the garden. Fresh air is good for them, but they should never be left

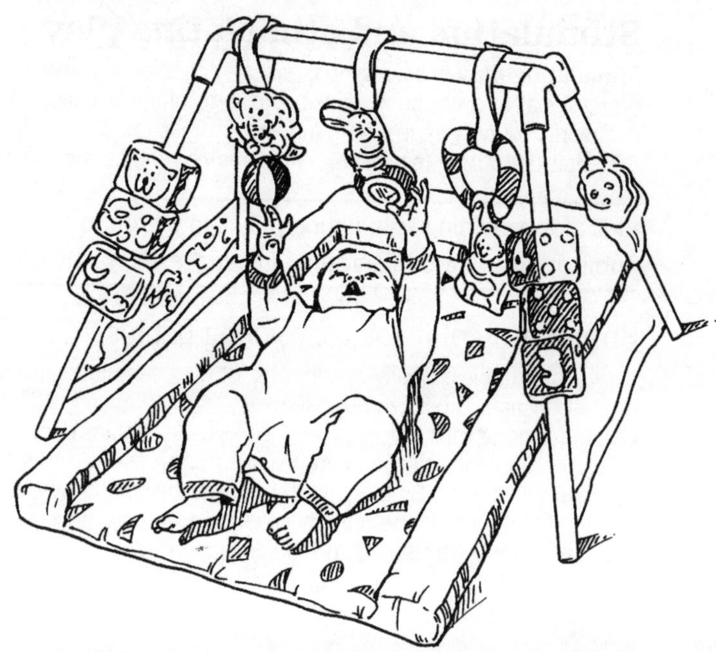
Fig 2.39 An activity frame encourages babies to focus visually and aurally on the items in front of them

remember It is important to monitor the movement of the sun to ensure that a baby's pram which was in shade is not now in sunlight.

unsupervised and care should be taken to ensure that prams are not positioned in the sun, as a baby's delicate skin burns extremely quickly. Whenever possible, allow a baby to lie out of doors in warm weather without a nappy on, as exposure of the nappy area to fresh air is healthy and stimulating for their skin too.

Although most professionals agree that taking a baby out each day is a good idea, this does not apply if the weather is particularly cold or foggy.

Stimulating play for older babies

As they develop, older babies will be interested in a range of household articles. Sturdy boxes can be handled easily, being passed from hand to hand from about six months and knocked together when the baby's movements become more controlled. Babies will also enjoy banging things in order to make a noise. A useful item is a wooden spoon to bang on a saucepan lid or on the tray of the baby's highchair.

Treasure baskets

Babies enjoy activities which enable them to explore through all of their senses, and an excellent resource for this is a treasure basket. A **treasure basket** includes a range of

Fig 2.40 From the age of about six months, a baby will enjoy exploring a treasure basket

objects that are made of natural materials and can be easily handled by the infant. The items should be selected carefully to **stimulate** all the senses and should be completely safe. Nothing in a treasure basket should be made of plastic or any other manufactured materials.

Infants of about six months will enjoy exploring a treasure basket. Ideally, they need to be able to sit up securely in order to benefit from the freedom to explore. They should be allowed to focus on the objects they are handling without distraction from adults or older children.

case study 2.11

Nasreen and Claire

Nasreen and Claire have been asked to prepare a treasure basket. They have selected the following items:

- a silk hankie
- a sheet of sandpaper
- an orange
- a natural sponge
- a wooden clothes peg
- a bag of lavender
- a wooden 'egg' permeated with lemon scent
- a wooden spoon
- a large shell
- a loofah
- a fir cone
- corrugated cardboard
- a glass paperweight
- a large cork

activity
INDIVIDUAL WORK

1 Are all the items suitable, do you think?
2 Would you remove any of the items? If yes, which ones and why?
3 What else would you add to the basket if you were preparing it?
4 Have Nasreen and Claire provided stimulation for all the senses?

Professional Practice

- The objects included in a treasure basket must be kept very clean.
- They should not have sharp or rough edges or be at risk of coming apart, and none should be small enough to be swallowed or put up noses.
- The infant will need supervision whilst exploring their treasure basket – but not direct adult intervention. The adult's role is to provide, to oversee and to allow freedom of exploration.
- Some older children with a special need may also benefit from exploring a resource prepared along the lines of a treasure basket.

For additional discussion of how to plan a suitable environment to stimulate a baby's all-round development, refer to Unit 3, page 159.

Stimulating play for toddlers

As they reach the toddler stage, children need opportunities to develop their large motor skills, particularly direction and spatial skills. Once they are walking, push-a-long toys will help them become more stable and co-ordinated. At this stage, children need space, and careful positioning of unavoidable obstacles around the nursery room will help them develop spatial awareness and control.

The use of boxes and tables and chairs as places to hide is common and rewarding for children of this age, and opportunities to learn to climb skilfully will be beneficial. Indoor slides and mini climbing frames are ideal.

Interest in boxes and placing items in and taking them out is gradually replaced by the building of towers; grading toys enhance both manipulative dexterity and early problem-solving.

remember Outdoor play needs careful supervision.

Outside play

Wheeled toys are enjoyed, including ride-along toys and tricycles. Whilst possible to use indoors, balls and beanbags are a real asset in the garden. Controlling large and small balls requires different skills, and paired games with an adult or an older child help develop physical as well as social development.

Stimulating play for older children

Activities should be planned to meet the needs of all children in the group or class, taking into account differentiation of need. Many children will be ahead of the 'norms', and some will still be developing towards them. An environment in which there is too little stimulation will result in children who are bored and potentially disruptive to others in the group. An environment in which there is little opportunity to achieve will result in frustrated, disappointed children whose self-esteem could be adversely affected.

Refer to Unit 3, pages 116–150, for stages of development, but remember that these are only a guide.

Outside play

As children become more independent, they sometimes take risks; therefore, play out of doors needs careful supervision. The wish to climb higher, run faster and so on often outstrips the child's ability to carry the activity out safely. If climbing frames and other large items of play equipment are provided, these must be supported by safety surfaces.

Maintaining and promoting the healthy development of children includes consideration of their diet and daily routine, the development of self-esteem and independence appropriate to their age, the safety of the environment, and also ensuring that they are clothed appropriately for the time of year and the activities they are engaged in.

Refer back to page 42, for information on safe play surfaces.

Care of equipment and toys

Children, like adults, value and enjoy equipment and resources that are clean, complete and well maintained. Part of the role of early years practitioners is to maintain a safe, clean environment for all children.

Refer to page 34 for information on how to care for the early years environment.

A stimulating learning environment contributes to their all-round well-being, and a range of ideas for this are set out in Unit 7, pages 361–363.

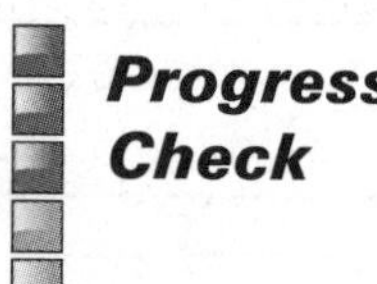

Progress Check

1 What is the purpose of a risk assessment?
2 List as many points as you can about kitchen hygiene.
3 List at least five safety precautions that should be considered when taking children on an outing.
4 How many qualified first aiders should be on duty in an early years setting?
5 How regularly should first aid training be updated and reassessed?
6 What does the A stand for in the ABC procedure? What does this involve?
7 What does the B stand for in the ABC procedure? What does this involve?
8 What does the C stand for in the ABC procedure? What does this involve?
9 How does the recovery position differ between a young baby and a child?
10 Why is it necessary to have a specific person responsible for the first aid box?
11 Give three important points regarding emergency exits.
12 At what temperature should a baby's room be kept?
13 Why are a baby's feet and hands sometimes cold even when their temperature is considered to be normal?
14 What body temperature indicates a potential fever?
15 List five points to remember about clothing for babies.

Promoting Children's Development

This unit covers the following objectives:

- Understand the expected patterns of development from 0–16 years
- Know how to promote development across age ranges
- Understand objectivity and ethics when observing children
- Understand the use of observation
- Be able to use techniques of observation to carry out a longitudinal child study

The study of growth and development involves looking at the processes and sequences of change within a human life, and the influences upon them. As you read this unit, you will develop your understanding of what are considered to be the 'normal' expectations of a child's development. This understanding is important as it will enable you to decide whether an individual child's development is following the expected rates and patterns, or whether it is delayed or impaired in any way.

The unit starts by looking at some principles of development and at the nature–nurture question. It considers growth and development, including some of the factors that affect development up to the end of the first year. You will then be introduced to some of the major theories of child development, before examining factors that affect the development of young children and in some cases lead to developmental delay.

The final sections will help you to understand why and how observations are carried out and familiarise you with a range of techniques for observing children. You will learn how you can record your observations and how to put together an observation portfolio.

grading criteria

To achieve a **Pass** grade the evidence must show that the learner is able to:	To achieve a **Merit** grade the evidence must show that, in addition to the pass criteria, the learner is able to:	To achieve a **Distinction** grade the evidence must show that, in addition to the pass and merit criteria, the learner is able to:
P1 describe the expected patterns of development from 0–16 years and the factors affecting development page 155	**M1** explain the expected patterns of development from 0–3 years and the factors affecting development page 155	**D1** analyse observations to show how these can be used to promote different aspects of development page 183
P2 describe how development can be promoted across the 0–16 years age range page 159	**M2** explain how development can be promoted across the 0–3 years age range page 159	**D2** evaluate the observational techniques used including the longitudinal method. page 190
P3 explain the importance of objectivity and the consideration of ethical issues when observing children page 163	**M3** interpret observations to show how observation can be used for assessing, recording and planning page 171	

To achieve a **Pass** grade the evidence must show that the learner is able to:	To achieve a **Merit** grade the evidence must show that, in addition to the pass criteria, the learner is able to:	To achieve a **Distinction** grade the evidence must show that, in addition to the pass and merit criteria, the learner is able to:
P4 explain the use of observation of children page 179	**M4** interpret longitudinal study, assessing, recording, and planning for the child. page 189	
P5 describe own use of four observational techniques to observe children page 180		
P6 describe own longitudinal study of a baby or young child. page 188		

Understand the expected patterns of development from 0–16 years

Conception to the end of the first year of life

The journey from the moment of conception to the birth of a baby approximately 38 to 40 weeks later is complex. Prenatal (before birth) development can be divided into three stages.

Fig 3.1 Prenatal development

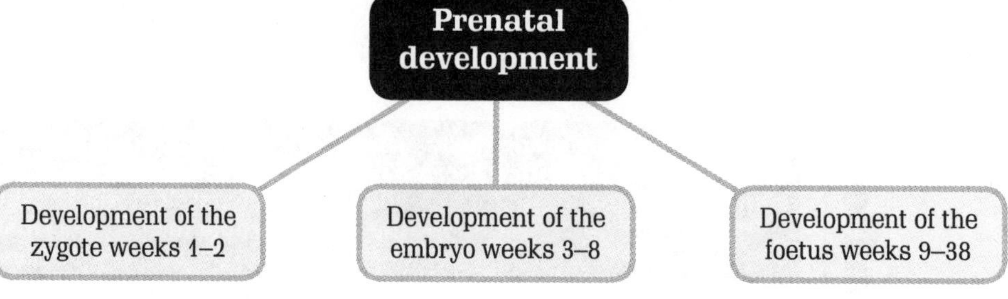

Chromosomes

The nucleus of each cell in our body contains a set of 46 **chromosomes**, arranged in 23 pairs. These control not only the development of our individual characteristics but also shared growth patterns. One pair of chromosomes is responsible for determining sex; in males, this pair is made up of one X chromosome and one Y chromosome, whereas females have two X chromosomes.

Whenever a new cell is needed for growth or tissue replacement, an existing cell duplicates. This process is called mitosis – both the old and the new cell will each contain the full 23 pairs of chromosomes.

Role of the gametes

The sperm and the ovum, which combine to produce each new being, are called gametes (or germ cells). These differ from other cells in that they each have just 23 chromosomes, rather than 23 pairs of cells.

In the earliest stages they divide by mitosis, but the final stage is quite different and is called meiosis. In meiosis only one member of each pair of chromosomes is passed on to the new cell.

In men, all four cells survive, and help to replace the millions of sperm used during each ejaculation. In women, the final stage of meiosis only occurs at ovulation during the monthly menstruation cycle, and only one of the four gametes survives. The other three disintegrate.

Development of the zygote (first two weeks)

- This starts with the release of the egg cell from the fallopian tube approximately midway through the menstrual cycle. Fertilisation usually takes place in the upper portion of the tube within 24 hours of ovulation.
- Conception takes place when the male's sperm cell fertilises the female egg (ovum), which implants itself into the wall of the uterus. Between 24 and 30 hours after fertilisation, the male and female chromosomal material join, and the egg cell divides for the first time. The ovum contained an X chromosome; the sperm could contain either an X or a Y. Thus, the sex of the conceived child is determined: XX = a girl; XY = a boy.
- At 36 hours post-fertilisation there are now two cells, dividing again to four cells at 48 hours. By four days, there will be a cluster of about 100 cells; this is called a morula.
- At approximately four to five days, the zygote enters the uterus and then, over the next two days, starts to embed within the wall of the uterus. It is now referred to as a blastocyst.
- At 14 days, the blastocyst is firmly attached to the uterine wall.
- Cells have already begun to differentiate to become the support system for the body of cells that becomes the embryo.

Development of the embryo (weeks 3–8)

- The main feature of the embryonic period is the development of the structures of the body and the internal organs.
- Three layers form in the embryo – the ectoderm (outer layer) becomes hair, the external layer of skin and the nervous system; the mesoderm (the middle layer) becomes bones, muscles and the circulatory system; the endoderm (inner layer) becomes the digestive and respiratory system.
- The embryo floats in a sac of amniotic fluid that protects it and keeps it at a constant temperature. Two major structures link the embryo to the mother – the umbilical cord and the placenta. These allow the exchange of oxygen, nutrients, vitamins and waste products between the embryo and the mother.

Foetal development (weeks 9–38)

- This is the final and longest phase of development when the increase in size and complexity of development is astounding.
- Rapid growth of all the body systems continues, and most of these systems are now functional.
- Between the 13th and 24th weeks, the foetus will be big enough for the mother to feel it moving. The foetus is now covered in a protective, greasy layer called the vernix.
- Most systems function well enough by 22–28 weeks of gestation for the foetus to be capable of survival if born prematurely, although intensive support will be needed.
- Developmental changes can be seen not only in growth but also in the behaviour of the foetus; foetuses have been observed reacting to stimulation such as music and other sounds.

This has been an extremely brief overview of a complex and fascinating area of development.

Further information can be found in most major texts on development. An ideal text is *A Child is Born* by Nilsson and Hamberger (2003), or refer to the chapter on prenatal development in *The Developing Child* by Bee (2004, 10th edition).

Factors influencing embryonic and foetal growth

A woman planning to have a baby should consider the effects on a potential pregnancy of her current:

- diet
- level of exercise
- smoking habits
- alcohol consumption
- use of drugs (prescribed as well as recreational)
- social life
- relationship.

Planning ahead can enable a woman to give up smoking or using drugs before conceiving and reduce or eliminate her intake of alcohol. It can give her time to assess whether her relationship is stable, and to begin to eat a healthy diet if this is not currently the case, eliminating foods which are not considered to be completely 'safe'. If a woman knows that she is unprotected against rubella (German measles) it is wise to be vaccinated, but she should then avoid becoming pregnant for at least three months after the vaccination.

Any woman with a long-standing medical condition or disorder should consult her doctor before planning a pregnancy to ensure that any medication she has to take regularly will be safe for her developing child. Her doctor may need to change her medication, either because it could harm the foetus or because it could make conception more difficult to achieve.

Table 3.1 Foods to avoid during pregnancy

Food	Possible outcome
Soft cheeses	Listeria, which can cause miscarriage
Pâté	Listeria, which can cause miscarriage
Raw egg	Salmonella, which causes food poisoning
Raw meat	Toxoplasmosis, which is a mild infection in adults but can cause serious harm to an unborn child

In recent years, it has been recommended that women take a supplement of folic acid, starting before conception up until 12 weeks into the pregnancy, as this contributes to the optimum development of the baby's central nervous system.

Screening in pregnancy

Some conditions can be identified by tests carried out during pregnancy; the process is known as **screening**. Specific tests are offered to some women depending on their circumstances, for example older women and women with a family history of certain inherited disorders are offered additional screening.

Blood tests

Routine tests on blood can screen for low iron levels, venereal disease and rubella. Low iron levels may need to be boosted by supplements, and venereal disease will be treated as appropriate. A pregnant woman who is not immune to rubella will be advised to avoid contact with the infection during the early months of her pregnancy as it can cause serious defects in the unborn infant, affecting hearing and vision.

Ultrasound scan

An ultrasound scan is a routine procedure carried out at around 20 weeks' gestation to note the development levels and measurements of the foetus. Measurements are taken of main bones such as the femur (thigh bone), the head circumference is noted and the heart chambers carefully examined. Further scans are carried out as necessary by the midwife or obstetrician.

The foetus shown on page 109 is developing within the normal range. The measurements and examinations made included the thigh bone, head circumference, spine, heart chambers, brain and amniotic fluid. The outcome showed that the foetus (now named Jasmine) had bone development and a head circumference that indicated 19+5 weeks' gestation; amniotic fluid was associated with 19+1 weeks' gestation. These results showed that the foetus was developing well within normal limits, as Jasmine's mother's pregnancy was at 19+3 weeks, according to her dates.

Serum alpha-fetoprotein (SAFP)

This test is used to identify the possibility of the foetus having spina bifida. It is taken at 16 weeks' gestation and is offered to women who are considered to be at risk.

The triple blood test

The triple blood test takes into consideration the woman's age and measures the levels of human chorionic gonadotrophin (HCG), serum alpha-fetoprotein (SAFP) and the placental hormones (oestriols). The combined outcome gives an assessment of the risk of the foetus having Down's syndrome. Again it is offered to women in the high-risk group, usually those over 35 years.

Fig 3.2 A scan of a 20-week-old foetus

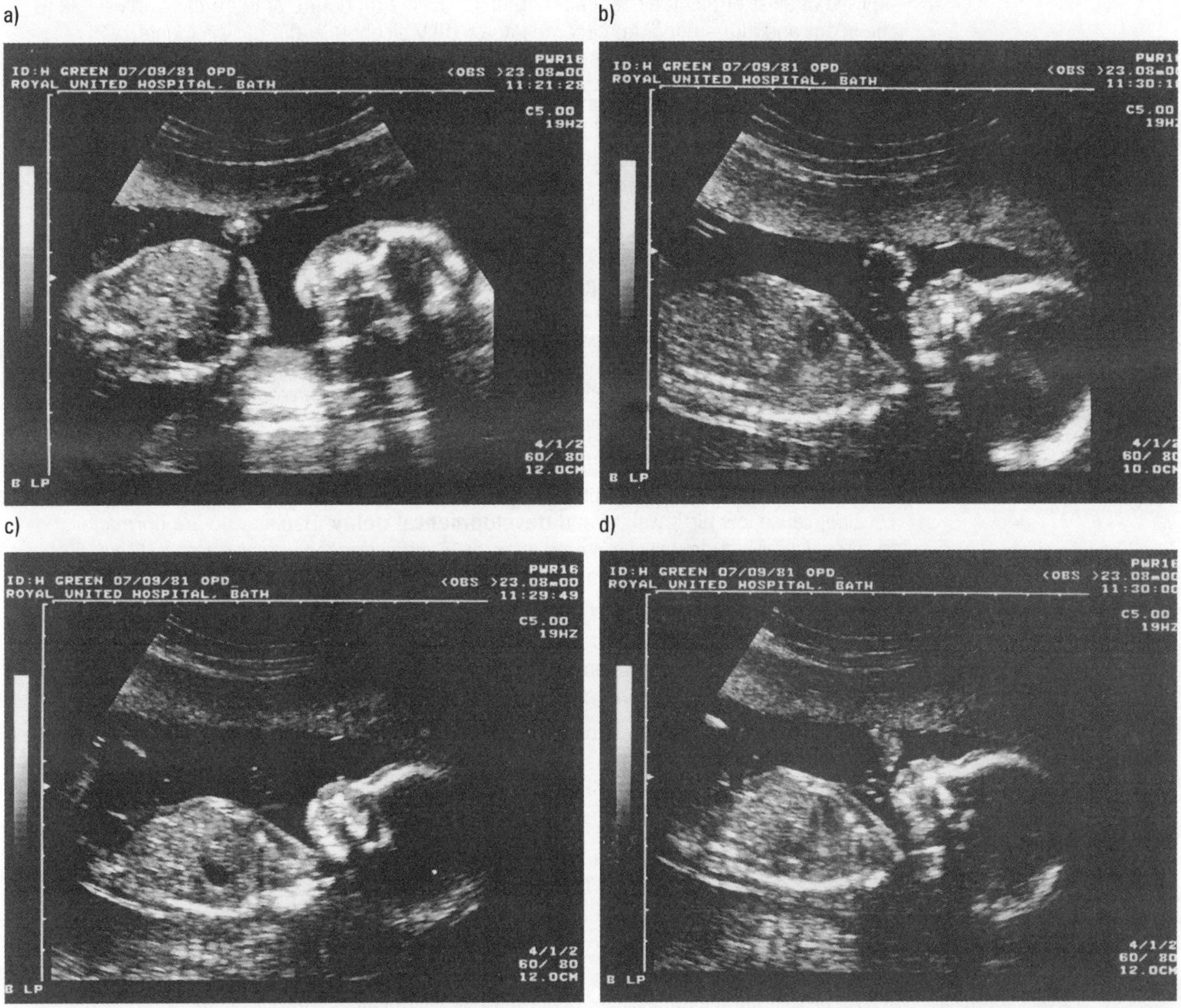

a)

b)

c)

d)

Amniocentesis

This test checks for chromosomal disorders, such as Down's syndrome; it usually takes place between 16 and 18 weeks' gestation. It involves the sampling of the amniotic fluid from the amniotic sac whilst the woman is linked up to an ultrasound machine. The link enables the procedure to be carried out with as much visibility as possible, but there is still a slight risk of miscarriage occurring with this procedure.

Chorionic villi sampling (CVS)

The CVS test involves the removal of a tiny amount of tissue directly from the placenta. It is usually carried out between 8 and 11 weeks' gestation and it can help identify a range of inherited disorders but, as with amniocentesis, it carries a risk of miscarriage.

Refer to Unit 9, page 406, for a summary of other screening programmes: neonatal, infant and childhood.

Environmental effects on foetal development

Even before birth, an infant can be adversely affected by environmental influences, for example the effects of alcohol, smoking and both illegal and (some) prescribed drugs.

Alcohol

Foetal alcohol syndrome (FAS) results from the woman continuing to consume alcohol, usually in considerable amounts, throughout her pregnancy. It was declared to be the leading cause of 'mental retardation' in America by researchers in 1991. It affects the development of the infant, causing delay, deformities and learning difficulties. Pregnant women are now advised against drinking alcohol altogether, as even a moderate amount can carry a risk to the infant and judgement can become impaired by alcohol, leading to accidents.

Poor nutrition

Inadequate nutrition in the pregnant woman is thought to have an adverse effect on the foetus and is associated with a higher rate of low-weight or premature infants. Neural tube disorders such as spina bifida appear to be more prevalent in women whose diet is low in folic acid; this incidence is lowered when folic acid supplements are taken both preconceptually and during pregnancy.

Smoking

Smoking (tobacco as well as illegal substances) affects birth weight owing to the release of nicotine and other substances into the body. It can also lead to learning difficulties in the child. There is a suggestion that infants born to smokers are at a higher risk of being affected by sudden infant death syndrome (also known as SIDS or cot death) and of developing respiratory conditions later. Passive smoking is also thought to contribute to respiratory problems in infants and older children.

Drugs

Any non-essential drug should be avoided during pregnancy. Illegal drugs, such as crack cocaine, cause low birth weight and **developmental delay**. Babies who are born addicted to drugs suffer withdrawal symptoms after birth and experience great distress. Many of these babies suffer all-round developmental problems and some develop epilepsy.

Prescribed drugs are only issued to pregnant women with extreme care, as some have been known to cause deformity and developmental problems. The most well-known example of a drug that caused problems is thalidomide, which was prescribed to women in the 1960s to combat severe vomiting in pregnancy. Their babies were born with severe limb deformities.

It should be remembered that cough and cold remedies are also drugs, and these should be treated with the same caution as any other medication. A pregnant woman should always check their suitability with her GP or a pharmacist before taking them.

Infections

Infections in pregnancy may also affect the developing embryo/foetus and, whilst some infections cannot be prevented, there are known sources of infection that can be avoided. This is especially relevant to the first trimester of pregnancy when the embryo is known to be particularly vulnerable to infection.

- Rubella (German measles) is the most well-known example and, if transmitted to a non-rubella-immune woman, can result in a baby with sensory impairments and congenital heart disease.
- HIV may be transmitted to the developing baby via the placenta, resulting in HIV-positive status for the newborn and the resulting disease process, although this appears to be more likely if the mother shows signs of AIDS during pregnancy.
- Cytomegalovirus is a virus in the herpes group that can lead to severe learning problems, delayed physical and motor skills, and problems with the liver.
- Toxoplasmosis is a parasitic infection which, if contracted in pregnancy, can lead to visual impairment, damage to the central nervous system, seizure disorders, and learning difficulties.
- Listeriosis is caused by a **pathogen** found in food, soil, vegetation and water and may be present in some packaged and raw foodstuffs. It can be the cause of premature labour.

Genetic effects and genetic disorders

Each chromosome in the human body is made up of thousands of genes, and our genetic inheritance is determined by the influences and combination of the genes present in the chromosomes of our parents. The term **genotype** is used to describe the complete genetic inheritance of one person, and the term **phenotype** refers to the visible arrangement of the characteristics that the person has inherited.

Genetically inherited disorders can be due to either autosomal recessive, autosomal dominant or X-linked transference. There are many other disorders that occur following conception; these are termed congenital disorders. Congenital disorders differ from genetically inherited disorders in that their origin is not from the gene bank of the parents.

Autosomal recessive disorder

This type of disorder can occur when both parents are carriers of the defective recessive gene. There is a one-in-four chance of offspring being affected, and a two-in-four chance of their being carriers. Disorders include Batten's disease, cystic fibrosis, phenylketonuria (PKU), sickle cell anaemia and thalassaemia.

Autosomal dominant disorder

This disorder occurs when the carrier is also affected by the disorder. If one parent is an affected carrier, there is a two-in-four chance of the offspring also being affected. If both parents are affected carriers, the incidence rises to a three-in-four chance. Disorders include Huntington's chorea, Marfan's syndrome and osteogenesis imperfecta (brittle bones).

X-linked disorders

The X-linked disorders are carried on the X chromosomes of the mother. As the mother has two X chromosomes, the defective X acts in a recessive way in female offspring and in a dominant way in males, making male offspring more likely to be affected than females. X-linked disorders include Duchenne muscular dystrophy, fragile-X syndrome, haemophilia and Lowe's syndrome.

For details of each of these and many other disorders, a good source of reference is *A–Z of Syndromes and Inherited Disorders* by Gilbert (2000). This is an excellent publication, written in an informative and accessible way.

Refer to Unit 27, *BTEC National Children's Care, Learning and Development*, Book 2, by Green (2007) for an overview of several conditions that affect development.

Birth

The experience of pregnancy and birth should be an exciting and positive one for the expectant parents and with effective preconceptual and antenatal care should result in the safe delivery of a healthy baby. The expectant mother will have met with her midwife regularly during the course of the 40 weeks (the average duration) of pregnancy. They will have discussed what sort of birth the mother would like, and her wishes are usually formalised in a birth plan. Birth may take place at home or in hospital, but the stages and processes of birth remain the same.

The process of birth

Signs of the start of labour

- Some women experience a 'burst of energy' and may feel the urge to start clearing out cupboards or cleaning under the stairs – sometimes called 'the nesting syndrome'.
- A 'show' of mucus (often bloody) from the vagina can happen just before labour starts or several days before.
- The waters break – the bag containing the amniotic fluid either breaks naturally or can be artificially ruptured by the midwifery staff.
- Contractions of the uterus become regular and very different in strength from the mild Braxton Hicks contractions that the mother may have experienced in late pregnancy.

For a much fuller discussion of the experience of pregnancy, labour and birth, see Great Ormond Street Hospital's *New Baby and Child Care Book*.

The first stage of labour

- This is the beginning of labour when the cervix is beginning to soften, thin out and dilate. The cervix has to 'ripen' from closed to 10 cm dilation by the beginning of the second stage.
- The muscles of the uterus will also have pulled the opening of the cervix into a central position, ready for the descent of the baby's head into the birth canal.
- Contractions become stronger and a regular pattern emerges. Most women prefer to remain active in this first phase of labour and will consult their midwife as to when the latter's presence at home is required, or when the woman needs to attend the maternity unit for delivery.

- This is the stage when waters may break naturally or be artificially ruptured, resulting in stronger and more painful contractions.

Second stage

- The stage starts with the full dilation of the cervix to 10 cm; it ends with the baby's birth!
- Contractions become very powerful in order to move the baby down through the birth canal and this transitional stage may make some women distressed.
- As the baby moves down into the birth canal, pressure on the woman's back may be intense and she may feel the urge to push or 'bear down'.
- As the baby's head crowns, the woman may be asked to stop pushing and give panting breaths.
- After delivery of the shoulders, the rest of the body emerges more easily and, if all is well, the baby is given to the mother to be held, comforted and put to the breast.

Third stage

- This lasts from the birth of the baby to the delivery of the placenta and membranes.
- This stage can last for up to 20 or 30 minutes.
- In most cases, the woman is given an injection of syntometrine to ensure that the uterus contracts effectively.

The role of hormones

Hormones are chemical messengers produced in the endocrine glands; they play a very important part in controlling the menstrual cycle, as well as in establishing and maintaining pregnancy, birth and breastfeeding.

- Oestrogen is the female sex hormone and is responsible for the development and general function of the female sex organs.
- Progesterone is the pregnancy hormone that helps the uterus to receive the fertilised egg and maintain pregnancy.
- Oxytocin stimulates the uterus to contract during labour.
- Prolactin controls the production of breast milk.

The role of the midwife

The midwife is an autonomous professional who specialises in the care of the woman in normal pregnancy and childbirth, being able to refer to medical colleagues in complex cases or emergencies. Midwives are highly educated and skilled and often undergo postgraduate training in specialities such as advanced neonatal practitioner status, scanning or acupuncture. Their primary role is to care for and support the woman during the experience of pregnancy and birth, and, although they function as independent practitioners, they also support medical staff during invasive or operative procedures. Many women will need only the care of a midwife in a normal pregnancy.

After delivery

Birth is physically very demanding for both mother and child. The type of birth can affect the level of stress experienced by the infant and, therefore, how well they appear immediately after delivery. All infants are assessed immediately after birth using a benchmark known as the **Apgar score**. This was devised by Dr Virginia Apgar in 1953 and assesses the vital signs of initial health, indicating whether an infant needs resuscitation or medical treatment. The five features of the assessment are scored at one minute after birth and then again at five minutes, continuing at five-minute intervals as necessary until the infant is responding satisfactorily. The higher the infant's score, the less likely it is that they will need any treatment. Most healthy infants have a score of 9 at one minute. They often have discolouration of their hands and feet because their circulation is not yet functioning fully. Infants who are preterm, of a low birth weight or who have experienced a difficult delivery are more likely to score lower – a score below 5 indicates a very poorly baby. Infants who fall into this category make up a large percentage of those who do not survive and those who have ongoing problems.

A premature, difficult or traumatic birth, particularly if either mother or baby is ill and in need of special care, can have an effect on the **bonding** process, owing to separation and lack of physical contact. Health professionals work hard to encourage and maintain links between mothers and their babies in these circumstances.

Fig 3.3 An Apgar chart

Sign	Score		
	0	1	2
Heart rate	Absent	<100 beats per minute	>100 beats per minute
Respiration	Absent	Slow, irregular	Good, regular
Muscle tone	Limp	Some flexion of extremeties	Active
Response to stimulus (stimulation of foot or nose)	No response	Grimace	Cry, cough
Colour	Blue, pale	Body oxygenated, bluish extremities	Well-oxygenated, completely pink

Main principles of children's development

A range of terms is used in the context of development. This unit will help you to understand:

- growth
- development
- rate
- sequence
- delay.

Growth can be most easily defined by changes in measurement such as height, weight, skeletal frame, or size of feet, all of which can be represented visually, through graphs and **tables**.

Development refers to the increase in abilities and to changes that occur within the body's whole structure, for example the closing of the fontanelles in an infant or the ossification of the skeleton (how the cartilage in a newborn infant is gradually replaced by bone). Different organs and tissues within the body have their own pattern and rate of development; and these processes trigger notable changes throughout the lifespan, such as the onset of menstruation in girls, sperm production in boys, the development of secondary sexual characteristics during puberty and, in later life, physical events such as the menopause in women.

The expectations are often referred to as the **developmental norms** or **normative development**. It should be noted, however, that these 'norms' do not accurately reflect all racial and cultural differences. Parents may be concerned if their child does not reach the same milestones as other children of the same age at a similar time. Part of your role, as an early years professional, will be to reassure concerned parents that 'benchmarks' are simply a guide and that all children develop at their own pace.

Return to the above list of terms once you have finished reading through the unit and note how far your understanding has developed.

The human lifespan

During an average lifespan, we each move through a range of developmental stages. There are a number of different ways to split the lifespan into stages, which you will discover if you read other texts. This book focuses on the ages up to 16 years. The categories are as follows:

- the prenatal stage – from conception to birth
- the neonatal stage – from birth to one month
- infancy – from one month to one year
- the toddler – from one to two years
- early childhood – from two to five years
- middle childhood – from 5 to 12 years.
- adolescence – from 12 to 20 years (with puberty being a physiological stage that can cross middle childhood and adolescence).

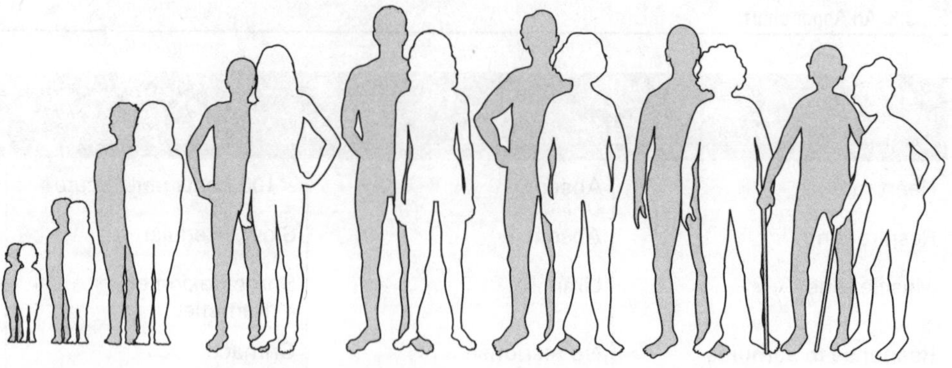

Fig 3.4 The continuum of life – from infancy to adulthood

A useful video is *The Human Body* (BBC, 1998). Originally a television series, this offers a very accessible view of development across the whole lifespan.

Erikson's model of psychosocial development

As you think about development in general, you may find it useful to refer to Erikson's model of psychosocial development, noting the links between age and developmental stage. It can be useful to consider where you see yourself in this model and in others familiar to you.

Table 3.2 Erikson's model of psycho-social development

Stage	Approximate age range	Developmental stages	Personality features	Negative aspects
1	0–1½ years	Basic trust versus mistrust	Sense of hope and safety	Insecurity, anxiety
2	1½–3 years	Self-control versus guilt	Learning self-control and independence	Dependent and unable to control events
3	3–7 years	Initiative versus guilt	Direction and purpose in life	Lack of self-esteem
4	6–15 years	Industry versus inferiority	Building skills competence and positive self-esteem	Feels inferior and lacks confidence
5	13–21 years	Identity versus role confusion	A developing sense of self confidence and security	No direction in life. Negative self-esteem
6	18–30 years	Intimacy versus isolation	Building relationships, loving commitment	Unable to build relationships
7	20s–60s	Generativity versus stagnation	Caring for others – reaching out in the community	Introverted – looking inwards – concentrated
8	Later life	Ego-integrity versus despair	Sense of meaning to life	Loss of sense of achievement

Holistic and interconnected development

Children's growth and development should be studied within a holistic framework that acknowledges the interconnections between all the areas of development, for example physical, social and emotional, cognitive and language. What happens in one area of development will almost certainly affect one or all of the other areas as will the influence of the child's environment and culture. Normative measures such as developmental milestones enable us to benchmark individual patterns of growth, development and behaviour. You may already have been introduced to acronyms such as:

- PIES (Physical, Intellectual, Emotional, Social)
- PILESS (Physical, Intellectual, Language, Emotional, Social, Spiritual)

- SIMPLE (Social, Intellectual, Moral, Physical, Language, Emotional)
- SPICE (Social, Physical, Intellectual, Communication, Emotional).

You may find it easier when beginning your studies to consider these areas of development separately, but remember to see the 'whole child' and what that child can do rather than just what milestones or competencies they have achieved.

Development occurs in broadly the same sequence, and control tends to be gained from head to toe, and from the inner body towards the outer body.

Refer to page 127 for more on the development of bodily control.

Theories of development

There are three principal types of **theories** of development:

- biological theories
- learning theories
- ecological theories.

When looking at the theories of child development, it is important to remember that no one theory alone can explain the complexity of the developing child. Theories, like children, need to be understood within their wider social, environmental and cultural contexts, so try to be 'critical' when using theoretical perspectives.

Biological theories

According to these theories, nature influences development through genetic programming, thus predisposing individuals to develop in certain ways. An example of a biological theory is Arnold Gesell's **maturational** theory. Maturational theory explains development as a genetically programmed pattern of **sequential** changes that are universal and found across cultures.

Learning theories

These theories propose that individuals acquire their skills, knowledge and responses through learning and experience of the environment. Some learning theories focus solely on the role of reinforcement, but Albert Bandura's social learning theory explains how individuals learn social behaviour from observing models.

Ecological theories

These types of theory explain an individual's development within the context of external factors such as their family and social environment. An example of this is to be found in Uri Bronfenbrenner's ecological theory, which has been used to understand the complex nature of the assessment of vulnerable children and families.

Nature–nurture debate

You will have seen that the three main types of theory differ as to whether a child's development is mostly influenced by genetics and biology (nature) or by learning and their family and wider social environment (nurture). This issue – whether it is heredity and genetics that shape our personalities and behaviour or the influences of our parents, family and

Fig 3.5 Family, friends, teachers, pets – do you think we have been moulded by experience?

our environment that are more important – is referred to as the **nature–nurture debate**. **Nativists** support the idea that human infants have innate (inborn) abilities that predispose them towards developing in certain ways, whereas **empiricists** believe firmly that we are moulded by experience. Early studies of child development and developmental psychology tended to see the nature–nurture question from one fixed position or the other, but most modern-day theorists take a combined approach, accepting that genetic influences interact with experiences to influence development.

A useful publication to help you explore the nature–nurture debate further is *The Foundations of Child Development* by Oates (1999).

case study 3.1

Lucy

Simon and Nina are clarifying the plans for next week's activities in their nursery class. 'I don't know what to do with Lucy,' said Nina. 'She just wants to talk non-stop, she rarely lets anyone else get a word in, and some of her language is pretty awful too. What with her tearing around all the time, it is difficult to get her to listen as she is hardly ever still for more than a few seconds.'

'She probably inherited it from her mother,' said Simon. 'Whenever I speak to her, I hardly manage to complete a sentence without her interrupting me. I've noticed that she is the same when she speaks to the other parents.'

'I'm not sure I agree with you about Lucy inheriting her behaviour,' replied Nina. 'I think children are more likely to learn by the way they are brought up. As Lucy lives in such a noisy and lively household, what else can we expect?'

activity
INDIVIDUAL WORK

Consider the conversation.

1 Who was taking a nativist view?

2 Who took a more empiricist view?

Stages and sequences of development

The various stages and sequences of development that are expected in children without any identified additional problems are often referred to as milestones. In new born infants there are a number of general expectations regarding appearance, **reflexes** and sensory responses. Each of these helps to confirm good health and well-being. Each individual child's progress is monitored though the use of percentile (or centile) charts.

Examples of percentile charts can be found on page 130.

Growth and development in children aged one to eight years

The period from one to eight years represents a time of growth and maturation in all areas of development and, although patterns and sequences of development will be similar for many children, development is not merely a linear continuum.

Table 3.3 Principles of growth

Age	Principles of Growth
Toddler (1–3 years)	■ Growth slows considerably ■ Average weight gain is 1.8 to 2.7 kg per year ■ Rate of increase in height also slows and usually increases by increments of 7.5 cm each year ■ Steady growth curve should be seen and is likely to show step-like growth spurts rather than linear pattern ■ Toddler often appears to be squat and 'pot-bellied' due to short legs and relatively poorly developed abdominal muscles
Pre-school (3–5 years)	■ Rate of physical growth slows and stabilises ■ Average weight gain remains 2.3 kg ■ Growth in height remains constant at between 6.75 to 7.5 cm ■ Physical proportions of the pre-schooler no longer similar to toddler – able to maintain an erect posture, sturdy and agile ■ Muscle development and bone growth still far from mature
School age (6–12)	■ Growth in both height and weight are slow but steady with average increase in height of 5 cm per year ■ May double in weight between 6 and 12 years ■ Girls and boys similar in size but boys tend to be slightly taller and heavier than girls ■ Body outline is slimmer than that of pre-schooler and posture is improved ■ By 12 years, both boys and girls will have increased their strength, physical capabilities and refined their coordination ■ In spite of an increase in strength, muscles are still relatively immature and easily damaged

The neonate and development up to one year

An infant during its first month is known as a **neonate**. At delivery, babies are wet and covered to some degree in mucus, maternal blood and body fluids. Their skin colour varies due to ethnic origin and their state of health, with black babies appearing pale at birth, as the skin pigmentation melanin does not reach its full levels until later on. Most infants are delivered onto their mother's abdomen and the umbilical cord is clamped and cut shortly after birth. Depending on the type and duration of the delivery, infants vary from being alert and wide awake to drowsy and unresponsive; medication given to the mother during labour can affect this.

General appearance of the neonate

- In the period after birth, the neonate will sleep most of the time, mostly waking for feeds and changing and often falling asleep during these routines.
- The neonate is unable to control the head and needs to be supported during handling.
- Vernix caseosa may be present; this is a creamy white protective substance which covers the body of an infant during the latter stages of pregnancy. It is usually seen in preterm infants and often in full-term infants too. It lubricates the skin and should be left to come off on its own, rather than be washed or rubbed.
- Some of the soft downy hair that covers the infant during pregnancy may also be present. It is called lanugo, and traces are often found on the back, shoulders and ears at birth.
- There are two fontanelles. The posterior fontanelle is a small triangular area near the crown which closes within a few weeks of birth. The anterior fontanelle is near the front of the head and is diamond shaped. It closes over by 18 months of age and can often be seen pulsating slightly. A sunken appearance can indicate insufficient fluids, whereas a bulging appearance can indicate an unacceptable level of pressure around the brain or an infection and should always be investigated.
- Newborn infants often have a flattened or misshapen head, and it can take some weeks for the natural shape to appear. Causes are pressure during the passage down the birth canal, delivery by forceps or ventouse suction, and, in a multiple birth, lack of space in the womb.
- The most usual sign of the neonate is the umbilical 'stump'. The umbilical cord is clamped and cut at birth, and the stump will be left to drop off on its own, usually between 7 and 10 days after birth. The stump should be kept dry and clean, although actual cleaning of it is not usually recommended.

- Some infants show signs of swelling or bruising, normally due to a difficult birth. This tends to disappear within a few days.
- Sticky eyes are a common occurrence in the first few days, and uncoordinated eyes are usual. All babies are born with dark eyes; permanent eye colour is not established until later.
- The posture of infants is very flexed and movements tend to be jerky. The extremities (feet and hands) are often bluish in colour due to poor circulation.
- Genitalia appear to be swollen in both boys and girls, and blood loss from the vaginal area in girls is quite common. This is caused by the mother's hormones crossing the placenta.
- The breasts of both boys and girls may leak a little milk. Again, this is due to the mother's hormones crossing the placenta.
- The stools (faeces) of the neonate are a dark, greenish black because they contain a tarry substance called meconium, which is very sticky. The colour and consistency change within a few days, as the mother's milk arrives.
- Spots and rashes are very common in the first few days, but the infant's skin soon settles down. A particularly common type is 'milia', which are tiny white spots often known as milk spots.
- Peeling skin is quite common on the hands and feet but usually only lasts two or three days.
- Some infants suffer from **neonatal jaundice** where the skin and eyes become yellowish due to the infant's immature liver function and a subsequent rise in levels of bilirubin. Bilirubin is formed when red cells break down, and the liver is unable to cope with its workload. It usually occurs (if it is going to) on about day three after birth. Jaundice occurring before the infant is three days old needs particular investigation, as liver disease or sepsis may be present and the infant's life could be in danger. On occasions, jaundice can be a sign of galactosaemia, rubella or cytomegalovirus.

Birthmarks

- Port wine marks are a permanent, dark-red mark, often on the face or neck. In the past they were often a permanent disfigurement, but many can now be successfully removed or reduced with laser treatment.
- The strawberry naevus is quite common. These are raised marks full of blood vessels; the marks are not actually present at birth but develop in the first few days or weeks. They usually disappear by eight years of age. The full name for this type of naevus is haemangioma.
- Another common mark is the 'stork bite'. These tiny red marks, found on the eyelids, the top of the nose and on the back of the neck, disappear gradually and are not usually a problem.
- Mongolian blue spots are dark marks found at the base of the spine on non-Caucasian infants. On occasions, these marks have been wrongly attributed to **physical abuse**. They are usually 'mapped' by health professionals in the early weeks. Early years workers need to be aware of these marks.
- Most people have moles, but some moles can be large and unsightly, for example congenital melanocytic naevus (CMN). CMNs get progressively darker as the infant grows but can sometimes be successfully removed or reduced with laser treatment or plastic surgery.

Neonatal reflexes

The primary reflexes can be defined as 'automatic body reactions to specific stimulation' (Bee, 1992, page 105). These reflexes include:

- blinking reflex – the neonate reacts to sudden lights, noises or movements in front of the eyes
- rooting reflex – the neonate turns their face towards their mother to locate the breast
- sucking reflex – infants will usually suck a clean finger, placed gently in the mouth
- palmar grasp –the infant holds firmly to whatever touches the palm (gently stroking the back of the hand will usually release the grasp)
- plantar reflex – touching the sole of the infant's foot with a finger will result in the flexing of the toes towards your finger
- stepping reflex – the neonate's foot responds to contact with a firm surface, resulting in a small step being taken

- moro reflex – a sudden movement of the neck is interpreted by the infant as falling; they will throw out their arms with open hands and reclasp them over their chest
- startle reflex – the infant throws out their arms at a sudden noise or movement, but the fists remain clenched
- asymmetric tonic neck reflex – when the infant's head is turned to one side, they will respond by straightening the arm and leg on the same side, whilst flexing the limbs opposite.

Fig 3.6 Infant rooting

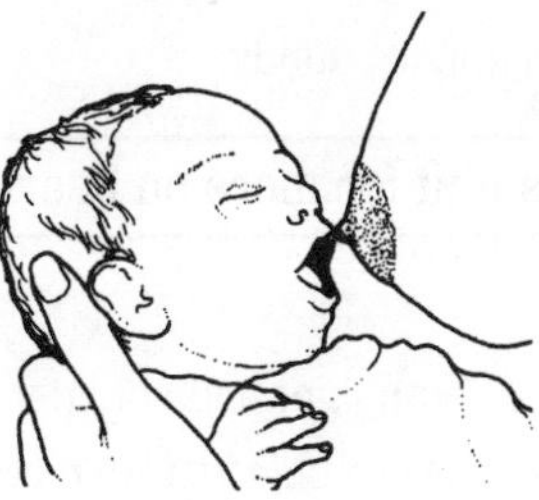

Fig 3.7 Infant sucking

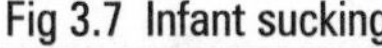

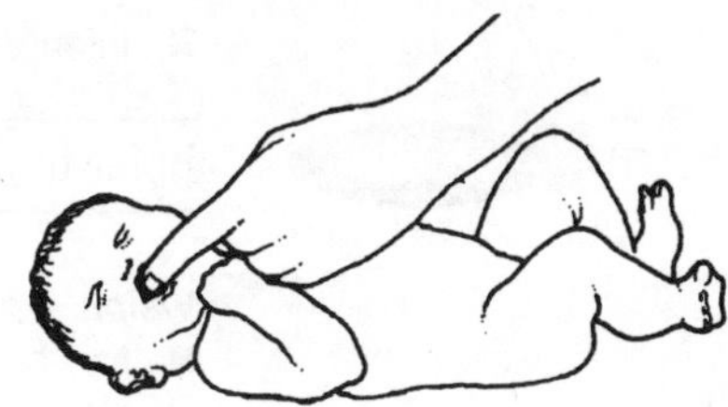

Fig 3.8 Palmar grasp

Fig 3.9 Stepping reflex

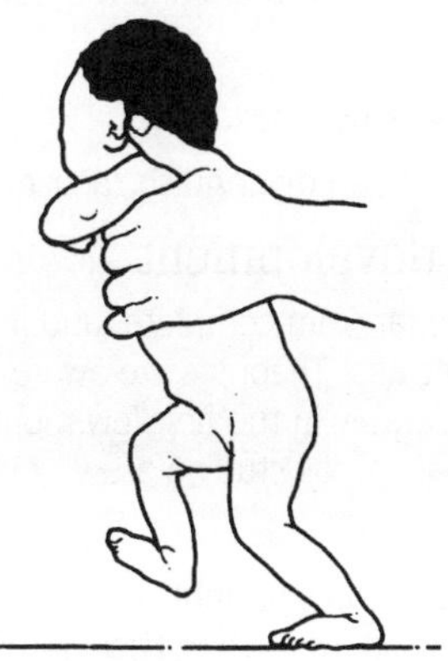

Fig 3.10 Moro reflex

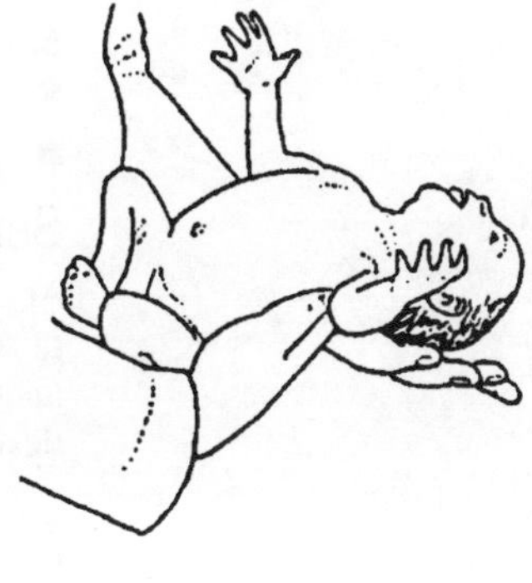

Some reflexes stay with us for life, for example blinking, but some are lost after the first few weeks (the primitive reflexes). The presence of reflexes is an indicator of an infant's neurological well-being. As the brain gradually takes over the body's responses, the primitive reflexes disappear.

The BBC's *Human Body* video is a good source of reference; the reflexes are clearly demonstrated.

Posture and motor skills

Immediately after birth, many infants naturally curl into the foetal position with their head to one side. Their limbs are kept partly flexed and are hypertonic (have tension) and they tend to display jerking movements. The head and neck are hypotonic (weak) and there is no head control, so full support of the head and neck is needed whenever the infant is handled.

Based on research findings, it is recommended that infants are always placed on their back to sleep to minimise the risk of sudden infant death.

The senses in a neonate

Hearing

- The hearing of infants is acute.
- They blink in response to sound.
- The neonate can discriminate the voice of their main carer almost immediately.
- Noisy objects can only roughly be located.
- Sudden noises distress the infant.
- Infants respond to soothing rhythmic sounds.

Refer to pages 121–122 in this unit for more on hearing and its development.

Vision

- Newborn infants are sensitive to both light and sound.
- Vision is diffused and limited initially to objects within about a 30 cm radius.
- Eyes initially do not work together and they often 'cross' or 'wander'.
- Eye-to-eye contact with the main carer (usually the mother) is an important means of establishing a bonding relationship.
- Infants show a preference for human faces.
- Infants will turn towards a light.

Refer below for more on vision and visual development.

Touch

- Skin-to-skin contact is important to the bonding process.
- Most infants are delivered onto their mother's abdomen.
- Contact and handling soothes a distressed infant, but may be contraindicated in a premature baby (handling may distress them and they thrive better with minimal handling).

Smell

- Infants can identify their mothers by smell.
- Research has shown that infants can distinguish their mother's milk on a breast pad.

Sensory and perceptual development

At birth, the nervous system is still far from complete, and it is not easy to understand the level of sensory awareness that an infant has. Theorists are aware that the visual system is not strong initially and that it develops considerably in the first few months, whereas hearing is quite well developed right from birth. The main areas studied are vision, hearing and **perception**.

Vision

From birth, infants turn to look at sources of light, and the eyes of the newborn infant may be seen to move in the direction of sounds. They show interest in the human face and spontaneous and imitative facial expressions are observed within a few days of birth. The early visual interaction between infant and carer strengthens the process of bonding and therefore enhances emotional security in the long term.

An ideal source of further reading on this area of development is *The Foundations of Child Development* by Oates (1999).

Stages of visual development

Birth

- The infant turns to the source of light.
- Imitative facial expressions are seen.
- The human face evokes the greatest level of attention.
- The eyes do not at first move co-operatively.

One month

- The infant turns to light sources.
- The infant stares at face of adult carer.
- The eyes now usually work in co-operation.
- Vision is held by bright mobile or similar object.
- The infant can track the mother's face briefly.

Three months

- The infant is now visually alert.
- The eyes move in co-operation.
- The defensive blink has been present for some time.
- The infant follows the movement of their main carer.
- There is more sustained visual tracking of face or similar.
- The infant may now be demonstrating visual awareness of own hands.
- Anticipation of feeding is demonstrated by responses to visual clues.

Six months

- The infant is visually very alert.
- The infant appears visually insatiable.
- The infant's eyes and head move to track objects of interest.

12 months

- Hand–eye co-ordination is seen as small objects are picked up using pincer grasp (index finger and thumb).
- The eyes follow the direction of fallen or dropped objects (based on Sheridan, 1997).

Concerns relating to vision

The following would cause concern:

- lack of eye contact with main carer
- no social smile by six weeks
- lack of visual tracking of carer's face or a bright mobile by two months
- lack of visual response to impending breast or bottle feed
- lack of co-operative eye movement after three months
- lack of signs that infant reaches out for toys in response to visual stimulus
- lack of mobility or directed attention by 12 months.

Hearing

At birth, the hearing of infants is acute as their auditory perception is as yet uncluttered by the sounds of everyday living. They can be seen to respond to sound by blinking and through startled movements (startle reflex). Newborn infants respond to the sound of their mother or main carer. They also show signs of auditory awareness by turning towards other sounds. Many infants are settled by calming or familiar music, often first heard within the safety of the womb.

Stages of auditory development

Birth

- The infant shows startle reactions to sound.
- Blinking is common in response to sounds.
- The infant may 'still' to ongoing gentle sounds.
- The infant turns towards sounds, including mother's voice.

One month

- The infant is still startled by sudden noises.
- They stiffen in alarm, extending limbs.
- They usually turn towards the sound of a familiar voice.
- The infant is usually calmed by the sound of a familiar voice.

Three months

- The infant turns their head or eyes towards the source of sound.
- They often appear to search for the location of sounds.
- They listen to musical mobiles and similar sounds.

Six months

- The infant shows considerable interest in familiar sounds.
- They turn to locate even very gentle sounds.
- They vocalise deliberately, listening to self.
- They vocalise to get attention, listen and then vocalise again.
- The infant can usually imitate sounds in response to carers.

12 months

- The infant responds to own name.
- Their behaviour indicates hearing; they make appropriate responses to carers (Sheridan, 1991).

Concerns relating to hearing

The following would cause concern:

- lack of response to sudden or loud noises in the first few months
- lack of response to familiar sounds, either listening or by being calmed
- no tracking of gentle sounds by nine months
- no indication of turning to the sound of a familiar voice
- limited changes in vocalising from about six months
- no obvious response to carer's simple instructions at a year.

From one year onwards, the development of speech is the greatest indication of a child's hearing levels although health issues can have an impact on hearing, for example repeated ear infections or glue-ear.

Infant perception

Perception is the process whereby the brain makes sense of information reaching it via the body's senses, helping us to understand what is happening both to us and around us. Visual perception and auditory perception are two early indicators that physical and perceptual development is progressing as expected. Vision and hearing affect language and cognitive development and are both assessed at regular intervals during infancy and early childhood.

Refer to Unit 9, page 406, for screening techniques.

Perception of faces

Researchers (for example, Robert Fantz in the 1950s) have repeatedly shown that the human face invokes a greater level of response than a range of other similar options.

Depth perception: the visual cliff investigation

Among studies carried out on infant perception are those of Gibson and Walk who, in 1960, devised a visual cliff to investigate depth perception. Infants who had gained a degree of mobility were placed on the visually 'safe' (chequered floor) side of the table and encouraged to crawl across the clear glass surface above the visually 'unsafe' cliff towards their mothers. Out of 27 infants, aged 6 to 12 months, only three crawled across the surface over the cliff. The remaining 24 showed a marked reservation in relation to crossing from the 'safe' to the 'unsafe' side, even though they would be moving towards their mothers, who would normally be a safe haven for them.

Under the age of six months it is clearly not possible to investigate depth perception in the same way, owing to infants' lack of mobility. However, Campos *et al.* (1970), monitored the heart rate of infants when placed first on one side and then on the other of the visual cliff. At just 55 days (approximately eight weeks) the heart rates were different, indicating that even at this young age a degree of depth perception is present.

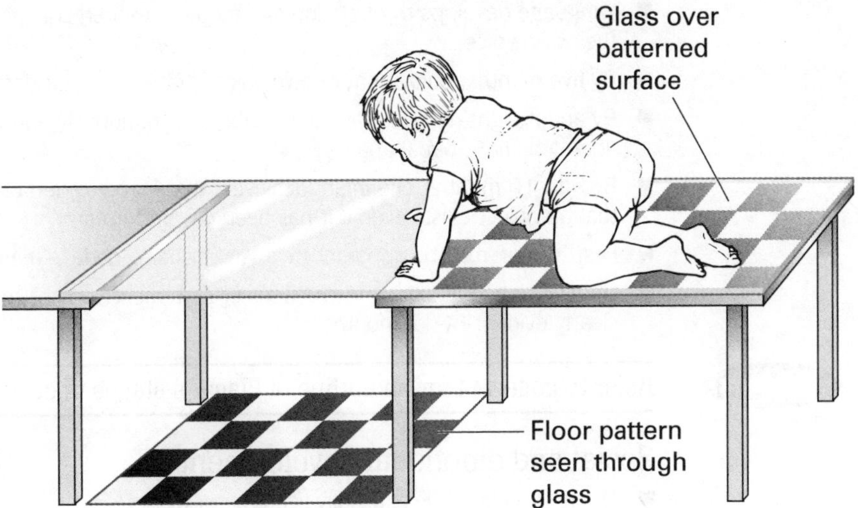

Fig 3.11 The 'visual cliff' experiment by Gibson and Walk

Infancy: one month to one year

Physical development (gross motor)

- Movements remain jerky.
- Head lag gradually decreases, and head control is usually good by five months.
- Rolling over is first seen between four and six months (from back to side), and then from front to back by about eight months.
- Reaching for objects begins at about four months with the transference of toys from hand to hand from about seven months.
- At four months, the infant discovers their feet and manages to sit with support.
- Sitting alone commences at about seven to eight months, with greater balance gradually developing.
- Crawling can start from six months (commando crawling) and traditional crawling from about eight months. Some infants bear-walk or bottom-shuffle.
- Some infants miss out the crawling stage, and move straight to pulling themselves up on furniture at around 8 to 10 months.
- Standing alone can occur any time from 10 months but is more usual at around 12 months, when generally balance is more established.
- Walking is normally achieved between 12 and 16 months.

Physical development (fine motor)

- Hand and finger movements gradually increase, from the grasping of the adult's fingers in the earliest months, through playing with own fingers and toes, to handling and then holding toys and objects from three to four months.
- Everything is explored through the mouth.
- At about seven months, the infant will try to transfer objects from one hand to the other with some success. Pincer grasp is emerging.
- By about 10 months, pincer grasp is developed.
- The infant will pick up small objects.
- Toys are pulled towards the infant.
- Pointing and clapping are deliberate actions for most infants by 10 to 12 months.
- Controlled efforts are made when feeding, with some successes.

Cognitive and language development

- The infant continues to explore orally throughout most of the first year. Piaget called this the sensorimotor stage.
- By about four months, recognition of an approaching feed is demonstrated by excited actions and squeals.

- Language develops through cooing, gurgling, excited squealing and changing tones of their own voice.
- By five months, enjoyment of own voice is obvious. Chuckles and laughs are evident.
- By about eight months, the infant babbles continuously and tunefully, for example 'mamamama', 'babababa'.
- By 9 to 10 months, the infant achieves what Piaget called object permanence; they know that an object exists even if it has been covered up and is out of sight.
- First 'words' may be apparent by a year, usually 'dada', 'mama', 'baba'.
- Understanding of simple instructions or statements begins from about nine months and is clearly evident by 12 months.

Refer to page 144 for an outline of Piaget's stages of cognitive development.

Social and emotional development

- The first social smile is usually seen by six weeks.
- Smiling is first confined to main carers and then occurs in response to most contacts.
- The infant concentrates on carers' faces.
- Pleasure during handling and caring routines is seen by eight weeks.
- From about 12 weeks, expressions of pleasure are clearly evident when the child gains another person's attention.
- Social games, involving handling and cuddles, elicit chuckles from four to five months onwards.
- Infants enjoy watching other infants.
- Sleep patterns begin to emerge from about four months onwards, although these will continue to change.
- From about 9 or 10 months, the infant may become distressed when the main carer leaves them and wary of strangers.
- Playing contentedly alone increases by one year, but the reassuring presence of an adult is still needed.

Toddler: one to two years

An engaging mixture of growing competencies, inquisitiveness and emerging personality, the toddler has frequently been incorrectly labelled as 'a terrible two'. Toddlerhood heralds a period of intensive exploration of the environment, during which the child will acquire a wide range of fine and gross motor skills. Great developments will also be seen in social and language skills, as well as in being able to differentiate the self from others.

Physical development: a summary

- Standing alone is achieved but, at first, toddlers are unable to sit from being in a standing position without help. They begin to let themselves down in a controlled manner from about 15 months.
- When walking, the infant takes uneven steps and has difficulty in stopping; the hands are held up for balance.
- Toddlers can creep upstairs quite safely (not advisable without an adult supervising).
- They begin to kneel.
- By 18 months, walking should be well established, and the arms are no longer needed for balance. The toddler can now back themselves into a small chair and climb forwards into an adult chair.
- Squatting when playing is now common.
- They can usually walk upstairs holding an adult hand.
- Manipulation skills are developing: pages of books can usually be turned quite well, and pencils can be held in a clumsy grasp.
- By two years, the child can run safely, starting and stopping at will.
- They are able to pull wheeled toys, with some understanding of direction.

Fig 3.12 By 18 months the toddler can climb forwards in to an adult armchair

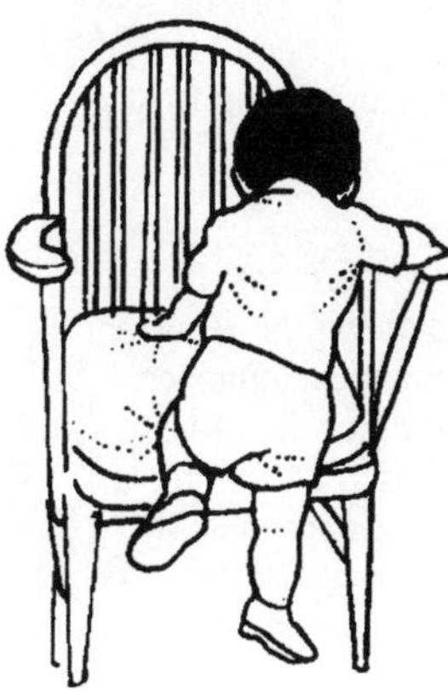

- They are able to control a ball to throw forwards.
- Walking up and (usually) down stairs is possible, holding on and two feet to a stair.
- They cannot yet kick a football without falling into it.
- They cannot usually pedal a tricycle.

Early childhood: 2 to 5 years

Physical development: a summary

- Walking up stairs alternating the feet is usually achieved by three years. Going securely up and down on alternate feet is seen by three and a half.
- At two and a half, a child can kick a football gently, by three years with force.
- Pushing and pulling of large toys is achieved by two and a half.
- Locomotor skills improve rapidly during this stage of development.
- Use of pedals is often achieved by three years, and a child can steer around corners.
- Balance improves gradually, and by four years a child can usually stand, walk and run on tiptoes and can navigate skilfully when active.
- From three years, ball skills increase (catching, throwing, bouncing and kicking).
- Manipulation skills improve.
- Scissor control is developing and greater pencil control is achieved by three years.
- By four years, threading small beads and early sewing is achieved.
- Adult pencil control is usually present by four years.

Fig 3.13 From three years, ball skills increase

Middle childhood: 5 to 12 years

Physical development: a summary

Physically, emphasis is now on practice and further development of the skills already gained. Large motor skills will be increased, for example, how fast a child can run, as will their stamina when playing group games and their ability to climb and manoeuvre more difficult objects in more challenging circumstances. The child's ability to balance also improves. Hand–eye co-ordination develops allowing a more adult level of control when writing, drawing, sewing and so on, and greater skill is seen during ball games and in activities involving manual dexterity.

For girls, the pre-pubescent stage can begin from nine years onwards. Height develops rapidly now with the thigh bone growing at a faster rate than the rest of the body.

Fig 3.14 Hand–eye co-ordination develops in middle childhood

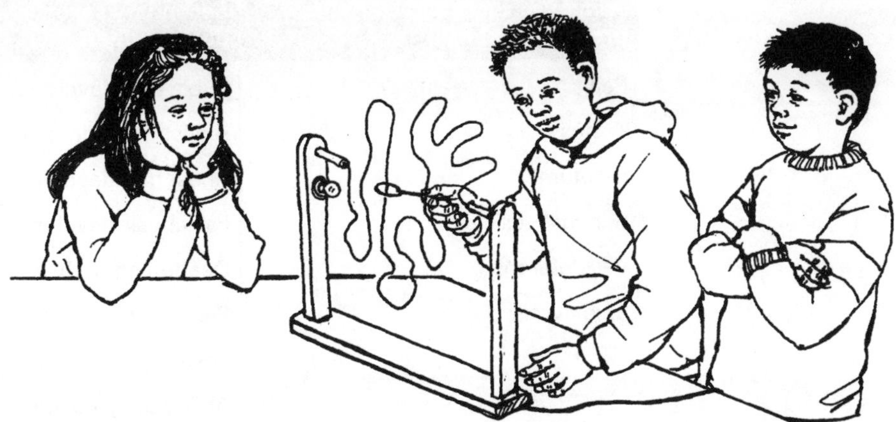

Adolescents: 12 to 16 years

Physical development

The main physical changes that occur during adolescence begin with the onset of puberty. Puberty is a physiological stage that can cross middle childhood and adolescence, and the age at which it actually begins varies from person to person.

Early adolescence is marked by a variety of changes:

- the adolescent growth spurt
- the maturation of the reproductive system
- the development of secondary sexual characteristics.

Both boys and girls have a tendency for oily skin throughout adolescence, leading to skin problems such as acne.

Development of secondary sexual characteristics

For girls, the most important change is the onset of menstruation (their periods). This can start as early as 10 years, but ages vary considerably; some girls are 15 or 16 when menstruation starts. Ethnic group, heredity, exercise levels and health can all influence individual biological timings. Breast development starts with the budding of the breasts, followed by enlargement; full breast maturity is reached with the formation of the areola. Once menstruation has begun it usually continues for approximately 35 years, only being interrupted by pregnancy.

Table 3.4 Sexual characteristics: girls

Primary sexual characteristics (from before birth)	Secondary sexual characteristics (develop during puberty)
Vagina	Breast budding preceding full breast maturity
Uterus	Pelvis widens (in preparation for childbirth)
Ovaries	Pubic hair develops
Fallopian tubes	Axillary (underarm) hair develops
	Ovaries start to produce eggs
	Onset of menstruation

In boys, puberty starts a little later (girls are on average two years ahead of boys in their development during this stage of life). The first signs of puberty in boys are usually pubic hair growth, followed by a slight increase in the size of the scrotum and testes. The texture of the scrotum changes, and when the penis develops it first increases in length and then in breadth. Deepening of the voice also occurs during this phase of development.

Table 3.5 Sexual characteristics: boys

Primary sexual characteristics (from before birth)	Secondary sexual characteristics (develop during puberty)
Penis	Pubic hair develops
Testes	Axillary hair develops
Scrotum	Chest hair develops
Seminal vesicles	Facial hair develops
Vas deferens	Deepening of the voice (voice 'breaks')
Epididymis	Penis increases in size and length
	Testes grow and begin to produce sperm
	Ability to ejaculate

Summary

- By 18 years of age puberty is usually passed and the genitals and reproductive ability of both boys and girls are fully mature.
- Overall physical strength and stamina is increased.
- Shoulders broaden and full height is reached.
- Body image is important.

- Eating disorders are not uncommon, with severe disorders such as anorexia nervosa causing secondary amenorrhea (the absence of menstruation) in girls.
- Secondary amenorrhea can also be linked to high levels of exercise, and is quite often noted in athletes, gymnasts and dancers.

Physical development

Having read through the earlier summaries of physical development on pages 123–126, you should find that this section will enable you to develop your understanding further.

Motor development

Motor skills, which can be gross (large) or fine, include movement and balance and can be either precise or casual. Movement can involve the whole body or just one part of it.

Development becomes increasingly more complex, and children acquire more difficult physical skills as it progresses. The maturational changes can be described as moving:

- *From the simple to the complex*. A child learns simple actions, such as standing, before learning the more complex actions involved in walking.
- *From* ***cephalo*** *(head) to* ***caudal*** *(tail)*. Physical control starts at the head and gradually develops down through the body. For example, head control is attained before the spine is strong enough for an infant to sit unsupported, and sitting unsupported is achieved before the child is able to stand.
- *From* ***proximal*** *(near to the body) to* ***distal*** *(the outer reaches of the body)*. A child develops control of actions near to the body before they develop control of the outer reaches of the body. For example, a child can hug and carry a large teddy bear (requires arm control) before they can fasten its clothing (requires finger control).
- *From general to specific*. Generalised responses give way gradually to specific ones. For example, when recognising a favourite carer, an infant shows the generalised physical responses associated with excitement, but in the same situation an older child would make the specific facial response of smiling.

Fig 3.15 Motor development in children

a)

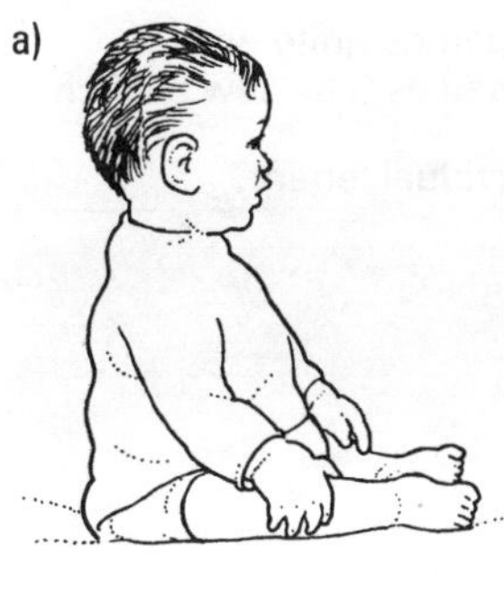

b)

c)

d)

The table below shows how motor skills can be categorised as:

- locomotor, which involves the body moving forward in some way (e.g. walking, running)
- non-locomotor, which describes large physical movements which take place whilst stationary (e.g. bending, pulling)
- manipulation, which involves dexterous actions (e.g. throwing and catching a ball).

The table places these three physical areas sequentially, according to the developmental norms.

Table 3.6 The sequence of motor skills

Age	Locomotor skills	Non-locomotor skills	Manipulative skills
1 month	Stepping reflex	Lifts head; visually follows slowly moving objects	Holds object if placed in hand
2–3 months		Briefly keeps head up if held in a sitting position	Begins to swipe at objects within visual range
4–6 months	Sits up with some support	Holds head erect in sitting position	Reaches for and grasps objects
7–9 months	Sits without support; rolls over in prone; crawls		Transfers objects from one hand to the other
10–12 months	Crawls; walks grasping furniture, then without help	Squats and stoops	Some sign of hand preference; grasps a spoon across palm but poor aim of food to mouth
13–18 months	Walks backwards and sideways	Rolls ball to adult	Stacks two blocks; puts objects into small containers and dumps them
18–24 months	Runs (20); walks well; climbs stairs – both feet to a step	Pushes and pulls boxes or wheeled toys; unscrews lid on a jar	Shows clear hand preference. Stacks four to six blocks. Turns pages one at a time. Picks things up, keeping balance
2–3 years	Runs easily; climbs up and down from furniture unaided	Hauls and shoves big toys around obstacles	Picks up small objects; throws small ball forward while standing
3–4 years	Walks upstairs one foot per step; skips on both feet; walks on tiptoe	Pedals and steers a tricycle; walks in any direction pulling a big toy	Catches large ball between outstretched arms; cuts paper with scissors; holds pencil between thumb and first two fingers
4–5 years	Walks up and down stairs, one foot per stair. Stands, runs and walks well on tip-toes		Strikes ball with bat; kicks and catches ball; threads bead, but not needle. Grasps pencil maturely
5–6 years	Skips on alternate feet; walks a thin line; slides and swings		Plays ball games quite well. Threads needles; can sew a stitch
7–8 years	Skips 12 times or more	Rides two-wheeler bike, short distances	Writes individual letters
8 years +	Skips freely	Rides bike easily	

Source: Helen Bee, *The Developing Child*, 6th edition, 1992, © Allyn & Bacon, reprinted by permission

Fig 3.16 The development of locomotion

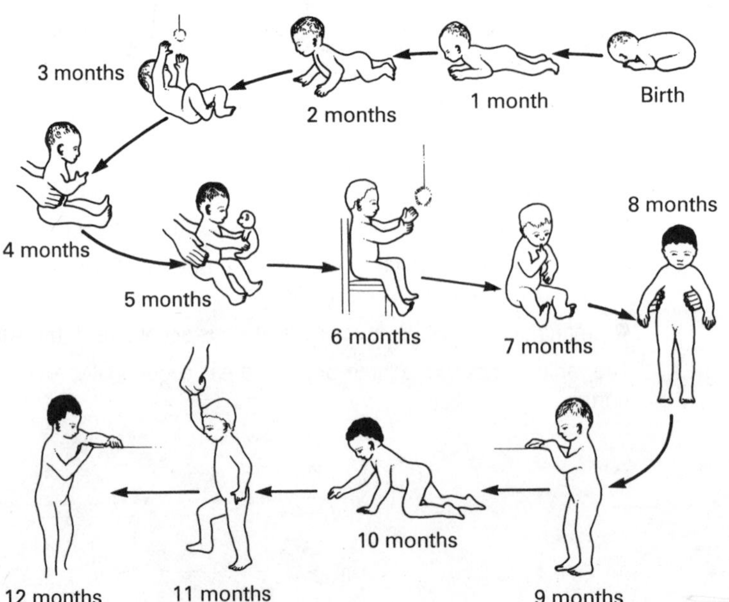

Monitoring physical development and health

An infant grows rapidly during the first year and then at a more steady rate from the toddler stage onwards. As puberty arrives, the growth rate rapidly increases once again, easing up in the latter years of adolescence. Full height is usually acquired by 18 years, whereas bone density continually develops, and old bone is replaced with new until around age 35, when the body ceases to continue replacing bone at the same rate.

Centile charts

The physical development of babies and young children is screened by health visitors and paediatricians using a centile chart to measure and monitor growth.

Different centile charts are used for boys and girls because there are slight differences in the growth expected of girl infants and boy infants – boys, on average, are slightly heavier than girls at birth. The 50th-centile line is the central line on the centile charts. It indicates the average at each age. The upper and lower lines represent the boundary within which 80 per cent of children will fall. A child who falls outside these boundaries will be monitored closely and may need further investigation into their development at some stage. The pattern (or line) formed as a child's measurements are plotted on the centile chart is known as a growth curve.

How centile charts are used

The centile charts overleaf show Jasmine's measurements at birth and the first nine months' measurements of her weight. We can see from these that, as a full-term baby, she was 'small for dates' at birth, weighing 2.780 kg (6 lb 2 oz), and was placed just below the 9th centile. Her length at 54 cm was considered to be long and reached the 98th centile; her head circumference, at 34 cm, was placed just above the 25th centile. Jasmine's weight gain progressed very slowly, and she remained below the norms of development for an infant of her age and birth weight.

Any infant who falls below the 0.4th centile is closely monitored by health professionals, and an infant who moves downwards across two centile lines is referred to their GP, or to a paediatrician, for close monitoring. At four months old, there was concern that Jasmine would need to be referred, although she was both healthy and alert. By five months, however, her weight began to increase more steadily; she moved above the 2nd centile for the first time at seven months. Jasmine is a very active baby, of petite build like her mother, and therefore there is no serious concern about her. She has always been healthy and alert and by eight months was walking around the furniture, crawling very fast and rarely still. Her weight gain trailed off again at this stage, but this was attributed to her high level of activity.

Health screening

Health screening of children takes place at specified ages, across the whole population. It enables parents and health professionals to identify problems sooner rather than later, giving the opportunity for early intervention and treatment. Screening is carried out at and after birth and throughout early childhood and schooling. It focuses mostly on the general physical development of individual children, with specific attention being given to hearing and vision.

Milestones of social and emotional development

Toddler – a summary

- By about 15 months, the toddler will indicate a wet or soiled nappy.
- They co-operate (help) with dressing.
- They are dependent on an adult's presence.
- Frustration leads to toys being discarded in anger.
- By 18 months, feeding themselves with a spoon is usually very successful.
- They can handle a cup confidently, but do not put it back down (they give it to the adult).
- They remove hats, shoes, etc. but can rarely replace them.
- They produce urgent vocalisations when making a demand.
- Bowel control is sometimes attained by 18 months and is usually attained by two years.
- By two years the child will play parallel alongside others.
- They can be rebellious and resistive and get frustrated when trying to make themselves understood.
- They can be easily distracted from their tantrums at this age.

Fig 3.17 Centile charts for a child

a)

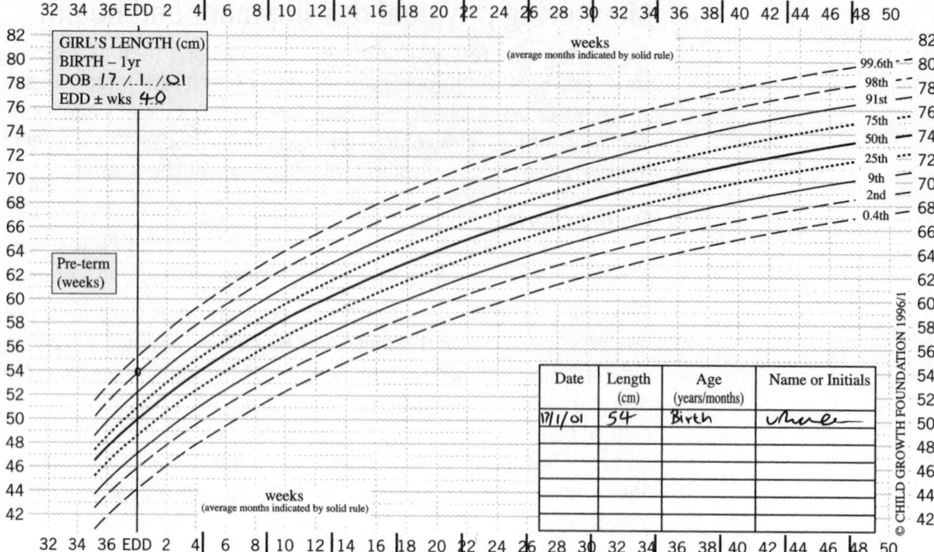

b)

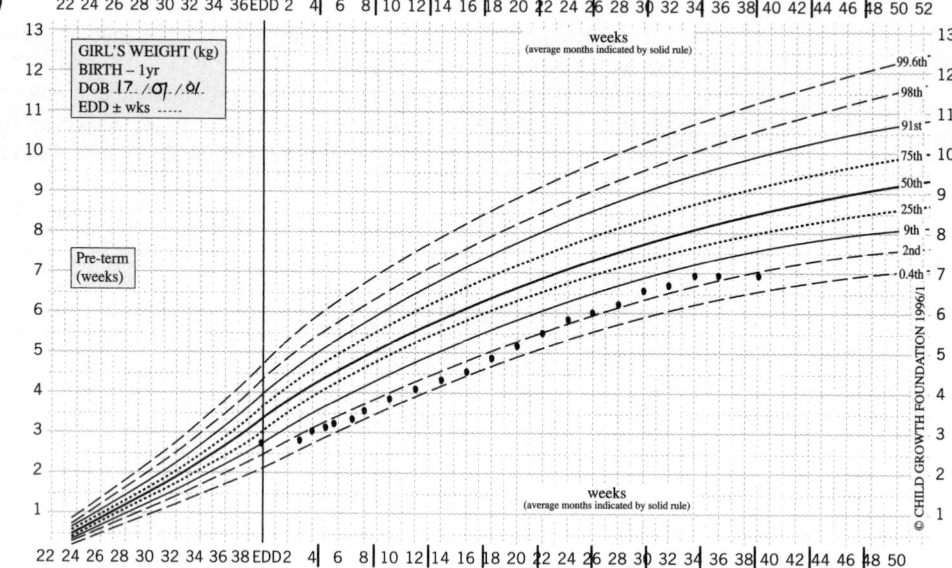

c)

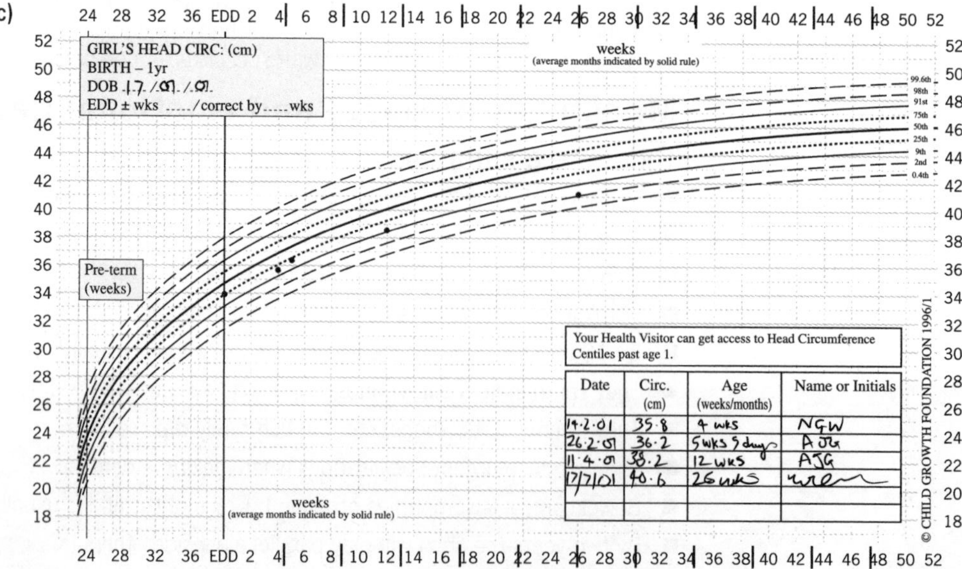

- It is normal for there to be no idea of sharing and no understanding of the need to defer their wishes.
- They follow adults around. They need reassurance when tired or fearful.
- They can now put on hat and shoes and can reposition a cup on a surface.

Early childhood: 2 to 5 years – a summary

- At two and half, tantrums are common when needs are thwarted. A child is less easily distracted from them now.
- They are very resistive of restraint.
- They mostly still watch others or play in parallel, occasionally joining in briefly.
- This is a generally more independent age; by four years, a child can eat skilfully and can dress, wash and clean their teeth (with supervision).
- They co-operate with others but can also be unco-operative if wishes are refused.
- They can be very strong willed.
- At five years, behaviour is noticeably more sensible and controlled.
- They understand sharing and turn-taking and the need for fair play.
- **Co-operative play** is constant at five years.
- They choose own friends and play well and are very protective towards younger children, pets and distressed playmates.

case study 3.2 Maya, Toby and Max

Maya, Toby and Max are looked after by the same childminder, Kahira. Maya is in Kahira's care every day, and either Toby or Max is usually present too. Maya is crawling and pulling herself up on the furniture. Max can walk now but is still unsteady, using his hands held high to balance himself. Toby can walk well and loves to play in the garden with a football. He can sometimes kick it without falling forward and is becoming steadier when climbing stairs but still needs to hold an adult's hand.

Toby talks to himself in long monologues as he plays, and adults nearby are able to identify some of his words, linked to his play. Max also talks to himself in play but little of his 'speech' is recognisable. Maya babbles and chuckles to herself as she roams around the floor, exploring all that she can find. She appears to get enjoyment from watching Max and Toby, but no child attempts to play with another.

activity
INDIVIDUAL WORK

1. What ages would you assume Maya, Toby and Max to be?
2. What else would you expect them to be doing?
3. Which of them would you expect to be able to feed themselves?
4. Would you expect any of the children to have gained bowel control?

Middle childhood: 5 to 12 years – a summary

- Co-operative play is frequent and sustained.
- Gender awareness is strong.
- Co-operative play is mostly with same-sex peers.
- Individual friendships are very important.
- Children make definite decisions about their friends.
- Parents are less openly important, but their continued support is needed.

Adolescents: 12 to 16 years – a summary

- Forming relationships becomes of great importance.
- Interest in the opposite sex develops.
- Sexual identity becomes an important focus.

- Confusion regarding sexuality is common.
- Forming own self-identity can at times be difficult.
- Mood swings and hormonal imbalance can cause emotional upheaval.
- Peer pressure is intense and can cause difficulties in maintaining beliefs.
- Depression is common at this stage.

Emotional development

Children can usually describe how they are feeling physically, although in very young children this may only be in a generalised way, for example a 'tummy ache' may refer to a range of pain experiences, but it is far harder for them to explain how they are feeling emotionally. Emotional development involves the child's development of **self-awareness**, sense of security and personal identity, and their learning to understand and express feelings towards other people. Emotions can be both positive and negative; they are our inner feelings which we often find difficult to explain. We should allow children the opportunities to express their emotions and reassure them that it is acceptable to have strong feelings, explaining that adults have them too.

Conditions for secure emotional development

Emotional development is not simply a maturational process; it needs the appropriate conditions to nurture it in the way that a flower needs sun, soil and water.

You would find it useful, here, to reflect for a moment on the placement experiences that you have had and think of situations where professional practice supported emotional development particularly well and also those where improvements could have been made.

Fig 3.18 Conditions for secure emotional development

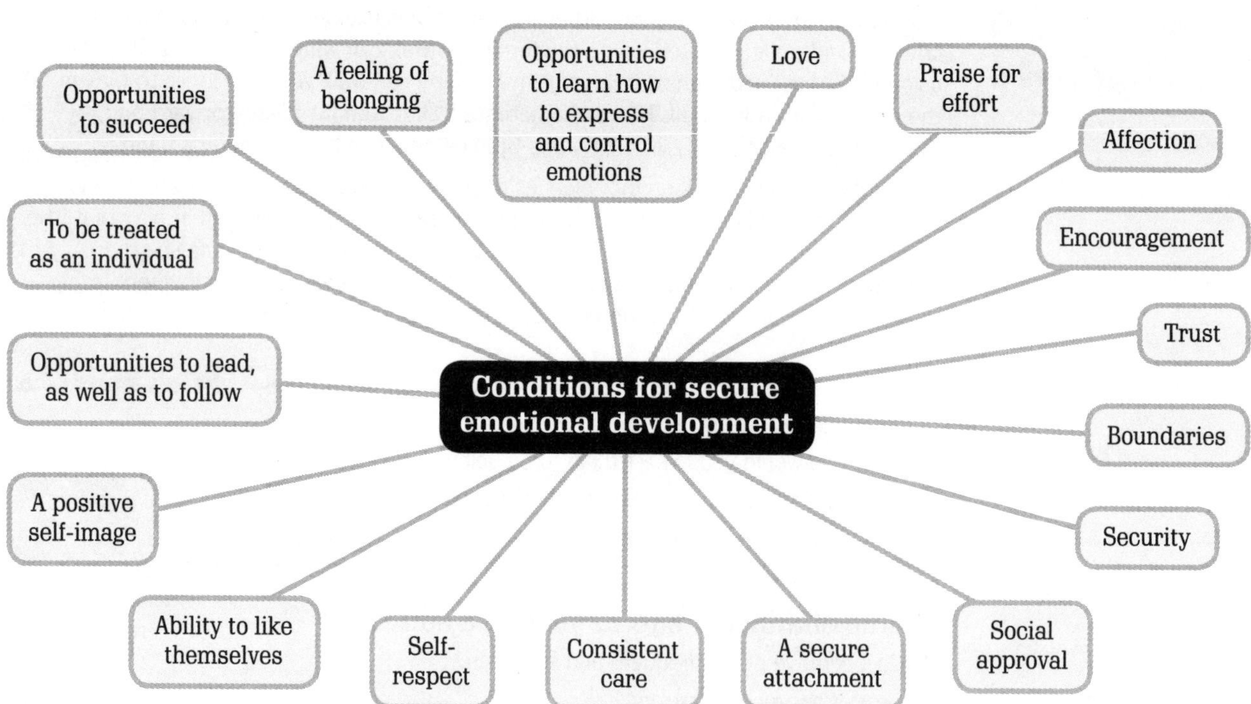

Emotional disturbance

Many children go through a phase of **emotional disturbance**. It is not usually serious and, with sensitive handling by parents and carers, is usually overcome quite quickly.

Emotional disturbance does not refer to the extremes of behaviour found in some developmental phases, such as temper tantrums in toddlers or mood swings in adolescence. It describes the more unusual and worrying behaviours that occur from time to time and which sometimes need professional referral to support and help the child through.

Emotional disturbance can manifest itself in many ways:

- A child may become withdrawn and insecure, clinging to a familiar adult and lacking confidence.
- Antisocial behaviour may be displayed by children who are trying to draw attention to themselves.
- Phobias may occur when a child is anxious about a situation; the child may display a pseudo (artificial) fear to draw attention to the real problem.
- Lonely or neglected children may develop physical habits such as hair-chewing or excessive nail-biting.
- Emotional distress can cause physical symptoms such as tummy upsets, tics and skin irritations.
- Severe emotional disturbance can result in regressed or impeded development, both physical and cognitive.

Emotional disturbance can be triggered by many situations as summarised in the spidergram below.

Fig 3.19 Triggers for emotional disturbance

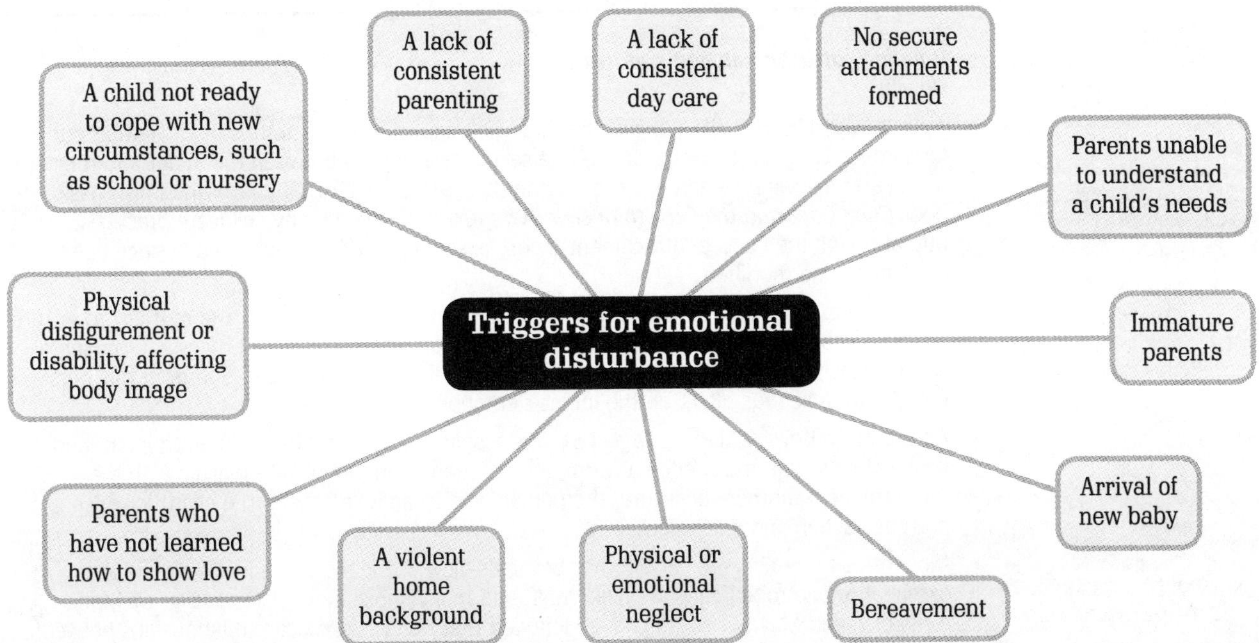

Patterns of emotional development

It is usual for young babies to show distress at sudden noises, as these disturb their sense of security. The passive acceptance of the caring routines that is established by a few weeks of age shows how their sense of security is well established, as does the way in which they cease to cry when they are picked up. In older babies, the soothing effect of their main carer's voice and the contented patting of breast or bottle both demonstrate emotional security.

At around the age of nine months, babies begin to show fear of strangers and become fretful when separated from their parent or main carer. This is a classic milestone of development, but it is also linked to the quality of the attachment bond that has been established between the parent, or carer, and the child. The behaviours that accompany separation anxiety may include crying and looking for the 'missing' adult.

As the infant approaches the toddler stage, emotional responses may be more negative because of their **egocentricity** (their self-centred view of the world), and the onset of tantrums may occur at around two years. This stage can last until the more socially aware and emotionally mature age of three years, when children begin to develop an understanding of how to defer their needs and share.

The early building-blocks of emotional security have been established by the time a child enters day care or a preschool setting. These new experiences should enable a child to continue to value themselves as an individual through the images they see and the opportunities they are given. Both experience and opportunity will have a further impact on a child's self-perception, affecting their self-esteem and self-image.

Refer to Unit 1, pages 2–8, for issues of children's behaviour and how to manage some of the difficulties that may arise.

Theories of emotional development

Several theories deal with aspects of emotional development, including theories of bonding, attachment and separation; **self-concept** and personal identity; and temperament. A brief summary of each of these is given below.

For detailed information about these theories, read *Angles on Child Psychology* by Jarvis (2001).

Bonding, attachment and separation

Bowlby

John Bowlby (1907–90) is one of the most well-known theorists in this field. He first put forward his views on the importance of a secure relationship between the infant and their main carer following research carried out in the 1950s. In 1953, he published his classic book *Child Care and the Growth of Love*. This text influenced many childcare practices but, although the basis of attachment theory is still upheld, his theories have since been challenged and modified.

Bowlby considered that all infants needed one main care giver (usually the mother) to ensure a secure attachment. He used the term '**monotropy**' to describe the process of forming a strong attachment to just one person. Bowlby believed that any separation from this person would have a serious effect on the infant's emotional development.

According to Bowlby (1953, page 13), it is essential for mental health that an infant and young child should experience a warm, intimate, and continuous relationship with the mother (or permanent mother substitute, the person who steadily 'mothers' the child) in which both find satisfaction and enjoyment.

Modern-day theorists are certain that Bowlby's view of the mother figure's role as the essential (monotropic) carer was incorrect, and many subsequent studies (e.g. by Mary Ainsworth and Michael Rutter) have identified that successful, secure relationships between infants and a range of other caregivers (multiple attachments) are possible and that the carer's ability to respond to the infant's needs is the greatest influencing factor in the attachment process.

Schaffer

Rudolf Schaffer also believed that babies can have multiple attachments. They build up interest in responding to and receiving responses initially from their parent or main carer and then from other adults who provide stimulation, interaction and a sense of security for them. These secure relationships are usually linked to day-to-day care, but this is not always the case. A secure attachment can be formed between an adult and infant when contact is regular but not necessarily frequent. The quality of the relationship is an important factor.

You may find it interesting to read *Mothering* by Schaffer (1977). A useful text to refer to for further examples is *Personal, Social and Emotional Development of Children* by Barnes (1998).

Self-concept and personal identity

A child begins to recognise that they are an individual quite early on. From the age of about 18 months, the growing toddler establishes that the person they see reflected in the mirror is actually them.

Dowling (2000, page 2) suggests that even babies build a picture of themselves, based on the way their care is given and the manner in which their carers respond to them. It is generally accepted that close members of the family, particularly the mother, are instrumental in this process; the baby sees the loving acceptance that the mother gives them as the first signal that they are an individual who is loved and who matters.

Once a child understands that they are an individual and what they, as that individual, are like, they move on to understand how they are perceived by others.

Theoretical perspectives on self and identity

The emergence of the awareness of self and identity has been of great interest to early psychologists such as Freud, Cooley and Mead and, of course, to later developmental psychologists such as Schaffer and others.

Sigmund Freud proposed that our personality is composed of three separate parts but we are not born with all three parts; some develop as we mature. He proposed that these parts are the:

- Id – this is the part of our personality that drives our basic wants and needs such as hunger and thirst. The id wants immediate satisfaction and Freud proposed that young babies personify the id as they demand the adult's attention until their needs are gratified.
- Ego – Freud suggested that the ego developed from the id in order to work out how the id's needs could best be met. The ego guides the id, helping it to learn from situations where behaviour can be modified in order for needs to be met quickly or when gratification has to be delayed.
- Superego – this part of our personality develops later in childhood and acts as our 'conscience', trying to restrain and control the ego. If we misbehave, the superego prompts our conscience to punish the ego, resulting in a feeling of guilt. However, the superego will also reward the ego in cases of good behaviour and this explains our feelings of confidence and pride.

C. H. Cooley and G. H. Mead were social philosophers who were interested in the development of the self.

- Both referred to the concept of the 'looking glass self', which means that an individual's understanding of their own identity is a reflection of how they think others see them.
- Cooley thought that children developed concepts of themselves from the 'looking-glass self'.
- Mead, however, saw the development of the self as a social product, in that we develop different aspects of ourselves as we interact with a variety of people.

You may find it useful to explore your college resource centre, to update yourself regarding contemporary studies on the development of self. You will find useful information in Chapter 2 of *An Introduction to Psychology*, edited by Roth (1990).

Fig 3.20 Developing a personal identity: 'I'm good at making models; my friends say I'm good at making models'

Temperament

Every individual has their own character, disposition and tendencies, and children are no exception to this. A child is sometimes referred to as being an 'easy' child or a 'difficult' child, but these terms are not helpful – they become labels which can lead to the prejudging of an individual and eventually become a 'self-fulfilling prophecy'.

Children can also be balanced, impulsive or reserved in their actions: an impulsive child may experience more accidents or 'near misses', and a reserved child's temperament may limit their experience. Temperament is seen even in very young babies; it is part of their natural personality make-up. When you lift up some babies, they mould towards you, taking pleasure in the cuddle, whereas others will remain tense and wary. The same applies to adults. You can probably think of individuals to whom these descriptions apply.

> 'A child's temperament is about:
> - emotionality: the child's feelings – fearful, anxious, enthusiastic
> - activity: whether the child does things impulsively or slowly
> - sociability: whether the child likes company or not.'
>
> (Bruce and Meggitt, 1996)

Again, this applies to adults too.

case study 3.3

Stanislas and Pradeep

Stanislas is an outgoing boy who is always eager to try out new activities and experiences. He is always on the go at nursery and flits from one activity to another, rarely spending long in one place. By contrast, Pradeep likes to spend time on everything he does, making sure that he has all that he thinks he will need (various colour pens and so on) before he starts. Pradeep rarely hurries to see anything new but will eventually try it out or join in when the rush is over. In this way, he often has the opportunity to spend more time than Stanislas enjoying the new experience.

activity
INDIVIDUAL WORK

1 How do you think the temperaments of Stanislas and Pradeep might affect their learning?

2 What long-term issues do you see for each of them if they continue in the same way?

Each of us can be categorised as a personality type, but we also display various personality traits. These predispositions towards certain behaviours are part of us as a general type of person, but some of us have a greater number of some traits than of others. Psychologists who study trait theory can be divided into:

- idiographic theorists, such as Allport (1897–1967) who focused on individual personality traits
- nomothetic theorists, such as Cattell (1905–1998) and Eysenck (1916–1998) who studied the more general laws of personality.

You can find out more about personality trait theory by referring to *Psychology for You* by Cullis *et al.* (1999).

It is easier for most of us to interact with others who are happy and easy going. They give us a positive extension of themselves that we can relate to. This is often referred to as having 'goodness of fit'. In the early years setting, it is important that the smiling, happy child is not given more of your attention than the reserved, quiet child. Similarly, the tearful, discontented child should not be dismissed as miserable and be left to their misery.

You need to understand that temperament is part of the personality we are born with and to accept the need for differing approaches to the children in your care. You cannot treat all children in the same way – you would not be meeting their individual needs. Childcare workers need to find a way to achieve 'goodness of fit' with every child with whom they are in contact.

Refer to Unit 1, page 29, for suggestions on managing personality clashes and encouraging co-operation within settings.

Learning theory

Ivan Pavlov and B. F. Skinner believed that all learning can be explained by conditioning.

Pavlov and classical conditioning

Pavlov carried out experiments on responses to stimulus. His famous experiment demonstrated **classical conditioning** with dogs and involved the use of a bell (the neutral stimulus) and food (called the unconditioned stimulus because it elicits a reflex response). When the bell rang, the dogs were fed, and the (unconditioned) response of salivating occurred. After several pairings of food and bell, the sound of a bell ringing would elicit the conditioned response (salivating) without the production of food.

Initially: Neutral stimulus (bell) + unconditioned stimulus (food) > unconditioned response (salivating). Eventually: Conditioned stimulus (bell) > conditioned response (salivating).

Classical conditioning can be used to explain some examples of childhood learning, such as learning not to touch a hot surface because doing so is painful. In some circumstances, it only requires one pairing of the neutral stimulus and the unconditioned stimulus for conditioning to occur.

Skinner and operant conditioning

In **operant conditioning**, learning takes place through the reinforcement of behaviour; in positive reinforcement, the learner is given a reward for performing the desired behaviour.

Skinner developed the Skinner box in which he trained rats to perform various tasks, such as pressing a lever. At first, the rat pressed the lever accidentally; when it did so, the rat received a food pellet as a reward (positive reinforcement). The rat soon learned to keep pressing the lever to get the reward. Other rats were given a mild electric shock if they pressed the lever (punishment); they learned not to press it. On some trials, a mild electric current was put through the floor of the box and pressing the lever switched off the current (negative reinforcement); in these trials, the rats learned to press the lever to avoid the electric shock.

Skinner was a behaviourist; he argued that stimulus–response learning moulds all behaviour and that this is how children learn. For example, he said that language develops by operant conditioning, with parents and carers giving praise for 'correct' speech and pronunciation.

Refer to Unit 1, page 3, for a discussion of strategies for positively reinforcing children's behaviour. Bandura's social learning theory, which developed out of learning theory, is described on page 140. See also page 148 for the behaviourist theory of language development.

Social development

Having read through the earlier summaries of social and emotional development on pages 129–132, you should find that this section will enable you to develop your understanding further.

Social development of babies

Babies appear to have an instinctive capacity to relate to other humans. This is referred to as **intersubjectivity**, and opportunities to meet with and relate to other humans, both babies and older age groups, are important to develop socialisation further. Social skills start to be developed through the earliest interactions with the mother or other primary carers following birth, and these turn-taking experiences, in which the mother and infant learn to 'mesh' with each other, form the basis for building later relationships. Infants can be seen imitating certain adult actions, such as tongue poking, mouth shaping and hand movements from shortly after birth.

As the mother–infant relationship develops (sometimes referred to as a dyadic relationship), the mother tends to anticipate the responses of her infant and react accordingly. This precipitating response is known as *a priori* imitation, and plays an important part in the development of a young infant's early relationships. There is a link between *a priori* imitation and Bruner's concept of **scaffolding**.

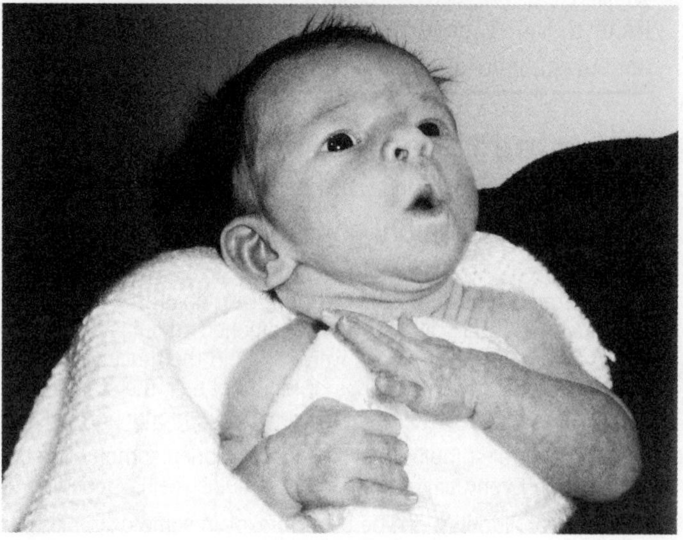

Fig 3.21 Infants can be seen to imitate adult actions, such as mouth shaping, from shortly after birth

Refer to page 147 for more about Bruner.

Socialisation

Socialisation refers to the process by which the individual learns about the social groups or society to which they belong. According to socialisation theory, there are two types of socialisation:

- primary socialisation, which takes place as a child understands and develops the customs and practices of their family
- **secondary socialisation**, which involves the wider influences of other adults and social groups in the community with whom the child has regular contact.

Bandura's theory of socialisation is outlined on page 140.

Prosocial behaviour

Prosocial behaviour is concerned with:

- empathy
- being altruistic
- having moral awareness
- the development of understanding of how other people feel
- knowing what is right and what is wrong and acting accordingly.

Giving children opportunities to share, to take turns, to care for others, pets, plants, the environment, etc. helps them to develop a prosocial approach to life, rather than an antisocial approach. It is important that adults act according to the behaviours they ask of the children in their care. A 'do as I say, not as I do' attitude will help no-one.

Prosocial behaviour is an aspect of morality.

A useful discussion of prosocial behaviour can be found in *Understanding Child Development* by Lindon (2005).

Moral development

Moral development involves learning what is right or wrong, good or bad. Each person develops their own moral code, which they strive to live by. According to Kohlberg's theory, young children's moral reasoning is initially defined by obedience in order to avoid punishment, whereas later it becomes important to them to uphold certain rules, because they feel that this is expected of them (conventional morality). The final stage of moral reasoning is only reached when the individual understands that at times rules need to be broken in order to achieve justice and develops a respect for the 'universal value and dignity of human life' (Cullis *et al.*, 1999).

Table 3.7 Kohlberg's six-stage theory of moral development

Level 1	**Pre-conventional morality (based on external authority)**
Stage 1	Child acts to avoid unpleasant consequences (punishment)
Stage 2	Child acts to gain rewards. You should behave fairly and honour deals
Level 2	**Conventional morality (based on judgements about the expectations of others)**
Stage 3	Child wishes to please others and be thought of as 'nice' – a 'good boy' or 'good girl'
Stage 4	Child respects social rules. It is good to uphold the law and do one's duty
Level 3	**Post-conventional morality (based on self-chosen ethical principles)**
Stage 5	Involves recognising rules or laws may be unjust, and so can sometimes be broken
Stage 6	Reasoning is based on universal principles which show profound respect for life

(Adapted from Cullis *et al.*, 1999, p. 118)

remember: Skinner would have argued that moral behaviour is learned through operant conditioning.

Cullis *et al.* (1999) go on to explain that:

- Level 1 reasoning is common until the age of 11 years.
- Level 2 reasoning is often seen between the ages of 12 and 15.
- Level 3 reasoning develops from 15 years onwards.

But many people do not reach the higher level of reasoning, with the majority of adults remaining at stage 4, only 10 per cent reaching stage 5, and very few individuals reaching stage 6.

Peer pressure

During adolescence, peer pressure becomes an increasingly important factor. No one likes to be different, or outside the main crowd; and it can be hard for individuals to maintain their moral thinking and beliefs in the face of pressure to conform to the activities of a social group.

Peer pressure can lead individuals into situations they know are wrong, causing conflict within themselves, and this in turn can affect their self-esteem and personal values.

Peer groups are important in that they can have a significant effect on attitudes as well as on actions. The effect can be both positive and negative. Dealing with negative peer pressure becomes easier as the individual gains in self-confidence and develops a clear sense of right and wrong.

Stages of social play

Social development can be clearly seen in the way in which children play, as demonstrated in Figure 3.22.

You may find it helpful to refer back to the summaries of development on pages 129–132, noting how children develop socially.

As you can see from Figure 3.22, social behaviour develops as a child's play moves from the solitary actions of the toddler absorbed in their own world through to the complex games involving rules seen in the infant school playground. The ability to co-operate with others moves through stages, which are dependent on the maturational stage of the individual child and the opportunities and experiences that have been made available to them.

Solitary play

The first stage of play is referred to as **solitary play**. The child plays contentedly on their own but still needs the reassurance of the adult. This play is typical up to two years of age. It is frequently imitative, demonstrating a basic understanding of the actions of others within a child's social world. An example of solitary imitative play is the child pretending to brush the hair of a doll or teddy, usually very briefly.

Fig 3.22 The development of play shows clearly how children develop socially

Co-operative play, over 3 years
Shared enjoyment, making joint decisions about play

Associative play, from 3 years
Watch other children
May copy their actions

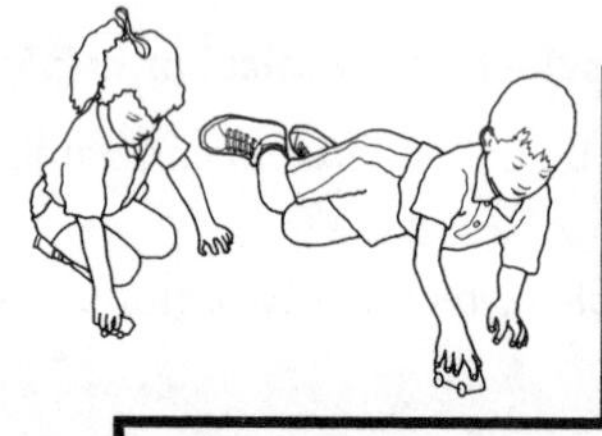

Parallel play, 2–3 years
Play alongside another child
Aware of other games, but does not co-operate

Solitary play 0–2 years
Play alone
Need adult reassurance

Parallel play

The next stage is **parallel play** in which a child finds enjoyment playing alongside, but not with, another child. The children do not necessarily even acknowledge that the other exists and make no reference to what the other is doing. This is true parallel play, one child playing parallel to the other. It usually begins to emerge between two and three years of age.

Associative (looking-on) play

At this stage in social play, the child begins to watch the actions of others, enjoying their play from a distance. They are not yet ready to play with others but learn a great deal from their observations. This stage of play is typically seen between three and four years of age.

Joining-in play (simple co-operative)

By four years old, most children are ready to play co-operatively with others. This simple co-operative play begins in an uncomplicated manner, involving the shared enjoyment of a similar activity. There are no rules and no restrictions; it is simply a pleasurable play experience with others. A good example is a group of children all dressing dolls together.

Co-operative play (complex co-operative)

During this, the last and most developed stage of children's play, children interact as a group. This can entail physical co-operation to complete a joint task or play that includes complex rules, involving the taking on of agreed (although 'evolving as they go') rules.

Social learning theory

Possibly the most well-known example of a theory of socialisation is social learning theory, which was put forward by Albert Bandura in 1965, based on his research. In his studies, he showed a film with three different endings to children to see how they could be affected by what they had seen.

Three groups of children were each shown a different version of the film, which involved an adult hitting and shouting at a Bobo doll (a large inflatable toy weighted at the bottom that always rights itself – you cannot knock it over).

- Group 1: the film ending showed the adult being rewarded for hitting the doll.
- Group 2: the film ending showed the adult being punished for hitting the doll.
- Group 3: in the film they saw, nothing happened to the adult after they hit the doll.

After they had watched their particular version of the film, the children in all three groups were given Bobo dolls to play with and were observed by the researchers. The children who had seen the adult rewarded for hitting the doll showed the highest tendency to hit the doll.

This study could not claim evidence of a direct cause and effect, but its results certainly suggest that the children in Group 1 may have been influenced by observing the rewarding of negative behaviour.

The following illustrates an example of learning where the reinforcement is direct (given to the learner), not vicarious (given to another person).

In the playground one dinner time, Jake was playing with a tennis ball, kicking it at the wall. His aim was taking the ball closer and closer to the windows, so Mrs Baker, the school meals supervisory assistant on playground duty, explained that he would need to keep away from the windows or he would not be allowed to continue playing ball. Jake took no notice of Mrs Baker and, eventually, his ball was taken away from him. Jake felt very cross with Mrs Baker at the time.

The next day, Jake again played ball, but this time he played over by the fence. He did not want to lose his ball again.

How would Skinner have explained Jake's learning?

Development of aggression

When does boisterous play become aggression? This is something most early years practitioners find hard to judge. Many settings ban weapons, play fighting and superhero play because it is felt that it leads children into combat-style actions. However, many children soon use imaginary or symbolic 'props' instead of 'real' ones. and the games go on. In *Understanding Child Development*, Jenni Lindon (2005) provides a useful discussion, citing the work of Paley who, having removed a ban on superhero-type play, was pleased to observe that the children's play did not become aggressive. Although there were issues of space within the setting, there was 'no justification for treating the games as problem behaviour'.

Within all aspects of play and learning, it is valuable if adults model acceptable and preferred behaviour, such as polite responses, patience, turn-taking, etc. This helps children to identify ways of negotiation that they can adopt themselves if faced with a situation of conflict.

Refer back to pages 138 and 139. Reading these sections on moral development and peer pressure will help you think about the pressures faced by older children and teenagers, some of which lead potentially to conflict and aggression. Refer also to Unit 1, page 29, for strategies on communication and dealing with conflict, and to page 5 for a discussion of managing behaviour.

Effects of stereotyping on development

Social development and play are affected by various experiences, one of which is **stereotyping**. To stereotype an individual is mentally to place them into a specific compartment according to a preconceived idea. It ignores the person's individual character and temperament and simply treats them as part of a group. In generalising in this way, we are likely to make serious errors of judgement about the world we live in and the people we interact with.

Children learn about social behaviour, including how to react to others, from watching and imitating other people. They are particularly influenced by the adults they admire. As an adult working with young children, you are a role model, and you should be aware of how your actions and words can affect the children in your care so that you do not reinforce social stereotypes.

Gender stereotyping

In the earliest years, children learn which sex they belong to. This is known as sex identity and it refers to body shape and biological make-up. Children also learn to behave in certain ways according to their sex identity; this is known as the gender role. Learning one's gender role contributes to the development of gender identity. Generally, when girls know they are girls, they tend to play with other girls and the same applies to boys. When children fully understand that their sex is set for life, they have reached the state of gender stability.

Socialisation not only affects children's behaviour, it also affects their perceptions of gender. Research has shown that gender roles are influenced by the parents and carers of children.

When adults interact with babies, they handle babies in different ways according to the baby's sex. This also applies to the tone of voice and language that are used. For example, most people have heard comments such as 'What a beautiful girl she is!' or 'He's a real bruiser, isn't he?' These are classic comments, which are used widely and are very gender specific.

In a study of 32 boy babies and 32 girl babies, each aged around six months, Goldberg and Lewis found that girl babies are held for longer, spoken to in a softer tone and cradled gently, whereas boy babies are approached in a more 'robust' manner. Goldberg and Lewis observed the same infants again at 13 months in a laboratory setting, with a limited selection of toys available to them. The girls were observed to choose the quieter toys and to stay near to their mothers, whereas the boys chose the more active toys and appeared to be more independent. Goldberg and Lewis drew the conclusion that the earlier experiences had affected the later actions of these babies.

remember

Messages can be portrayed by actions, words, attitudes and non-verbal behaviour. They can be positive or negative.

Interactions with older children have also been seen to influence gender. Beverley Fagot carried out **observations** in the homes of many families with children approaching two years. She particularly noted which behaviours were encouraged and discouraged by the parents and found that, on the whole, girls were encouraged to stay near to the parents, to ask for help and to take an interest in stereotypical 'girls'' activities (dolls, clothes, dancing). They tended to be discouraged from active play (jumping, running around, rough-and-tumble games) and from being aggressive. Boys, on the other hand, were encouraged to use their bodies actively and to explore construction toys and play with cars; they were discouraged from playing with dolls and other stereotypical 'girls'' activities. They were also discouraged from asking for help. The boys who tended towards 'girls'' activities were more strongly criticised by the parents than the girls who tended towards 'boys'' activities.

Working with children requires a clear understanding of the importance of **equality** and awareness that all children should be encouraged to use all of the available activities and experience all situations in the setting. You need to think about the messages that you are giving the children with whom you work. These messages have a direct impact on their social learning.

case study 3.4 Paul and Patrick

Paul and Patrick were playing outside with balls and hoops, when Rachel, an early years worker, called out for 'a big strong boy' to help her get the mats out. Paul and Patrick both ran to help her, but Patrick got his foot caught in one of the hoops and fell heavily. He began to cry. Paul helped him up saying, 'Come on, Patrick, big boys don't cry. Quick, let's help Rachel.'

activity
INDIVIDUAL WORK

1 What messages were being given here?
2 How could Rachel have made both situations more positive?
3 What could be the long-term implications for social learning for Paul and Patrick?
4 What personal learning can you take from this case study? How might it affect your practice in the future?

Cultural and racial stereotyping

We live in a pluralist society (one which is made up of a variety of groups each with its own distinctive ethnic origin, culture or religion). Culture is an important part of the family's way of life and affects ways of parenting. It is therefore important to have an understanding of a broad range of cultures, religions and beliefs and be willing to value and explore differences with the children in your care.

remember

The impact of adult actions and words can have long-term effects.

A child should be accepted first and foremost for themselves. Their background, ethnicity and religion are simply part of what makes them who they are. The individual child's personality is what you should focus upon as you build up a relationship with them. The influences of primary and secondary socialisation will have given them a sense of belonging within their own culture.

Refer to Unit 6, pages 282–301, for a more detailed discussion of equality, **diversity** and rights.

Milestones of cognitive and language development

Toddler – a summary

- The toddler is very curious, investigating everything they can; they are interested in all that happens around them.
- Able to use a precise pincer grasp, they enjoy putting objects into containers.
- They take toys to mouth less often now.
- They enjoy activities that need fitting together.
- The toddler will place an object on another – two-object tower.
- They know approximately six words at 15 months and up to 20 recognisable words by 18 months.
- By 18 months, they talk continuously as they play (mostly, this is unintelligible).
- There is brief imitation of everyday activities (e.g. the feeding of a doll).
- They are contented to play alone.
- They talk to themselves in long monologues (much is incomprehensible to others).
- They can put two or more words together (e.g. 'daddy gone').
- They refer to themselves by name (e.g. 'Danny shoes').
- Echolalia (repeating the last word they hear) is almost constant.
- They verbalise their needs (e.g. drinks, toilet or food).
- Simple role play is demonstrated.

Early childhood: 2 to 5 years – a summary

- By two years, more than 50 words are clearly recognisable.
- At three years, the child has a large vocabulary that is understood by others but still includes unconventional grammar and infantilisms (the child's personal 'baby talk').
- During play, they still talk to themselves in long monologues.
- By three years, they can build six to eight objects into a tower.
- They can follow simple instructions (e.g. 'Fetch your shoes, please').
- They can successfully complete simple jigsaw puzzles.
- They can draw vertical and horizontal lines.
- By four years, speech is usually grammatically correct.
- They can usually draw a person with the main details.
- Role play is frequent and detailed by five years.
- Floor play is very complex.
- Understanding of time, linked to routine, is emerging.

Middle childhood: 5 to 12 years – a summary

Children between these ages develop from Piaget's pre-operational stage to the concrete operations stage of thinking. They develop the ability to think logically, for example adding up, subtracting, reading and ordering. Co-operative play from age five onwards becomes very involved, with role play that requires accuracy and detail.

By the age of 11, an average child has a vocabulary of 11,000–12,000 words. They are usually fluent readers with substantial reading stamina. Girls have a tendency to read more than boys.

Refer to page 144 for Piaget's stages of cognitive development.

Adolescents: 12 to 16 years – a summary

As children reach adolescence:

- The emphasis is on learning and developing career options for the future.
- Understanding of abstract concepts has developed.
- Colloquialisms and 'peer' talk is frequently displayed.
- Conflicts arise, particularly with parents and figures of authority.

- Family values are frequently challenged.
- Moral reasoning becomes important.
- There is a need to develop problem-solving skills as greater independence is attained.

Theories of cognitive development

Having read through the summaries of cognitive and language development, you should find that the following sections will enable you to develop your understanding further.

Cognitive development involves the development of concepts, thinking, problem-solving and memory. This section discusses in some detail the theories of three influential theorists of cognitive development, Jean Piaget, Lev Vygotsky and Jerome Bruner.

Table 3.8 The main theorists in cognitive development

Jean Piaget	Lev Vygotsky	Jerome Bruner
Particularly associated with: ■ constructivist theory ■ stages of cognitive development ■ schemas ■ assimilation and accommodation ■ conservation ■ discovery learning.	Particularly associated with: ■ zone of proximal development (ZPD) ■ social constructivist theory.	Particularly associated with: ■ the three modes of representation: – enactive – iconic – symbolic ■ discovery learning ■ scaffolding.

Piaget's stages of cognitive development

Piaget believed that a child's way of thinking changes as they get older and that all children pass through four stages of cognitive development in the same order, although the age at which they enter and leave each stage may vary considerably. The four stages are:

1 sensorimotor stage – birth to two years

2 pre-operational stage – two to seven years (preconceptual stage – two to four years; intuitive stage – four to seven years)

3 concrete operations stage – 7 to 11 years

4 formal operations stage – 11 years onwards.

Schemas

Piaget believed that children develop knowledge and concepts by using and building on previous experiences. He considered that they gradually adapt their concepts, which he called **schemas**, to establish new understanding. For example, a child recognises a dog as something which is 'larger than themselves and has four legs' – this is a schema.

Assimilation

The child uses the previously learned schema to make sense of a new situation. For example, using the schema 'a dog is larger than themselves and has four legs', the child refers to a goat as 'dog'. Piaget's term for the process of trying to fit new experience into existing knowledge is **assimilation**.

Accommodation

When this misunderstanding is corrected by an adult – the goat is large and has four legs, but it is a goat, not a dog – the child will be moved towards a new schema – 'goats *and* dogs can be large and have four legs'. Piaget called this process **accommodation**.

The ongoing development of schemas

As the child comes into contact with different animals, they will continue to learn new schemas, for example that a dog can be large or small, black, white or brown. They will also eventually have schemas that tell them that other animals can be large or small, and can also be black, white or brown.

Fig 3.23 An example of a child developing a schema for bricks

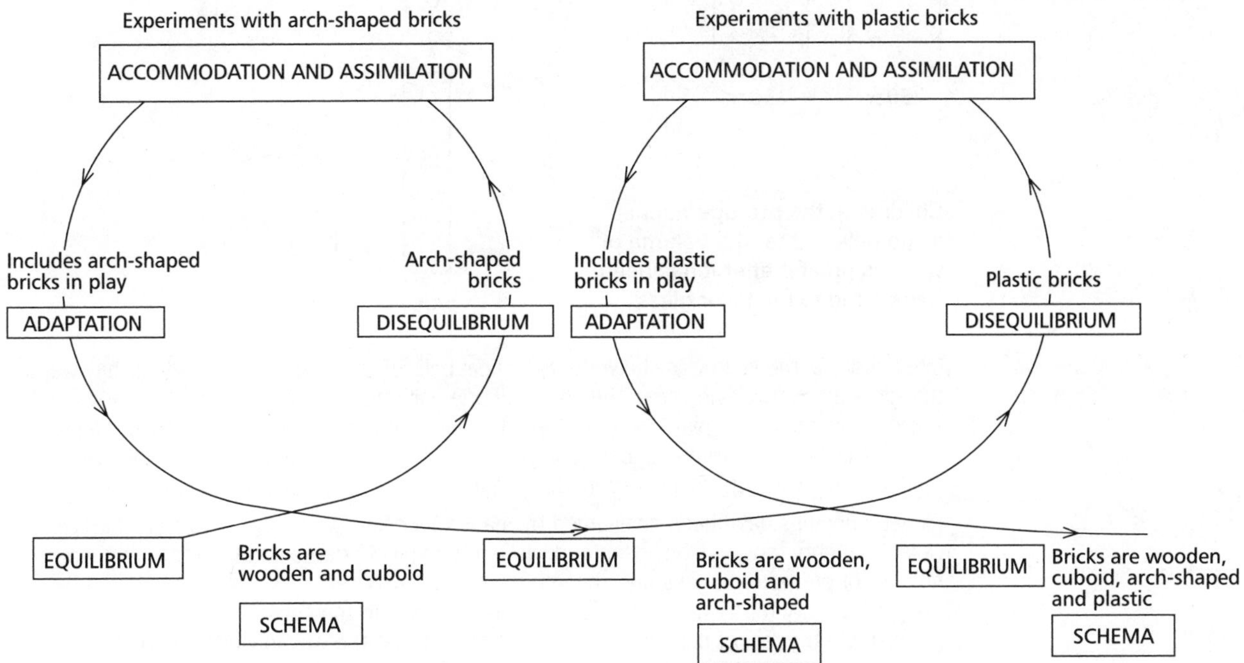

Disequilibrium

When a child is unable to make sense of new information (unable to assimilate) they are considered to be in an unbalanced state, which Piaget called **disequilibrium**.

Equilibrium

As the child accommodates new concepts, they reach a point of equilibrium where they are able to understand the new information:

Assimilation > Disequilibrium > Accommodation > Equilibrium > Assimilation.

Conservation

Piaget is also renowned for his studies of **conservation**. He believed that children under the age of six would not be able to conserve (i.e. understand changes in quantity, size and number). He used a variety of tasks to explore this. Below are examples of the three that are most well known.

In Example A, the child was shown two identical rows of coins and was asked if there were the same number in each row. The coins in the second row were then spaced further apart and the child was asked if the number of coins in each row was still the same. If the child was able to conserve, they would answer that there were the same number. If the child could not conserve, they would answer that there were more coins in the longer row.

Fig 3.24 Conservation – Example A

Children at the pre-operational stage say that the two rows contain the same number of pennies ...

... but also that there are more pennies in the more spread-out, second row.

In Example B, the child was shown two identical beakers of liquid and asked if they contained the same amount. After watching the adult pour the liquid from one beaker into a taller beaker, the child was asked if the amount of liquid in the beakers was still the same. If the child could conserve, they would answer that the amount of liquid remained the same. If they could not conserve, they would state that the amount was different – there was more liquid in the taller beaker.

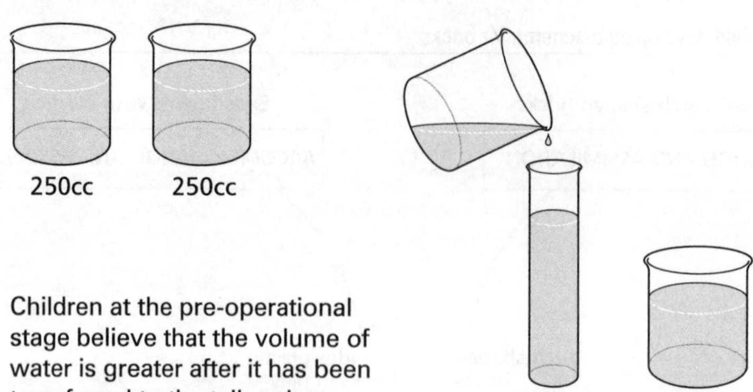

Fig 3.25 Conservation – Example B

In Example C, the child was shown two identical balls of play dough and asked if they were the same amount. Having seen the adult roll one ball into a sausage shape, the child was asked if the amount of play dough was still the same. If the child could conserve, they would answer that the balls were still both the same size. If they could not conserve, they would think that the sausage shape was made from a greater amount of play dough.

Piaget's findings have been challenged by many theorists. For example, using a character called 'naughty teddy', Donaldson and McGarrigle (1974) demonstrated that a higher number of pre-operational stage children were able to conserve than had been found by Piaget. Naughty teddy was used to 'accidentally' mess up the conservation experiments, for example the row of pennies. The researchers felt that the way in which the questions had been phrased by Piaget had led children to assume that the adult was indicating that a change had occurred in the number of counters, amount of liquid, and so on. When teddy was involved, the children were able to see that it was simply teddy being 'naughty', and that no alteration had been made.

case study 3.5 Cerys and Claudia

Cerys was being 'mummy' in the role-play house. She was getting her baby ready to go shopping. She put on a pair of play shoes and picked up a shopping bag. When she was halfway across the room, she shouted, 'My baby, I've forgotten my baby', and rushed back to collect the pram. Cerys was learning about responsibility through her play.

Claudia was playing with the magnetic train set. She was trying to link up each of the carriages to the engines, but one carriage would not stay linked up. Claudia tried it at the end of each train she had made, but to no avail (the magnets at one end attract and at the other repel). Eventually, she turned the carriage around and this time it linked up successfully. Claudia was very pleased with herself and continued with her game happily.

activity INDIVIDUAL WORK

1 Which of the two girls gives the better example of discovery learning?
2 What examples of discovery learning have you seen in your current placement?
3 Does your current placement allow opportunities for discovery learning, or do staff step in to help out whenever a child is seen to be having difficulties?

Discovery learning
Children learn best by being given opportunities to find out for themselves. According to Piaget's constructivist theory of play, children are active learners who enjoy using a range of materials, objects and situations from their everyday life to help them develop their play and learn about the world.

Vygotsky's social constructivist view of play

Like Piaget, Vygotsky believed that children need to have access to a range of objects, materials and situations to develop their play. However, unlike Piaget, Vygotsky placed considerable emphasis on the child's need for adult input into their play in order for the child to realise their potential through play situations. His **social constructivist theory** has been influential in education.

Zone of proximal development (ZPD)
Vygotsky developed his concept of a **zone of proximal development (ZPD)** by studying what a child can achieve playing alone, and what they can achieve with some sensitive input from an adult. The ZPD is particularly relevant when a child is attempting to achieve a new aim, perhaps using a new piece of equipment or a more complex jigsaw puzzle. An adult can enhance the development of a child's understanding, affecting their subsequent thinking and actions. (It would be useful to think about occasions when you have observed an adult helping a child in this way.)

Refer to Unit 7, page 322, for a diagram illustrating Vygotsky's concept of the ZPD.

Jerome Bruner and discovery learning

Bruner believed that children enjoy finding out new things for themselves; like Piaget, he felt that children learn through the use of materials that are freely available to them.

He suggested that there are three ways or modes of thinking that children use internally to represent the world to themselves as their thinking develops.

Enactive mode
Bruner emphasised the importance of first-hand experiences and believed that the simplest thinking involves manipulating aspects of the environment. He referred to this as the **enactive mode of representation**. It has links with discovery learning.

Iconic mode
The **iconic mode of representation** involves the child's development of mental images, such as remembering what somebody or something looks like.

Iconic representation shows that the child is extending their memory and is not relying purely on active learning (enactive mode). A photograph, for example, will remind a child of someone they have met and enable them to think about the person further. Similarly, the smell of onions may remind them of cooking a barbecue with granny and granddad.

Symbolic mode
Thinking using symbolism, including language, number, music and art, is what Bruner termed the **symbolic mode of representation**. It enables older children to extend their thinking and express themselves through a variety of media.

Refer to Unit 7, page 323, for information on Bruner's concept of scaffolding.

Fig 3.26 Bruner's three modes of thinking

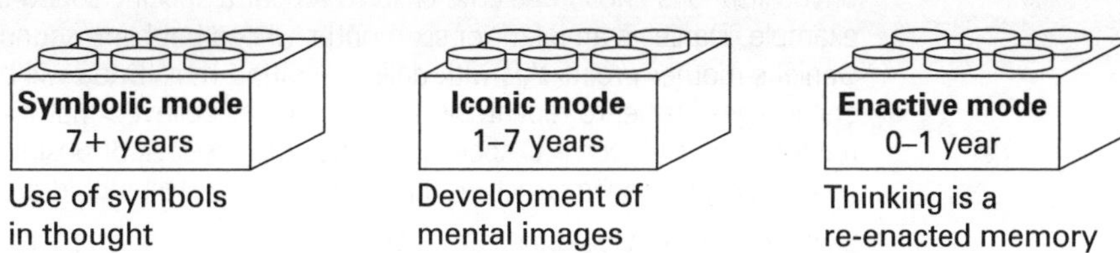

Language development

Language is the main way in which humans communicate with one another. It involves expression of meaning through the use of words or symbols and, when spoken or signed, it is often assisted by facial expressions, tone of voice and body posture.

Language is:

- Rule-governed – grammatical rules are present in each language (syntax).
- Structured – there is a system of speech sounds (phonology).
- Symbolic – words have meanings, building into phrases, and so on (semantics).
- Generative – it is the basis of the sharing of knowledge (pragmatics).

Prerequisites for language

The normal, unimpeded development of language is affected by other areas of development. For example, not only are the physical abilities of vision, hearing and speech vital, but there are also social and intellectual prerequisites, such as an understanding of the benefits of communicating with others. Children learn the basis of their culture through communication (during socialisation), and develop understanding of themselves and how they fit within their peer and social groups (goodness of fit). Psychologists believe that language plays an important part in all aspects of human development, with some theorists arguing that language is the basis of learning. An important debate involves two questions:

- Is language dependent on thought?
- Is thought dependent on language?

What are your first thoughts on this language vs. thought debate? Do you think understanding is needed in order to develop linguistically? Or do you think that language enables understanding to develop? Come back to these questions when you have read the theories outlined below.

Theories of language development

The theories described below offer some very different ideas about how language develops. As you read them, consider which you could accept and which do not seem possible.

A detailed discussion of the theories of language can be found in *Psychology for You* by Cullis *et al.* (1999).

Theories of language development include:

- association theory
- behaviourist theory
- biological theory
- maturational theory
- interactionist theory.

Association theory

This theory proposes that a child gradually builds their language by associating words with what they see. This theory works well up to a point, but does not take into account how we learn all aspects of language, for example those words used to describe feelings or emotions.

Behaviourist theory

Theorists such as Skinner proposed that a child's language is shaped by the responses given to them by their parents or main carers (operant conditioning). The positive reinforcement of vocalisations encourages the child to repeat a specific sound over and over again. For example, Daniel is an infant of six months whose babbling sounds have become 'dadadada'. Daniel's mother greets this with delight, stating that 'Dada will be home soon', and this encourages Daniel to repeat the sound. Skinner believed that the continuous positive reinforcement of 'correct' speech sounds, and the lack of positive response to sounds or (eventually) sentence structure that is not correct, will mould a child's language.

Skinner's theory would indicate that children have to go through a trial-and-error process for every aspect of speech, but this is clearly not the case, although it is accepted that infants are encouraged by the positive reactions of adults. Skinner's theory was challenged by many psychologists and consequently the nativist theories set out below became an inviting alternative.

Refer back to page 115, if you need to remind yourself about the nativist view.

The principles of social learning theory can also be applied to language, that is, that humans repeat behaviour that they see being rewarded (remember the Bobo dolls). If, for example, a child sees an older brother or sister being rewarded for speech, the younger child may try to imitate that behaviour.

Biological theory

Biological theory states that infants are born with an inbuilt programme for language, which Noam Chomsky (a nativist) calls the infant's **language acquisition device (LAD)**. He considered that this LAD enabled children to absorb the language that they heard, decode it and then develop an understanding of its rules and grammatical structure. It has been shown that children of all cultures develop language at much the same time and this gave support to the theories of Chomsky and others favouring this view.

Maturational theory

Lenneberg, like Chomsky, considered that, as long as children were exposed to language, they would simply pick it up. Lenneberg argued that a child's language development progresses as other aspects of their development advance. (This should not be confused with the Gesell's maturational theory which is concerned with other aspects of maturation.)

remember

As you move through the various placements that will make up your professional practice experience, observe and note the differences in speech intonation, questioning and grammar of children at different ages and stages.

Interactionist theory

According to interactionist theory, children's language reflects what they have experienced and what they understand. This theory sees language as a reflection of cognitive development: the schemas that children develop subsequently facilitate language development. In other words, children first experience and then talk about their experiences. Piaget, Vygotsky and Bruner took this interactionist approach in their thinking on language development.

Other research

It is interesting that research carried out with hearing children born to deaf parents has shown that, while a child may learn words from what they hear around them (e.g. radio, television, videos), they need to be actively involved in conversation in order to develop their understanding and use of grammar. In the cases of some children, speech therapy resulted in a sudden improvement in their language structure which soon brought them up to the expected level of language development for their age. This indicated that they had previously been ready to learn the grammatical rules associated with their culture's language, but needed active involvement with others in order to facilitate their learning.

Stages of language development

As with every aspect of development, children develop language at differing rates within what is considered to be the 'normal' range. This process of language development can be divided into 10 basic stages:

1. non-verbal communication/expression
2. speech-like noises
3. controlling sounds, using mouth and tongue
4. imitating sounds
5. first words
6. development of vocabulary (50 words is usual at 2 years)
7. putting words together to form simple phrases and sentences
8. use of grammar
9. use of meaning
10. using language to develop other skills, for example early literacy.

These 10 stages can be linked to approximate ages as shown in the following table.

Table 3.9 The stages of language development

Age	Understanding	No. of words	Type of words	Average length of sentence
3 months	Soothed by sound	0	Cooing and gurgling	0
6 months	Responds to voice tones	0	Babble	0
1 year	Knows own name and a few others	1	Noun (naming word)	1 word
18 months	Understands simple commands	6–20	Nouns	1 word
2 years	Understands much more than they can say	50+	Verbs and pronouns (action + name)	1–2 word phrases

cont'd

Table 3.9 continued

Age	Understanding	No. of words	Type of words	Average length of sentence
$2\frac{1}{2}$ years	Enjoys simple and familiar stories	200+	Pronouns I, me, you; Questions what, where	2–3 word phrases
3 years	Carries out complex commands	500–1,000	Plurals; Verbs in present tense; Questions who	3–4 word phrases
4 years	Listens to long stories	1,000–1,500	Verbs in past tense; Questions why, where, how	4–5 word phrases
5 years	Developing the ability to reason	1,500–2,000	Complex sentences with adult forms of grammar	5–6 word phrases

The development of speech sounds in the English language

Speech sounds are made up of consonants, vowels, syllables and words.

Consonants

Consonants are 'closed' sounds. This means that, for a consonant sound to be produced, the airflow is obstructed by parts of the mouth coming into contact with each other or almost touching. For example:

- To pronounce the 'b' in 'book', the lips need to come into contact.
- To pronounce the 's' in the word 'sand', the tip of the tongue touches the ridge just behind the top front teeth.

There are five main types of consonants:

- plosives
- nasals
- fricatives
- affricates
- approximants.

Table 3.10 The approximate sequential development of consonants in the English language

At 2 years	*m, n, p, b, t, d, w*
At $2\frac{1}{2}$ years	*k, g, ng* (as in *sing*), *h*
$2\frac{1}{2}$–3 years	*f, s, l, y*
$3\frac{1}{2}$–4 years	*v, z, ch, j, sh*
$4\frac{1}{2}$ years onwards	*th* (as in *thin*), *th* (as in *the*), *r*

Double consonants such as *sp*, *tr* and *fl*, and also the sounds *r* and *th*, can develop as late at $6\frac{1}{2}$ years in some children.

These are examples of how the obstructions are made.

Table 3.11 English consonant sounds 'at a glance'

	Bilabial	Labio-dental	Dental	Alveolar	Post-alveolar	Palatal	Velar	Glottal
Plosive	*p, b*			*t, d*			*c/k, g*	
Nasal	*m*			*n*			*ng*	
Fricative		*f, v*	*th, th*	*s, z*	*sh, zh*			*h*
Affricate					*ch, j*			
Approximant	*w*			*l*	*r*	*y*		

remember Exploring your own pronunciation to see how each sound is produced will help you understand the difficulties that children face.

How we pronounce sounds is quite complex. It is, however, a useful exercise for early years workers to explore their own pronunciation to gain a better understanding of how the parts of the mouth work together and how each sound is subsequently produced. This helps with understanding the difficulties faced by some children when developing speech sounds.

Plosives

Plosives are produced by a complete obstruction of the airflow at some position in the mouth, for example, the lips coming together. Air builds up behind the temporary obstruction, and when the obstruction is removed (e.g. the lips part) the air rushes out (a plosive).

Plosives can be voiceless (produced without the involvement of the vocal cords) or voiced (involving the vibration of the vocal cords). They occur in pairs:

- First pair: 'p', 'b' – the two lips come together to form a complete obstruction. These are known as bilabial plosives (two lips). Try pronouncing them.
- Second pair: 't', 'd' – these involve the tip of the tongue contacting the gum ridge (alveolar ridge) just behind the top front teeth. (Run your tongue over your alveolar ridge to identify where it is). These are known as alveolar plosives. Try pronouncing them.
- Third pair: 'c'/'k', 'g' (as in 'goat') – the back of the roof of the mouth is known as the soft palate (velum). Velar plosives are sounded when the tongue is in contact with the soft palate.

Try pronouncing these three consonant sounds.

Nasals

When a plosive sound is made, the soft palate is raised so that it touches the back of the throat and stops air from escaping through the nose. Nasals are similar in that there is complete obstruction of air flow in the mouth, but the air pressure does not build up. It is allowed to escape through the nose by lowering the soft palate.

There are three nasals:

- 'm' is a bilabial nasal where the sound is formed at the front of the mouth, with the lips coming together
- 'n' is an alveolar nasal, where the obstruction is between the back of the tongue and the soft palate
- 'ng' (as in 'sing') is a velar nasal; this sound never appears at the beginning of a word in English.

Try pronouncing these nasal consonants.

Fricatives

These sounds are formed by the narrowing of the mouth passage by any two of the articulators (lips, teeth, tongue, roof of mouth) coming into near contact. The air is forced through a narrow gap creating a friction sound, hence the name, fricative consonant. Each of these sounds can be prolonged by first taking a deep breath.

There are four pairs of fricatives:

- First pair: 'f', 'v' – these are articulated with slight contact between the bottom lip and the top front teeth. They are known as labio-dental fricatives.
- Second pair: 'th' (as in 'thin'), 'th' (as in 'that') – these fricatives involve the tongue nearly contacting the top front teeth. The sounds are quite hard for young children to pronounce and they often use alternatives, for example: 'f' instead of 'th' and/or 'v' instead of 'th'.
- Third pair: 's', 'z' – these are formed when the tongue is almost in contact with the alveolar ridge. They are known as alveolar fricatives.
- Fourth pair: 'sh', 'zh' (as sounded in the middle of the word 'measure') – these post-alveolar fricatives are formed further back in the mouth when the middle of the tongue comes into contact with the roof of the mouth, just behind the alveolar ridge. The 'zh' sound is never found at the beginning of a word in English.
- The final fricative is 'h'. It is a glottal fricative. It is made deep down in the throat (the glottis). This sound is never found at the end of a word in English.

Try pronouncing these fricative consonants.

Affricates

The affricates are the sounds that combine both a complete obstruction with a partial obstruction. They start with a complete obstruction formed by the tip of the tongue contacting the alveolar ridge, but then the air is released slowly with friction, behind the alveolar ridge. No air is released in an explosive way.

These sounds are 'j' and 'ch'. They are post-alveolar affricates. Try pronouncing them.

Approximants

The term 'approximant' is used for the sound made when the mouth passage is not completely obstructed, as it is with the plosives and the nasals, nor is it restricted so that friction is developed. Two articulators (tongue, teeth, etc.) approximate closely together.

The approximants are:

- 'w', formed by the two lips approximating closely (bilabial approximant)
- 'l', made by the tongue approximating to the alveolar ridge (alveolar approximant)
- 'r', sounded by the tongue being behind the alveolar ridge (post-alveolar approximant)
- 'y', articulated with the middle of the tongue approximating closely to the palate (palatal approximant).

Try pronouncing these approximants.

Refer back to the 'at a glance' table on page 150 to help consolidate your understanding.

Vowels

The basic vowel sounds are 'a', 'e', 'i', 'o' and 'u', but there are other vowel sounds too. These include the double sounds such as 'ee', 'oo', and so on. Vowels are 'open' sounds. There is no obstruction to the airflow during pronunciation and each sound differs according to the position of the mouth. For example:

- If the lips are spread widely, the sound 'ee' is produced.
- If the lips are rounded, the sound 'oo' is produced.
- Vowels can be long sounds as in the word 'more'. They can also be short sounds as in the word 'pack'.
- There are simple vowels such as 'o' as in 'pot', 'u' as in 'put', 'a' as in 'pat'. They are simple because, once the mouth is set in position, it does not need to alter in order to produce the sound.
- There are also more complex vowel sounds such as 'oy' as in 'boy' and 'ow' as in 'cow'. With these sounds, you need to change the mouth and/or tongue position for the full sound to be made.
- All vowels in English are 'voiced'. This means that they involve the vibration of the vocal cords.

Syllables

Speech sounds combine together to form syllables. A syllable is made up of a combination of consonants (c) and at least one vowel (v). There can be up to three consonants before a vowel and up to four consonants after a vowel in the English language.

Examples of syllables are:

- be = cv (one consonant and one vowel)
- and = vcc (one vowel and two consonants)
- plot = ccvc
- strip = cccvc
- tempts = cvcccc.

The more consonants in a syllable, the harder it will be for a child to pronounce, because it requires greater ability to co-ordinate the articulators.

Words

Syllables combine together to form words. Some words have just one syllable, for example 'cat', 'dog' and 'hen'. These are called monosyllabic words. Words that have more than one syllable are known as polysyllabic words.

Even in adulthood, some people have difficulty in pronouncing some polysyllabic words. For example, common difficulties are found in pronouncing:

- 'laboratory' (often mispronounced as 'labroratrory')
- 'certificates' (often mispronounced as 'cerstificates').

There may be words that you find difficult or stumble over on occasions. Think why this might be. Also, which words have you noticed other adults having difficulty with and how complex are the syllable combinations of these words?

Concerns regarding language development

The following are causes for concern:

- lack of communication with parents and carers in early weeks
- significant feeding difficulties (speech therapists are often involved at this early stage)
- lack of vocalisation from three months onwards
- no babbling from eight to nine months onwards
- lack of verbal responses to play
- vocalisation completely out of line with the developmental 'norms'.

Factors that can affect language development include medical problems such as glue ear. This is a condition of the middle ear in which sticky mucus is formed which is unable to drain away through the Eustachian tubes in the normal way. If severe and left untreated, it can lead to permanent hearing loss.

Cleft lip and palate can affect speech. A child born with one or both of these physical conditions will automatically be referred to a speech therapist, to ensure that the most appropriate feeding positions are established from birth.

Disordered or delayed speech

Many children have phases of unclear speech, but they do not all need to be seen by a speech therapist.

When expressing themselves, language disordered children may:

- have difficulty in finding appropriate words
- display word-order confusion
- have difficulty in giving explanations
- use confused grammar
- omit grammatical word endings
- use confused sounds within individual words.

Fig 3.27 Language disorder

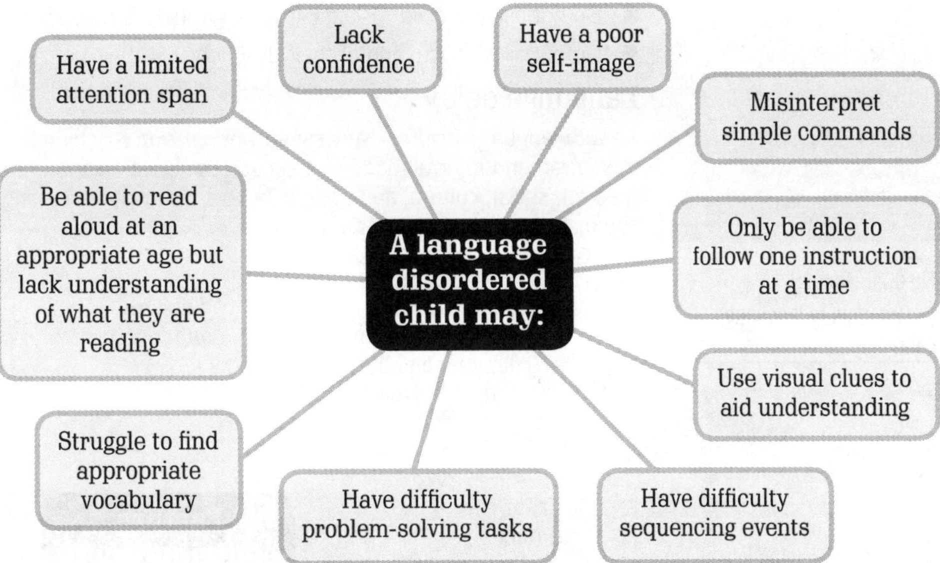

Elision

When a child regularly misses out part of a speech sound altogether, this is referred to as 'elision'. It is a common occurrence, particularly with the second consonant of a cluster of two, for example:

- The 'st' in the word 'postman' would become 'pos'man'.
- The 'pt' in the word 'slept' would become 'slep''.

In young children, this is part of the maturational development of speech patterns. In older children and adults, elision is more likely to be habit!

Dysfluency

Many temporary disorders occur because the child hastens to say something and stumbles over it in their eagerness and excitement; this is common and is known as dysfluency.

Hesitation is another type of dysfluency; it is often associated with the child's attempts to use more complex language structure. Speech therapists refer to this as 'normal developmental dysfluency' as it does not usually need professional intervention.

If a child's dysfluency continues for more than a short period of time, or if the parents or the child appear to be worried by the dysfluency, a referral to a speech therapist will usually be made. The British Stammering Association has drawn up the following guidelines to help decide if there should be referral. A referral is made if:

- the child has dysfluent speech and one or more of the following factors are present:
  - a family history of stammering or speech or language problems
  - the child is finding learning to talk difficult in any way
  - the child shows signs of frustration or is upset by his speaking
  - the child is struggling when talking
  - the child is in a dual-language situation and is stammering in their first language
  - there is parental concern or uneasiness
- the child's general behaviour is causing concern (Mukherji and O'Dea, 2000).

remember Language disorder and language delay can affect other aspects of a child's learning and development.

When conversing with a dysfluent child, it is important to give them time and attention to minimise the affect of the dysfluency. Also:

- Do speak steadily and clearly yourself.
- Do give the dysfluent child your full attention.
- Do avoid interrupting the child whenever possible.
- Do focus on what they are saying, and try to ignore the dysfluency.
- Do not ask the child to repeat it or to start again.
- Do not tell the child to 'take a deep breath' before they speak.
- Do not tell the child to slow down.
- Do not ask the child to 'think it through' before they speak.
- Do not allow discussion of their dysfluency in their presence.

Language delay

As with language disorder, any significant delay in reaching the expected 'norms' would be monitored and referral made to a speech therapist as appropriate. There are environmental, medical, social, cultural and genetic factors that can affect language development, as summarised in the spidergram below.

Fig 3.28 Factors contributing to language delay

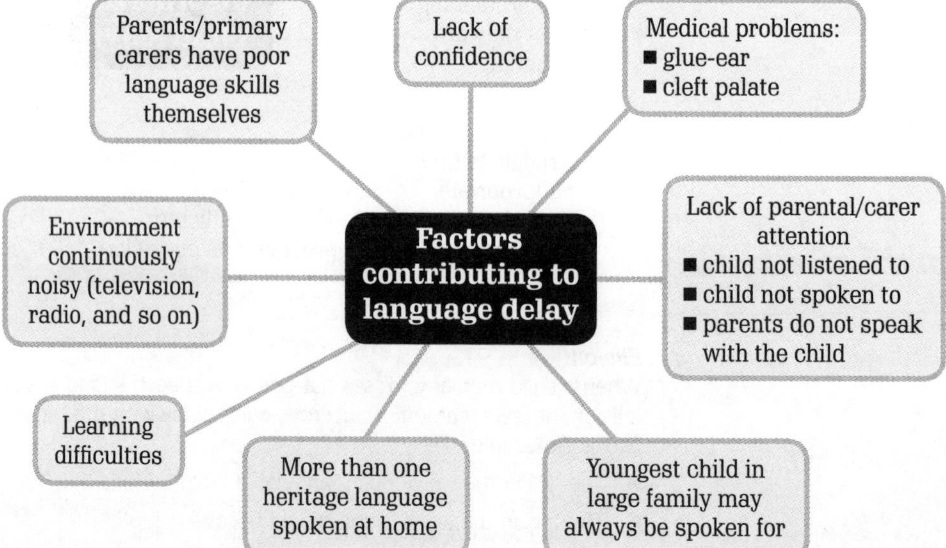

To extend your understanding of language development, a useful source of further reading is *Understanding Children's Language and Literacy* by Mukherji and O'Dea (2000).

Language as a means of communication

Language is essential to humans so that we can communicate our needs, express our feelings and extend our experiences beyond our own environment by interacting with others. These interactions enable us to enhance our thinking and learn new skills. Spoken language is our most important means of communication. It is enhanced by facial expression, tone of voice and body language. Communication is an important aspect of early years professionalism.

Refer back to Unit 1, pages 11–24, to remind yourself about communication and interpersonal skills in early years work.

1 Produce a large poster, clearly labelled, setting out the main patterns of development from birth to 16 years.
2 Display your poster and be ready to answer questions on your knowledge and understanding.

1 Taking a specific part each, as a group, produce a 'magazine' on baby and toddler development from birth to three years and the factors affecting it.
2 Divide the material into appropriate sections and ensure that you use clear labelling and visual images and explain any difficult terminology.
3 Ideally, your magazine will be word processed, or produced using a desk top publishing programme.

Factors affecting growth and development

Development can be affected by any of the following:

- social and economic factors
- health
- housing, environment and social circumstances
- stimulation
- motivation
- adult expectations
- gender
- genetic factors.

An understanding of these factors will enable you to place children's growth and development within a wider social context and identify areas of concern that may require intervention. As your experience in working with children and families grows, you will note how some children's development may be compromised by one or many of the factors above and that some children will be seriously disadvantaged.

Social and economic factors

A child raised in poverty is less likely to thrive than a child who enjoys an economically stable life. It is unlikely that a family on a low income will be able to have a diet that is varied and provides all the nutrients needed for optimum growth and healthy development. Inadequate or barely adequate household equipment, particularly with regard to safety features, can increase the possibility of accidents. If there are limited funds to pay for heating, children may be persistently unwell, particularly in winter.

Fig 3.29 Proportion of children living in households below median income

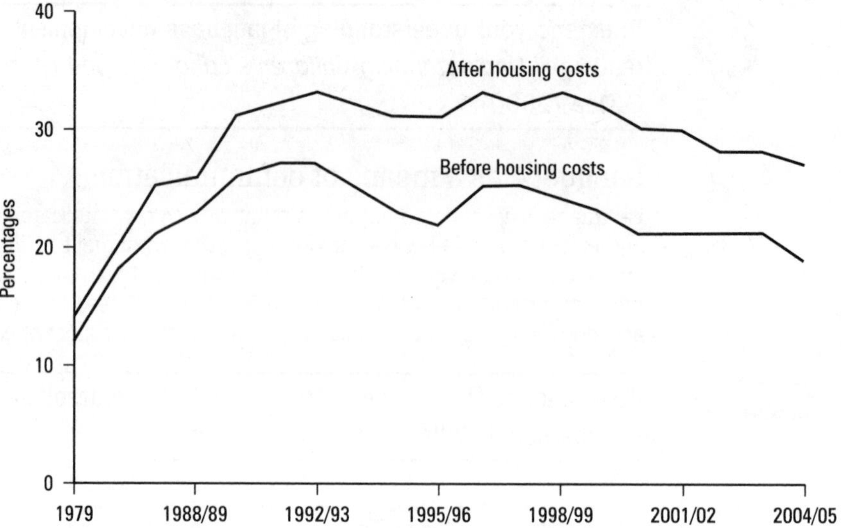

Social Policy and Welfare by Walsh *et al.* (2000) offers a useful source of further information on the effects of poverty.

Health

All aspects of a child's development can be affected by illness, especially their capacity to learn and maximise their personal potential. We also know from seminal studies such as the Black Report (1980) and the Acheson Report (1998) that health and other inequalities continue to widen the gap between the health of the wealthy and the health of the less advantaged. There are well-documented links between poor, or inadequate, diet and health. Poor diet and poor health may adversely affect a child's physical growth and development, as well as their ability to learn. The improvement of children's health is a key target in the *Every Child Matters* agenda, and it is imperative that early years workers are familiar with the indicators of ill health, so that early interventions can be initiated and possible effects on development ameliorated.

Refer to Unit 9, page 411, for further information on the effects of health on children's development.

Housing, environment and social circumstances

Children living in poverty and disadvantaged circumstances are often accommodated in old or inadequate housing stock. Living in poor housing is linked to a higher incidence of respiratory illnesses and an increased rate of accidental injuries, both of which will affect a child's development generally, or may result in serious trauma or chronic ill health. Poverty also makes it more likely that children are living in environments that are densely populated and polluted by traffic or industrial fumes. Lack of open spaces and clean air may limit opportunities for physical development.

Cramped living conditions are stressful to most people. The opportunities for cross-infection are greater because of the close proximity of family members. Temporary accommodation, such as bed and breakfast facilities, affects families in that they have no secure base; this is stressful for the parents, which has a subsequent effect on the children, with older children often worrying about their parents and feeling powerless to help them.

By contrast, when children live in privileged circumstances and have parents and an extended family able to give them time in a stress-free environment, they often feel more settled and have fewer worries. They are better able to enjoy childhood.

Family and cultural practices also affect a child's development. Some cultures place great emphasis on the importance of older generations, and members of the extended family share in the upbringing of the children.

Stimulation

A stimulating environment offers greater opportunities for learning, helping the child to reach their potential. Stimulation has been shown to start in the womb, and some women choose to maximise this by playing music and reading to their unborn child. However, at times parents overstimulate their children (known as '**hot-housing**'). This can be counterproductive in that the children may become tired and irritable and, eventually, uninterested in learning.

Refer to Unit 2, page 101, for more about setting up stimulating environments for children.

Motivation

Most young children seem automatically motivated. They are enthusiastic about new experiences and tend to enjoy the whole learning process. However, as they get older and face more challenging learning situations, motivation can wane as the immediate reward of success may occur less often. The adult needs to encourage, praising effort, and showing enthusiasm themselves. Motivation is often directly linked to the expectations of the adults who influence the child.

Adult expectations

Expectations of children should be high. To expect only a little will often result in the child's only attaining a little. Children take their cue from adults; if they are not expected to achieve, they are likely to give up sooner than they might have done if the adult's expectation had been greater, and thus a 'self-fulfilling prophecy' occurs. Expectations should, however, also be realistic: a child's age, stage of development, temperament and prior experience should all be taken into account.

Most adults usually have high expectations and help children develop strategies to meet them, for example by positively reinforcing good behaviour and by modelling actions and responses to help shape ways of managing conflict resolution, etc. The same approach should be applied to learning, with the adult modelling actions, talking through alternative strategies for achieving an aim and using positive reinforcement.

Refer to the work of Vygotsky, page 146, and Bruner, page 147.

Gender

Gender can also affect development. Physically girls tend to be slightly taller than boys by about age six or seven, and the onset of puberty in girls is usually around two years ahead of its onset in boys. The nature–nurture debate continues to rumble on in relation to what is innate in play and learning and what is due to influence, but boys on the whole do have a tendency towards more active play, and girls often tend to have a more caring streak and also to enjoy books and 'quieter' activities.

Professional Practice

- It is important that children are given the same opportunities and enabled to make choices based on current interests whenever possible.
- On the whole, if children are interested in what they are doing, they are likely to do it well, enjoy a positive sense of achievement, and therefore feel motivated towards further learning.

Genetic factors

Genetic factors were discussed earlier in the unit, and this should have helped you understand how additional difficulties can be faced by some children and families. The development of children with an inherited or congenital condition may be generally or specifically affected and early years workers may well be involved in the assessment of their development.

Refer back to page 110 for more information on genetic effects on development and genetic disorders.

Developmental delay

Although all children will follow the same pattern and sequence of development, some will 'hit' the normative milestones relatively on target, but other children may display one or more elements of delayed development. There may be specific delay in developing one or more motor or other skills, or delay may be more global. The likelihood of developmental delay may be identified at the baby's birth if a hereditary or congenital condition is obvious. However, it may not be identified until much later, and this can be a source of great stress for the family.

Possible reasons for developmental delay

Reasons for developmental delay are often complex and occasionally remain unknown, but certain factors are known to be implicated:

- prenatal and perinatal factors
- congenital or inherited conditions
- postnatal factors
- family and social factors.

Prenatal and perinatal factors

Development may be affected or delayed by substances which the mother ingests during pregnancy or from an illness that she contracts. Problems during or shortly after birth that result in lack or oxygen may also have a lasting effect on cognitive and motor development, as may prematurity, postmaturity and complicated deliveries.

Refer back to page 107 for information on factors influencing embryonic and foetal growth.

Congenital or inherited conditions

There are many congenital, inherited or chromosomal conditions that may affect one or more areas of development.

Refer to page 70 for information on a range of conditions and to Unit 27 of *BTEC National Children's Care, Learning and Development* Book 2, by Green (2007).

Postnatal factors

Delays in development may be caused by a wide range of postnatal factors including accidental injury and trauma; the complications of infections; childhood cancers and malignant tumours. Children's physical and motor development may also be affected by the social and emotional consequences of medical treatments and periods in hospital.

Family and social factors

It is possible for delays in emotional and social development to be observed in situations of extreme family stress and dysfunction. This type of delay may also occur when there are frequent changes of key carers in a child's earliest years, problems with positive parenting or when any type of abuse or emotional deprivation is present.

See *Good Practice in Caring for Young Children with Special Needs* by Dare and O'Donovan (2002) for a fuller description of delays in development and the associated problems. You will also find a table on page 11 that outlines the major types of additional needs that are likely to result in some form of developmental delay.

remember

It is important to enable the child to meet their social and educational potential by providing a welcoming and inclusive environment and ensuring that the child has access to stimulating and supportive care and activities.

Independence and lifelong learning

Early years workers are in a key position to identify and support children with delayed development, as well as working in partnership with parents and other professionals.

Developmental delays of any kind will necessitate that particular attention is paid to fostering skills for independence and promoting an ethos of lifelong learning. Early years workers will collaborate with parents and other professionals in the multidisciplinary team to maximise a child's independence and sense of mastery in whichever area of development is delayed. Practice will be enhanced if an anti-oppressive and anti-disablist stance is taken and if a positive and enabling attitude towards the area of delay is evident. Workers may need to act as an advocate for the child or parent on occasions, but the emphasis should be on empowering children and parents. Lifelong learning is of relevance to child, parent and practitioners, and regular professional updating should facilitate high-quality, evidence-based care.

remember
Like children, we learn best through direct involvement.

Play

Play is an integral part of how children learn. This statement should be kept at the forefront of our minds as we plan and prepare activities, lessons and outings. The more inviting, interactive and enjoyable an activity can be made to be, the more likely it is for the learning aim to be retained and therefore for it to be of value. Children almost always learn better by being directly involved.

For example, think about the difference to a child in actually handling pine cones, horse chestnut cases and holly, compared with looking at pictures of them and hearing someone else describe them. The direct contact is so much more meaningful. They can feel the textures, smell the differences between them, note how smooth, spiky, hard, flexible and so on each item is. This learning cannot be established fully just by looking at pictures.

As adults we also play as we explore new items. For example, think about your first experience of using items such as an iPod or MP3 player, when you were finding out how best to use them. As adults we delight in the increased level of interaction offered us through computer programs such as Skype, and we try a new one out several times as we familiarise ourselves with its uses and limitations.

Refer to page 139 for more on the stages of play, and, for a fuller discussion, see Unit 7, page 331.

Know how to promote development across age ranges

activity
INDIVIDUAL WORK 3.3
M2

Look on the Nelson Thornes website for a poster giving examples of how to support and promote development in children aged birth to three years. There are five main headings:

- environment
- meeting physical needs
- encouragement
- supporting learning
- communication.

Using the same headings, and referring to the poster and to relevant sections of this course text, as well as drawing on knowledge and understanding gained from placement experience and classroom learning, prepare a booklet on supporting and promoting development that could be given to a parent enquiring about a placement for their child. Use the information on the poster simply to get you started. Many more examples could have been given.

See the Nelson Thornes website for the poster 'Promoting development' and refer to the section on birth to three years.
www.nelsonthornes.com/btec

activity
GROUP WORK 3.4
P2

1 Having read through the unit so far, and using the poster 'Promoting development' as starting points, prepare a presentation on ways to promote development across the four age ranges:
   - birth to 3 years
   - 3 to 7 years
   - 7 to 12 years
   - 12 to 16 years.

2 Use a different form of presentation for each age range.
3 Present your information to another group of students.

Look on the Nelson Thornes website for the poster 'Promoting development'. www.nelsonthornes.com/btec

Understand objectivity and ethics when observing children

Objectivity not subjectivity

Objectivity

It is important to consider your own feelings, **attitudes and values** when you carry out observations of children as these can affect **objectivity** if not taken into account.

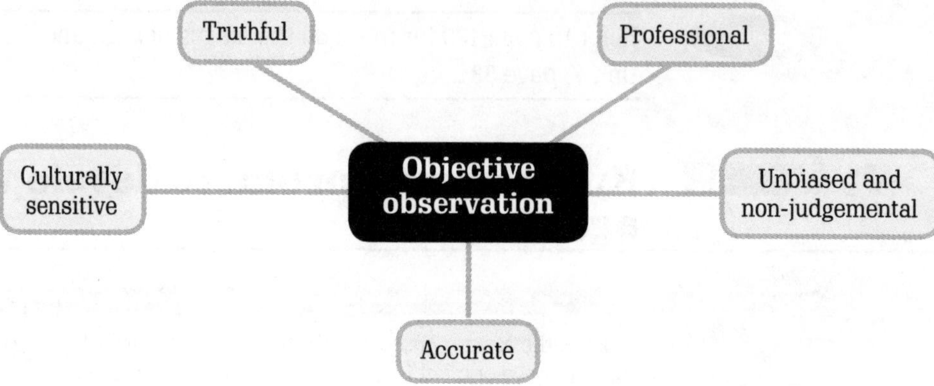

Fig 3.30 Objective observation

An objective observation can be summarised as being:

- truthful
- professional
- unbiased
- non-judgemental
- accurate
- culturally sensitive
- valid
- reliable.

Truthfulness
It can be very difficult when beginning to observe children to remember that the aim is to record only what you see and hear. This must be done without making assumptions about the children or what you think is taking place. It can be tempting to 'embroider' what appears to be a short observation where nothing much seems to be happening, but this is not acceptable practice.

Accuracy
Accuracy is always important when recording your observations. For example, imagine that you were not absolutely sure that you heard a conversation correctly and wrote up your notes with inaccuracies; as a result, misleading information about a child might be recorded. Accuracy and sensitivity are particularly essential when, for example, an observation is being made of a child who is thought to be displaying signs of disturbed behaviour. Accuracy is also important when recording times and events. It is good practice to ask your placement supervisor or another member of trained staff to countersign your observation. They can then confirm that you have presented an accurate observation.

Cultural sensitivity

Assumptions about practices or behaviours in a cultural group that differs from your own must not be allowed to affect objective observations. This means that you should think carefully about the way in which you approach observations and the instruments that are used to record data. For example, Tassoni *et al*. (2002, page 26) note that normative developmental charts are frequently culturally biased and do not account for individual differences in childrearing or cultural practices.

Refer to Unit 8, page 368, for further reminders on objectivity, and to page 393, for the relevance of validity and reliability to any form of research.

Perception and subjectivity

Perception is the organisation and interpretation of information received from the senses. One person's perception of something may be different from another's, even when they are looking at the same situation at the same time. At times, our brain tells us what it thinks it sees, based on preconceived information, ideas and expectations.

There are various illustrations in which the object seen can be viewed in two different ways. We cannot perceive both images at the same time; and one person may see one image first, whereas someone else may see the other.

Fig 3.31 Ambiguous figures

remember If you are unsure whether your perception of a child or what is happening may differ from those of other workers, ask them to check your observations for you, or observe the same situation or child with you.

Our individual perceptions will also be a powerful influence on how we carry out and record our observations of children. Perceptions of how a child is behaving or how well a planned activity suits the needs of a group of children may vary from practitioner to practitioner, according to their point of view, because perceptions are founded not only on what we 'see' but also on our values and beliefs, making them **subjective**.

As with any other area of professional practice, our work in observing children should be free from bias and personal perspectives. Our perceptions and knowledge of children can sometimes hinder objective observation, as it can be difficult to stop personal feelings getting in the way. We all see the world differently, and we may, owing to our background and upbringing, understand things slightly differently. However, early years workers share a common set of values and principles, including working within an anti-discriminatory framework. By checking that our perceptions are similar to those of others, we can promote good practice.

Attitudes and subjectivity

It is important that we do not let our personal feelings and beliefs intrude into our observations of children, as these cloud objectivity, introducing subjectivity and therefore bias. Lay and Dopeyra (1977) refer to this as 'sorting out "you" from what you view'; it is easier said than done, as we need to have some awareness of potential **prejudices** and stereotypical assumptions in order to put them aside when observing. Allport (1897–1967) considered that we each have several personality traits and that these affect our approach to what we do. It is therefore important to identify the 'us' in ourselves to help us maintain a sense of objectivity.

The dangers of discrimination and stereotyping are discussed in Unit 6, pages 288–292.

Preventing bias from influencing observation

- Be aware of your own potential for stereotyping or unintentional prejudice.
- Acknowledge that you may feel more positively about some children than others, as this may result in your paying too much or too little attention to certain aspects of their behaviour.
- Make sure that you find out about any cultural differences that might influence the objectivity of your observation.
- Be sensitive to children's social and cultural backgrounds when recording information and make sure that perceived differences in behaviour, appearance and cleanliness do not cloud your objectivity.
- Make yourself familiar with cultural differences in facial expressions and body language. Ask trained, experienced staff for help in interpreting this important area of communication.
- Try to ensure that you do not replicate any gender or other biases when undertaking an observation. What you expect may be what you see, but, if you are looking through biased eyes, you may not be seeing a true picture.
- Try to use an appropriate observational technique and be aware of the external factors that can influence observations.
- Discuss any worries about potential bias with your tutor or placement supervisor.
- Take advice when choosing a child to study unless you are absolutely certain that your choice is appropriate.
- Consider the timing of your observation and whether this might affect the outcome. A child may lack energy and enthusiasm at the end of the day, and an observation done then could produce a very different outcome from one carried out early in the morning.

remember

It can be a useful exercise to think about the types of bias or stereotypical judgements that might be encountered when observing children. This will help you avoid them yourself.

Ethical practice

Ethical protocols

Like any other area of childcare practice, the observation of children must be undertaken ethically and in line with any protocols that your college or setting may have. Your behaviour when you are in a setting, whether or not you are observing children, should conform to the highest standards as you are there as a representative of your college or course provider. You are also working with a potentially vulnerable client group, and you need to act in a child's best interests at all times.

You need to take into account:

- getting all necessary permissions
- whether you need any explicit authorisation
- level of consultation needed
- what information should be given to the participants or their parent/teacher/guardian.
- what information you are actually trying to obtain, i.e. why you need it and whether it is appropriate to seek it
- getting full approval from tutors and placement
- issues of negotiation, i.e. meeting the needs of participants and sticking to any agreed amendments to your original plans
- how you will report the information.

Refer to pages 166–168 for an example of these protocols.

Maintaining confidentiality

It should go without saying that confidentiality is of prime importance when undertaking observations. Children and practitioners should not be identified by name, neither should the setting in which they are being observed. The information that you derive from observing children should only be shared on a professional basis with those people who 'need to know'; and all observations should be carefully and securely stored. You may be asked to discuss your observations with your tutor, but you will not be expected to refer to children or settings by name. There are few occasions when confidentiality should be broken: one is in the case of suspected or actual child abuse.

Professional Practice

- The Data Protection Act 1998 covers information kept on paper and on computer. This Act is relevant to all early years settings, and it is relevant to you as a student too. Ensure that all information you use, record and refer to meets the requirements of the Act.
- Remember never to discuss children, parents, staff or settings in public places or disclose information to friends or family.

Refer also to the section on confidentiality in Unit 1, page 28.

Rights

Observing children also raises issues of rights: the right of a parent not to have their child observed by students and the right of a child not to participate. This area must be approached with sensitivity and your supervisor should advise you of any child that it would be better not to use for your observations. If you are at all unsure, ask before starting your observation.

Professional Practice

- You should always have written permission from the parent or carer before undertaking an observation.
- Ask permission from the setting and comply with any policies or protocols.
- Consult staff if you sense that a child is not happy with the observational process – even young infants can show their unwillingness to participate.
- Write your observation in a professional manner and ensure that you respect children's and parents' rights at all times. Remember that the language that is used also needs to be professional and you should avoid subjective descriptions or slang.
- Store your observations securely and ensure that you do not disclose the names of children, settings or staff.
- Ensure that you behave in an ethical and professional manner at all times.

Imagine that you are going to be carrying out a range of observations on children in your placement. You have gained outline permission from your placement supervisor, and she has asked you to draft a letter for her to send out to all parents, explaining what you wish to do and asking their permission. In your letter, outline briefly why carrying out the observations is important to you and explain how you will ensure objectivity and observe ethical practice, including the rights of individuals.

Understand the use of observation

Observation and recording of children's development are important to the work of early years practitioners. Learning the techniques of observation will therefore be useful to your future role as a professional.

Observation forms part of the assessment process within early years courses and is therefore also a requirement in order to obtain your qualification.

Purpose of observing children

An observation may be carried out for the reasons listed below.

Fig 3.32 Reasons for observation

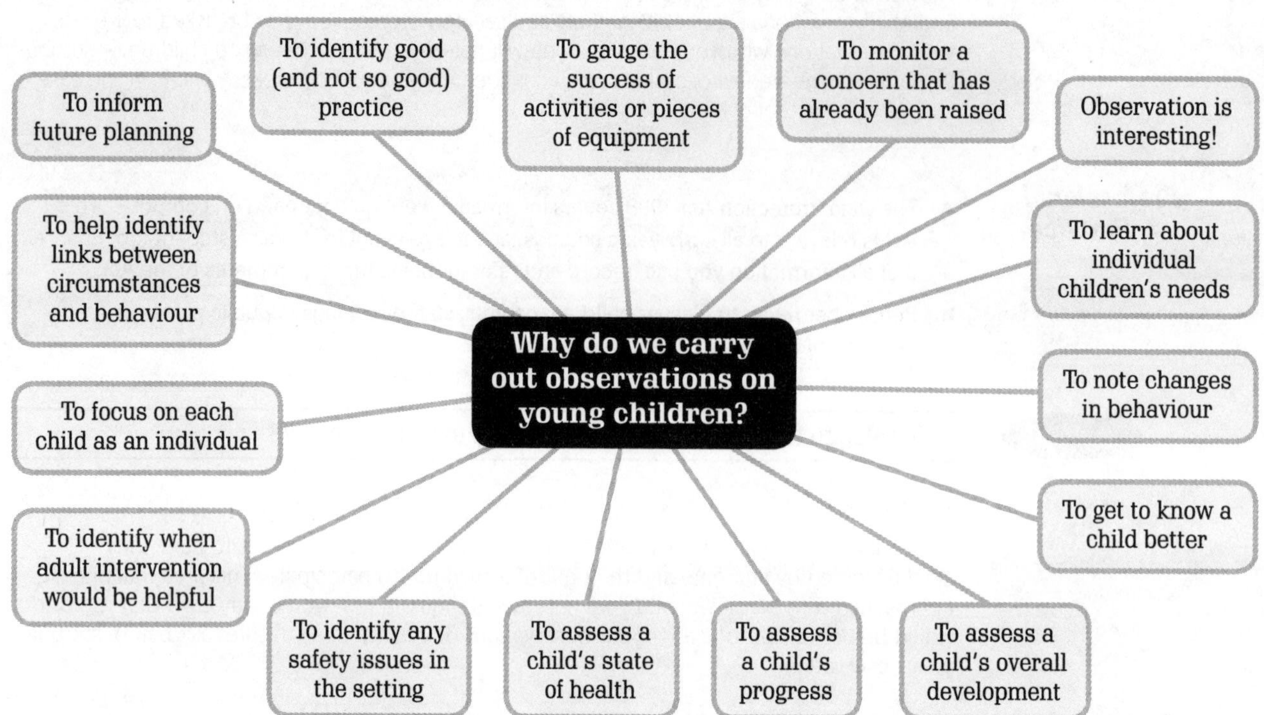

To learn about individual children's needs

Through observation, you may identify that a particular child is reluctant to socialise with others or is not accepted by the group and is consequently on their own for much of the time. Developing strategies with the child, to encourage them to play initially alongside others and then more co-operatively, gradually helps to involve them in interactive play without adult intervention.

To note changes in behaviour

Observation is a useful means of identifying any significant change in how a child is behaving. For example, a previously happy and bright child who is suddenly very quiet and withdrawn, or possibly aggressive, should raise concerns. Taking time to observe if the behaviour is generalised or only occurs in isolated situations would aid you in developing a strategy to help the child back to their former self.

To get to know a child better

Particularly when a child is new to the setting, an outline assessment of their stage of development helps staff to understand the child's needs and offer an appropriate programme of care and education.

To assess a child's overall development

Assessment is routine in most settings, and an initial assessment is likely to take place when a child joins or moves from one setting to another. It helps identify the rate of progress that a child is making and enables the setting to plan an appropriate programme to meet the child's needs.

To assess a child's progress

Once an overall assessment has been made, subsequent observation of the child can be useful in identifying if they are progressing. Any area of concern can be picked up and used as a focus for planning.

To assess a child's state of health

In a busy early years setting, a tired child will struggle to achieve and enjoy the facilities offered. Observation can help you monitor a situation and decide whether a child is simply tired or has a medical need. Young children are usually full of energy, particularly at the start of the day, but those who have only recently given up a daytime sleep may need rest times built into their daily programme.

To identify any safety issues in the setting

Observation can highlight areas within the setting where supervision is insufficient, or where potential hazards could arise. Observation should be used, in conjunction with reflection on past accidents or incidents, to inform decisions regarding changes in safety policy.

To identify when adult intervention would be helpful

Some children benefit from sensitive adult input into their activities. Observing adults in the nursery or classroom can help you learn when to intervene and when to hold back. As a student, you should feel able to ask (at a suitable time) why a decision was made either to intervene or to leave a child to their own devices. This will develop your understanding of using observation skills.

Refer to pages 146–147 in this unit and to Unit 7, pages 322–323, to remind you of the work of Vygotsky and Bruner.

To focus on each child as an individual

Most settings have quite high numbers of children; if they are observed as a group, the louder and more active child is likely to figure far more centrally in the observation than the quiet child who has been unobtrusively engaged throughout the session. It is quite likely that, even with a series of such observations, the same children will be prominent and the same children will be 'missed'. Focusing on an individual child ensures that that particular child's development can be assessed and that staff can see if they are happy within the setting.

To help identify links between circumstances and behaviour

An observation aimed at identifying what triggers a regular tantrum in a child is looking for a link between circumstance and behaviour. Identifying such links is also the main focus of event sampling, see page 172.

Refer to Unit 1, page 6, for the antecedent behaviour in the ABC behaviour management strategy.

To inform future planning

Observation can identify aspects of developmental need that can be incorporated into future plans. For example, a child who is unable to hold a pencil sufficiently well to meet their needs may be disadvantaged as they move into a more formal educational setting that requires regular use of pencil skills. Activities to encourage development of the finer skills in general would help such a child develop better pencil control. Similarly, a child who has not as yet developed an understanding of the need to share can be encouraged to do so by being involved in a range of adult-supervised 'shared' activities.

To identify good (and not so good) practice

Observation can reveal examples of excellence in a setting, but it can also raise concerns regarding the practice. A manager or supervisor may use observation as part of a staff appraisal scheme.

Refer to Unit 1, for pointers on the importance of interactions with children.

To gauge the success of activities or pieces of equipment

At times, certain activities may not seem to be as popular and well used as expected. This can be for many reasons. For example, the farm set may be too near to a doorway, so the animals regularly get knocked over; this might discourage children from playing with it. A simple solution would be to move the farm to a less busy area of the setting, where the children can enjoy the activity without being interrupted.

To monitor a concern that has already been raised

When a child has been identified as having a particular need, it is likely that their progress will continue to be monitored. This may be by the early years staff within the setting, or it may be by a professional who visits specifically to observe and assess the child in a 'natural' environment.

Fig 3.33 What might the observer gain from studying this group of children?

Observation is interesting!

It is to be hoped that the majority of early years workers and students are developing a career in the field of early years because of their interest in, and love of, children. Although quite time consuming, observation offers a fascinating insight into their world. If for no other reason, you should observe the children in your care for the pure pleasure that it will bring you.

A useful source of further reading on the importance of observation is *Closely Observed Infants* by Miller (1997). This book sets out exemplary observations, accompanied by critical discussion.

remember Check whether your setting has a policy for observing children and ensure that you adhere to it closely.

remember Always have a small notebook or 'post-it' notes and a pen or pencil in order to capture spontaneous **snapshots**.

Planning and preparation

Before beginning to observe babies or children, it is useful to plan what you will be doing.

Permissions

Making observations involves gaining formal permission from the parents and the person in charge of the setting; to carry out observations without permission would be an infringement of rights. Some adults are uncomfortable being observed by students, and some parents are unhappy if their child is focused upon. This is why permission to observe is needed in advance. Permission should preferably be given in writing and stored securely. You also need to re-check on the chosen day that your supervisor is willing for you to go ahead with the observation.

Preparation of documentation

Before starting to observe, it is wise to identify your aims and objectives for the observation. This will help you to focus effectively and use your time wisely. Make sure that you have the equipment that you need as some methods require pre-prepared templates.

See Chapter 2 in *How to Observe Children* by Sheila Riddall-Leech (2005) for further information and guidance on aims and objectives. She also provides clear examples of how observations may be presented or set out.

Decisions about aim, method, activity

You will be able to ask your tutor and trained staff about the most appropriate methods to use and which children are the most suitable to use as the focus of an observation. Decisions will also be influenced by:

- Areas of development to be focused on – are you going to look at a child's overall abilities or focus on one area, such as fine motor skills?

- The required number or types of observations needed to meet course requirements – you will be required to use a variety of techniques covering children of different ages.
- The individual child – trained staff may suggest a suitable child or children to use for an observation, or they may indicate which children should be avoided for personal reasons. This could be due to a sensitive family situation or because the child is unwell or tired.
- The timing of the observation – this needs to be thought about and negotiated so that you are not asking to be spared at a busy time of day. Remember, too, that small babies will need rest and sleep periods, so observations should fit in with these, and also that babies (and older children) do not respond as positively when they are tired as when they are rested and alert.

remember You do not usually need to observe children interacting with an adult, unless for a specific purpose.

What to observe

This choice depends on the aims and objectives of your observation and may be dictated by the requirements of your course, or by your personal interests. You may find it useful to use the Birth to Three Matters framework to guide your choice of activities for observation, as this framework is not **underpinned** by a linear model of development. Alternatively, you may be asked by the staff in a setting to observe a child undertaking a particular activity or displaying certain behaviour.

Practical considerations

When planning to observe, certain practical issues have to be taken into account, as the following list shows:

- Always gain permission to carry out observations of a specific child.
- Agree with your supervisor a convenient time for observing.
- Be unobtrusive – avoid eye contact with the child you are observing, while remaining within a range that enables you to hear their use of language.
- Try not to catch the attention of the children in the setting.
- Be prepared – have pen, paper, charts, and so on to hand.
- Know what you are aiming to achieve; set objectives – spontaneous activity, planned activity, and so on.
- Try not to be drawn into a child's activity as this will be likely to hinder your observation.
- Start with children who appear within the normal developmental ranges; **evaluation** will be easier.
- Observe for short periods initially and gradually build up the length of the observational period.
- Try out a variety of observational styles in different situations.
- Keep pen and paper handy for those 'spur of the moment' observational opportunities.
- If using a timed technique, ensure that you have easy access to a clock.
- In the event of an emergency, you will have to abandon your observation until another time.

Refer to page 181 for more detailed information about planning an observation.

Professional Practice

- **Observations should only be carried out if there are sufficient other adults present to meet safely the required adult:child ratio of the setting. Students are officially exempt from these ratios, but at times they are relied upon to be an additional adult in the supervision of a complex activity.**
- **Make sure that you inform your placement supervisor that you have a number of observations to complete and agree mutually satisfactory times.**

When and where to observe

During your training you will visit a range of settings, and each of these will offer opportunities for observation. National Children's Care, Learning and Development students are required to undertake a minimum of 800 hours' assessed placement experience involving each of the following age ranges:

- birth to one year
- one to three years
- three to five years
- five to eight years.

In special needs settings, placement experience can include older children too. It is accepted that at times the age ranges within some settings will differ, and the above guidelines can occasionally be adjusted slightly. You will therefore be able to have placement experience in at least four of the following settings:

- the home
- childminder
- voluntary preschool
- statutory preschool
- private nursery provision
- nursery school/class
- primary school
- hospital
- special needs provision.

Fig 3.34 Situations and behaviours to observe

Undertaking observations

Observation is only valuable if it is carried out appropriately. It is not something that can be done half-heartedly. In college, your tutors will introduce observational techniques to you and will most likely suggest that you practise before you start your portfolio. Many tutors will assess your first observations and offer feedback on their strengths as well as guidance as to how they can be improved for the future.

> *remember* Unobtrusive observation will give a truer picture of what is really happening as both adults and children react differently if they know that they are being observed.

Your tutor and qualified practitioners will give you guidance about the most suitable method to use in a given situation. Although you may concentrate on one method until your confidence and skills improve, do try to use as many methods as you can as this will help you to link theory to practice and ensure that appropriate methods are used.

As you observe, you will get better and more accurate results if you work unobtrusively and minimise any distraction to the observed child or to any other children in the group or class. A child who knows that they are being watched is unlikely to be completely natural in their actions and in their level of interaction with peers and/or adults. They may also try to draw you into their activity because they can see that you are interested in them.

During the course of some observations, you may actually be involved with the activity. This is known as **participant observation**.

Participant or non-participant observation?

Participant observation can be carried out whilst being involved in an activity with children, but this is not ideal. It is far better to observe children from a short distance (**non-participant observation**), as you can focus completely on what you are observing and are not distracted by your own involvement. You may, however, feel that participant observation is a useful approach if noting language is important, and the child you are focusing on speaks very quietly.

One of the first decisions to be made is whether you will observe from a distance or whether you will conduct your observation whilst engaged in the situation. Both methods have advantages and disadvantages.

Non-participant observation

- This method is ideal for an inexperienced observer who can note down what is happening without the distraction of being involved in the activity.
- Non-participation may help the observer to be more objective.
- Non-participation means that most techniques can be used.
- However, you may find it difficult to take time out from planned activities or care routines to sit away from the action and undertake your observation.
- Children may not do or say what you were hoping to observe, or you may simply not be in the right position to see and hear what is of interest to you.

Participant observation

- The participant observer can give instructions to a child in order to observe the type of behaviour that is desired.
- This method may be more effective in terms of time available for observations, as less time is spent waiting for spontaneous events to happen.
- However, it may be difficult to capture all that is happening if the observer is involved.
- Not all methods are suitable for participant observation, particularly if a narrative of an episode is required.
- Children may be influenced by the pressure of the situation or the presence of an unfamiliar adult, or their behaviour may be altered from a desire to please the adult observing them.

remember

Checklists or tick lists are useful methods of recording behaviour, as are 'post-it notes' and quick jottings.

Observational techniques for individuals and groups

There are many methods of observing children although no one method is preferable to another. The aim is to select the correct method for the type of situation or behaviour that you intend to observe, and to be aware of the advantages and disadvantages of each one. The major types of techniques are listed in the table below, as well as the methods that are most appropriate for observing individual children or groups.

Table 3.12 Observation techniques for individuals and groups

Individual	Group
Written record	Target child
Target child	Sociograms
Event sampling	Movement & flow charts
Movement & flow charts	
Checklist	
Sociogram	
Child study (longitudinal)	

Techniques for recording information

Methods of observing children vary as to the type and breadth of information that is studied: some enable the observer to record individual behaviours, whereas with some the information is more general.

A Practical Guide to Child Observation and Assessment by Hobart and Frankel (2005) is an excellent source of further reading; it provides examples and discussion of each of the methods mentioned below.

Naturalistic observation (using a written/narrative record)

This is likely to be one of the first observational methods that you use. It is useful as it requires no specific preparation, you simply need to be able to make a **written record**, writing down as clearly (and concisely) as you can what you are observing. It can, however, be repetitive and long-winded to write the record out neatly afterwards. As children are so active, you may find that with this method you miss out on recording some of what they are doing.

This method:

- is ideal when beginning to observe children
- is useful when time is short as it is usually only possible to use this method for short periods of time
- can provide 'open' data
- helps the observer to practise objectivity as the point is to record what the observer sees and hears, without interpreting (at this stage)
- gives the observer the opportunity to make a structured or unstructured observation and is ideal for capturing snapshots of a child's interests and abilities
- can require intensive concentration to capture details, so is not suitable for lengthy observations.

Example of an unstructured written observation

Sarah, Fliss and Abi are in the role-play corner with Megan (student). Sarah and Fliss are leaning over the cot; Megan is standing at the entrance to the role play corner, and Abi is sitting at the table. Sarah says, 'I want to go shopping. Shall we take our babies out with us?' Fliss says, 'All right, can Megan come with us?' and moves to the back of the role-play corner where she pulls out the pushchair and puts her baby doll into it. Sarah walks over to Fliss and pats the baby doll on the head. She then picks up a shopping bag and hands this to Megan, saying, 'You can buy the food for dinner'. Abi is now standing at the side of the bookcase, looking at the other girls. Megan asks Abi, 'Do you want to come shopping?' and then she helps her to find another pushchair for her doll. Megan and the three girls then come out of the role-play corner, and Sarah and Fliss walk in front of Abi and Megan.

Movement and flow chart

These are also sometimes called 'tracking' observations. Using a **movement and flow chart** enables you to monitor the movements of a particular child. The simplest way to do this is to produce a rough sketch of the setting, noting where each activity is positioned and then track the child's movements, adding in the times and duration of use for each activity. Observations using movement and flow charts enable the setting to monitor a child's particular choices of activities and review the layout of activities to maximise use.

A movement and flow chart:

- can be helpful in matching a child's needs to the learning and play opportunities provided in a setting
- allows staff to observe a child's particular interests over a specified time period
- can produce data that are difficult to analyse unless the chart is clearly laid out
- provides 'closed' data
- limits spontaneity because the observer will need to have previously drawn a template plan of the area where the observation takes place.

Example of a movement and flow chart

In the example below, the movement and flow chart tracks Jenny's movements.

Summary of Jenny's movements:

Jenny arrives at Little Lambs Nursery at 8.30 a.m.

8.30 She moves straight to the drawing and writing table (8.30–8.40)

8.40 Jenny moves to the dressing up clothes (8.40–8.55)

8.55 Jenny plays outside (8.55–9.15)

9.15 She returns to the dressing-up clothes to change her outfit (9.15–9.20)

9.20 Jenny enters the role-play corner (9.20–9.40)

9.40 Jenny returns the dressing-up clothes to the box (9.40–9.45)

9.45 Jenny now moves to the jigsaw puzzle area (9.45–10.10)

10.10 From the puzzles Jenny moves to the book corner (10.10–10.30)

10.30 She goes outside to play again (10.30–10.50)

10.50 Jenny now returns to the jigsaw puzzles (10.50–11.00)

11.00 Jenny plays a board game (11.00–11.15)

11.15 Jenny goes to do some drawing (11.15–11.30)

11.30 Jenny joins the whole group for a story and singing (11.30–11.50)

11.50 Jenny is collected by her dad.

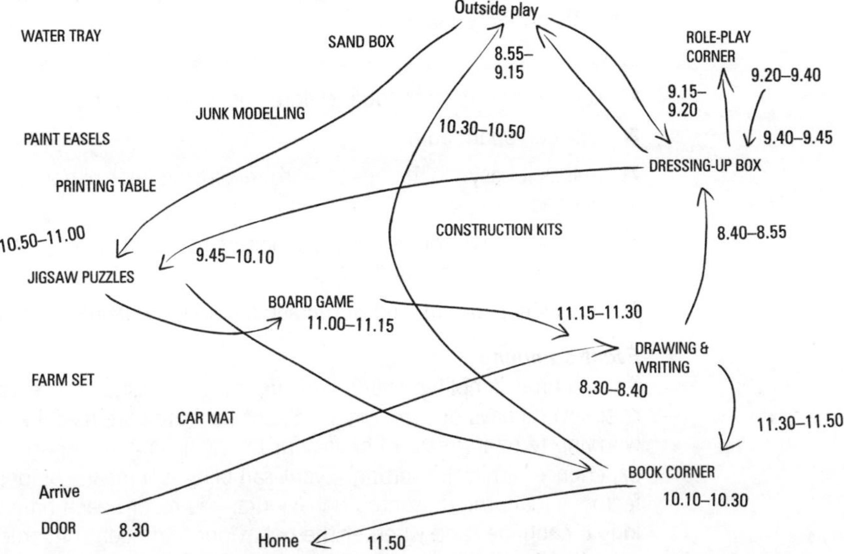

Fig 3.35 Jenny's movement and flow chart

activity
INDIVIDUAL WORK 3.6
M3

Study the information in the example above.

1 What does it tell you, and what might be missing?

2 How might the observation have been used by staff for further planning?

3 Would you have used a different observational method? If so, why?

Comment on Jenny's movement and flow chart

The example observation would be of limited use to you without further details. To be able to see if Jenny is interacting and playing as is usually expected for her age group, you would need to know:

- Jenny's age
- for how much of the morning she was playing alone
- whether she interacted with another child as a pair
- whether there were times when Jenny was playing in a small group
- whether there were times when she was playing in a large group
- whether Jenny interacted with adults during the morning.

Without this information, it is hard to know whether Jenny was having as positive an experience as she could have had. She clearly kept herself fully occupied, but did you notice anything about her choice of activities?

At no time did Jenny involve herself in any 'messy' activities. This may not be an issue, as she may simply not have wanted to take up those opportunities on that particular day, but if it were also observed in other observations, Jenny's behaviour would be considered unusual. It would also have been useful to include details of how long Jenny has been at the setting, as this could have some bearing on how well she interacts with others and her confidence in involving herself in some activities.

Time sampling

Time samples are used to observe a particular child at regular intervals throughout a planned period of time, usually on more than one day. This method can be especially useful if there is some concern about the child; perhaps they have suddenly become withdrawn and no longer seem to interact with other children. Your observation can help identify whether there is a major cause for concern, or whether the child's behaviour simply needs monitoring for a short while. As you observe, you should be as unobtrusive as possible to ensure that you obtain a true record.

By observing a particular activity at regular intervals rather than focusing on a specific child, time sampling observations can also help to identify whether activities or equipment are being under- or inappropriately used. Time sampling can give accurate information which is easily understood, but it is a time-consuming method and takes a member of staff out of the adult:child ratio equation.

The method:

- can be used for individual children as well as groups
- collects 'open' data
- makes it easy for the observer to record the information, although clear focus on timing is needed.
- However, help from other practitioners may be needed at times, so all need to be familiar with the aims and method.
- Events may be 'missed' if the activity occurs outside of the pre-set timings.

Event sampling

As with time sampling, event sampling may necessitate observations being carried out over several days or even longer. **Event samples** are useful when a child is displaying worrying (e.g. aggressive) behaviour that is having an impact on their own and others' daily experience within the setting. Event sampling is a means of identifying whether any trigger factors initiate the unwanted behaviours: you record each time the behaviour occurs, how long it continues and whether the behaviour had been triggered by anyone or by any specific situation. The advantage of this method is that data are clearly timed and recorded and easily understood but, as with time sampling, the method is also time consuming. It may also require all staff to be involved in the recording of events.

Event sampling:

- is straightforward to use
- collects 'open' data
- allows observer and practitioner to identify and understand a focus of anxiety and plan an intervention
- needs a pre-prepared template and may require co-operation from others.

If an observation is undertaken to look at a particularly serious case of behaviour disturbance, the event samples may need to be shown to other professionals who become involved with the child's welfare; they may also visit the setting in order to observe and assess the child for themselves.

Table 3.13 Example of an event sampling record sheet

Child's initials _______	The concern you have:				
Date	**Time**	**Was reaction provoked?**	**Duration of 'incident'**	**Emotions/ behaviour displayed**	**Staff observing**

Target child

The target child method is one of the most widely used methods of observation. It was first developed by the Oxford Preschool Research Project, led by Kathy Sylva, and was originally aimed at identifying which activities and situations helped children to develop their concentration. It is also useful for identifying aspects of socialisation in children and gives opportunities for noting their language, in particular when they initiate conversation.

- The method can be used for a variety of different purposes and timescales.
- Once the observer is familiar with the format and codes used, it is relatively straightforward to use.
- This method can result in a narrow focus of information but is not limited to 'closed' data.
- Spontaneous use is precluded because pre-prepared templates are needed.

The target child method involves the remembering, understanding and recording of pre-coded information. The codes are recorded in a table under the following headings:

Table 3.14

Min	Activity record	Language record	Task code	Social code

The coding is set out minute by minute, usually for up to 10 minutes at a time. The minutes are recorded in the first column of the table.

Activity record

The activity record column is a brief comment on what is happening with the activity being used by the target child. The codes used are:

TC = target child (the child's name or initials are not used)

C = child

A = adult.

Table 3.15

Min	Activity record	Language record	Task code	Social code
1	TC & C on car mat pushing cars on road			

Social code

The codes in the social code column (showing who the child is with) are:

SOL = the target child is playing on their own (solitary)

PAIR = the child is with one other person, child or adult

SG = the target child is within a small group (three to five children)

LG = the target child is within a large group (six or more children).

If the target child is playing with the same activity as others, but not interacting with them in any way (parallel play), you would write one of the following codes:

PAIR/P = the target child is playing parallel to one other child

SG/P = the target child is playing parallel to a small group

LG/P = the target child is playing parallel to a large group.

If there is an adult interacting with an activity, there would be a circle drawn around the social code.

Fig 3.36 Example of a social code

Table 3.16

Min	Activity record	Language record	Task code	Social code
1	TC & C on car mat pushing cars on road			PAIR

Task code

The entries in the task code column (showing what the child is doing) include the following codes:

LMM = large muscle movement

LSC = large-scale construction

SSC = small-scale construction

MAN = manipulation

SM = structured materials

PS = problem-solving

SVT = scale version toys

IG = informal games

SINP = social interaction, non-play

DB = distress behaviour.

There are many more task codes covering the complete range of actions displayed and activities enjoyed by children. Most colleges have complete lists.

Table 3.17

Min	Activity record	Language record	Task code	Social code
1	TC & C on car mat pushing cars on road		SVT	PAIR

Language record

To record language (what the child is saying), you would simply write: TC>C if the target child is speaking to another child, or TC>A if they are speaking to an adult.

Table 3.18

Min	Activity record	Language record	Task code	Social code
1	TC & C on car mat pushing cars on road	TC>C 'That my car' TC>'brmm brmm' TC>C 'Mine!'	SVT	PAIR
2	3 Cs now playing	All Cs > 'brumm brmm'	SVT	SG
3	A joins them	A>'What a lot of cars' TC>A 'Mine a red car'	SVT	SG

The target child method can be useful for 'at a glance' monitoring of a child's social development, because a quick glance at the social codes will indicate whether the child plays mostly with others or alone. This information, together with the child's age, indicates whether they are following the norms for social development.

Using the target child method, an observer can identify occasions when the intervention of an adult enables a child to extend their understanding of the activity they are using and work within the zone of proximal development. The Nelson Thornes website has two examples of target child observations. The first example shows that sensitive input from the adult has raised the achievement of the child from what they could achieve alone.

Refer back to page 147, for Vygotsky's zone of proximal development, and to the Nelson Thornes website for 'Target child observation' A and 'Target child observation B'. These are useful examples to help you.
www.nelsonthornes.com/btec

Checklists

Assessments of children are a routine part of most early years settings and involve the regular observation of children to ascertain what they are currently able to achieve. An example of an assessment programme is the Sound Learning Preschool Record System, which includes assessment records for all ages of preschool children; it is suggested that the assessments can be completed on monthly, three-monthly or termly bases. However, it should be noted that reliance on checklists alone tends to promote a 'deficit' model, showing what children cannot achieve rather than identifying what they can.

A checklist:

- is relatively simple and quick to use
- can be used for one child or adapted to cover or compare several children
- can be used on subsequent occasions, as long as the date of each observation is clearly recorded
- can result in a deficit model as it only records what the child can do, not what they might be near to achieving with support or time
- requires a pre-prepared template.

Table 3.19 3–36 month development

3–36 MONTH DEVELOPMENT RECORDS

Name ______________________

Date of assessment						
Colour code						

PHYSICAL DEVELOPMENT (1)		**R**	**S**	**U**
Can lift head and shoulders when lying on front.	Waves arms and kicks legs vigorously			
	Has little or no head lag when pulled to sit			
	Can lift head and shoulders when lying on front			
	Sits with firm back when supported			
	Can hold head steady when supported			
	Can hold head steady when upright			
When held standing, takes weight on feet and bounces up and down				
Can roll from front to back				
Can roll from back to front				
Can sit without support				
While sitting can reach forward for a toy without falling over				
Moves around slowly by crawling or bottom shuffling				
Moves around rapidly by crawling or bottom shuffling				
Can pull self to standing position using furniture				
Can get from a lying down to a sitting position				
Walks around room holding onto furniture				
Walks well alone.	Stands alone			
	Walks with adult help			
	Crawls up stairs			
	Walks a few steps alone			
	Walks across room when held by one hand			
	Without help gets up off floor and stands alone			
	Walks pushing large wheeled toys			
	Can climb onto a low chair or step and sit down			
	Walks well alone			

COMMENTS

Key to code:
R – Rarely
S – Sometimes
U – Usually

For older children working to the **Foundation Stage Curriculum**, the codes are:

E = emerging C = consolidating
W = working on A = achieved.

Table 3.20 Older children development record

LEARNING AREA RECORD **Communication, Language and Literacy (1)**

Name ____________ **Assessment date**

D.O.B. ________ **Colour code**

	E	W	C	A
Enjoys listening to stories, songs, rhymes and conversation between others				
Incorporates elements of what he/she has seen and heard into her/his everyday play and learning experiences				
Enjoys participating in conversations, sharing experience and ideas with others				
'Talks' to self during play and during imaginative play with figures or puppets				
'Talks' to miniature figures, or puppets, recreating conversations and experiences				
Recreates conversations and recounts experiences during imaginative and role play				
Experiments with mark making equipment such as pens, pencils, crayons, brushes, sponges, fingers, sticks				
Incorporates shapes, symbols and letters in his/her free writing				
ELG: is able to enjoy listening to and using spoken and written language, and readily turns to it in play and learning				
Explores sounds in a variety of ways such as: sounds in the environment				
sounds made by everyday objects				
sounds and words made by voices				
Responds to a range of sounds by: imitating				
identifying their source				
linking to make sound patterns				
Recreates words she/he hears and incorporates in own language usage				
Makes up new nonsense words e.g. rhyming nonsense words 'cap, hap, dap, zap'				
Makes observations such as 'that sounds like', 'that sounds the same as'				
Sounds out familiar letters in a simple text				
Sounds out familiar words in simple text				
ELG: Explores and experiments with sounds, words, text				

COMMENTS

Key to code:
E – Emergency
W – Working on
C – Consolidating
A – Achieved

Many early years settings, and some local authorities, have developed their own style of recording sheets. For the youngest children, these may reflect the use of the Birth to Three Matters framework; the Foundation Stage Profile may be used for the older children. Ask at your current setting to find out what is used there.

Sociograms

A **sociogram** gives an 'at a glance' record of the social behaviour of a group of children. It can be used to identify friendship groups and secure pair-relationships and also for establishing when a child lacks friends within the setting. The observer should always be aware how quickly friendship groups change, particularly when children are under the age of five, and, for this reason, the method has limited use. If the observation shows that a particular child's relationships are cause for concern, strategies can be established to help the child to integrate better.

A sociogram:

- is quite easy to use
- can be useful for looking at a group of children
- captures a relative 'moment in time' rather than a long-term perspective
- requires skilful interpretation.

Refer to Unit 8, page 391, for an example of a sociogram.

Audiovisual recordings

With the increased use of technology within early years settings, it may be possible for you to record the activities of children using a camcorder. This can enable:

- assessment and interpretation to take place at a more leisurely pace
- a group of staff to interpret the video record
- the observers to gather clear, factual material, which is objective and not based on memory or one person's interpretation.

Professional Practice

- **If children are to be filmed, permission must be obtained in advance.**
- **The storage and distribution of any material must comply with the policies and guidelines of the setting. This helps maintain the privacy of the children and their families.**

Longitudinal studies

In a **longitudinal study**, the observation is carried out at intervals over a considerable length of time. You will use this method for a baby or child study. Such studies need written parental permission before the study starts and involve regular visiting and observing of the child's development and progress over a preset period. For example, a baby study may involve weekly visits for three months, whereas a child study is likely to require fortnightly visits for six months or more.

Longitudinal studies should be approached in an objective manner, and it is important to ensure the confidentiality of the family.

The longitudinal approach will enable you to:

- get to know the child and the impact of their family life on their development
- understand the needs of the child more fully
- identify and record changes in the child's development
- comment on each area of development and how the rates of development vary
- chart the child's development according to a chosen screening process.

remember

A longitudinal study of a child will benefit from the inclusion of other observational methods.

Potential drawbacks of longitudinal studies are that:

- visits to a child's home can sometimes feel intrusive
- family holidays, illness and visitors can sometimes affect your planning
- objective observations are not always welcomed by the parents
- a house move by the family may end your study prematurely.

Refer to the section on longitudinal studies on page 186 for more information as to what elements are usually expected in a longitudinal baby or child study.

See *A Practical Guide to Child Observation and Assessment* by Hobart and Frankel (1999) for further details of what is expected in a child or baby study.

activity INDIVIDUAL WORK 3.7

P4

Select three different observational methods and give examples of how each can be used when observing children, explaining how each of the three chosen methods could be of value to a child's key worker who is drawing up activity plans.

Comparison of methods

When selecting a method of observation, you will need to consider various situational variables, including time, space, and whether or not you will be participating in the observed activity. You will also have to take into account what each method offers in terms of scope. The following table will assist you to choose.

Table 3.21 Comparison of methods

Method	Benefits
Written records ■ Structured ■ Unstructured ■ Snapshots ■ Individual child or baby studies ■ Open data	■ Simple to use ■ More suitable for one child ■ Short time span but can be repeated sequentially ■ Can provide detailed information about individual
Movement and flow charts (tracking) ■ Closed data	■ Can be used to match interest to provision ■ Gives a full picture of child's movements or interest ■ Clearer data if used with one child
Time sampling ■ Open data	■ Can be used for single child or group ■ Pre-set form allows easy collection of data ■ Longer recordings can be made
Event sampling ■ Open data	■ Simple to use ■ Can identify area of concern ■ Best used with individual children
Target child ■ Mostly open data	■ Simple to use when familiar with method ■ Can be used with one or more children ■ Allows observation over longer periods
Checklists ■ Closed data	■ Easy to use with one or more children ■ Can be used to compare children ■ Can be repeated at intervals
Sociograms ■ Closed data	■ Simple to use ■ Can be used with group of children

Limitations of observational methods

There will, of course, be limitations to any of the methods mentioned, some of which have already been highlighted. One observer may have a better memory than another, but rarely can any one person recall the amount of detail that is needed when observing children (either within a professional role or as a student compiling an assessed portfolio). There is no one ideal method for any situation, and it is not only important to be familiar with the use of the pro forma; checklist, timing sheets, etc. but also to be aware of the differences between the methods and the advantages and disadvantages of each one. The table below summarises the limitations of each method.

Table 3.22 Limitations of each method

Method	Limitations
Written records	■ Difficult to use for long periods of time ■ Intense concentration needed to 'capture' all the data ■ Notes need to be written up at the time or shortly afterwards
Movement and flow charts	■ Spontaneous use limited ■ Clear recording necessary or data can be difficult to interpret
Time sampling	■ Help from other practitioners may be needed ■ Events may be missed if they occur outside the time frame
Event sampling	■ Requires a pre-prepared template and understanding of coding categories ■ Help of other practitioners may be needed
Target child	■ Difficult to use spontaneously ■ Requires a pre-prepared template and understanding of coding categories ■ Help of other practitioners may be needed
Checklists	■ Do not allow effort or potential to be noted ■ Can result in deficit model ■ Only skills observed are assessed and much may be missed ■ Pre-prepared template needed
Sociograms	■ Capture a limited moment in time ■ Can be difficult to interpret
Longitudinal studies	■ Require careful planning of visits ■ Family may find it intrusive or may move away ■ Notes must be written up after each visit or relevant data may be forgotten

Limitations of recording methods

Sometimes, little will happen within the timeframe of your planned observation, but on other occasions the observed child could be extremely active. It is therefore sensible to consider how easily you find it to write notes at speed. You may wish to record the child's use of language; whether that is possible will depend on the observational method that you choose. The **validity** of the observation may be lost if the wrong observational method has been used or the observational record is incomplete. Consider the following:

- Can you write quickly enough for the method you are using to be effective?
- The legibility of your notes is an issue, particularly if you are using the written narrative method. Will you be able to read your notes later?
- Will your writing be sufficiently legible for another person to read and interpret your record?

1 Select four examples from your portfolio of observations carried out during your placement experience; you should choose your observations to include examples from at least two different age ranges.

2 Describe how each observation was carried out, i.e.

(a) the observational method used

(b) your evaluation of the observation

(c) its success in meeting your aim

(d) any changes that you would make if you were carrying out a similar observation.

Writing up your observation

It is essential that your observations are presented in a clear and coherent manner, and you may be expected to use an agreed format for your documentation. Most observations will have a front or title page which outlines where the observation is taking place; who is involved; and the aims and objectives. Your file should also include a reflective record of your developing observation skills. The figure below shows an excellent template for a reflective record page.

Table 3.23 Pro forma for a reflective record page

Method	Start	Midway	Limitations
Ability to evaluate			
Ability to negotiate time to observe			
Ability to note detail			
Ability to plan			
Ability to take notes and record information			
Communication skills			
Confidence to make a start			
Interpersonal skills			
Knowledge of child development			
Knowledge of observaton techniques			
Listening skills			
Maturity			
Objectivity			
Patience			
Sensitivity			
Time management skills			
Understanding of aims			
Unobtrusiveness			

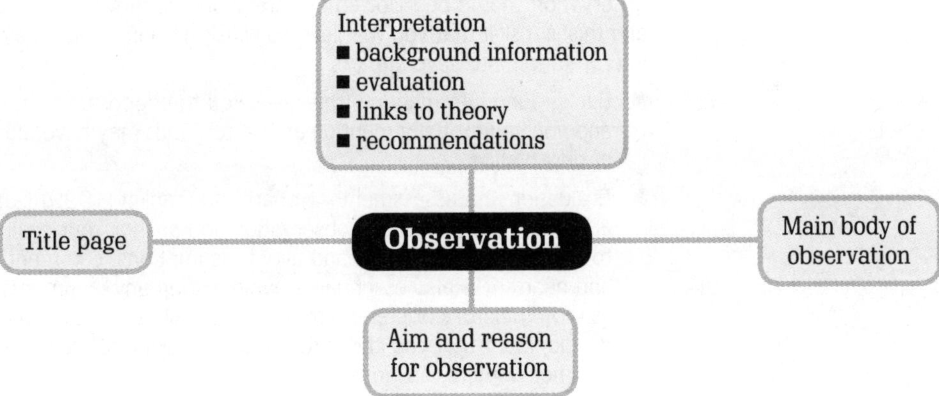

Fig 3.37 Format of an observation

Stating the aim

- It is important to have a clearly stated aim for your observation: this will usually be to look at a particular aspect of a child's development or behaviour. Other focuses of observation may be on a child's health or additional needs or part of the Birth to Three Matters Framework or the Foundation Stage Curriculum. Your reason (sometimes called a rationale) for undertaking the observation should also be clearly stated, as both will help you to provide a coherent evaluation and interpretation.

Recording and reporting information

Whichever observation method you are using, you will need to include some or all of the following:

- an identifier – name, initials, number, etc.
- age of child/children
- date of birth

- date of observation
- reference number in your portfolio
- type of observation
- the type of setting – nursery, preschool, classroom, home, etc.
- the situation – lunchtime, on arrival, during drama session, etc.
- the permissions needed
- any specific link with parents
- any need to share your findings (this should always be in accordance with the procedures of the setting)
- any identified concerns which should be referred on (e.g. particular difficulties, suspected **neglect** or abuse)
- any potential psychological evidence that you have observed
- any potential legal evidence that you may have gathered.

See pages 184–190 for guidance on setting out your observations, linked to the mandatory longitudinal study of a baby or young child, and page 186 for information about sharing material obtained from observations.

Interpretation

Once you have carried out your observation, you need to interpret what you have seen and, if language was involved, what you have heard. You may have observed a significant stage in the child's learning or a specific achievement or perhaps you will have noted changes in a child's behaviour. Alternatively, your observation may have been done to establish if a change to the provision is required.

Have a look at the example given on page 183.

Whatever the observational method that you selected, the write-up of the main body of the observation should be followed by careful and sensitive interpretation of what was observed, and this is a skill that you will develop with experience. You may wish to divide your interpretation into several parts:

- Background information – this gives you the opportunity to put the observation in context and you could briefly mention any factors that may have affected the child or the process of observation.
- Evaluation and assessment – Hobart and Frankel (1999) suggest that you look back at the aim and reason for observation and anchor your evaluation firmly in this. Try to use objective language and avoid assumptions, commenting only on what you saw and heard. It is also essential to avoid writing any comments that could be interpreted as discriminatory or stereotypical. You should evaluate and comment on the area of development that you chose to observe, making reference to appropriate theory but not to other workers' opinions.

It is important to reflect on what you have learnt from the process of observation, and interpretation is a valuable aspect of professional practice. Questions that you might ask yourself to help this process include:

- Did I choose the right method?
- If I were to repeat this observation, would I do anything differently?
- What did I do well and what might I want to improve upon?
- What did I learn about this child and how did theory link to what I observed?
- How could I improve my practice based on what I have observed?

Links to theory

These may be woven into the body of your evaluation or written as a separate section. Whichever method you adopt, it is expected that you will refer to a range of normative milestones of development and information from appropriate textbooks. These should be correctly referenced and should help you to compare the child's development or behaviour to accepted norms.

Recommendations

You may find it difficult to make recommendations when you undertake your first evaluations, but, as your experience and confidence grow, you will be able to show your understanding of the process of observation.

Refer back to pages 163–166, and think about links between the reasons for observing children and making recommendations.

activity
INDIVIDUAL WORK
3.9

D1

Using the example below, write out possible aims and a rationale for this observation and then outline what factors you might include in an evaluation of this visit.

A visit to a child as part of an ongoing child study

Date_____ Type of visit: General visit to observe how JM has recovered after her recent illness

JM was having her lunch but ate little of what was put in front of her. She ate a quarter of an egg sandwich, but left a banana and small yoghurt. She also had a drink of diluted fruit juice. She smiled when she saw me but remained on her mother's lap. I asked her mother how JM was feeling now that her recent illness has resolved and she reported that she is still 'not quite her old self'.

After washing her hands (which she can now do quite well by herself), JM played with her doll's house. She busied herself putting the people to bed, and then getting them up again to have their breakfast. She talked to herself all the time in a monologue; most I could understand, but at other times she was not coherent. JM showed understanding of the roles of family members and where domestic events occur, e.g. washing up in the kitchen, getting dressed in the bedroom, adults dressing the children, etc. She played like this for almost 20 minutes.

I then asked JM if she would like me to read her a story, but she said, 'No, mummy will read a story for me before bed time'. JM's speech is now becoming clearer, and I was able to understand most of what she was saying to me, although I could see some change in her behaviour towards me since I last saw her but this was before her illness.

JM's grandparents arrived at this point and I felt that it was appropriate for me to leave. On previous visits JM had given me a hug, but today she clung to her mother and just waved me goodbye. As I left, it was clear that there was a change in JM's behaviour since the last time I saw her, and I think that this may have been linked to her illness. Next time I visit, I plan to ask her mother whether she showed any other signs of reaction to being ill, other than the clinginess that I observed today.

1 What are your first thoughts?
2 Read the observation through again and reflect on what you can 'lift' from it to analyse.
3 Make a list of what you think is good about the observation.
4 Make a list of what you think would have improved this observation.

Depending on the age of the child being studied, you would be able to comment on how well they are developing according to the developmental norms, making specific comments with regard to how recent illness may have affected her social and emotional development, language use in her small-world play and her reaction to you on this occasion.

Assessment of progress

Assessment is an integral part of the planning cycle, and all school-age children will be regularly assessed via the **Standard Attainment Tasks (SATs)**. Formal assessment starts with the Foundation Stage Profile, which is a statutory assessment undertaken at the end of the Foundation Stage. It is based on the Early Learning Goals but the aim is to record what a child can do, rather than highlight deficits. It also provides a baseline assessment for the child's transfer to Key Stage 1. SATs are used as assessment tools at the end of each key stage of the **National Curriculum** and should provide an accurate picture of a child's ability.

Refer to Unit 7, page 350, to learn more about the links between assessment and the curriculum.

When observing a child to assess their progress or stage of development, your write-up may need to refer to:

- former assessments already recorded
- accepted charts of developmental milestones
- the thinking and guidance of developmental theorists
- where the child falls within curriculum objectives.

You could then use the outcomes of your observation:

- as a basis for future planning of play and learning activities
- for identifying additional support needs
- to contribute to a report on developmental delay
- towards a formal assessment.

Presenting your observations

You may be asked to set out your observations as a separate portfolio, or you may be required to submit them as part of your professional practice portfolio. Whichever way you will be presenting your observations, it is likely that you will be asked to make comparisons between the observations you make, noting similarities and differences between the behaviour of children of different ages in similar situations.

This should consolidate your understanding of how children develop at different rates across all the areas of development, while still remaining within 'normal' boundaries. It will also help you see the benefits of the developmental norm charts, while recognising that, if used simply as a snapshot of an individual child, the charts can at times be misleading.

Your portfolio will need to include a chart recording the dates, times and outline details of each observation you make; this would usually cross-reference to a matrix. This will enable you and your tutors to see at a glance that your observations have included children from all age ranges and placement settings experienced during your training. If the majority of your observations are part of your professional practice portfolio, you will still need to 'signpost' your evidence in the same way.

It is helpful if you give all observations a number. This helps with cross-referencing and ensures that you and your tutors are referring to the same observation during any discussion.

remember You have to complete 800 assessed hours of placement experience in four separate settings.

An 'at a glance' matrix

A matrix is often used to give an 'at a glance' reference to your observations. This helps to ensure that you do not inadvertently miss out any one age range or placement setting (doing so would make it difficult for you to complete your portfolio at the end of your course). Alternatively, you may want to include a separate matrix for each part of your professional practice portfolio.

Table 3.24 An 'at a glance' matrix

	Home setting	Childminder	Voluntary preschool	Statutory preschool	Private nursery setting	Nursery school/class	Primary school	Hospital	Special needs setting
0–1 year									
1–2 years									
2–4 years									
4–8 years									

Refer to page 168 to check the range of settings that are suitable for your professional practice experience.

The chart below provides an example of how you could record your observations in numerical order. It shows the date, age and gender of the child you have observed, together with the setting details (for example, day nursery – painting activity) and the method of observation used. A chart like this would help you to ensure that you have used a range of observational methods and observed a range of different activities; it could also be used as a contents page for your observation file.

Table 3.25 Example of a record of observations

Observation	Date	Age of child	Gender of child	Setting details	Method of observation
1	9.06.06	3.6	M	Day nursery – construction	Target child
2	16.06.06	4.1	M	Day nursery – painting	Time sampling
3	23.06.06	3.9	F	Day nursery – clearing up	Target child
4	30.06.06	3.7	F	Day nursery – role-play area	Written record
5	6.07.06	3.6	M	Day nursery – painting	Target child
6	13.07.06	4.2	F	Day nursery – in general	Movement and flow chart
7	20.07.06	4.2	F	Day nursery – water play	Target child

Table 3.26 Matrix of development

	Age			
Area of development observed	0–1	1–2	2–4	4–8
Gross motor skills				
Fine motor skills				
Spatial awareness				
Simply co-operative play				

Table 3.27 Matrix of activities

	Age			
Activity area observed	0–1	1–2	2–4	4–8
Threading				
Pencil skills				
Shared storytime				
Small scale construction				
Emergent writing				
Role play				

A Practical Guide to Child Observation and Assessment by Hobart and Frankel (1999) is an accessible text with explanations of each observational method and plenty of relevant examples.

remember

Observing children is an important way in which you can identify and meet their needs.

Sharing information from observations

A very important aspect of observing children is the use that is made of what has been observed. On a personal basis, you may feel at first that the most important use of the observations is to fulfil your course requirements, but their use goes far beyond this aspect.

Refer to Unit 4 to remind yourself how children's individual needs are identified and met across a range of age groups.

It is also important to consider with whom the information is likely to be shared. As you gain experience in working with babies and children of different ages and have the opportunity to work alongside skilled practitioners, you will observe how children react to routine care and learning activities. You should share the findings of a child's observation with their key worker and take the opportunity to discuss the findings and implications. Your observations play an important part in planning care, and may even contribute to the identification of a child in need. The results of observations will almost certainly be shared with parents as part of an ongoing process of **sharing information**, and sensitivity should be shown when recording and reporting information.

See Chapter 5 of *Observing Children: A Practical Guide* by Sharman *et al*. (2004) for a comprehensive discussion of sharing information from observations and the assessment process in general.

Reporting concerns from observations

Findings from observations will occasionally be shared with other professionals and can contribute to multidisciplinary care planning. Students may occasionally be asked to make an observation of a child who is thought to be at risk and, in these circumstances, the observation may be used as part of the safeguarding procedures. If, during the course of any observation, you identify something that concerns you or that you think may identify a child protection issue, you must report it to your supervisor immediately. It may be that your concerns can be allayed, but you may have been instrumental in identifying a vulnerable child.

Refer to Unit 5, page 256, for the procedures to be followed when child abuse is suspected.

Be able to use techniques of observation to carry out a longitudinal child study

Your centre will let you know the stage of your training at which you start your study and the centre's requirements as to the length of the study, and how frequently you will be expected to visit the child and in which contexts.

Situations

Ideally, you will have opportunities to observe the child in a variety of situations. This could include their day-care setting (often your placement setting), at home with their family, or out with their family, perhaps on a visit to a park or soft-play centre. Very occasionally, however, it is only possible for observations to take place within one situation, for example your placement setting or the child's family home. In these cases, it is important that consideration is given to ensuring a good range of timings and environments, such as in the garden, during adult-led activities, during free play, at lunchtime, on waking up, on arrival, and so on. This will ensure that you gain as broad a picture of the child as possible.

Number and type of observations

You tutor will guide you on the requirements of your course programme with regard to how many observations you will need to carry out. Specific numbers of observations for each observational method may be required; or you may be given more flexibility as to the methods you choose to use (even so, a minimum number may be stipulated).

However many observations you carry out, it is always important to cross-reference them so that they can easily be found within your study.

Refer back to the matrix examples on pages 184 and 185.

Baby or young child?

A mandatory criterion for this study is that the child to be studied is under the age of three years.

Often, the choice of child within the age range is left to you, but do not make a hasty decision. Listen to, and seek the advice of, your tutors and placement supervisors regarding the age and suitability of the child.

Should a placement supervisor guide you away from studying a particular child but not be able to give you the reason why, you must accept this guidance and respect the supervisor's advice as sound. You must also uphold any confidentiality issues to which you may have become privy.

Planning

You may particularly enjoy working with babies and feel that this is the age that you would like to observe, but be aware of restrictions such as those in relation to infant sleep patterns and needs.

Fig 3.38 Choose your child carefully

Once you have chosen your child, you should:

- gain permission from the child's parents in writing, and
- if the child is based at your placement, you must gain agreement from your placement supervisor to take time to observe them and to make extra visits as needed.

Initial information gathering

It is important that readers of your longitudinal study have a full and rounded picture of the child when you first started. This provides a clear baseline starting point which will also be important to you when you come to assess the child's development over the period of the longitudinal study. Without having information on a child's development at the start, it is impossible to comment accurately on how far they have developed.

Within your study you are likely to include information such as:

- an identifier – name (you could use just their first name, or use a substitute name to uphold confidentiality, but retain a sense of reality), or initials; ask the parents which they would prefer.
- exact age of child or baby
- their weight

- eye colour (this may change in a young baby during the course of the study)
- height (child), or length (baby)
- head circumference (baby)
- shoe size (child)
- clothing sizes
- position in family (e.g. first child, middle child, youngest child)
- any specific health issues (e.g. asthma, eczema, regular ear infections)
- any identified developmental problems, (e.g. Were they premature? Any delay?)
- sleep needs and sleep pattern at onset of study
- any crying pattern (babies who suffer colic often do so at the same time each day)
- feeding pattern (baby)
- usual eating pattern for meals and snacks (child)
- favourite toys, activities and games
- favourite books
- favourite foods
- people they are most content and secure with
- current stage of social development (e.g. sharing, stage of playing, etc.)
- current stage of intellectual development (e.g. has object permanence been established?)
- current physical skills (e.g. fine motor skills, locomotor skills, etc.)
- current level of language ability (e.g. clarity of speech, number of words, use of phrases, etc.)
- any obvious issues linked to emotional development (e.g. temperament traits, issues of security, clinginess, etc.)
- photo (only with parent's written permission).

What else can you think of?

Refer back to the relevant sections of this unit to help you assess stages of development.

remember

All observations should be appropriate to the child you are studying and their immediate environment.

Range of observational techniques used

You will be expected to use several methods of observation, ensuring that they are relevant to the child and situation and to your overall aim or rationale. Remember to take into consideration the benefits and drawbacks of each method, and the suitability and relevance of including both participant and non-participant observations.

A method should not be used simply to prove you can use it. You will have had an opportunity to demonstrate your observational skills through your main observation file, or within your placement portfolio.

Refer back to pages 179–180 to remind yourself of observational methods and the benefits and drawbacks of each; it is important that you refer to them as you plan your study.

activity
INDIVIDUAL WORK 3.10

P6

Imagine that you have been asked by the parents to tell them about the study you have carried out on their baby/child.

1 Write out how you would explain the study to them. Use the following headings as a guide:
   - Your planning
   - Gathering the initial information
   - Your choice of observational methods
   - The number of observations made

cont'd

- The ethical issues you have taken into account
- How, by using graphs, percentile charts, etc., you have shown clearly how their child's development has progressed
- Why objectivity is important

2 What else will you include?

Organising your time

Having identified the types of activities and observational methods that you may want to include, you will need to organise your time effectively, allowing extra time for family holidays, illness or other unexpected interruptions to your planned schedule of visits.

Considerations

Ethical considerations

Ethical considerations include:

- awareness of the ethics involved and the need for confidentiality
- gaining written permission from the parents and ensuring that they understand what the study involves; thereafter keeping to the specified timeframe
- only making relevant observations and measurements
- adhering to ethical protocols.

Other considerations

Others include:

- referring to normative benchmarks of development
- keeping to the specified timeframe and making the required number of visits
- making relevant observations and measurements of all areas of the baby's or child's development
- describing and explaining the baby's or child's individual needs and how these are met through daily routines and procedures
- giving details of play activities that can be implemented to stimulate development and learning
- giving an explanation of the role of significant adults in the baby's or child's life and that of any professionals involved
- identifying the safety and security measures needed and anticipating those needed in the near future.

You will need to take all the above into account. Without clear adherence to these simple protocols, your study could easily be considered unacceptable, which could impact on whether you pass this unit.

M4

Your tutor has asked you to attend an individual tutorial and give an update on your longitudinal study. The tutor wants to know both how you carried out your study and what you have learned from it.

1 How will you explain this to them? Use the following headings as a guide:

- Your planning. How did you approach planning the study? Do you consider your planning to have been sufficiently thorough? Would you do anything differently another time?
- *Gathering the initial information*. Did you get all you needed? If not, why not? Where, when and how did you obtain your information? Would any other source have been better? Has there been a negative impact on the overall study?
- *Your choice of observation methods*. On what did you base your choice?
- *The number of observations made*. Explain your reasons for deciding how the observations were allocated.
- *The ethical issues you have taken into account*. Explain what ethical protocols you upheld (when, how and why).

cont'd

activity
CONTINUED

- *How you have made clear how the child's development has moved on*. Identify the visual material that you have included, the accuracy of the information and what you can interpret from each graph, chart, etc.
- *An explanation of objectivity and why objectivity is important.* Give examples from the write-up of your study.

2 What else will you include?

remember

Objectivity is absolutely vital when observing children.

You will already have carried out observations as part of your professional practice. It may well be helpful to refer to the feedback that you were given by your tutor or placement supervisor as to how well you have chosen, implemented and interpreted your observations.

activity
INDIVIDUAL WORK 3.12

Plan a presentation on the observational methods used during your longitudinal study. You will need to:

1 Explain each observational method.
2 Outline how and when each method was used.
3 Explain your reasoning for deciding how the observations were allocated and the success of these decisions.
4 Talk through the outcome of each observation, including what you learned about the child at that point, in that particular situation.
5 Highlight the observations carried out that you consider worked very well, giving your reasons why.
6 Identify the observations that were less successful, detailing in what way they were less successful, any identified or potential impact on the interpretation of the situation at that time and any identified or potential impact on the overall outcomes of the study.
7 Clarify which observation methods you feel would have been better in certain instances, giving your reasons why.

Progress Check

1 What signs would give you concern regarding an infant's visual development?
2 What would raise your concern regarding their auditory development?
3 What does the term 'perception' mean?
4 What is meant by object permanence?
5 Explain the difference between locomotor and non-locomotor skills.
6 List the conditions needed for secure emotional development.
7 What is meant by the term 'goodness of fit'?
8 Give an example of social learning that could be explained by social learning theory.
9 What does the term 'gender stability' mean?
10 What is echolalia?
11 Explain the difference between constructivist and social constructivist theory.
12 Which of Bruner's modes of thinking involves the development of mental images?
13 What is meant by normal developmental dysfluency?
14 What are the benefits of carrying out observations?
15 What are the main factors in interpreting observations?

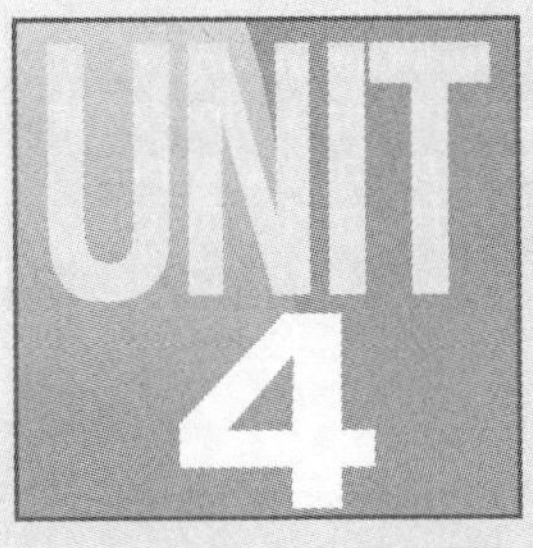

Reflecting on and Developing Practice for Children Aged 0–8 Years

This unit covers the following objectices:

- Understand roles and responsibilities within the Children's Care, Learning and Development sector
- Be able to observe and identify the individual needs and skills of children
- Know how to respond to children's needs through care routines and procedures
- Know how to promote a stimulating learning environment for children
- Be able to reflect on own practices in work placement experiences

This unit is designed to help you achieve the core skills, attributes and competencies that are needed by everyone who works in an early years setting. Using the underpinning knowledge and understanding set out in Unit 3, you will focus on your current role as a student and on how you can support the individual needs of a child or group of children appropriately in practical everyday situations within different types of setting.

The environment and activities that support learning and development are described, and you will learn about the importance of health and safety and codes of practice.

The unit begins with a look at what is expected of a professional early years worker and towards the end you will be encouraged to reflect on and evaluate your own practice.

grading criteria

To achieve a Pass grade the evidence must show that the learner is able to:	To achieve a Merit grade the evidence must show that, in addition to the pass criteria, the learner is able to:	To achieve a Distinction grade the evidence must show that, in addition to the pass and merit criteria, the learner is able to:
P1 describe own adherence to codes of practice for each placement setting page 197	**M1** compare policies and practices at different placement settings page 210	**D1** use the observations and interpretations to make recommendations for further action with respect to the skills and needs of the child/children concerned page 208
P2 observe and identify the physical, social, emotional, cognitive and communication needs and skills of children in each age range and in four different settings page 218	**M2** interpret the observations undertaken in relation to children's skills and needs page 208	**D2** evaluate each activity in terms of its effectiveness in promoting children's development page 229

To achieve a Pass grade the evidence must show that the learner is able to:	To achieve a Merit grade the evidence must show that, in addition to the pass criteria, the learner is able to:	To achieve a Distinction grade the evidence must show that, in addition to the pass and merit criteria, the learner is able to:
P3 observe and identify the individual needs of children with additional needs page 226	**M3** explain the importance of different care routines to the child/children, and the organisations/settings page 212	**D3** evaluate own effectiveness in each placement. page 233
P4 describe four different routines within each placement setting, including own role page 212	**M4** analyse each activity and suggest how each could be improved to increase the child's/children's learning and understanding page 229	
P5 plan, consult on, prepare and implement five activities for a child/group of children to promote specific areas of development within each placement setting page 210	**M5** produce a personal development plan and explain how it will potentially support own development. page 232	
P6 review own performance in each of the work placements and identify areas for further self-development page 230		
P7 describe the role of continuing professional development for workers in the Children's Care, Learning and Development sector. page 233		

Understand roles and responsibilities within the Children's Care, Learning and Development sector

Professional practice

The term 'professional practice' describes the practical working life of any professional person. Being professional is to be competent, efficient and skilled in your work and appropriately qualified to carry it out. When you come into contact with, for example, teachers or doctors, you probably have certain expectations of them and how they do their job, and you expect them to be professional. You will be striving to gain this professionalism yourself as you work towards your qualification.

Another term used regularly in the care sector is '**vocational**', which means learning through practical experience as well as theory. The BTEC National Children's Care, Learning and Development (CCLD) is a recognised vocational qualification for anyone working with children from birth to eight years of age.

Placement experience is built into all BTEC National CCLD programmes, usually commencing soon after the start of the course. Preparation for placement usually takes place during the course induction period. Both Diploma and Certificate students need a minimum of 800 hours of assessed practical experience. It is important that placements are arranged well in advance to ensure that you can maximise the time available to you. Some colleges have placement officers who take on this responsibility for you; in other colleges, you will be asked to arrange a placement for yourself. If you leave this important arrangement until the last minute, you will have less choice of suitable placements and possibly a less satisfactory placement experience.

remember

The student supervisor's role is to help you gain as much from your placement experience as possible. You can ask them questions and seek their advice.

In each placement there will usually be a member of staff allocated the role of student supervisor. This person's function is to help you gain as much from your placement experience as possible. Together with other staff, your supervisor will try to make you feel comfortable in the setting, but they will also expect you to be responsive and willing to learn. Most members of staff will have been students at some point in their lives and will understand the importance of a good supportive environment in which to develop your practical skills and build on your understanding.

Professionalism

As a professional or trainee within the field of early years, you will be expected to conform to a range of expectations. These will be dependent upon your status (student, nursery nurse, deputy manager and so on) within the setting. Many of these expectations will be assessed during your training, and will continue to be refined once you have qualified. Most aspects of professionalism will directly affect your working practice, with some having a considerable impact on how you are judged by others.

Let us begin by looking at what will be expected initially before we go on to examine professional expectations in more detail.

Initial expectations

Professionalism brings with it expectations. The following checklists can be used as starting points for considering what will be expected of you in each placement setting you attend.

Checklist: what you need to know

Before your first placement day, you will need to have answers to the following:

- What is the address and telephone number of the setting?
- What time do you need to arrive and leave?
- Who do you report to?
- Who will be your placement supervisor?
- Are there any dress codes?
- Are students expected to eat with the children at mealtimes?
- Do you need to pay for meals, coffee, etc.?
- Is there an information booklet about the setting that you can read in advance?

These are practical, easy-to-answer questions. A visit to the setting or a telephone call before you begin your placement will enable you to arrive on your first day feeling confident. Some placement settings have special requirements, and it is important that these are clarified in advance. Whenever possible, visit the placement in advance; this demonstrates commitment, and it can be helpful for both you and the staff to put a face to a name. It can also give you an opportunity to discuss what will be expected of you.

case study 4.1 Merryfields Day Nursery

Merryfields Day Nursery sends students the following dress code before they start their placement experience with them.

Fig 4.1 Dress code

MERRYFIELDS DAY NURSERY STAFF DRESS CODE

Dear ....

Whilst at Merryfields Day Nursery, you are politely requested to comply with the following:

Staff and students will ...

- wear tidy trousers or skirts
- wear low-heeled shoes
- wear plain rings and small earrings
- always be clean and tidy
- keep hair tied back
- keep nails short.

Staff and students will not ...

- wear jeans
- wear untidy clothes at any time
- wear heavy make-up
- wear excessive jewellery
- have visible body piercings.

Thank you

activity
INDIVIDUAL THEN GROUP WORK

1 Do you think the above requirements are:

(a) acceptable

(b) important? Give reasons for your answers.

2 Do you disagree with any of them? If you do, why is this? Discuss your reservations with other students. What do they think?

3 What else would you add to the lists?

remember

Just as you need information before starting at a new setting, it is useful for the setting to know something about you and your needs. This will help them make your induction and time at the placement as useful and enjoyable as possible.

Checklist: what the placement needs to know

Before you start the placement, the setting will need the following information:

- your course details and placement paperwork
- your college address and telephone number
- the name of your placement tutor/course tutor
- your home contact number
- emergency contact details
- any relevant medical information (allergies, asthma, epilepsy, etc.)
- an outline of your previous experience (if any).

The first day in any placement can be quite daunting, and it helps if you enter with a smile. It can give you an air of confidence (even if you do not feel it) and encourages others to respond positively to you. The staff will probably remember what it was like to be very new and unsure. They will not expect you to know everything, or remember everything straightaway. Figures 4.2 and 4.3 summarise what will be expected of you. Follow these guidelines and ensure that you understand why each point is important. This will give you a good start in developing yourself as a professional, helping you gain, and maintain, confidence in yourself.

Fig 4.2 Professional expectations: the first day of placement

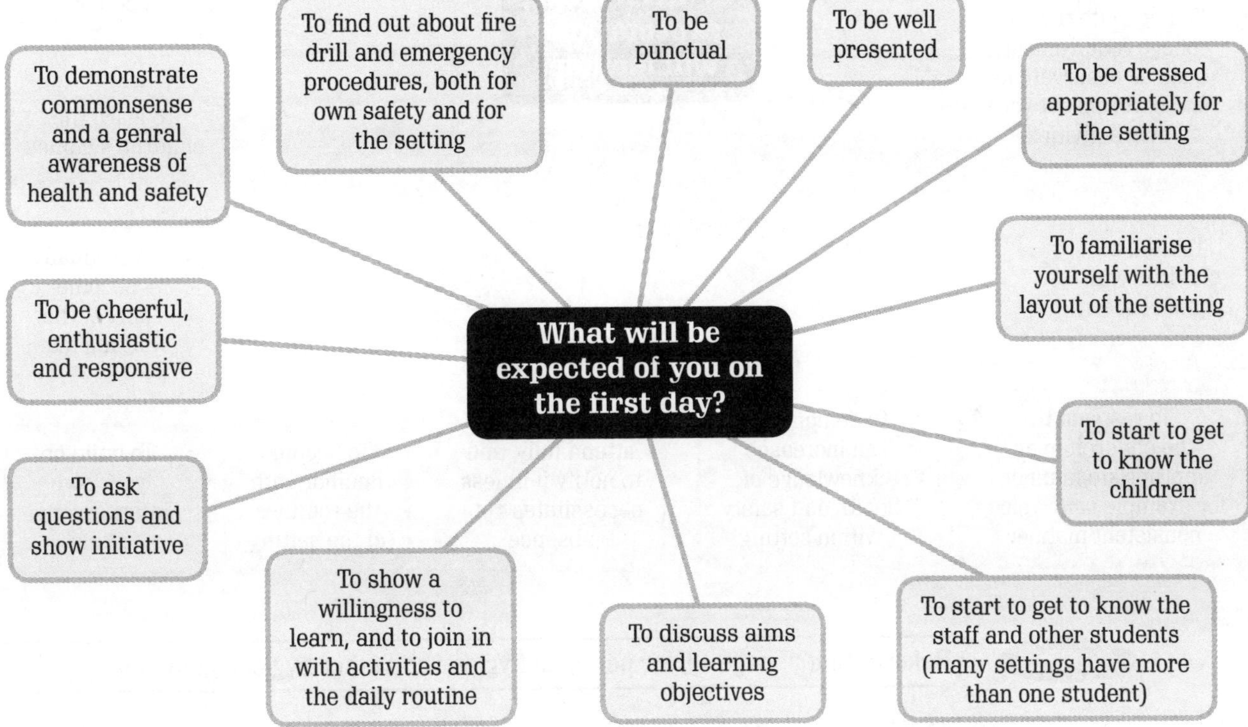

remember

To be professional is to reflect on your working practice, your level of training and the subsequent responsibility of your current role.

Attendance and punctuality, reliability and commitment

Children need stability and routine in order to feel secure in their environment. A member of staff who is unreliable, or who regularly has time off work unnecessarily, can adversely affect this. It is an important point to consider.

Expected standards of behaviour, particularly personal presentation and hygiene

Children learn by example, and as individuals we are judged initially by what people see (their first impressions of us). **Personal presentation** is therefore important. When a student or member of staff is not well presented or behaves inappropriately, it is unacceptable and may have a detrimental effect on the working environment. This does not mean, however, that individual expression cannot be allowed, as sometimes our confidence is linked to how we feel we look, but each of us as individuals should consider the impact of our personal contribution to the overall setting.

Fig 4.3 Professional expectations: week by week

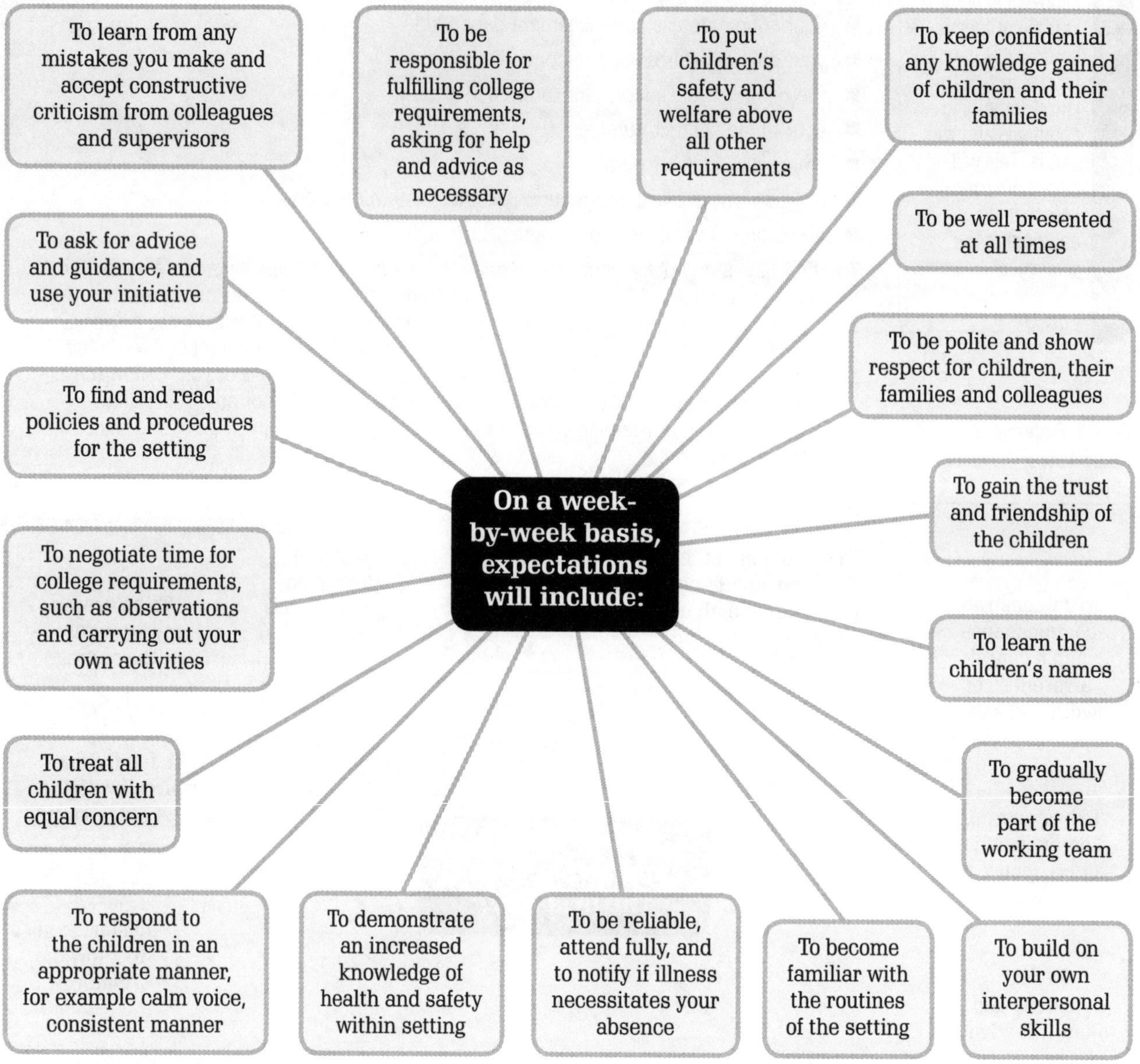

On a week-by-week basis, expectations will include:

- To learn from any mistakes you make and accept constructive criticism from colleagues and supervisors
- To be responsible for fulfilling college requirements, asking for help and advice as necessary
- To put children's safety and welfare above all other requirements
- To keep confidential any knowledge gained of children and their families
- To be well presented at all times
- To be polite and show respect for children, their families and colleagues
- To gain the trust and friendship of the children
- To learn the children's names
- To gradually become part of the working team
- To build on your own interpersonal skills
- To become familiar with the routines of the setting
- To be reliable, attend fully, and to notify if illness necessitates your absence
- To demonstrate an increased knowledge of health and safety within setting
- To respond to the children in an appropriate manner, for example calm voice, consistent manner
- To treat all children with equal concern
- To negotiate time for college requirements, such as observations and carrying out your own activities
- To find and read policies and procedures for the setting
- To ask for advice and guidance, and use your initiative

Refer to Unit 2, page 49, for personal hygiene and other hygiene guidelines.

Maintenance of own safety

Although the managers of any setting hold overall responsibility for the safety of the working environment, staff and students have a responsibility for their own individual safety, taking into account commonsense decisions and the needs of the setting. Each individual is expected to identify and address any safety issues as they occur and is expected to work both safely and sensibly at all times. Commonsense decisions may be needed in a variety of situations, for example, if:

- an accident occurs
- the potential for an accident is identified
- health and safety precautions are lacking
- exposure to infectious material is a possibility
- you are faced with aggressive or violent behaviour
- you are being subjected to verbal abuse.

remember If you are not yet confident that you have this information for your current placement, it is important that you ask your placement supervisor.

As part of taking responsibility for your personal safety, it is important that, in each placement, you know the following:

- the fire drill procedures for the setting
- the health and safety policy
- who the first aiders are
- where the accident book is kept and who writes in it
- what is in the first aid box, where it is and who is allowed access to it
- the procedure if a child becomes ill
- when and how equipment and furniture should be cleaned and by whom
- what happens if unplanned visitors arrive.

P1

1 What does the term '**personal safety**' mean to you?

2 In what ways do the **codes of practice** at your current placement and any past placements help ensure safety?

3 Draw up a list of where you might need to be responsible for your own safety in college, in your placement and whilst travelling to and from each.

Codes of practice are discussed on pages 202–203.

Roles and responsibilities

In any setting, it is the staff team as a whole which makes the setting successful, and this **teamwork** should not be underestimated. Each individual will have their own role to play, but no single person can carry the full weight of responsibility or of the organisation, although clearly the nursery/setting owner and/or manager holds ultimate responsibility for safety within the setting and for its smooth running; they will also be responsible for ensuring that appropriate standards are met.

As individuals, staff and students need to consider their place within the staff team, reflecting on how well they co-operate with each other, how flexible they are willing (and able) to be, and whether they are using their skills and abilities appropriately. Clearly, it does not make sense for someone who is good at carrying ideas through to completion to be involved only in the suggestions or planning stage of a project. Most settings have regular planning meetings at which staff contribute ideas and decide who will take on what responsibility. Identifying your strengths and where you best fit into a team will enable you to work within your capabilities and help you feel valued as a person.

remember Some staff members work better together than others; that is human nature. There should be opportunities for internal movement of roles and responsibilities in order to ensure the greatest level of cohesive teamwork.

According to Sadek and Sadek (1996), a good team will:

- work together
- share a common aim
- co-operate with each other
- share/communicate/support its members
- have motivation for the task in hand
- have catalytic relationships so that new ideas are extended
- be committed to the task and the team
- be composed of members who each understand their own role in the team and are reliable in it
- complete the task.

Refer back to Unit 1, pages 11–31, for more on communication.

The need for confidentiality and its parameters

Each setting will keep records of the children in its care. These records are private, and any information you are given, or you hear about, should be regarded as strictly confidential. You will be expected to refrain from sharing anything with other people at home or in a social situation. This is all part of being professional.

At times, it may feel appropriate to refer to something from your placement in a class discussion led by your tutor. This should only take place if you are certain that no individuals can be identified, or that the information you are sharing in no way contravenes the confidentiality of your placement setting. The same approach applies to your **professional practice log**. You will need to give evidence of your dealings with children, parents and staff in your professional practice log, but it should not be possible for them to be identified by any reader, even your tutor. It can be permissible to use initials, or sometimes a first name, but be aware of how much more easily some names are identified than others.

case study 4.2 Colleen

Colleen has recently started a placement in a local authority nursery. A child in the nursery lives near to her home; Colleen had often thought the child looked poorly and undernourished, and her own mother had commented on this too. Colleen has now discovered that the child has a place in the nursery because her parents find the responsibility of parenting difficult. The child has been neglected and always eats ravenously whilst at nursery. The family is regularly visited by a family support worker.

activity GROUP WORK

1 If you were Colleen, would you pass this information on to your mother?
2 Would you discuss the case in college?
3 What are the confidentiality issues here?

case study 4.3 Briony

Briony overhears a parent from the nursery where she is on placement gossiping in the supermarket queue about another parent's discipline methods. The parent concerned tries to draw Briony into the conversation as she checks through her shopping.

activity GROUP WORK

1 How should Briony respond?
2 Should Briony do anything about this afterwards?
3 What are the confidentiality issues here?
4 Are there any circumstances in which you would consider it permissible to pass on information that you have overheard or received in such a manner? Discuss this question with other students and check your thoughts with your tutor.

Professional Practice

- Any child protection issues of which you become aware should never be kept to yourself.
- If you have a concern, or you overhear comments that concern you, you should ask to speak to your supervisor, the manager of the setting or your college tutor. If no cause for concern is found, no harm will have been done. Your supervisor (or tutor) will be pleased that you have used your initiative and discussed your concerns appropriately. If the concern is subsequently substantiated, your actions will be proof in itself of the importance of speaking up.
- Delays or reluctance to talk about concerns can potentially lead to further harm for a child.

Refer to Unit 5, page 263, for more on confidentiality and child protection.

Appropriate interpersonal skills

remember Good interpersonal skills are crucial to working effectively with other people.

Expectations are made of you according to your role or position, but at times parents may not understand your role, expecting more of you than you are able to give them. The ability to interact and communicate on different levels is important, and you will develop your own style of communication within an ethos of courtesy, consistency and appropriateness. Your communication style will affect your interpersonal skills and therefore how well you relate to and empathise with others.

When supporting children and their families, communications should be age-appropriate and understood by all concerned, and you need to be able to initiate and sustain relationships. It is also important to recognise that there are different approaches to parenting.

Communication

Communication can be both verbal and non-verbal; it includes speech, looks and gestures.

Refer to Unit 1, pages 13–24, for a detailed explanation of the communication process.

Communicating with babies and young children

The earliest stage of pre-verbal communication starts shortly after birth and comprises the eye contact and turn-taking that takes place between an infant and its parent or carer. When an infant cries, to express need, and the parent responds, this begins to establish for the infant that crying produces a response. When the carer talks to the baby and murmurs comfort during care routines, this encourages communication.

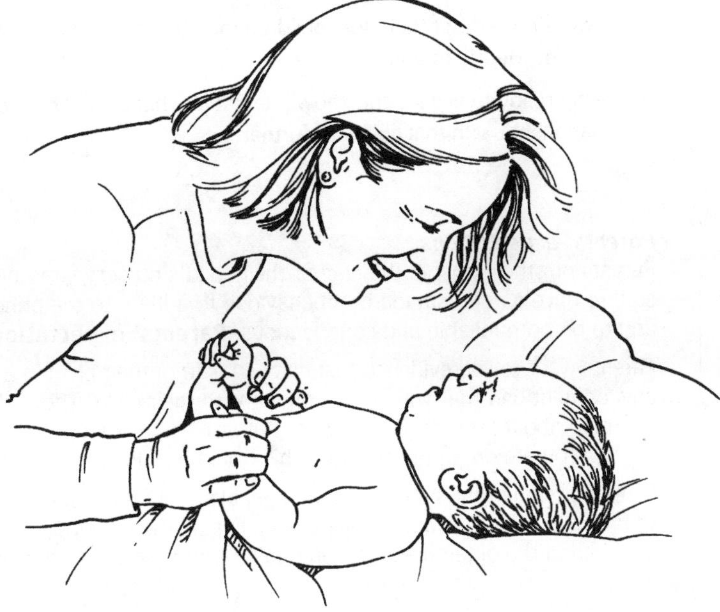

Fig 4.4 Eye contact and turn-taking between an infant and its parent or carer is the earliest stage of pre-verbal communication

In children, communication is developed through the use of symbols. With very young children, opportunities for expression and communication need to be given through **symbolic play**. This allows them to learn and share meanings as they explore new ideas, and to practise and consolidate understanding by using the familiar.

Communication barriers

It is important to establish communication between you and the main carers of the children with whom you work. Some barriers to communication are social or cultural; others are emotional.

Refer to Unit 1, page 19, for more about barriers to communication and to page 12, for more on interpersonal skills.

Range of contacts

When considering interpersonal skills, you will need to think about:

- the range of people you will interact with as an early years professional
- the expectations and demands that are likely to be made of you
- the type and level of contact an early years professional would usually have with:
  - children
  - parents
  - colleagues, including support staff
  - other professionals (those within the immediate setting and those outside).

Children's expectations

Very young children are non-judgemental. They will like you for yourself. It does not matter if you cannot sing in tune, build a good model or catch a ball properly. They will simply expect you to play with them, give them your time, talk to them and be interested in what they do. Slightly older children will also enjoy having your time and attention. They may already have formed ideas about adult capabilities and may expect all adults to have the same level of skills and knowledge. At times, they may expect more from you than you are able to give them.

Professional Practice

- **Know where you would turn for advice when you feel out of your depth, for example if a child were to demand answers or a demonstration from you that you cannot deliver.**
- **Patience and clear explanations are needed in these circumstances.**
- **There is no need to feel shame or embarrassment in admitting that you do not know something.**
- **The age of the child is not the main factor here. The child's levels of understanding and ability should be the main criteria in determining your responses.**
- **Always remember that older children may be able to demonstrate a skill or introduce new knowledge to you.**
- **Being ready to accept and show interest in what a child can teach you may enhance your relationship with that child still further.**

remember

Early years staff are caring for someone very precious to parents, their child.

Parents' expectations

Parents put their trust in the staff at their child's nursery, preschool or school. They expect staff to have a good standard of behaviour, to adhere to the principle of equal opportunities and to be both reliable and conscientious. **Parents' expectations** are not always voiced.

Parents want to see evidence that care is taken of their child in a safe and stimulating environment and that you enjoy working with their child. They will expect not only to be kept informed about their child's progress but also that someone will have time to discuss their child with them on a regular basis. This would usually be the child's key worker.

Parents assume that staff are knowledgeable about early years issues and may from time to time ask questions about their child's health and development. They will not always understand the difference between qualification levels and may unwittingly consult a junior member of the team on a matter requiring the attention of someone more senior. It is important that staff realise this and know how to respond to the situation positively, guiding the parent to someone more appropriate in a way that maintains the parents' faith in the staff member's ability to perform their current role.

Colleagues' expectations

Your colleagues will expect you to contribute to discussion and to the planning of the setting's environment. They will expect evidence of knowledge appropriate to the level of your training, qualification and experience, and the ability to put it into practice. It will be assumed that, if you take on a team role, you will be able to fulfil it. Time is in short supply in early years settings, and no one will be happy with a team member who does not contribute fully. It is always important that you are honest about your ability and level of understanding before taking on extra responsibilities.

Support staff play an important role in the running of any setting. They have the right to be treated with the same level of consideration as qualified staff and to be consulted about any changes that involve their contribution to the running of the day, for example when changes to snack time are made to allow for a specific activity. It is important to remember that, although some staff may not hold the same qualification as you – or may have no formal training at all – they may well have years of experience. Everyone has a role to play and should be valued as part of the team.

Professional Practice

- **If you pretend to have knowledge and understanding when you do not, you could put children at risk, through lack of awareness, lack of supervision, or by taking staff away from where they should be, so that they can help you. It could also lower your self-esteem and lose you the respect of your colleagues.**
- **It can be helpful to reflect regularly on the different roles of the adults within each setting. (You might like to consider the impact of not having staff specifically carrying out certain roles and how your current role might be affected if there were no support staff.)**

Expectations of other professionals

Many different professionals work within early years settings, including those who are permanently employed, some who visit occasionally and those who have a peripatetic role, visiting the setting at a specified, regular time. These include:

- health visitors
- educational psychologists
- speech therapists
- social workers
- play therapists
- physiotherapists
- music therapists
- Portage workers
- family support workers.

Each of these professionals works with specific client groups. They may be linked through the **primary health care** team, through the local social services departments or through the local education authority. Support may be offered on a daily or weekly basis for some children and through regular ongoing programmes for others.

Some children will be individually supported alongside their peers, within the main room of the setting, while other children will be given one-to-one support in an alternative room or quiet area. The only expectation made of you by the professionals will be to support the child in continuing with any programme that they set.

Refer to the Nelson Thornes website for case studies relating to professional intervention.
www.nelsonthornes.com/btec

remember Issues of confidentiality are very relevant when dealing with other professionals.

Respect for the knowledge and contributions of others

The breadth of staff experience, both professional and acquired from life in general, enriches an early years setting. Students and newly qualified staff are encouraged to observe carefully how their more experienced colleagues perform their work. Different ways of doing things are not necessarily right or wrong, simply different. Your attitude to the viewpoints of others is an important part of your professionalism; it should be positive and welcoming.

Diversity of opinion, language, culture and religion should be celebrated as one of the setting's strengths. Staff, students, children and their parents should benefit from diversity as it helps to broaden knowledge and understanding of people and the issues of society.

Without equality of opportunity for all children and their families, an early years setting will not be meeting the needs of all client groups. Equality means not simply treating everyone the same, but giving everyone the same opportunities, taking into account their differences and differing levels of need.

Diversity and equality are discussed in Unit 6, pages 282 and 288.

Knowledge base

The BTEC National CCLD course will give you a good grounding in how to work with, provide for and understand the needs of children and their families.

A sound knowledge base will enable you to take the initiative in planning, resourcing and implementing activities and care within whatever setting you are working. Successful completion of the course will mean that others will have expectations of you, regarding how you act, what you know and how you initiate actions. At times, you will be involved in **referral procedures**, individual action plans and situations needing diplomacy and sensitivity. The knowledge gained during your training should help you respond to each situation competently and confidently.

Your knowledge will stem not only from the subjects that you have studied in your course but also from what you learn about the legislation and recommendations that relate to working with children. Such knowledge informs appropriate interventions, and future employers may well expect you to have developed an understanding of:

> **remember** It is important to know about these important documents and to understand the principles of each and their relevance to your future role and responsibility.

- The Birth to Three Matters framework
- Sure Start programmes and provision
- The Foundation Stage and the National Curriculum
- *Every Child Matters* (DfES, 2004)
- *What to Do if You're Worried a Child Is Being Abused*
- The Framework for the Assessment of Children in Need and their Families.

Link

You may find it helpful to refer to Unit 5, page 255, for information on referral procedures.

You should also have developed an in-depth awareness of the needs of children and families in differing circumstances and the appropriate routes of referral that may be required. Nobody will expect you to know everything when you start work as a qualified early years professional, but do make sure that you ask more experienced staff for help when you are unsure.

You will have developed a variety of skills, knowledge and attitudes that will help you begin your practice as a qualified practitioner, but learning does not stop with gaining the qualification. You may find that, although you now have a range of strategies for everyday practice, you want to develop more specialised knowledge in order to become a reflective and effective practitioner. This will mean planning your training and learning needs in response to areas identified for development, and you may well have started this process during the final months of your course.

Codes of practice and policies

> **remember** It will be useful to gather information on the codes of practice, statements and policies of each setting that you attend as part of your placement experience.

Each setting will have its own codes of practice, together with a range of policies, contacts and possibly a mission statement too. These are drawn up to serve a range of client groups. For example, settings may have a mission statement or philosophy that sets out their values, beliefs and aspirations. The statement may be corporate if the setting is part of a large organisation, or it may be the result of staff consultation in a smaller setting. You should make sure that you are familiar with any such mission statement.

Settings may also have behaviour contracts, outlining the professional behaviour expected from staff and students. It is important to comply with these whilst in placement and also with the policies of the setting. Such policies are the day-to-day expression of compliance with legislation and government guidance and underpin high-quality care and education. Under the recommendations of the Children Act 2004, settings are obliged to have certain policies; others are merely advisable.

In accordance with good professional practice, settings also have policies and statements covering behaviour, disability, child protection and equal opportunities. Most will of course have many more.

Issues covered by policies include:

- the need to balance the needs, rights and safety of the individual with those of others and the provision of effective care and learning
- individual staff roles and responsibilities
- agreed ways of responding to certain behaviours
- provisions that may need to be made in order to meet children's additional needs and to ensure equality of opportunity
- ways in which children will be safeguarded from harm and protocols for ensuring this
- resources that are needed to reflect diversity and to meet the needs of all children.

Adherence to codes of practice

When you start your placement in a setting, you will be shown the policies and codes of practice, and it is important to ensure that you comply with them. This is not only to ensure safe working practices for the children you will be caring for, but also to promote the concept of the 'safe learner'. You will be given further advice on this during your course, as well as receiving advice from the practitioners that you encounter in settings. Policies are not there simply to regulate the provision of care and learning, but also to promote and protect important principles such as equality, health and safety, appropriate behaviour and fair employment.

The safety of children and the smooth running of a setting depend on all staff and students working to the same codes. An important aspect of this is in ensuring that parents are supported in their parenting, and in knowing how to seek help and when to make a referral onwards if there are difficulties.

Supporting families

Supporting and promoting parenting

Support for parents can be a significant element of the staff–parent relationship. Early years staff can often become a stabilising part of a child's life. They offer a reliable environment at times when life at home for a child may be confusing or disrupted through life events, such as bereavement, illness or relationship difficulties between parents. Staff need to initiate and sustain good relationships to ensure the best joint care of the children.

This is not always easy: conflicting views on parenting and how to deal with challenging behaviour can be a barrier.

Rights and responsibilities

The **UN Convention on the Rights of the Child** was adopted by the United Nations General Assembly in 1989.

Refer to Unit 5, page 253, for more about the UN Convention on the Rights of the Child.

Parents also have rights, but with rights come responsibilities. Under the Children Act 1989, the term 'parental responsibility' was introduced into legislation. It relates to the term previously used in legislation, 'legal custody', and is defined as follows:

> '"Parental responsibility" means all the rights, duties, powers, responsibilities and authority which by law a parent of a child has in relation to the child and his property.'
>
> (Allen, 1996, page 13)

remember: The Children Act 1989 has been superseded by the Children Act 2004.

This definition replaced the unofficial list of parental rights and duties which, whilst not being linked to any one specific piece of legislation (they were taken from a range), were used by the courts as guidelines prior to the implementation of the 1989 Act.

Refer to Unit 6, page 292, for more about children's rights.

Developing strategies of support

Staff can be role models for families, demonstrating how to build up positive and caring relationships with others, both adults and children. Showing respect for and being interested in the children is a natural part of your work as a professional. It is not always instinctive in some families and, at times and for a number of reasons, parents might not share the ethos of the setting in which you work. For example, a court order may have initiated the family's attendance at the setting; in such a case, there is the potential for an atmosphere of resentment to build, making communication difficult.

case study 4.4

Jamie

Jamie is aged three years and four months. In the nursery he is always very boisterous, to the point where children are wary of him as he rushes past them. He is used to climbing on chairs and tables at home and frequently tries to do the same in the nursery room.

activity
INDIVIDUAL WORK

1 How would you manage Jamie's boisterousness?
2 Would you refer to his opportunities to climb at home? If so, how would you approach this, ensuring that you remain supportive of his parents?

Professional Practice

- **As an early years professional, you will need to ensure that communication continues between yourself and parents, whatever the circumstances. A warm smile or a welcoming comment on arrival could be used to keep some contact, even if opportunities for conversation are currently limited.**
- **It is imperative that you do not compromise parents' choices, provided of course that these choices are not detrimental to the development, well-being or security of their child.**

Awareness of differences in parenting

Every parent makes decisions with regard to how their child is brought up. Some parents take an autocratic approach, monitoring their child's behaviour very strictly. Others are more laissez-faire, allowing their child much freedom of expression and giving little correction or guidance. The majority of parents fall somewhere between the two styles: they allow their children an element of freedom to challenge and explore but set boundaries that incorporate safety and guidance. The differences in the ways families live are what give our society its sense of richness.

A family's lifestyle may be influenced by cultural practice, and this may also affect how children are parented. Terminology can be important, for example in one of her case studies, Jackson (1996, page 51) refers to a father of Caribbean background using the term 'beating of a child'. To many white-English people, this term would suggest a far harder punishment than is denoted by the term 'smack', but, to the father referred to by Jackson, they meant the same. Whether or not you agree with parents smacking their own child, the cultural difference in connotation is significant, and could lead to confusion and, possibly, unwarranted concern for the child's welfare.

Managing the effects of abuse

Sadly, most early years workers will, at some point, care for children who have been abused, whether that abuse is physical, emotional, sexual, or through neglect. The knowledge and understanding of development that form such an important element of early years courses enable early years practitioners and others to identify when a child's development or behaviour strays from the norms, possibly denoting abuse.

Refer to Unit 5, pages 244–250, for details of the signs and symptoms that may indicate abuse. These form a useful guide, and you should familiarise yourself with them. See also page 266, which deals with managing the effects of abuse.

Clearly there can be many reasons for a child's development or behaviour to stray from the norms. Emotional disturbance, such as moving house, or a burglary at the child's home, can cause changes and possibly regression in development. Usually, any change would be temporary and, with careful handling and plenty of reassurance, would be alleviated within a reasonable length of time.

Any progressive signs of change in a child's behaviour or regression in development need careful consideration and observation.

Supporting children who disclose

Young children are not able to invent stories of events that they would not usually experience. They should receive the unconditional acceptance of early years staff. All staff (and students) should know who to talk to if they have any concerns about a child. Most settings have a nominated person who is the setting contact with regard to child protection issues.

Ensure that you know the procedures and contact person for each setting you attend. If you are the person a child chooses to disclose to, you do not want to waste precious time finding out who needs to be informed.

This should also ensure that information is only shared on a 'need to know' basis.

Confidentiality is paramount in child protection cases. However, an adult should never make a promise to a child that they will not tell anyone what the child has disclosed. They are legally and morally obliged to tell the appropriate person in the setting.

Making a promise to a child and then breaking that promise is likely to compound the child's lack of trust in others. You will have let the child down, as did the abuser, and many people would consider it another form of abuse.

Refer to Unit 5, page 262, for information on supporting children who disclose.

The role of play therapy

Play therapy is one way of helping children come to terms with what they have experienced. It encourages expression of feelings and ideas and helps to rebuild a child's self-esteem and self-image, thereby aiding the healing process. Play therapy is not a strategy that anyone can simply 'have a go at'. It takes specialist training and must be undertaken carefully, usually in conjunction with other professionals. Sadly, play therapy is not available to all children who might benefit from it.

Refer to Unit 5, page 279, for more about play therapy.

Potential impact of abuse on the child and the family

Abuse not only affects the child. Dealing with its effects can be extremely difficult for family members, who, prior to disclosure, may have been unaware of what was happening to the child. Sensitivity is clearly needed here. Early years professionals can help by encouraging the family to develop new strategies for meeting children's needs and coping with challenging behaviour.

remember To support families effectively, it is important to establish good channels of communication.

Advice on local groups that the family can attend with their children can be useful (e.g. family centres, drop-in centres or a community bus that stops nearby). Phone lines, such as Cry-sis, provide useful support when a situation gets too much and the parents risk 'losing it'. These lines are often staffed 24 hours a day.

Home visiting and co-operation with professionals

Visiting children and their families in their own homes has become more commonplace in recent years, although health visitors now make fewer home visits of a general nature. Other professionals, such as family support workers employed by social services, now undertake this role as part of the general support available to children and parents.

Refer to Unit 5, page 275, for an outline of the roles of professionals who become involved in family problems such as child protection.

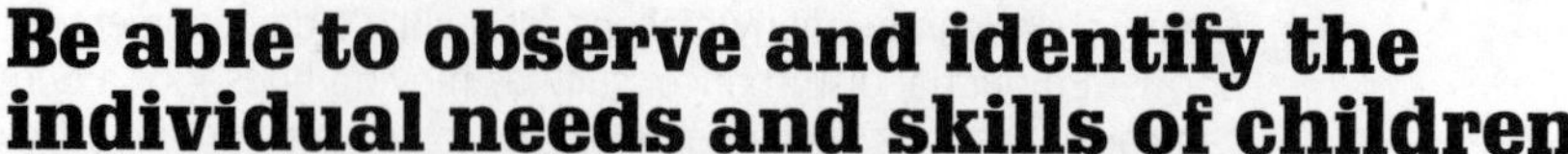

Be able to observe and identify the individual needs and skills of children

Observing and identifying ages/stages in the development of children

Observation is one of the primary methods of identifying the care and educational needs of babies and young children, and you will use observational skills each and every day to understand the needs of the children in your care.

The acquisition of observational skills is an important aspect of your early years training. To complete the BTEC National CCLD courses successfully, you will have to provide evidence of your ability to monitor and plan for children's individual needs through the use of observation. There are many different ways of observing children, with some methods being more appropriate to certain situations than others. Your tutors will teach you about the practical aspects involved in observing children. You will also learn about how observations are written, interpreted and used, and how information is shared with parents and other professionals.

You will need to observe and identify ages and stages of development of children in the following age ranges:

- birth to one year
- one to three years
- three to five years
- five to eight years.

You will be expected to consider:

- milestones of development
- social development
- emotional development
- physical development
- intellectual (cognitive) development
- language development and communication needs.

Refer to Unit 3 for an outline of development in each of the above areas, including the expected milestones.

It is rare to find a child who develops according to the norms in all developmental areas. It is therefore important to accommodate the advances and delays in individual children when you plan activities or give them instructions. Taking their developmental level into account in relation to the responses you expect from them is equally important.

Growth and development mean very different things.

- Growth refers to the measurable elements of how children change, for example their height and weight.
- Development refers to the stages of change in a child. Although the age at which each stage is reached may differ slightly between children, the stages are usually reached in the same order. For example, the action of walking is mastered before the more complex actions of hopping and skipping.

At times a tall, large-framed child may appear older than their actual age and some people will have greater expectations of their ability and behaviour because of this. Similarly, less may be expected of a small, petite child. These examples show why understanding the difference between growth and development is important.

Children with particular needs

You will be expected to observe and interpret any particular needs an individual child may have. **Identifying needs** involves carefully considering each aspect of the child's current level of development. This may include identifying where they are placed on development charts, how they interact within the setting, how they manage to communicate or what limitations they currently face in everyday activities.

Once a child's particular needs have been identified, the appropriate professional intervention and support can be arranged. This may include:

- strategies for behaviour management
- encouragement of physical skills, either general or specific
- emotional support
- encouragement to interact socially
- supporting cultural differences.

There are also a number of government recommendations and frameworks that practitioners should use to consider children's holistic needs and to structure appropriate interventions. One key document is *Every Child Matters* (DfES, 2004).

Childcare settings

Your observations will take place in a range of different settings. These will usually be your main placements, but one-off visits may also provide opportunities. You may find yourself in any of the settings described below.

Day nurseries

Day nurseries provide full-time or sessional care and education for children between the ages of six weeks and five years of age. Day nurseries may be found in the statutory and the private sector, and provision is usually linked to parental working hours. Statutory (provided by the state) day care is now to be found within Sure Start centres or neighbourhood nurseries, as well as within children's centres. Not all nurseries care for babies. Children are offered age-appropriate care and learning that is informed by the Birth to Three Matters Framework and the Foundation Stage Curriculum, and regular inspections will be carried out by Ofsted.

Nursery schools and nursery classes

These provide childcare and early education for children from three to five years of age. Nursery schools are free if they are part of the state education system, but fees are payable if the class or school is classed as private provision. A substantial amount of most children's fees is now covered by funding from the government in the form of the Nursery Education Grant. Children are offered play and learning opportunities that are suitable for their age and development, and the staff team will include a qualified early years teacher. The Birth to Three Matters framework and the Foundation Stage Curriculum will underpin care and learning, and settings will be regularly inspected by Ofsted.

Preschools or playgroups

Preschools or playgroups usually offer sessional care and provide early education for the three to fives. They are usually organised by the community or by private individuals on a not-for-profit basis and often use the help of parents and other volunteers. Sessions are often restricted to term times and may be run every day or on certain days of the week. Children will be offered age-appropriate learning and development activities based on the Birth to Three Matters framework and the Foundation Stage Curriculum. These settings are also regularly inspected by Ofsted. Again, funding is supported through the Nursery Education Grant.

Crèches

A crèche offers short, sessional care and tends to be used on an occasional basis. Crèches offer care and play facilities for children under eight and may be found in sports centres, shopping complexes and in conference and exhibition halls. A crèche needs to be registered if it runs for more than two hours each day. Crèches are unlikely to be suitable for Diploma-level placement experience, owing to their limited hours.

Children's centres

Children's centres are usually, but not always, part of a Sure Start scheme. They provide full day care and education for children under five. Children's centres offer integrated services across early years care and education, health and social services and provide family support and outreach work. Most are open for 10 hours each day and for a minimum of 48 weeks a year. All centres are inspected regularly by Ofsted and may have developed from previous local Sure Start programmes.

Paediatric hospital unit

Many general or specialist hospitals will have a paediatric unit that offers a range of children's services; these may include inpatient care; outpatient care; a neonatal and baby unit; intensive care; developmental assessment centres; paediatric physical, occupational and speech therapy;

play room and **therapeutic play** facilities; and a hospital school service. It may be possible to undertake placements in some of these, but priority may be given to nurses in training.

Childminding

Registered childminders look after small groups of children, usually in the childminder's home. They may care for up to six children under the age of eight years including their own, but only three may be under-fives. Hours offered depend on the childminder, and hours, terms and conditions are negotiated with the parent. Not all childminders will have childcare qualifications, although they will be registered with Ofsted and have received a police check, as will all adults over the age of 16 years living in the home.

Nannies

Nannies and other home-based carers are employed by parents and usually care for children in the family home. Hours, terms and conditions are negotiated to suit individual circumstances, and work may be full time, part time or shared with another nanny. Duties may include living in the family home, and some positions may require light household duties as well as childcare. Many nannies will hold a recognised childcare qualification, although this is not compulsory.

Observational methods

As a student you will be asked to carry out a range of appropriate observations, using a variety of methods. The portfolio of observations that you build up throughout your programme of study will be assessed by your tutors. This portfolio is likely to include some or all of the following:

- written record
- target child
- baby study
- child study
- movement and flow chart
- time sampling
- checklist.

Refer to Unit 3, pages 168–179, where the above methods for observing children are discussed, with examples.

Interpreting observations

Interpretation will be the most important aspect of your observations. It provides the information that you will use to inform your planning and care, and at times may also alert you to a concern about a child.

The interpretation of observations is discussed in Unit 3, page 182. It will be helpful to refer back to that section.

activity
INDIVIDUAL WORK 4.2

M2

D1

Using knowledge and understanding of observations taken from:

(a) the practical experience gained within your placements

(b) studying the relevant section of Unit 3, carry out the following tasks:

1 Take four observations from your portfolio. Preferably, these will be of children of different ages or at different stages of development.

2 Write a clear explanation of what you learned about each child's current skill level and support needs, noting whether or not these were being met appropriately during the activities observed, with the resources and level of adult input provided.

3 For each observation, outline how the child could have been supported further and how the additional support could have met their needs more fully and built on their skill development.

Know how to respond to children's needs through care routines and procedures

The following section refers to the responses that will be expected from you as you work with children across your placement experience. Each aspect is covered in much greater detail in Unit 2, so the material here should be read in conjunction with that indicated in the links.

Health and safety issues

Health and safety awareness is crucial in all settings and, in order to comply with standard requirements, it is important that all those involved are clear as to the meaning of the term 'health and safety'. Each adult working in the early years field has a responsibility to ensure that children are protected from hazards and infection whilst in their care. This applies to daily activities, visits outside the setting, and whilst travelling with children. Every setting must have a qualified first aider present, and colleges offering the BTEC National CCLD include a first aid qualification as part of the course.

Refer to Unit 2, page 33, for the main discussion of health and safety issues.

Without the security of knowing that their child will be safe, most parents would not leave the child in the care of your setting. Issues of health and safety in early years settings can be divided into four main areas:

- supervision
- policies and practices
- safe use of materials and equipment
- hygiene.

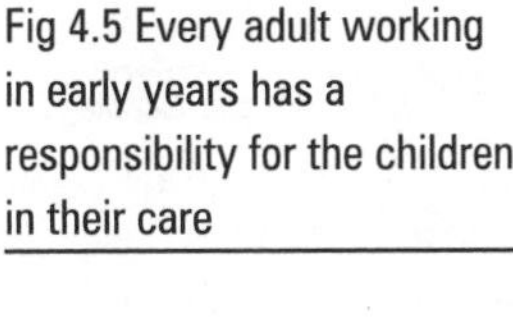

Fig 4.5 Every adult working in early years has a responsibility for the children in their care

activity
GROUP WORK 4.3

M1

1 Collect examples of health and safety policies from your placement.
2 Consider which aspects of health and safety are relevant to each of your current settings.
3 Are there any differences? If yes, how do they differ?
4 What common factors are there?
5 Copy out the table below and place each health and safety issue discussed by your group into the appropriate column or columns (some may need to go in more than one).
6 Compare the policies you have collected. How clear are they? Draw up a list of reasons why policies help support safe practice.

Table 4.1

Supervision	Policies and practice	Safe use of equipment and hygiene

Once your table for the above activity has been checked and agreed with your tutor or placement supervisor, it will serve as a useful reference for the future.

activity
GROUP WORK 4.4

P5

Donna and Marlene are classroom assistants planning a display on autumn with a group of Reception class children. They have selected a range of books and posters and have collected a variety of cones, leaves, berries and plants. Their aim is for the children to go to the park to enjoy a walk, collect more autumnal objects and make bark rubbings from the trees to add further interest to their display.

1 If you were Donna and Marlene, what would your aim be for the children's development and learning?
2 What would you need to consider and do in advance and who would you need to consult?
3 What are the relevant health and safety issues?
4 How else could Donna and Marlene extend the topic? Draw up a list of ideas, linking them to areas of development and learning.

remember
Keep in mind the four main areas of health and safety.

Professional Practice

- For children to reach their developmental potential, they need opportunities. However, many activities require boundaries. For example, learning to climb needs an adult on hand to give guidance on limitations, and learning to cook needs adult guidance and support with using sharp implements and heat.
- When setting boundaries, it is important to take into account the developmental stage of the child or children concerned. Appropriate boundaries make a vital contribution to their overall safety and security, whilst enhancing their development.

Care routines

Care routines involve the safe provision of a regular programme of activity within a secure environment.

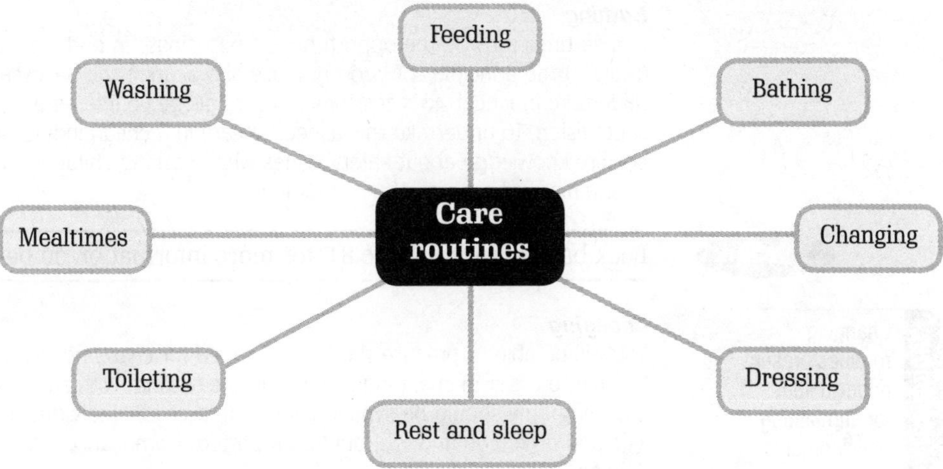

Fig 4.6 Care routines

Role of early years workers

Working with children involves being in constant close contact with adults and children. Personal hygiene is therefore extremely important. Attention to personal hygiene procedures ensures that staff smell fresh and pleasant as they carry out personal care routines where these are appropriate, thereby providing children with positive role models.

The sterilisation of equipment for babies may also be your responsibility. It is crucial to control for potential bacterial infection, and all equipment must be washed regularly to prevent cross-infection. All childcare workers should be aware of the signs of infestations, for example head lice and threadworms. Observation and identification of potential problems are a vital part of the role.

Refer to Unit 2, page 33, for a discussion of the main issues of health, safety and hygiene and to page 63 for the identification of signs and symptoms of illness and infestation.

Professional Practice

- **Settings should have procedures for recording when and how cleaning processes have taken place and who was responsible for checking them. Ask to see an example at your placement.**
- **If you are not yet confident that you have all the information that you need to take responsibility for your personal safety while at your current placement, it is important that you ask your placement supervisor.**

Care routines – for children

Care routines include the physical and personal care of children. It is important that you understand your role in these care routines and also your limitations. As a student, you will not be allowed to change babies and toddlers unsupervised. This is part of the child protection strategy for the setting. It is in no way a reflection of how staff view you as a person or as a childcarer. It is simply putting the safety of the children first.

Feeding and mealtimes

You will gain experience of preparing food and drinks for babies and children and so will be able to participate in helping to provide a balanced and healthy diet. You will learn about the importance of meeting the individual child's nutritional needs and the significance of mealtimes as opportunities for developing skills and learning. You will also learn about specific dietary needs and conditions, safety and hygiene in food preparation and storage, and the influence of cultural and social customs.

Look at Unit 9, pages 435–442, for information on nutrition and diet and to Unit 11 of *BTEC National Children's Care, Learning and Development*, Book 2, by Green (2007).

Bathing

Few settings provide the opportunity to participate in bathing children, but you should still be aware of the principles of good practice and acquire the necessary skills. You will be able to undertake practical skills sessions in your college course, and it may be possible for you, with supervision, to undertake this aspect of care in a childminding or family setting. You will also acquire knowledge about safety issues when bathing children and how bath time can be used to stimulate all aspects of development.

Look back at Unit 2, page 81, for more information on bathing routines.

remember Changing routines present opportunities for stimulating development.

Changing

You will be able to practise the skills required for changing routines in college, and you may be able to assist in changing routines in the setting, with supervision. You will learn how changing time should be synchronised with a child's individual needs and why alterations in skin and other conditions should be reported. Compliance with cultural and parental practice is important.

Look back at Unit 2, pages 79 and 81, for more information about changing routines and skin care.

remember The role of the early years worker is to meet the needs of the individual child and provide personalised care that is developmentally and culturally sensitive.

Dressing

Most settings will provide supervised opportunities for you to participate in some aspects of helping to dress children. You will also be able to support children in mastering the skills involved in learning to dress themselves and in selecting appropriate clothing and footwear.

Look back at Unit 2, pages 96 and 97, for more information on dressing, clothing and footwear.

Rest and sleep

To be appropriate, sleep and rest routines should be in tune with the individual child's needs, and you will be able to participate in supporting these needs. You will learn about the benefits of sleep, rest and quiet times and about the need for safety and supervision during these periods.

Look back at Unit 2, page 84, for more information on rest and sleep.

remember You will need to write about different routines in each placement for inclusion in your professional practice log.

Toileting and other hygiene routines

You will be able to participate, with supervision, in assisting children with their elimination and hygiene needs. Certain aspects of this care may be carried out by a baby's or child's key worker, and you should not feel excluded when this happens. These routines also provide the opportunity to support older babies and young children as they master the skills needed for independence.

Look back at Unit 2, page 84, for more information about toileting and other hygiene routines.

activity
INDIVIDUAL WORK 4.5

P4

M3

1 Make a list of the various routines that you have identified as taking place within the setting of your current placement.
2 From the list, select four different routines that you have been part of and describe them in detail. Ensure that you include issues of staffing and supervision, the rationale of the routine, who benefits and how, timing issues, any recording involved, etc.
3 Make clear your role within each routine.
4 Explain the importance of each routine to the children being cared for. Make reference to their ages, stages of development, etc.

You will find Activity 4.5 a useful one to carry out in every placement. It will help you to identify best practice as well as how best to meet the needs of young children.

Know how to promote a stimulating learning environment for children

Setting

Children learn through stimulus. The verb 'to stimulate' means to encourage, to inspire or to act as an incentive. This refers not only to the provision of activities, but to the ways in which you interact with children, using body language, eye contact, and giving encouraging looks and smiles. Early years professionals should understand the importance of ensuring that all children have an appropriate share of their time and attention. You need to recognise that some children are more demanding than others, but that the less demanding child should not lose out because of this. You should deal with a demanding child by positively reinforcing acceptable behaviour, making it clear what your expectations are and setting clear, consistent boundaries.

Refer back to Unit 1, page 2, for setting goals and boundaries in early years settings.

Age groups

It is important that children are grouped appropriately to ensure that their needs are met as fully as possible. It is usual for babies either to be looked after separately from the other children or to be with the youngest age range of toddlers. Typically, nurseries group children in the following way:

- baby room – babies from six weeks can be found here, along with crawlers and standers, and the youngest of the walkers
- toddler room – toddlers approximately between one and a half years and two and a half years are likely to be found here
- preschool room – all children working towards the Early Learning Goals in the Foundation Stage Curriculum will be in this group, plus a few of the rising-threes
- and in school, where reception children will either be in a specific reception age group or combined with the youngest of the children from Year 1.

Aims

The aims of every setting should be clear. These are written down, are given to parents when they take up a place for their child at the setting, and will be available for inspection and reflection. Written plans should be in place for all age groups, linked to curriculum or guidance strategies as appropriate.

Refer to Unit 7, pages 338–341, for information on the Birth to Three Matters strategy, the Foundation Stage Curriculum and the National Curriculum.

Staffing and structure

Staff hold a range of qualifications. Schools are, of course, staffed by qualified primary teachers, usually supported by nursery nurses or classroom assistants who often hold a level 3 qualification in early years.

In day-care settings – nurseries, crèches, preschools, and play groups – staff are qualified to either level 2 or level 3, as are childminders and nannies. Those staff holding supervisory posts will be qualified to at least level 3.

The numbers of children in any group or room will usually determine the numbers and qualification levels of staff. More senior or experienced staff will often be key workers, liaising with the parents of the group of children for whom they have greater responsibility.

Each early years setting has its own aims, practice and structure. Most settings for three- to five-year-olds follow the Early Learning Goals set out in the Foundation Stage Curriculum; some, however, follow a particular school of educational thought, for example **High/Scope**, **Montessori** and **Steiner,** each of which, despite their differences, emphasises play and experiential learning.

Refer to Unit 7, pages 325–329, for more about High/Scope, Montessori and Steiner philosophies.

Professional Practice

- If you are fortunate enough to have a placement in a setting using the High/Scope, Montessori or Steiner educational methods, take the opportunity to learn as much as possible about it, using this first-hand knowledge to compare and contrast differing schools of thought.
- This can be invaluable experience for assignment work on educational theory; it will help you to contribute usefully to classroom discussion and inform other students too.

remember

The type of setting, and the ages of the children catered for, as well as the curriculum followed, will by necessity have an impact on the structure of the day and the scope for activity planning.

As set out on page 168, there are many types of provision, each with the general aim of providing a safe and stimulating environment for the children in its care.

Whatever the type of provision, staff must be aware of the routines and procedures for the setting in which they work. These will vary according to the type of provision and the ages of the children being cared for. Changes to routines and procedures should be agreed in advance, and all staff, students and any parent-helpers should be kept informed. Although routine is necessary in order to provide security for the children and to avoid chaos or confusion, it should not be so rigid that it cannot embrace sufficient flexibility to allow staff and children to enjoy spontaneous experiences or opportunities. There has to be a balance.

Provision

Resources

Resources available in early years settings can be broadly described as either **human resources** or **physical resources**. It is important that consideration is given to what resources are available within the setting itself and what is available in the wider community. This will ensure not only that the talents and experience of the staff are fully utilised but that the children are also able to benefit from facilities and individuals that are available locally.

Human resources

The human resources within the setting itself comprise the staff, students and, possibly, parent-helpers. Jointly, they are likely to have an array of experience and talent. Good teamwork will enable this talent and experience to benefit the children, encourage individuals to share their expertise and further individual staff members' development.

Among possible visitors from the wider community are dental hygienists, police officers, and road safety officers. Visits to shops or to a local farm, for example, will enable children to interact with a range of adults in their natural working environments and learn about their roles in context.

Physical resources

The physical resources within the setting comprise the equipment that is available, as well as the space used for play, both indoors and outdoors. In a school, there are likely to be additional spaces that can be utilised, such as a hall, library or technology room.

The wider community contains a vast array of physical resources (see below).

Materials

As the main focus is on learning through play, each setting has to offer an extensive range of resources and materials, including equipment and replica objects and creative resources derived from natural materials and household waste. Much of this will be bought by the settings, but some will be acquired from factories and offices in the community and possibly from the organisation Scrapstore, if there is one locally.

Parents can, of course, also be a valuable source of interesting objects and artefacts, particularly for the role-play area or for interest tables or themed interest boxes.

Outings

As already mentioned, the children could be taken to visit a shop or a farm, or to the park, on a nature ramble or a 'listening' walk. A trip out, even if it is simply a local walk, offers many opportunities for young children to build on their knowledge and understanding, opening up additional avenues for exploration, discussion and learning.

Refer to Unit 2, page 43, for guidance on planning a safe outing.

Professional Practice

- Drawing a plan of your current setting, and adding your comments and suggestions for change could form part of your professional practice log, evidencing your understanding of how to respond to the needs of children and contribute to the provision of a stimulating environment.
- Any planning should take into consideration policies on permission and safety, and the impact on all concerned (e.g. implications for staffing).
- A range of activities is needed to keep a child's interest; consolidate and extend the familiar; give them the incentive to try something new; and enhance their experience through the introduction of new ideas.

Fig 4.7 Children's play provides opportunities for them to develop and explore their understanding of the world

Curriculum activities

Part of the role of a professional early years worker is to respond to children in an appropriate manner. This includes providing appropriately stimulating activities in socially appropriate circumstances. The use of positive body language, voice intonation and eye contact is essential, to ensure that each child feels focused upon and valued.

When on placement, you will be expected to support the setting's provision by planning and implementing a range of stimulating activities appropriate to the needs of the children. When working with older, preschool age groups, plans must be linked to the Foundation Stage Curriculum, set up by the Department of Education and Skills' Qualifications and Curriculum Authority (QCA) in 2000. This curriculum is divided into six areas of learning.

In primary schools, plans must work within the framework of both the Foundation Stage Curriculum, for children in reception classes, and the National Curriculum for children in Years 1 and 2. The six main areas of learning that make up the Foundation Stage Curriculum (Early Learning Goals) are:

- personal, social and emotional development
- communication, language and literacy
- mathematical development
- knowledge and understanding of the world
- creative development
- physical development.

remember

You will need to become familiar with these aims.

The Department of Education and Skills' aims for the Foundation Stage

The Department of Education and Skills has published its aims for the Foundation Stage; these are set out below.

'The curriculum for the Foundation Stage should underpin all future learning by supporting, fostering, promoting and developing children's:

Personal, social and emotional well-being: in particular by supporting the transition to and between settings, promoting an inclusive ethos and providing opportunities for each child to become a valued member of that group and community so that a strong self-image and self-esteem are promoted;

Positive attitudes and dispositions towards their learning: in particular an enthusiasm for knowledge and learning and a confidence in their ability to be successful learners;

Social skills: in particular by providing opportunities that enable them to learn how to co-operate and work harmoniously alongside and with each other and to listen to each other;

Language and communication: with opportunities for all children to talk and communicate in a widening range of situations, to respond to adults and to each other, to practise and extend the range of vocabulary and communication skills they use and to listen carefully;

Reading and writing: with opportunities for all children to explore, enjoy, learn about and use words and text in a broad range of contexts and to experience a rich variety of books;

Mathematics: with opportunities for all children to develop their understanding of number, measurement, pattern, shape and space by providing a broad range of contexts in which they can explore, enjoy, learn, practise and talk about them;

Knowledge and understanding of the world: with opportunities for all children to solve problems, make decisions, experiment, predict, plan and question in a variety of contexts, and to explore and find out about their environment and people and places that have significance in their lives;

Physical development: with opportunities for all children to develop and practise their fine and gross motor skills and to increase their understanding of how their bodies work and what they need to do to be healthy and safe;

Creative development: with opportunities for all children to explore and share their thoughts, ideas and feelings through a variety of art, design and technology, music, movement, dance and imaginative and role play activities.'

(Qualifications and Curriculum Authority, *Curriculum Guidance for the Foundation Stage*, 2000)

Professional Practice

- You will need to provide evidence of your understanding of what you consider to be stimulating activities. This evidence should be applied to a range of ages and stages of development during your various placement experiences.
- Your ability to provide stimulating activities will be evidenced through your professional practice log and also by the practical assessments that you undertake in the workplace, set by either your placement supervisor or by a tutor.

The main discussion of development can be found in Unit 3, pages 113–159.

Fig 4.8 Providing stimulating activities

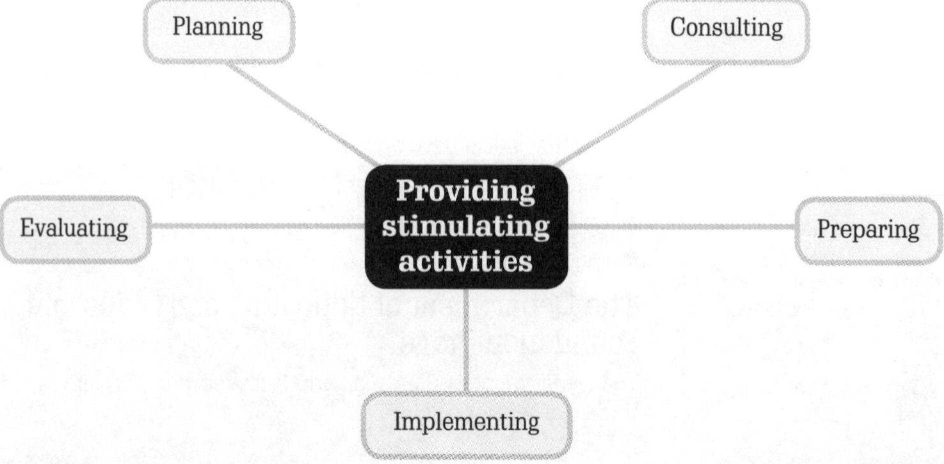

Planning

Planning care routines, play or learning activities is at the heart of good-quality and effective provision. Whether the plan is being made for care, play or learning needs, it needs to be structured; and informed by appropriate frameworks such as the Birth to Three Matters Framework or the Foundation Stage Curriculum. It should also be flexible, inclusive and responsive to the needs of the individual.

Refer to Unit 7, page 353, for more on planning and to the Nelson Thornes website for examples.
www.nelsonthornes.com/btec

Consulting

Consultation with parents and other members of staff may be instrumental in planning effective care and, most importantly, children should also be consulted. Consultation is important when identifying additional needs as well as for planning culturally and developmentally sensitive care.

Preparing

Preparation should be linked to careful planning in order that care and activities can be successfully implemented. This means not only preparation of the items and resources required for the activity or care routine, but also preparation of the environment.

Refer to Unit 7, pages 353–364, for guidance on planning and preparation.

Implementing

Implementation must be carefully planned.

In this pivotal phase, the care routine or activity is put into action with the identified individual or group. Implementation may involve some element of instruction, demonstration and questioning as well as observation and assessment of how children react to the care or activity.

Evaluating

Implementation of care, play or learning activities should be followed by careful evaluation of how successfully the needs of babies and children have been met. Observation and assessment are involved in the evaluation process, and evaluation is also an integral part of reflective practice. Evaluation includes asking questions of children, other staff and oneself, such as:

- Did all of the children enjoy and benefit from this activity? If not, why?
- Did the activity meet the set learning objectives?
- Was care effective in meeting children's needs? If not, what modifications should be made?
- Was the preparation for this care or activity effective, and were all the health and safety aspects considered?
- How could this activity be developed further?

Refer to pages 230–235 for more on evaluating and reflection of own practice.

Play activities

It is useful to consider everyday activities, evaluating how they enhance each aspect of children's development. Initially, you should consider the basic opportunities that each activity provides. As you progress through your course of study, you will develop an understanding of how to extend activities. The following section outlines just a few of the many play activities that you will enjoy with children during your training and career.

activity
INDIVIDUAL WORK 4.6

P2

1 Take time to observe the children in your placement over a period of time.
2 Think about their developmental needs and skill levels, together with the vast array of potential play activities that you have seen them enjoy, or could offer them.
3 Using a table like the one below, place the listed activities under the headings that you consider to be appropriate: i.e. indicating the developmental areas that the activities would be likely to enhance.

NB Some will come under several (or all) of the headings.

Activities:

role play corner/imaginative play
games involving more than one child
sand, water, clay, wood (natural materials)
dough
group story times
group discussion times
lotto games
circle time
activities to encouage repsonsiblity and taking turns
drama
music and movement
setting out the weather chart
books and stories
puzzles
construction activites
interest tables
farms, car mats, dolls houses an so on (small world play)
balls, hoops, beanbags, and so on
bikes
climbing frames
threading toys
pencil skill activities
painting easel
gardening

Table 4.2

Social development	Intellectual development	Moral development	Physical development	Language development	Emotional development

Most of the above activities can be both child led and adult led. Whenever possible let children initiate the use of materials. They will learn through planning, consulting, experimentation and reflection.

Painting

Fig 4.9 Painting

Painting is a very popular medium for self-expression and communication and is usually a favourite activity with children of all ages. Paints can also be used with other media; for example, wax crayons or candle wax can be used to make wax-resist painting. Children can be encouraged to experiment with different painting styles and techniques, as well as with styles and techniques from other cultures.

Setting up

- Set up painting activities in a clearly defined space.
- Set up on an easily cleaned surface or floor.
- Ensure that provision has been made for drying wet paintings.
- Make sure that each child wears a protective overall.
- Provide a wide variety of paint, brushes, string, wax crayons, sponges, etc.
- Ensure that all materials are non-toxic and that children are supervised.

Benefits for physical development

- Painting encourages some fine motor skills and manipulation skills.
- It aids the development of manual dexterity as the child uses and explores different materials and tools and learns how to control the brush.

Benefits for intellectual development

- Painting helps children to recognise concepts such as size, shape and colour.
- It encourages experimentation when mixing and creating new colours.
- It teaches that properties and textures of liquids and objects change.
- It helps children to gain confidence in choosing colours, the subject of the painting, etc.
- It encourages language skills when textures and colours are being discussed.
- Painting supports the child in identifying and talking about ideas, intentions, and the finished product.

Benefits for emotional and social development

- Children can share their ideas with others although many children choose to work independently.
- Painting is satisfying and non-competitive, allowing the child free expression of their ideas and feelings.
- It can encourage an apprehensive child to join in messy activities as there is no 'right' or 'wrong'.
- Self-esteem and confidence are boosted if the child sees that their work is valued.

Water play

Fig 4.10 Water play

Water is an essential element of children's lives, and water play is a popular activity that offers many valuable and pleasurable learning possibilities. Although it is a fun activity, safety and supervision must be a priority as accidental drowning could easily occur when adult vigilance is relaxed.

Setting up

- Make sure that the container used for water play is easy to fill and empty.
- The number of children using the water play area may have to be limited for safety and to ensure adequate supervision.
- Remind children to behave safely.
- Spillages must be wiped up immediately.
- Children should wear protective overalls.
- Provide a wide range of containers, scoops, funnels and other equipment, as well as items that will float and sink.
- Remember to change the water after each session, and remind children to wash their hands.

Benefits for physical development

- Children will be able to develop their hand–eye co-ordination when pouring water into a container or from one container to another.
- Water play offers opportunities to increase fine motor skills and control over body movements.

Benefits for intellectual development

- Water play offers valuable learning opportunities as children experiment with texture, feeling and properties.
- It enables development of concepts such as volume, capacity, sinking, floating, full, and empty.
- It encourages experimentation and discussion of ideas.
- Language development can be stimulated by asking children questions and encouraging description.
- It may encourage the use of imagination.

Benefits for emotional and social development

- Water play is therapeutic and relaxing as the play tends to be solitary or parallel; parallel play also fosters shared enjoyment of the activity.
- Self-esteem and confidence can be boosted as there is no right or wrong way to play with water (as long as play is safe!).
- It facilitates the expression of pleasure and excitement.

Sand play

Fig 4.11 Sand play

Sand play, like water play, is a popular activity in most settings and an absorbing and pleasurable play medium for children and adults alike. Whether indoors or outdoors, children can involve themselves in sand play at whatever level they like, as there is no right or wrong way to play with sand.

Setting up

- Provide plenty of props to use with the sand: for example, different-sized cups and containers, spades, spoons, ladles, scoops, moulds, plastic biscuit cutters, toy people, toy cars, toy animals, shells, pebbles, colander, rakes, funnels, sieves, measuring cups and spoons, scales, magnifying glass.
- Store props where children can have easy access to them.
- Put sand play area near other active areas.
- If the sand tray is outside, the sand must be carefully checked for contamination from animal faeces.
- Ensure that the correct type of sand is used and change it regularly.
- Supervise closely and limit the number of children in the area at any one time.
- Provide protective covering – some settings provide head covering as well as overalls.
- Make sure that children do not throw sand and that spilt sand is swept up promptly in order to prevent falls.

Benefits for physical development

- Playing with sand improves fine motor skills and manual dexterity.
- It helps with hand–eye co-ordination.

Benefits for intellectual development

- Sand play encourages sensory experiences as children explore the properties of wet or dry sand.
- It increases vocabulary as children use words like 'wet', 'dry', 'mould', 'sift', 'pour', 'trickle'.
- It encourages children to talk to other children and adults as they play and experiment.
- It allows children to explore and experiment with concepts such as volume, capacity, and cause and effect, as children pour sand into and out of containers.

Benefits for emotional and social development

- The activity is usually soothing and may be used therapeutically for some children.
- Children's confidence can be built through co-operation and interaction with others.

Role play

Fig 4.12 Role play

Most children enjoy the role-play area (some settings call it 'the home corner'). Regardless of the name, it must be an area that reflects the home life, experiences and abilities of all children and should contain culturally diverse equipment and props. The children's role play will benefit from regular changes to the layout and emphasis of the play area', and a wide range of resources will support creativity and lessen the chance of repetitious play.

Setting up

- The area should be set up with sufficient space and resources for several children to play at the same time.
- Resources should be checked for safety, suitability and ability to stimulate play and development.
- Children may need adult support to explore new concepts and topic areas.
- Dressing-up clothes should be easy to use and should represent a wide variety of cultures.
- Clothes should be washed regularly.
- Some limitations may have to be imposed on the use of role-play clothes and hats if children have contagious skin conditions or head lice.

Benefits for physical development

- Fine motor skills can be practised when using the dressing-up clothes – dexterity and control will develop as children fasten buttons, manipulate zip fasteners and use equipment and props.

Benefits for intellectual development

- Depending on what the area is being used for, children will be able to understand and explore different roles and processes, for example going to the garage and writing a bill for repairs.
- Concepts relating to number and money may be explored through pretend shopping.
- There are opportunities for sorting, grouping, matching and pairing, for example cups and saucers, knives and forks.
- Role play stimulates language through conversations and use of role-specific language.
- There are opportunities for using writing skills when, for example, children write menus for the café, bills for the garage or tickets for the bus.

Benefits for emotional and social development

- There is no right or wrong way to undertake role play, so it provides children with the freedom to use their imagination and understand another's role.
- Whilst planning roles, exchanging ideas and deciding on costumes, children learn to co-operate and share.
- Role play encourages expression of social greetings and conventions, such as 'hello', 'please', and 'thank you'.
- It promotes confidence in interacting with others.
- Children are helped to understand unfamiliar situations, such as going to the doctor or hospital, or having a new baby.
- Role play and play in the home corner can be used therapeutically with a vulnerable child in order to explore feelings and anxieties.

Construction play

Children find construction play to be stimulating and satisfying, and it enables them to experience the excitement of building something from assorted components. Many different types of construction toys are available, varying in the materials used and orientation. For example, settings may have wooden train sets, plastic interlocking bricks, puzzles, all of which could be called construction toys.

Setting up

- Minimal time is needed for setting up construction play, but space to allow several children to play and spread out the equipment is necessary.
- Equipment should be age appropriate in order to counter frustration and ensure safety.
- Make sure that all children are encouraged to engage in construction play regardless of gender.

Fig 4.13 Construction

Benefits for physical development

- Handling the components develops manipulation and dexterity.
- Hand–eye co-ordination and motor development improve as children fit pieces together and use large boxes, tables, chairs, etc.

Benefits for intellectual development

- Construction play helps children to develop planning and intention skills.
- It aids development of concepts such as shape, size, colour, height and weight, as children learn to sort and group by size, weight and shape.
- Construction play develops the ability to sustain concentration and effort.
- It helps children develop new vocabulary; they can use language to give instructions as well as for discussing ideas.

Benefits for emotional and social development

- Construction play encourages co-operation and sharing, as well as the social conventions involved in requesting resources and thanking others.
- It allows the child to experience and express elation and frustration when efforts succeed or fail.
- The achievement of intentions will aid self-confidence and promote independence.
- Co-operative play can be encouraged although large groups may be less successful.

Books and stories

Fig 4.14 Children having a story read to them

Books and stories offer rich opportunities to develop and extend children's language and literacy skills, as well as the chance to share a special time with adults and other children. There is no age limit on the use of books and stories; these should be regularly offered to babies as well as to older children. A variety of types, sizes and formats of books should be offered, as well as dual-language texts and books with children's heritage languages and alphabets. All resources should reflect cultural diversity and contain **positive images** of gender, ability, ethnic origin, etc.

Setting up
- Very little formal setting up is required, but care should be taken with the size of the book if more than one child is to be read to.
- The environment should be conducive to quiet reading or story time.
- Props can be used to bring the story alive and to help the children engage with the story.

Benefits for physical development
- Manipulation skills are developed when turning pages and handling books.
- Hand–eye skills improve when following direction and orientation of text.
- Actions can be used with some stories.

Benefits for intellectual development
- Books and stories offer rich opportunities for the development of language and literacy skills – from learning how books 'work' to appreciating the different forms and properties of language and learning new vocabulary.
- Learning and understanding are enhanced by repetition and imitation.
- Children learn to understand the differences between factual books and fiction.

Benefits for emotional and social development
- The child can enjoy a solitary or shared experience.
- It helps understanding about the social world and wider environment.
- The child can explore a range of situations that may cause anxiety such as a new baby in the family or going to the doctor.
- It allows the child to experience and express a range of emotions, and children may find favourite stories comforting.
- Storytelling can be used therapeutically with a vulnerable or anxious child.

Clay and dough play

Fig 4.15 Playing with clay and dough

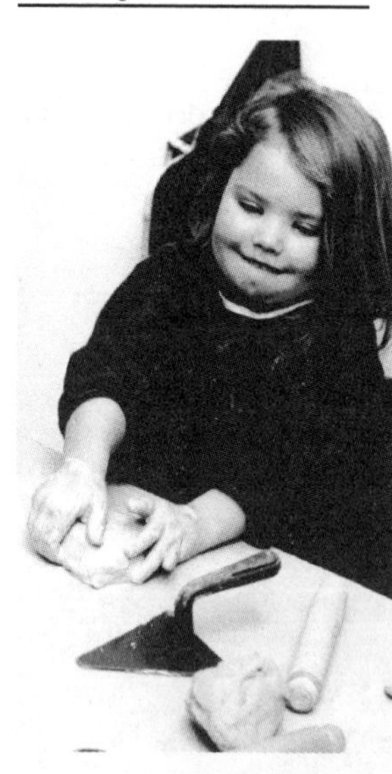

Most children enjoy playing with clay, dough and other malleable materials, and this type of play offers valuable learning opportunities. It provides freedom for creative expression as well as giving the child the opportunity to explore the properties and possibilities of these media.

Setting up
- Most settings will use a table with a wipeable top for this kind of play, although a tray could be used if a child is confined to bed.
- The activity can be incorporated with other areas, such as the home corner.
- Safety and hygiene must be considered – dough should be replaced regularly, and children with allergies or intolerances may need materials that are free from gluten or other known allergens.
- Children must be encouraged to wash their hands before and after using malleable materials, and those with sensitive skin or infectious skin conditions may need to take precautions when playing, such as wearing gloves.
- A range of equipment should be offered (e.g. plastic cutters, blunt knives, rolling pins, stamps, boards, garlic presses).

Benefits for physical development
- This type of play promotes hand–eye coordination and dexterity as the child manipulates the malleable material and the equipment. Manipulation skills can be practised when using cutters etc.
- It allows the child a range of sensory and tactile experiences.

Benefits for intellectual development

- Children are able to explore properties and textures as well as concepts such as malleability, shape, mass, etc.
- It helps children to understand what tools are appropriate for which actions and helps link planning to intentions.
- New vocabulary can be learned, and the child can describe textures, actions and intentions.

Benefits for emotional and social development

- Play is satisfying, and there is no right or wrong way to play with malleable materials.
- The child can express strong emotions through squeezing, squashing and then remaking.
- Play can be undertaken as a solitary activity, but it also provides an opportunity to work and share with others.
- It can help children develop social conventions, such as please and thank you, as equipment is passed and shared.

Promoting development and supporting learning

Learning and development can be supported in many ways. Hands-on experience, together with display work and visits, can make a subject more real to children than simply hearing about it or looking at pictures, although, clearly, both of these media are valuable information sources in their own right.

Displays can involve children and their families in contributing objects and information. Parents and other family members may be able to demonstrate a skill or recount personal experience of the subject matter. The list of possible activities to be enjoyed with children is almost endless.

Unit 7 focuses on learning activities and play. It will be helpful to refer to the relevant sections on pages 332–336 and 361–363.

For information on setting up play activities, refer to the Ready, Steady, Play! Series, edited by Green (2004/5) and to *Planning Play and the Early Years* by Tassoni and Hucker (2000).

Promoting and supporting physical skills

An individual child's physical needs will be met by evaluating their current level of development and their main interests. All types of play promote some aspect of physical development.

The development of large motor skills is easily supported by outside activities in dry weather, but more ingenuity is needed to do so within the confines of a small room. Fine motor skills can be developed anywhere, for example in domestic and learning activities.

Physical exercise helps to build strength and improve general health; it also helps with the practice and extension of large motor skills; in addition, activities requiring co-ordinated movements using these skills help the child to develop spatial awareness. Fine motor skills are enhanced by more dexterous activities.

Children who live in cramped conditions, or who have little access to outside play at home, benefit in particular from opportunities to exercise their bodies through play.

The adult's role in helping and supporting physical development is often to be innovative. It is easy to provide plenty of opportunities for practising large motor skills on a fine day, when there is a safe outdoor playing area, but more imagination is needed to encourage the use of these skills indoors. Drama, dance and exercise are important, as are activities for encouraging the development of fine skills in children with limited dexterity or concentration spans. Careful planning is needed to ensure that all children have sufficient, and equal, access to each type of activity.

activity
INDIVIDUAL WORK 4.7
P3

1 Consider the general physical development of children aged around three years and plan three ideas to support large motor skills development indoors, and three ideas to support fine motor skills.

2 At your placement, observe the children aged around three years old. Which of them have additional needs that you would have to take into account if implementing your activities?

3 What adjustments do you need to make to ensure that they can participate fully in the activities?

Promoting and supporting emotional development

remember
A child suffering emotional stress is less likely to be as receptive to learning as one who is emotionally stable.

A withdrawn or unhappy child may require additional adult support; the insecure child may need extra reassurance and sensitive settling in, involving both the parent and the professional.

Children need opportunities to come to terms with their feelings; at times, they may be confused or even frightened. They need to be reassured that it is alright to have negative feelings, such as jealousy and anger, and to be helped to learn how to manage these feelings. It is important, also, that children understand that others, adults included, have these feelings too. This is all part of their emotional development.

remember
Being made to feel unvalued can potentially have long-term as well as short-term effects.

Common family events, for example moving house, starting nursery or the arrival of a new baby, are all potentially disturbing situations. The adult's role in helping and supporting emotional development is one of observation and empathy, supporting the anxious child and providing a range of opportunities through play, books and discussion (and at times using puppets) to help them work through their feelings and concerns in a safe environment.

Self-esteem can be closely associated with emotional stability, and you can probably think of situations where you have been made to feel unvalued. No doubt this had an impact on your sense of self-worth, even if only temporarily.

Self-esteem can be boosted through the use of circle time.

Refer to Unit 3, page 132, for more on the emotional development of young children, and to Unit 6, page 312, for circle time.

Promoting and supporting social development

A child who has not learned to share, to interact with others or to respond appropriately to social situations may need adult involvement to help them find their way. Having other children as role models will help, as will adult encouragement and support, such as giving praise when acceptable social interactions take place and clear explanations when behaviour is not acceptable.

Children need to develop self-confidence and be able to make and sustain friendships; they need to understand the ways of others and to value the differences between themselves and their peers. Society expects us to conform to some basic social rules, which have to be learned, enabling us to respect the needs of others, to win and lose gracefully and to behave appropriately in whatever circumstances we find ourselves.

When supporting social development, the adult's role is at times one of mediator, helping children to learn to share through the use of games, books and discussion, encouraging turn-taking and the apportioning of materials in play. Adults also have a responsibility to introduce new experiences, such as cultural events and religious festivals, to enhance learning and to help avoid the development of prejudice.

Refer to Unit 1, page 2, for information on setting goals and boundaries in early years settings, and to Unit 3, page 137, for more on the social development of children.

remember

Staff should not assume that all children have the same day-to-day experiences; by making this assumption, they may be excluding some individuals.

Promoting and supporting cultural differences

A child's culture is significant to them as an individual; it is part of their social identity. It is important that the setting they attend recognises this and enables the child to take part in and benefit from all opportunities within the setting. Sometimes, this may necessitate a slight adjustment to ensure that the child's cultural requirements are fully acknowledged. Cultural issues of diet and health care should be taken into consideration as well as aspects of resources, equipment and communication.

Promoting and supporting cognitive development

The need to achieve high academic standards is emphasised in today's society. In early years this does not mean a formal education; it means 'developing key learning skills such as listening, speaking, concentration, persistence and learning to work together and co-operate with other children' (Hodge, 2000).

All this can be achieved through play, as advocated in the guidance set out by the Plowden Report in 1967, which gave 'central status' to the role of play in the education of young children.

remember

Opportunities for conserving, measuring and estimating occur naturally in many activities.

Undoubtedly, children need opportunities to explore within their play, using all of their senses. They need opportunities to conserve, to measure, to estimate, and to predict, and activities designed for understanding concepts such as volume, capacity, weight and length. But perhaps most of all, children need opportunities to develop thinking skills and the power of concentration.

The adult's role in supporting cognitive development can be as general as the setting-out of stimulating materials and activities, and as specific as noting when to intervene in the experiential process in order to enhance learning. The psychologist Lev Vygotsky (1896–1935) called the difference between what a child can achieve alone and what they can potentially achieve with adult intervention the 'zone of proximal development' (ZPD). As you develop your observation skills you will increasingly develop your understanding of when it is appropriate to join in with a child's play in order to enrich the learning process. This is a skill which develops over time and will be an important aspect of your professional practice.

Refer to Unit 3, pages 144–147, for a discussion of learning, including the thinking of Vygotsky.

Promoting and supporting language development

Your time is the most important gift that you can give to a child to enhance their language development. The adult's role is to supply opportunities for conversation, introduce the child to literature and let them write using a variety of media. Ideally, children should be surrounded by language from birth. They need to be both spoken to and listened to. They need to be encouraged to talk, for example discussing what they are doing and what they have already done.

remember

Children need to be surrounded by spoken and written language, for example in the role-play area, so that they gain an understanding of the purpose of reading.

There are opportunities for writing within imaginative play, if appropriate props are supplied to enhance the children's playing at shops, café, and so on. Familiar articles, pictures and objects can be labelled to help make links between spoken and written language.

Language is our main means of communication, without which it is less easy to express ourselves or make our needs known. The development of spoken language enables a child to describe and to explain and offers opportunities to question and to clarify instructions, thereby furthering their opportunities for learning.

Refer to Unit 3, page 147, for more on language development.

Promoting and supporting moral development

Children need moral guidance too! Moral development is closely linked to social development. A child's understanding of socially acceptable behaviour is essential to their building of successful relationships. Developing an understanding of sharing and of what is right and what is wrong is helped by having well-defined boundaries within the setting and a positive approach to addressing any problems that arise. Valuing other cultures and religions is particularly important in our multicultural society; equality should be both recognised and respected.

Learning self-value helps us to cope with peer pressure, to stand firm and maintain our beliefs and moral conduct.

The professional adult can support moral development by acting as a role model for good behaviour and by setting clear boundaries with regard to what is acceptable within the setting and what is not. It is also important that the adults within the setting are prepared to challenge unacceptable behaviour, whether a child's or another adult's.

Factors that affect development

As well as considering how best the developmental needs of children can be met, it is important to look at what influences development and what early years professionals can do.

Fig 4.16 Factors that affect development

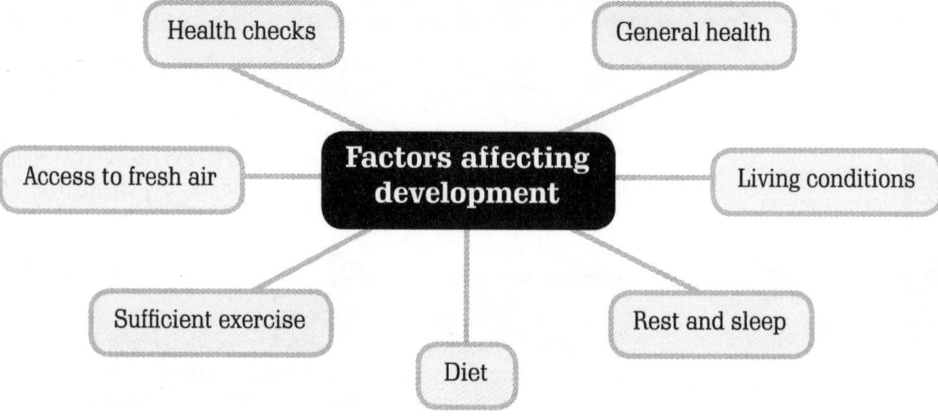

Health

The **World Health Organization (WHO)** stated in 1946 that: 'Health is the state of complete physical, mental and social well-being, not merely the absence of disease and infirmity.'

This definition has been updated to include a more general description: 'The enjoyment of the highest attainable standard of health is one of the fundamental rights of every human being without distinction of race, religion, political belief, economic or social condition ...'.

Refer to Unit 9, page 404, for further information on health and to Unit 3, page 155, for more on factors that affect development.

Opportunities for healthy development are based on good health, physical care and emotional well-being. The nutrition required for the growth, maintenance and development of the body is found in the food that we eat; it helps us to maintain and repair our body tissues and keeps muscles and organs functioning. Food also helps to prevent infection and supplies the body with its energy needs.

Refer to Unit 9, page 435, for information on nutrition and dietary needs.

remember A balanced diet contains a range of vitamins and minerals and is divided into four main food groups.

Children need not only a balanced diet to achieve their potential but also to be in full health. To monitor a child's health, health professionals carry out routine examinations, assessments and immunisations.

Children need to feel cared for and loved unconditionally; they need sufficient fresh air and opportunities for exercise, rest and activity; they also need protection from harm and they need security. Without the right balance of these, a child's health and development are likely to suffer.

As an early years professional, you will be one of many adults contributing to the well-being and development of the children in your care. Think about the different people who influence children's health choices and attitudes, and the various ways in which they have influence.

You will also be a role model for children, as they develop their own attitudes towards health choices. How positive are your influences?

Issues to be considered when supporting learning

Positive/negative effects of images

All books, posters, games, puzzles, toys and similar resources should be carefully evaluated for the types of image they portray. Those that are considered to offer **negative images** should be removed and, when funds allow, replaced with materials depicting positive images. There is no advantage to having a large range of resources if they include negative images. The children will not benefit from them and may absorb the wrong messages. It is far better to have a smaller range which will enhance children's understanding of equality, be it gender, race or disability.

Fig 4.17 Toys should be evaluated for the images they convey

Positive/negative effects of language and labelling

It is important that you use language appropriately. Take note of how colleagues address children and their parents, and value the diversity of the languages spoken within your setting. Encourage children to use their heritage language as well as the language used most commonly within the setting. Settings can demonstrate to families that their language is valued by translating notices appropriately. Asking parents to help with the translations will also demonstrate that their involvement is valued.

activity
INDIVIDUAL WORK 4.8

M4

D2

Carry out an **audit** of the resources in your setting. This involves looking carefully at the materials and activities offered and making a judgement on their suitability with regard to development, learning and positive messages. Ask yourself the following questions:

1 Is the range of books, toys, posters, and so on, adequate?
   (a) Do they cover a sufficiently broad range of learning?
   (b) Do they support all areas of development?
   (c) Are all the activities and equipment suitable?
   (d) Do any of them promote unacceptable images?
   (e) Who should you talk to if you have identified any negativity?
2 Select 10 activities and note how each promotes development and supports learning.
   (a) How does each support children as individuals?
   (b) How does each support paired or group learning?
   (c) How could each activity be altered or improved to support development or build further on learning?

Refer to Unit 6, page 224, for discussion of the importance of diversity, and to Unit 7, for learning and play.

For further reading on equal opportunities, refer to *A Practical Guide to Equal Opportunities* by Malik (2003).

case study 4.5

Jolene

Jolene attends a family centre with her mother. She is aged three years and three months. Jolene struggles to complete 12-piece jigsaw puzzles; she tries to put pieces together at random. Jolene's mother is unsure how to help her complete the puzzles successfully and asks you for advice.

activity
INDIVIDUAL WORK

1 What approach would you suggest that Jolene's mother takes? Explain this clearly to a partner.

2 How might your suggested approach differ if the child were a different age or at a different stage of development?

Professional Practice

- The term 'developmentally appropriate' is a significant one. It is rare to find a child who develops according to the norms in all developmental areas. It is therefore important to accommodate the advances and delays in individual children when you plan activities or give them instructions. Taking their developmental level into account in relation to the responses you expect from them is equally important.
- Careful planning is needed to ensure that all children have sufficient, and equal, support in, and access to each type of activity.

Health and safety

Issues of health and safety have already been touched upon in this unit, but are discussed fully in Unit 2, page 33. You may find it useful to refer to that unit now to think through the implications for:

- choice and use of a range of materials, tools and equipment both inside and outside the setting
- restrictions on numbers and staff:child ratios
- hygiene and cleanliness.

Each of these is important to supporting development and learning.

Be able to reflect on own practices in work placement experiences

Self-appraisal and monitoring own progress

Evaluation and self-appraisal are vital skills for every professional, and, as you progress through the BTEC National course, you will be required to reflect upon and evaluate both your assignment work and your professional practice. This reflection might be part of a verbal appraisal, by your tutor or supervisor, which could be either formal or informal. It could also be in writing. Reflection is often included as part of the submission process for assignment work.

Your reflection should add value to the learning process. There is little benefit in stating in an evaluation that 'I could have improved upon my assignment had I started it earlier'.

It would be far more useful to reflect upon your time management and how you could develop strategies for spacing your work out more appropriately. Similarly, it is pointless to state that 'I was unable to give as much time to this assignment as I would have liked, as I also had three other assignments needing attention'. All students have the same number of assignments to complete. Tutors do not expect more from you than is reasonable. The workload does not, however, take into account that a student might need to work every evening after college, or be a parent with several children to care for. This may at times seem hard, but the requirements of a full-time course assume a full-time commitment to the course, and the workload required will have been made clear to you at the outset.

Reflection

Reflection is the consideration and evaluation of:

- what you have done
- the impact your actions may have had
- feedback you have been given
- questions you ask yourself and others
- how open-minded you have been
- how you compare actions and outcomes
- how you could have done something better, i.e. challenging your own practice in order to become a better practitioner.

remember
Reflection is particularly relevant to the assessment criteria in Units 3 and 8.

Your 800 hours' placement experience will take place in several different types of provision. Most of the more general skills that you will use will be the same for each setting, but at times an additional skill will be required. There will always be things that you could have done differently, and often better.

You may also set yourself specific targets, or targets may be set for you by your tutor or your placement supervisor. You will use reflection to evaluate how well you have met any such targets.

Targets

Any targets set should be meaningful. They will often be linked to the acronym SMART. This stands for:

- Specific
- Measurable
- Achievable
- Realistic
- Timed.

Example

An example of a SMART target would be:

Specific – I will build on my observation skills.

Measurable – Each day in placement I will carry out at least one observation.

Achievable – Each week I will use a different observational method.

Realistic – I will re-read college notes and the relevant section of Unit 3 to consolidate my understanding of each method.

Timed – I will ask my tutor to comment on my observations during personal tutorial sessions.

activity
INDIVIDUAL WORK 4.9
P6

1. At the end of each placement, think back over your time there. Make a list of the highlights and also note the times you found hard going.
2. Ask yourself what made things good or difficult? How did each situation link to your own actions or responses?
3. What have you learned about yourself from this reflection?
4. What areas of further self-development have you identified?

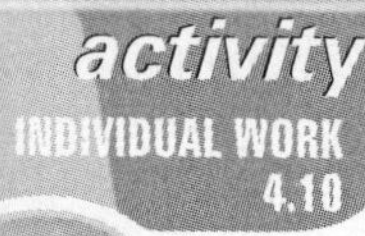

Building on Activity 4.9 above and using the blank chart that is available to download from the Nelson Thornes website, write SMART targets for yourself, based on each aspect of further development that you have identified.

Look on the Nelson Thornes website for the blank chart 'Setting SMART targets'. www.nelsonthornes.com/btec

Evaluation of professional practice

Evaluation of (or reflecting on) professional practice will form an important part of your professional practice log. You will need to consider each of the following points:

- your use of initiative and self-direction, and its importance
- your ability to meet changing needs and situations
- issues of responsiveness and adaptability
- reflecting upon own attitudes and relationships
- recognition of own knowledge, skills and contribution to team work
- how well you set targets for future development
- how well individual professional qualities have been developed, including:
  - interpersonal skills
  - verbal and non-verbal communication skills
  - professionalism
  - your knowledge base
  - level of understanding of the needs of children and families
  - knowledge of resources
  - knowledge of how to make referrals
- how well your personal management skills have developed, regarding:
  - roles and responsibilities within early years teams
  - organisational requirements
  - self-management in relation to:
    - timekeeping
    - dress
    - personal hygiene
    - punctuality
    - commitment
- how effective your individual problem-solving has been, including:
  - analysis of information
  - decision-making
  - prioritisation
  - evaluation of outcomes
- issues of self-appraisal, including:
  - self-awareness
  - ability to review own performance in all relevant activities.

Professional Practice

- Self-awareness is needed in order to reflect clearly on your abilities and achievements.
- Evaluation includes plans, actions, using feedback and outcomes. It requires acknowledgement of your strengths and also the areas that you need specifically to work on – your further development plan.

activity
GROUP WORK 4.11
P7

In a small group, explore the opportunities for continuing professional development that you could take up. Prepare a short presentation on each, outlining:

- how each could be of benefit
- who can access each opportunity
- from where relevant information can be obtained
- what is involved
- how different opportunities can build upon and support each other.

Remember to include local opportunities and national opportunities, short courses, longer periods of further study and one-off opportunities.

Evaluating effectiveness

This last section of the unit is primarily set out as a series of questions linked to the following topic areas:

- use of initiative and self-direction
- the need to be adaptable
- the effects of your attitude
- the need to work within a team
- identifying your personal needs
- developing professional qualities
- developing personal management
- current self-management
- the effectiveness of your problem-solving skills.

The questions below may seem daunting, but you will find it helpful when building up evidence for your professional practice log if you answer them honestly. The questions will enable you:

- to reflect more clearly on your skills
- evaluate your current level of knowledge
- analyse your understanding
- identify where there are gaps in your knowledge and understanding
- plan for continuous improvement
- to build on your professionalism.

As an early years student (or as a newly qualified early years professional), you would be expected to identify areas in which you feel you need to develop, so do not be concerned if you recognise gaps in your knowledge or practice. You are not failing if you are working to fill them in – you are simply developing.

remember

This ability to identify and acknowledge your own personal development needs is what makes a good professional. It also helps you plan for the future and for your development as a professional early years practitioner.

activity
INDIVIDUAL WORK 4.12
D3

Using the questions in Sections 1 to 9 on pages 234–235, reflect upon your professional practice and evaluate your own effectiveness in each placement that you have attended.

Section 1 question

Use of initiative and self-direction

Throughout placement experience you will increasingly be expected to use your own initiative. You should not have to be constantly guided as to what to do next. However, a student on placement for the first time will clearly not be expected to be as proactive as a student in their final term before qualifying. Taking into account where you are currently in your training and/or placement experience, answer the following:

How well do you use your initiative? Give examples.

Section 2 questions

Early years workers need to be adaptable to an ever-changing environment.

1 How well have you met the need for change? How flexible have you been?

2 When have you been less accommodating to the needs of the situation than you could have been? Why was this?

3 Have you always been responsive? Or do you need coaxing or reminding?

4 How adaptable are you? Give examples of your adaptability.

Section 3 questions

Attitude can greatly affect what you do, and how you go about it.

1 Is your attitude always positive? If not, why is this? What affects your attitude?

2 How well do you build relationships?

3 Are your relationships with others generally good? OK? Or are they poor? Why is this?

4 With whom do you form your best relationships? Why is this?

5 With whom do you find it hardest to form a good relationship?

6 What are the most significant factors affecting the quality of your relationships?

Section 4 questions

All early years workers need to be able to work within a team.

1 How well do you contribute knowledge to teamwork? Give examples.

2 How well do you utilise your greatest skills? What are they?

3 In your opinion, how well do you contribute to teamwork generally? Give examples.

Section 5 questions

Professional development involves identifying personal development needs (or targets).

1 Do you usually set yourself targets for the future? If yes, give examples.

2 How useful do you find this to be?

3 If you have not set targets before, set some now. What would they be?

4 How will they benefit your professional development for the future?

Section 6 questions

Development of individual professional qualities is essential.

1 How good are your interpersonal skills?

2 Give examples of situations when your interpersonal skills have been particularly important.

3 When communicating verbally, how successfully do you communicate with children? With parents/carers? With colleagues?

4 What messages does your body language give out? Are they always positive?

5 Give examples of good body language that you use. What effect does this have?

6 Give examples of unhelpful or negative body language that you have used. What effect did this have?

7 How would you rate yourself as a professional? Support this with examples.

8 How sound is your knowledge base? Where are your strengths best evidenced? In placement? In your assignment work? In classroom discussion? Anywhere else?

9 Give examples of how your knowledge base has been evidenced.

10 How well do you understand the needs of children and families? Use examples from your placement experience to illustrate this.

11 In what ways have you demonstrated your knowledge and understanding of resources? Give examples from your placement experience and your assignment work.

12 How could you demonstrate your knowledge of making referrals?

Section 7 questions
Personal management skills will develop with experience.

1 What roles and responsibilities have you had within early years teams/placements to date? Make a list and evaluate how successful each has been.

2 How well have you been able to meet the organisational requirements of your placements? Give examples showing where this has worked well and where this could have been improved.

Section 8 questions
Current self-management

1 How good is your timekeeping at the placement?

2 What effect does this have on you as a professional?

3 Does it have a positive or negative effect on the placement?

4 How does this affect your contribution to the placement?

5 How good is your timekeeping at college?

6 What effect does this have on you as a professional?

7 Does it have a positive or negative effect on the course and your contribution to it?

8 How good is your timekeeping generally?

9 What effect does this have on your life? For example, are you always thought of as reliable? Or as late?

10 Do you usually dress appropriately? Give examples of both appropriate and inappropriate dress for placement.

11 How do you ensure your personal hygiene is always good?

12 How good is your attendance record? How does this affect what you do?

13 Are you committed to what you are doing? How is this evidenced?

14 Would college tutors describe you as committed? If not, why?

15 Would your current placement supervisor describe you as committed? If not, why?

16 Would past placement supervisors have described you as committed? If not, why was this?

17 What has changed in your level (or demonstration) of commitment?

Section 9 questions
Effectiveness of individual problem-solving is an important aspect of your role as an early years professional. The decisions that you make can have a significant impact on the provision for the children in your care.

1 How good is your ability to analyse information? Give examples of where (a) a good analysis and (b) a poor analysis have been made. What impact did these analyses have?

2 What important decisions have you had to make? In college? In placement? Give examples to illustrate.

3 What was the impact of your decisions? Have there been any negative outcomes? What were these? How could they have been avoided?

4 How do you prioritise your actions? What do you take into consideration?

5 How do you prioritise your time? What are the most important factors?

6 How good are you at evaluating the outcomes of your work?

7 How well do you plan? Can you see how your plans impact on your outcomes?

8 Give examples to show how planning has affected the outcomes of your actions.

9 How self-aware are you? Are you able to identify your own limitations? Give examples from your placement experiences.

10 Do you review your own performance in all the activities, events and presentations that you are involved in? Give examples of good (and not so good) performance.

Key skills

As you move through the BTEC National CCLD course, you will use oral skills, written skills, information technology skills and numeracy skills. You will develop personally, academically and practically. The overall level and structure of the course will enable you to apply your newly acquired or enhanced learning to further your academic development, taking it into the workplace on qualifying and into your life in general. These areas of development are linked to the key skills qualification, which you will most likely have opportunities to take alongside your main qualification. Key skills are available at levels 1 to 4 (and to level 5 in personal skills development); they will contribute to your professional development and may be used as evidence in your professional practice log.

Students start the course with differing levels of knowledge, skills, experience and qualifications. Your tutors will guide you to the level most appropriate to your current stage of development in each key skill that you are taking.

Professional Practice

- As you read through the other units, your knowledge and understanding will develop further and this will have a positive impact on your practical skills.
- Evaluating your professional development regularly will be a valuable process. It will enable you to see clearly how you are progressing and help you to decide on your personal targets for the future.

Progress Check

1. What is meant by the term 'professionalism'?
2. What expectations are likely to be required of you in placement?
3. How might an unreliable staff member affect an early years setting?
4. What forms might your professional practice log take?
5. What is important about teamwork?
6. What is meant by 'being responsible for your personal safety'?
7. Define the term 'confidentiality'.
8. What is meant by the term 'need to know'?
9. What is meant by 'human and physical resources'?
10. Give a brief summary of the six main areas of development.
11. What does 'developmentally appropriate' mean?
12. Give examples of how you can contribute to the safety of children.
13. What is meant by 'evaluating your own performance'?
14. What does 'reflective practice' mean?

Protecting Children

This unit covers the following objectives:

- Understand indicators of potential child abuse
- Understand the requirements of legislation, regulation and codes of practice for safeguarding and protecting children
- Understand the principles of responding to disclosure
- Understand strategies for supporting children, their families and other adults

Child protection is one of the most difficult and sensitive areas of work for early years professionals; responsibility for the protection of children is an essential requirement of anyone working in an early years setting. At some point in your career you are likely to be involved with a child who has been abused or is in danger of being abused, and it is, therefore, important that you have an understanding of child protection procedures and of different types of child abuse and that you learn how to support the children in your care.

This unit introduces and defines the term 'abuse' and discusses how those working with children should respond to incidents of abuse or suspected abuse. It also discusses the support available to parents and carers of abused or at-risk children, both within the local community and through the legal system. Issues of safety within individual childcare settings are explored and opportunities are given for evaluation.

grading criteria

To achieve a **Pass** grade the evidence must show that the learner is able to:	To achieve a **Merit** grade the evidence must show that, in addition to the pass criteria, the learner is able to:	To achieve a **Distinction** grade the evidence must show that, in addition to the pass and merit criteria, the learner is able to:
P1 describe four physical and four behavioural indicators of possible child abuse page 250	**M1** compare four theoretical models of child abuse page 252	**D1** evaluate four theoretical models of child abuse page 252
P2 describe four theoretical models of child abuse page 252	**M2** explain reporting procedures in childcare settings page 260	**D2** evaluate child protection strategies to support children, their families and other adults. page 273
P3 outline the legal framework relating to the protection of children page 258	**M3** explain child protection strategies to support children, their families and other adults. page 274	
P4 describe the reporting procedures in a childcare setting page 260		

To achieve a **Pass** grade the evidence must show that the learner is able to:	To achieve a **Merit** grade the evidence must show that, in addition to the pass criteria, the learner is able to:	To achieve a **Distinction** grade the evidence must show that, in addition to the pass and merit criteria, the learner is able to:
P5 describe the principles of responding to disclosure page 262		
P6 describe child protection strategies to support children, their families and other adults. page 261		

Understand indicators of potential child abuse

Historically, children have suffered a great deal of abuse, partly due to general lack of understanding and acceptance that children should have rights and protection as individuals. Social attitudes have thankfully moved on, although the process has been slow and haphazard, progressing from the seventeenth-century thinking, which was that 'children's inherent [natural] badness needed disciplining' (Reder *et al.*, 1993), through phases in which childhood was essentially denied and children were considered to be extensions of their parents rather than individuals in their own right, leading eventually to the **paramountcy principle** set out in the Children Act 1989.

Encompassing the development of society's attitudes, together with a multitude of parliamentary Acts, the Children Act 1989 is one of the most important pieces of legislation ever for children in the UK.

The paramountcy principle gives priority to the welfare, safety and protection of children; any decision taken about children must be in their best interests. It demonstrates that children are at last being considered as people in their own right, who can contribute to decisions about their own futures.

The Children Act 1989 has been superseded by the Children Act 2004, and these will be referred to many times during this chapter. A copy of the Children Act, or volumes drawn from it, is usually available in college libraries; it is also available from Stationery Office bookshops or from the Internet.

Historical perspective on abuse

It is useful to adopt a **historical perspective**, looking at how what has happened in the past has implications for today.

Table 5.1 sets out the historical developments in the UK, outlining changes in thinking from medieval times through to the implementation of the Children Act 1989 in 1991.

Sadly, there have been many more cases like the ones shown in the table since the implementation of the Children Act 1989, and in many instances failure of communication between the various agencies was condemned. However, the findings of the Laming Report into the death of Victoria Climbié in 2000 fed into the reorganisation of children's services in the government's *Every Child Matters: Change for Children* agenda. This wholesale revision of services for children is underpinned by the legislation of the Children Act 2004; the aim is to change and improve the quality, accessibility and coherence of children's services, whilst maximising opportunity and minimising risk.

Table 5.1

Year/s	Transitional event	Prevalent social attitude	Professional involvement
Medieval	Poor Law Act	Childhood denied; caring problems caused by moral failings; communality of life	
17th century		Children's inherent badness needed disciplining	
18th century		Family life more private	
19th century		Influence of private philanthropists	Child maltreatment observed but denied
1833	Factory Act	Children's need for protection recognised	
1834	Poor Law Reform Act	Family's moral failings needed correction	
1872	Infant Life Protection Act	Children recognised as individuals	
1880	Education Act	Children's developmental needs recognised	
1889	Prevention of Cruelty to and Protection of Children Act	Child cruelty considered a crime	Emphasis on prosecution of perpetrators
1889	Poor Law (Children) Act		Poor Law Guardians for children introduced
1890			NSPCC established
1904	Prevention of Cruelty to Children Act		Local authority empowered to remove child from their family
1908	Children Act		Special courts for juveniles
1920s			Child's emotional life acknowledged; child guidance clinics established
1933	Children and Young Persons Act	Welfare of the child emphasised	Care proceedings introduced
1940s			Child abuse 'rediscovered'
1945	Denis O'Neill inquiry		
1948	Children Act	Children's best interest paramount	Attempts to keep families intact
1950s		Sanctity of the biological family	Attachment theory elaborated
1963	Guardianship of Infants Act		Local authorities to undertake preventative work to keep families intact
1969	Children and Young Persons Act		Local authorities given clear powers to remove children from their families
1970			At Risk Registers and Area Review Committees introduced
1974	Maria Colwell inquiry	Blood-tie re-evaluated; media interest in child abuse	
1975	Children Act		Permanency policy
1980s			Child sexual abuse 'rediscovered'
1985	Jasmine Beckford inquiry		
1987	Kimberley Carlile inquiry		
1988	Cleveland inquiry	Media interest in child sexual abuse	
1989	Children Act	Parental responsibility emphasised; ambivalence to family vs state	

Having read the information in Table 5.1, you might find it useful to read further about past attitudes and legislation that you are not familiar with. This will help you build a fuller understanding of the historical development of child protection.

Every Child Matters: Change for Children
www.everychildmatters.gov.uk
Chapter 3 of *Child Abuse* by Carver (1980) is an accessible text about past legislation, although you should bear in mind that it was published before the Children Act 1989 came into being.
Child Abuse: A Study of Inquiry Reports 1980–1989 (Department of Health, 1991) provides a summary of some of the most high-profile cases during the 1980s.

Risk of abuse

Children can be at risk from abuse both from within and outside their own family. Although the media frequently publicise concern about the abuse and 'grooming' of children by **paedophiles**, the incidence of abuse and the potential for its occurrence are in fact higher within families for a number of reasons. Abuse can also take place within care settings, and practitioners should work to the good practice guidelines set out by each setting where they work.

Refer to page 242 for predisposing factors and to page 264 for guidance for staff on safe working practice.

Risk of exploitation

Today's technological environment, with its greater use of communication systems such as the Internet, has given rise to a new potential source of abuse. Pornography and uninvited contact from persons with abusive intentions can be a real threat to children's safety. Most computer software includes the facility to block certain websites and contacts. This is often called the 'parental controls'. Any early years setting or provision for children of any age should have these controls in place.

Another cause of concern is the media's increased use of highly graphic images; again, it is important to monitor what the children in your care have access to.

Family functioning

Families are a central force in society and, for most of us, a positive influence on our lives. They provide much of our learning, emotional support and physical and health care needs. For some people, however, the family can be a source of violence, crime, neglect and abuse, and these are the families that are most often known to local authority social services departments.

Family types and partnership arrangements

Family structures include:

- the nuclear family – a heterosexual couple and their children
- the extended family – more than one generation of the nuclear family living together or very close by
- the lone-parent family – a single parent (most often the mother) plus the children
- the reconstituted family – adults forming new relationships, which include their children from a previous relationship.

When parents live apart, the access agreements are often complex. At times, for a variety of reasons, often relating to concern about the safety and well-being of the child, supervised access is the only situation in which a parent sees the child.

remember
Abuse occurs in all social classes, in all family structures and within all cultures.

The changing face of the family

As the structure of families continues to develop, with reconstituted families now being openly headed by heterosexual, lesbian or gay couples, the changing face of the family should be recognised. These 'new' families continue to fight prejudice in some areas of society, seeking to gain equal rights with 'traditional' families.

A useful discussion on the definition and diversity of the modern family can be found in *Social Policy and Welfare* by Walsh *et al.* (2000).

Social disadvantage

The **cycle of disadvantage** increases the pressure on families and often lowers self-esteem as financial problems increase. This in turn can make it far harder for parents to focus on their child's needs, leading to **emotional abuse** and neglect, and to maintain self-control, leading to more physical forms of abuse.

You may find it useful to refer to Unit 6, page 287 for the cycle of disadvantage.

Different concepts of discipline

Families and cultures have different ideas about what is a suitable form of discipline for their children. In some, discipline is left to the father, as he is seen as having the most power within the family group. Think about situations where discipline is left to the father in a family and what message this is likely to give to children and how it might confuse them.

Children often attend a variety of care settings, and differences in settings' expectations can cause confusion and lack of understanding as to what constitutes unwanted behaviour and how it should be managed.

A consistent approach to discipline, promoting adherence to clear boundaries, will provide children with the greatest level of security.

Cultural variations

remember

It is important to consider cultural differences and practices before jumping to conclusions about a situation that raises concerns for you.

Terminology varies and the meaning given to the word 'beat' in one culture is not the same as in another. Whatever your views on smacking children, if a child told you that their father 'beat them last night' what image would this conjure in your mind? In British culture, most people would immediately think of forceful, heavy-handed hitting. In Caribbean culture, however, the term 'beat' is used in place of 'smack' and means the same. The difference in understanding here could be crucial.

Some cultural practices, which are considered a normal part of life or a rite of passage, are considered to be acts of abuse in others. A well-documented example is that of female circumcision, which is common in those African cultures where it is seen as necessary so that a bride can be presented 'unblemished' to her groom on their wedding day. Western societies condemn the practice, considering it to be barbaric; it has been illegal in the UK since 1985, but it is suspected that the practice still continues, either covertly or by sending young girls on a 'cultural' visit back to their family's country of origin. As a result of the genital mutilation, many of the girls suffer constant pain and experience problems with menstruation, urination and childbirth in later years. Anyone caught perpetrating female circumcision in the UK faces prosecution.

Pressures on some cultures regarding what is acceptable 'behaviour' prior to marriage can also have an impact on a child's or young adult's ability to disclose the abuse they have suffered.

case study 5.1 Sophie and Sungita

Sophie is 14 years old and has been sexually abused by her uncle since she was nine. She has recently disclosed the abuse to a trusted adult and is now being supported by her parents in bringing charges against her uncle.

Sungita is also 14 and has also been sexually abused by her uncle since she was nine. She is trying to raise the courage to disclose her abuse to her family. Sungita's family culture considers sexual contact before marriage for girls to be the ultimate disgrace for a family, and any girl known to have lost her virginity before marriage is disowned by both her family and the community.

activity
GROUP WORK

1 Clearly, both girls have suffered from the physical abuse but what extra pressure do you think Sungita faces as she considers disclosing?

2 Find out what support networks there are in your area for young people such as Sophie and Sungita.

For an in-depth look at the particular issues faced by children in minority cultures who are abused, refer to *Racism and Child Protection* by Jackson (1996).

remember Abusers can be male or female, of any age, culture, social class or religion.

Abuse within families

It should be remembered that, in most cases, the abuse of a child is by someone they know well, often a parent. Sadly, children too at times abuse, as discussed below.

It is equally important to remember that abuse takes place across all cultures, at all levels within society and within all religions.

Predisposing factors

It is not easy to predict when a child may be at risk of abuse, but research has suggested that some factors may predispose individuals to abuse. These **predisposing factors** can be related to the past and current experiences of parents and to the child or children in a family unit.

Predisposing factors in relation to the abuser

These include:

- parents who may not have had good role models to follow themselves
  - this may affect their parenting practices and ability to manage their children's behaviour in a positive manner
  - they may have lowered self-esteem and a poor image of themselves
  - they may also have been abused themselves as a child
- parents who may be very young or immature
  - they may not have as yet developed the skills to cope with difficult circumstances
  - they may have unrealistic expectations of their child's rate of development
- separation at birth through maternal illness, which can result in disruption of the bonding process
- lack of support
  - from a partner resulting in lone parenting
  - from extended family
  - through discord within a reconstituted family
- illness either of parent or child
  - parental illness may result in inability to care for the child appropriately
  - illness in the child may cause resentment in the parent
  - mental illness may prevent the adult fully recognising their responsibilities
- bereavement – any form of stress can lessen a person's ability to cope, particularly bereavement
- learning difficulties – parents whose understanding is limited may make inappropriate decisions and cause suffering unintentionally
- social problems, such as:
  - unemployment, poverty and housing problems, which can cause high levels of stress
  - substance and alcohol abuse, which cloud judgement and alter the adult's priorities.

Predisposing factors in relation to the child

Such predisposing factors might include:

- prematurity
  - caring for such a vulnerable child increases a new parent's anxiety
  - premature and low-birth-weight babies are more difficult for parents to learn to care for
  - sometimes a child is born before the parents have fully prepared themselves
  - separation at birth may affect the bonding process
- disability
  - difficulty in feeding and general caring routines can cause resentment

remember The cycle of abuse is not automatic – many people who have been abused as children become caring and loving adults and parents.

- at times, parents feel that they have lost the child they thought they would have and need help in learning how to care for, and enjoy, their disabled child
- children with communication difficulties are less likely to be able to seek help and can be more vulnerable.

The young abuser

From time to time, we hear reports in the media of abuse or murder perpetrated on a child by another child, and this is met with shock and horror by society. A high proportion of these children have been abused themselves or have had less-than-ideal parenting and need help in addressing their behaviour. Children abuse sexually, physically and by bullying. Many people find it hard to believe that **sexual abuse** can take place between children, but, as with all other aspects of development, children learn by example.

Well-known cases of children abusing and/or murdering other children include the Mary Bell case in Newcastle in 1968, and the Robert Thompson and Jon Venables case in Liverpool in the 1990s. These are well documented and raise serious questions about how children are both supported and failed by society. A more recent case occurred in 2005, when a 12-year-old girl was arrested by police on suspicion of trying to murder a five-year-old boy. The boy was found alone and in a state of distress with ligature-type marks around his neck, leading police to suspect that some attempt to hang him had been made. Several other children were also arrested but released without charge.

In *Cries Unheard: The Story of Mary Bell,* Sereny (1999) charts the 'terribly damaged life' of Mary Bell and follows her years of trial, detention and imprisonment. The book raises serious questions about the roles of adults and of society in supporting children.

Types of abuse

Across society (and indeed across the world), there are varying definitions of what constitutes discipline and what constitutes abuse. Some people consider that smacking a child is a harmless and effective form of managing unwanted behaviour, but others regard smacking as an offence. In most parts of the UK, however, parents are still able, by law, to smack their own child with a bare hand, but are not allowed to use any kind of implement. This continues to be a controversial issue. In Scotland, recent legislation has now declared it an offence to hit any child under the age of three and any child of any age around the head. This is seen by many childcare organisations as a starting point for greater legal protection of young children.

Early years professionals consider smacking to be both unacceptable and ineffective, and early years trainers promote the use of a range of alternative strategies in the management of children's behaviour, including the establishment of clear boundaries. In day-care settings, physical punishment of children is not allowed in any form, but, controversially, the old *National Standards for Under-eights Care for Childminders* (reference criteria 11.4–11.6) did allow children to be smacked by a childminder with the written agreement of parents. This has now been amended (revised Standards 11.4 and 11.5).

The organisation **EPOCH** campaigns for changes to be made to the law in relation to the physical punishment of children.

If asked to define the term 'abuse', you would most likely respond by referring to the four main categories: physical abuse, neglect, sexual abuse and emotional abuse. As a general summary, it can be said that abuse of a child occurs when any avoidable act, or avoidable failure to act, adversely affects the physical, mental or emotional well-being of a child.

Table 5.2 Types of abuse

Physical abuse	Physical neglect	Bullying
Emotional abuse	Emotional neglect	Harassment
Intellectual abuse	Intellectual neglect	
Social abuse		
Sexual abuse		

Professional Practice

- You should be aware that abuse can be both deliberate and non-deliberate. The physical effects on the child are the same, but at times the intentions and understanding, or limitations in understanding, of the parent/abuser will be taken into account when a situation is investigated.
- Cultural practices should be understood and taken into consideration, particularly with regard to the terminology used within some cultures.

Defining abuse

Kempe (1992) defined the four main categories of abuse. His definitions are useful, although each local authority will have its own definition set out in the literature given to early years providers; you may also find it useful to refer to these. Kempe's definitions are shown below.

Physical abuse
'Physical abuse implies physically harmful action directed against a child; it is usually defined by any inflicted injury such as bruises, burns, head injuries, fractures, abdominal injuries, or poisoning.'

Neglect
'Neglect can be a very insidious form of maltreatment, which can go on for a long time. It implies the failure of the parents to act properly in safeguarding the health, safety and well-being of the child. It includes nutritional neglect, failure to provide care or to protect a child from physical and social danger.'

Sexual abuse
'Sexual abuse is defined as the involvement of dependent, developmentally immature children and adolescents in sexual activities they do not truly comprehend, to which they are unable to give informed consent, or that violate the social taboos of family roles.'

Emotional abuse
'Emotional abuse includes a child being continually terrorised, berated, or rejected.'

For definitions of bullying and harassment, refer to page 248.

remember Researching the definitions drawn up by the authority in which you work or study will help you consolidate your understanding.

Indicators of abuse

This section sets out a range of **indicators of abuse**, that is, signs that could alert professionals that a child may be suffering abuse or may be at risk of being abused. It is important that the indicators are not used in isolation – they should be noted carefully and any concerns considered, together with recent observations of the child and discussions with management or senior staff, with decisions for further investigation being made where applicable. Naturally, there can be times when one specific sign or injury is considered to be significant on its own, in which case immediate action will need to be taken.

Accidental injuries

It is important to remember that all children injure themselves from time to time, and it is common to see toddlers with blackened eyes or bruised foreheads as they tend to fall over or run into furniture such as coffee tables. Older children learn to ride bikes and climb trees and fences, tumbling in the process and scraping knees, grazing legs and arms, and on occasions suffering more serious injuries, such as concussion and bone fractures. It is important that you consider the age and stage of development of the child, when you make a judgement as to whether an injury is a cause for concern, and take into account the circumstances of the injury.

Although children regularly have physical marks following accidental falls, the site of the injury can be the easiest indicator of the need for concern.

Physical abuse

Possible indicators of physical abuse

- bruises on the soft areas of the body (inner arms, thighs, buttocks)
- bald patches
- unexplained injuries, including bruises, burns, bone fractures
- bite marks – remember that a dog bite will look very different from a human bite and that an adult's bite mark is considerably larger than a child's

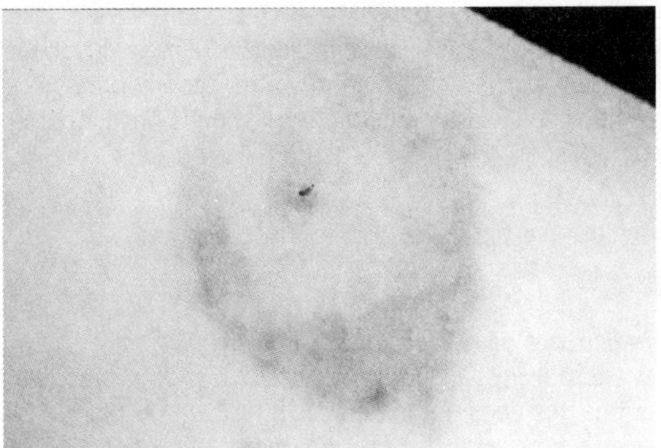
Fig 5.1 How do you think this bruise was caused?

- finger-tip bruising on the face – this could be caused by forced bottle feeding of a baby or young toddler
- unusually shaped bruises – consider how a child might show non-accidental bruising other than by being hit with an implement such as a stick or a lash
- thumb and finger-tip bruises each side of the torso, which can indicate that a child has been shaken or held forcefully
- pin-point haemorrhage in the ears, which can be caused by shaking
- scald and burn marks – an accidental scald (caused, for example, if a child pulls over a kettle of boiling water) will have different signs from a scald caused, say, by a cup of tea deliberately thrown
- evenly spaced scald marks which can indicate the deliberate placing of hands or feet in hot water – these will often have the appearance of socks or glove marks
- repeated black eyes or injuries which should start to raise alarm bells.

Fig 5.2 Severe scalding on a baby and a cigarette burn

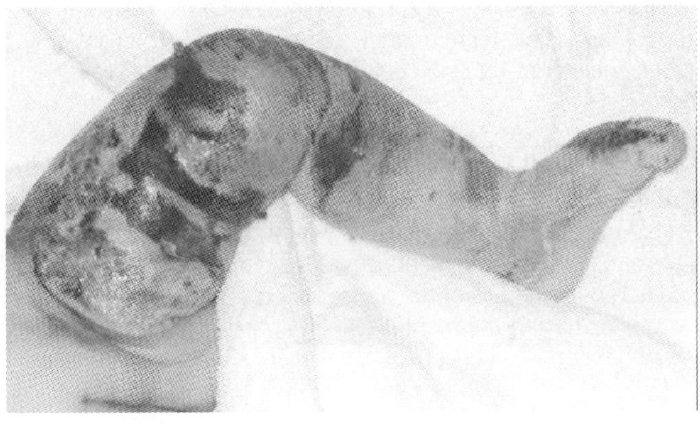

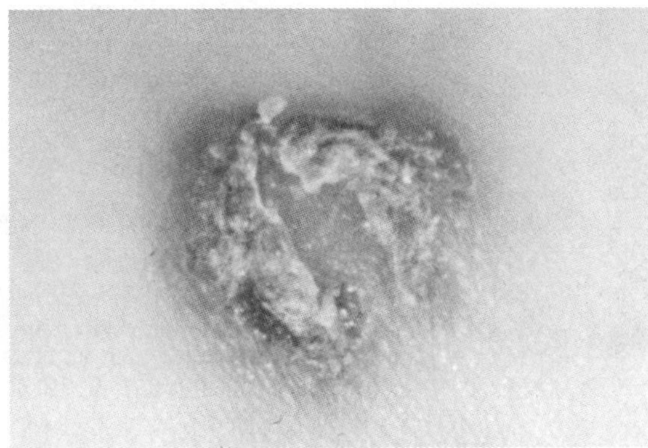

Professional Practice

At times innocent injuries can be misinterpreted. Examples include:

- the condition impetigo, which can be mistaken for cigarette burns
- the 'hidden' condition osteogenesis imperfecta (brittle bone disease or Lobstein's syndrome), which can be mistaken for non-accidental fractures.

Behaviour

Physically abused children may display changes in behaviour, which can vary considerably from child to child. One child may become withdrawn and quiet, while another may become aggressive towards others. Children may show reluctance to go home or to be with particular adults, parents or carers. They may show physical signs of discomfort such as difficulty in moving when dressing, or during changing or physical activity.

As children grow older, their bodies are less often seen by the adults who care for them. Be aware of a child who wishes to remain covered up or who always arrives at the setting in long-sleeved tops and long trousers, whatever the weather.

> **remember**
> The explanation of how and when a bruise occurred can at times be important.

Bruises

Bruises are damaged blood vessels where the skin has not been broken. They develop in stages, appearing purple or blue shortly after the injury has occurred. Gradually, they become yellow and they usually disappear within 10 to 12 days. Therefore, a yellowing bruise has not 'just appeared'. Similarly, a dark-blue bruise is unlikely to have been there for more than a couple of days.

Bruises often appear darker on dark-skinned children.

Neglect

Possible indicators of neglect

Neglect can stem from parental ignorance and lack of practical childcare skills. It is not always intentional, but this does not lessen the physical effects for a child. A neglected child may:

- be underweight, possibly emaciated
- be hungry, and may scavenge for food or wolf food down at mealtimes
- be dirty and unkempt, with poor personal hygiene
- suffer frequent minor injuries
- appear to have no regular bedtime pattern – the child may indicate that they watch late, and unsuitable, television programmes
- suffer from frequent minor infections, such as colds and coughs, due to inappropriate nutrition, and subsequently become run-down
- lack experience of common childhood activities such as looking at books and using creative materials
- be left unsupervised on a regular basis – the child may indicate this in conversation
- lack parental interest in the child's progress in school or at nursery
- display self-comforting behaviours, such as rocking and head banging.

Behaviour

Neglected children often seem constantly tired from going to bed when they choose. They may display lack of concentration and lack of attention due to tiredness. Often, the child may be hungry and steal food. Frequent, excessive masturbation for self-comfort is common. Neglected children frequently display low self-esteem and low self-confidence. They are likely to be fearful of new situations and can at times be over-friendly to any adult available, indicating their need for attention.

Sexual abuse

Possible indicators of sexual abuse

Sexual abuse often goes undetected; research has shown that two-thirds of all children who are sexually abused do not tell anyone about their experiences. These children may suffer long-term physical harm (depending on the nature of the abuse suffered, there may be medical effects in adulthood), as well as having the mental scars that abuse brings generally. It is more often the child's behaviour that raises concerns, rather than actual physical signs.

Sexual abuse includes:

- the use of pornographic material – showing it to children or involving children in the making of it
- **incest** – an incestuous relationship is one which involves sexual activity between family members who are too closely related to be able to marry, for example between father and daughter, or brother and sister.

Physical signs of sexual abuse

- bruises on areas such as the inner thighs and genital areas
- soreness in anal or vaginal areas, or in the throat
- vaginal discharge in girls
- swollen penis or discharge in boys
- sexually transmitted diseases and urine infections, sometimes found if medical examination takes place
- distress when having nappy changed (babies and toddlers)
- difficulty or reluctance to pass urine or faeces, often resulting in constipation

- difficulty in walking, and in standing up or sitting down
- pain on movement generally
- poor personal hygiene
- obsession with sexual matters
- having unexplained sums of money on a regular basis (older children).

Behaviour

A sexually abused child may cling on to a parent or trusted carer and may avoid certain individuals or show distress at being left with certain adults. The child's development may regress, for example bed-wetting may start again when the child has previously been dry at night. The child may become withdrawn and appear saddened, and concentration may suffer leading to poor progress at school.

> **remember** Not all cases of anorexia or bulimia are linked to abuse. Such cases do, however, need to be investigated and the appropriate support offered.

Some children display sexually inappropriate behaviour towards adults. Also, their drawings may not fit with what is expected for their developmental stage; they may include explicit body parts, for example an erect penis.

As children get older, they may want to talk about their 'friend's' problems and hint at secrets. Abused children tend to isolate themselves from their peers and do not form relationships which would involve inviting friends home. Eating disorders such as anorexia or bulimia are common, as is frequently running away from home. Poor hygiene or obsessive cleanliness can be present.

Paedophiles

Sometimes abusers are known as paedophiles. The true definition of a paedophile is a person who is sexually attracted to children. However, the term is commonly used to describe adults who sexually abuse children. These abusers come from all walks of life and are often considered to be pillars of the community, holding posts of responsibility and trust and taking on roles that will bring them into regular contact with children, such as scout group leaders, sports coaches, youth workers and teachers.

> **remember** If an individual person begins to be closely involved with a child or family other than their own it may be appropriate for the situation to be monitored closely.

Paedophiles spend a great deal of time and effort setting the scene for their abuse, often building up relationships with a child's parent or parents, increasing their level of trust. Children of single mothers can be particularly vulnerable as the mother may be pleased to encourage a male role model for her children, particularly if they do not see their father. This process is known as 'grooming'.

As the paedophile gains the trust of the family, closer physical contact develops, gradually moving towards sexual contact or involvement in pornography. Intimidation, bribes and threats often follow, in return for promises that the activity is kept secret.

As reported in Elliott (1992), a study by Abel showed that a small group of compulsive child abusers can create a huge number of victims and that the victims are either silent about what happened or are not believed if they tell.

Refer to the Nelson Thornes website and read about Abel's study of 232 'first-time' abusers.
www.nelsonthornes.com/btec

Paedophiles are devious people and many operate for many years before being caught. They are skilful in identifying vulnerable children, such as a child who:

- is a loner
- lacks confidence
- is very trusting of adults
- craves love and attention.

> **remember** Motivation + Opportunity = Abuse

Paedophiles have the motivation to abuse. They seek opportunities to abuse the children they have contact with. Early years staff can play a part in reducing their opportunities.

Emotional abuse

Possible indicators of emotional abuse

Emotional abuse accompanies all other experiences of abuse. Children quite understandably become bewildered and confused when a person they love or trust begins to abuse them. Emotional abuse is rarely cited as the main type of abuse in official reports; the term is used if emotional abuse is clearly defined as the only form of abuse suffered by the child concerned. This would perhaps occur if a child was cared for physically but was denied love and was constantly rejected, or put down and ridiculed, by the abuser.

These children may:

- have low self-esteem and lack confidence
- have a poor concentration span
- show developmental delay
- be fearful of new situations
- be concerned about their parents being contacted
- respond inappropriately to situations
- have speech disorders
- find it hard to build social relationships with their peers
- use self-mutilating behaviours, such as head-banging and pulling out their hair.

remember Practitioners need to pay careful attention to body language, physical signs of discomfort, and any unusual responses to individuals, whether that be parents, staff or other adults.

Behaviour

Emotionally abused children learn from their abuser that they are not of value, and their feelings of self-worth can disappear. For example, Helen felt that her mother only liked the children that she supported through her charity work; these children were emaciated and deprived, so Helen began to dress in her oldest clothes to become more desirable to her mother and gain her love (Doyle, 1990).

Recognition of abuse where children cannot communicate

When children are unable to communicate, it is harder for them to let others know if they are suffering in any way, for example if they are in pain, are hungry or generally feel unwell. Clearly, this also applies to situations involving abuse. A child who cannot tell can be a useful target for the abuser.

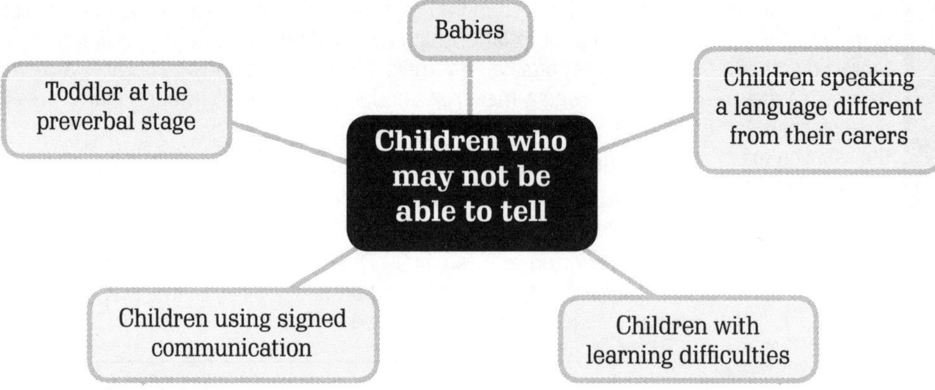

Fig 5.3 Children who may not be able to tell

Bullying and harassment

Bullying and harassment can take a number of forms; the common factor is that they cause lasting harm to children and young people, leading to self-harm and to suicide in some cases. Bullying and harassment encompass a wide range of abusive behaviours such as physical and verbal hostility and aggression; extortion of goods or property; isolating or excluding a child from peer groups; discriminatory behaviours; and many other offensive verbal and physical acts. Verbal teasing and 'joking about' quickly get out of hand. Practitioners should be aware when children use these strategies and should step in to explain the effect they may be having and, most importantly, to reassure and support the victim. Bullying and harassment are serious problems in the lives of many children and should be dealt with quickly. The bully will often have problems of their own which have led them to bully others, and strategies to support them in changing their behaviour also need to be in place. In preschool environments, bullying is only occasionally seen, but the possibility should not automatically be disregarded.

Refer to Chapter 11 of *Good Practice in Child Protection* by Hobart and Frankel (2005) for more information.

Behaviour that may indicate that a child is being bullied

- school or nursery refusal
- frequent complaints of general malaise early in the day
- returning home with clothes in disarray or torn; appearing to be hungry if food has been stolen
- showing signs of emotional distress
- disturbed sleep patterns
- starting to behave in an aggressive manner to others.

Consequences of abuse

No child remains unscarred by the abuse they suffer, but some are able, or are enabled, to deal with some of what they experience and move on to lead fulfilling and positive lives. For those who are not so lucky, the future can be far bleaker.

The consequences of childhood abuse can be both short and long term, affecting the choices that the children make as adults and the levels of achievement they reach, and limiting their feelings of self-worth.

The spidergrams below summarise the **short-term consequences of abuse** and the **long-term consequences of abuse**. Bear in mind that the effects on individual children will vary greatly and not all consequences will be experienced by all children.

Fig 5.4 Short-term consequences of abuse

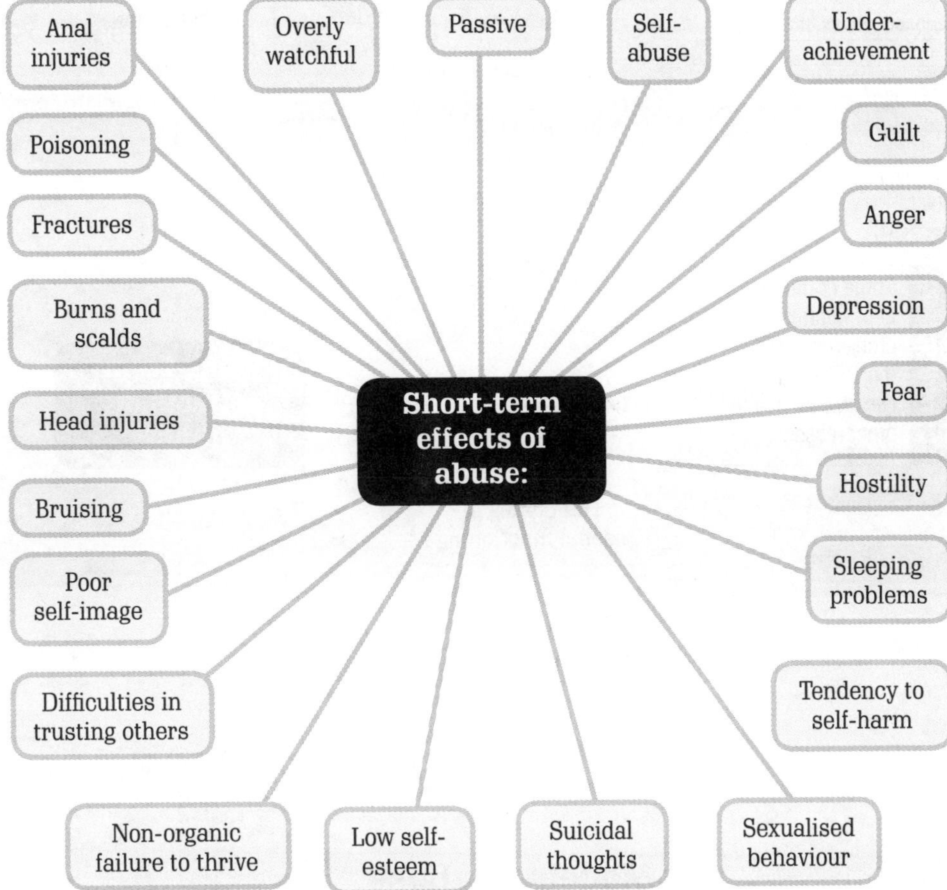

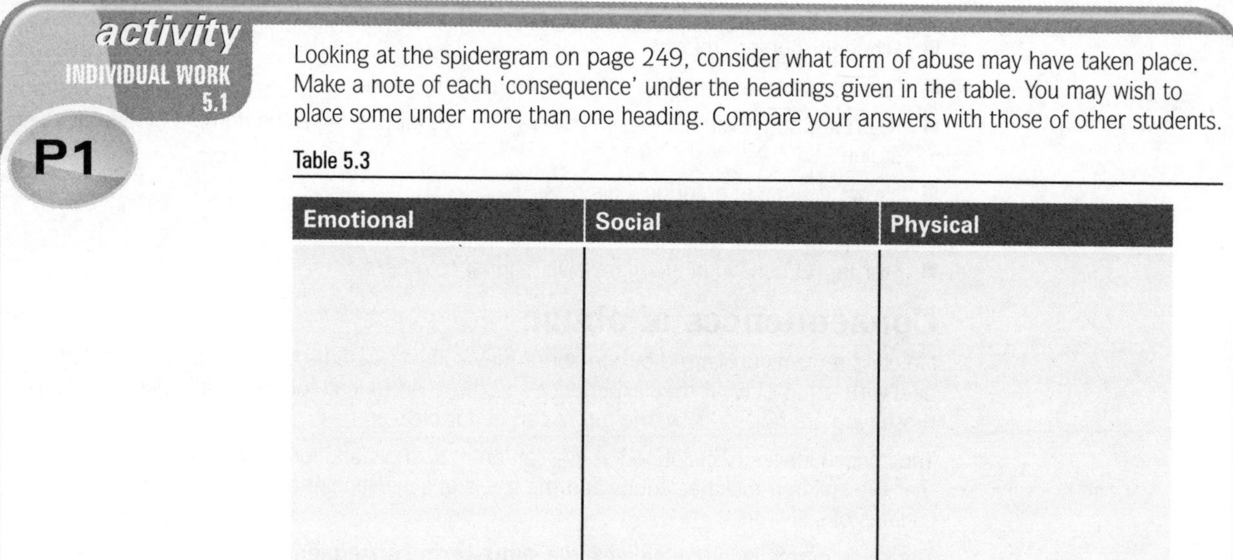

activity
INDIVIDUAL WORK 5.1

P1

Looking at the spidergram on page 249, consider what form of abuse may have taken place. Make a note of each 'consequence' under the headings given in the table. You may wish to place some under more than one heading. Compare your answers with those of other students.

Table 5.3

Emotional	Social	Physical

Fig 5.5 Long-term consequences of abuse

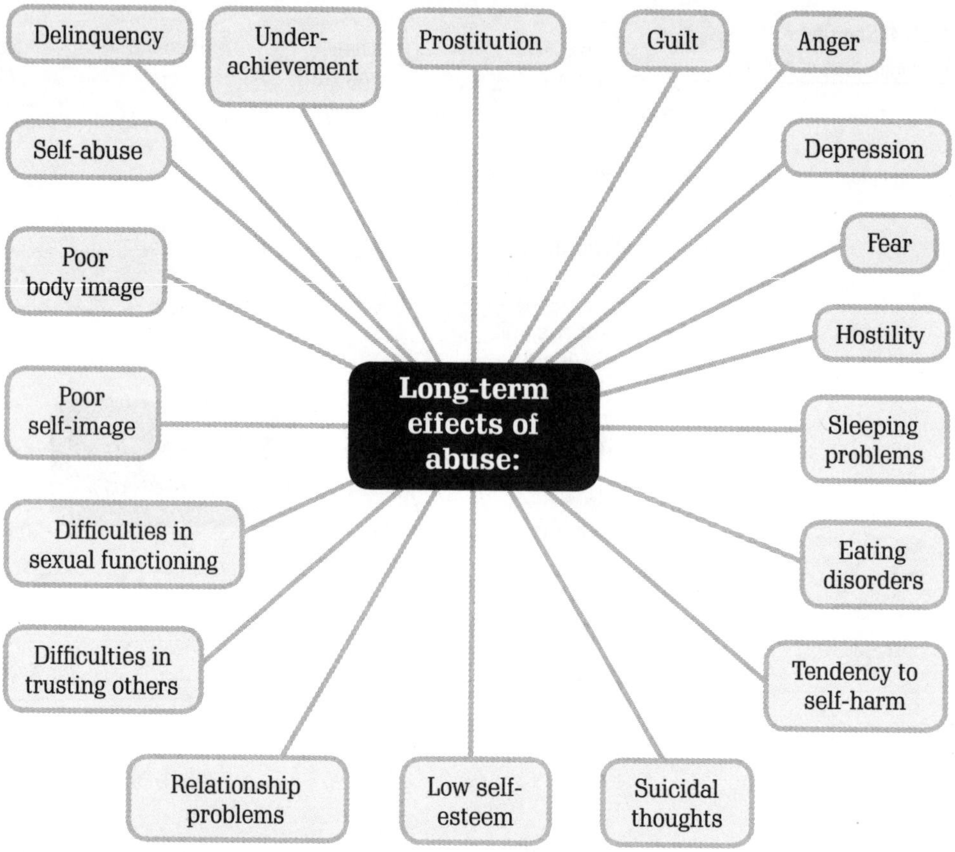

Long-term effects of abuse:
Delinquency
Under-achievement
Prostitution
Guilt
Anger
Self-abuse
Depression
Poor body image
Fear
Hostility
Poor self-image
Sleeping problems
Difficulties in sexual functioning
Eating disorders
Difficulties in trusting others
Tendency to self-harm
Relationship problems
Low self-esteem
Suicidal thoughts

remember Some of the behaviours and problems noted in the spidergrams can also be due to other reasons.

Models of abuse

Parental experience can influence the way in which children are treated. The family's circumstances, both financial and environmental, and any medical complications can also have an effect.

There are different theories as to why abuse occurs; the four main models of abuse are:

- the **medical model**
- the **sociological model**
- the **psychological model**
- the **feminist model**.

The medical model of abuse

The medical model sees the abuse as an underlying physiological condition, i.e. an illness which needs a cure. In some cases, there is thought to be the potential for an ongoing cycle of abuse: the abusive parents' ability to parent appropriately may have been adversely affected by poor attachments with the main carers in their lives, and this pattern may be repeated with their own children. With regard to sexual abuse, there are medical treatments to reduce arousal, which are sometimes successful if used together with more generalised behavioural approaches.

The sociological model of abuse

The sociological model links abuse to the social environment, the support structures that are either available or absent and the family make-up (extended, reconstituted, and so on). This model includes poverty, unemployment and lack of suitable housing as potential reasons for abusive situations and relationships to develop.

The psychological model of abuse

The psychological model links abuse to the abuser's previous experience. It includes the abuser's own upbringing, the role models the abuser had, the effects of the bonding process with both the abuser's parents and now with the abuser's children, and any problems regarding attachment to the abuser's main carer. It also recognises that the abuser's ability to understand the care needs of an individual child may be a factor.

The feminist model of abuse

The feminist model looks at the role of women and how they have always been perceived as carers and, in particular, as the main carer of the family. The model focuses on how women and children are offended against and ignores the offences that are perpetrated by some women, both alone and in conjunction with men. Many people find it inconceivable that a woman, for whom maternal instincts are seen as inherent, could harm a child, but this is a dangerous misconception. As long as this view is held, society will continue to deny the full potential of women to injure, damage and exploit the children that they give birth to or care for.

Factitious illness (this was formerly known as Munchausen syndrome by proxy (MSBP))

Factitious illness is relatively uncommon but is an example of abuse that is mostly carried out by women. It is often referred to as 'factitious illness by proxy'. It involves parents (most often mothers) fabricating illness in their child and seeking repetitive medical investigations, often moving from doctor to doctor. This can result in the child's being subjected to unnecessary medical intervention and prolonged periods of monitoring and even hospitalisation.

The adult perpetrator of factitious illness abuse tries to mirror in the child the symptoms of various conditions. The abuser often has a degree of knowledge of medical matters. Examples of falsely creating symptoms include:

- altering temperature charts or warming up thermometers
- giving a child laxatives to instigate diarrhoea
- adding blood (often their own) to a child's urine sample
- inducing vomiting by giving the child salt or an emetic (vomit-causing) drug
- simulating apnoea attacks (temporary inability to breathe) by partial suffocation.

The syndrome is a psychological condition in which adults seek attention themselves, or want to be seen as a good, caring parent. It can be very difficult to detect, and the child usually suffers for a considerable length of time before a diagnosis is reached. In many cases, other children in the family will have suffered abuse of some kind too.

On rare occasions, children have been deliberately made ill (or more seriously ill) by a nurse on the ward in which they are already being treated. A well-documented case illustrating factitious illness by a medical professional is the investigation and subsequent conviction of Beverley Allitt, a nurse on a children's ward. Reading reports on this case will help consolidate your understanding of how subtle the approach of such perpetrators can be.

Useful further sources of information on the models of abuse can be found in *Female Sexual Abuse of Children: The Ultimate Taboo* by Elliott (1993) and *Child Abuse and Child Abusers* edited by Waterhouse (1993).

A graphic account of factitious illness can be found in the autobiography *Sickened* by Julie Gregory (2003).

In groups of four, take turns to explain the four main 'models of abuse' to each other in your own words. Discuss the similarities and differences between each model, and, using the media or the Internet, find examples to illustrate your understanding.

activity
INDIVIDUAL WORK
5.3
D1

Using the examples found in the above activity, evaluate the extent to which you feel that each of the main models of abuse has impacted on each case.

Understand the requirements of legislation, regulation and codes of practice for safeguarding and protecting children

Legislation/legal framework

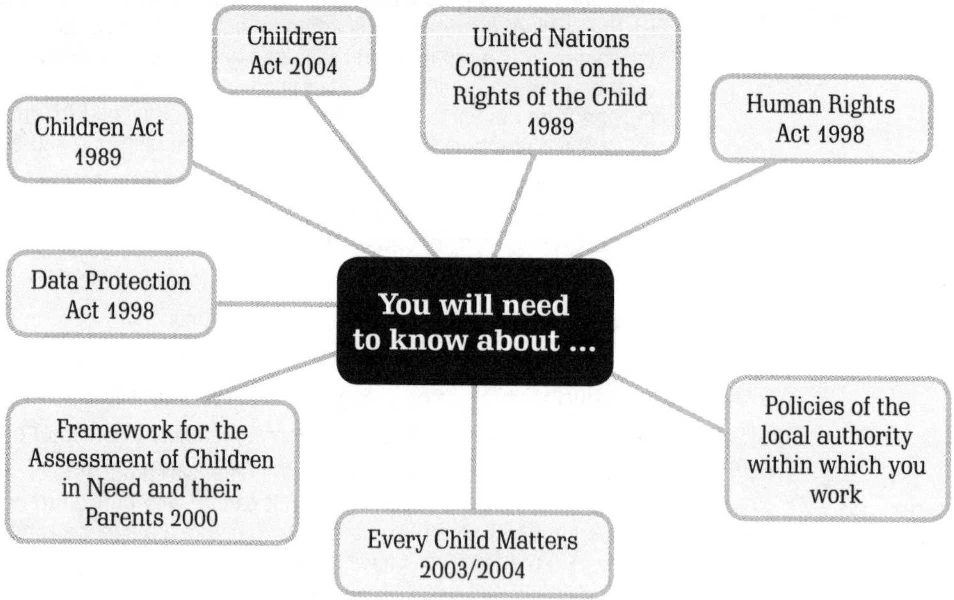

Fig 5.6 You will need to know about ...

Children Act 1989, 2004

The main aspects of law affecting child protection were set out in the Children Act 1989, which brought together all the legislation relevant to children; it has subsequently been updated by the Children Act 2004.

The implementation of the Children Act 1989 in October 1991 placed emphasis on parental responsibility, rather than parental rights. This responsibility for children refers to the 'collection of duties, rights and authority' which parents have regarding their child. Parental responsibility is automatically acquired by married couples and by unmarried mothers. Unmarried fathers can acquire it if they are made a legal guardian by the mother or by applying to the courts.

Where it is in the interests of a child, parental responsibility can be granted to other adults, such as grandparents, step-parents or the local authority when a **care order** or **emergency protection order** has been obtained. The responsibility would automatically end when the order ends, or in the case of step-parents, where responsibility is gained through a residency order, if that order ends.

The Children Act lays emphasis on parental responsibility continuing after the separation or divorce of the parents unless otherwise stated by a court of law.

The publication *Working Together under the Children Act 1989* (Department of Health, 1991) sets out clearly the procedures, roles and responsibilities of all those who may become involved in child protection cases.

Data Protection Act

The Data Protection Act 1998 covers the security and confidentiality of information held about individuals on paper and in computer-held records. One of the perceived tenets of the Act is that security of information is sacrosanct. In the case of the murder of Holly Wells and Jessica Chapman, police failure to share vital information about Ian Huntley was criticised. The Bichard Report (2004) confirmed that the Data Protection Act does not prevent information about a suspected sex offender being shared with the relevant authorities, but made recommendations about how information is stored and shared.

United Nations Convention on the Rights of the Child

Children have rights, and the United Nations Convention on the Rights of the Child, adopted by the United Nations in 1989, includes a range of rights directly relevant to child protection. For example:

- Article 3 – The best interests of the child should always be taken into account.
- Article 12 – The child's viewpoint should always be considered in conjunction with an assessment of the child's age and level of understanding.
- Article 16 – Children have the right to privacy.
- Article 19 – Children have a right to be looked after properly, and protected from violence and kept safe from harm.
- Article 37 – Children should not be punished cruelly.
- Article 39 – A child who has suffered ill treatment should be helped to recovery.

In *The Participation Rights of the Child*, Flekkøy and Kaufman (1997) offer a useful discussion of children's rights; Appendix 2 includes an 'unofficial' summary of the main provisions of the UN Convention on the Rights of the Child and is a helpful point of reference.

The Framework for the Assessment of Children in Need and their Families

This valuable document was published by the Department of Health in 2000 as a partner to *Working Together to Safeguard Children* (DfEE, 1999) and recommended that child protection services would benefit from a wider perspective on what the term 'children in need' constituted. The framework advocates:

- looking at children in need and their families from the viewpoint of their strengths as well as their weaknesses
- safeguarding children within a wider social framework that includes responding to their developmental needs
- a common assessment process shared by all professionals concerned with the child in need.

Fig 5.7 Assessment framework triangle

Chapter 4 in *Protecting Children: Working Together to Keep Children Safe* by Flynn and Starns (2004) gives a clear and comprehensive overview of the framework.

Every Child Matters 2003, 2004

The Laming Report (2003) into the death of Victoria Climbié resulted in the publication of a Green Paper entitled *Every Child Matters*. The circumstances involved in Victoria's death revealed a catalogue of missed opportunities on the part of social services, health services and the police to save her. The government response outlined in *Every Child Matters* was that the concept of safeguarding children should be embedded within a wider social context. Hobart and Frankel (2005) summarise the proposals as follows:

- statutory child-safeguarding boards to replace Area Child Protection Committees
- a Children's Commissioner for England
- the establishment of 150 Children's Trusts by 2006
- the amalgamation of children's services such as education, health and social services.

Local Safeguarding Children Boards

Under the Children Act 1989, each area was required to have a joint forum for developing, monitoring and reviewing child protection policies. This was the responsibility of what was then known as the Area Child Protection Committee (ACPC).

These ACPCs were made up of those persons who have contact with a child whose case comes before them, for example:

- social workers
- police officers
- medical practitioners
- community health team workers
- school teachers
- voluntary agencies.

An interagency approach to each case ensured that relevant information was passed on to all who need it. However, with the implementation of the recommendations of the Laming Report into the death of Victoria Climbié, the ACPCs were given a more statutory position and were replaced by **Local Safeguarding Children Boards (LSCBs)**, although the primary purpose remains largely the same.

Human Rights Act 1998

Refer to Unit 6, page 292, for discussion of the Human Rights Act.

Megan's law: its implication for human rights

In the state of New Jersey in the USA, a young girl named Megan was sexually abused and killed. Following her death, a campaign was successfully carried out to change the law regarding sex offenders. Courts in many states in the USA now have to inform local communities when a convicted sex offender moves into their area.

Many people have called for a similar law to be passed in the UK, claiming that it will improve the safety of all children. Others argue that it infringes the human rights of the offenders and will cause social unrest in communities, with the risk of vigilante-style ousting of the offenders and the wrongful identification of innocent people as abusers of children.

Sequence of events leading to registration on the child protection register or to a legal order being put in place

Referral

Investigations into cases of abuse or suspected abuse, or where there is a concern that a child may be at risk, are carried out following a referral. Referrals can be made to the police, social services departments or to the NSPCC. Anyone can make a referral, and the impetus to do so may result from disclosure by a child to the individual making the referral, or it may be made by the child's representative (early years settings and schools have a designated person who takes on this responsibility) or by a concerned individual or a group of people represented by the individual. Referrals are also made by neighbours, family members and concerned members of the public. It is always preferred if individuals identify themselves when making a referral, but referral procedures allow for anonymous referrals to be accepted and investigated as necessary.

It is a misconception that following a referral the 'authority' goes immediately to the family and takes away the child. This only happens on rare occasions when there has been a clear case of abuse and the child faces imminent risk of further abuse. Most cases go through a set procedure to establish if the concern is justified, to explore the concerns raised with all those who are in contact with the child, or who might have relevant information, and to establish the level of risk to the child. An example of a situation in which immediate action may be needed to remove the child to safety would be if physical violence is likely to increase following the referral being brought to the family's notice. If a child is not allowed to leave voluntarily, an emergency protection order can be obtained.

Child protection register

In the mid-1970s, **child protection registers** were set up within each local authority. The child protection register is a list of children considered to be 'at risk'. A child's name is put on the register if there is concern about the safety of that child or their family. An unborn baby can be placed on the register, if there is a known abuser in the family.

The register contains relevant information (see below) about the child, so that the child's situation can be monitored and appropriate action taken when necessary. The child's case and inclusion on the register is reviewed regularly.

A senior professional with a concern about a child can ask for a check to be made of the register for the name of that particular child or the family. These registers are now computerised and held centrally, enabling checking to be done quickly. The information is not readily given out, and professionals wishing to consult the registers have their details and authority to apply to the register checked before information is released to them.

Deregistration can take place when a child's case is reviewed, if it is thought appropriate. Deregistration can occur if:

- the original points that led to registration no longer apply
- the child reaches the age of majority (18) and is no longer termed a 'child'
- the child dies.

There are a variety of care and protection procedures, linked to specific legal orders, which may lead to a child being added to the child protection register. These are summarised below.

Table 5.4 The investigation procedure in cases of suspected child abuse

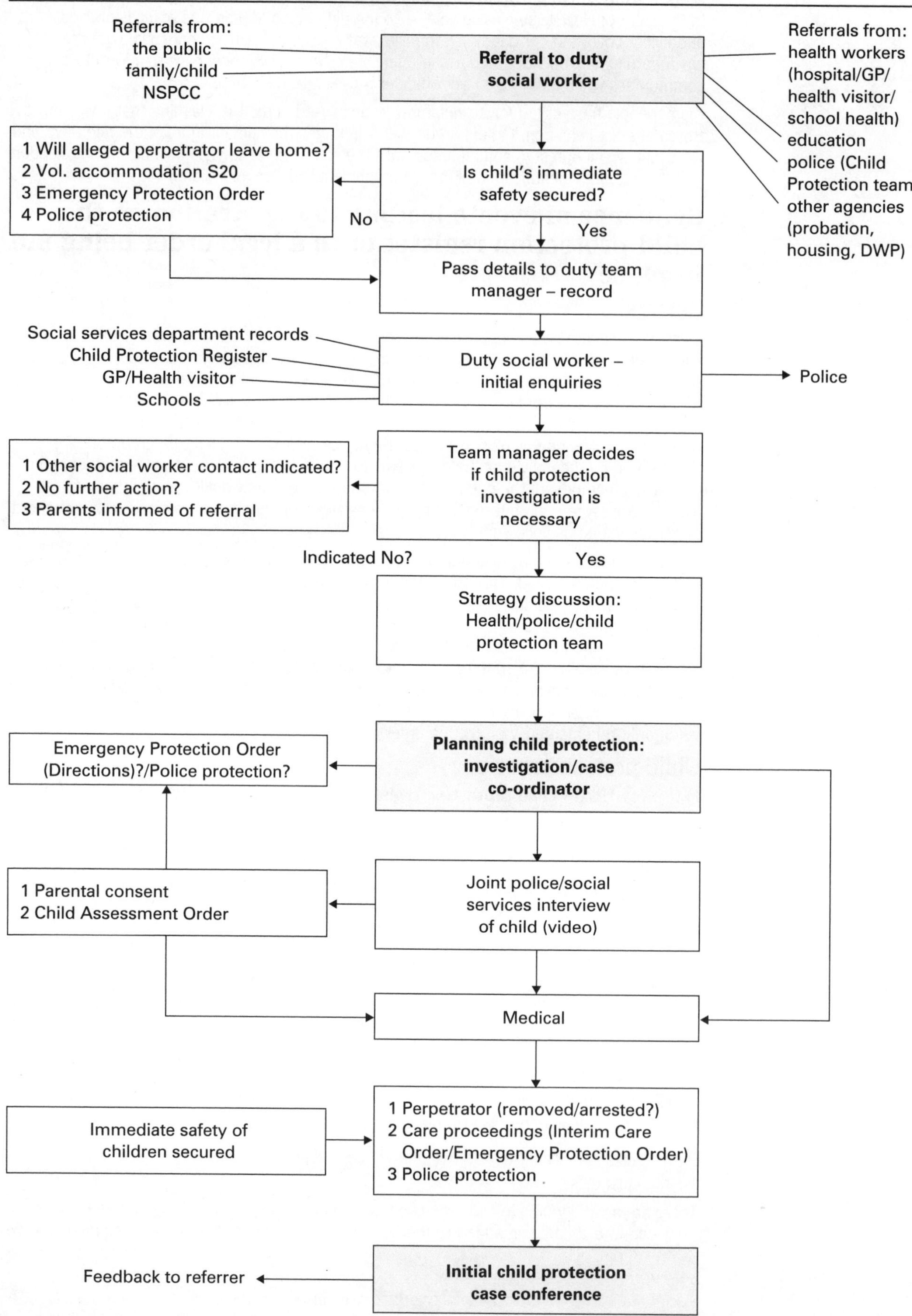

Details recorded on a child protection register

The information held on a child protection register includes:

- the child's name (and any other names the child is known by)
- the child's address, gender, date of birth, culture and any known religion
- the name and contact details of the child's GP
- the name and details of the main carer
- details of any school or other setting the child is known to attend
- if applicable, the name and details of any person who has parental responsibility for the child (if different from above)
- outline details of any court orders
- an outline of the alleged or confirmed abuse that has previously occurred
- the date the child was placed on the register
- the name and details of the professional responsible for the child's case (the child's key worker)
- the date of the proposed review of the child's situation.

Police protection

A child may be taken into **police protection** for up to 72 hours, during which time the applicant can apply for an emergency protection order (EPO, see below).

Child assessment order

A **child assessment order** can only be applied for through the courts by the local authority or the NSPCC. It is applied for when a child's parents are unlikely to give permission for an assessment of their child's state of health or level of development, when a concern is raised that a child is already suffering harm, or is likely to suffer significant harm. A child assessment order can only last for seven days.

The *Framework for the Assessment of Children in Need and their Families* (Department of Health, 2000) provides practice guidance for the assessment of children in need and recommends that all professionals working with the child are involved in the assessment process. It is also recommended that the assessment is made in collaboration with the child and family.

Emergency protection order

An application for this short-term order can be made by anyone and, if the order is granted, the applicant subsequently takes on parental responsibility for the child for the duration of the order. The order is usually issued for eight days, with one opportunity to extend the order for a further seven days. An applicant taking on parental responsibility 'must take (but may only take) action which is reasonably required to safeguard or promote the child's welfare' (*Children Act 1989, Guidance and Regulations*, Volume 2).

There may be an assessment of the child or decisions about how much contact or who has contact with the child.

An emergency protection order is always followed by an investigation by the local authority.

Recovery order

A **recovery order** is designed to provide a legal basis for recovering a child who is the subject of an emergency protection order, a care order or who is in police protection. It is used in situations where a child has been unlawfully taken away, or is being kept away from the person who has parental responsibility for the child. It also applies if the child runs away from the 'responsible' person or is considered to be missing.

The recovery order directs anyone who is in a position to do so to produce the child concerned, if asked to do so, or to give details of the child's whereabouts. The child will then be removed by the local authority. Police are authorised under the order to enter and search any premises as is necessary, using reasonable force.

Supervision order

On occasions, a child is placed under the supervision of the local authority (for up to one year) if it is not felt that there is sufficient co-operation from the parents to ensure that the child is fully protected. Although the child continues to live at home, the local authority has right of access to the child. The **supervision order** can be extended if deemed necessary.

Care order

As with the supervision order, a child continues to live at home under a care order. The local authority has shared responsibility for the protection of the child, and its decisions hold the greater balance of power in any disputes between the authority and the parents. At any time the authority can remove the child from the parents' home without the need to apply to the courts for any other order. The care order can last until the child reaches the age of majority (18 years old).

Setting procedures

Policy of the setting

Each setting caring for children of any age will have its own policy and procedural plan to ensure that children are kept safe. These documents will most likely include:

- what information is kept on an individual child and where (in line with the guidance of the Data Protection Act 1998)
- who has access to the information
- guidance on the security of records
- appropriate reporting procedures
- who co-ordinates any concerns within the setting, making any referrals as needed
- clear guidance regarding writing accurate and factual reports
- safe practice guidance for staff
- safe practice guidance for the inclusion of students within the setting
- safe practice guidance regarding visitors
- guidance on the use of accident and incident books for reporting injuries and illness during time at the setting, and (ideally) any injuries or concerns on arrival
- an outline of the process leading to a potential referral.

Although some procedures may vary slightly, all will be founded on the principles laid down by the Local Child Safeguarding Board and they are informed by *Every Child Matters* and *What to Do If You're Worried a Child Is Being Abused*. You must ensure that you are wholly familiar with the policy in your setting and that you know the appropriate lines of communication and reporting.

Clear guidance for writing accurate and factual reports

It is important that any signs of possible abuse are clearly recorded in a signed and dated statement that outlines what has been noticed. This needs to be done within 24 hours of the observation being made. Hobart and Frankel (2005) advise that it may be good practice to discretely ask a senior colleague to confirm your findings before the report is made to the manager or designated person for child protection.

activity
INDIVIDUAL WORK 5.4
P3

Using your college resource centre, find the *What to Do If You're Worried a Child Is Being Abused* document online and print the flow charts that outline actions to be taken. Write a brief guidance sheet suitable to be discussed with a group of your peers about relevant child protection legislation.

Professional Practice

- You may find it helpful to contact the appropriate address to request your own copy of *What to Do if You're Worried a Child Is Being Abused*.
- If, during your placement experience, you are concerned about a child for any reason, you should talk to your placement supervisor or, if you do not yet feel comfortable doing this, talk to your college tutor. Either will help you to explore your concerns further and take action appropriately.
- It is never appropriate simply to talk to your friends about a concern, as confidentiality is of utmost importance in all cases, and information about any suspected case of abuse should only be discussed on a 'need to know' basis.

Security of records

In early years settings, clear record keeping and report writing help to provide all the details that may be asked of the setting in the event of an enquiry. Each setting should have an accident book, where all accidents and incidents are recorded, witnessed and signed by at least two members of staff. Many settings use body maps to record marks and bruises that have been identified. Body maps should be dated and can be useful supportive evidence in a case involving physical abuse. It is important that staff are able to identify signs and symptoms of abuse on different skin tones.

Fig 5.8 A body map

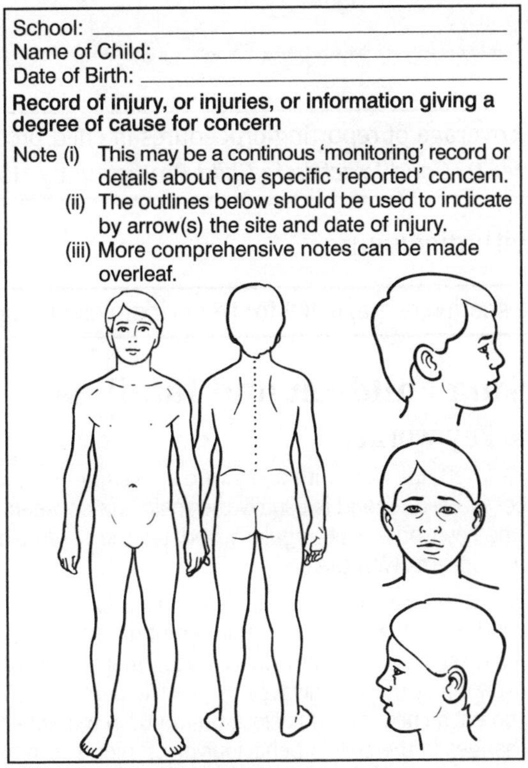

School: ____________________

Name of Child: ____________________

Date of Birth: ____________________

Record of injury, or injuries, or information giving a degree of cause for concern

Note (i) This may be a continous 'monitoring' record or details about one specific 'reported' concern.

(ii) The outlines below should be used to indicate by arrow(s) the site and date of injury.

(iii) More comprehensive notes can be made overleaf.

remember

Each setting should have a child protection procedure which follows the guidelines provided by the local authority.

case study 5.2

Kieron

Kieron arrives at nursery one morning with a bruise developing above his left eyebrow. Several staff members notice it, but no one mentions it to Kieron or to his mother. At home time, Kieron's mother asks what has happened to Kieron for him to get such a nasty bruise. Staff are astounded at this and protest that he arrived with the bruise in the morning. His mother denies this emphatically and is angry with the staff, raising her voice and shouting her concerns about the quality of care and levels of safety in the nursery.

activity
GROUP WORK

1 How could this situation have been avoided?
2 What should happen now?
3 How differently might staff view Kieron's mother and her relationship with Kieron from now on?

Building up good relationships with parents is important in order to provide the best care possible for the child. If the setting has a policy on child protection which states exactly what will happen in the event of any concerns, this lets parents know that you are making the welfare of their child of paramount importance, as set down by the Children Acts 1989, 2004. This policy could include a clause stating that, if any child arrives at the setting with an injury, a note will be made in the accident/incident book. This will offer added safety for the child and for the staff, avoiding the situation described in the case study.

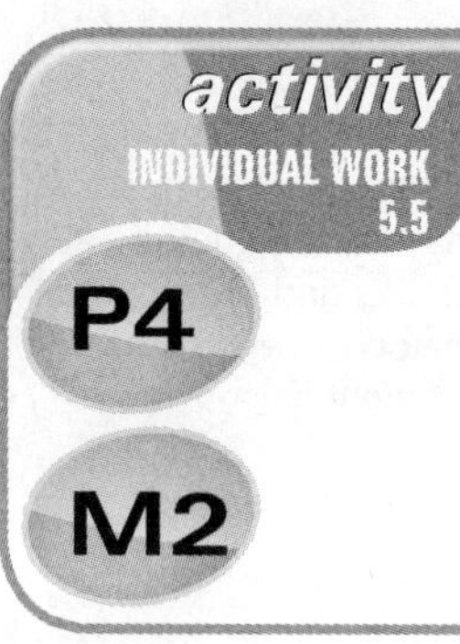

1 Ask to see a copy of the child protection guidelines and reporting procedures specified by your local authority and those specified by your work placement or place of employment.
2 If the guidelines are not clear, ask for an explanation.
3 Try explaining the guidelines and procedure to another person. If you can explain them clearly, it is likely that you understand them.

For further coverage of reporting procedures in child protection cases, it would be useful to refer to *Good Practice in Child Protection* by Hobart and Frankel (2005).

Dealing with disclosure

Refer to the section on page 262 for the principles of responding to disclosure.

Supporting children and families

Role of the key worker

Most early years settings work with a key worker system. Each key worker is responsible for a small number of children and is usually the main link between the setting and the child's parents; it is the key worker who regularly updates the parents on their child's progress and who raises any concerns with them.

The advantages of this system are that a relationship of trust can be built up between the key worker and the child, and between the parent and the setting, and consistency of staffing helps to maintain security. A system where a staff member has responsibility for a set group of children ensures that there is always one specific person keeping records and making observations on each child, and this close relationship will enhance that person's ability to pick up any changes in the child's behaviour or problems with their development. The key worker will also be more likely to build up a good relationship with the child's parents and be more likely to feel able to ask if there is anything troubling the child or to raise a concern with them. This will be less easy if no relationship has been established.

Key workers are also ideally placed to act as advocates for vulnerable children and their parents, and, in terms of assessing children in need, they are usually well informed about the family's circumstances. More importantly, the key worker represents a stable figure in the child's life during a period of stress, offering consistency of care and unconditional support. This can be of great value to a child when inconsistency of parental care results in feelings of uncertainty, self-blame and anxiety.

remember The best interests and safety of the child must always come first.

Working in partnership

Working in partnership with parents is an integral part of early years practice, and this holds true more than ever when issues of safeguarding children arise. The need to work closely with parents is established by:

- the Children Acts 1989, 2004
- *Working Together to Safeguard Children* (DfES, 1999; revised DfES, 2006)
- *Framework for the Assessment of Children in Need and their Families* (DoH, 2000).

It is possible for early years workers to contribute to the safeguarding of children from abuse by enabling vulnerable parents to take adequate care of their children and by teaching and role modelling positive parenting skills. The central aim of working with parents of abused children is to ensure and promote the welfare of the child in need, and this is not always an easy process. Some parents will not be amenable to advice and support and may resent professional assessment of their childcare and parenting abilities. However, this attitude should not be allowed to compromise the care of the child and every effort should be made to work with parents, however difficult that might be.

1 The term 'good-enough parenting' does not have a specific definition.
   (a) What does the term mean to you?
   (b) Discuss what factors you consider would be good-enough aspects of parenting and what would not.
   (c) Consider what you are basing your ideas on.
   (d) How well did you agree within your group?
   (e) Discuss the differences in your ideas and what may have influenced them.

2 Sometimes, parents need support to help them parent their children. Look at the spidergram below. In what ways do you think each form of support would help parents develop better parenting skills?

   As you consider each point, think:
   (a) about the impact on the child or children
   (b) how the parent might feel about themselves as a parent
   (c) how they might feel about themselves as a person
   (d) how early years settings can contribute.

Fig 5.9

Supporting children and parents
- Providing feedback to parents about their parenting
- Involving parents in the early years setting
- Helping parents to relate to their children positively
- Helping parents adapt as their child develops
- Helping parents to modify their children's behaviour
- Offering ideas to parents for developing play and stimulation for their child
- Offering general parenting skills training
- Helping parents develop practical caring skills
- Keeping parents informed about childcare and their child's development

Good-enough parenting

A term that is used from time to time is '**good-enough parenting**'. Few people would describe themselves, or be described by others, as 'perfect' parents, nor is perfection necessary for a positive parent–child relationship to develop, or for children to feel cared for and loved. Overall, it is consistency of care and being valued and supported by parents that counts, providing that it is 'good enough'.

Understand the principles of responding to disclosure

When a child discloses abuse to an adult, i.e. tells an adult about it, the child is likely to have chosen that person for a reason and it will have taken a great deal of time and courage to speak out. It is therefore crucial that, when disclosure takes place, the child is given an appropriate response. Disclosure can be either direct or indirect.

Direct vs. indirect disclosure

If, as described above, a child actually tells a trusted adult about their abuse, that is a direct disclosure. Often, however, the child does not know how to tell, cannot put it into words, or does not have sufficient ability to communicate. In such cases, disclosure may be made through changes to the way they behave; they may refuse to take part in things, or be reluctant to be with certain people, and so on. This is indirect disclosure. It can either be conscious or subconscious on the part of the child. Practitioners should be alert to these non-verbal signs.

Refer back to page 244 for further guidance.

Principles of understanding and responding to disclosure

The main principles of understanding and responding to disclosure are:

- to listen carefully and attentively
- to communicate at the child's own pace and without undue pressure
- to take the child seriously
- to reassure and support the child
- not to promise confidentiality when the disclosure cannot remain confidential
- to follow procedures correctly
- to deal with your own feelings and emotions appropriately.

1. Imagine that, during the course of your work, a child discloses to you that they have been abused. You are in a busy environment, with many other children nearby. How would you respond to the child, both initially and on an ongoing basis?
2. How might you, or another adult, feel in this situation? Horrified? Shocked? Anger at the abuser? Scared about what to do? What other emotions do you think that you might feel?

Listening carefully and attentively

It is important to anticipate and explore your thoughts and emotions in order to think through how you might deal with them if the need arises. The most important initial response to a child should be one of unconditional acceptance. By listening to the child, showing that you believe them and responding to them positively, you will have provided the first stage of help.

Responding

In responding to disclosure you need to:

- reassure the child that they have done the right thing by telling someone
- assure the child that you will help in whatever way you can
- explain that you understand how hard it is for the child to tell you this information
- find a more appropriate setting, or make arrangements to talk to the child somewhere else as soon as you can if you are not in a suitable place (e.g. if there is no privacy)
- do not ask leading questions; it is important that you do not influence the disclosure in any way
- remain calm
- keep your facial expressions and body language positive
- give the child time
- be a good listener
- be patient; the child will most likely need to pause to sort out their thoughts
- reassure the child that, whatever the situation, they are in no way to blame
- ensure that you do not make promises that you cannot keep; i.e. you cannot keep disclosed information a secret, and the child cannot come to your house to live
- explain that there are other people whom you may need to contact
- explain that these people will also want to help the child
- ask the child if they have told anyone else
- ask the child who else they think they could tell – a parent, aunt, etc. – it may be appropriate to offer to help the child tell that person
- maintain strict confidentiality, working on a need-to-know basis
- follow the reporting guidelines for your setting
- write up a report of the disclosure immediately afterwards and date and sign it
- let the child know what will happen next
- keep the child informed until the situation is out of your hands.

Professional Practice

- Often, disclosure comes 'out of the blue'. It is important that you are prepared to deal with it if it arises.
- It is essential that you do not ask the child leading questions. These can invalidate a child's statement if there is a subsequent prosecution.

Confidentiality

All information that you receive about children and their families, verbal or written, is confidential. You have been trusted to receive it and, as part of your professional role, you must respond to that trust. To break confidence may put a child at further risk. It could have an impact on an investigation, and it could cast a slur on a person's character if the concern is subsequently unfounded. However, there is sometimes a fine line between maintaining confidentiality and failing to share vital information. In terms of safeguarding children, it is permissible to disclose confidential information if the parent or child gives consent for information to be disclosed. Disclosure can also be made without consent if legislation requires it.

Professional Practice

- The primary duty of all those working with children is always to put the child's best interests first.
- Confidentiality is always important, but within child protection it is essential. Information should only be shared on a need-to-know basis, and sharing of information should be in accordance with local policies and protocols.
- You should never discuss a parent with other parents.
- You should work with facts, not with gossip.

remember

If the abuse disclosed by another adult is current, consideration must be given to any children who may also be at risk.

Support after disclosure

Support for children who disclose

Children who have disclosed abuse need the continued support of early years workers who care for them; who may, for example, support them through the process of giving evidence in court, act as an advocate for a child in care proceedings, or support a child on supervised access visits. Children who have disclosed abuse are often in need of specialist support; they may be referred to counselling services or to psychologists if needed, or they may self-refer to services such as ChildLine (now supported by the NSPCC).

ChildLine
www.childline.org.uk

Refer back to page 261 for guidance on how to respond to disclosure of abuse.

Support for adults who disclose

Disclosure can also come from an adult who has grown to trust you. This may be a friend or a work colleague. The same approach is needed here as it would be for a child. The adult may have waited a long time to speak out and your response will be as important to the adult as it would be to a child. You may feel shocked, or even guilty that you had not been aware of what had been happening. These are natural responses, but you should remember that your level of understanding and awareness has developed further, and you were less equipped in the past to identify signs of abuse.

The impact of abuse on families

Families are not always aware of what has been happening to a child even if the perpetrator lives within the same house. A significant percentage of abuse is carried out by close relatives or persons known to the child and the family. In some families, violence may be commonplace and adults dealing with their own suffering may not perceive the suffering of their children, or may not have the physical or emotional energy to deal with it.

As an early years worker, you will be interacting with the parents on a daily basis. If they are the subject of an enquiry instigated by the setting, you may have to face anger and hostility.

If they had been unaware of the abuse and are in no way responsible, they are likely to feel distressed, guilty and saddened. They may wish to talk to staff who know their child well and may require more feedback than usual on their child's welfare and progress.

Parents who abuse are often in need of help and support themselves. This can be a difficult area to cope with. It is important that staff continue to interact with the parents positively, offering opportunities to talk where appropriate and acting as good role models in their interactions with children.

case study 5.3

Isobel

Isobel, who has mild learning difficulties, is the single mother of James and was supported by staff at her local family centre while she was learning to look after James in his early weeks. They showed her how to prepare suitable foods for him when he was ready for solids and offered advice on developing a routine for him. Isobel has attended the family centre only occasionally since then as she often goes to stay with her mother, some distance away. In conversation with Isobel when she arrived today, it has become clear that she is very proud of the way that she has managed to care for James, but you can see that she has not really moved James on very far in his development. James is now 11 months old and is still only being fed puréed foods, mostly from jars, with bottles of formula throughout the day. His playthings are still mostly rattles and soft toys, and he is a very passive baby, showing no real interest in moving. There does not seem to be any cause for concern regarding James's weight. As Isobel has been away a great deal, she has not had recent contact with her health visitor.

activity
GROUP WORK

1 What support and advice do you think Isobel needs first for James?
2 How could you help her develop more stimulating play for James?
3 What should be most important in your approach to Isobel?
4 What concern might there be for James's future if his mother does not have support offered to her?

Understand strategies for supporting children, their families and other adults

As a practitioner, you need to be aware of the many strategies used within society to support children and their families.

Refer to the Nelson Thornes website for the poster 'Strategies for support', which summarises strategies which help childcare workers and others too. Relevant points were addressed in an earlier section concerning the requirements of legislation. As you read through the information on the poster, you may find it helpful to refer back to that section.
www.nelsonthornes.com/btec

Safe practices that protect children and adults who work with them

Police screening of staff

It is obligatory that all staff working with children in statutory or voluntary settings, or who are on premises where children are cared for, be screened for their suitability to work with children. The Protection of Children Act 1999 enabled the Criminal Records Bureau (CRB) to release data on those people who are identified as being unsuitable to work with children. CRB checks for students are likely to be standard checks whilst qualified staff will be required to undergo enhanced checks. However, nannies working in private homes are often not screened so carefully.

Visiting and access rights

Some parents or family members may only have access to their children in a supervised setting such as a family centre or other designated place. This is to ensure the child's continuing safety and is often also to comply with a court order. It is important that staff are aware of any children to whom these circumstances apply so that inappropriate access is not granted. Such situations must be treated with sensitivity so that the child is able to see the parent or family member in positive circumstances.

Building security and access

Security of early years settings has had to be reassessed in recent years after a number of incidents involving unauthorised entry into buildings, on occasions resulting in children being harmed or even killed (for example, at Dunblane Primary School in March 1996, when 16 children and their teacher died). Security is increasingly being made a high priority by local authorities and private owners, with staff teams having to consider how easy it might be to gain access to the premises and redefining who is allowed access.

Asking for proof of identity from visitors, such as course tutors or health visitors, should now be mandatory, and children should only be handed over to known adults or others if there have been prior instructions from the parent who usually collects them. Most preschool settings allow parents to stay for a short while to settle their child, but some degree of control over the numbers of visitors should be in place to ensure that staff can maintain a safe level of supervision at all times.

Visitors should never be allowed to take children anywhere on their own, and they should not be involved in intimate care routines. Any child who is reluctant to work with a visitor should not have to do so, and staff should monitor the effect that visitors have on the children in their care. If it is found that visitors disrupt the session to unacceptable levels or that children appear insecure, the frequency and level of involvement of visitors in the setting may need to be reassessed.

As an early years student, you too are a visitor, particularly in the early weeks of your placement. You will need to build up a rapport with the children and will not be involved in intimate care routines without supervision.

Outer doors should ideally be kept locked at all times. If parents have to have access (e.g. if having a staff member leave the room to answer the door would be the greater risk), their arrival should be indicated by an alarm, and staff should ensure that they know who has arrived and where they have gone. Any visitors who are staying for a specific length of time should be signed in and out of the setting and issued with a visitor badge, to be handed in as they leave.

A clear policy should be developed about not accepting visitors 'off the street'. All prospective visitors should make an appointment in advance, and anyone interested in the welfare and safety of children will not have a problem with this. Unexpected visitors can interfere with staff:child ratios and can cause disruption to the planned structure of the session. They should be politely asked to return at a mutually convenient time unless the manager is supernumerary to numbers and it is practicable for the manager to accommodate unexpected visitors at that time.

case study 5.4

Sarah

Sarah is a BTEC National student, currently on placement at Greenwood Primary School. It is mostly an open-plan site, with the classrooms along three sides of a square, and side areas for creativity, music and PE along the fourth. Sarah was preparing materials for a creative activity in one of the side areas when she became aware of a man walking slowly along the outside wall, looking through the windows. She watched him for a few minutes, but, as he did not seem to be making any attempt to get into the building, she did not do anything about it.

activity
INDIVIDUAL WORK

1 What would you have done if you had been Sarah?
2 What might this tell you about the security of the school building?
3 What would you do if you were trying to get into a school on the first day of your placement but were unable to find an open entrance?

It is always a good idea to report any suspicious individuals or occurrences and it is better to be proved wrong than to miss an opportunity to keep a child safe. In hindsight, the school perimeter should have been securely enclosed to deter intruders and to ensure that children were not able to be observed by anyone inappropriate. Schools usually have a security code to enable access to entrances; in the case of a student who is unable to gain entry on arrival, a prior phone call could have ensured that a member of staff was there to greet the student.

Carrying out a safety audit of the setting

Early years staff should, from time to time, reassess the safety of the setting, asking themselves:

- What possibilities for abuse exist within the setting?
- What risks can be identified and how can they be reduced?
- How can the children be helped to lower the risk?
- What can the staff do?
- What external factors might have an impact on safety from abuse?

Strategies with children and young people

Promoting confidence and self-esteem

Children develop confidence and a healthy feeling of self-esteem if they experience praise, encouragement and love. Not all children receive this at home, but in care settings staff should be aiming to work within a framework that praises children for their efforts and interests, encourages them to explore, to try, and to investigate, and enables them to feel valued as an individual. Games can be played and activities developed to explore situations and problems that might be faced by children, giving them confidence in their ability to cope.

Empowering children

remember It is important to help children build their confidence.

Working with abused and potentially vulnerable children can call on all of an early years worker's skills and knowledge, but one of the key aims should be to foster a sense of resilience and empowerment. Past experiences may have taught a child that adults are not to be trusted, or they may have made the child feel guilty or ashamed. All children have the right to enjoy their childhood without fear of harm and should be encouraged to be aware of their rights and be taught ways in which they can be treated with respect. This can be done by:

- teaching all children assertiveness skills and how to say no
- encouraging their participation in decisions about their care and ensuring that the child's voice is heard
- helping them to identify what is acceptable behaviour and what behaviours are unwanted
- building trusting relationships with adults
- providing them with skills and strategies for personal safety.

Fig 5.10 Personal safety

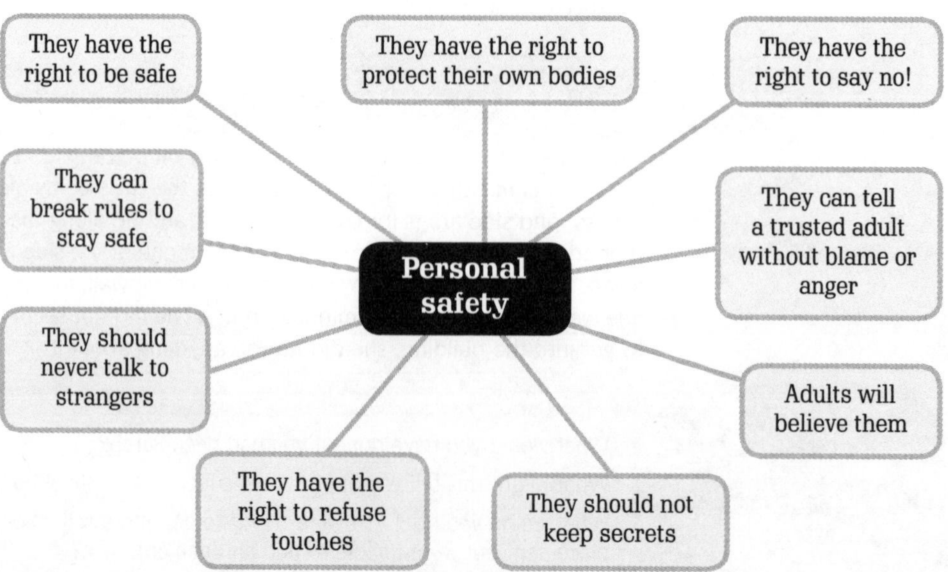

Personal safety and self-protection

Teaching children about personal safety can be one way of empowering them, as long as they do not feel that they alone are responsible for keeping themselves safe. There are many areas of personal safety that are relevant for young children and these can be taught through age and developmentally appropriate activities. It is important that children are provided with effective **self-protection strategies** and that they know that help is available to them.

Children can be taught self-protection strategies.

Strategies suggested by Karp and Butler (1996) include:

- the 'private triangle'
- 'colour in the personal space'
- 'people I trust' – the child draws a picture of someone they trust.

Fig 5.11 The private triangle – dot to dot

• Connect the dots and colour your picture.

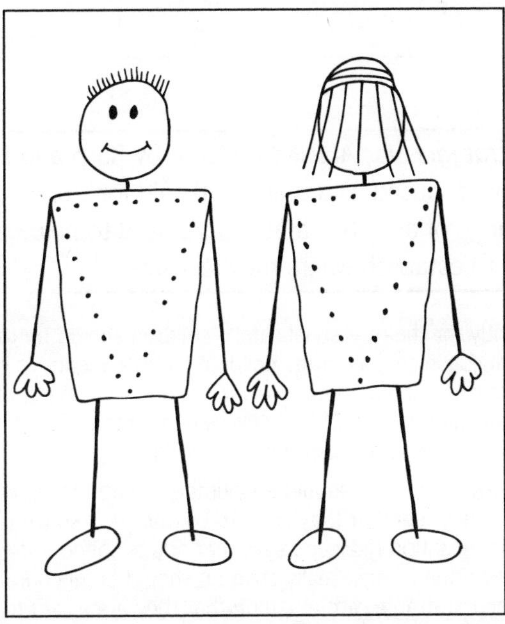

Fig 5.12 The private triangle – cut and paste

• Cut out the triangle and paste it on the picture, showing where the private triangle should go.

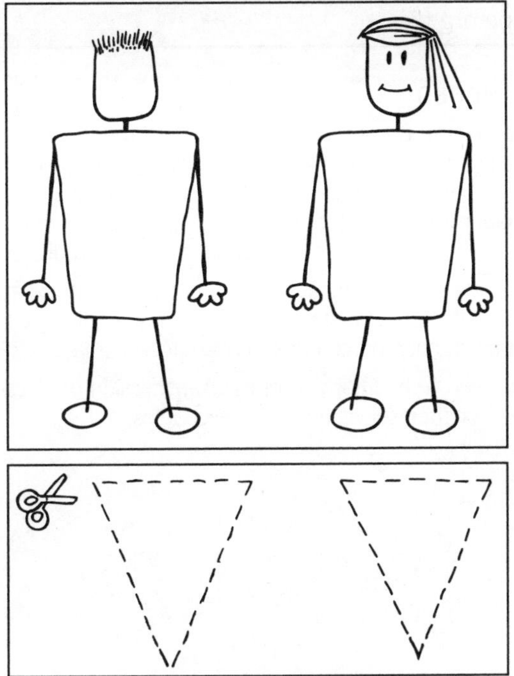

Fig 5.13 Colour in the personal space

• Colour in the personal space.

Treatment Strategies for Abused Children by Karp and Butler (1996), which was originally produced as a therapeutic aid for children who have been abused, includes a range of activities that can be used to help define boundaries for young children and to establish where they feel safe.

Most importantly for their personal safety, children should be taught to speak out when they need to. Activities which encourage children to take a lead, to demonstrate, illustrate or describe something will help them grow in confidence. Giving praise for effort rather than just for achievement will boost children's self-esteem, and giving them small responsibilities will make them feel valued and worthwhile as individuals.

Parents and early years staff should encourage children to be open and honest and to learn to say no when they feel that they want to or that their space is being intruded upon. Michele Elliott of the organisation Kidscape says that adults spend a great deal of time teaching children to obey adults, when really children should be encouraged to say no when they are unhappy or uncomfortable with anything that they are asked to do.

The children's organisation Kidscape provides excellent downloadable resources and ideas on its website.
www.kidscape.org.uk

Body awareness

Children need to learn that their bodies belong to them and that no one has the right to touch their body if they do not want them to. They can learn that the areas of their body covered by their bathing suit are private to them and should not be touched by anyone else. It would be inappropriate to state simply that these are areas that 'should not be touched' as this implies that the child also should refrain from the natural exploration of their own body.

They need to know that this applies to all adults, but with exceptions for medical treatment (e.g. a doctor listening with a stethoscope or a nurse taking a blood sample or giving an injection; to a child, such procedures may be unwelcome).

Older children need to be informed of the transmission of disease and helped to develop a healthy respect for themselves and for their bodies.

Fig 5.14 Everywhere under your bathing suit is private

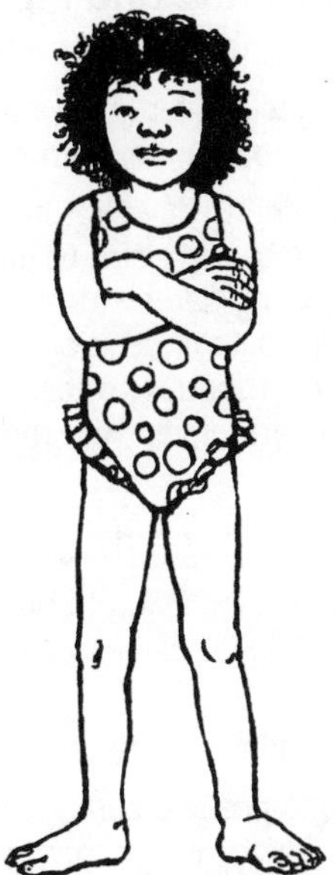

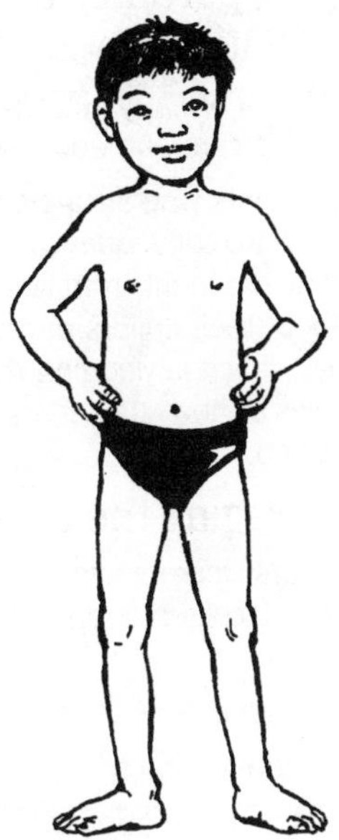

Secrets

When supporting the learning of self-protection, it is important to explore the issue of secrets with children. Secrets should be pleasurable and exciting, linked to birthdays, festivals and surprises, but for some children secrets mean abuse, with the abuser telling them, 'This is our little secret' or 'Make sure you don't tell anyone about this, because ...'. You need to be able to help children understand the difference and to know when they should tell their parents about a secret that they have been asked to keep.

Activities relating to secrets can be introduced within the general planning of the setting.

The television characters Cosmo and Dibs are featured in a useful video addressing safety issues, including safe and unsafe secrets.

Working with parents and families

Partnerships with parents

Communication is an important aspect of supporting children and their families. Good parent–staff relationships create a level of trust and respect that promotes honesty and openness and allows concerns to be raised more easily. It is important to share information about the setting's child protection procedures with parents, so that, were an issue to arise, it could be dealt with effectively.

Professional Practice

- In cases of child abuse, you need to be aware that (non-abusing) parents can sometimes be embarrassed to talk to early years staff if they feel that they have let their child down by not protecting them.
- You will at times need to continue to communicate with a known or suspected abuser. This will not always be easy. Personal feelings must never be allowed to affect your professionalism.
- You can help parents by being a good role model in how you interact with children.
- Keeping communication open between staff and parents is an important part of supporting both the child and their family.

Refer to Unit 1, pages 11 and 23, to refresh your understanding of communication and the barriers that can exist.

Helping parents recognise the value and significance of their contributions

Each school or early years setting has strategies for involving parents in the different aspects of a child's care and education, thereby helping parents to feel valued.

Many parents who struggle with their parenting have not had good role models to learn from, and they are consequently not always able to recognise when they are doing well and when they would benefit from some support. Giving parents positive feedback, inviting them to talk about their child's progress and participate in decision-making and listening to them are all ways of acknowledging that they are contributing to their child's development. These are examples of how the setting can work in partnership with the parents, helping them feel valued.

Encouraging the development of parenting skills

Early years workers can also support parents by trying to understand some of the problems that they face and initiating evidence-based strategies to develop their parenting. These may cover:

- developing a positive and realistic relationship with their children
- developing practical childcare skills and positive parenting
- sharing information about children's behaviour and development
- helping parents to enjoy playing with their children and supporting their children's learning.

Some settings, particularly schools and children's centres now offer parenting classes to support positive relationships with children, behaviour management, etc.

Supporting positive relationships with children

There is some evidence to suggest that parenting programmes based on the principles of 'positive parenting' and anger management have some success in helping parents to relate more positively. Staff may find it helpful to role model positive attitudes and ensure that parents have access to any supportive services and benefits they may need.

Helping parents develop practical caring skills

Some parents may not possess the skills and knowledge required to care for children effectively. Parents may find it intimidating to have their care questioned by what they regard as 'authority', and it may take some time to gain their trust. It can be useful to discuss how children's behaviour is affected by tension or stress in the family, or how to manage everyday behaviour problems. Parents in need of support often find that they harbour unrealistic expectations of children's development and behaviour, or that they do not know how to offer appropriate care. Sensitivity is required when working with parents to increase their knowledge of nutrition and practical caring skills, and role modelling can be valuable. Supporting parents by helping them to respond positively to the changing demands of their developing child, or react with equanimity to a child's challenging behaviour, is an inherent part of working with children in need and their families. More specialist or intensive support may be needed for some parents whose tolerance levels are low or whose idea of appropriate discipline is skewed.

Access to Basic Skills sessions may be offered, as well as the opportunity to learn more about child development and care.

Helping parents to offer play and stimulation

Some parents may not have had positive experiences of childhood; they may not know how to have fun and may have little knowledge of how to play with their children. They may not know what will stimulate interest and learning at what age. They may not have the income to support a wide range of play and learning activities, but they can be directed to resources such as toy libraries and Books for Babies schemes. Practical art and craft sessions may also be of use, as may 'coaching' in joint parent-and-child sessions, where staff involve parents and model good practice in how to play and have fun.

Cultural and social variations

Parenting support should not be undertaken without due regard to social and cultural variations. Patterns of behaviour and discipline will inevitably vary from family to family, and some children may be confused when they experience different approaches in settings other than home. Staff should be aware of the different cultural and child-rearing practices of the families they care for and use supportive services as needed. These may include the use of advocates, translators and interpreters.

Refer to Unit 1, page 23, for information on advocates, translators and interpreters.

Local support networks

Help and advice can be given to parents by:

- known professionals (e.g. day-care providers, teachers, playgroup staff)
- other professionals (e.g. health visitors, social workers, family support workers)
- family members
- friends.
- support groups.

The level of support available to parents can make a huge difference, tipping the balance between good-enough parenting and the need for intervention. Many of the same agencies are able to offer support informally as well as through specific case involvement. Sure Start schemes are an example of how these agencies are now working collaboratively to support children and parents.

Sure Start and Sure Start programmes

Government funding has been provided to focus on areas that have been identified as having an unacceptable level of poverty and social deprivation. The initiative is called Sure Start. The Sure Start ethos is to work with local communities to improve and increase the range of support and provision for young children (under three) and their families. Sure Start programmes and policies apply to England only, as responsibility for early care and education in Scotland, Northern Ireland and Wales rests with the respective devolved administrations.

- Sure Start has created 45,000 affordable day-care places for children under five in the most deprived areas of Britain.
- Neighbourhood nursery projects have been developed in 142 local authorities in the most deprived electoral wards in England.
- There are Early Excellence Centres across the UK, which offer high-quality integrated services from education, health and social services.
- The government is committed to providing a Sure Start children's centre in every neighbourhood by 2010 as part of its 10-year childcare strategy.

Information on projects incorporating Sure Start in your area is available from the local authority Family Information Service, which was set up by the Early Years Development and Childcare Partnership (EYDCP).

remember

Drawing up a list of addresses of parenting support groups in your area and website addresses for national societies will enable you to offer practical sources of help and advice for parents if the need arises.

Family centres

A family centre is usually staffed by a multidisciplinary team and offers a range of support. Centres can be used as access points for parents who have restricted or supervised access visits to their children. Many family centres receive funding through the Sure Start initiative. Some family centres run separate support sessions for fathers, with life skills, parenting skills, health, education and counselling being available to all family members. Families are mostly referred by health professionals, and there are strong links with the family support workers who are part of the social services' team for children and families.

Many family centres have now been amalgamated into Sure Start children's centres or neighbourhood nurseries.

Procedures, roles and responsibilities where abuse is suspected or confirmed

Refer back to page 255 for information on procedures to be taken when abuse is suspected or confirmed.

Formulating a child protection policy

Each setting needs:

- a copy of the local authority guidelines
- a person specifically responsible for child protection
- setting guidelines for all staff with regard to behaviour, responsibilities and recording procedures
- police screening of all staff
- whenever possible, police screening of students.

Local authority guidelines

Most local authorities will have similar guidelines that centre on their duty to safeguard and promote the welfare of children in need within their designated area. Most will be developing a multi-agency response to safeguarding children following the Laming Report's recommendations that children's services should be co-ordinated. Guidelines will also closely follow the guidance given in *What to Do if You're Worried a Child Is Being Abused*. All staff should be aware of the guidelines that apply in their area and the content of their setting's policy and lines of reporting.

Guidelines for staff behaviour

It is a sad fact that abusive behaviour against children can sometimes happen in the settings that are mandated to care for and protect them. To ensure that this does not happen, staff should behave in appropriate and sensitive ways that demonstrate integrity and an awareness of their moral and professional duty.

- Do not shout at children or talk in an aggressive tone of voice.
- Do not threaten them with frightening stories of what will happen to them if they don't behave.
- Do not use humiliating punishments for unwanted behaviour.
- Do not express any discriminatory or oppressive statements or opinions.
- Do not leave children inappropriately supervised or neglect routine aspects of care.
- Do make sure that the language you use is appropriate, anti-discriminatory and anti-oppressive.
- Do make sure that children are treated with unconditional, positive regard.
- Do use touch and affection appropriately and respect children's rights to refuse inappropriate touch.
- Do make sure that all aspects of care are delivered in a sensitive and respectful manner without any element of coercion or force.
- Do talk to somebody if you think that you might need support with any aspect of your practice.

Ensuring good working practice with children means ensuring that physical care is always appropriate. Ask yourself:

- How much can children do for themselves when dressing?
- How much can children do for themselves in the bathroom?
- How much privacy should I be giving them?
- Is it appropriate for the children to kiss me goodbye?
- Is it appropriate for the child to be having cuddles?
- Is it appropriate for the child to be sitting on my lap?
- Is the contact I have with the children fulfilling their need, or mine?

You will probably find that your answers will partly depend on the ages of the children and their stage of development. It will also be determined by the environment in which you are working, and the role you have in the children's lives, as a nanny, nursery manager, key worker, teacher, nursery nurse or student on placement.

remember

Physical contact is permissible when a child needs comforting, during intimate care routines and at times when physical restraint might be required (such as when a child is about to run into a road).

Professional Practice

- Children deserve respect at all times; you should not, for example, sit the child on a potty in full view of a multitude of other people or ask the child to undress in front of a crowd.
- Children should not be photographed partially clothed.
- Any photographs that are taken in early years settings must be shown to parents before being displayed. This is particularly important if any items are likely to be published in local newspapers.

Abigail is three years old and has recently joined Little Monkeys Preschool, which is situated in a large village on the outskirts of a country town. It has recently had a very successful fundraising event and wishes to advertise this in the local press. A member of staff contacted the local newspaper who sent along a photographer. All the children lined up and had their photo taken, and it was subsequently printed in the local free newspaper. Abigail's mother was very upset when she found out about this. She has recently moved to the area, having left a violent relationship with Abigail's father, and is living in a safe house supported by the Women's Refuge Organisation. She is very worried that he might see the photograph and trace them, as the paper is also distributed in the area in which he lives.

1 What should have been the procedure here?

2 Were the preschool staff wrong, do you think?

3 Should Abigail have been missed out of the photograph?

4 How could this issue have been resolved satisfactorily?

5 What other strategies to protect children do early years settings take, and how effective are they likely to be?

Record-keeping

Any records made of children should be kept safely, and only the appropriate member of staff (key worker, senior staff, manager, etc.) and the child's parents should be allowed access to them. It is not usually appropriate for children's records to be shared with students, although in some settings this may be the case. As a student, you must be aware of the responsibility of being privy to this information and should ensure that you in no way pass any of it on.

Where there is a child protection concern, the records should make it clear what has been directly observed by staff and what information has been gathered from other sources. Records of any kind must always be dated and signed, and then witnessed by another person, usually a senior member of staff.

Accurate records

It is very important to keep **accurate records**. On occasions, 'hearsay' evidence may be accepted and included in a child's case. If a child has disclosed to you, it is important that you include the full details in your report. This must include any questions that you asked, the details of the disclosure and any non-verbal communication relevant to the disclosure, such as indicating a body part by pointing.

The facts will be the most important aspect of your report. However, a comment, such as the example below, may be appropriate if you are an experienced practitioner raising a concern following your own observations.

'In my professional judgement, following 18 years as a senior nursery worker working with children aged 0–5 years, I consider the overt sexual nature of Joseph's interactions with both staff and children to be beyond what would be expected of children of his age, taking into consideration the natural curiosity and exploration of the age group.'

In this example, the opinion of an experienced professional early years worker is based on developmental norms and what has been observed.

remember
The safety of the child is paramount.

Professional Practice

- Early years settings have a duty to report any concerns about a child.
- If you have a concern, discuss it with your line manager or designated member of staff. The worst situation that can arise is that your concern is unfounded. You may be embarrassed, but you will know the child is safe. You would feel worse if you had not raised a concern and a child suffered further.
- It takes courage to raise a concern, but it is part of your professional role as an early years worker.

Allegations against staff

A vetting procedure will usually have been carried out prior to members of staff joining the setting; however, this only indicates when someone has been investigated and convicted. It does not tell you for certain that the new staff member is a 'safe' person. As found in Abel's study (cited in Elliott, 1992), most convicted abusers have been offending for a long time prior to their conviction. Many of these individuals will have applied for posts working with children. Any teacher who is convicted of inappropriate conduct with children, or who is no longer considered safe to work with children, is placed on a list known as List 99. This list can be accessed by employers.

To prevent false allegations being made against innocent members of staff, early years settings must look at ways in which staff can safeguard themselves. These safeguards should form part of the setting's child protection policy, for example:

- Avoid unnecessary intimate care.
- Record all accidents or incidents and have them witnessed by another member of staff.
- If a child acts or talks in a sexually inappropriate way to you, record it and tell your manager.
- Avoid spending time alone with individual children.

activity
INDIVIDUAL WORK 5.9
M3

What other guidelines could be included? Consider this in the light of:

1 working with preschool-age children
2 working in a primary school
3 working in residential care
4 taking part in an organised trip.

Professional Practice

- The same rules of confidentiality apply to staff facing an allegation as apply to parents.
- Information will be given on a need-to-know basis.
- Speculation and gossip is never helpful.
- Any discussion with, or reassurance of, parents should be the responsibility of the manager of the setting or of a designated senior member of staff.
- You should pass any enquiries on, rather than deal with them yourself.
- You should ask for guidance and support if you are unsure about your role or about what action should be taken.

Support for staff

Dealing with the feelings that arise when children are abused is never easy, as it is often difficult to remain distanced from the experience. It is common to feel a wide range of emotions, ranging from anger and revulsion to sadness and disbelief, but objectivity is an essential component of a professional response. However, that is not to say that other feelings should be ignored or suppressed, merely that they should not hinder acting in the child's best interests.

Staff involved in the safeguarding of children may find it of great benefit to have regular supervision with a senior and experienced staff member, in order to maintain a professional response and discuss reactions and feelings. In some cases, referral to professional counselling services may be needed. Confidence in dealing with such situations and the feelings they engender will also be helped by professional development activities linked to safeguarding children and supporting parents.

Refer to page 244 to refresh your understanding of signs and symptoms of abuse, and to page 261 for guidance on disclosure.

Sources of information and support

The multi-professional, multi-agency approach

Working in collaboration with other agencies and sharing information has been recommended by most of the reports into child abuse fatalities. It was legitimised in *Working Together to Safeguard Children*, the Children Acts 1989 and 2004, and *Every Child Matters*. It cannot be stressed too highly that interagency working and the effective sharing of information is vital to the work of safeguarding children. The Laming Report into the death of Victoria Climbié noted that there were 12 occasions when she could have been saved if information had been shared and acted on.

Information concerning the safety of children who may be at risk of harm must be shared with the appropriate agencies. This would include social services, education and early years services, police, health services, and any other agencies involved.

Sharing information, initiating and sustaining contact

The procedures for initiating and sustaining contact with the other agencies involved in safeguarding children will, to some extent, be governed by local guidelines and policies. Referrals about a child at risk may be made by practitioners in schools or nurseries, health care professionals, parents, other members of the extended family, or neighbours. In early years settings, it is customary for the referral to be made through either the named person for child protection or the manager; they will make the initial contact with social services.

Professional Practice

- Respect the contribution and role of other professionals.
- Act within professional boundaries.
- Undertake regular professional training and updating – preferably multidisciplinary.
- Communicate clearly, effectively and in a timely manner with members of other agencies.
- Share information about children who are, or who may be, at risk of harm, according to agreed policies and protocols.

Boundaries of confidentiality

Refer to page 263 to remind yourself of confidentiality issues.

Range of professionals and community support networks

The professionals and agencies that may become involved in a child protection case are set out in Figure 5.15, followed by a summary of each.

Fig 5.15 Professionals and agencies providing support in the community

Professionals and agencies providing support in the community
Coroner
Guardian *ad litem*
Teachers/early years staff
Social services child protection worker/key worker
School nurse
NSPCC (RSSPCC in Scotland)
Health visitor
Police officers
GD/Paediatrician

Teachers/early years staff

- A designated person with responsibility for child protection issues should be named in each setting.
- Concerns should be taken to the designated person who will notify social services.
- Staff are trained in child development and are able to monitor signs of change or regression.
- Training in recognising and responding to signs of abuse should be undertaken.

School nurse

- School nurses have close and regular contact with children.
- They are particularly involved with children with special needs.
- They are aware of child development and the signs of abuse.
- Some, but not all, are trained children's nurses.

Health visitor

- Health visitors have ongoing contact with families, particularly those with very young children.
- They are specialists in child development; their main concerns include the welfare of children and the monitoring of their development.
- Most early years settings have an established health visitor link.
- Health visitors will refer suspected cases of abuse to the police or social services.

GP/paediatrician

- Children may be presented with injuries or health concerns either at their local GP surgery or at a hospital's casualty department.
- Community paediatricians may identify causes for concern during screening programmes for young children.
- Referrals will be made to police or social services.

Police officers

- Police officers uphold the law.
- Referrals can be made directly to the police.
- They have a duty to protect children and to follow up any referrals or concerns brought to their notice.
- Police officers have responsibility for the safekeeping of any evidence in cases which may end in a prosecution.
- The police have emergency powers to remove a child to a place of safety.

NSPCC (RSSPCC in Scotland)

- Both organisations have qualified social workers who have powers to investigate cases of abuse.
- Referrals can be made directly to the NSPCC and to the RSSPCC.
- They can apply to remove a child to a place of safety or to start care proceedings.
- Both organisations have family support workers who work with families both during and after cases have been investigated.

Social services child protection worker/key worker

- The social services social worker who takes on the case will be the key worker for the child or family.
- Staff can apply to remove a child to a place of safety or to start care proceedings.

Coroner

- The coroner is an independent officer of the law who is involved in all cases of violent or unexplained death.
- Many coroners are also medical practitioners.
- They investigate a death to establish its cause.
- They are not involved in the prosecution of any perpetrator of abuse.

Guardian ad litem

- A guardian *ad litem* is an independent person who is appointed by the court.
- The guardian *ad litem* speaks on behalf of children, ensuring that their welfare remains paramount.
- Where the child is sufficiently able, the guardian *ad litem* will help the child to understand the proceedings.

Alternative forms of care

Alternative forms of care are considered when, even with the full support available within the community, a decision eventually has to be made to remove a child from the direct care of their parents. This decision is not taken lightly. The child's age and situation is always assessed before they are placed in an alternative form of care. Some children are better placed as the youngest or only child within a family, while others will benefit from having other children around. Whenever possible, and appropriate, siblings are placed together.

Care alternatives can be either temporary or permanent, depending on circumstances.

- Temporary care, for example foster care, applies when a child needs emergency or short-term care, for example as a result of a care order or the ill health of the main carer.
- Permanent care, for example adoption, is needed if a child is orphaned, where there is no alternative option available, or where parental responsibility is permanently removed by law for any reason.

Foster care

Foster carers undergo considerable assessment and in most areas receive training through the local authority. They need to have a high degree of emotional stamina, as many of the children they care for will have suffered trauma caused by abuse.

Respite care

Respite care is offered to parents when they need regular breaks from their children in order to cope with their parenting requirements. The parents may be struggling to cope generally, or the family may be facing specifically difficult circumstances. Respite care is also offered to families who care for a child with extreme physical needs or very challenging behaviour.

Adoption

Adoption is the permanent handing over of all responsibility for a child to permanent replacement parents. Adoptions can be either closed or open.

- A closed adoption involves the total breaking of ties between parent and child, although children can apply for information to trace their parents when they reach 18 years of age.
- An **open adoption** means that limited contact is kept between the child and the birth family. They may exchange letters and cards, and even meet on occasions, although this does not alter the permanency of the adoption. The birth parents have no responsibility for the child and are not entitled to any say in their upbringing.

Residential care homes

It is now very unusual for young children to be placed in residential care; they are usually placed with foster families. Residential care no longer consists of dormitory-style wings in large centres; children are more likely to be cared for in small family-sized units.

Family support workers

Wherever possible, children are helped to stay in their own homes, sometimes with the support of a family worker. These workers may spend time in the family home at times that are proving difficult for the parents to manage. For example, they may be present at mealtimes to establish good eating habits, or at bedtime to help introduce an accepted regular bedtime routine. The support worker may also be involved with the child and/or the family in day-care settings or family centres.

Alleviating the effects of abuse

Short-term effects of abuse include injuries; long-term effects of abuse may be more subtle.

Children who have been abused or had to face trauma need to be helped to counteract the effects of what they have experienced. This help may come from parents, child care practitioners and (for older children and young people) their peers, or there may be more structured and longer-term input from professionals who specialise in supporting children in these circumstances.

Children need opportunities to express themselves when they are ready to do so. Usually their self-esteem is low and feelings of worthlessness and lack of value can lead to a downward spiral if help and support is not available to them. Professional counselling is offered to some children. Early years staff can support children by giving them time, space and praise. Another approach to helping children is play therapy.

Fig 5.16 Alleviating the effects of abuse

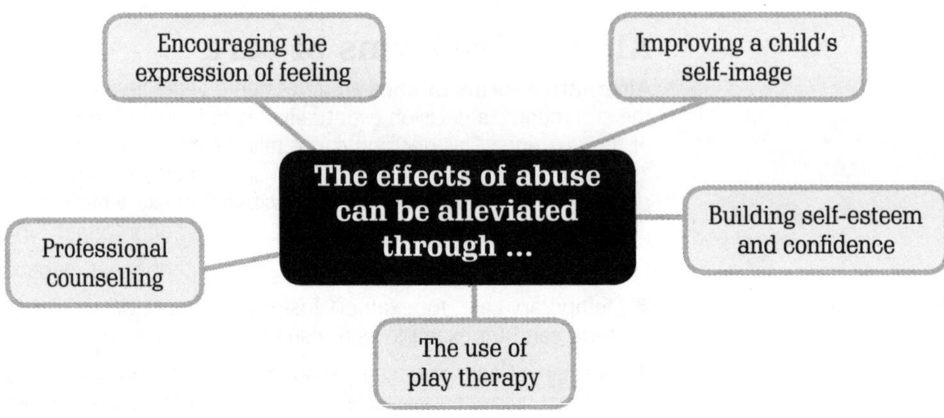

remember Child protection, whilst being a difficult and sensitive area of the early years profession, is very rewarding. If, through your knowledge, understanding, observation or support, you are able to help lessen the trauma for just one child by your words or actions, it will have been an important element of your professional career.

Encouraging expression of feeling

- There are many books dealing with various traumatic experiences, including abuse and bullying. Children often find these helpful, as they can see others in – and coping with – situations that they can relate to.
- Creative activities can help children to express how they are feeling, through drawing, the use of colour and the freedom to simply 'do'.
- Children can be helped to manage anger and resentment through 'non-fail' activities (e.g. activities using clay, dough, sand, water) and can 'let off steam' through drama and by making loud music (e.g. with cymbals, drums and blocks).
- Doll play, dolls' houses and puppets can all enable a child to 'act out' scenes that worry them and at times allow them to give the play the ending that they wish it to have.

Improving self-image

- Many story books focus on image.
- Make a book with each child, highlighting all their positives.
- Circle time helps all children to have a turn at speaking and being listened to.
- **Persona dolls** can help the whole group to focus on the positive aspects of a range of backgrounds, disabilities and situations. This can be beneficial for a child who has perhaps moved house a lot, been in foster care, etc.
- Dressing up and role play can help children not only be the person they want but also be acknowledged and admired for the person they are.

remember It is important that cultural diversity is acknowledged and provided for.

Building self-esteem and confidence

- As with self-image and expressing feelings, stories can be helpful.
- Giving praise for small achievements works wonders for a child's confidence, encouraging them to try new tasks and, usually, achieve even more. A positive cycle of self-esteem building often naturally follows.

- Encouraging children to take on small responsibilities (e.g. feeding the birds each day or looking after a newcomer) will help them feel valued; and being valued builds confidence.

Counselling

Counselling is sometimes offered to children who, it is felt, will benefit from talking things through with a professional counsellor who will listen and help them affirm how they feel. Counsellors do not suggest, guide or coerce. They use active listening and reflective listening skills, offering a calm environment for the child.

Refer to Unit 1, pages 18 and 19 to remind yourself about active and reflective listening skills.

Sometimes additional therapies are used to help children explore issues, and raise self-esteem and improve body image. For example:

- play therapy
- art therapy
- music therapy.

Play therapy

Play therapy is the most commonly used therapy. It shows children that they are valued and helps them to continue to value themselves as they move through the healing process. Children have always re-enacted familiar situations through their play, exploring and making sense of roles and events so, on this basis, providing therapy through play makes good sense. Following abuse, the purpose of therapy is to help children move on from being victims and become survivors. It needs to be a non-threatening experience for the child, be relevant to their age and stage of development and be carried out by people who understand what they are doing and the limitations of the therapy that they are providing. It is not something that untrained individuals should attempt to involve themselves in, although early years settings are an excellent source of creative opportunities for children, as they can express themselves through paint, clay, role play, and so on.

The timing of structured play therapy sessions should be carefully considered. Sometimes a child will have a greater need that must be met before successful therapy can begin. For example, it may be desirable to establish a more settled home life or increase the involvement of the child's family. Play therapists need to build up a trusting relationship with a child, and time for this will be incorporated into any programme that is devised. Trust is all important in helping children relax, feel safe and understand that they are able to express themselves in safety. Most often, sessions with a play therapist take place weekly for an hour at a time. Children are (within safety limits) able to direct the play, deciding what they will do and how they will go about it. Therapy sessions are the child's own special time, and the therapist, while being present throughout, is often subsidiary to the play, remaining alert to what is happening and ready to respond where it is felt to be appropriate.

A useful definition of play therapy was drawn up by the British Association of Play Therapists:

> 'Play therapy is the dynamic process between child and Play Therapist in which the child explores at his or her own pace and with his or her own agenda those issues, past and current, conscious and unconscious, that are affecting the child's life in the present. The child's inner resources are enabled by the therapeutic alliance to bring about growth and change. Play therapy is child-centred, in which play is the primary medium and speech is the secondary medium. Play Therapy encompasses many approaches but the foundation of all approaches is child-centred.'
>
> (British Association of Play Therapists, Code of Ethics and Practice, 1996)

This definition encompasses the main focus of play therapy, in that it is largely a non-verbal experience. Play is the most natural way in which children express themselves. Babies make sense of their world exploring through play, and a similar process occurs for traumatised children. Play therapy gives them the opportunity to express and make sense of what they have experienced, supported by the experience and understanding of a specialist adult.

Typical resources provided by play therapists

Some therapists will work from a room that has been specially set out and will ensure that aspects of the room remain constant for the child to give added security. Others work peripatetically and may find themselves having to use a range of suitable (and barely suitable) places; many of these therapists will establish a safe area for the child by using a rug or mat to define a special space, thereby endeavouring to give some consistency to the sessions.

Puppets form an important part of most therapists' resources. Puppets can be used to represent victims and survivors; and dominant and passive individuals, giving opportunities to demonstrate strength and power (and how power can be overthrown). Animal puppets may offer a less personalised way for some children to symbolise their lives and experiences.

Dolls of different sizes, cultures, genders, and states of dress are also common, with or without dolls' houses and vehicles. These offer scope for children to illustrate their family members, and the other significant adults in their lives, within their play. Many children will have had a transient lifestyle with multiple homes; providing a considerable number of 'people' will allow these children greater scope to explore their experience.

remember The trickling sensation of sand can be very calming.

Monsters, bizarre creatures, snakes and worms are common items, allowing children to explore and deal with 'nasty', 'wicked' and 'evil' individuals.

Creative materials such as drawing, painting, collage, face painting and clay offer children the chance to immerse themselves in their chosen medium and communicate some of their feelings; sand play and water play are always therapeutic giving children pleasure and opportunities to express themselves.

The following two titles give an interesting and accessible introduction to play therapy, offering examples drawn from experience: *Play Therapy with Abused Children* by Cattanach (1992) and *Introduction to Therapeutic Play* by Carroll (1998).

For general accounts of the work of therapists, the following books are wonderful examples: *Poppies on the Rubbish Heap: Sexual Abuse – The Child's Voice* by Bray (1991); and *Dibs: In Search of Self* by Axline (1964). These two books are, however, quite explicit in content and you should be aware that they can at times be quite distressing.

remember Compiling a list of voluntary organisations would be helpful as a source of information for you for the future and will also enable you to pass on details to the families you work with, if appropriate.

Role of voluntary organisations

In most areas of Britain there are voluntary organisations that support children and families with many of life's crises. Voluntary organisations play an important part, as the level of funding available for statutory services rarely meets local needs. Examples include NSPCC, NCH and ChildLine.

Progress Check

1. What is meant by the term 'predisposing factor'?
2. Give at least five examples of indicators of physical abuse.
3. Give at least five examples of indicators of neglect.
4. Give at least five examples of indicators of sexual abuse.
5. Why is it important to understand how paedophiles operate?
6. Give at least five examples of indicators of emotional abuse.
7. Why is confidentiality important?
8. What is the child protection register?
9. In what way can the key-worker system contribute to the safety and welfare of children?
10. List 10 examples of how you should respond if a child discloses abuse to you.
11. What examples can you give of teaching children self-protection strategies?
12. Why is it important to gain permission from parents before taking and displaying photographs?
13. Explain the importance of clear records in early years settings.
14. What should you consider when involved with a child's physical care?
15. How would you explain the difference between the short-term and long-term effects of abuse?

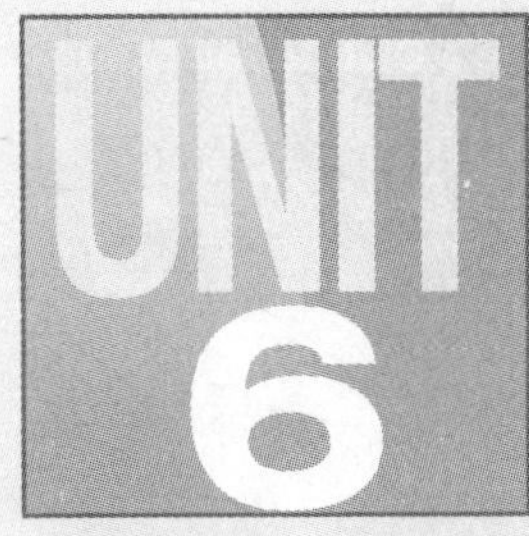

Promoting Children's Rights

This unit covers the following objectives:

- Understand the meaning of diversity in today's society
- Understand the importance of equality, recognising diversity and rights in services for children
- Understand the ways in which services for children recognise and promote equality, diversity and rights
- Know the ways in which the individual worker can promote inclusion in their own practice

Good practice in early years work addresses all issues of prejudice, racism and discrimination. This unit explores the principle of equity and considers how early years settings can promote equality and rights. It begins by describing some of the cultural and other differences in people that contribute to the diversity of British society and then looks at why it is important that the individual early years worker is aware that prejudice and inequality can adversely affect children's opportunities for development, before examining the ways in which legislation, policies and settings promote diversity and equality and protect the rights of children and their families.

You will be encouraged to explore your personal values, your own practice and that of others. Reviewing your own practice and identifying how you can promote equality of opportunity and diversity will help you to develop professionally and will have a positive effect on much of your work during your course of study.

grading criteria

To achieve a **Pass** grade the evidence must show that the learner is able to:	**To achieve a Merit grade the evidence must show that, in addition to the pass criteria, the learner is able to:**	To achieve a **Distinction** grade the evidence must show that, in addition to the pass and merit criteria, the learner is able to:
P1 describe the meaning of diversity in today's society page 283	**M1** describe the implications for children's settings of addressing issues of diversity page 283	**D1** analyse the value of diversity in today's society and its relevance for children's care, learning and development practice page 285
P2 explain causes of economic diversity and potential effects on children, their families, and society page 284	**M2** explain how one policy from a children's setting meets the requirements of a piece of legislation page 297	**D2** analyse the role of children's care, learning and development practitioners in ensuring the promotion of inclusive practice. page 312

To achieve a **Pass** grade the evidence must show that the learner is able to:	**To achieve a Merit grade the evidence must show that, in addition to the pass criteria, the learner is able to:**	To achieve a **Distinction** grade the evidence must show that, in addition to the pass and merit criteria, the learner is able to:
P3 explain the importance of recognising equality, diversity and rights in providing children's services page 290	**M3** use examples to explain how practices in children's services can promote equality of opportunity, inclusion and rights page 304	
P4 identify how legislation promotes equality of opportunity, inclusion and rights page 295		
P5 describe how practices in children's services can promote equality of opportunity, inclusion and rights page 305		
P6 explain how the individual worker can promote inclusion. page 312		

Understand the meaning of diversity in today's society

Diversity in contemporary British society

In contemporary British society, we need to consider diversity within each of the following areas.

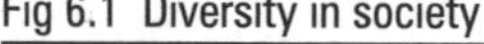
Fig 6.1 Diversity in society

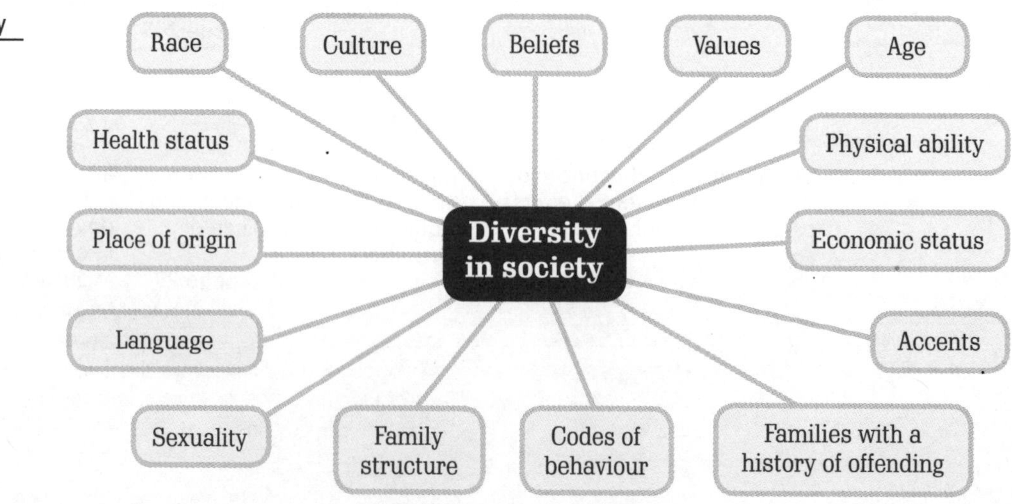

P1

M1

Having looked at the spidergram above, consider what diversity means.

1 Explain diversity to a friend. How fully do you both understand your explanation?

  Often, in explaining something to another person you can identify how well you understand it yourself.

2 Describe how each aspect of diversity can be supported within early years. The following examples will get you started. You will also find it helpful to read through the rest of this unit:

  (a) Physical ability: this can involve the variety of skill levels reached by children within any given age range and applies to children with and without a specific need. It also applies to adults: staff, parents and other carers. The layout of the environment may need adjusting to enable access for some individuals. Specific equipment may help others to achieve greater independence. What examples can you find in your placement?

  (b) Language diversity: this applies to children and adults for whom English is not their first language, children with identified speech difficulties, and children with delayed speech, including those with hearing loss. Consideration of language diversity will be needed in relation to notices, letters and general information, books, posters, and methods of personal address. Where have you identified the support of language diversity within your placement?

Economic diversity

Economic diversity refers to having or not having sufficient finances to enable you and your family to live healthily, without hardship. The distribution of wealth and income in Britain indicates clear differences across the population. For example, the Institute for Fiscal Studies states that 'the richest 10% of the population now have as much income as the whole of the poorer 50% of households' (Gregg *et al.*, 1999).

Social inequality

The life chances of an individual are likely to be linked to their social group, age, gender and ethnicity. (This division of people into social 'groups' or 'classes' is sometimes referred to as 'social stratification'.) However, individuals who are talented or intellectually able can frequently be found in positions of more influence or power than would have been predicted from those factors. This positive outcome is often referred to as a 'system of meritocracy'.

Having a disability can impact on health, and often also on economic status. Families within the working class group will usually live and work in environments different from those of the upper and middle classes. Income levels tend to differ considerably, and some families are unable to afford to buy the better (and often healthier) foods. Also, on the whole, people from the upper and middle classes work in better environments and are less likely to be affected by factors such as chemicals and noise, found in many factory workplaces, or the boredom and repetition often associated with many factory and manual positions. A greater number of working class adults smoke, and so the risk of passive smoking in the home increases for their children and close contacts.

Inequality is discussed further on pages 286–288.

Concepts of poverty

Poverty can be described as absolute or relative.

Absolute poverty

Absolute poverty is having the basic necessities that are needed to live. Absolute poverty will be defined differently across the world according to the level of social and economic development of the area concerned. If you think about the living conditions in Britain, you will easily be able to draw up a list of what you consider necessary in order to live healthily and avoid poverty. Now think about the circumstances of people living in a developing country, such as the Sudan; their definition of poverty is likely to be different from yours.

The Rowntree Foundation has compiled a list of what is considered necessary in our society to be above the 'poverty line'.
www.jrf.org

Relative poverty

Relative poverty refers to how restricted or deprived one person is in comparison with other similar people. For example, a person may consider themselves to be impoverished compared with their neighbours when there are differences in the cars they can afford, the quality of the clothing they buy, their choice of restaurant, and so on. Another person, whose neighbour also has a better car etc., may not perceive themselves as deprived. Even within the same street, one person's definition of poverty can differ widely from another's.

The effects of poverty on children, families and society

Poverty can affect all aspects of well-being. Health, growth rate and ability to concentrate will be affected in a child who is under-nourished, or who is living in a cramped, unheated or damp home. Parents who are struggling to manage financially are often worried and distracted, giving children less attention than is ideal. They may be unemployed, depressed and have low self-esteem. Negative feelings in parents can easily cause children to be worried, and at times neglected.

Ideally using the area in which you live, produce an information sheet suitable to be given to local counsellors explaining how economic disadvantage is potentially affecting children in their constituency. Make clear the economic diversity of the area and how this impacts on children and on their families and wider society.

Advantages of diversity

A pluralist society is one which consists of groups of people of distinctive ethnic origins, cultures or religions. The UK is a pluralist society and therefore offers us the opportunity to explore differences in customs and ways of living. Its diversity also enables us to socialise and work with people with disabilities, owing to the improved accessibility of places of recreation (although still inadequate in places) and the greater recognition rightly given to disabled people in the workplace. There are more opportunities to interact with older people because the population is living longer.

A diverse culture enriches our lives by opening up new experiences, enabling us to learn about the wider world and to explore and appreciate the distinctions and similarities between cultures, races and religions. Our personal understanding is further enhanced by recognising that minority and vulnerable groups face hurdles not experienced by the rest of us and by our working to address these difficulties.

Professional Practice

- It is of even greater importance to introduce diversity into early years settings where few cultures are represented. This will extend children's knowledge and understanding of alternative languages, religions and ways of life.
- This preparation will aid children in forming values that will help them deal with any discrimination and prejudice that they may encounter later in life.

An excellent resource for understanding discrimination and legislation, in particular, is *The Equal Opportunities Handbook* by Clements and Spinks (2000, 3rd edn).

Fig 6.2 Advantages of diversity in the UK

Advantages of diversity in the UK

- Diversity of family make-up helps us to understand the particular importance of the extended family in some cultures
- Opportunities for new knowledge and experiences of the rest of the world
- Opportunities to learn a variety of languages
- Social, moral and ethical understanding is enhanced by witnessing perseverance
- Patience shown by people facing restrictions gives a positive role model
- Clothing and costumes from various cultures adds a richness to life
- Foods from around the world are explored and enjoyed by many different cultures
- Diverse lifestyles demonstrate how different cultures can live successfully within a joint society
- Festivals and celebrations throughout the year offer enrichment and opportunities for shared cross-cultural experiences
- Opportunities to learn about other religions help us identify the similarities and appreciate the differences between religions
- Increased knowledge of religions etiquette and relevant rituals helps us understand the needs of people who follow that religion

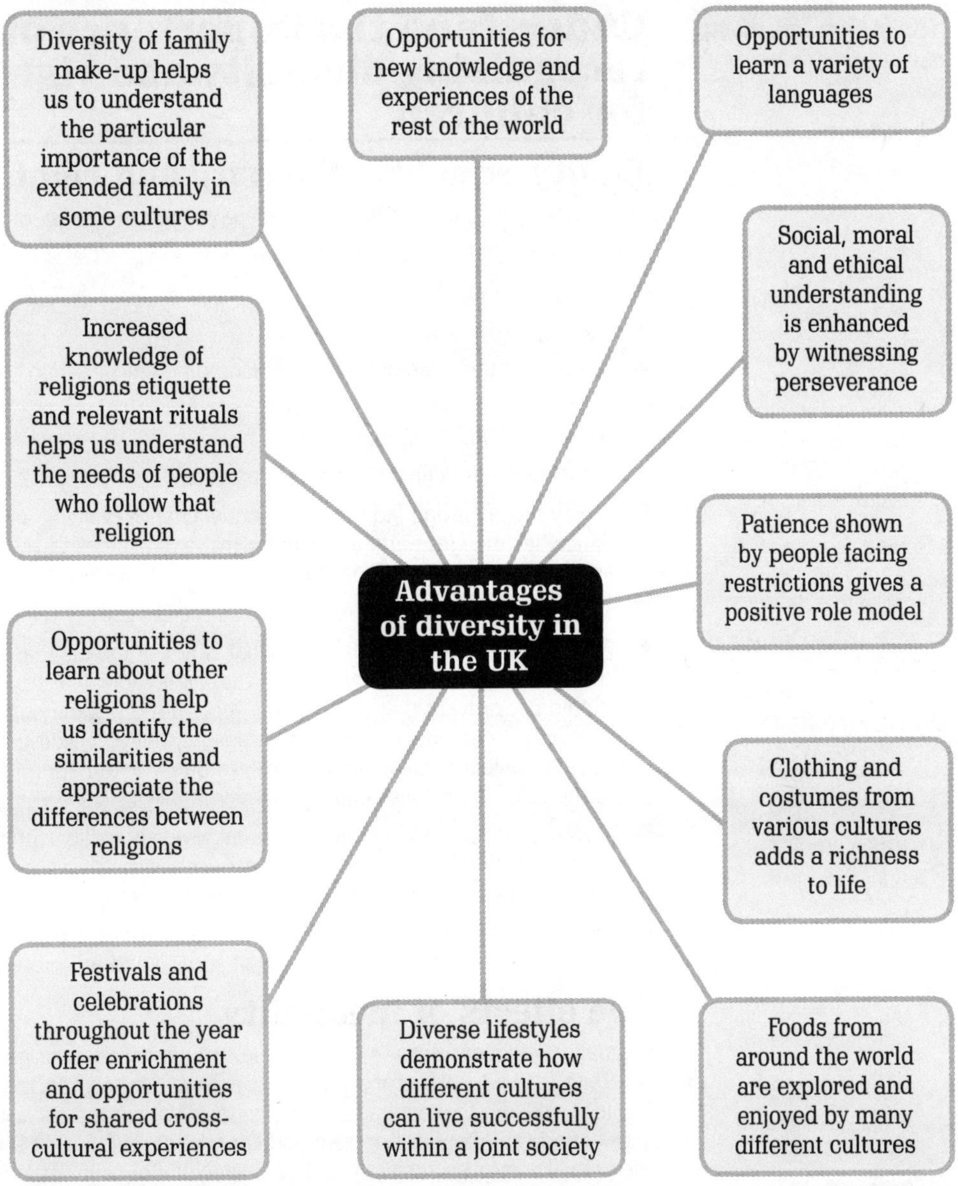

remember

As individuals we each have rights.

Link

Refer to pages 292–293 for information on human rights and, specifically, the rights of children.

activity
GROUP WORK 6.3
D1

Identify ways in which multicultural and mixed ability teaching enriches life in contemporary society. Analyse how this richness impacts on early years practice, for example through:

1 the personal experiences of parents and staff
2 the 'shrinking' world in relation to travel opportunities
3 various media images, such as television, books and magazines

Understand the importance of equality, recognising diversity and rights in services for children

Equity, equality, diversity and rights

The terms equity, equality, diversity and rights are used often, but what do they actually mean? The dictionary definitions of these terms are:

- equity – 'an impartial or fair act, decision, etc.'
- equality – 'the state of being equal'
- diversity – 'the state or quality of being different or varied'
- rights – 'any claim ... that is morally just or legally granted as allowable or due to a person' (*Collins Dictionary*, 1991).

But what do these definitions mean in practice?

- Equity means giving individuals an equal chance, valuing and acknowledging the difficulties they face and allowing for those difficulties in your planning for, dealing with, and tolerance of, each individual.
- This would sometimes be referred to as the concept of tolerance.
- Equality refers to what is fair and what is not. It means that an individual's family or cultural background, the way they live, or the individual's past or current state of health should not prevent that person from receiving the same opportunities as anyone else in society. Intervention is needed to ensure that all children have an equal chance to achieve, to learn, to join in activities, to be parented appropriately and to live according to the cultural practices chosen by their families.
- Diversity refers to the range of different levels of ability within any group of individuals, to the variety of cultures and religions, each with its own experiences, which make up a group or society, and to the age range of any group.
- Rights are the entitlements of each individual to receive the same opportunities as others. Many rights are linked to standards of service and are protected by legislation (laws).

The effects of inequality

Inequality within any society can result in some individuals or groups being less able than others to take advantage of the benefits available in their society, and they may consequently feel less valued. This can lead to a feeling of isolation and exclusion from mainstream society and can affect self-esteem and confidence. Within our society, some children and their families may be subject to certain types of inequality that may affect their health, development and well-being on a short-term or even permanent basis. It is important that early years workers are aware of these differences so that children and families in need can be identified and interventions planned.

Fig 6.3 Inequality within society

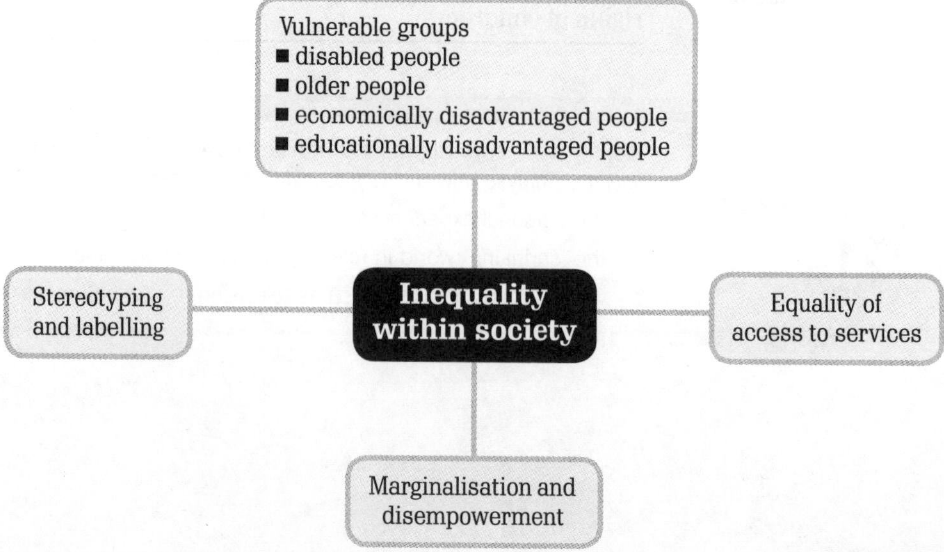

For a fuller discussion of equal opportunities in society in general, look at the 'Equal opportunities' chapter in Stephen Moore's *Social Welfare Alive* (2002, 3rd edn).

Marginalisation and disempowerment

Owing to oppression, discrimination or inequalities, certain groups may find themselves at the edges of mainstream society or even excluded from it. Members of such a group may feel isolated and less able to participate in the activities of daily life. People belonging to a **marginalised** group may be denied opportunities to take control of their lives and make choices. This disempowerment can have far-reaching effects. People who are disempowered see themselves as being 'less than equal' in society.

Vulnerable groups and equality of access to services

Certain groups may be more vulnerable to inequality than others, owing to disability, poor health, age, gender, poverty, nationality, religious beliefs or lack of educational opportunities. Being treated less fairly because of vulnerability may result in the individuals in a group becoming trapped in a cycle of disadvantage from which it may be difficult to break free. Disadvantaged and vulnerable groups may then find that they are less able to obtain or gain access to services that may help and support them – this is known as the 'inverse care law'.

The cycle of disadvantage

A cycle of disadvantage can occur. Children can be disadvantaged whatever their ethnic background, religion, language, social class or gender; However, when children are members of social or cultural groups which are already marginalised by society it is harder to break out of this cycle. As children move through life, they experience the consequences of their family's lifestyle, type of housing and employment opportunities. Some will, of course, adopt different lifestyles as they grow older, but others will not and the situation may well be perpetuated for their own children.

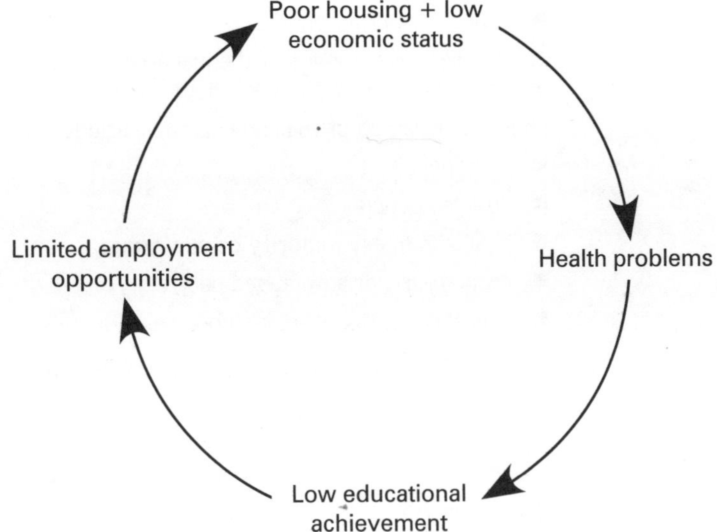

Fig 6.4 The cycle of disadvantage

case study 6.1 Traveller families

A travelling group of five families was heading for an authorised traveller site near a maternity unit as two of the women were due to give birth. On arrival, they found that the site was completely full and so they moved on to an unauthorised site at which they had stopped in the past. Whilst the first woman was giving birth in hospital that night, the five men were arrested and charged with unauthorised occupation and ordered to move on and not return to the authority. They waited until the second woman had given birth two days later; she returned to her trailer almost immediately. When the community midwife went to visit the next day, both women and all the families had gone.

activity GROUP WORK

1 What inequalities can you identify here?
2 In what ways were these families facing disadvantage?
3 Do you consider these families to be a marginalised group?
4 What rights do you think these families were entitled to?
5 What might be the long-term health issues for these new babies?
6 What are the implications for the education of children who are moved on like this?

In the case study above, there were examples of:

- inequality
- marginalisation
- disempowerment
- vulnerability
- potential economic disadvantage
- educational disadvantage.

The families were being denied equal access to services, as the men were likely to be imprisoned if the group did not move on.

Other marginalised or vulnerable groups include:

- older people
- disabled people
- people from any **minority ethnic group**
- economically disadvantaged people
- educationally disadvantaged people.

The value base of the early years care sector

The overriding values in early years support the all-round welfare of a child, in partnership with the child's family.

The effects of inequality on people can be summarised as follows:

- Certain groups may be regarded as less able or less valued than others, owing to ethnic origin, gender, age, ability, income, social class, etc.
- Members of these groups may find it harder to obtain the social benefits that the majority enjoy.
- This can lead to short- or long-term effects on health, education and employment, as well as affecting emotional and social well-being.

Stereotyping and labelling

Belonging to a group that is seen as 'different' or experiences unequal treatment can lead to stereotyping and labelling. Stereotyping involves treating members of a group as if they are all the same and prejudging an individual on the basis of their group membership. Stereotyped judgements are frequently both inappropriate and incorrect. Upholding stereotypes takes away people's individuality or personal identity.

Fig 6.5 The welfare of the child

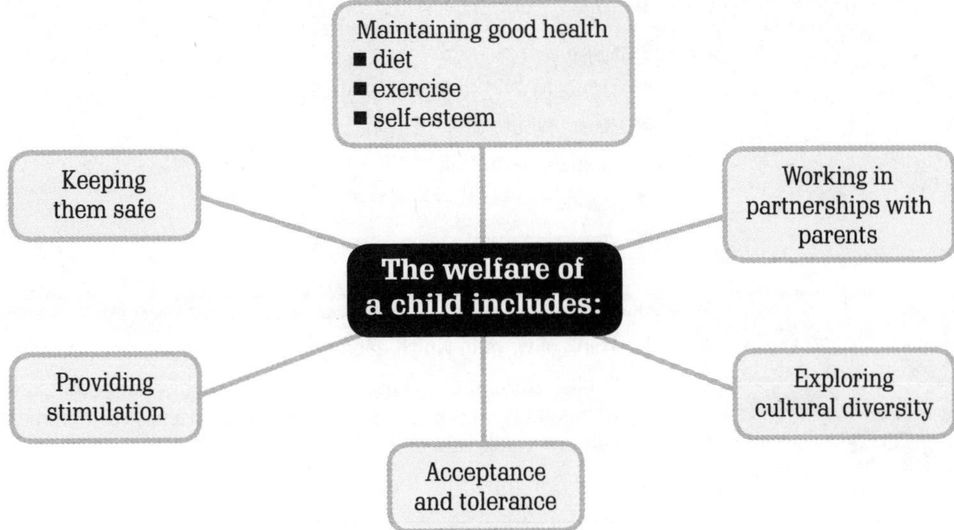

Stereotypical images can be positive or negative and, although they are sometimes built up by personal experience, they are more often due to the influences of others, including the media.

An example of a stereotyped idea might be that 'all students are nightclubbers'. While many students do, of course, enjoy nightclub life, many do not, but students in general are a good example of a social group who are 'lumped together' for many stereotyped assumptions. You can probably think of many other examples of stereotyping. It is important to remember that:

- Stereotypical judgements are frequently both inappropriate and incorrect.
- Upholding stereotypes takes away people's individuality or personal identity.

Discrimination and prejudice

To discriminate means to give favourable or unfavourable treatment to someone or something because of a specific factor. There can be:

- **institutional discrimination**, where the policies or practices of a workplace result in treating certain groups of people differently
- or individual discrimination, where the prejudice (an opinion formed in advance) is the personal bias of one person.

Discrimination can be:

- direct, where people are told that they are not allowed to do something because of their race, sex, situation or disability
- indirect, by excluding individuals who are unable to take part in or do something because of their race, sex, situation or disability. For example, a school which refuses to allow hats or headgear to be worn will be indirectly discriminating against those who traditionally wear them as part of their cultural dress. This would include Jewish boys who wear a yarmulke, Sikh boys who wear a turban, and Pakistani girls who wear a hijab.

Groups of individuals can become marginalised by society through prejudice and discrimination, making them feel unable to initiate change or make their voices heard, and making them feel disempowered.

remember

Prejudice	+	Power	=	Discrimination
(a pre-formed opinion)	+	(the practice of the setting)	=	(certain individuals may not receive equal opportunities

A number of groups face discrimination in society. These include people who are the victims of prejudice on the grounds of their:

- age
- class
- disability and differing abilities
- race, culture and religion
- sexual orientation
- gender
- marital status.

activity
INDIVIDUAL WORK 6.4
P3

1 Think of ways in which each group listed above faces discrimination.
2 Explain how, in each case, there might be discrimination in early years settings. Remember to consider issues of staffing, access, communication, economics, clothing, cultural rituals and diet.
3 Why is it important that these issues are addressed?

It is important to be aware of the possibility that, in early years settings, there could be discrimination based on, for example:

- age – adolescent parents/older parents
- class – 'wrong' class from the wrong area/not good enough/too 'posh' for 'us'
- disability, differing abilities – inaccessibility/not asked to help out/avoided/limited
- race, culture, religion – only one culture catered for/devaluing or non-recognition of other cultures and religious festivals
- sexual orientation – homophobia (a dislike of homosexual people)/suspicions
- gender – fathers not encouraged/stereotyping of 'help' (men to fix toys, women to cook)
- marital status – values attached to marital status/meetings not accessible to single parents.

Professional Practice

- **The points raised above indicate the need for policies. A strong equal opportunities policy is essential to monitor and maintain equality.**
- **It would be useful to consider any early years setting that you are familiar with to see if any element of practice could be classed as prejudiced or discriminatory.**

Refer to page 296, where the importance of policies and the contents of a policy are discussed.

Supporting vulnerable groups

Being in a minority often makes the individual more vulnerable to all negative aspects of society. This can include prejudice, discrimination and disempowerment. Being the target of prejudice and discrimination causes a multitude of negative feelings in an individual, including vulnerability, hurt, devaluing of self, confusion, disempowerment and uncertainty. It is an intolerable situation which must be addressed. As an early years professional, you have obligations to protect the rights of the children in your care, by speaking up for them when they are unable to do so for themselves, and to support their value as a person.

You need to consider how you will address negativity when you come across it, because, if you fail to speak out when you hear or see an act of prejudice or discrimination, you will be failing the children or families you are supposed to be supporting. To ignore an offensive comment made to one child by another will be to passively condone the comment. This passivity will compound the hurt for the child receiving the comment (as you will not have stepped in to correct the 'wrong' and to give support) and will fail to help the child making the comment develop more positive values (sometimes children simply need guidance in how to speak and act). It is pointless having a 'correct' range of resources available to explore and promote positive attitudes to cultural differences and disability if negative incidents are ignored.

Help in addressing prejudice and discrimination

At times, you may feel you need support in redressing prejudice and/or discrimination. Your supervisor or tutor will be able to advise you. Alternatively, there are a variety of organisations, written materials and online sources that may help you.

Help and advice about combating prejudice or discrimination can be found through the:

- Race Relations Act 1976 as amended by the Race Relations (Amendment) Act 2000. These Acts make it unlawful to discriminate against anyone on the grounds of race, colour, nationality (including citizenship) or ethnic or national origin. The newest legislation also gives public bodies and authorities the power to promote racial equality.
- Commission for Racial Equality (CRE). The CRE monitors the way in which race relations legislation is working; gives advice to those who think they have been discriminated against and aims to promote equality of opportunity and promote good relations between people from different racial and ethnic backgrounds.
- Sex Discrimination Act 1985. This makes sex discrimination against men or women illegal and is monitored by the Equal Opportunities Commission.
- Commission for Equal Opportunities. This deals with sex discrimination and inequality issues related to gender.
- Disability Rights Commission. This independent body aims to stop discrimination and promote equality of opportunity for disabled people.

Commission for Racial Equality (CRE)
www.cre.gov.uk
Commission for Equal Opportunities
www.eoc.org.uk
Disability Rights Commission
www.drc-gb.org

Where does discrimination stem from?

Much discriminatory practice comes from ignorance and lack of understanding; it is sometimes accidental but often intentional. As a professional in the early years sector, you need to become informed in order to avoid the accidental, and to address any personal prejudices in order to remove the intentional.

Historical perspective on racial prejudice and discrimination

The UK has been a diverse society throughout history, beginning with the Bronze Age and the Neolithic migrants who settled in northern Europe 5000 years ago. There have been invasions by the Romans, Saxons, Vikings and Normans, and many refugees have come to the UK, for example from France, Ireland, Russia, Uganda and Eastern Europe, fleeing war, persecution or famine in their own countries.

Significant groups of immigrants include the following:

- Jews first came at the invitation of William I (William the Conqueror) in the eleventh century. They were the founders of banking and financial services in the UK. Throughout history they have been persecuted, discriminated against and even expelled from the country at times.
- From the fourteenth century, Flemish and French weavers, German mining engineers and Dutch canal builders came, bringing with them new skills.
- In the sixteenth and seventeen centuries, Protestant refugees (Huguenots) came from France; they played a major role in British society.
- African slaves were brought to the UK by the slave trade to work as servants (the slave trade was abolished in 1807 and slavery in 1838).
- Irish refugees, fleeing poverty and famine in the 1830s–1850s, worked in the new industries, in the mines, docks, canals and railways.

Other significant groups of immigrants have come from Italy, China and the Indian subcontinent. In fact, according to the Commission for Racial Equality, most people in the UK today have origins somewhere else and can probably trace the immigrants in their family histories. Only about seven per cent of the British population were not born in the UK, but immigrants have been met with hostility and resentment.

Black people, in particular, have suffered prejudice and discrimination in the UK. They were expelled by Queen Elizabeth I in 1601 and attempts were made to return them to their country of birth at various times during that century. As recently as 1925, laws were passed which prevented black people from working on British ships, and anti-black riots were seen in areas of the UK in 1919 and 1948.

When the UK suffered a serious shortage of labour after the Second World War, the British government encouraged immigration, first from European refugees, then from Ireland and the Commonwealth. In 1948, the first of these immigrant recruits arrived, being employed to do the low-paid, unskilled jobs that British workers had not filled. However, tension arose between the ethnic minority groups and the white population, resulting in race riots. Some people claimed that the large numbers of immigrants that had relocated to the UK were causing greater economic problems for the country. In 1962, the Commonwealth Immigrants Act was introduced, with entry into the UK allowed only if certain criteria were met: for example, if the applicant had a job arranged.

Since that time, the UK has continued to see large numbers of black and Asian workers employed in lower-paid and unskilled jobs, and this has continued to reinforce the message of lower values for these groups of people. There are, however, greater numbers of people from ethnic minority groups than ever before achieving positions of management and power in the UK, indicating that acceptance and equality is developing. As an early years professional, you will need to uphold and promote this thinking too.

An ideal source of information about the historical perspective on racial discrimination and prejudice is *Sociology: Themes and Perspectives* by Haralambos and Holborn (2000).

Best practice

Human Rights Act 1998

The Human Rights Act 1998 focuses on the individual's right to a life free from torture, loss of liberty, unfair punishment or discrimination. It also refers to respect for private and family life (Article 8), freedom of thought, conscience and religion (Article 9) and the freedom of expression (Article 10). The Act is linked to the drawing-up of no-smacking policies and is also relevant to female circumcision.

Refer to Unit 5, page 241, for discussion of these issues.

UN Convention on the Rights of the Child 1989

This is an international agreement on human rights which has been ratified by 191 countries. It consists of 54 articles (statements) and its four main principles are:

- *Non-discrimination*. All children have the same rights and are entitled to the same treatment.
- *Children's best interests*. The best interests of the child should be placed as highest priority when making decisions about the child's future.
- *Survival and development of children*. Children have the right to survive and the right to be able to develop to their full potential.
- *Rights to participation*. The views of children should be taken seriously and they should be able to take part in what is going on around them.

The Convention is important because it brings together in one document all the rights of children; adults are asked to view children as individuals with all human rights being applied to children everywhere (based on a paper by Save the Children, 2000).

Examples of articles set out within the Convention have been unofficially summarised by Flekkøy and Kaufman in *The Participation Rights of the Child* (1997) as follows:

- Article 2 – all rights apply to all children without exception, and the state is obliged to protect children from any form of discrimination. The state must not violate any right and must take positive action to promote them all
- Article 22 – special protection to be granted to children who are refugees or seeking refugee status, and the state's obligation to co-operate with competent organisations providing such protection and assistance

- Article 23 – the right of handicapped children to special care, education and training designed to help them achieve greatest possible self-reliance and to lead a full and active life in society
- Article 30 – the right of children of minority communities and indigenous populations to practise their own culture, their own religion and language.

Children Acts, 1989, 2004

Best practice ensures that the best quality of care is provided and supports the directive of the Children Act 2004, that local authorities provide day-care provision that is staffed appropriately.

As individuals we each have rights

> 'People working with young children should value and respect the different racial origins, religions, cultures and languages in a multi-racial society so that each child is valued as an individual without racial or gender stereotyping. Children from a very young age learn about different races and cultures including religion and languages and will be capable of assigning different values to them. The same applies to gender and making distinctions between male and female roles. It is important that people working with young children are aware of this, so that their practice enables the children to develop positive attitudes to differences of race, culture and language and differences of gender.'

(*Children Act 1989, Guidance and Regulations*, Volume 2, Section 6.10)

See page 295 for more on the Children Act.

Supporting identity

In *Supporting Identity, Diversity and Language in the Early Years*, Siraj-Blatchford and Clarke (2000) state that the first two foundations of learning are:

- 'The child needs to be in a state of emotional well-being and secure.
- The child needs a positive self-identity and self-esteem.'

(Siraj-Blatchford and Clarke, 2000).

The aim of all early years staff should be to build up a child's self-identity and self-esteem by providing them with positive images of their lives and people and job roles with which they can identify. If you do not acknowledge and place value on the diversity within your working environment, you will not be fulfilling your professional role adequately and the children's sense of identity will be less positively reinforced.

Refer to Unit 3, page 134, for information on self-identity and emotional development.

Professional Practice

- **Working to the principles of the Children Act will ensure that your professional practice is consistently good, rather than consistently adequate, and that the children you care for benefit holistically.**
- **It is important to remember that acknowledging difference is not the same as being prejudiced. It is the value that you place on difference that indicates whether prejudice exists or not.**

Provision and services

With the move in recent years towards achieving integration whenever possible, more children with additional needs have had greater access to a broader range of facilities. Local authorities work with parents to decide what is best for the child. This may be an integrated place within a mainstream setting or a separate placement where specialised support and equipment is more readily available and the environment is more suited to the child. Decisions are based on assessments and observation of the child, medical reports and the outcomes of a statement of educational need. The child's needs are then set out in an individual education plan (IEP).

Issues that are taken into consideration include;

- the child's assessed needs (e.g. medical assessment etc.)
- personal choice of parent and/or child
- negative implications of segregation (e.g. separation from siblings, stigma, etc.)
- any difficulty in accessing a certain provision and what has to be done to overcome this (e.g. distance from home, issues of transport, funding, etc.)
- the resources available in the local community to support equality of access (e.g. specialist training of staff).

Sources of information for children and their families

All local authorities have an Early Years Partnership, and part of this partnership includes a Children's Information Service (CIS). Anyone can access the CIS. It typically holds information on mainstream schools, specialised schools, preschools, nurseries and childminders, as well as information on interpreters, advocates and translators. Most CIS centres can also provide contact details for a range of support groups and organisations.

This service helps both parents and professionals find the most suitable placement and support for children as individuals.

Understand the ways in which services for children recognise and promote equality, diversity and rights

Settings should recognise and promote equality, diversity and rights. The promotion of equality and rights by any organisation can be considered in terms of:

- legislation
- policies and practice
- individual rights.

As we shall see, however, there are some reasons why it is considered beneficial to override an individual's rights.

Legislation

Legislation involves a range of charters and Acts of Parliament which control and monitor the treatment of individuals. These Acts form the basis for many of the policies and procedures on which early years practice is based.

Examples include:

- Children Act 2004
- Human Rights Act 1998
- UN Convention on the Rights of the Child 1989
- Disability Discrimination Act 1995, 1997 and 2005
- Special Education Needs and Disability Act 2001
- Code of Practice for Special Educational Needs 2001.

This is the legislation most relevant to your role as an early years professional.

More about legislation can be found on page 295.

It would also be useful to know about the following legislation:

- Race Relations Act 1976
- Race Relations (Amendment) Act 2000.
- Sex Discrimination Act 1975, 1976
- Criminal Justice Act 1994
- Mental Health Act 1993
- Equal Pay Act 1970
- Equal Pay Act (Amendment) 1983

- Citizen's Charter
- Patient's Charter.

P4

1 Find out what you can about each of these Acts and Charters to build up an overall picture of the legislative rights of all people in society.
2 On a large poster, make clear the main aspects of each.
3 Be prepared to talk through and answer questions on your poster.

Copies of all government legislation are available from HMSO bookshops and on UK government websites.

The legislation most directly relevant to early years professionals is described below. This legislation may affect the children in your care either directly, with regard to their own rights or needs, or indirectly, through the rights or needs of their families.

Children Act 2004

The principles of the Children Act 1989 (and now the Children Act 2004) include the following points:

- The welfare of the child is paramount and should be safeguarded and promoted at all times by those providing services.
- Children with disabilities are children first with the same rights to services as all children.
- Parents and families are important in children's lives. Local authorities should support them in carrying out their responsibilities.
- Parents should be valued as partners with local authorities and other agencies such as health and education services.
- Children have a right to be consulted and listened to when decisions about them are being made. Their views and the views of their parents must always be taken into account.
- Health, education and social services for children with disabilities should be co-coordinated (Dare and O'Donovan, 2002).

Volume 2 of the Children Act specifically covers day care and states that parents have a right to influence the quality of education that their child receives; therefore they have the right to make enquiries about what is available and to be able to understand the information that they receive. Parents with limited use of English are often disadvantaged in this and may require the help of an advocate or interpreter.

Section 22(5)(c) of the Children Act states that local authorities must give consideration to the religious persuasion, racial origin, cultural and linguistic background of any child within their care. Any provider of care for children can be deregistered if these needs and rights are not properly cared for, as they would not be considered to be a 'fit' person to care for children, under the Act.

Professional Practice

- **Early years settings can help parents by, whenever possible, presenting information in languages other than English.**
- **Visual information will also help to some extent. Involving an advocate or interpreter will show that you value the family's heritage language and their need for information.**

Refer to Unit 1, page 23, for information about advocates and interpreters.

Gillick competence (now known as the Fraser ruling)

Although it does not form a part of the Children Act, children's rights are sometimes considered under the principle of **Gillick competence**. This is based on a child's ability to make their own decisions and give informed consent. This principle was first drawn up in connection with the issue of giving medical treatment (contraception) without the agreement of parents. It is a principle that is not applied at any one particular age, as each child and the relevant situation is considered individually, to ascertain whether the child is considered to be 'Gillick competent'. The principle of Gillick competence has been used in connection with Section 8 of the Children Act (particularly the prohibited steps order) in which a child may challenge the directive of the courts, for example in the contact the child is allowed to have with a parent. A child does not have an automatic right to appeal under Section 8, and Gillick competence is determined by health professionals, together with others relevant to the case, such as a child psychologist, to decide whether a child has sufficient understanding of all the relevant circumstances. The term 'Gillick competent' has now been replaced by the term 'Fraser ruling'.

Disability Discrimination Act 1995, 1997

This Act is directly relevant to early years in that it supports the ethos of the Education Act 1993 which underlines the necessity to provide all children who have a special need with an appropriate education at a suitable school. All settings should have a special educational needs co-coordinator (SENCO) who is responsible for ensuring that the special needs of children are met. In schools, this would be a member of the teaching staff who liaises with parents and other staff and keeps records of the special educational needs within the school.

The Special Educational Needs and Disability Act 2001 (SENDA) and revised Regulations

This Act and its associated Regulations came into force in January 2002 and clarified the duties of local education authorities (LEAs) and early years settings with regards to the needs of children with additional needs. Part II of SENDA emphasised the additional duty of LEAs and settings to ensure that children with special or additional needs are not discriminated against and are treated as favourably as those children who are not disabled.

The Special Educational Needs Code of Practice

The Special Educational Needs Code of Practice also came into force in January 2002, replacing the 1994 Code. It contains detailed guidance for early years practitioners in order to ensure that children with additional or special needs are supported to reach their potential.

Further discussion of legislation and special educational needs policies and the role of the SENCO are set out in *Good Practice in Caring for Young Children with Special Needs* by Dare and O'Donovan (2002, 2nd edn).

Policies and practice

An equal opportunities policy is a plan of how a setting will put its legal responsibilities for promoting equal opportunities into action. The policy should give clear guidelines to follow should an incident or concern arise. All staff at the setting should comply with the policy.

All early years settings must have an equal opportunities policy and many will also have statements linked to anti-**racism**, gender and the code of practice for special needs. There should also be policies for staff development, recruitment of new staff and training; these should be drawn up and agreed by all members of staff. When staff have been involved in drawing up a policy they are more likely to feel 'ownership' of it, understanding it fully and supporting it openly. A copy of relevant policies should be given to parents when they first take up a place for their child at the setting. A written policy that has been agreed by parents and staff provides a point of referral, if challenging a breach of the setting's policy seems difficult to face.

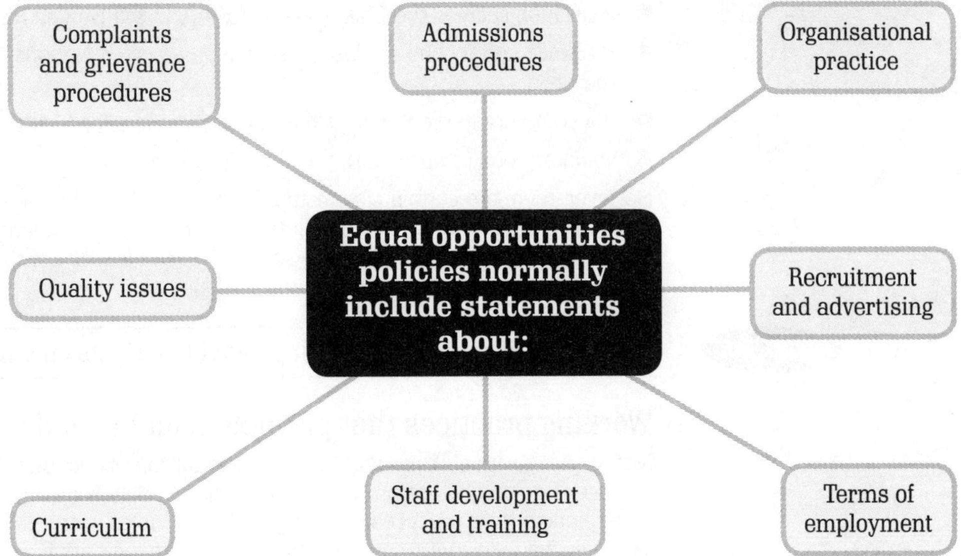

Fig 6.6 Equal opportunities policies

Implementing the policy

Training is important, to ensure that the policy is fully understood. It will need to be monitored and reviewed to ensure that it meets the needs of the setting. A named person should take overall responsibility for its implementation.

activity
INDIVIDUAL WORK 6.6
M2

1 Ask your placement supervisor and either your college's day-care setting (if there is one) or another early years setting for a copy of its equal opportunities policy and any accompanying statements or separate policies for anti-racism, special educational needs, recruitment or sex discrimination.
2 Make a comparison of the two settings' policies, noting the similarities and differences.
3 Does either policy, or set of policies, seem more comprehensive than the other? If so, why is this, do you think?
4 Do the policies include all the statements listed in the diagram above? What else is included?
5 Write an explanation of the ways in which the policies meet the requirements of legislation?

For policies and equal rights legislation, refer to *Good Practice in Nursery Management* by Sadek and Sadek (1996).

remember

A policy should set out clearly the grievance and complaints procedures step by step. The process should be available to all, and people should feel able to raise a complaint or concern without anxiety or risk of harassment. The procedures should help to raise and maintain quality of provision and should be viewed as a positive aspect of the overall framework of the setting.

Individual rights

Promoting the rights of the individual is one of the core principles of the care value base and early years workers have a moral and legal responsibility to protect and promote children's rights. Children's rights are protected by:

- legislation such as the Children Act 2004 and the Human Rights Act 1998
- guidance and recommendations such as the United Nations Convention on the Rights of the Child
- government interventions such as Commissioners for Children's Rights
- voluntary bodies such as the Alliance for Children's Rights.

However, there are certain circumstances in which the rights of a child or parent may need to be overridden in their own best interests. The factors that lead to such an action are often complex, and intervention must be sensitive to the feelings of those involved and to the consequences, as well as the legal implications.

Refer to the section on overriding individual rights on page 300.

Working practices that promote equality and individual rights

Staff working with children and families have a professional duty to ensure actively that their practice is guided by the promotion of equality and individual rights. They can do this by underpinning their practice with the guiding principles of the care value base and by ensuring that they are fully conversant with the appropriate legislation and guidance. This will mean much more than just treating people equally; aspects of a setting where equality and rights are promoted will feature:

- good practice in data protection and confidentiality
- acknowledgement of the inherent tensions to be found in challenging discrimination and promoting equality of rights
- creating an inclusive and anti-oppressive environment that acknowledges the rights of the individual and which has a clear and accessible complaints procedure
- fair employment and recruitment practices that promote equality and diversity
- regular opportunities for staff to undertake development and training in equality, diversity and rights.

Confidentiality

Maintaining confidentiality is one of the cornerstones of good practice and the care value base, and so it is important that early years workers recognise the professional aspects of confidentiality and how it relates to practice. However, some practitioners may be uncertain as to which aspects of information about children and families should be kept confidential and which information can be shared. Knowing the difference between the two can be a key to good practice and can be the foundation for trusting relationships with parents and carers.

Fig 6.7 Confidentiality

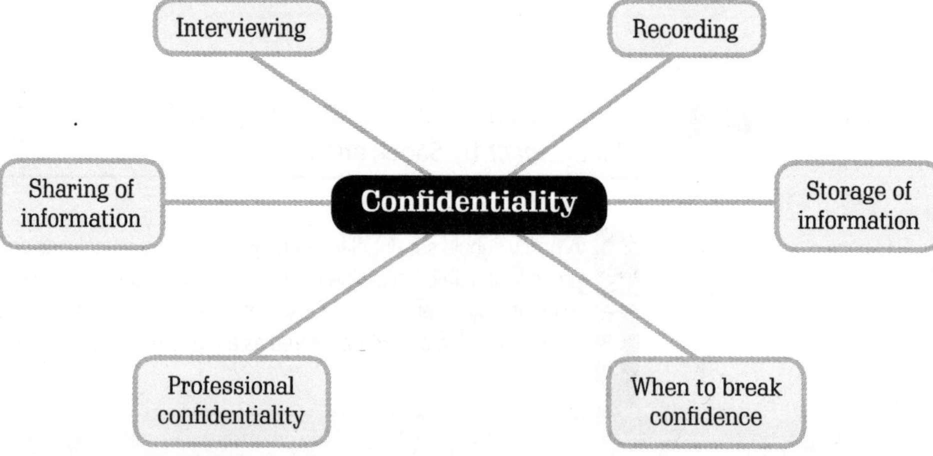

Professional Practice

- As an early years professional, you will at times have access to information that should be kept confidential. You will need to take this responsibility seriously. Confidentiality is linked directly to rights.

Interviewing

Early years workers gather and record data about children and families all the time, and information is often collected during interviews when a child enters a setting or when circumstances warrant discussions between the staff and the parent or carer. Practitioners should regularly review the categories of information that they request at interview and consider the relevance of the data and the issues of confidentiality that may be important.

Recording and storing confidential information

All information that is held on children and families should be recorded accurately and stored securely, in accordance with the requirements of the Data Protection Act 1998. Senior staff may be aware of individual circumstances which dictate that even 'basic' information such as a child's address is held securely and not made public, for example in the case of domestic violence. This may mean that some information is withheld from support staff, students or volunteers, whereas other agencies involved with the child or family may have access to confidential information. Written information that is sensitive or confidential must be kept in a secure, locked facility that is only accessible to those staff with a 'need to know'.

Disclosing confidential information

If information is disclosed inappropriately, parents may lose trust in individual workers or the setting in general, and this can be detrimental to the setting's ability to work in partnership with parents. However, there will be circumstances when information has to be disclosed or shared in order to safeguard a child or to promote their health, development or well-being. Cases of actual or suspected child abuse come under this heading, and those working with children have a professional duty to break confidentiality in these circumstances.

The requirement to maintain confidentiality of information about the children and families in your care is also governed by legislation that is designed to uphold their rights to privacy.

For a clear discussion of practice issues in confidentiality, see *Good Practice in the Early Years* by Kay (2004, 2nd edn).

Refer to Unit 5, pages 259 and 263, for further information on record-keeping and confidentiality.

Fig 6.8 Legislation that affects confidentiality

Legislation that affects confidentiality

1 Data Protection Act 1998 – designed to protect the rights of an individual not to have confidential information about them passed on without their permission. Updates to this Act now cover any information held on paper or computer and passing on information about children or families without their permission would be in breach of the Act.

2 Access to Personal Files Act 1987 – gives individuals rights to access computerised and paper-based files of personal information held on them. Rights to see this data comes from the Data Protection Act 1998 (DPA) and includes medical records, social work, housing, and school records.

3 Access to Medical Reports Act 1988 – individuals also have rights of access to records of their physical and mental health under data protection legislation. Records held by any registered health professional may be accessed and, in some cases, copies made.

Partnerships with parents/legal guardians

Throughout your training and future career there will be a common thread – partnerships with parents. The level of rapport that is built between practitioners and children's parents/carers is crucial to how successfully and smoothly the care of a child is managed. If parents are fully included in decision-making, are asked to contribute ideas and share experiences, and also

> **remember** A family's needs may be cultural or social and/or there may be specific parental or communication needs.

receive regular feedback from their child's key worker or similar, then it is more likely that the needs of the family will be met.

If parents are marginalised by practitioners, they are likely to find it difficult to understand fully their child's progress and needs, or make their cultural preferences known.

Practitioners who marginalise parents lose one of the most valuable sources of information about the children in their care. As a result, they may have to spend additional time observing, assessing and researching to ensure that the child's needs are fully met.

If a child's parents are not kept fully involved and informed, there is the danger that the child will grow up thinking that their parents are not interested. They may lose opportunities to share experiences with their parents because the parent does not fully understand what they are being told.

Imagine you are a parent, leaving your child at a day-care setting for the first time. Consider the level of interaction that you would hope to have with the staff. You may well expect to:

- have opportunities for regular discussion and feedback concerning your child
- feel welcomed by the staff
- feel that your role as parent is valued and respected
- feel that your requests/suggestions/ideas are valued
- feel that your cultural practices and beliefs are respected and upheld with regard to your child's care
- have opportunities to be involved with the setting and your child's care.

There are many ways in which each of the above expectations can be supported, for example:

- through initial printed material and visits
- via a home–setting diary
- through notices to parents
- within the curriculum activities
- through the setting's key worker system.

Communication

To ensure equality of opportunity, it may, at times, be necessary to involve an interpreter or translator. Some parents will benefit from the support of an advocate.

Signing can be a useful and important skill in early years work. You might consider learning to sign.

Refer back to Unit 1, pages 19–23, for information on reducing communication barriers.

Overriding individual's rights

The rights of an individual may be overridden in certain circumstances.

Fig 6.9 Overriding individual rights

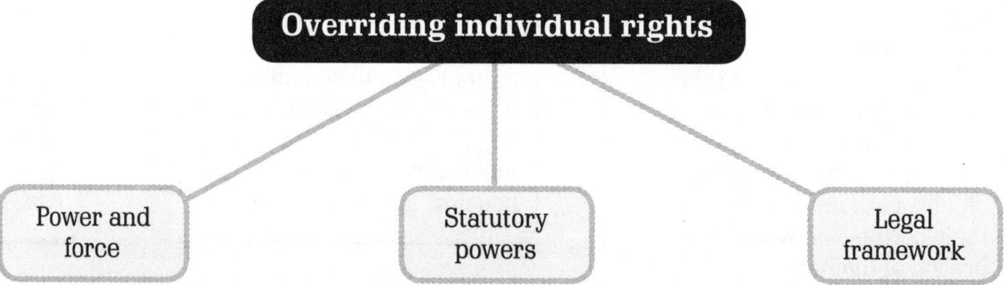

Children's or parents' rights may need to be overridden:

- in cases of actual or suspected abuse – this is one instance when issues of confidentiality or parental rights must be overridden in order to safeguard a child's health, development and well-being
- when a child's behaviour threatens their own safety or well-being, or that of others

- when custody or access issues fail to acknowledge a child's best interests or wishes
- when, owing to mental health problems, a child or parent is a danger to themselves or to others
- when a child's offending behaviour makes the child liable to statutory powers of redress, such as ASBOs (antisocial behaviour orders) or secure accommodation.

Power and force

- Early years workers should be aware of the power that adults have over vulnerable children and ensure that their work with children respects children's autonomy and individuality, whilst acknowledging their right to protection.
- Children need to feel that their wants and wishes are respected and that they are actively consulted and involved in choices and decisions that concern them.
- Children should never be subjected to force although the boundaries of safe practice may sometimes curtail some elements of choice or behaviour.

Statutory powers

- Legislation protects an individual's rights but may also be used to override those rights in certain circumstances.
- Children's rights are not always promoted or respected by adults, and legislation and guidance can enforce these rights on their behalf.
- Statutory powers can be used to protect children from harm and from adults who are not acting in the child's best interests.

Legislation

- The Mental Health Act 1983 and Mental Capacity Act 2005 can be used to detain an individual against their will when their mental health poses a threat to themselves or to others.
- The Children Act 2004 covers many aspects of best practice for children, and it enshrines their right to grow and develop in a safe environment where their best interests are paramount. The Disability Discrimination Act 2005 also promotes the best interests of the child. At times, this is in conflict with parental wishes.
- Children's rights are often interpreted and mediated by the adults who care for them, and so early years workers need to be aware of the appropriate legislation and of an individual child's ability to make informed decisions and choices.

Know the ways in which the individual worker can promote inclusion in their own practice

Personal awareness

remember

You are a role model!

Personal awareness involves identifying one's own beliefs and prejudices and avoiding stereotyping and labelling.

Children learn values and attitudes at a very young age from those of us who are their role models.

Role modelling

When they are unsure about a new person or a new experience, children look to their role models for guidance, approval or encouragement, and therefore absorb their attitudes. These role models include their families (part of their primary socialisation) and their friends, adults and peers, early years staff, teachers and health professionals (secondary socialisation).

As an early years student you need to consider:

- what you do (your actions, gestures and behaviour)
- what you say (the terminology you use and its suitability for the situation of the person you are talking to)
- how you communicate (your attitude, gestures, eye contact, tone and language level).

remember

Children are learning from you all the time. Make sure that they learn positively, never negatively.

As an early years student, you will work with a diverse range of children and families. It is therefore important that you understand stereotyping, prejudice and discrimination, and that you are clear in your mind as to what is good practice. You might find it helpful to explore how you initially formed your own views and who or what influenced them.

Refer back to pages 288–292, to remind you about stereotyping, prejudice and discrimination.

Identifying and changing one's own beliefs and prejudices

To explore how your own views were shaped, you will need to think back to your childhood. Consider the following questions.

1 Who had most influence over you? This almost certainly included your parents, teachers and any nursery or preschool workers.

2 Who else would you include and how did each of them influence you?

3 Were the influences on you positive or negative? What made them so?

4 Have you ever challenged a negative comment or action?

5 Have you ever felt you wanted to but not done so? When was this and what stopped you?

Developing personal values is just the first step. Upholding them when others have different views is often hard, and it can sometimes seem easier to keep your views quiet and go along with what others say or do. You need to be aware that this could mean that you are not working to best practice and are compromising your own values.

Professional Practice

- By exploring issues of prejudice, you come to understand the effects that it can have, which will help you to consider your personal values. If you find that your views are not free from prejudice, you should think through how you might deal with this.
- If your views have been influenced by your parents, you could find yourself confronting the values of your family. This can be difficult.
- Changing your viewpoint is not easy. It will only change by exploring alternative views and ideas and re-evaluating your own thoughts and feelings based on new information and understanding.
- Exploring your thinking, obtaining information and becoming better informed about the effects of stereotyping, prejudice and discrimination will help you work to best practice.

remember

You cannot force your views on anyone, and similarly the views of others cannot be forced upon you.

Challenging oppressive and discriminatory behaviour

It is unlikely that individuals would change their beliefs simply because they were told to. They need to experience at first hand the alternative and identify for themselves what the advantages of the alternative are likely to be, and who would benefit.

For most of us, it is only by exploring the impact of words or actions and how they affect others that we can begin to see fully the power of what we say and do.

Refer to the Nelson Thornes website for case studies that examine the concept of tolerance in the context of values promoted by the early years sector. www.nelsonthornes.com/btec

Links between discrimination and behaviour

Discrimination can be directly linked to behaviour; children often live up to adults' expectations of them; labelling can produce a self-fulfilling prophecy.

Add into this equation a prejudiced belief (e.g. 'girls are no good at playing football' or 'boys never read') and it is easy to see how such negativity can have an impact on both learning and behaviour.

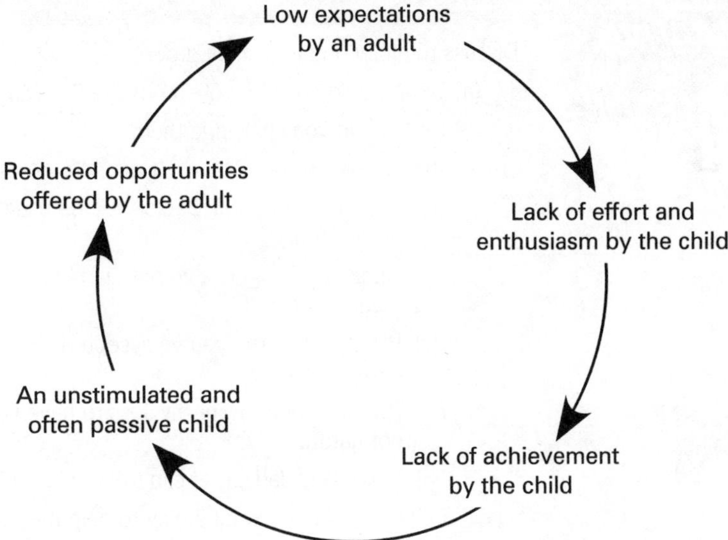

Fig 6.10 Expectation/achievement cycle

Appropriate use of language

In an early years setting, it is important not only to provide appropriate resources and opportunities but also to use appropriate terminology. It is outdated, stereotypical and wrong to use such statements as 'big, strong boy' and 'quiet, little girls'. Most importantly, such statements give confused messages to children about what is expected of them. It is also important to address a family's ethnicity correctly. If you are unsure about any terms, ask. Most people would rather you asked, and addressed them correctly, than continue to address them inappropriately.

Application of the early years care value base

Ensuring that you demonstrate respect for individual differences, identity and the dignity of children and families requires you to work to the overriding values of early years care. You need to:

- Keep children safe at all times.
- Help children maintain good health through:
  - diet
  - exercise
  - self-esteem.
- Work in partnership with parents.
- Provide a stimulating learning environment.
- Model acceptance and tolerance.
- Promote and provide experiences of cultural diversity.

Hopefully, working through this unit will help you understand how to achieve much of this.

You will also find it useful to refer to Unit 2 for information on safety, to Units 2 and 9 for information on children's health, and to Unit 7 for ideas on suitable play provision.

To improve your understanding of equality and therefore your professional practice, it can be helpful to explore a range of scenarios. This section is designed to help you think and reflect on your ability to work to good practice. Try the following activities.

activity
GROUP WORK 6.7
M3

Discuss the following in a small group.

1 (a) What would concern you about the following statements?
(b) How would you challenge them?
(i) Nursery nurse: 'We can't ask Mrs Jones to help because she's got five kids.'
(ii) Nursery nurse: 'Mr Daniels will be useful to have around as there'll be plenty of heavy lifting.'
(iii) Nursery manager: 'I've put Darren on bathroom duty, but always with another member of staff.'
(iv) Parent: 'Is it true you've accepted a child with HIV? If it is, I'll take my Michael away, you know.'
(v) Parent: 'I don't want my Jess to have Darren as a key worker. He's a man; it's not natural.'
(vi) Child: 'My dad says I can't play with Ephraim anymore. He's black.'
(vii) Child: 'I don't want Jenny to help me, her arm's all funny.'

2 (a) Which of the comments below (or similar) have you heard being used?
(i) 'The girls are sitting lovely and quiet as always!'
(ii) 'Would a strong lad come and help me with the construction box, please?'
(iii) 'Which of you girls will look after the new children?'
(iv) 'Whose dad has got an electric drill?'
(v) 'Can you all ask your mummies if they would have time to help us sew the costumes for the play, please?'
(b) What stereotypes were being reinforced here?
(c) Rephrase each comment more appropriately.

3 (a) Which of the following statements will be more likely to ensure equality of opportunity in an early years setting? Explain the reason for your answer.
(i) All staff are entitled to staff development training.
(ii) All staff are entitled to equal amounts of staff development training.
(b) What might be the long-term implications of each statement?

Inclusive practice

Inclusive practice applies to:

- communication
- care routines
- play
- curricular activities
- the environment
- equipment and materials
- seeking and respecting the views and preferences of children
- working within the context of the UN Convention on the Rights of the Child.

Staff, children and parents should promote and encourage the ethos that all children should experience all activities. At times, parents will be uncertain about letting their child take part in particular activities, and sensitivity and encouragement will be needed. A common example is parents' concern over their son ironing in the role-play area or dressing up in a nurse's uniform. It should be sufficient to explain to the anxious parent that in many households men undertake a share of the cleaning tasks and, hopefully, their son will too. However, where possible, obtain dressing-up clothes for both genders when a role is common to both; for example, having male as well as female nurses' uniforms will establish the correct dress code while still promoting the role of male nurses.

A useful way of exploring how successfully your setting is meeting its commitment to equality is to carry out an audit (a type of inspection) of the various activities that are offered, looking at how many depict positive messages, supporting a positive self-image; how many are simply neutral, neither particularly promoting diversity nor causing offence or confusion; and, most importantly, considering if any depict negative messages through the images portrayed or the resources provided. Any negative images found should be brought to the setting manager's notice.

Fig 6.11 Does your setting convey positive messages?

activity
GROUP WORK 6.8
P5

1 In a small group, draw up a checklist of points to use when carrying out an audit of an early years setting. Think about:
   - policies
   - staffing
   - equipment
   - resources
   - accessibility.
2 When you have drawn up your checklist, discuss it with your tutor, explaining the importance of addressing issues of diversity, and then arrange to carry out an audit of a setting. Remember to ask permission of the setting supervisor first.

Tokenism

You will need to be aware of **tokenism**, which is the pretence at being committed to diversity and equality. Settings which have only a tokenistic approach may have a few items depicting positive messages in prominent places but, when you explore the resources further, a less positive picture of equality emerges. One example would be for the setting to have black dolls, which are simply a 'black' version of a 'white' doll and do not represent the normal facial features or hair type of many black people.

The tourist approach

The **tourist approach** is taken by settings that focus on the diversity of other cultures and festivals as a 'tourist experience' but do not have equality fully embedded in their practice. For example, it can be a wonderful experience for children to explore the Diwali festival of light in late autumn, but the dietary and belief requirements of families who celebrate Diwali also need to be valued and supported throughout the year, together with any communication needs of those learning English as an additional language.

Curricular activities

remember Books and stories should give positive messages about equality and diversity.

Books and stories

To truly represent society, positive messages within books should include:

- boys in caring roles or carrying out household tasks
- girls involved in activities or occupations involving strength or occupations where managing people and power are attributed to the role
- minority ethnic groups depicted in both traditional cultural situations and occupations where managing people and power are attributed to the role
- illustrations showing mixed cultural activities or the sharing of each other's festivals by a group of children or adult
- disabled people carrying out the same tasks as everyone else and joining in activities alongside able-bodied people
- different family groupings – nuclear, extended, stepfamilies, mixed-race families.

It is important to have some dual-language books. These will help to involve parents who speak those languages, and give all children an opportunity to see the written word in an alternative script.

Fig 6.12 Cover images of dual-language books

case study 6.2 Katya

Katya is in her first term of her nursery nursing course and is currently on placement in the reception class of the local primary school. She is enthusiastic and keen to be involved and asks the teacher, Mrs Davis, if she can read to the class on her placement day next week. Mrs Davis agrees and suggests that she reads a book that she is very familiar with. Katya says she will bring a book that she reads regularly when she is baby-sitting. The following week Katya settles down to read a home-time story to the children, while Mrs Davis sorts out the paintings. Mrs Davis is horrified when she realises that Katya is reading a story about a naughty black golliwog. She lets Katya finish the story as she is unsure what to do. The children then go home.

activity GROUP WORK

1 What are the problems here?
2 Should Mrs Davis have checked what Katya was going to read?
3 What form of discrimination is depicted here?
4 How should Mrs Davis broach the 'error' with Katya?
5 What would you do tomorrow, if you were Mrs Davis?

remember The examples of positive and negative images given for books and stories apply to all resources and activities that involve illustrations.

It is important that negative incidents are dealt with promptly. Mrs Davis needed to talk to both Katya and the children.

Negative messages within books include showing:

- boys as always physically stronger than girls, in 'macho' roles or positions of power
- girls as cute, pretty and clean, only as carers, in supportive occupations
- minority ethnic groups inappropriately or negatively characterised, in manual occupations or only in traditional cultural situations
- disabled people in wheelchairs only, seated to the side of activities, on a different level from others in the illustration
- family groupings always of the nuclear type (two parents and two children).

Fig 6.13 Encourage all children to enjoy all the resources

Professional Practice

- Having the right resources does not in itself ensure that equality and diversity is being promoted. It needs positive language and attitudes on the part of staff to place the correct values on the resources and activities that are provided.
- It is acceptable for there to be a range of images, some neutral and some positive, as long as there is an overall emphasis on the positive.
- It is never acceptable for a setting to continue to include negative images within its resources.

remember

Parents of children from different cultures will usually be pleased to help with improving the resources of the setting.

Role play

In the role-play area, issues of gender are mostly found in the use of the resources rather than in the resources themselves. A way to address gender stereotyping here is to encourage all the children to enjoy all the resources, taking different roles within their play. An array of artefacts, clothes and foods from a range of cultures will enhance the learning of all children and positively promote the self-image of children from those cultures.

Which cultures are portrayed by the dolls in your placement? If they are all pink skinned, blonde haired and stereotypically English, they are likely to support a racist message as to who is important and needs caring for.

case study 6.3

Children playing 'at home'

A group of children are playing 'at home' when you overhear the following:

'Get the baby, mummy, she's crying.'

'You get it.'

'No! I'm reading the paper and I've had a hard day at work.'

'I'm cooking tea.'

'So what!'

activity
GROUP WORK

1 Would you interrupt the play? Explain your answer.
2 Is discrimination taking place here?
3 What can be the issue with 'correcting' what some children think of as normal (because they see and hear it at home each day)?

The illustration below shows a readily available range of resources for depicting other cultures through role play.

Fig 6.14 A range of resources is available to depict other cultures through role play

Professional Practice

- Where finances are limited, many cultural costumes can easily be made – dyeing and printing materials appropriately
- 'Foods' can be made from salt dough, copying real items or pictures.

Construction materials

Children often consider construction kits to be boys' toys. Encouraging both boys and girls to use construction materials will help dispel stereotypical views, but be aware of who dominates the construction area. At times, it can be appropriate to encourage girls to use construction materials without the 'help' of the boys; this will ensure that girls have the opportunity to plan, predict, experiment and achieve on their own.

Fig 6.15 Encourage both boys and girls to use construction materials to help dispel stereotypical views

remember
It is easy to change gender-specific pictures on the boxes of the construction kits in your placement. Simply remove the construction material from its original box and place in a more suitable container.

Creativity

This is an area where children can experiment and be involved in a non-competitive way, as you cannot paint a 'wrong' picture. Opportunities for creative expression involve the use of a range of media and a range of utensils.

Brushes or alternatives need to be suitable for all hands. A child with limited manual dexterity will benefit from chunky brush handles (lightweight wallpaper brushes can be useful), and all children will enjoy the experience of painting with (thoroughly cleaned) roll-on deodorant containers (plastic) or large sponge rollers.

When children have skin problems such as eczema, the irritation can be exacerbated if they have direct contact with paint and other 'messy' media. Finger painting under a length of cling film can keep them involved without risking infection or further discomfort, but should be done under supervision. Using large bubble-wrap as an alternative can add to the sensory experience. Disposable gloves can be a useful resource here too.

Enormous scope for creative activity is offered by the range of festivals celebrated by people of different religions and cultures throughout the year, for example:

- Diwali, the Hindu festival of light
  - Rangoli patterns – a decoration laid at the entrance to the home to welcome the goddess of fortune, Lakshi
  - Diwali cards – a popular design would be to use a hand shape and decorate it in the traditional mehndi patterns
- Chinese New Year, the first day of the lunar calendar each year
  - Teng Chieh, the lantern festival, denotes the end of the new-year celebrations; decorated sheets of paper are cut and made into lanterns
  - money envelopes (lai see) – it is traditional for children to receive money in red envelopes decorated with gold writing
  - dragons, one of the 12 animals in the Chinese animal years; making a huge dragon can be a super whole-group activity, culminating in the 'dance of the dragon' – such activities allow every child to contribute, working together towards a joint goal.

remember
A range of skin-tone colours in both paints and crayons will enable all children to represent themselves and their families accurately in their pictures.

> **remember** Just because a child needs large pieces to meet their physical need does not necessarily mean that they cannot enjoy a challenging picture. Physical and cognitive needs are not always parallel with each other.

Puzzles

Puzzles can be for table or floor use and can have large or small pieces. Consider differentiation of control and manipulation: large pieces will help the less-able child, as will puzzles with sturdy knobs that make it easy to lift and replace pieces. Issues of positive images apply in the same way as with books and stories.

Music, movement and singing

It is very easy to include diversity in this area of the curriculum. An abundance of musical instruments is available from a vast array of cultures and to suit most physical needs. A musical instrument box should not simply hold tambourines, drums and cymbals, as this is limiting for expression and restricts opportunities to explore the multitude of other options available.

Fig 6.16 It is very easy to include diversity in music activities

In dance children can be encouraged to explore and communicate through a range of expressions and movements. Dance can be combined with the use of instruments, with children accompanying each other and building co-operation and appreciation of each other as equal partners in a joint activity.

Electronic musical activities and those involving vibration offer a multiple-sensory experience and are particularly useful for children with severe hearing loss.

Hand and body signs for musical notes can be used with older children. The Addison body notation and Curwen hand signs are two examples. Curwen hand signs are similar to Addison body notation but do not involve the whole body (as their name suggests) – see Figure 6.17.

Professional Practice

- Tapes and CDs of world music can be borrowed from music libraries.
- Children can enjoy a range of songs from around the globe, learning to sing in different languages and experiencing rhythm and dance from other cultures.
- It could be helpful for your future practice to make a list of songs and music from cultures other than British. (You will probably hear some in your placements.) Examples might include: 'Kookaburra sits in an old gum tree' (Australia) and 'Frère Jacques' (France).
- It is important to look at the content of traditional nursery rhymes and songs. For example, 'Taffy was a Welshman; Taffy was a thief' is not a good example for promoting cultures and raising self-esteem.
- Inviting musicians into the setting allows children to hear a variety of instruments for real. Musicians from various cultures can explain links between the instruments and festivals and special occasions.

Fig 6.17 Addison body notation

Cooking activities

What food-related activities have you seen, and what are planned for the future at your placement? Ask your supervisor to let you see the plans for the full academic year, as this will enable you to gain a more accurate picture.

There are medical, practical and cultural issues to be taken into account when planning activities with food. Consideration must be given to the needs of children who have medical conditions such as:

- diabetes
- coeliac disease
- cystic fibrosis.

You must also think about the needs of children with food allergies, particularly those who have an anaphylactic response.

Some children have ethical and/or cultural dietary needs; such children might be:

- vegetarian
- vegan
- from cultures where certain foods, or combinations of foods, are not allowed.

Refer to Unit 2, pages 63–76, for more information on common childhood illnesses, and to page 95, for a table setting out dietary requirements related to culture and religion.

Festivals lend themselves to a range of cooking activities, for example:

- Baisakhi – the Sikh festival to celebrate the start of Guru Nanak's travels; people provide vegetarian foods, such as dahl and chapattis, both of which are good foods for children to help make
- Lent – the Christian period of 40 days leading up to Easter which Christ spent in the Wilderness; pancakes are traditionally made on Shrove Tuesday, the day before the start of Lent

- Raksha Bandhan – the Hindu festival of protection and care between siblings and close friends; a traditional offering is coconut barfi, similar to coconut ice, which needs no actual cooking so is an ideal cookery activity.

Professional Practice

- **Parents are the ideal people to involve in cooking recipes from their own cultures.**
- **Make a list of festivals that would provide opportunities for cooking activities and add it to your placement portfolio for future reference.**

activity
INDIVIDUAL WORK 6.9
P6

Pete, a classroom assistant, is making pancakes with small groups as part of the exploration of the Christian festivals of Lent and Easter. The children join him eagerly and clamour to be next. Pete chooses his next helpers and turns to Sammy, saying, 'You can make them, Sammy, but you won't be able to eat them, as they have wheat in them'. Sammy, who has coeliac disease, looks disappointed but joins in anyway.

1 How should Pete have dealt with this situation?
2 What form of discrimination is described here?
3 Are there any problems with letting Sammy cook with wheat-based flour?
4 What could Pete have done to enable Sammy to be fully involved in the activity?

activity
INDIVIDUAL WORK 6.10
D2

1 Think about the importance of inclusive practice.
2 Select six examples where inclusion might not be fully supported by all practitioners. You may use examples you have observed.
3 Write an explanation setting out:
   (a) the ways in which inclusive practice was supported
   (b) the ways in which each example did not fully promote inclusion
   (c) what the practitioner's role should have been in each example
   (d) potential outcomes, in both the short and long term, for any specific child; for children in general; and in relation to the overall ethos and reputation of the setting.

remember
Promoting self-esteem in all children is part of inclusion, and can be promoted during circle time, a specific time which gives each child an opportunity to speak and be listened to.

Persona dolls

Promoting a child's self-esteem is an important way of making them feel valued, and persona dolls can be used to help promote self-esteem. The dolls represent children from various cultures and with a range of disabilities. A persona doll can be provided for any individual need and can be an ideal way of encouraging children to accept difference and of paving the way for a child to settle and integrate easily into the group or class.

When using a persona doll, the adult explains the doll's background and tells a special story which can lead to discussion with the children, exploring, for example, difficulties that can be faced by an individual, bias that can be experienced and the hurt that can be felt.

For information on using persona dolls, refer to *Persona Dolls in Action* by Brown (2001).
For information on circle time, see *Quality Circle Time in the Primary Classroom: Your Essential Guide to Enhancing Self-esteem, Self-discipline and Positive Relationships*, by Mosely (1998).

Fig 6.18 Persona dolls

Professional Practice

- Working positively will encourage the promotion of equality in others: colleagues, parents and children.
- Being a role model for children is a privilege and should be taken seriously.
- You should always remember that your actions and words could have a lasting impact on the development of the values and self-esteem of the children in your care.

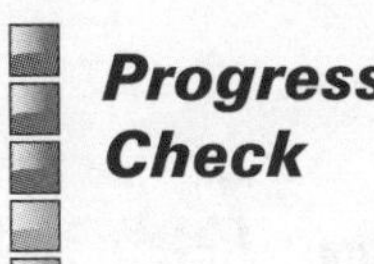

Progress Check

1 Define 'institutional discrimination'.
2 What is prejudice?
3 Give an example of tokenism.
4 What is meant by the term 'tourist approach'?
5 Why is it not enough simply to have a range of resources giving positive messages?
6 Explain one way of helping a child with a medical dietary need be involved in cooking.
7 Which religions celebrate Diwali?
8 How could a deaf child's enjoyment of music be enhanced?
9 What is a persona doll?
10 What are the likely long-term effects of an early years setting which does not promote inclusive practice?

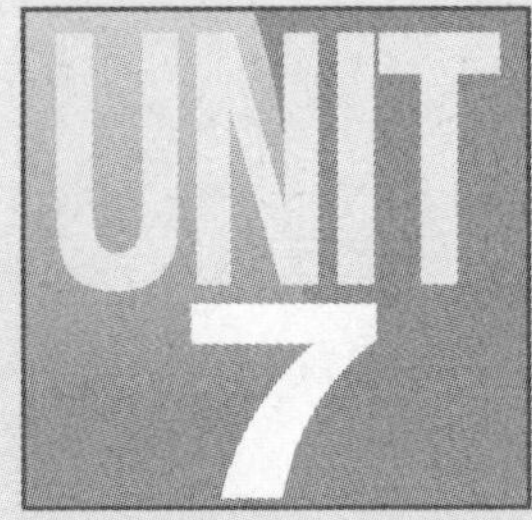

Children's Learning Activities and Play

This unit covers:

- Understand the major theories of how children develop and learn
- Understand the role of play in the development of children
- Understand the role of the adult in all aspects of the provision and implementation of play and learning activities for children
- Know how to identify and promote learning opportunities for children aged from 0 to 8 years of age
- Be able to plan, implement and evaluate learning activities for children aged from 0 to 8 years of age
- Be able to provide play situations for children

This unit focuses on how children learn from birth to eight years, the period covered by preschool provision and the first years of school. Any setting which receives government funding must provide evidence of a high standard of care and a planned environment in which appropriate learning can take place. An understanding of how children learn is a mandatory requirement for all professionals working in the early years field.

This unit describes a range of theories on the development of learning and looks at the work of several important early years educators, examining how their theories influence current thinking and practice.

The value of play is discussed, and consideration is given to choice and presentation of activities. Advice is offered on when to introduce new learning to children and how to extend and identify appropriate opportunities for learning, enabling differentiation of need within any group of children.

grading criteria

To achieve a **Pass** grade the evidence must show that the learner is able to:	To achieve a **Merit** grade the evidence must show that, in addition to the pass criteria, the learner is able to:	To achieve a **Distinction** grade the evidence must show that, in addition to the pass and merit criteria, the learner is able to:
P1 describe the ways in which children learn with reference to the major theories of learning page 320	**M1** with reference to the major theories of learning, explain how children learn page 320	**D1** evaluate the major theories of learning, using examples from work placement page 323
P2 describe the potential value of play in the development of children page 328	**M2** explain the potential value of play in the development of children page 332	**D2** with reference to the major theories of learning, evaluate the two learning activities and the two play situations. page 364

To achieve a **Pass** grade the evidence must show that the learner is able to:	To achieve a **Merit** grade the evidence must show that, in addition to the pass criteria, the learner is able to:	To achieve a **Distinction** grade the evidence must show that, in addition to the pass and merit criteria, the learner is able to:
P3 describe the role of the adult in all aspects of the provision and implementation of play and learning activities for children page 334	**M3** analyse the role of the adult in children's learning page 334	
P4 use examples to describe how early years settings provide learning opportunities for children from 0–3, 3–5 and 5–8 years of age page 339	**M4** explain the value of the two learning activities and the two play situations. page 363	
P5 plan and implement two learning activities in early years settings page 347		
P6 set up and review 10 different play situations. page 363		

Understand the major theories of how children develop and learn

Early years education has seen many changes in recent years as the learning needs of young children have gained greater status. The earlier stages of a child's learning are now recognised as important in their own right, rather than simply as a springboard for learning in later years.

Across the world, children's experiences of early learning vary considerably, and the starting age for formal education differs quite significantly between countries. Until recently, in the UK, learning opportunities across the range of settings offered also varied a great deal. Government input, both educational and financial, has tried to address some of the imbalance between settings by introducing a comparable learning experience for all children of similar ages.

Development and learning

As with general development, a child's rate of learning is influenced by a range of factors. Development can be described as a progression or expansion of past achievements, building on previously set foundations, for example walking before running or sitting before standing, whereas learning is the process of acquiring new knowledge or a skill through a certain set of circumstances, for example being able to roll a ball and then learning to play the ball game, boules.

Children's development and learning is most usefully seen as a continuum, along which they progress according to the influences and opportunities available to them. Each stage of development is a defined part of the overall human lifespan. It should not be seen merely as a prelude to the rest of life. The term 'lifelong learning' is commonly used to describe how we all continue to develop our knowledge, understanding and skills throughout our lives, whether formally or informally.

The findings of neuroscience and brain studies

According to recent neuroscientific research, the quality of the young child's environment and experience is important for brain development in the early years. Consistent and loving care from responsive adults appears to be of vital importance, as does a stimulating and supportive environment.

These research studies also support the concept of sensitive periods for brain development during which particular skills or functions are being refined. The ability of the brains of infants and children to 'wire' themselves depends on optimal prenatal and postnatal environments, as well as the amount of stress that the individual is exposed to. It has also been noted that engaging children in formal learning at too early an age can lead to a child's disengagement and shutting off from the experience.

Professional Practice

- **It can be useful to read about the findings of research into early brain development, to help you identify the factors that may be relevant both prenatally and following birth. It will also help you to consolidate your understanding of the importance of high-quality organisation and delivery of early years services.**
- **It is important to remember that not all the current findings about factors affecting brain development in infancy and childhood have been scientifically proven; therefore, if you refer to findings, make sure that they are from reputable research studies and are not just media 'hype'.**

For a clear explanation of the importance of neuroscience and brain studies, refer to pages 71–73 in *Essential Early Years* by Dryden *et al.* (2005), or 'Research into brain development' in *How Children Learn* by Pound (2005).

Prerequisites for learning, development and growth

Babies and children will not learn effectively unless their basic needs are met and certain conditions are favourable. There are certain basic physiological needs that must be met in order to ensure healthy growth, development and learning. Meeting these needs entails:

- unconditional love and affection
- consistent and appropriate care
- balanced and healthy nutrition
- being kept safe but allowed to explore and learn to take responsibility
- appropriate warmth, shelter and clothing
- protection from ill health and infection.

Refer to Unit 4, page 209, for a description of children's basic needs.

In order to learn, children also need:

- a stimulating environment that is rich in play and learning opportunities
- opportunities to take part in care routines and activities that are designed to stimulate development
- knowledgeable early years practitioners who are aware of evidence-based practice and the frameworks and curricula that support care and education
- encouragement and support to play and learn from parents and carers
- timely interventions which are developmentally and culturally sensitive.

Factors that may influence development and affect learning

Development is affected by a variety of factors within the individual child, the family, and the wider social environment.

Refer to Unit 3, pages 151–157, for the factors that affect development.

The following factors are particularly important to learning:

- timing
- genetics
- environment, including support
- health factors.

Timing
Offering children opportunities at appropriate times ensures the best learning experiences. In the past, some theorists believed that children have critical times for learning and that learning can be missed altogether if it does not occur at a certain point in a child's life. Modern theorists do not generally agree with this, preferring the idea that there is a 'sensitive period' when acquisition is easier and acknowledging that most children are able to catch up on lost time once they have learned a new skill or been introduced to a new experience. However, these children may lack confidence and self-esteem owing to being slightly 'behind' their peers. Children who have been pushed on too fast at too early an age (hot-housing) are at risk of losing interest in learning (**burn-out**). The most successful approach to providing positive learning experiences for children is to direct the learning to each child's individual stage of development.

Professional Practice

- **A child who is tired will gain less from a new experience than a child who is fresh and alert.**
- **The end of the day is not a suitable time to introduce an exciting new activity: some children may be going home; others may be too tired to appreciate the potential of the activity.**

Genetics
Biological factors (e.g. chromosomal make-up and dominant and recessive genes) strongly influence the characteristics of each individual and play a role in our achievements and in the choices that we each make. However, the line between nature and nurture is often blurred, making it difficult to distinguish biological effects from the effects of social factors. Consider foetal alcohol syndrome (FAS) and maternal drug use: both can give rise to malformations, impaired cognitive development and either hyperactivity (associated with FAS) or lethargy (associated with drug use), with consequent impact on learning.

At times, adverse circumstances, either social or familial, do not have a negative effect on development, and, in some cases, the adverse effects that present in the early years can be reversed later on in life with relevant support.

Refer to Unit 3, page 157, for information about genetic effects on development, and to page 109 for foetal alcohol syndrome.

Environment and support
Most modern-day theorists take a nature-plus-nurture approach to learning, considering that the genetic start (nature) is enhanced by experience (nurture). Most agree that the environment in which children are brought up and educated has an effect on the rate at which they develop and learn and how well they achieve their potential. Factors such as a stable home life, parental interest in their children, encouragement, provision of resources, opportunities for new experiences and emphasis on raising self-esteem are all seen as important.

Health factors
The health of a child has an impact on both development and learning: a child who is unwell, undernourished or who has a chronic health problem, is likely to be at a disadvantage because of repeated health care needs. A hungry child will lack the energy usually associated with young children. Chronic health needs include asthma, diabetes, sickle cell anaemia or severe eczema. To be fully able to learn, a child needs to be physically and mentally alert. Therefore, children who are distracted by discomfort or pain will be less able to assimilate learning at the rate of their peers and will move more slowly along the developmental continuum.

case study 7.1

Stewart

Stewart is five and has chronic asthma. He often needs to sit quietly and uses his inhaler several times during an average school day.

activity
INDIVIDUAL WORK

1 How might this affect Stewart in the classroom?
2 How might he be affected in the playground?
3 What impact might this have on Stewart's learning overall?

Refer to Unit 9 for information on child health and to page 426 for information on asthma.

Major theories

Nature–nurture debate

Genetic inheritance and how it influences children's learning has been much debated, with nativists proposing that genetic factors influence behaviour and learning and that we are born ready primed for what we will achieve. Empiricists, however, claim that **environmental factors** are the main influences on learning and that the circumstances we are born into and raised within will determine our achievements. This is the nature–nurture debate.

Refer back to Unit 3, page 115, for more about the nature–nurture debate.

Models of learning – an overview

There are three main models of learning:

- the **transmission model**
- the **laissez-faire model**
- the social constructivist model.

Table 7.1 Advantages/disadvantages of models of learning

Model	Advantage	Disadvantages
Transmission ■ Learning takes place without inherent abilities (nurture)	■ Behaviour can be modified ■ Learning comes from experience ■ Child may learn though imitation and observing others	■ Oversimplifies children's learning ■ Inhibits exploration ■ Not child centred ■ Child takes a passive role in learning
Laissez-faire ■ Environment does not affect learning (nature)	■ Child centred ■ Makes use of developmental scales ■ Identifies favourable periods for learning ■ Encourages a well-resourced environment	■ Normative benchmarks may label child if not achieving ■ Disregards cultural influences on development ■ Children are passive learners ■ Opportunities for learning may be missed due to limited adult support
Social constructivist ■ Development and learning are linked (nature *and* nurture)	■ Child centred and child is seen as active learner ■ Sees play as important part of learning ■ Adult support extends opportunities for learning ■ Recognises importance of family, community and cultural links to learning	■ Expensive operating costs due to resources needed and high levels of adult support

Transmission model of learning

The seventeenth-century philosopher John Locke, an empiricist, considered that children were a blank page to be written on by adults. His view was that when children are born they differ in their potential for intelligence and temperament but have no facilities for innate learning. Therefore, Locke believed solely in the influences of nurturing. Classical conditioning (the process whereby learning results from the association of a neutral stimulus with a reflex response) and operant conditioning (the process of learning voluntary behaviour by association with reinforcement or punishment) reflect this philosophy.

The transmission model of learning is one in which adults keep control of the situation. Adults determine what learning will take place by their own direct involvement, controlling the learning process and suppressing the children's initiative. Children remain passive in these situations and in the long term are less likely to try out new experiences because they are concerned about failing.

The main theorists linked to this model of learning are

- Ivan Pavlov – classical conditioning
- B. F. Skinner – operant conditioning.

Pavlov

Ivan Pavlov was most famous for an experiment he undertook with dogs in which he demonstrated that a neutral stimulus (a bell) elicited a response (salivation) when it was paired with an unconditional stimulus (food). Put simply, he conditioned his dogs by stimulating them with a bell before they were fed. The dogs produced saliva when they saw the food, but, after a while, started to salivate when they heard the bell. Classical conditioning is one form of learning from experience.

Refer back to Unit 3, page 137, for a fuller explanation of classical conditioning.

Skinner

B.F. Skinner's work is based on behaviourism, which is a theory of learning that was popular in the first half of the twentieth century and was influenced by Pavlov's work. Skinner believed that we learn to behave in certain ways by being either punished or rewarded. According to this model of learning, adults can shape or modify children's learning by reinforcing wanted behaviours. You may observe some elements of this approach used in behaviour management in settings where rewards such as stickers or stars are used to reinforce wanted behaviours.

Refer back to Unit 3, page 137, for a fuller explanation of operant conditioning.

Laissez-faire model of learning

The laissez-faire model of learning is based on the thinking of Jean Jacques Rousseau (a nativist) in the eighteenth century. He considered that children learn naturally, following pre-set biological processes, and that these biological processes are best developed if supported by caring adults, who oversee what children are doing but do not intervene in the learning process.

The laissez-faire model of learning allows for exploration and choice. However, the lack of adult input limits any extension of the learning, by example or by scaffolding. It is possible that with this approach children may not reach their potential because the adult hesitates to 'interfere' in the learning.

Refer to page 322 for more about scaffolding.

The main theorists loosely linked to this model of learning are:

- Noam Chomsky
- Sigmund Freud.

Chomsky

Noam Chomsky is an American linguist who believes that children have a mental language acquisition device that enables them to acquire and decode language simply by hearing it spoken. He thinks that the decoder allows children to recognise and understand the complexities and grammatical constructions of language, no matter what language it is they are hearing. Other theorists have disagreed with Chomsky.

Refer to Unit 3, page 147, for further information on language development.

Freud

Sigmund Freud's theories, which are complex and have been fiercely debated, centre on psychoanalysis and personality development. He believed that the individual's unconscious mind is responsible for shaping their life, as are unresolved emotional conflicts with parents. Freud, who is only loosely linked to the laissez-faire model, inspired many modern developmental psychologists. Others disagree strongly with his views.

Social constructivist model of learning

According to this model, a child learns by interacting with the environment and through practical experience. This model of learning is still in favour today and underpins many curricular developments. The social constructivist model has its roots in the work of Immanuel Kant (1724–1804) and combines elements of the transmission model which views the child as an empty vessel and the laissez-faire model which suggests that learning is, to some extent, pre-programmed. The social constructivist model of learning is the one that you are most likely to encounter in early years settings.

Theorists linked to the social constructivist model include:

- Jean Piaget
- Lev Vygotsky
- Jerome Bruner.

Piaget

Jean Piaget (1896–1980) was a Swiss psychologist who originally studied biology and became interested in knowledge and its origins, which he called the 'embryology of intelligence'. He was particularly interested in the way that children think, and he concluded that their thinking was different from the thinking of adults. Piaget considered the interaction between the child and the environment to be the main factor in influencing cognitive development (the development of learning through thinking and problem-solving). According to Piaget, the child is actively involved in their learning and through interaction with the environment acquires a series of schemas (principles). Piaget considered that these schemas changed and developed through the processes of assimilation and accommodation.

Refer to Unit 3, page 144, for an explanation of assimilation and accommodation.

Piaget proposed four stages of cognitive development:

1 sensorimotor stage (birth to two years)
2 pre-operational stage, comprising the pre-conceptual (two to four years) and the intuitive (four to seven years)
3 concrete operations stage (7 to 11 years)
4 formal operations stage (11 years onwards).

P1

M1

Donovan is two years old. He is using clay and is trying to squeeze it in his hands. He says the word 'ball' twice. Eventually, Donovan leaves the clay and moves to play with the salt dough. Again, he tries to squeeze the material in his hands. He smiles as he is successful.

1 Which of Piaget's stages of cognitive development do you consider Donovan to be in? Use the chart on page 321 to help you.
2 Explain your reasons.
3 Give examples of play for each of Piaget's stages of cognitive development for children under the age of eight years. Again, use the chart on page 321 to help guide you.

Refer to Unit 3, page 144, for more about Piaget.

Table 7.2 Piaget's first two stages of cognitive development

Source: Neaum and Tallack (2000, p. 24)

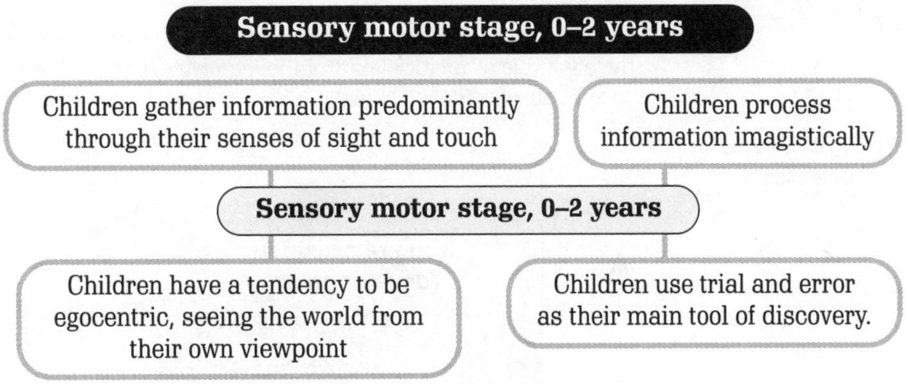

Sensory motor stage, 0–2 years

Children gather information predominantly through their senses of sight and touch

Children process information imagistically

Sensory motor stage, 0–2 years

Children have a tendency to be egocentric, seeing the world from their own viewpoint

Children use trial and error as their main tool of discovery.

Children in this age range have a limited language ability, therefore senses other than hearing are predominant in gathering and processing information. Sight and touch are vital senses in enabling a child to gather the information in his or her environment. This information is then processed as images, similar to, but more sophisticated than, pictures or photographs. This processing system is inflexible and has limited use. For example, how would you store the concept of justice in this way? Children, therefore, need to acquire language. It thus becomes immediately obvious, even at this early stage, that there is an important link between language and intellectual development. It is an interdependent relationship.

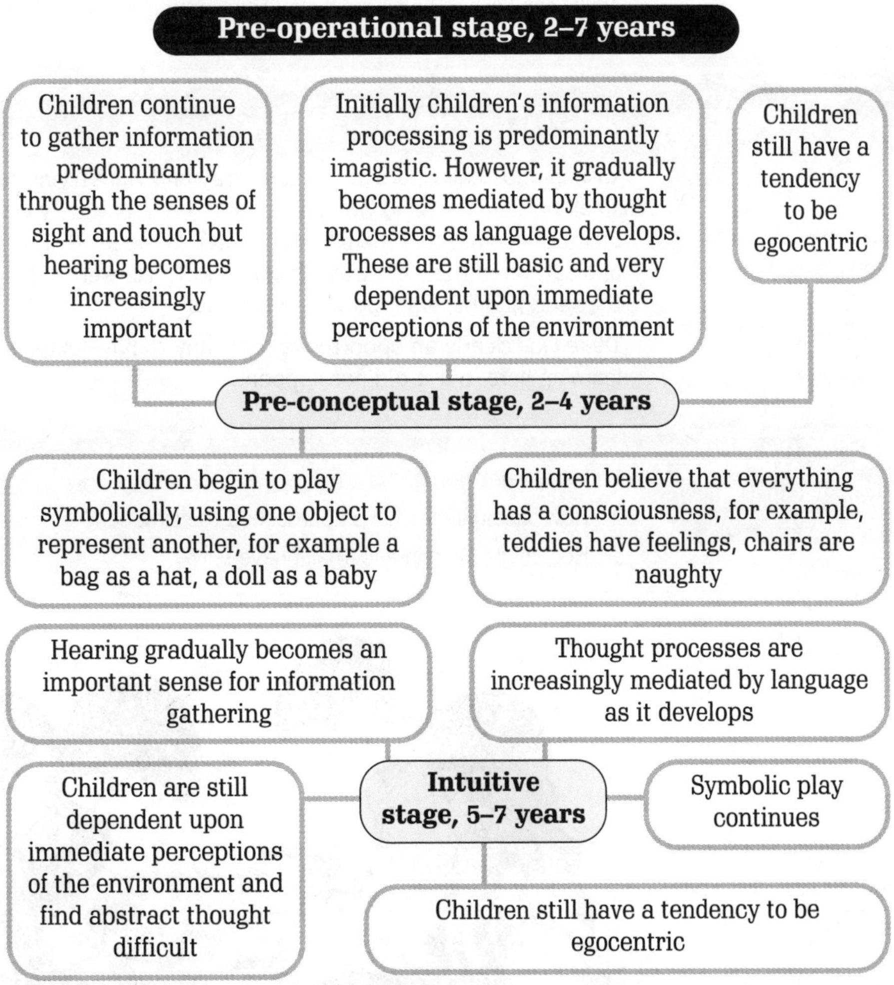

Pre-operational stage, 2–7 years

Children continue to gather information predominantly through the senses of sight and touch but hearing becomes increasingly important

Initially children's information processing is predominantly imagistic. However, it gradually becomes mediated by thought processes as language develops. These are still basic and very dependent upon immediate perceptions of the environment

Children still have a tendency to be egocentric

Pre-conceptual stage, 2–4 years

Children begin to play symbolically, using one object to represent another, for example a bag as a hat, a doll as a baby

Children believe that everything has a consciousness, for example, teddies have feelings, chairs are naughty

Hearing gradually becomes an important sense for information gathering

Thought processes are increasingly mediated by language as it develops

Intuitive stage, 5–7 years

Children are still dependent upon immediate perceptions of the environment and find abstract thought difficult

Symbolic play continues

Children still have a tendency to be egocentric

As language develops children increasingly use this to gather and process information. Language is a complex system of representation and therefore enables a child to develop more complex ways of gathering and processing information. Again the link between language and intellectual development is shown to be vital in children's learning.

Vygotsky

Lev Vygotsky (1896–1935) also believed that children learn by active involvement. He saw the adult role as a crucial part of the learning experience, and central to his theory is the zone of proximal development (ZPD), see the diagram below.

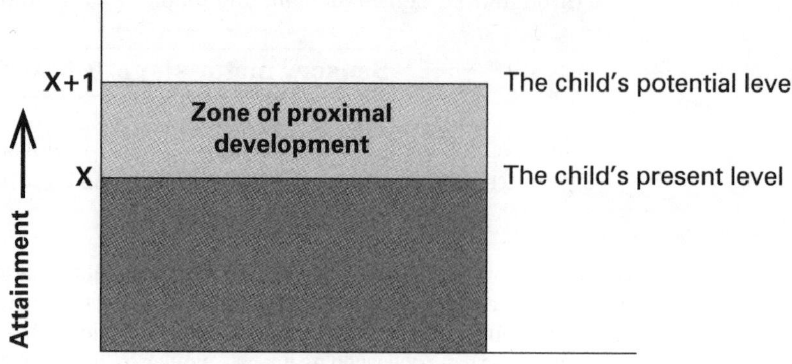

Fig 7.1 Vygotsky's zone of proximal development

Vygotsky argued that children can often understand more than they demonstrate and that, while they are able to show understanding of some concepts through their play, they have the potential to develop further understanding, for example of more abstract concepts, if helped by an adult (or an older child). Children can therefore achieve more than if there had been no adult involvement. This highlights the important role that a (more able) individual (usually an adult) can have in helping develop the learning of a (less able) individual (usually a child) by extending opportunities for experience.

case study 7.2

Yasmin and Thalia

Yasmin and Thalia were at the sand tray and were trying to make sand pies with a small bucket. The sand was very fine and dry, and they were not succeeding. Jenny, a member of staff, told them to add water to the sand. This they did, in large quantities, and saturated the sand tray. Yasmin and Thalia were still unable to make a sand pie as the sand had become too wet to turn out.

There was clearly an opportunity for Jenny to have extended Yasmin's and Thalia's learning here, but it did not happen.

activity
INDIVIDUAL WORK

1 What went wrong?
2 How should Jenny have approached the situation?
3 How might Yasmin and Thalia have felt?

Fig 7.2 Sand play

Refer to Unit 3, page 146, for more about Vygotsky.

Bruner

Jerome Bruner (1915–) was influenced by Vygotsky's ideas, particularly the concept of the ZPD; he believes that scaffolding contributes to the child's learning. In scaffolding, the adult supports the learning experience, enhancing the child's learning through the introduction of manageable levels of information, thus enabling the child to solve a problem or to achieve further.

Bruner believes that children use three modes of representing (or ways of thinking about) experience; the modes develop sequentially:

> **remember**
> When planning an activity for children, consider the level of adult involvement required and include it in your planning.

1 Enactive mode of representation – information is recorded mentally and linked to physical activity; this is the stage of most infants under one year old.

2 Iconic mode of representation – the mental images are linked to the senses; this stage is associated with children aged one to seven years.

3 Symbolic mode of representation – a range of representative forms, such as language and number, is used to demonstrate the child's learning; this stage is seen mostly from seven years onwards.

Refer to Unit 3, page 147, for more about Bruner.

Use examples from your placement to illustrate how you have seen the ideas of Piaget, Vygotsky and Bruner demonstrated through the actions of children and staff.

Make clear which theorist you are referring to in each example and explain in detail how the example shows learning.

A useful source of information about current research linked to early years learning is the journal *Early Childhood Practice: The Journal for Multi-Professional Partnerships*, edited by Professor Tina Bruce.

Implications for early years education

Early years education is affected by the ability of workers to understand the models of learning, the main theories of education and how to implement them effectively.

There are times when adult direction is needed in early years settings. As a student, you will see many examples of good practice during your placement experience. This is an important learning opportunity for you. However, on occasions, less ideal practice may be evident, which is unfortunate but will add to your knowledge base as a professional early years worker, reminding you how not to approach certain situations.

Think of situations in which you have identified particularly good examples of high-quality practice. What made it good practice, do you think?

With the regular inspections of settings and the **quality assurance** accreditation processes that are developing within early years, there should be fewer instances of below-standard practice. The quality assurance process is led by a government initiative; the aim is that a significant proportion of all providers of early years care and education should gain accreditation with a nationally recognised quality assurance scheme 'kite mark'.

How children learn

Children learn through:

- first-hand experiences and stimulation
- play
- being active
- using language
- working with others

- doing meaningful activities
- feeling secure
- appropriate adult intervention.

First-hand experiences and stimulation

First-hand experiences are pivotal to learning, and all children have a right to take an active role in a stimulating learning environment in which their competence is recognised and encouraged. Practitioners should acknowledge that play, developmentally appropriate care routines and experiential learning are all important to the provision of a stimulating and dynamic learning environment. Children must also be given the freedom to learn in their own way and to make mistakes without feeling under pressure.

Play

Children have a right to enjoy play opportunities from the earliest age and the adult should support this with encouragement and appropriate care and stimulation. Play is an essential part of children's lives and learning and it should not be seen as a passive activity that keeps children 'busy'. If learning is to take place, play opportunities should be purposeful, innovative and worthwhile.

Being active

Children learn by being actively involved in the exploration and discovery of their environment. Even the youngest infants are curious about their environment and make use of all of their sensory abilities to explore and learn. Children may need support, encouragement and opportunities to become competent and active learners, and adults should make use of appropriate resources and frameworks to facilitate 'learning by doing'.

Using language

From the earliest days, children learn from being in a language-rich environment. They will benefit from a wide variety of activities and resources that promote and celebrate spoken and written languages, but the importance of the role of the adult in speaking and listening to a child cannot be overemphasised. Routine care activities offer many opportunities for stimulating language, as do stories, nursery rhymes, music, poetry and singing. Babies and young children need the opportunity to hear and learn to use language, and this demands a practitioner who is willing to talk and listen. They will also learn from non-verbal communication, and this may involve the adult in helping the child to recognise facial expressions, gestures and signs.

Working with others

Children learn many useful skills from working with other children and with adults. They will learn how to co-operate and share, as well as how to take turns and wait. They benefit from the opportunity to share play and learning experiences with other children and may need adult support to help them negotiate social boundaries and behave in accepted ways.

Doing meaningful activities

Activities need to be meaningful in order that children are actively engaged and learning, rather than being passively amused or occupied. It is the adult's responsibility to provide high-quality activities that involve and engage the child. Activities should be developmentally appropriate and culturally sensitive and centred on the needs of the individual child.

Feeling secure

It is impossible for a baby or child to flourish and learn in an atmosphere where they do not feel secure. Emotional security is crucial to a positive learning experience, and practitioners must consider the 'emotional security' of the learning environment as carefully as health and safety. Routine care and learning activities should acknowledge a child's individual personality and changes to their needs and circumstances, as well as the day-to-day events that affect children's emotional stability. Key-worker systems are essential in providing consistency of care and responsiveness to children's changing needs.

Appropriate adult intervention

Adults rightly support children's care, play and learning, but there may be times when it is necessary to consider the nature and timing of adult intervention. There should be a balance between allowing a child the freedom to explore and experiment and providing support to facilitate the next stage of learning.

Influences on practice: early years educators

A number of early educators have had a significant influence on the practice of modern early years professionals, enabling a greater understanding of how children learn and what affects the learning process. This section summarises the contributions of some of the most influential early pioneers.

Friedrich Froebel (1782–1852)

Friedrich Froebel considered parents to be the main educators of their children. He founded the first kindergarten in 1840; the children who attended were given the opportunity to learn through **exploratory play**, particularly with natural materials. Froebel emphasised that children learn best when they are well motivated, and he focused on offering opportunities for developing a positive relationship between the child's home, school and the wider community. Froebel encouraged symbolic play and what is known today as free-flow play. He developed a set of learning materials which he called 'the gifts' (these materials influenced the work of Maria Montessori). Froebel's emphasis was always on the linking together of materials, and learning by their differences in a non-directed way.

Table 7.3 Froebel: key concepts

Key concepts	Types of play	The 'gifts'
Parents as the main educators of their children Interaction between home, school and the community Non-directed learning Focus on the whole child No formal learning under seven	Exploratory play Learning through nature Symbolic play	Materials and resources

Refer to page 332 for more about free-flow play and to page 326 for Maria Montessori.

Rudolph Steiner (1861–1925)

According to Rudolph Steiner, the child has to pass through three developmental stages on the way to adulthood. He proposed that:

- up to 7 years of age, the emphasis of learning should be on the will (the active stage)
- from 7 to 14 years old, the emphasis moves to the heart (the emphasis is now on feelings)
- from 14 years onwards, the head is of greatest importance (the cognitive stage).

Like Froebel, Steiner considered the child holistically (as a whole), maintaining that each stage of learning was fostered by the interaction of prior experience.

He firmly believed that formal reading and writing should not be introduced at an early age but should occur naturally at a child's own pace, fostered by opportunities for creativity. He also encouraged the use of natural materials and felt that learning should be initiated by the child – it should come from within. Steiner settings offer a carefully structured environment which particularly fosters non-pressurised personal and social learning. Steiner promoted what was known as curative education for children with emotional, behavioural and learning difficulties. The main emphasis of the Steiner approach is on learning from life's experiences. Textbooks are only used as a support to the learning that is already developing; textbooks are not used to initiate it.

Steiner Waldorf schools are run as private schools, but parents usually pay according to their means. Some (but not all) children are integrated back into the state sector when they reach the GCSE and post-GCSE stages of their education.

Table 7.4 Steiner: key concepts

Key concepts	Types of play	The 'gifts'
Three stages of learning: ■ the will ■ the heart ■ the head Learning at own pace Focus on the whole child	Free play Exploratory play Learning through nature	Natural materials

The Steiner setting places great emphasis on imaginative play and creativity. There are many opportunities for self-expression through music, dance, drama and art. Various objects are provided to encourage imagination, and there is a marked lack of commercially produced artefacts.

The role of the adult is to guide and supply materials to enhance the child's creativity. Play is child initiated and adults join in as appropriate.

Professional Practice

- **Although the Steiner philosophy attracts a significant following, there are limited opportunities for placement experience.**
- **If you are fortunate to gain a place in a Steiner setting, remember to share your experience with others, enhancing their learning too.**

Fig 7.3 Children can often be seen concentrating hard on what they are doing

You may find it interesting to refer to *Bringing the Steiner Waldorf Approach to your Early Years Practice* by Nicol (2007).

Maria Montessori (1870–1952)

Maria Montessori believed that, given the right stimuli, children are naturally self-motivating. She saw children as active learners in much the same way as Piaget did, but she did not value play in its free-flow sense, believing that children became independent learners if they are encouraged to work alone.

Montessori thought that children needed to work through the range of learning materials that she developed before they were ready to express their own ideas. This range of materials particularly encouraged dexterity, and, as they worked with them, children were guided from the simple to the more complex tasks. These included activities designed to enable children to learn particular skills. Montessori believed that each activity should only be used for the purpose for which it was designed and she did not value imaginative play.

She encouraged children to learn to form letters through sand and finger play, and no methods involving the formal learning of reading and writing were seen in a Montessori nursery, although great emphasis was placed on the richness of literature and the use of language. Montessori encouraged independence and considered that children have reached the highest point of their learning when they are silently absorbed in their activity. She referred to this as the 'polarisation of the attention'.

Montessori believed that the adult's role is to 'follow the child'. She based her theories on extensive observation of children, and today's acceptance that children are eager learners from birth is often attributed to her theories.

Table 7.5 Montessori: key concepts

Key concepts	Types of play	The 'gifts'
Children are self-motivating Independent learning was encouraged Planned environment Adult should follow the child	Free-flow play not valued Sensory learning Encouraged dexterous activity	Developed own range of equipment

The Montessori philosophy initiated the need for child-sized equipment, including display tables and storage facilities, to allow children to select and return their chosen activities (this is similar to the High/Scope approach). Montessori settings also favour rugs, mats and cushions for the children to use at floor level, and children will often be seen selecting an activity, for example a grading board, and taking it to a mat (or carpet square) to explore it. In line with Montessori thinking, each activity is to be used for its intended purpose, and imaginative play is not actively encouraged in most settings.

The adult role within a Montessori setting is to observe and guide, using understanding of a child's needs to indicate when adult intervention is needed.

The materials that Montessori produced to encourage dexterity are still used in Montessori settings today, although the overall curriculum is generally more varied.

You may find it interesting to refer to *Bringing the Montessori Approach to your Early Years Practice* by Isaacs (2007)

Margaret McMillan (1860–1931)

Margaret McMillan was influenced by Froebel and like him she was interested in allowing children to learn both freely and naturally. She considered that play helped children demonstrate their knowledge and understanding of materials and situations, and she emphasised manual dexterity and manipulation, which were also later favoured by Montessori.

McMillan was the pioneer of nursery schools, school meals and medical services. She was the first to recognise that, as a hungry or sick child will be unlikely to reach their potential, feeding children and monitoring their health is crucial to the learning process.

She considered that children expressed what they had learned through their play and pioneered working in partnership with parents, encouraging them to learn alongside their children. McMillan's later work promoted the importance of training adults to enable them to work with young children in an informed manner.

Table 7.6 McMillan: key concepts

Key concepts	Types of play	The 'gifts'
Emphasis on manipulative dexterity Pioneer of nursery schools Initiated school meals and health services Partnership with parents No formal learning before seven Promoted training for adults	Free-play Natural play Exploratory play	No special resources

Susan Isaacs (1885–1948)

Also influenced by the work of Froebel, Susan Isaacs believed that children should not enter formal learning situations before the age of seven. She considered that children should be allowed to learn through free play and individual experience, and she placed great emphasis on the need for movement in their play and learning. Isaacs also believed in the role of parents as the main educators of their children and, influenced by the work of Melanie Klein (a psychoanalyst), she was also interested in children's feelings and emotions. According to Isaacs, children are able to move in and out of reality during their play, as they learn to cope with their feelings, and that this is important to their emotional security.

Table 7.7 Isaacs: key concepts

Key concepts	Types of play	The 'gifts'
Emphasis on need for movement Play fundamental to learning No formal learning before seven Parents as main educators Emotional regression common on entering school	Free play Active play	No special resources

Isaacs recorded her observations of children before and after they had left the nursery. She noted that a marked regression in development was common when children entered formal schooling.

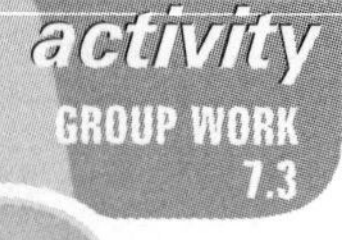

1 Using outdoor play as your basis, plan activities for children in your current placement that could be directly relevant to the thinking of each of the five early educators.

2 Answer the following:

(a) How might the activities differ?

(b) How might they be similar?

(c) In what ways do they help children learn?

Other influences on practice

Other influences on early years practice include

- curriculum models outside mainstream practice
- the organisation of the environment
- the role of the adult and how they interact with children
- resources.

Curriculum models outside mainstream provision

Although approaches to education outside the main curricula are more often found in privately funded settings, elements of these approaches may be incorporated into the curriculum and planning of maintained settings. Approaches include:

- Steiner Waldorf
- Montessori
- High/Scope
- Reggio Emillia.

> **remember** Both Steiner Waldorf and Montessori were early years pioneers and are referred to in the previous section.

High/Scope

The High/Scope curricular model derives from work done in the USA and was originally intended to be used in areas of deprivation, in tandem with the Head Start schemes. Designed to meet perceived deficits in children's learning and life experiences, it was well resourced and involved parents. Parents were visited at home in order to ensure that the learning experiences in the High/Scope setting were consistent with those offered at home. Results from the USA appeared to show that there were reasonably good long-term benefits from this approach: children enrolled in these programmes appeared to have better long-term development and learning. Evidence from its use in the UK is less convincing.

The High/Scope curriculum encourages children to take responsibility for their own learning, making choices, planning their activities and reviewing them collectively at a set point. High/Scope is associated with the principle: '**plan, do and review**'.

Plan

Children decide, often with an adult, what they will do during the session. There are different ways in which children can relay their plans to others in the group; it could be through words, actions or simple gestures. The session often starts with circle time, in which the whole group sits together, perhaps for weather-board or news time. The group then divides into smaller groups for planning. In many settings, you would, as a student, simply observe at this stage until the student supervisor is confident that you are able to support the planning process appropriately.

Do

> **remember** It is important that you ask for advice and guidance when you are unsure. You will not be expected to know everything and will be respected for your honesty.

Children select, use and put away their planned activities during the main 'work' time. The equipment is made easily accessible to the children and is clearly labelled to enable them to identify and select for themselves. Independent learning is encouraged; adults assist and encourage the children but do not direct them, and the children develop responsibility. Selecting and replacing resources becomes part of each day, adding to the child's development of social skills and their sense that they are part of the setting.

The High/Scope curriculum promotes active learning: the children make choices, exploring their environment freely and initiating ideas based on their interests and prior experiences. The adult role is to support those choices by providing an appropriate overall framework. As an adult working within this curriculum, you will encourage children to question and to find the answers for themselves wherever possible. The High/Scope curriculum requires a well-balanced level of child–adult interaction and many decisions are left to the child, which you may at first find strange. Joint child–adult-led interaction, in which you join the child at their level, is an important aspect of the High/Scope philosophy. Use of observational skills will enable you to identify when it is appropriate to involve yourself in a child's activity, to extend their learning, and when to hold back.

> **remember** The plan, do, review approach is regularly incorporated into non-High/Scope schools and nurseries.

Review

At the end of the High/Scope session, each child describes what they have been doing, often displaying the creative outcomes. This time of recall and reflection is led by an adult, usually in a small group setting. The key worker responsible for a group of children keeps a written record of each individual child's plans. This helps identify aspects of the setting that the child does not particularly enjoy and areas of special interest.

You may find it interesting to refer to *Bringing the High/Scope Approach to your Early Years Practice* by Holt (2007).

Reggio Emilia

Reggio Emilia is a region of Northern Italy where Loris Malaguzzi developed an innovative approach to early years care and education over 40 years ago. The Reggio approach separates care from education, which differs greatly from the British system. However, it is not only this that makes the Reggio approach unique: care and education are woven together and offered in custom-built environments where the expressive arts are embedded into every aspect of the curriculum. It is loosely based on social constructivist theories of learning, drawing on the work of Vygotsky and Jerome Bruner and on Howard Gardner's Multiple Intelligences theory. There is no set curriculum in these schools; instead, children are encouraged to undertake a variety of projects that will give them first-hand experiences and the opportunity to form hypotheses. All of the child's project work is fully recorded in writing and images, and all levels of work are valued.

In a Reggio setting, the child is at the centre of all that happens; the belief is that it is a child's fundamental right to realise and expand their potential and to be loved, valued and listened to. Children are perceived as active contributors to their learning and not empty vessels waiting to be filled. They are considered to have immense potential, strength and competence and to learn best by being able to develop their own ideas and use adults to test these ideas out.

The role of the adult is crucial to the Reggio approach. It is one of facilitation rather than transmission: it is not intended that the adult lets the child do completely as the child desires, but the child is free to explore and learn within an ordered and stimulating environment. Adults using this approach must be willing to let the child take measured risks and make mistakes in order to form hypotheses and learn from experimentation. The Reggio approach places great importance on the contribution that parents and grandparents have to make; this is valued by parents, children and staff and ensures that the whole community feels a sense of ownership of the learning that takes place.

The learning and care environment is of utmost importance in this approach and, although well known anecdotally, this is often misunderstood. The environment is not divided into separate spaces where discrete groups of children are taught in fixed groups; rather, the schools have a series of interconnected spaces that all open into a central space. Furniture and equipment are designed to be multifunctional, and children are encouraged to move around freely. The environment in a Reggio Emilia setting is considered to be the 'third' teacher.

Various expressive activities are provided in the central 'atelier' space of the school, where there is a qualified 'atelierista' to facilitate. Resources that are likely to be found in a setting that uses the Reggio approach include:

- shells
- beads
- stones
- pulses
- clay and other materials for ceramics
- paper
- cardboard
- wood
- musical instruments
- paints, pastels, crayons, batik and other craft supplies
- cloth, wool and a variety of other materials
- open spaces
- different sensory resources – as well as more 'traditional' teaching and learning resources common to many settings.

You may find it interesting to refer to *Bringing the Reggio Approach to your Early Years Practice* by Thornton and Brunton (2007).

The organisation of the early years environment

Children will learn well in many different environments, and early years care and education takes place wherever children are to be found. The home is the traditional place where learning begins, as appropriate care routines and play stimulate all areas of development and learning. Outside the family home, current provision of early years environments is influenced by external factors, such as:

- government legislation, policies, guidelines and recommendations – for example, the Birth to Three Matters framework and the Foundation Stage Curriculum
- provision linked to initiatives such as Sure Start programmes – for example, children's centres and neighbourhood nurseries
- the drive to integrate children's services in response to the Every Child Matters agenda and the National Service Framework
- organisational and cultural factors to be found in individual settings, such as the underlying philosophy or approach that influences care and education. There would, for example, be differences found in settings offering the approaches described above.

The role of the adult and how they interact with children

Various factors, internal and external to the setting, influence the way that the adult's role is interpreted and the way in which adults interact with children. Examples of factors that may influence the role of the adult include:

- The approach of the setting – the learning style that is used (transmission, laissez-faire, etc.) will largely determine the adult's role.
- Staff training and qualifications – it is generally accepted that effective learning environments require a high ratio of trained staff.
- The philosophy of the setting – for example, the involvement and input of adults in a Waldorf Steiner setting will differ from what is seen in a High/Scope setting.
- An adult's individual personality can impact on the level of interaction between adult and child.
- External factors, such as budgeting, can influence staff numbers and also numbers of qualified staff.

Resources

Here again, the philosophy of the setting will be a major influence. As outlined above, in Reggio Emillia settings there is great emphasis on natural materials. This also applies particularly to Steiner Waldorf settings. Most early years settings include a range of both natural and manufactured resources, with Montessori settings incorporating many of her specially designed pieces of equipment.

Most settings will have child-sized furniture (e.g. tables, chairs, storage units). For practical reasons, many will use plastic cups, plates, and so on. However, in a setting promoting the philosophy of Reggio Emillia or Steiner Waldorf, there is likely to be greater emphasis on real items (e.g. china cups); the thinking is to foster appreciation of the feel and enjoyment of the more natural material in preparation for life in general.

Understand the role of play in the development of children

The nature of play

There have been many definitions of play put forward over the years:

- Susan Isaacs (1933) stated that: 'Play is a child's life and the means by which he comes to understand the world he lives in'.
- According to Janet Moyles (1989), play should be 'viewed as a process'. She makes reference to Bruner who wrote: 'For the main characteristic of play – whether of child or adult – is not its content but its mode. Play is an approach to action, not a form of activity.'

Moyles has written extensively on the importance of children's play. The following title may be of interest: *The Excellence of Play* (ed. Moyles, 1994).

Moyles referred to the idea of 'playing at our work' and 'working at our play'. Children can often be seen concentrating hard on what they are doing, with their tongue sticking out as they focus their attention. They are indeed 'working' at their play. If, as adults, we enjoy our work and it is stimulating, interactive and challenging, it is likely to be fulfilling the same desires and needs as our leisure activities, i.e. our play. When adults buy a new 'toy', for example a camcorder, iPod or home music system, they experiment with it, testing it out, seeing how it works and discovering its limitations. Basically, they are playing with it, learning about it in much the same way as children experiment and learn with a new toy or resource.

Motivational value of play

Children clearly enjoy and respond to activities and situations that raise their curiosity, amuse and stimulate them, and that are simply fun. Ensuring that all aspects of play provision acknowledge cultural diversity helps children to appreciate other cultures and contributes to the self-esteem of children across the range of cultures represented. This in turn increases motivation to play and therefore to learn. As adults we need to be aware that play is ideally spontaneous and led by the child's own interests. When planning learning activities for children we need not only to make them fun but also take into account how the children

remember

Ask yourself: are the children at present fascinated by creative activities, using IT, or being outside?

are best motivated, including their current main interests. Tapping in to what is currently considered great fun by the children is likely to ensure a greater level of success for the activity, and therefore for the children's learning. Whenever possible, we should also build in freedom to explore, investigate and initiate.

Developmental stages of play

Play is developmental, and the **stages of play** can be seen as children develop socially from solitary play (playing alone), to parallel play (playing alongside other children), to **associative play** (watching and copying other children) and finally to co-operative play (playing with other children).

Refer to page 335 and also to Unit 3, page 139, where the development of play is discussed as part of social development.

Types of play

There are many different types of play. Understanding what each type of play involves and how it supports development is important. They can broadly be described as shown in the spidergram.

Fig 7.4 Types of play

Refer also to the table on page 354.

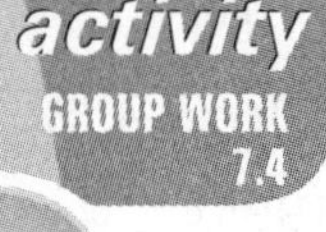

activity GROUP WORK 7.4

M2

1 With others, research the terms used in Figure 7.4 and explain to each other the potential value of each type of play to a child's development.
2 Produce a chart of activities, resources and ideas to illustrate each type of play.

Many play activities are referred to at other points in this unit, for example pages 354–355, and in Unit 4, page 217. You may find it helpful to refer to them for this activity and from time to time as you read through the unit.

Free-flow play

Free-flow play is described by Tina Bruce (1991) as the only true concept of play. It is often referred to as imaginative, pretend or ludic play – it allows children to learn by discovery.

> 'Games help children to understand external pressures and constraints; free-flow play helps children to see the function of rules for themselves.'
>
> (Bruce, 1991).

Bruce illustrates her definition of free-flow play as follows:

Fig 7.5 Free-flow play

Free-flow play	=	Wallowing in ideas, feelings and relationships	+	Application of competence and technical prowess that has already been developed

Bruce's 12 features of free-flow play are summarised as follows:

- It is an active process without a product.
- It is intrinsically motivated.
- There is no external pressure to conform.
- It is about lifting the 'players' to their highest levels of functioning, involving creativity and imagination.
- It involves reflection, the 'wallowing in ideas'.
- It actively uses previous first-hand experiences.
- It is sustained and helps us to function ahead of our real-life ability levels.
- It allows control, using competence previously attained.
- It can be initiated by child or adult, but adults need to be aware of not imposing rules, or directing activity.
- It can be a solitary experience.
- It can be in partnership with others.
- It brings together what we learn, feel and understand (Bruce, 1991).

In *Time to Play in Early Childhood Education*, Bruce (1991) offers a detailed and fascinating explanation of play, bringing together the thinking of many theorists and educationists.

remember If children are continually led by an adult, they are likely to be less involved in the process of their play, and some opportunities for learning will be missed.

remember Children learn through stimulus. They need a range of activities that will keep their interest and enhance their experience.

remember When explaining to someone else, you will be able to check your own understanding.

Structured play

Structured play is planned and led by an adult, who may or may not work alongside the child during the activity. Most people agree that children benefit from a degree of structure, and every setting has its constraints regarding time, space and staffing which lead to the need to 'frame' the daily routine. This should not, however, result in lack of flexibility and lack of opportunity for play to flow. A balance has to be achieved with the structured introduction to a new experience leading the child to further (free-play) exploration of the material or subject.

Spontaneous play

Spontaneous play allows children to develop their play ideas for themselves, with the adult providing a range of resources and materials. Children learn successfully if they are allowed to 'seize the moment' and this is where adult flexibility is vital. The child who unexpectedly brings a jar of snails into the nursery offers the opportunity for an on-the-spot discussion of minibeasts, life forms, houses, bodily needs (food, water, and so on). The interest of the children will be captured by the excitement of the snails' arrival, and therefore opportunities for learning are high. Similarly, the child who makes a pretend kite (perhaps triggered by observation of kites elsewhere) and runs around the garden trying to fly it will be learning the basis of aerodynamics, as well as having fun and fulfilling a spontaneous need to try something new.

Combining types of play

Moyles developed the play spiral (see Figure 7.6). The spiral incorporates free play with directed (structured) play, showing how children move in and out of each mode as their learning develops, leading to the development (accretion) of knowledge, understanding and new skills. When you feel that you understand the play spiral, try to explain it to another person.

Fig 7.6 Moyles's play spiral

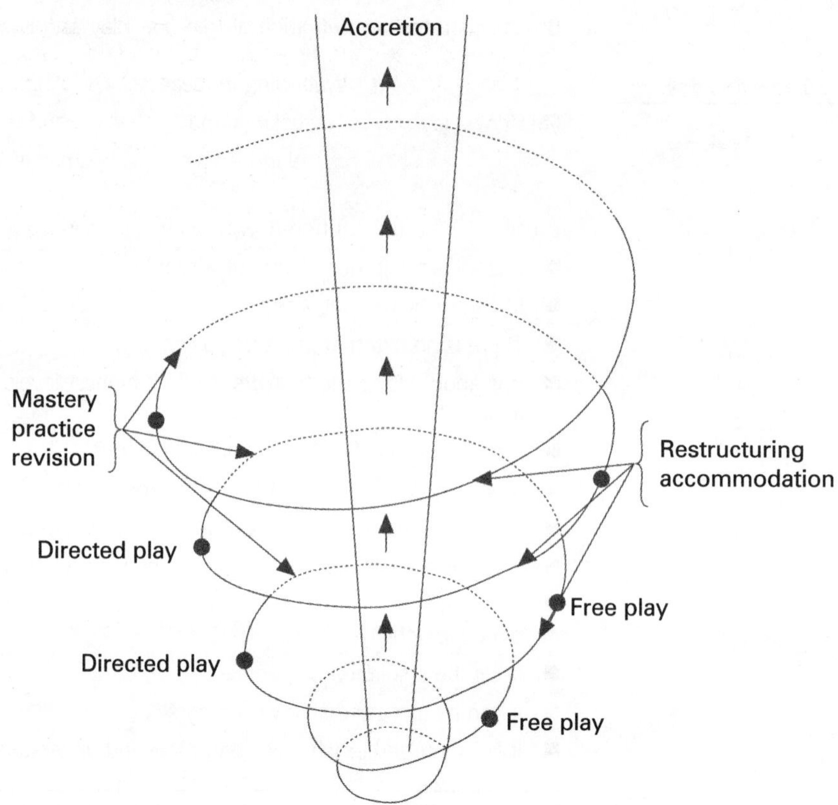

activity
INDIVIDUAL WORK 7.5

P3

M3

With reference to Moyles's play spiral:

1 Identify and describe a child in your placement whom you have observed developing in this way.
2 Explain how their development has moved on, using the spiral illustration as part of your explanation.
3 Ensure that you fully explain the adult's role in the child's learning process.

Therapeutic play

There is a fourth main type of play – therapeutic play or play therapy; this helps children who are troubled in some way to begin to explore their problems and work through them. It is also a medium of play used in preparing children for health care interventions and procedures, and with children who have a life-limiting illness who may need to act out negative emotions, such as fear or stress.

Refer to Unit 5, page 279, for information on play therapy.

The role of play

As you read through this unit you will notice how many of the play activities and ideas can be linked to various areas of development. A brief overview of play's role in each main developmental area follows.

Play's role in physical development

To support physical development, children need to take part in activities that encourage them to:

- Use their bodies to move forward, backwards, sideways, to express themselves to music and creative ideas – these actions come under the headings of locomotion and gross motor skills.

- Use their bodies to stretch, reach, bend, balance, curl up, be still, sway, etc., also to dress themselves, putting on and taking off shoes, coats, hats, scarves, etc. – these are non-locomotion actions but mostly use gross motor skills.
- Use their hands and fingers in precise actions, to draw, paint, mould clay and dough, handle sand and water, thread and sew, to position puzzle pieces and construction materials, to learn to feed themselves and hold cups securely, to fasten clothing (e.g. zips, toggles, buttons) – these are all fine motor skills.

Play's role in social and emotional development

To support social and emotional development, children need to take part in activities that encourage them to:

- share, take turns, develop an awareness of the needs of others
- express themselves both verbally and non-verbally
- feel wanted, valued, part of the group, equal to their peers
- express and understand their own emotions, knowing that it is OK for them to feel this way
- feel safe
- be able to trust those around them.

Play's role in language development

To support language development, children need to take part in activities that encourage them to:

- use books for pleasure, to gain information, to support topic work
- share storytelling experiences with others, one to one, in pairs and within both small and larger groups
- talk to others, one to one, in pairs, and within both small and larger groups
- name, explain, suggest, describe, question, predict, etc.
- notice the written word around them, at home, within the setting and in the wider environment
- make marks, write, draw, paint, label, etc.
- use language within context, both verbal and written, and through gesture.

Play's role in intellectual development

To support intellectual development, children need to take part in activities that encourage them to:

Fig 7.7 Benefits of play

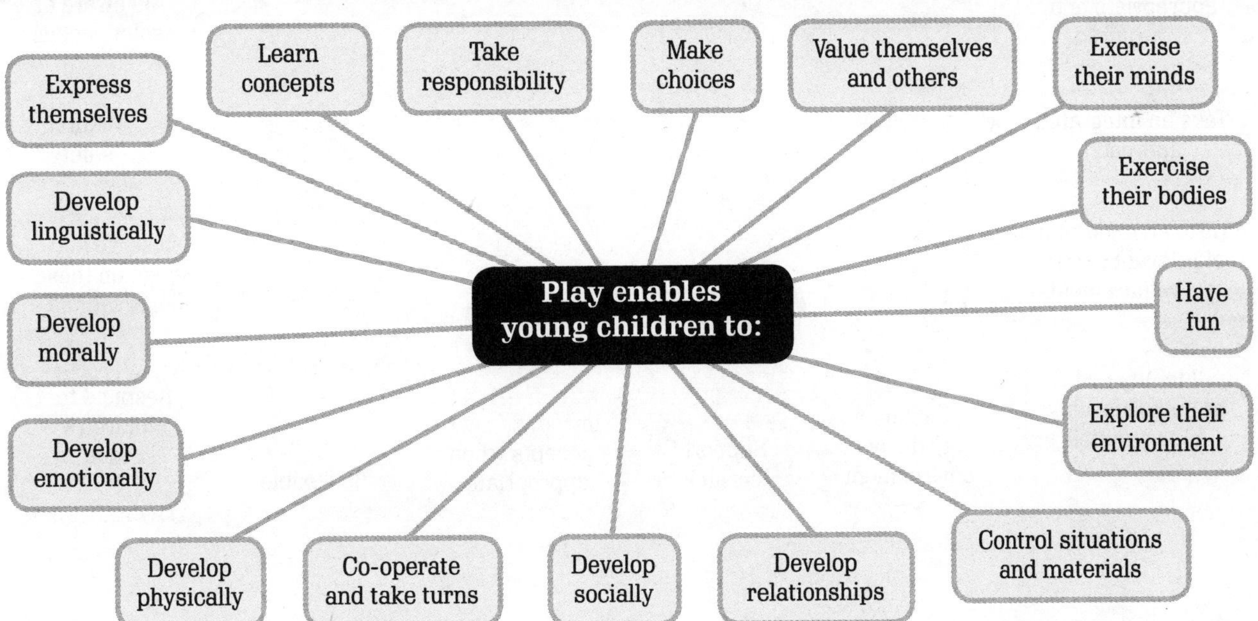

- think, remember, consider, etc.
- refer back to past experiences, to build on previous knowledge
- use their imagination
- to be creative
- to plan, implement and reflect.

Figure 7.7 is another useful way of summarising play's value.

Understand the role of the adult in all aspects of provision and implementation of play and learning activities for children

Role of the adult

The spidergram below demonstrates the various roles that adults have in supporting learning and play.

Fig 7.8 The role of the adult

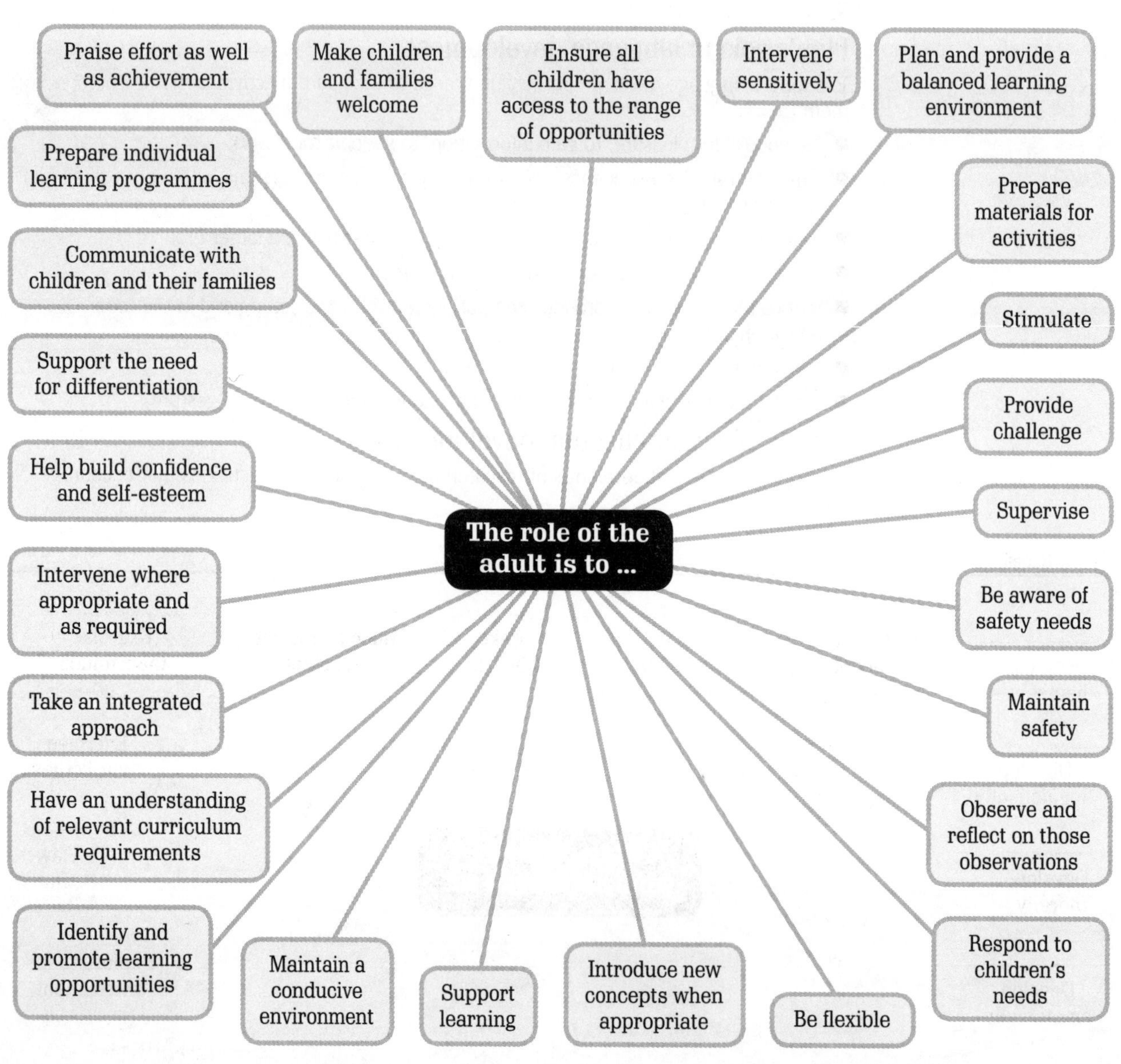

You will find it helpful to refer back to the spidergram as you read through the section on planning activities to support early learning, pages 347–350.

A well-planned setting is usually a successful setting and one in which the effective deployment of adults has a positive effect on the children's development. Whatever the approach to play, directed or non-directed, careful adult supervision is always necessary, and childcare workers are responsible for the safety of all situations, including the range of equipment and resources. Successful experiences for children are based on suitability and good planning. It is crucial that practitioners understand the levels of development of the children they work with to ensure that they plan and prepare appropriately. The adults should have realistic expectations of what the children can achieve and should put in place any additional support that is required, including opportunities for extension. Acknowledging and implementing differentiation is central to meeting in full the needs of all children in a group.

Each of us needs to hear and feel that we are valued by others. It gives us a sense of self-worth and helps build confidence. Many children do not get this at home, as some parents simply do not understand the importance of taking time to talk with their children, play with them, read to them, give them praise for effort, and so on. Giving children your time will often be the most important part of your role as a practitioner.

Refer also to Unit 1, and to Unit 4, page 200.

remember

Safety awareness involves assessing the suitability of resources for the age groups present, removing small articles from the environment of the youngest children and giving guidance on safe use of utensils and materials to all children.

Adult–child relationships

The relationship between adult and child has an impact on the overall experience for the child. As you develop professionally, you need to consider how you build your relationships with the children in your care.

Table 7.8 Adult–child relationship

Adult role	Child role
Conductor	Orchestra
Chef	Ingredients
Sales representative	Customer
Police officer	Citizen
Sergeant Major	Soldier
Gardener	Flower
Parent	Child
Potter	Clay
Teacher	Student
Performer	Audience

To remind yourself about using observation, refer to Unit 3, pages 163–180 and, for communication skills, to Unit 1, pages 11–23.

Curriculum

Implementation of the curriculum is a particular feature of the adult role. Curriculum guidance and frameworks to support all-round health, education and well-being cover not only the whole period of compulsory schooling but also the time before that begins. At present, these frameworks include:

- Birth to Three Matters
- Foundation Stage Curriculum
- Every Child Matters
- National Curriculum.

From September 2008, there will be changes, as the Early Years Foundation Stage (EYFS) framework becomes mandatory, building on the current curriculum guidance for the Foundation Stage, Birth to Three Matters and the National Standards for Under Eights Day-care and Childminding. The EYFS has as its aim the five intended outcomes of the Every Child Matters strategy, i.e. young children will:

- be healthy
- stay safe
- enjoy and achieve
- make a positive contribution
- achieve economic well-being.

Details of the EYFS can be downloaded from its website; information is likely to continue to be updated until the framework's full implementation.
www.dfes.gov.uk

In Wales there will also be changes, with the new Foundation Phase curriculum also being in place in 2008.

Details of the Foundation Phase can be found at:
www.wales.gov.uk.

Research has shown how important the first three years of life are for a child's development.

Birth to Three Matters (DfES, 2003)

The Birth to Three Matters framework is not intended to be a formal curriculum as such but was designed to support effective practice. The framework is designed to inform the practice of anyone working with the under-threes regardless of the nature of the setting; it has four main aspects:

- a strong child
- a skilful communicator
- a competent learner
- a healthy child.

Each aspect is further broken down into key components that inform the delivery of care and early learning.

A strong child
The components are:

- me, myself and I
- being acknowledged and affirmed
- developing self assurance
- a sense of belonging.

A skilful communicator
The components are:

- being together
- finding a voice
- listening and responding
- making meaning.

A competent learner
The components are:

- making connections
- being imaginative
- being creative
- representing.

A healthy child
The components are:

- emotional well-being
- growing and developing
- keeping safe
- healthy choices.

These aspects and components should be used to inform and structure innovative and imaginative care for the very youngest children. Babies are 'born to learn' and benefit from a rich, stimulating and emotionally supportive environment. Most provision for young babies is to be found within baby units or separate baby rooms. There is some evidence to suggest that they benefit from time spent with older babies and young children, but they also need a discrete and appropriate environment where there is a high ratio of qualified staff. The different aspects and components of the Birth to Three Matters framework can be used as a basis for daily care activities as well as for more structured learning opportunities. It can be used equally by practitioners in day nurseries, family homes and children's centres, and by childminders.

1 Using your college resource centre, research the Birth to Three Matters framework.
2 Discuss with others how the activities and care routines that you have seen in practice fit with the four aspects and the different components.

A useful series of books to also refer to is *From Birth to 3* by Roberts and Harpley, (ed. Green, 2006/7).

Foundation Stage Curriculum

The early year's curriculum is one part of a range of connected strategies for children's services and is based on six main areas of learning:

- personal, social and emotional development
- communication, language and literacy
- mathematical development
- knowledge and understanding of the world
- physical development
- creative development.

Environments that implement the Foundation Stage Curriculum successfully will centre their practice on play and the holistic development of the individual child. Each of the areas of learning has Early Learning Goals that are measurable, but everything that a child does in the setting is valued as the curriculum includes 'everything children do, see, hear or feel in their setting, both planned and unplanned' (QCA, cited in Drake, 2001).

All settings offering the Foundation Stage Curriculum and achieving satisfactory inspection outcomes from Ofsted receive funding for their three- and four-year-olds from a finance source known as the Nursery Education Grant.

The Foundation Stage Curriculum is offered from the age of three, up until the child begins to follow the National Curriculum and its principles should be the basis of all future learning by supporting, fostering, promoting and developing children's:

- personal, social and emotional well-being: in particular by supporting the transition to and between settings, promoting an inclusive ethos and providing opportunities for each child to become a valued member of that group and community so that a strong self-image and self-esteem are promoted
- *positive attitudes and dispositions towards their learning*: in particular an enthusiasm for knowledge and learning and a confidence in their ability to be successful learners
- *social skills*: in particular by providing opportunities that enable them to learn how to co-operate and work harmoniously alongside and with each other and to listen to each other
- *attention skills and persistence*: in particular the capacity to concentrate on their own play or on group tasks
- *language and communication*: with opportunities for all children to talk and communicate in a widening range of situations, to respond to adults and to each other, to practise and extend the range of vocabulary and communication skills they use and to listen carefully
- *reading and writing*: with opportunities for all children to explore, enjoy, learn about and use words and text in a broad range of context and to experience a rich variety of books

- *mathematics*: with opportunities for all children to develop their understanding of number, measurement, pattern, shape and space by providing a broad range of contexts in which they can explore, enjoy, learn, practise and talk about them
- *knowledge and understanding of the world*: with opportunities for all children to solve problems, make decisions, experiment, predict, plan and question in a variety of contexts, and to explore and find out about their environment and people and places that have significance in their lives
- *physical development*: with opportunities for all children to develop and practise their fine and gross motor skills and to increase their understanding of how the body works and what they need to do to be healthy and safe
- *creative development*: with opportunities for all children to explore and share thoughts, ideas and feelings through a variety of art, design and technology, music, movement, dance and imaginative and role-play activities (QCA, 2000, pages 8–9).

There is a single assessment strategy for the Foundation Stage; it is known as the Foundation Stage Profile. The thirteen assessment scales that are used to assess the six areas of learning are usually completed by the end of the Foundation Stage, and observations of a child's progress will be made although the Early Learning Goals are not summatively assessed.

Refer to page 350 for an explanation of summative assessment.

National Curriculum

The National Curriculum is intended to be a broad and balanced framework to meet the learning needs of all children; its main principles are based on the Education Acts of 1988 and 1996. All state schools must offer the National Curriculum; although schools in the private sector can opt out, few do. It is considered to be a prescriptive curriculum in that it gives precise outcomes to be achieved at certain stages in a child's school career. Schools are also free to provide extra areas of learning in addition to the National Curriculum to reflect the particular needs and circumstances of the setting.

The National Curriculum is divided into key stages.

Table 7.9 National Curriculum key stages

Key stage	Age	Year groups
Key Stage 1 (KS1)	5–7 years	1–2
Key Stage 2 (KS2)	7–11 years	3–6
Key Stage 3 (KS3)	11–14 years	7–9
Key Stage 4 (KS4)	14–16 years	10–11

Key Stage 1 follows on from the Foundation Stage; you will usually work with children who are following the curriculum for this stage during placement experience in a Year 1 or Year 2 class.

At the end of each key stage, there are a number of tests known as Standard Attainment Tasks (SATs), which all children must complete. The purpose of SATS is to monitor each individual child's performance as they progress through school.

Key Stage 1

Key Stage 1 includes:

- English
- mathematics
- science
- technology (design and technology and information technology)
- history
- geography
- art
- music
- physical education.

The attainment targets at the end of Key Stage 1 are based around the following areas of learning:

- English – speaking and listening; reading; writing
- mathematics – using and applying mathematics; number and algebra; shape, space and measure; handling data
- science – experimental and investigative science; life processes and living things; materials and their properties; physical processes
- design and technology – designing; making
- art – investigating and making; knowledge and understanding
- music – performing and composing; listening and appraising.

For each of the other subjects, teachers make a decision about the level attained, which is based on the range of descriptions set out for each key stage level.

Details of these can be found in DfEE (1995) *Key Stages 1 and 2 of the National Curriculum*, or at www.dfes.gov.uk.

Planning and preparation

Environment

The environment for learning is just as important as the content of the curriculum and, although few children will experience the purpose-built environment found in settings working to the influences of Reggio Emillia, much can be done to enhance all areas in which learning takes place. It is essential that the environment is:

- safe – Does the area conform to Health and Safety regulations? Are routines and care activities carried out safely? Is the relevant protective equipment used when needed? Are COSHH regulations complied with? Do staff and children know what to do in case of emergencies?
- organised – Do children know what the expected pattern of the day is? Do they know where resources are to be found and stored? Do they know what they are supposed to do? Does the environment promote independence? Is it child friendly?

Resources

It is important that children have access to a wide range of stimulating resources, and these should be organised in such a way that children are able to select and use resources freely. Ask yourself:

- Are resources clearly categorised and labelled? Can children understand the labelling system? Can they reach and access resources? What modifications have been made to support children with additional needs?
- Do children have access to a personal storage or display space that they can call their own? Are they consulted about the resources and activities?
- Is there sufficient space for large-group activities such as circle time or dance? Are activities and resources linked in themed areas? Do the children have easy access to creative spaces and activities? Can they easily gain access to outdoor activities and equipment?
- Do the resources and activities reflect diversity and inclusion? Are there positive images of men and women, people with different levels of ability, different ethnic origins? Are there quiet areas for rest and reading?

Storage of resources

Good storage methods enable easy access to resources and keep them in good condition. A separate area is needed for 'messy' resources, such as paint, glue, clay, collage items and junk modelling boxes. Clay should be kept slightly moist: otherwise small hands will not be able to manipulate it. Paint pots and spatulas should be washed regularly and brushes need thorough cleaning to keep the bristles soft and pliable. Glue lids should be secured to prevent a skin forming. Ideally, surplus resources should be kept in a trolley or cupboard (most are now mobile). Items such as scissors are best kept in designated holders, and paper is ideally stored in a purposely designed storage unit. Storing paper flat will keep it free of tears and make it easier to handle.

You need to consider how you will store paintings and models. An old clothes horse can be useful, but a drying frame is even better, especially if it has a shelf or spare surface area for models.

Storage boxes for items such as dressing-up clothes, construction kits and puppets can be purchased quite cheaply and will encourage children to take responsibility for clearing away.

A multitude of small items can be stored in trays and placed in cupboards, and specially designed tray-storage units can be purchased.

Organisation of resources

When organising where resources and activities are placed within the setting, the following require careful consideration:

- the amount of space needed for the activity
- the number of children likely to use the activity at any one time
- the importance of a quiet area for the activity
- whether hand-washing facilities are required nearby
- the level of adult involvement needed (affecting deployment of staff)
- any interruption that could be posed to the activity by doorways, access points, etc.

case study 7.3

Fountain Park Nursery

Fountain Park Nursery is shortly opening in its new premises. Each member of staff has been asked to plan where they would position the range of everyday activities. They have been given the following list of what to include:

- water tray
- sand tray
- indoor slide
- mat for cars, farm, and so on
- area for puzzles, threading, and so on
- book corner
- painting easels
- a creative activity
- drawing and writing
- dough (or clay)
- role-play area with dressing-up clothes
- large-scale construction
- small-scale construction
- a topic table.

It is not necessary for all the activities to be available all of the time, but each is offered in some way every day.

activity
INDIVIDUAL WORK

Using a copy of the blank floor plan that is available to download from the Nelson Thornes website:

1 How would you set out the nursery if you were asked?
2 What would determine your decisions?
3 Which areas would you consider needed to be static, and why?
4 Which areas would you consider could be moved around?

Refer to the Nelson Thornes website for the 'Fountain Park Nursery floor plan'. www.nelsonthornes.com/btec

Involving children

Children's interests can change quite quickly and can be influenced by new experiences. Whenever practical, respond to current interests, involving children in decision-making and choice, and helping them take ownership of ideas and projects. This will make them feel valued both as individuals and as part of a group and will build their confidence and self-esteem.

Many learning opportunities can be found within daily routines. Simple examples include:

- encouraging counting as children line up at a door or lay a table for snack time
- encouraging children to group themselves by jumper colour, hair colour, etc. as they move from activity to activity, or from indoors to outside
- introducing new vocabulary as you discuss the weather (e.g. 'blustery', 'scorching', 'torrential').

Promoting independence

Promoting independence and mastery of skills is important. Even the youngest children can be encouraged to participate in their own care, although this may only be holding a flannel to the face for a brief moment or helping to pull up a zip fastening. As children grow and mature, it becomes more important for them to develop and master the skills needed for independence, and the early years worker has an important role to play in this respect. Children should be encouraged to take supervised and acceptable risks and be allowed to make mistakes on the journey from relative dependence to independence. This will foster a sense of autonomy and competence that will increase their self-confidence as learners.

Extension of activities

Adult intervention

Very young children need one key ingredient – a knowledgeable and enthusiastic practitioner who has a clear understanding of the child's holistic developmental needs. That practitioner will make sure that care and learning activities are offered in emotionally secure environments where key workers and the key-person concept ensure that individual needs are met. Older children will be more confident in their play and will, with appropriate support, make the most of learning opportunities. Environments for learning should be adequately resourced and staffed and underpinned by the required curricular frameworks.

Every adult is a potential human resource, extending learning and developing language by contributing to a child's play. Any curriculum for early years should be broad and balanced, involving a range of people, situations, values and resources. Learning takes place at all times, in all situations, and is enhanced by visits to places of interest and by visitors from the wider community.

Refer back to the thinking of Lev Vygotsky, page 322, and Jerome Bruner, page 323, to remind yourself about facilitating children's progress to the next stage in their understanding.

Refer also to the Nelson Thornes website for an example of an observation recording successful adult intervention (Target child observation A). www.nelsonthornes.com/btec

Broadening experience

Each time you plan an activity it is important to think through how it can be further developed. Simple, everyday experiences can often be easily extended to introduce a much greater breadth of experience. For example, try making playdough in your usual way but add scents and essences to different 'portions' and ask children to think about each smell and guess what it is. This activity offers opportunities to introduce new vocabulary (e.g. 'sour', 'bitter', 'perfumed'); you may also feel that it is relevant to make links to other senses. Another simple example is to prepare a fruit salad with children, observing all the usual food and hygiene preparations; learning opportunities here include:

- discussing the various features of each fruit (shape, size, skin texture, etc.)
- washing and sorting the pips and seeds according to a specified feature

- planting some of the pips and seeds, so the children can observe which will grow and under what conditions, and using halves of different fruits for making printed images
- making links to stories, games and rhymes (e.g. reading the story 'Oliver's Fruit Salad' by Vivian French; playing the ring game 'Oranges and Lemons', and so on).

Observation and inclusion

Observational skills will help you to identify the individual stage in each child's development. You will learn from your placement supervisor and colleagues how to use observations to ensure that all children can access the activities you have planned. At times, you will have to consider where additional adult support will be needed and if alternative resources would make a child feel more included and improve their experience. In the examples given above, some children may need pictures to help support them in identifying smells, or those with limited dexterity may need help in 'releasing' the aromas within the balls of dough. Hand-on-hand contact may be required so that children can cut and sort fruits, pips and seeds; giving children small trays to contain small parts may make sorting easier.

You will find plenty of examples of activities and ideas to extend them in the Ready, Steady, Play! series, edited by Green (2005).

Professional Practice

- Whatever you plan to do, health and safety must always be taken into account.
- You may find that another member of staff has a skill that would enhance the activity, so remember to discuss and encourage the sharing of ideas to ensure that everyone's expertise is used to the full benefit of the children.

Monitoring strategies

When monitoring the effectiveness of provision for children, you will use all or some of the following:

- discussion with colleagues
- setting criteria and referring back to set criteria
- documentation, either specific to your placement or materials that it uses
- feedback from tutors and placement supervisors
- observations of children.

You will be:

- monitoring levels of participation and learning
- evaluating children's enjoyment, reactions and responses
- reflecting on your own practice
- noting the practice of others.

Refer now to Unit 4, pages 216 and 230 where the monitoring and evaluation of the adult role, the promotion of opportunities and the implementation of activities are discussed.

Know how to identify and promote learning opportunities for children aged from 0 to 8 years of age

Supporting early learning

You will support learning through the promotion of key concepts, skills, attitudes and knowledge across a range of curriculum areas according to the early education framework relevant to the age group you are working with and linked to the guidance of your home country, for example England, Wales, etc.

Concepts

As children explore concepts they are developing their own ideas, trying out the ideas of others, testing theories (e.g. They will be thinking, 'I wonder if …'; 'If I do this, will such and such happen' and so on). You can support this development by setting up activities that allow them to plan, predict and make errors. They will learn a great deal from observing what worked and what did not. Play involving malleable materials, such as sand and clay, and construction activities of all types are good vehicles for concept development.

Skills

Both gross and fine skills will be developed as children handle resources, explore materials, construct, draw and write, dance, move about, etc. Every activity that you set up will involve physical skills in some form. An important aspect of linking your observations and assessment to your planning will be identifying the skills in which a child needs further support and planning activities to assist their development. For example, activities involving the positioning of objects and materials, and games involving matching and tessellation, will help a child develop the fine motor skills required to complete jigsaw puzzles. Similarly, regular free use of pencils, crayons, etc. will help the development of a sturdy pencil grip, although some children may need specific guidance on how to grasp each implement properly.

Attitudes

A child's attitude to learning can often be influenced by what is expected of them and how their efforts are received. It is important to show enthusiasm and pleasure for what children have been doing in order to encourage them to carry on, to try again, and to repeat the activity or experience another time. A child who receives limited feedback for their efforts is less likely to continue to be interested, or willing to try. Also, a child who is often reluctant to try new activities is likely to miss out on learning experiences if the adults working with them automatically expect them to show reluctance. Therefore, it is easy to see how as an adult you can help shape a child's approach to learning, i.e. their attitude, quite easily, simply by addressing your own attitude and level of interest in them.

Knowledge

Young children soak up knowledge like a sponge. This can be seen as they greet new experiences with enthusiasm and interest, asking questions, clamouring to have a go or to be the first to do something. Each activity you set up should have a clear aim; in other words, you should know what you want the children to learn from it. You will then be able to evaluate their learning and decide whether your aim has been met.

Whichever curriculum you work with, aims and learning objectives will have been specified, and many of your activities will be linked to these. Each curriculum framework also encourages practitioners to take an integrated approach to supporting children's learning, emphasising inclusion and anti-discriminatory practice.

Refer to page 348 for differentiation and IEPs.

Meeting the Early Learning Goals

As already discussed on page 339, practitioners in England work currently within the framework known as the Curriculum Guidance for the Foundation Stage.

You may find it helpful to refer back to Unit 4, page 215 to remind yourself of the main principles of the framework.

As we saw, the curriculum comprises six areas of learning, each having Early Learning Goals (ELGs). These ELGs are based on Stepping Stones – the Stepping Stones gradually lead a child through the ELGs and are colour coded in order that a child's progression can easily be tracked.

In order to help children meet the Early Learning Goals for communication, language and literacy, practitioners should:

- offer opportunities for children to take part in role play and other activities where they can practise speaking and listening
- ensure that the environment is language-rich

- support and encourage children to explore and enjoy books, stories, rhymes and poems
- support children in literacy activities and help them to delight in the written word and writing
- act as a positive role model by showing them how to listen, speak clearly and use language effectively
- provide a wide range of stimulating activities that provoke learning in communication, language and literacy.

For mathematical development, practitioners need to:

- provide children with a wide range of resources and activities that encourage numeracy and mathematical learning – this could include a wide range of materials and role play scenarios
- engage children in activities such as sorting, grading, weighing, and measuring, as these all underpin mathematical learning
- help them to see the 'pattern' of mathematics and number by the use of activities and games that encourage counting and number and shape recognition
- role model positive attitudes to numbers and maths and use mathematical language confidently
- support children to enable them to ask questions and form hypotheses by engaging in experiments.

For knowledge and understanding of the world, practitioners need to:

- ensure that children have access to real-world experiences
- facilitate children's knowledge of their immediate environment and a wide variety of environments with which they are not familiar
- provide opportunities for visits to appropriate venues such as museums, places of historical and geographical interest
- introduce children to a wide range of artefacts and objects that represent an understanding of a diverse world.

For physical development, practitioners need to:

- make sure that all children have regular opportunities to practise and develop their fine and gross motor skills
- encourage and support them to master skills of independence in dressing, personal hygiene and feeding
- give children space, time and permission to experiment, take carefully supervised risks and make mistakes
- provide challenging yet safe indoors and outdoors environments in which to practise the skills for physical development
- make sure that all children have access to opportunities to maximise their personal potential for physical development, regardless of ability.

For creative development, practitioners need to:

- provide a wide range of diverse, stimulating resources that encourage creativity
- allow children to enjoy the expressive arts in their own ways and not confine them to prescribed media
- ensure that the environment is arranged in such a way that there are provocations to creative learning and expression
- provide children with access to a range of experiences and people that represent the whole spectrum of expressive and creative arts.

In order to foster these goals, children need opportunities to work both alone and in groups of different sizes. They need to develop independence and be able both to lead and to follow.

Planning and evaluating activities to support early learning

As a practitioner you will need to provide children with a wide range of activities to support their learning, and these will mostly be informed by curricular frameworks. Planning should not only be for immediate use but also for the short-term and longer-term future. Each school or early years setting will have their own style and method. There is no one correct way of planning, but planning should always be meaningful and fully understood by all practitioners needing to use it.

You will probably find that you need to refer to the planning sheets (daily and/or weekly) at your placement when you are planning an activity, to ensure that what you aim to do fits in with the current overall learning theme. Sometimes there will be separate plans for small-group activities and whole-class activities, and there would usually be space to make reference to any previous assessments made either by you or by other practitioners. Some settings will break down the planning even further, providing planning sheets for creative activities, physical activities, and so on.

Look on the Nelson Thornes website for the following examples of planning: weekly planning for Key Stage 1 (Being explorers in the Arctic); Small group activity (Learning Intention – To know that darkness is the absence of light); and two blank planning sheets (whole class activity; physical activity). www.nelsonthornes.com/btec

Here is another example.

Table 7.10

Learning Intention	Resources	Child's Activity	Adult's role	Language
Show a strong sense of self as a member of a setting or a family Differentiation Make connections between different parts of their life experiences Cross-curricula CLL1 P+S 3+4 K+U 4	Books *Just as well really* *Za-Za's Baby Brother* *The Nursery Collection* *A Quiet Night In* *John Joe and the Big Hen* *Will there be a lap for me?* *Billy & Belle* *My Mum is so Unusual* *Something Special*	Listen to stories about different families Listen to story and sit appropriately Begin to understand that everyone has different families Relate stories to their own family life and talk about it at end of story Talk in a small group – talking about family (relating to story) i.e. about new baby	To read story – stopping and asking questions to encourage children to use picture clues and relate story to life at home/ feelings etc. Lead discussion about family – relating to story in book	Listen Look Sit Family Names of family members Grandma Grandpa Granny Grampfer Nanny etc.

activity
INDIVIDUAL WORK 7.7
P5

Part A – Foundation Stage Curriculum

Individual work

1 Using planning sheets of your choice, plan two learning activities for children in your current placement. Make clear your intentions for the children, the resources you will need and any specific links, vocabulary to be introduced, etc.

2 Carry out the activities at times agreed with your placement supervisor.

3 Evaluate the learning outcomes and overall success of each activity.

activity
GROUP WORK
7.7

P5

Part B – Birth to Three Matters Framework

The blank table below links to the Birth to Three Matters framework.

Working in a small group, select an area of learning and set out appropriate care routines and learning experiences to support the four main areas of the framework:

- a strong child
- a skilful communicator
- a competent learner
- a healthy child.

NB. You will need to refer to a copy of the framework to complete this activity.

Table 7.11

Months
Heads Up, Lookers and Communicators
Sitters, Standers and Explorers
Movers, Shakers and Players
Walkers, Talkers and Pretenders

Differentiation

Differentiation should be an integral part of all curricular planning in order that experiences and activities can meet the learning needs of individual children. Differentiation is part of short-term planning and provides the fine detail, showing how the activity may be altered or developed to meet the needs of specific individual children or groups. It will identify:

- activities
- experiences
- resources that may be needed
- teaching strategies that may be used
- support that may be required.

An effectively planned educational provision will include:

- high-quality staffing, planning and resources
- positive relationships between adults and children
- opportunities for children to build on what they already know
- equality of opportunity with regard to ethnicity, culture, religion, disability and gender
- differentiated plans to incorporate all children's developmental levels
- a balance of adult- and child-initiated activities
- adults who are able to intervene appropriately in the learning process to help extend learning.

Individual education plan (IEP)

When a child has an additional need, an individual education plan (IEP) needs to be drawn up and the focus placed on removing as many barriers as possible so that the child can have access to the mainstream curriculum. Early years settings will either have, or be linked to, a special needs co-coordinator (SENCO) who will oversee the IEPs and support children and their families. The SENCO will usually have a link to an educational psychologist and other members of the multidisciplinary education and health care teams.

IEPs should:

- assess the level of a child's difficulty
- give an overview of what intervention is needed
- outline what special educational needs provision is required
- identify who is currently supporting the child
- suggest timescales and review dates.

An IEP should include:

- short-term targets set for or by the child
- specified teaching strategies
- exactly what help needs to be put in place for the child
- when the level of help is to be reviewed
- criteria to help judge the success of the IEP
- criteria to help decide when the help is no longer needed
- outcomes, which are recorded when the IEP is reviewed.

There is a five-stage code of practice for special needs:

- Stage 1: a concern is expressed by parent, teacher or health professional
- Stage 2: involvement of a SENCO and the development of an IEP
- Stage 3: outside help from an educational psychologist is required
- Stage 4: a detailed assessment is made by the local authority in conjunction with parents and school
- Stage 5: a binding document (the statement) is drawn up by the local authority, setting out the agreed provision for the child.

Children with English as an additional language

The curriculum of any setting will need to plan for supporting children in developing their English and, where possible, enabling children to use their home language too. This should help both languages to develop alongside each other.

Supporting Identity, Diversity and Language in Early Years by Siraj-Blatchford and Clarke (2000) is an excellent source of reference.

Professional Practice

- Remember that children learning a new language will usually understand a considerable amount of what they hear before they attempt to speak the new language.
- You will need to support spoken language, with visual cues such as pictures, signs and artefacts.

Fig 7.9 Learning English alongside a home language

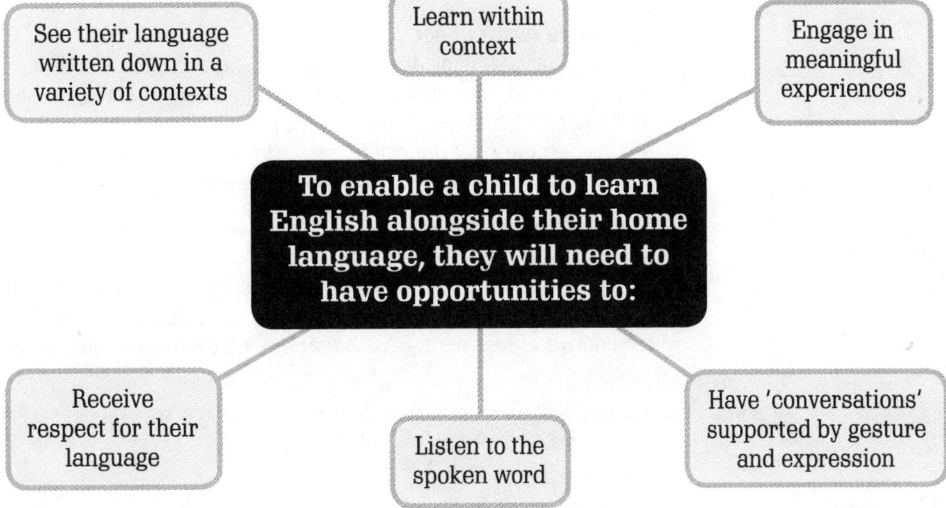

remember

Anything you record about a child must be based on what you have seen or what has actually taken place. It is not appropriate to make assumptions about what they 'meant' to say or 'intended' to do.

Use of observation

Observation is the key to identifying how children learn best. Providing a range of resources and facilitating children to work in their preferred style whenever possible will ensure that they are able to gain the most from the opportunities around them. Using observation as part of daily practice, i.e. recording children's efforts, successes, skill development, and any particular points that will help other practitioners understand a child better, supports the child's overall development.

Refer back to Unit 3, page 169, for an overview of observational methods.

Professional Practice

- **Resources include individual practitioner skills, parents, and other adults within the wider community as well as specialist equipment and the use of ICT. You should be aiming to make use of as many different resources as you can to provide the greatest range of opportunities for the children.**
- **Providing appropriate resources to support the learning environment includes planning, storage and organisation of resources, as well as the actual resources themselves.**

Monitoring progress

A natural part of working with children is the monitoring of their progress. As adults we look at what they can do, how they do it, and what interests them and provide resources, activities and opportunities to move them forward to the next stage. Monitoring is important, but relatively low key in the earliest years, becoming more formal as children develop and reach the age of compulsory education.

In baby units and toddler rooms, the child's progress is monitored not only so that further activities can be planned for the child but also so that the information can be shared with the child's parents. Once children reach the age covered by the Foundation Stage Curriculum, their progress is monitored and assessed in relation to the Stepping Stones that lead to the Early Learning Goals of the six areas of learning. A record of how far they have progressed is kept by their key worker and passed on whenever the child changes to another setting (e.g. from nursery into reception class). This record is called the Foundation Stage Profile.

Assessment

Assessment is usually carried out at regular intervals. It can be:

- formative or
- summative.

Formative assessment

Formative assessment of children's learning and progress takes place every day as children play, learn and interact together. It usually involves careful observation of children taking part in a range of activities. Parents can also be involved in the formative assessment process, as they are not only the child's first educator but may be able to put a child's behaviour or learning pattern in context. Daily records would form part of formative assessment.

Summative assessment

Summative assessment is more structured and formal and is measured in graded scores. Judgements are made according to pre-set criteria which have been graded in numerical order in respect of levels of achievement. The Foundation Stage Profile is a form of summative assessment. SATs are another example of summative assessment.

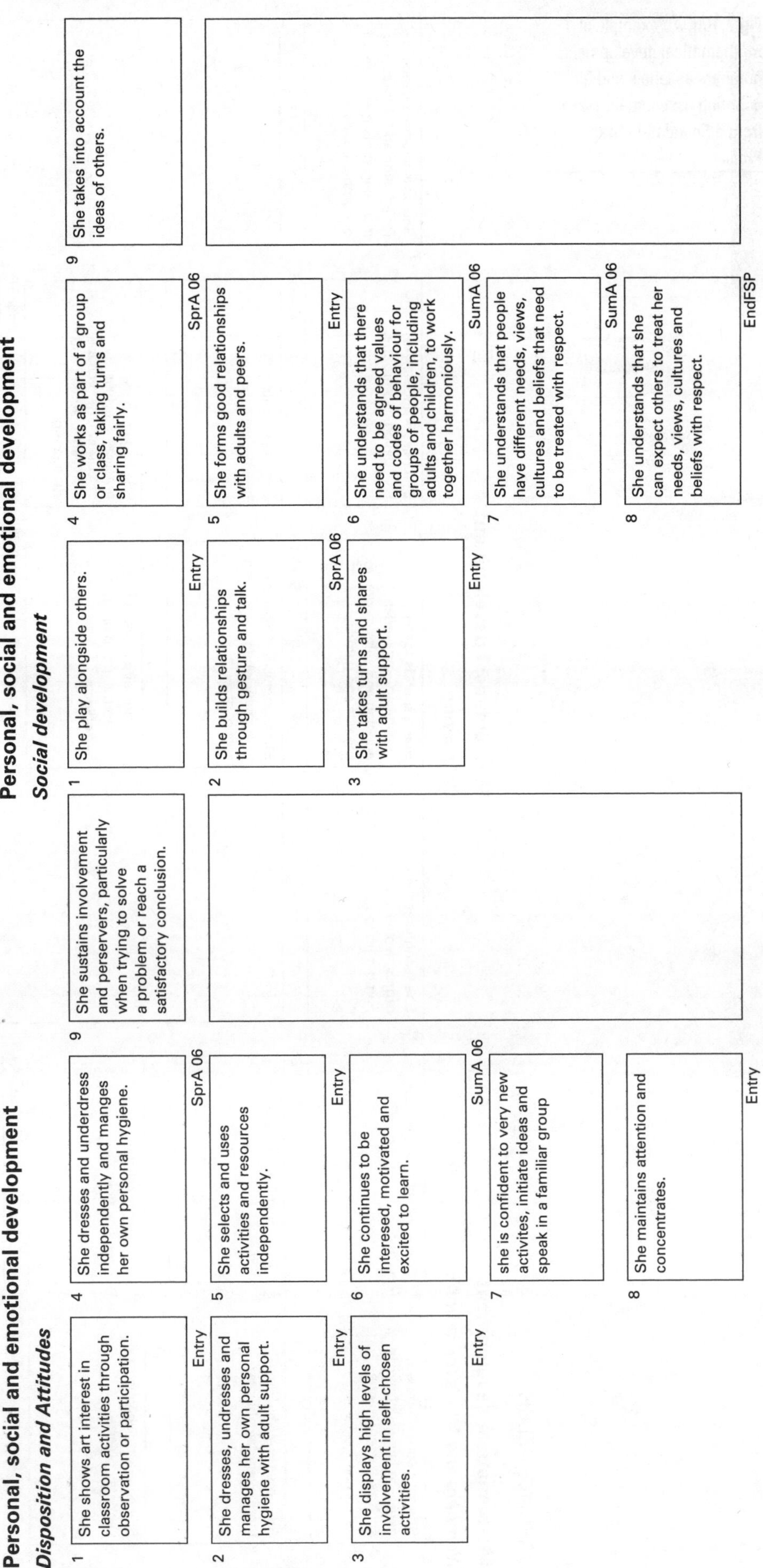

JASMINE BEECH

Personal, social and emotional development

Disposition and Attitudes

1 She shows art interest in classroom activities through observation or participation. Entry

2 She dresses, undresses and manages her own personal hygiene with adult support. Entry

3 She displays high levels of involvement in self-chosen activities. Entry

4 She dresses and underdress independently and manges her own personal hygiene. SprA 06

5 She selects and uses activities and resources independently. Entry

6 She continues to be interested, motivated and excited to learn. SumA 06

7 she is confident to very new activites, initiate ideas and speak in a familiar group

8 She maintains attention and concentrates. Entry

9 She sustains involvement and perservers, particularly when trying to solve a problem or reach a satisfactory conclusion.

Personal, social and emotional development

Social development

1 She play alongside others. Entry

2 She builds relationships through gesture and talk. SprA 06

3 She takes turns and shares with adult support. Entry

4 She works as part of a group or class, taking turns and sharing fairly. SprA 06

5 She forms good relationships with adults and peers. Entry

6 She understands that there need to be agreed values and codes of behaviour for groups of people, including adults and children, to work together harmoniously. SumA 06

7 She understands that people have different needs, views, cultures and beliefs that need to be treated with respect. SumA 06

8 She understands that she can expect others to treat her needs, views, cultures and beliefs with respect. EndFSP

9 She takes into account the ideas of others.

Fig 7.10a An example of personal, social and emotional development, disposition and attitudes assessment taken from a Foundation Stage Profile

Fig 7.10b An example of mathematical development, numbers as labels and for counting assessment taken from a Foundation Stage Profile

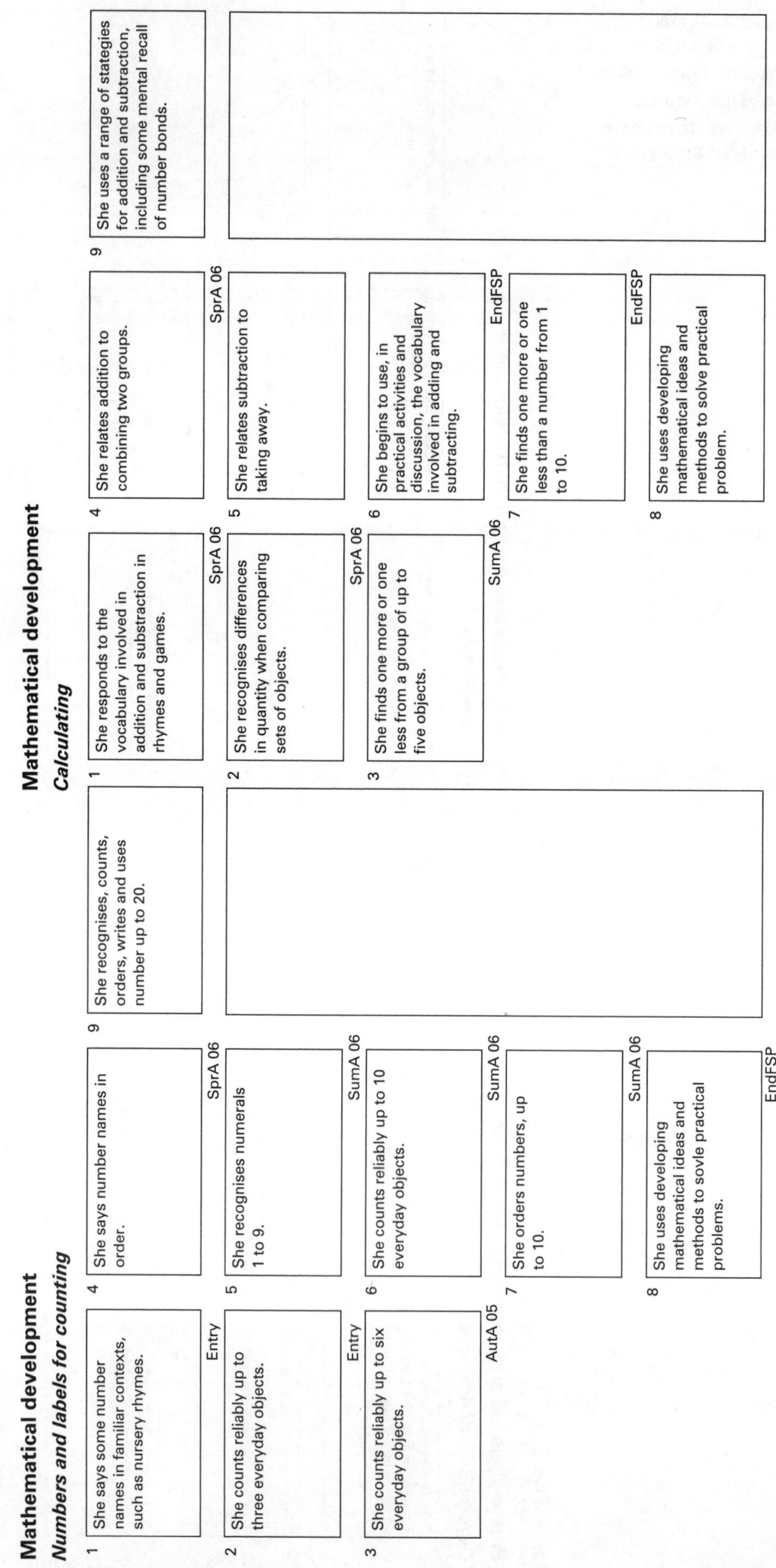

JASMINE BEECH

Mathematical development

Numbers and labels for counting

1 She says some number names in familiar contexts, such as nursery rhymes. Entry

2 She counts reliably up to three everyday objects. Entry

3 She counts reliably up to six everyday objects. AutA 05

4 She says number names in order. SprA 06

5 She recognises numerals 1 to 9. SumA 06

6 She counts reliably up to 10 everyday objects. SumA 06

7 She orders numbers, up to 10. SumA 06

8 She uses developing mathematical ideas and methods to sovle practical problems. EndFSP

9 She recognises, counts, orders, writes and uses number up to 20.

Mathematical development

Calculating

1 She responds to the vocabulary involved in addition and substraction in rhymes and games. SprA 06

2 She recognises differences in quantity when comparing sets of objects. SprA 06

3 She finds one more or one less from a group of up to five objects. SumA 06

4 She relates addition to combining two groups. SprA 06

5 She relates subtraction to taking away.

6 She begins to use, in practical activities and discussion, the vocabulary involved in adding and subtracting. EndFSP

7 She finds one more or one less than a number from 1 to 10. EndFSP

8 She uses developing mathematical ideas and methods to solve practical problem.

9 She uses a range of stategies for addition and subtraction, including some mental recall of number bonds.

The assessment process

Assessment can be a complex process but careful attention to the following can help:

- Who gathers the evidence needed? Who makes the observations? If untrained staff members are making the observation, are they confident in what they are observing? Are they aware of key learning intentions, behaviour, vocabulary, etc.?
- Assessments enable the observer to gather a wide range of information that will inform the planning of care and activities. If an observation is being made, does it have a clear aim? Does the observation cover all aspects of learning? What language does the child use? What skills and competencies have been identified? What strengths does the child show? What areas need to be developed?
- When assessing children's behaviour and learning, it is necessary to choose the method that is most suitable to meet the aim of the observation. Practitioners should ask themselves what method is most suitable. Do all staff have knowledge of a wide range of observational methods? Are there sufficient members of staff to allow time out for observations? Have staff accounted for potential bias? Has account been taken of the factors that influence observations?

Refer to Unit 3 for further information on observing children.

Links to planning

Planning and assessment are closely linked and depend on each other, although there is some debate as to which should come first in the cycle of planning, implementing and evaluating learning. As Gardner (1993) points out, children come into their learning settings with a very wide range of skills, attributes and competencies, and planning could start with the assessment of what children already know, using that as a baseline. Assessment informs all areas of planning, whether this is planning for a child's short-term or medium-term needs or longer-term curricular planning.

Be able to plan, implement and evaluate learning activities for children aged from 0 to 8 years of age

Planning and preparation

As already discussed, planning can be short, medium or longer term. You may be linking activities to a specified theme, or you may simply be setting out a diverse range of opportunities.

For every activity you plan, you will have similar considerations:

- how the activity fits into the overall day/session (if applicable)
- the environment where the activity will take place
- the type of facilities you will need (e.g. floor space, table-surface space, access to hand-washing facilities, use of ICT equipment)
- supervision levels and numbers of staff needed
- how many children can take part at one time
- the likely duration of the activity
- the aim of the activity, i.e. how it will benefit the children
- how you will evaluate the success of the activity
- how you will record the success of the activity and where you would note any recommendations for the future
- the resources you will need, and how much of each resource
- any potential health and safety issues and how they can be overcome
- any potential impact the activity could have on other groups of children or areas of the setting
- how much additional help and support younger or less able children are likely to need, and what form that support might take
- how the activity can be extended for the more able children within a group.

Table 7.12 Use this table to consolidate your understanding of how the listed activities link to the headings

Activity A	Personal, social and emotional development	Communication, language and literacy	Mathematical development	Knowledge and understanding of the world	Physical development	Creative development
Settling into a group						
Sand and water play						
Shape sorting						
Puzzles						
Cooking						
Role play and dressing-up						
Small world play						
Woodwork						
Sorting and classifying						
Sequencing games						
Handwashing and toileting						
Interest tables						
Music and movement						
Book corner						
One-to-one stories						
Group storytime						
Drawing and colouring						
Clay and dough						
Climbing frames and large equipment						
Bikes and sit-ons						
Using scissors						
Helping to clear up						
Construction resources – small-scale						
Construction resources – large-scale						
Turn-taking games						
Board games						
Circle time						

NB: This is not an exhaustive list.

Table 7.13 Use this table to consolidate your understanding of supporting these curriculum areas

Activity B	Literacy	Mathematics	Science	ICT
Settling into a group				
Sand and water play				
Shape sorting				
Puzzles				
Cooking				
Role play and dressing-up				
Small world play				
Woodwork				
Sorting and classifying				
Sequencing games				
Handwashing and toileting				
Interest tables				
Music and movement				
Book corner				
One-to-one stories				
Group storytime				
Drawing and colouring				
Clay and dough				
Climbing frames and large equipment				
Bikes and sit-ons				
Using scissors				
Helping to clear up				
Construction resources – small-scale				
Construction resources – large-scale				
Turn-taking games				
Board games				
Circle time				

NB: This is not an exhaustive list.

Role in formal learning

Each area of learning can be incorporated within most activities in some way or other. A range of play activities and resources are listed below.

As children enter mainstream schooling and follow the National Curriculum, their learning will be supported through the Primary National Strategy. This is a framework for the Foundation Stage, and Key Stages 1 and 2. It covers literacy and mathematics. There are 12 strands to the literacy strategy, which is divided into:

- speaking
- listening and responding
- group discussion and interaction
- drama
- word recognition: decoding (reading) and encoding (speaking)
- word structure and spelling
- understanding and interpreting texts
- engaging with and responding to texts
- creating and shaping texts
- text structure and organisation
- sentence structure and punctuation.

There are seven strands to the mathematics strategy, set out as:

- using and applying mathematics
- counting and understanding number
- knowing and using number facts
- calculating
- understanding shape
- measuring
- handling data.

The daily literacy and mathematics lessons may be stand-alone sessions or linked to a sequence. Adults should be working to a process of: review > teach > practice > apply > evaluate.

This process underpins the aim of the Primary National Strategy. On placement in a primary school, you will be able to observe the process of the strategy at first hand. Your main role here will be to support the literacy and mathematics activities planned by the class teacher, ensuring that you use appropriate language to explain, describe, encourage and inform.

Role in spontaneous learning

As well as being able to plan appropriately in advance you will also need to be able to make full use of the unexpected opportunities that will occur from time to time. Ensuring that you have a good all-round knowledge of the value of the resources, toys and equipment available at your school or preschool setting will help you.

Early Leaning Goals

Spontaneous learning can sometimes contribute to meeting the Early Leaning Goals.

Early Learning Goals for personal, social and emotional development

The Early Learning Goals for personal, social and emotional development are as follows.

By the end of the Foundation Stage, most children will:

- continue to be interested, excited and motivated to learn
- be confident to try new activities, initiate ideas and speak in a familiar group
- maintain attention, concentrate, and sit quietly when appropriate

- have a developing awareness of their own needs, views and feelings and be sensitive to the needs, views and feelings of others
- have a developing respect for their own cultures and beliefs and those of other people
- respond to significant experiences, showing a range of feelings when appropriate
- form good relationships with adults and peers
- work as part of a group or class, taking turns and sharing fairly, understanding that there need to be agreed values and codes of behaviour for groups of people, including adults and children, to work together harmoniously
- understand what is right, what is wrong, and why
- dress and undress independently and manage their own personal hygiene
- select and use activities and resources independently
- consider the consequences of their words and actions for themselves and others
- understand that people have different needs, views, cultures and beliefs, which need to be treated with respect
- understand that they can expect others to treat their needs, views, cultures and beliefs with respect.

(adapted from *Curriculum Guidance for the Foundation Stage*, QCA, 2000).

case study 7.4

Maya

Maya brought a jar of caterpillars into the nursery. Her key worker, Savita, showed immediate interest and placed them on a table to display them. Maya and the other children went into the nursery garden to find 'treats' for the caterpillars. They returned with some dandelions, daisies, grass and a few leaves. Savita helped the children to open the jar and to gently add a selection from the garden. She talked to the children about the caterpillars, asking Maya where she had found them. As a group, they explored the book corner to find information on caterpillars, which they looked at together. Later in the day, Maya let the caterpillars go in the shrubbery. When she was collected, she gave an excited account to her mother of what she had done.

activity
GROUP WORK

1. Which Early Learning Goals for personal, social and emotional development were supported here?
2. What other areas of learning were supported?
3. How well do you think Savita responded to the arrival of the caterpillars?
4. What else would you have done?

It would be useful to refer to a copy of the Early Learning Goals in your college library and identify which goals from the other areas of learning were also being supported in case study 7.4.

Once you have identified a child's learning needs, you need to link the activity to learning outcomes. Most activities will cover several areas of learning at once, and you will be taught to think this through by your tutors and by practitioners in placement settings. The following diagram will give you some idea of the areas of learning that an activity might cover. Please note that not all possible learning goals for each activity have been included.

Fig 7.11 Group cooking activity

Group cooking activity

Personal, Social and Emotional Development
- Be confident to try new activities, initiate ideas and speak in a group
- Maintain attention, concentrate and sit quietly when appropriate
- Work as part of a group or class, taking turns and sharing fairly
- Dress and undress independently and manage own personal hygiene
- Select and use activities and resources independently

Communication, Language and Literacy
- Use talk to organise, sequence and clarify thinking, ideas, feelings and events
- Interact with others, negotiate plans and activities and take turns in conversation
- Extend their vocabulary, exploring the meaning and sounds of new words

Mathematical Development
- Use language such as 'more' or 'less', 'greater' or 'smaller', 'heavier' or 'lighter' to compare two numbers or quantities
- Use language such as 'circle' or 'bigger' to describe the shape and size of solids and flat shapes

Creative Development
- Explore colour, texture, shape, form and space in two and three dimensions
- Respond in a variety of ways to what they see, hear, smell, touch and feel
- Express and communicate their ideas, thoughts and feelings by using a wide range of materials, suitable tools, imaginative play and role play, movement, designing and making a variety of songs and musical instruments

Knowledge and Understanding of the World
- Investigate objects and materials by using all of their senses as appropriate
- Select the tools and techniques they need to shape, join and assemble the materials they are using

Physical Development
- Recognise the importance of keeping healthy and those things that contribute to this
- Handle tools, objects, construction and malleable materials safely and with increasing control

At times, not all of each learning goal applies to a given activity. However, it will be beneficial to write out the Early Learning Goals in full when you are planning activities for children in the Foundation Stage to help both you and your supervisors identify it easily.

case study 7.5 Fircone Class

Fircone Class is cooking with a parent, Kamala's mother, Mrs Behera. The children are making chapattis and have each put on an apron and a cook's hat. Mrs Behera talks to the children about the process of kneading and flattening the dough and the importance of washing their hands. Kamala shows how she has brought chapattis in her lunch box, along with some dahl and fruit. Rajan says that he too brings chapattis for lunch. All the children are keen to try the chapattis when they are ready. They compare them to different types of bread (focaccia, rye bread, and so on), discussing the differences in texture and identifying the cultural origin of each food.

activity
INDIVIDUAL WORK

1 Which Early Learning Goals for personal, social and emotional development are supported here?
2 What other areas of learning were supported?
3 What is the particular significance of Mrs Behera leading the cooking activity?
4 How could the activity be extended into other aspects of the classroom?

It would be useful to refer to a copy of the Early Learning Goals in your college library and identify which goals from the other areas of learning were also being supported in case study 7.5.

Early Learning Goals for mathematical development

The Early Learning Goals for mathematical development are as follows.

By the end of the Foundation Stage, most children will be able to:

- say and use number names in order in familiar contexts
- count reliably up to 10 everyday objects
- recognise numerals 1 to 9
- use language such as 'more' or 'less, 'greater' or 'smaller', 'heavier' or 'lighter' to compare two numbers or quantities
- in practical activities and discussion begin to use the vocabulary involved in adding and subtracting
- find one more or one less than a number from 1 to 10
- begin to relate addition to combining two groups of objects, and subtraction to 'taking away'
- talk about, recognise and recreate simple patterns
- use language such as 'circle' or 'bigger' to describe the shape and size of solids and flat shapes
- use everyday words to describe position
- use developing mathematical ideas and methods to solve practical problems.

(adapted from *Curriculum Guidance for the Foundation Stage*, QCA, 2000).

case study 7.6

Sean and Callum

Sean and Callum are playing at the water tray with a range of graded containers. They are filling and pouring from one side of the tray to the other and are also filling up a large bucket.

activity
INDIVIDUAL WORK

1 Which Early Learning Goals for mathematical development are supported here?
2 Which other areas of learning were supported?
3 How can an adult enhance the learning still further?

It would be useful to refer to a copy of the Early Learning Goals in your college library and identify which goals from the other areas of learning were also being supported in case study 7.6.

The following case study gives an example linked to the National Curriculum. You will need to access a copy from your college library, or placement if you are in a primary school.

case study 7.7

Acorn Group

The Acorn group in Class 1 is growing beans in jars. Each child has their own bean.

activity
INDIVIDUAL WORK

1 Which elements of the National Curriculum could you link to this activity?
2 How could the activity be extended further?

remember Most activities at Foundation Stage and Key Stage 1 are cross-curricular, covering a range of learning intentions.

Encompass diversity

It is important for all children to understand the wider world and the differences and similarities between cultures and societies. Diversity should be acknowledged positively and integrated into daily routines and experiences.

Diversity can be supported by using the many vibrant and interesting festivals, celebrations and holy days as a basis for learning; these provide opportunities to support the children's investigations, using books, maps and the Internet, and promote their enjoyment of music and dance from around the world. These occasions will also provide opportunities for exciting creative experiences using a range of tools and resources. Displaying these creations, showing how they link to other experiences within the setting, helps to promote positive attitudes and anti-discriminatory practice.

Implementation and evaluation

Implementing learning activities within a remit of good practice means:

- ensuring that your interpersonal skills are appropriate at all times, taking into account who you are working or interacting with and what you are doing and aiming to achieve
- making full use of your observation skills, understanding how to interpret what you see and what to do with that information
- constantly monitoring children's activities, both planned and child-initiated, to pre-empt accidents and compensate for mistakes where practical
- having the knowledge, understanding and awareness with regard to when to intervene, either to ensure safety, or to support learning, development or a sense of achievement
- ensuring that children understand all aspects of play and learning activities, including the planning of activities where applicable, preparation of materials and the environment, and the need for involvement of all children in clearing away afterwards and tidying the environment
- being constantly aware of health and safety issues with regard to the resources used, the children's attitude to the activity, and the impact or potential impact on the immediate and wider environment.

Evaluation of learning activities within a remit of good practice means:

- *Reflecting on the monitoring strategies that were in place, and how effective they had been*. Did anything occur that was unexpected? Hazardous? Detrimental to the aims of the activity?
- *Reflecting back on how carefully the activity was observed by the supervising adults*. Was anything missed that should have been seen?
- *Thinking through the range of communications that took place.* Did all those involved appear comfortable? Were they able to participate in the conversation or communication? Did anyone dominate the communication? Was anyone prevented from putting their idea or point across?
- *Giving consideration to the strengths and weaknesses of those involved*. Were individual strengths utilised, supported and given the potential for further enhancement? Were individual weaknesses supported through an appropriate process, for example smaller steps to reach the overall aim of the activity, a greater number of shorter instructions, physical help such as modelling by the adult, hand-over-hand support for improving dexterity, and so on?
- *Reflecting on how valuable the activity was and how it has benefited the children*. Have they gained a new skill? Have they been able to practise a developing skill? Has their understanding of something been increased? Have they been encouraged to explore something further or initiate extended play ideas because of it?
- *Using the outcomes of this activity to help you consider further ideas to extend children's learning and development*. Could this be managed through direct extension of the activity itself? Or through greater understanding of the way that the children currently learn best or what they find exciting?
- *Reflecting on all aspects of the activity to identify where you could make improvements for the future.*
- *Constantly reflecting on all that you do, and embracing the ethos of 'reflective practice' in your day-to-day work as an early years practitioner*. This will be the best way to ensure

that you continue to build on and improve your own practice throughout your career. It should always be remembered that when you qualify at the end of your training, you are at the beginning of your career and your learning will only just have started.

- *Reflecting on what role you take when working with children*. Do you offer support at appropriate times? Do you understand when a child is struggling and needs adult guidance? Can you identify when to wait just a little longer to let achievement and the satisfaction that accompanies it take place? Can you judge how much freedom can be allowed before the balance moves to chaos?

Your understanding of each of the above will develop with experience. Many points have been discussed elsewhere too. You may find it helpful to re-read other relevant passages.

Be able to provide play situations for children

Types of play and play situations

Play can be structured and it can be free. To have structure does not mean that an experience is negative and restricted; in this context, structure indicates that there are some natural boundaries to the activity or experience. For example, jigsaw puzzles have structure; the pieces have to fit together within a set boundary in order for the puzzle to be completed. Both structured and free-flowing play have a place in the world of child development. The following table provides a useful overview of play in its various forms.

Table 7.14 Play types

Play type	Characteristics of play type	Examples of how this play type can be provided for by practitioners
Communicative play	This is play that uses words, gestures or nuances, including conversation, debate, jokes, singing, poetry, play acting	Through musical activities, group circle time/debate time, consultation activities, drama games and performances
Creative play	This occurs when children play in a way that allows them to transfer information, respond in new ways and develop an awareness of new connections with an element of surprise. An example of this would be to create a sculpture from clay or to paint a picture, for the sake of creation	Through art and craft activities such as drawing, painting, collage, chalking, sculpture with malleable materials and tools. Access to a broad range of materials both natural and man-made including wool, fabrics, cellophane, tissue paper
Deep play	This play occurs when children participate in experiences that are risky, perhaps even potentially life threatening. It allows children to conquer fear and to develop survival skills. Examples of this play include balancing on a high beam and skateboarding along a wall	Through exhilarating play within adventure setting – using zip wires, climbing trees, caving, mountain biking. Participating in sports/physical activities such as skateboarding, rollerblading or sledging. (As always, practitioners must carry out a risk assessment before these activities)
Dramatic play	This occurs when children dramatise events which they do not participate in directly. This includes playing TV shows or games based on cartoons or super-heroes, or the enactment of a religious/festive event, perhaps even a funeral	Through time and space for children to develop their own such games and activities. Practitioners can support this play by not interrupting unless play becomes dangerous, and allowing children to use resources and materials freely to develop 'sets' and so on
Exploratory play	This occurs when children gain factual information through manipulation or movement. This can include handling objects in a range of ways, such as throwing, banging or mouthing – this allows children to assess the properties of the object and to assess its possibilities. An example of this is the way in which children manipulate recycled objects to make a model	Provide interesting resources for children and regularly introduce new objects, both man-made and natural. This could include autumn leaves, for example. Allow children to find their own way of using tools and objects as long as this is safe – do not insist on showing them the 'right' or 'proper' way unless children ask for help

Table 7.14 continued

Play type	Characteristics of play type	Examples of how this play type can be provided for by practitioners
Fantasy play	This takes place when children rearrange the world in a way that is unlikely to occur, but that appeals to them. For instance, they may play at owning a zoo, or an expensive car, or play at being a pop star or pilot	Through allowing children the time and space to develop fantasy play and worlds themselves. Practitioners can support this play by not interrupting unless play becomes dangerous, or they are invited to participate. In this case practitioners should follow the child's lead, and not impose their own ideas or rules on the child's play. Practitioners should accept without question the rules children have devised
Locomotor play	This occurs when children move around in any and every direction for the sake of doing so. Examples of this include playing playground games such as tag and climbing apparatus and trees	Through allowing plenty of free-play time in large areas, so that children can develop their own games and travel around the play space spontaneously. Practitioners can also organise and join in with playground games such as Sticky Glue (also known as Stuck in the Mud)
Mastery play	This occurs when children's play controls the physical and affective ingredients of the environment. Examples include making fires, building dams, digging holes and creating shelters	Through activities that involve the elements, such as building a camp fire and cooking on it or making and flying windsocks or kites. If necessary (depending on the nature of the play space) practitioners can arrange visits/trips so that children can experience making shelters in the woods or digging trenches in the sand
Object play	This occurs when children handle an object using an interesting sequence of manipulations and movements. This includes examining properties of objects closely, or using items in a new or novel way – using a ruler as a twirling baton for instance	Through providing interesting resources for children and regularly introducing new objects likely to stimulate curiosity and imagination (both man-made and natural). Allowing children to find their own way of using objects as long as this is safe
Rough and tumble	This occurs when all children involved are obviously unhurt and enjoying themselves while they play chasing, wrestling or playful 'fighting' games. This 'close encounter play' is about discovering physical flexibility, gauging relative strength and the exhilaration of display. It involves safe touching	By not stepping in too soon if children are enjoying rough-and-tumble play – monitoring the play enables practitioners to step in if rough and tumble escalates to play which is outside safe or acceptable limits. Resources such as soft play equipment and soft play zones are helpful for facilitating this type of play in otherwise 'formal' areas – within a classroom used for an after-school club for instance
Social play	This occurs when children play together. Rules and criteria for social engagement and interaction between the children can be revealed, explored and amended (changed during play). Examples are activities where children involved are expected to stick to rules or protocols such as in games or conversations	Through allowing children plenty of time and space to develop rules and protocols for themselves. Practitioners should support children when the rules of play and interaction are explored or changed, as long as behaviour does not become unsafe. Team activities and opportunities for children to design their own board games can facilitate this type of play
Socio-dramatic play	This occurs when children act out experiences of an intense personal, social, domestic or interpersonal nature. The experiences acted out may have really happened to children, or they could potentially occur. Examples of this play include playing homes/families, playing shopping and even arguing	Through providing play areas such as home corners and the provision of prop resources such as play money, play telephones and so on. Older children may enjoy role play or moral dilemma games where they act out or describe how they would behave in certain situations – if they missed the last bus home, for example

Table 7.14 continued

Play type	Characteristics of play type	Examples of how this play type can be provided for by practitioners
Symbolic play	This occurs when children use an object to symbolise something else, e.g. a piece of wood may become a snake, or a piece of string may be used as a wedding ring. Symbolic play allows control, gradual exploration and increased understanding, without children risking being out of their depth	Through providing interesting resources for children, and regularly introducing new objects likely to stimulate curiosity and imagination (both man-made and natural). Allowing children free access to resources, so they can get out items they want to play with

Planning and preparation

Refer back to page 341 to refresh your understanding of planning and preparation and then carry out the following activity.

activity
INDIVIDUAL WORK 7.8
P6

Select two different types of play, then plan and carry out an activity at your current placement to support each type.

Ensure that you:

- obtain permission in advance from your placement supervisor and consult with all relevant staff
- provide written plans, with specified aims, and detailing how issues of differentiation and inclusion will be addressed
- identify any necessary equipment and resources (human or physical) that are likely to be needed
- make clear any health and safety issues
- identify appropriate supervision levels
- make clear the anticipated role of each adult.

Review

As a developing practitioner, the review process is crucial to your continued professional development.

Refer back to Unit 4, page 230 for further guidance.

activity
PAIR WORK 7.9
M4

Working with a partner, describe to each other the two learning activities and two play activities that you have each carried out in your placements.

1 Explain the value of each activity.
2 Explain any planned links to a specified curriculum.
3 Discuss the explained values of the activities. Do you both agree? If not, discuss why not.
4 Write a clear explanation for 1 and 2 for others to read.

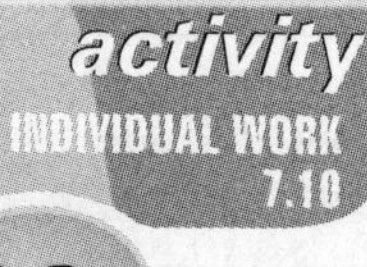

D2

1 Having carried out two learning activities and prepared and implemented two play situations, you now need to evaluate their success. Take the following into consideration:

(a) How successful were the outcomes of each for the children?

(b) How successful were the outcomes of each for you as a learner and developing practitioner? Did you meet your aims? Were your preparations, timings, supervision levels, etc. appropriate?

(c) How successful was each activity/situation from the relevant setting's point of view? What feedback were you given? Did your activities blend into the routine of each particular day? Did you cause any disruption?

(d) With regard to the major theories of learning, make clear which you had intended working within and which you now identify through your evaluation process. Give examples.

2 Identify and explain what you would do differently another time and why. Who would benefit, and in what ways?

You may wish to refer to several units of the course to support your work.

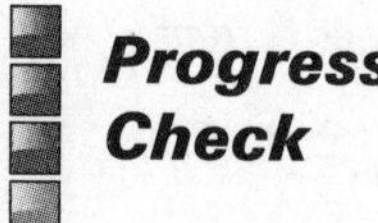

1 What is the difference between the transmission and the laissez-faire models of learning?
2 Name the three eminent theorists who support the philosophy of the social constructivist model of learning.
3 Which of the early educators supported learning through exploratory play?
4 Which curriculum model includes the plan, do and review process?
5 How would you describe free-flow play?
6 What does Moyles's play spiral illustrate?
7 In what ways can an adult have an impact on a child's learning?
8 What framework supports work with the under-threes?
9 What are the six main areas of learning in the Foundation Stage curriculum?
10 What should be taken into account when organising the positioning of resources and activities?
11 What is an IEP?
12 Give at least three examples of activities to promote mathematical development.
13 Give at least three examples of activities to promote personal, social and emotional development.
14 Why is it important to have written curriculum plans?
15 What is meant by formative and summative assessment?

Research Methodology for Children's Care, Learning and Development

This unit covers the following objectives:

- Understand the purpose and role of research within children's care, learning and development
- Understand the research methodology relevant to children's care, learning and development
- Be able to identify a suitable topic and produce a plan for a research proposal
- Be able to conduct the research and present the findings
- Be able to evaluate the research project
- Understand the implications of and ethical issues related to using research in children's care, learning and development

Research skills are important to achieving a BTEC National qualification in Children's Care, Learning and Development (CCLD); each unit that you undertake will require an element of personal enquiry, and many will demand considerable levels of independent research and study.

This unit will help you to understand the research process and will enable you to gain the practical, written and analytical skills that are required. You will learn how to describe and evaluate a range of relevant research methods, and use and present statistics.

The unit will also examine the importance of research to the professional practice of an early years worker and look at relevant ethical issues.

grading criteria

To achieve a **Pass** grade the evidence must show that the learner is able to:	To achieve a **Merit** grade the evidence must show that, in addition to the pass criteria, the learner is able to:	To achieve a **Distinction** grade the evidence must show that, in addition to the pass and merit criteria, the learner is able to:
P1 explain the purpose and role of research for the children's care, learning and development sector page 367	**M1** justify the choice of topic and hypothesis page 384	**D1** discuss how the methodology of the research project could be altered to reduce bias and error page 396
P2 describe the key elements of research methodologies page 373	**M2** review the research methods chosen in relation to the results obtained, any sources of bias or error and ethical considerations page 396	**D2** analyse the purpose and role of research in the sector, drawing on the piece of research undertaken. page 401

To achieve a **Pass** grade the evidence must show that the learner is able to:	To achieve a **Merit** grade the evidence must show that, in addition to the pass criteria, the learner is able to:	To achieve a **Distinction** grade the evidence must show that, in addition to the pass and merit criteria, the learner is able to:
P3 identify and plan a research topic and carry out a literature search page 384	**M3** analyse the findings of the research in relation to the original hypothesis page 396	
P4 carry out the primary research and collect and record appropriate data page 393	**M4** discuss the possible implications that the research results may have on the current practice. page 401	
P5 present and report findings in a relevant format, identifying sources of bias or error page 396		
P6 discuss the findings of the research in relation to the original hypothesis page 396		
P7 outline any possible improvements to the research, referring to any relevant implications and ethical issues. page 401		

Understand the purpose and role of research within children's care, learning and development

Purpose

Research plays an important part in the development of early years standards and provision. It enables comparisons to be made and needs to be identified. When considering the purpose of research, it is useful to think of research that has been undertaken in recent years in the field of early years health, care and education. Identifying research and evaluating its aims, its relevance and its outcomes will help you to focus on its necessity.

As you progress through the course, you will need to make reference to how thinking and practice in the field of early years has been improved due to the impact of research outcomes. An example is the improvement of practice relating to the care of children in hospital. During the 1950s and 1960s, child psychiatrists James and Joyce Robertson observed and filmed children separated from their primary carer (usually their mothers) during hospital stays or because they were in residential care. The Robertsons identified a pattern of distress which raised concern about the long-term effects such separations could have on children. In 1959, the Platt Report (initiated by the UK government) set out the welfare needs of children in hospital and as a result the National Association for the Welfare of Children in Hospital (NAWCH) was established (now known as Action for Sick Children, ASC). As a result of the Robertsons' research and the Platt Report, parents are encouraged to stay with their children when they are receiving hospital treatment.

Research can be used for many purposes, including to:

- identify a need
- provide further knowledge
- highlight gaps in provision
- obtain feedback on standards
- see what is happening currently
- find out why something is happening
- plan for future development.

remember If you take a more evaluative approach to reading the summary or outcomes of a piece of research, you will understand the research more fully.

Role of research

Its role is to:

- confirm policy or practice
- extend knowledge
- improve practice
- allow progress to be monitored
- examine topics of contemporary interest.

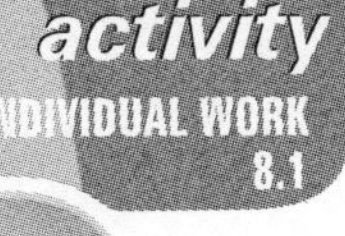

P1

1 What examples of research can you think of? Copy the table below and list as many as you can. Use newspapers, magazines and the Internet to help you. Examples have been given to get you started.

2 Explain in writing how each research example has benefited the CCLD sector.

Table 8.1

Child health	Early years care	Education	Behaviour
Immunisation Genetics	Sudden Infant Death Syndrome	Head Start EEL project	Relationships Attachment

Understand the research methodology relevant to children's care, learning and development

Research is the systematic investigation of a topic for a purpose, using orderly and scientific methods. An analysis of the outcomes of research can lead to the development of new ideas and improved practice.

Types of research

Methods of research vary considerably and can be divided into two types: **primary research** and **secondary research**.

Primary and secondary research

The significant difference between primary and secondary research is that:

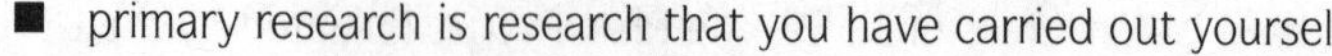

remember

Choose the method most suitable for your current assignment task or personal enquiry (e.g. when you undertake your own research project).

- primary research is research that you have carried out yourself
- secondary research is the use of material researched and presented by others.

In general assignment work, you will almost always use more secondary sources than primary sources, as you explore material produced by others to support your written work, interpreting (clarifying and explaining) your findings and analysing (evaluating) their relevance.

Primary research is needed, and is a mandatory requirement, in the project undertaken as part of this unit. It will also be expected in other specified assignment briefs. For example, a practical activity that could be linked to Unit 3 would be to replicate Piaget's conservation tasks within your current placement, presenting and evaluating the outcomes with reference to Piaget and his subsequent critics.

Refer to Unit 3, page 145, for an explanation of Piaget's conservation tasks.

Table 8.2 Examples of primary and secondary research methods

Primary	Secondary
Interviews	Literature searches
Questionnaires	Media analysis
Action research	Technology based research
Observation	Case studies
Case studies	Statistical analysis
Experiments	

Quantitative and qualitative research

Research can be either quantitative or qualitative:

- **quantitative research** produces results which can be expressed using numbers or statistics, exploring the extent to which something happens
- **qualitative research** explores individual viewpoints which are not so easily measured. Qualitative researchers wish to gain an understanding of their topic rather than make an analysis of statistics.

At times, a piece of research can involve both approaches.

In all research, the quality of the information you receive is directly linked to the questions that you ask. Unless your questions are well thought out, the resulting data will not be of any use to you. The wording of questions must be carefully thought through.

Refer to page 372 for more about questions in research.

Longitudinal, cross-sectional and cross-cultural studies

Research can include longitudinal, cross-sectional or cross-cultural studies:

- A longitudinal study is a study carried out over a given length of time, following the progress of something or someone (e.g. a child's development, as required within the BTEC National CCLD).
- A cross-sectional study takes a 'slice' (a cross-section) of its target group and its overall findings are assumed to be typical of the whole group.
- In a cross-cultural piece of research, the researcher would decide on the main focus of their research and then apply it to a range of cultures. The focus could be confined to a single community within each culture or could be applied across a range of communities.

Objectivity

In all research, objectivity (an impartial viewpoint) is important. Personal opinion, bias or prejudice can influence both the process of research and the interpretation of the results.

Maintaining objectivity will ensure that your research is 'value-free'. This is not always easy. The results of research will not always be what you expect, and it is important that you accept the outcomes of the research. Carrying out an honest analysis of the outcomes and producing an accurate report will ensure that your research is as objective as possible. Subjective research outcomes (a viewpoint influenced by your own opinions) will be of little value either to you or to anyone else.

Forming a hypothesis, an issue or research question

In any piece of research, the overall aim needs to be made clear. This will usually be in the form of:

- a research issue – a statement of fact or a concern that could be explored by the researcher
- a research question – when the researcher wishes to find out a specific answer
- a hypothesis – a statement, usually written in the form of a prediction, which the researcher sets out to test.

Forming a hypothesis is a requirement of your project for this unit. Your hypothesis will need to be both achievable and identifiable.

Types of hypothesis

A hypothesis can be either:

- Single-ended – 'Girls read more than boys' is a single-ended hypothesis because it suggests which way the outcome of the enquiry is likely to be; it will be supported if girls are found to read more than boys, and it will not be supported if boys read more than girls or if they read the same amount.
- Open-ended – 'Day care affects children's social skills' is an open-ended hypothesis; it simply suggests that one factor (day care) will affect another (children's social skills) and does not predict the direction of the outcome by, for example, saying that day care improves children's social skills.

A research question or issue can sometimes give a clearer aim for you to work towards, but setting a hypothesis is often more interesting and thought-provoking.

The research process

The research process can be summarised as follows:

- Research has a purpose: to inform and improve practice.
- Research enables society to develop new ideas based on enquiry.
- Research may involve a new line of enquiry (primary research method).
- A previous piece of research may be referred to (secondary research method).
- The results of research may be measurable (quantitative research).
- Research may simply give insight into a subject (qualitative research).
- Research can be used to compare, to explore a theory or to identify change.
- Research needs a specific focus, in the form of a hypothesis, an issue or a question.

Data collection – primary sources

Primary research involves carrying out a new line of enquiry.

Interviews

The interview is a common primary research method. Interviews can be either structured or unstructured, or they can be a combination of both. It is a particularly useful method if you are trying to find out people's individual opinions or experiences (a qualitative approach), although quantitative research can also be carried out in this way. Most interviews are planned in advance, but on occasions an interview can be carried out 'on the spot'. Interviews differ as to how structured they are; the level of structure to an interview can be drawn as a continuum:

Unstructured interview ———————————— Structured interview

Fig 8.1 An interview

Structured interviews

The interview's level of structure can usually be equated with the level of formality. The more formal approach usually follows a rigid course of pre-set questions which every participant is asked in the same order. Answers are controlled by forming questions which do not allow for expansion of the topic area. These are known as closed questions and can be particularly useful in quantitative research.

Table 8.3 Advantages and disadvantages of structure interviews

Advantages	Disadvantages
The questions are firmly set in advance.	There is no flexibility.
All participants are asked the same questions.	The additional information a participant may have available will be missed.
The structure and outcomes can be narrowly focused.	
The outcomes are easy to collate.	
Time management can be carefully controlled by the researcher.	

Unstructured interviews

In an unstructured interview, each participant is asked the same set of questions in the same order, but time is allowed for questions and responses to be developed further. It is often considered to be a far more relaxed process.

Table 8.4 Advantages and disadvantages of unstructured interviews

Advantages	Disadvantages
The questions set in advance are used simply as a guide or prompt	Not all participants are asked exactly the same questions
Flexibility is offered to explore points further if appropriate	Questions about the reliability of the outcomes may be raised
The structure and outcomes are not so narrowly focused	Time management cannot be so easily controlled by the researcher
	The interview can become simply a 'chat' if not carefully contained

A combined approach

A combined approach usually involves a list of pre-set questions, but the interviewer allows expansion where it is felt appropriate. This enables a degree of control to remain while giving flexibility. This would place the interview nearer the middle of the continuum:

Unstructured interview	Combined approach	structured interview

Length of interviews

Interviews should not be overly long, and it is usual for the researcher to impose a time limit. A structured interview would normally take less time than an unstructured interview, as participants are kept to a pre-set schedule. Your proposed time limit should be stated in advance. Consider how much time you would be willing to give up for someone else's research before you ask others to agree to your request.

You need to make a note of participants' responses throughout the interview, and so shorthand would be an advantage. It is important to be systematic, using the same approach to each set of interview notes to make it easier to compare participants' responses at the analysis stage.

Audio- or videotaping the interview is an alternative approach. It can be useful if you need to record answers verbatim (word for word). Videotaping also enables you to look at participants' body language, but transcribing tapes is time consuming and so these methods should be selected with caution. It is imperative that participants have agreed to the recording in advance and have had a genuine opportunity to refuse. It is completely inappropriate to covertly (secretly) record an interview, and you should always remember that confidentiality is of the utmost importance, as is the security of any recorded tapes.

Participants in your research

When selecting participants, you should consider if it really is convenient for them. If, for example, you choose to interview other students within your college, do not make them late for their classes.

Fig 8.2 Pick an appropriate time to carry out your interview

Surveys and questionnaires

Another primary method is the survey, usually carried out using a questionnaire. It tends to be a popular method with students. However, questionnaires are not as easy to produce as they may at first look. It is worth considering the following issues:

- the reason for using a questionnaire
- when to use a questionnaire
- how many questions to ask
- the order of questions
- writing open and closed questions

- piloting the questionnaire
- distribution and collection of questionnaires.

It is important that you are able to justify why and how a survey will enhance the outcomes of your work. Ask yourself:

- What extra information will it enable me to gather?
- Is the information available from another source? If yes, from where?
- How deficient would my project be without it?
- Will including a survey add quality to my work or just quantity?

Questionnaires can be an ideal method of gathering primary data if you are seeking the views of many people. If the subject area is sensitive, it can offer **anonymity** which may encourage participants to share information that they might otherwise have kept back. Time restrictions may mean that carrying out interviews would be impractical; questionnaires can be distributed and collected later, limiting the amount of time needed.

Questionnaires can be distributed by hand or they can be posted. Postal surveys often have a poor return rate and can be costly for the researcher to administer.

Fig 8.3 Postal surveys can be costly to administer and have a poor return rate

Questions

The questions you ask in a questionnaire must be relevant. They should flow into each other, following a logical sequence, and not jump from one topic to the next. Questions must be carefully thought through. They should not offend or pry into a participant's privacy. Your tutor will be able to offer advice as to whether any questions are inappropriate, and the piloting process will provide a check on the questions before the questionnaire is distributed.

Refer to page 374, for more information on piloting your questionnaire.

When devising questionnaires:

- The wording of questions must be clear.
- It is important to avoid ambiguities (double meanings).
- Keep your questionnaire as short as possible – a lengthy questionnaire can be very off-putting to your participants.

Open vs. closed questions

Broadly, there are two types of question: open and closed

- An open question offers opportunity for an individual answer.
- A closed question restricts each answer to one word or statement.

A combination of both types may well be appropriate for your questionnaire if you use one. A combination would give you control over some aspects of the questionnaire (e.g. closed questions could be used to obtain some 'core' information) while allowing participants to express their views more freely in response to open questions. Always ask yourself whether the questions being asked will elicit the information that you are seeking. If you are unsure, rethink your questions or ask your tutor for advice.

The level of language used in questionnaires should be appropriate for the target group. Participants may become indignant if your questions indicate that they have limited understanding, or they may be confused if your questions are inappropriately academic.

P2

1 With a group of other students, collect examples of questionnaires. These can be found in magazines, newspapers (results of opinion polls) or in books on research methodology (e.g. Green, 2000).

2 Consider each of the questionnaires that you have found and give written answers to the following questions:

(a) How would you feel if asked to complete them?

(b) How easy or complex did their completion appear?

(c) Did they make sense?

(d) Did you identify any ambiguities or irrelevant questions?

(e) Was it made clear how you should record your answers?

(f) Which would you be most happy to complete? Why is this?

(g) Which would you be least happy to complete? Why is this?

(h) How appropriate were the numbers of questions asked on each?

(i) Did the questionnaire include open or closed questions, or both? Did this seem appropriate?

(j) What influenced your answers to questions (a) to (i)?

Categories of response

You need to think carefully about how the questions will be answered. Instructions for this should be given at the beginning of the questionnaire and they should be very clear to the participants.

Questions can be answered in a number of ways, for example by:

- ticking a box
- writing in the space provided
- circling the chosen answer.

Responses should be kept as consistent as possible. There would not usually be more than two styles of response on any one questionnaire.

Responses can be:

- scaled – participants are given a choice of responses on a scale
- ranked – participants put a list of qualities in rank order according to importance
- by category – participants choose their answer from a range of given categories.

Scaled responses

Q1 How important is it for young children to see positive gender images?

Vital ____ Very important ____ Important ____ Quite important ____ Not important ____

Q2 Training in providing positive images is very important for all day nursery staff.

Strongly agree _____ Agree _____ Disagree _____ Strongly disagree _____

Q3 Circle the number on the scale below which represents how important you feel it is for day nursery staff to have had training in equal opportunities: 1 being the lowest and 10 being the highest importance.

1 2 3 4 5 6 7 8 9 10

Ranked response

Q4 Which of the activities listed below do you consider to be most important in the development of fine motor skills? Place them in order of importance, 1 to 5.

threading activities; opportunities for mark-making; construction materials; small world play; jigsaw puzzles

Which number did you think should be used to indicate the greatest importance: 1 or 5?

It is important that you always make this clear to the participant. It is better to say: 'Place them in order of importance 1 to 5, with 1 indicating the greatest level of importance'.

This will avoid any confusion, as you have indicated to the participant in which order your scale is set out.

Category response

Q5 How long is it since your last first aid training update?

0–3 years _____ 4–8 years _____ 9–12 years _____ 13–16 years _____

No training at all _____ Other (please specify) _____

This question would enable the researcher to consider links between how long it is since the respondent was updated and their responses to other questions.

Professional Practice

- **Always ensure that categories do not overlap (e.g. 0–3, 3–8, 8–12), as participants will be unsure which to choose.**
- **Overlap also makes it difficult to collate and present the findings, and the accuracy of the outcomes may be in question. Clear categories would be 0–3, 4–8, 9–12.**

Table 8.5 Advantages and disadvantages of surveys

Advantages	Disadvantages
Questionnaires can offer anonymity to participants which is not possible during an interview. The same questions are answered by all participants. The researcher's time can be used effectively. Participants are able to complete the questionnaire without time pressure. A good return rate is possible but not always achieved. Preparation time should not be under-estimated. Careful planning is important. Piloting of questionnaires is vital, but adds to the time allocation needed.	Return rates for postal surveys are often low (below 35 per cent). Postal surveys can be costly. Collection and distribution of questionnaires can be time-consuming. If questions remain unanswered on some questionnaires, it can affect the outcomes. Unless carefully set out, questions can be misunderstood.

Piloting your questionnaire

Piloting a questionnaire helps to identify any ambiguities in instructions and layout before it is distributed to your target group. It involves asking a small number of participants to complete the questionnaire and comment on the layout, the instructions for its completion and the clarity of the questions. The participants should be similar to those who will be asked to complete the final version.

You need to allocate time for the pilot to be completed, returned and analysed, as well as time for making any necessary alterations prior to the main distribution. This should be built into your time plan for the research process.

Choosing the target group
It is important to ensure that the intended target group is appropriate for your survey. It would be of limited benefit, for example, to ask for opinions from motor vehicle students about a range of books for two-year-olds. Similarly, early years students are unlikely to be the ideal participants in a survey on a range of car engine components. Ask yourself:

- Do your participants need to have a working knowledge of your chosen subject?
- Do they need to be from a particular:
  - age range
  - type of employment
  - culture
  - sex
  - geographical area, and so on?

Professional Practice

- Be clear what your questionnaire is trying to achieve.
- Match your questions to your target group.
- Always pilot your questionnaire.
- Make your instructions clear.
- Avoid ambiguity.
- Keep your questionnaire simple – you will have to analyse the outcomes.

Experimental research

Polit and Hungler (1991) define experimental research as: 'a research study in which the investigator controls or manipulates the independent variable and randomly assigns subjects to different conditions.'

Experimental research usually involves two groups of people: the experimental group and the control group.

- Participants in the experimental group are subjected to the variable that is being tested (the independent variable) to see if it has an effect.
- Participants in the control group experience the same conditions (the constant variables) as the experimental group, except that they are not treated with the independent variable; their results are compared with those of the experimental group to see if the independent variable has had an effect.

Fig 8.4 The control group and the experiment group should be as alike as possible

It is important that the two groups are as alike as possible at the outset so that, when the groups' results are compared, any difference is unlikely to have been caused by something other than the independent variable.

Experimental research is usually associated with laboratory testing rather than the more people/opinion-orientated focus of social research. It is unlikely that experimental research would be undertaken as a level 3 early years course research project.

Many experiments have been considered controversial, owing to ethical issues.

See page 385 for more on ethical issues affecting research.

Observation

Observation is rarely chosen as a research method by inexperienced researchers. However, when it is selected, observation is useful – while a participant may tell you that they would respond as X, during observation you may note that in practice they really respond as Y.

The aim of observational research is to see 'what really happens'. It is important to carry it out unobtrusively, because any interruption to normal events could change (and therefore invalidate) the outcomes of the research.

- Researchers using formal (participant) observation obtain their findings by joining in with the situation they are observing.
- Researchers using informal (non-participant observation) obtain information by observing from a distance.

Observation is an important research tool in childcare settings where it is already used as a routine part of early years care and education assessments.

Fig 8.5 Observation can be formal (participant) ...

Fig 8.6 ... or informal (non-participant)

Table 8.6 Advantages and disadvantages of observation

Advantages	Disadvantages
Behaviour is seen in a natural environment. The process of social situations can be observed – what preceded a certain factor or what resulted from it. Observation can either be direct (participant) or indirect (non-participant).	Observation is time-consuming. It is not always considered to be a reliable method as it can be subjective. The presence of the researcher can affect what is being observed.

It would be useful to make a note of three situations that could be researched through observation. In each case, which approach would be more appropriate, direct or indirect? You would need to ensure that there was no interruption to the usual routine.

Fig 8.7 Formal observation can sometimes be difficult

Action research

Action research is an excellent example of how the outcomes of research can have an impact on praxis (the practice involved in an area of study, for example in early years). In action research, the researcher studies an aspect of their own working environment. It could, for example, involve exploring how well staff in a preschool or nursery utilise certain equipment or resources. Alternatively, it could analyse how well the parents are involved with the setting.

You should consider carefully when deciding whether or not to use action research, as you will have to carry on working within the setting after the research has been completed. The possibility of there being negative as well as positive outcomes should be thought through at the planning stage, as outcomes from this type of research sometimes raise discontent in other staff. This is not a method usually used by students studying at level 3.

Case studies

The detailed study of a situation, an individual, a group or a family, in which the researcher looks at a range of factors, is often referred to as a case study. As the researcher, you would make an in-depth analysis of your findings, possibly making comparisons with other cases or examples.

This method is particularly useful in social research, and case studies are often used in academic texts to illustrate particular points. When using this method, it is unlikely that you will be able to claim that your outcomes are representative of society at large, but they may produce interesting ideas and thought-provoking material that can be explored further.

In a research project at level 3, it can be useful to include a case study to illustrate a particular point that you are trying to get across (as a secondary source). If you are unsure how best to do this, your tutor will be able to help you.

case study 8.1 Sonia

Sonia has chosen to look at examples of emotional disturbance commonly found in children's lives and intends to use the following case study as part of her discussion. Read through the case study and consider the questions that follow it.

Janine

Janine is seven and her brother, Alan, is five. They have recently moved from a two-bedroom house, the only home they have known, into bed-and-breakfast accommodation, following the family's financial difficulties and eviction for mortgage arrears. Alan is behaving unacceptably both at home and in school. Janine has begun to wet her bed at night, which is causing her a great deal of distress and significant laundry problems for her parents. She has become very quiet and withdrawn. The children's mother is tearful a lot of the time, and their father is short-tempered with everyone.

activity
INDIVIDUAL WORK

1 How might Janine and Alan be feeling?
2 How might their parents be feeling?
3 What help might be available to the children?
4 What might the role of a classroom support assistant be in this situation?
5 How useful do you consider this case study might be to Sonia's research project?

It is useful to look through some examples of past research projects. (There may be a section of these in your college library). How have case studies enhanced the projects?

Data collection – secondary sources

Secondary research is the use or presentation of material which has been researched or written by someone else. It will support your chosen topic area and your primary research findings (or data collection) for your own research project. Secondary research data will be used at some point in most assignments during your course of study.

Approaching a literature search

Every researcher should read around their subject area in order to broaden the scope for their research and to form a solid literature base. This base will include both technological and non-technological sources.

It is important to set yourself clear parameters. If your research becomes too wide, your coverage of the topic area may be thin and of limited value. A narrower, but more deeply considered, approach may give greater insight into your chosen topic area, thereby producing more valuable outcomes. The subject being explored will sometimes indicate natural parameters, but at other times you, as the researcher, will need to set them for yourself.

Deciding the scope of the research can be difficult. It is useful to set clear boundaries, for example by asking yourself:

- How far back shall I research – to the year 2005, to 2000, to 1990, to 1980, to 1950? You have to decide how much your decision will affect your outcomes. Will it be a mistake to limit your research to just the past year, rather than the past decade? Will you miss out on important historically relevant data by only focusing on recent years?
- Should I restrict my work geographically? Will focusing on the UK be appropriate? Would you benefit from including USA statistics, or would a comparison with Europe be relevant? Perhaps focusing on your own local area is sufficient. Tutors will be able to offer guidance on these questions.

Finding information

An initial literature search helps to establish where the most significant amount of material for a subject area is to be found and should help set the research parameters. You will need to consider local sources of material too. For example, if the subject to be researched is health related, you should be asking yourself what sources are available locally. There may be a **health promotion** office at your local hospital or surgery.

Ideally, you should start by identifying the general subject area appropriate to your chosen research topic. Is it:

- health?
- childcare?
- education?
- community provision?
- special educational needs? What else could it be?

The clearer the definition of the subject area, the easier it will be to establish sources of secondary data. In the field of early years, there is a wealth of places to look for information. These include:

- public libraries
- academic libraries (college and university)
- health promotion offices
- resource centres
- government offices
- support groups
- organisations
- GP surgeries, dentists, pharmacies
- bookshops
- the Internet.

Published (written) sources

These include:

- books
- magazines
- specialist journals
- newspapers
- information sheets and pamphlets

- government documents
- Hansard (transcripts from parliamentary debate).

Think through what other sources there might be and from where you might access them.

For more information about sources of information and guidance on how to refer to published sources in your writing, refer to *Research Methods in Health, Social and Early Years Care* by Green (2000).

Technological sources

Researchers today have the benefit of a range of technological resources, for example:

- CD-ROMs, which are usually held in college libraries, offer the opportunity to explore many avenues of enquiry quickly. Many national newspapers produce CD-ROMs of past articles, producing updates at regular intervals. There are also many specialist subject areas on CD-ROM too, for example menu planning for young children. CD-ROMs are often interactive, extending learning by exploration.
- The Internet provides online libraries and encyclopaedias. From the Internet public library you can access a collection of texts which can also be downloaded. Always check for copyright status – some are copyright-free, but others are not. Be sure that you do not break copyright laws. Details of these laws are displayed in all libraries, often beside the photocopier.
  - Search engines guide you through the mass of information on the Internet. Popular search engines are Google, Yahoo and Ask (see below). Staff will help you if you are unsure how to access these.
  - National newspapers are often on line too. Their website addresses can be found printed in each edition of the newspaper. Transcripts from parliamentary debate (Hansard) can also be accessed in this way; these would be particularly useful if your subject area is policy led.
- Microfiche is a database on film, used in many libraries, to store newspapers, books and other data.
- The Educational Resources Information Centre (ERIC), which is usually found in libraries in colleges of higher and further education, is a facility that searches for information from key words, to produce titles of books and articles. ERIC is only of use if you have access to the titles that it suggests.

Nelson Thornes, the publisher of this book, has a website and you may find it useful to explore what it offers.
www.nelsonthornes.com/btec

Using search engines

Search engines such as Google, Yahoo and Ask allow you to type in a key word, question or phrase. They then refine the material with each subsequent search that you make.

1. Type in the category you are studying, for example 'rashes'. A large index of relevant options will appear.
2. Select another category from this index. A further index will appear.
3. Continue to select and re-select until you have the information that you are looking for.

Media sources

Media sources include television, radio, newspapers, journals and magazines. Each offers current information on a vast array of subjects, and can be useful when discussing your subject area. However, it is important to remember that many media sources portray bias (a prejudice).

Fig 8.8 Researchers today benefit hugely from a range of technological resources, such as CD-ROMs and the Internet

Fig 8.9 It is important to remember that many media sources portray bias

remember

Many early years professionals write media articles, sharing their expertise and indicating current thinking. Their viewpoints can be particularly useful in discussing subject areas involving current policy or practice.

Television and radio programmes offer topical discussions, current affairs and documentaries. If any of these is to be referred to in a piece of research, the reference details should be set out using the Harvard method as described in Green (2000).

Newspapers and journals also cover current affairs and topical issues. They often include articles on controversial subjects, which may reflect the writer's bias. When examining points raised in articles, it is important to explore alternative views to obtain a balance. Being aware of the source or author can establish whether objectivity can be assumed. For example, an article on the benefits of disposable nappies written by an 'expert' working for a leading manufacturer of disposable nappies is unlikely to be completely objective. It would be likely that any reference to ecological or economic factors would be marginalised in comparison with the emphasis on convenience factors and benefits over rival products.

Case studies

Case studies published by a previous researcher can be used as a secondary source of data. You can use them in more than one way:

- as a point of discussion, analysing the main components of the case and discussing each part, making reference to your own primary research findings or to other outcomes discovered in your literature search;
- to identify differences and discuss comparisons in a number of case studies.

Statistical reports and sources

Statistics can make an important contribution to research. They may show how a trend relevant to a topic area has developed, for example the number of babies born to teenagers in 2005. It is important to use the most recent statistics that you can find; there is little point in discussing a current issue and using statistics from 1995 as an example. Using past statistics can be relevant, however, if a comparison is to be made, for example, between the numbers of babies born to teenagers in 1980 and in 2005. The subsequent discussion would usually explore what changes have occurred, and how and why they have done so.

A good source for social statistics (both national and regional) is the government publication, *Social Trends*, which is published annually by the Stationery Office. Most libraries hold copies.

Professional Practice

- **Research involves both primary and secondary sources of information. You will usually be expected to incorporate both research methods.**
- **Length and breadth of interviews can be controlled through questions and structure.**
- **Questionnaires should be clear, piloted and targeted appropriately. Avoid using leading questions.**
- **Observation, both formal and informal, must be as objective and unobtrusive as possible.**
- **The long-term impact of action research needs careful consideration.**
- **Secondary sources used to support research should be carefully selected.**
- **Issues of bias must be considered in all that you read and also in all that you write.**

Be able to identify a suitable topic and produce a plan for a research proposal

You should by now have identified how the general principles of research methodology are relevant to the whole process of your training. Throughout your studies, you will need to locate printed and technological sources of information, and each time you do this you are carrying out a form of research. Each assignment you prepare will require:

- planning
- a literature search
- decisions about scope and parameters, and validity
- referencing
- clear presentation
- reflection and analysis.

Each of these is part of the research process.

In your interactions with others during your research project, you will need to show respect and consideration, treating others both in college and in placement as you would wish to be treated yourself. You must also respect their rights and privacy.

The new thinking and practice that is introduced into the settings that you attend will most likely be based on research of some description and will enable you to witness at first hand how the practical application of the research process affects standards, achievement and professionalism.

Your chosen research project will enable you to bring together the breadth of knowledge that you have gained from studying this unit. Applying this knowledge practically will consolidate your understanding and enhance your personal development. It is a chance for you to explore an area of particular interest to you, and it can help you to formulate a career plan, by highlighting potential career opportunities in early years care or education. This section summarises the main points that you will need to consider.

For additional useful guidance in planning, presenting and evaluating your project, and in developing your personal research skills, look at *Research Methods in Health, Social and Early Years Care* (Green, 2000), on which the following summaries are based.

Planning, presenting and evaluating your research

To achieve the project unit you will need to:

- identify a suitable topic and produce a plan for a research proposal
- carry out a literature search
- conduct the research
- analyse and present the findings of the research, including the identification of bias or error
- identify and evaluate your own learning from the process.

You will need to produce a research project which shows:

- a relevant hypothesis for the research
- a range of primary and secondary sources
- your findings, analysed and presented using appropriate methods
- discussion of your findings which relate back to the hypothesis
- your planning and progress throughout the research
- the ethical considerations that you have taken into account
- your evaluation and conclusion
- comments on your own research skills and how these could be further developed.

Planning the research

To produce a successful research project, it is necessary to plan each stage carefully. This involves:

- choosing the subject area
- writing the aims and objectives
- setting out a hypothesis
- setting parameters
- selecting an appropriate approach to the research
- identifying ethical considerations
- managing time
- keeping records
- tutorial support
- avoiding common pitfalls.

Presenting the research

Presentation of the research is likely to involve both written and oral presentation skills. The written presentation would usually include the following:

- abstract
- introduction
- methodology
- presentation of data
- main text (discussion)
- conclusions and any recommendations
- evaluation
- bibliography
- appendices.

An oral presentation would usually include the use of some or all of the following:

- overhead projector transparencies
- audiovisual resources (tape recorders, videos, slides)
- tables, charts, graphs

- handouts
- questions from the audience.

More on each of these can be found in Green (2000).

Evaluating the learning process

When evaluating your learning from the research process, the following points should be considered:

- oral skills
- written skills
- information technology skills
- numeracy skills
- personal development
- academic achievement
- practical skills
- applying new skills to other situations.

Professional Practice

- **Research projects offer ideal opportunities for you to gain the key skills of Communication, Application of number, and Information and communication technology.**
- **If you are gathering evidence for the wider key skills (Working with others, Improving own learning and performance, Problem-solving, and Personal skills development), you will also find that the activities you carry out, and the decisions that you make, will contribute to your portfolio of evidence.**

activity
INDIVIDUAL WORK 8.3

P3

M1

In conjunction with the specific guidance given to you by your tutors, plan your research project, taking into account the following:

1 Choosing a suitable topic
 Consider:
 (a) your personal interests
 (b) any guidelines or parameters regarding topic set by your tutors
 (c) practicalities linked to the timeframe you have been given.
2 Issues of suitability
 (a) Identify a suitable topic and agree it with your tutor.
 (b) Ensure that you can form a relevant hypothesis for the research.
 (c) Ensure that you will be able to use a range of primary and secondary sources.
3 Getting started
 (a) Write your aims and objectives.
 (b) Set out a hypothesis.
 (c) Identify and set your parameters.
 (d) Identify the ethical considerations that you will need to take into account.
 (e) Plan how you will manage your time.
 (f) Plan how you will keep records of how the research is going.
 (g) Make sure that you know when and how much tutorial support is available.
 (h) Remind yourself of how to avoid the common pitfalls experienced by other researchers.
 (i) Carry out a literature search.
 (j) Keep details of all sources that you have referred to.
4 Write a justification of your choice of topic and the hypothesis around which you are basing your research.

Refer back to pages 367–378 as you consider which research methods you will use and identify suitable sources of information to guide, support and back up your work.

Be able to conduct the research and present the findings

Preparing the introduction

remember: The preparation for your project should include a written planning sheet to help you to manage your time, monitor your progress and regularly review how the project is going.

remember: You will need to have relevant statistics to hand to back up what you are saying or what you are questioning.

remember: Remember that some research methods take a great deal more time than others.

You will need to read around the subject well and familiarise yourself with all related research outcomes and views. Depending on any parameters you have set yourself, you will need to refer to both well-established and contemporary thinking, and, wherever possible, link these to your hypothesis.

The introduction to your project should be clear, concise and immediately gain the interest of the reader. It will be important to include a summary of any current research related to your topic and any other significant information. For example, if you are choosing to study an aspect of health, nutrition or children's diets, you will be expected to refer to some of the many recent media reports on, for example:

- Jamie Oliver's campaign to raise the nutritional quality of school meals
- the rise in the numbers of child obesity cases
- the introduction of free fruit for young children.

You may also wish to refer to media material such as:

- the film/documentary *Supersize Me* about a man who spent a month eating only food from a fast food chain and the impact that it had on his weight, health and general sense of well-being (you could relate this to the potential impact on children of a diet high in fast-food products)
- television programmes where parents are helped to improve their children's diet and life style and are shown the projected difference that living healthily would make both in the short and long term.

Method

When making your choice of research method, think about:

- the time you have available
- the relevance of each primary research method to the topic you are studying
- how your hypothesis will be researched most effectively
- how you will record your data.

As you make decisions during the planning stage of your project, refer to pages 367–378 for guidance on primary and secondary research methods.

Ethical considerations

You need to work ethically throughout your research project to ensure that you treat your participants correctly.

Refer to page 396 for a discussion of the ethical issues that you should take into account.

Results

A great deal of information is produced during a research project. **Raw data** are derived from primary research: questionnaires, interview notes, observations, and so on. Often, raw data are in numerical form.

Raw data should be kept in a logical order so that they can be understood and explained if a query is raised. It is particularly important that raw data are kept safely until after a piece of

remember Keep your data safe – you may need them as evidence of your research.

work has been read and graded by your tutors. The data may be needed as evidence of your research process.

There are many ways in which raw data can be analysed and presented. Tables and graphs are common, and in some subjects it can be appropriate to use a pictorial method. You need to become familiar with some forms of statistical analysis and with the different types of presentation and their uses, so that you can understand findings published by other researchers and know how to present the findings from your own research. You will find information in the next two sections about basic statistics and different forms of graphical presentation.

Some basic statistical tools

When you collect numerical data, you will usually need to manipulate or describe them in some way. Statistics is the area which deals specifically with the description and manipulation of numerical data. For the purposes of level 3 research, you need to understand the following terms:

- the **mean**, **median** or **mode** – three different kinds of statistical averages
- the **range** – the difference between the smallest and largest result in each collection of data
- the **standard deviation** – a measure of how widely the results in a set of data are distributed, taking the mean as a point of reference.

You also need to understand how to calculate percentages.

The mean

The mean is the score which is normally recognised as being the average. It is worked out by adding up all the scores that are being dealt with and then dividing that sum by the number of scores.

For example, in Oak class at Country Primary school, there are 24 children. Their reading ages are as follows:

two have a reading age of 6 years

three have a reading age of 7 years

fourteen have a reading age of 9 years

four have a reading age of 12 years

one has a reading age of 14 years.

If these reading ages are added together, it makes 221

(6 + 6 + 7 + 7 + 7 + 9 + 9 + 9 + 9 + 9 + 9 + 9 + 9 + 9 + 9 + 9 + 9 + 9 +9 + 12 + 12 + 12 + 12 + 14 = 221).

To obtain the mean, 221 is divided by 24 (the number of children): 221 ÷ 24 = 9.2.

The mean reading age of Oak class is therefore 9.2 years.

The median

The median is the point in the sequence of scores that divides the lower half from the higher half.

For example, in Oak class:

6 6 7 7 7 9 9 9 9 9 9 9   9 9 9 9 9 9 9 12 12 12 12 14

The median reading age is therefore 9 years.

The mode

The mode or modal score is the most common score in the set of data.

For example, as the most common reading age in Oak class is 9, the mode will also be 9 years:

6 6 7 7 7 9 9 9 9 9 9 9 9 9 9 9 9 9 9 12 12 12 12 14

The range

The range tells us about the spread of scores in a set. It is the difference between the lowest and the highest score. You would therefore calculate the range by subtracting the lowest result from the highest.

For example, in Oak class, the highest reading age is 14 and the lowest is 6; the 6 therefore needs to be subtracted from the 14: 14 – 6 = 8.

The range is 8 years.

Standard deviation

The spread of numerical data can sometimes be shown on a chart, known as a distribution curve, which shows standard deviations.

The size of the standard deviation indicates how widely the results are distributed around the mean, which is the centre of the distribution. A small standard deviation would see most of the results gathered in a narrow band either side of the mean. When the standard deviation is large, the results spread out further from the mean.

Fig 8.10 Standard deviation of reading ages in Oak class

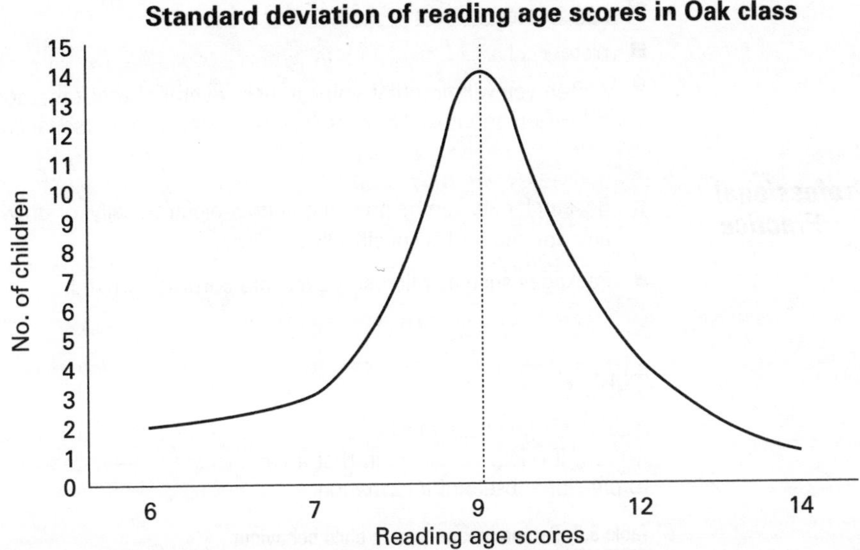

Calculating percentages

Per cent means part of a hundred. If your number is part of a total and you want to calculate the percentage, you divide the number by the total and multiply it by 100. This can be done quickly on a standard calculator. For example; if there are 100 children in a setting and 13 receive free school meals, it is easy to see that is 13% of children as the calculation involved is: 13/100 = 0.13, and 0.13 x 100 = 13%.

If there were 113 pupils in the school and 17 chose to join the Judo club, the percentage is worked out as follows: 17/113 = 0.15; 0.15 x 100 = 15%.

Using a computer for statistical analysis

Statistical Package for Social Sciences (SPSS)

There are software packages available to help you analyse and present your data using a computer. One example is SPSS, which is particularly helpful for:

- surveys and market research
- administration
- medical, scientific, clinical and social science research.

It will help you to:

- enter data and compute descriptive statistics
- compute an analysis of variance
- compute correlation and scatterplots.

It can often be accessed through your college library or resource centre. Your tutors or resource centre staff will be able to help you access and use it.

Microsoft Excel

Another popular package is Microsoft Excel. This will enable you easily to:

- produce spreadsheets
- produce graphs and tables from written data
- use formulae to make calculations.

Methods of presentation

Numerical data can be presented in a variety of ways, for example as:

- tables
- **bar charts**
- histograms
- **line graphs**
- **pie charts**
- sociograms
- pictographs.

Very often you will find that you can use several of these methods to present your data, and your decision about which to use will be a matter of personal choice.

Professional Practice

- Research data can be presented either electronically, or drawn. Your tutor will tell you if any one method is specifically required.
- Packages such as Microsoft Excel are commonly used.

Tables

A table is one of the most basic methods of presenting information, whether numerical or written. It offers versatility in that it can include a great deal of raw data and can also be used to present subsets of information.

Table 8.7 Parental responses to child behaviour

	% Positive response		% Negative response	
Type of behaviour	Boys	Girls	Boys	Girls
Playing with blocks	36	0	0	0
Manipulating objects	46	46	2	26
Transportation toys	61	57	0	2
Rough/tumble toys	91	84	3	2
Aggression	23	18	50	53
Climbing	39	43	12	24
Playing with dolls	39	63	14	4
Dancing	0	50	0	0
Asking for help	72	87	13	6
Dressing-up play	50	71	50	6

Source: Adapted from B. Fagot (1978), 'The influence of sex of child on parental reactions to toddler children', cited in Cullis *et al.* (1999)

Table 8.8 A factual table, offering an 'at a glance' comparison of a range of learning systems

	High Scope	Montessori	Steiner
Specific staff qualification	No	Yes	No
Specific training needed	Yes	Yes	Yes
Specific equipment needed	No	Yes	No
Particular daily routine	Yes	No	Yes
Particular teaching methods	Yes	Yes	Yes
Own terminology	Yes	Yes	Yes
Particular method of grouping children	Yes	No	No
Particular room layout	Yes	No	No

Source: Adapted from Jameson and Watson (1998)

When drawing up a table:

- It should have a title.
- All rows and columns must be clearly labelled.
- The source of your information should always be given below the table.
- For numerical data, all units of measurement must be given.
- If rows or columns are totalled, this must be clearly indicated in the table.
- For large or complex tables, shading or colouring may help to make information more accessible.

Bar charts

A bar chart is particularly useful for showing comparisons between sets of information where the data are discrete (not continuous). The length of each bar is clearly seen in relation to its neighbours.

Fig 8.11 A bar chart

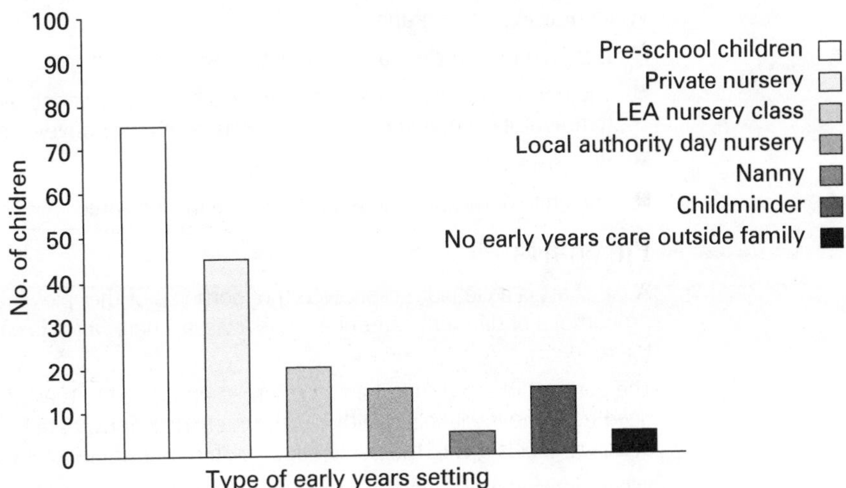

When drawing a bar chart:

- It should have a relevant and informative title.
- Both axes should be clearly labelled and the units of measurement clearly identified.
- Each bar should be clearly labelled and a key provided where necessary.
- The bars should be of equal width.
- The bars may be separated by a small gap or may butt up against each other.

Histograms

A histogram is quite similar to a bar chart in appearance and is for continuous data (e.g. age or temperature). The frequency of the class is indicated by the area of the column, and histograms are often used to represent grouped data. If the intervals along the horizontal axis of a histogram are the same width, for example a scale of children's ages ranging from birth to three years, with each interval representing six months, the intervals are the same and the frequency for each interval (in this case, the number of children of a certain age) can be read from the height. However, histograms are not as easy to use or interpret as a bar chart as the width of the columns may vary in line with the size of interval they are meant to convey, meaning that, in some histograms, the area of each column has to be calculated in order to reach a conclusion.

Line graphs

A line graph gives clear 'at a glance' understanding for the reader. They show trends or changes in quantity and are particularly useful for displaying information which changes over a period of time. The horizontal axis indicates the continuously variable aspect of the data being presented.

You cannot plot a line graph unless you have quite a lot of data. Trying to join just a few points plotted from sketchy data may give an unreliable impression.

Fig 8.12 A line graph

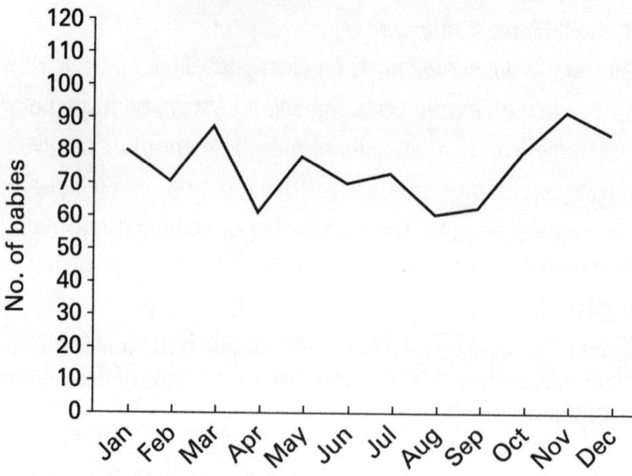

When drawing a line graph:

- It should have a clear and informative title.
- The horizontal axis should represent a continuously variable quantity, such as age, time or temperature (i.e. it should not be discrete or descriptive categories).
- Both axes should be clearly labelled.
- The units of measurement should be clearly indicated.

Pie charts

A pie chart is a circular graph, with the 'portions' of the 'pie' showing clearly the relative proportions of different categories. It is a visual chart which is easily understood by the reader.

The portions of a pie chart can be coloured or shaded to make the data clear but they also need to be clearly labelled, either with simple descriptive labels for each category or, for more accuracy, labels giving the percentage share of the whole for each category.

When drawing a pie chart, the angle at the centre of the circle (360°) is shared between the different categories in proportion to their size using a mathematical calculation. It is worth learning how to draw a pie chart, although software programs are available which can do this for you.

Fig 8.13 A pie chart

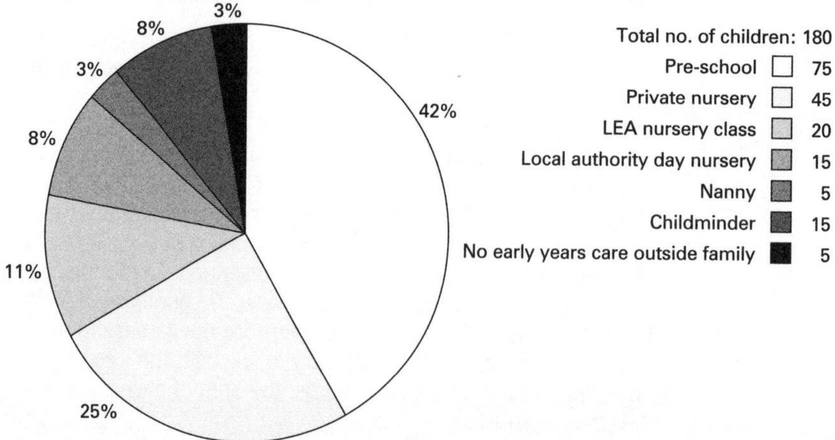

The advantage of pie charts is that they are especially useful for showing, at a glance, the relative proportions of different categories. Their disadvantage is that they are quite difficult to draw. The more categories you are trying to represent, the more difficult it is to draw the chart.

When drawing a pie chart:

- It should have a clear and informative title.
- Each slice or segment should be shaded or coloured to distinguish it from the others.
- Each segment should be labelled to indicate which category it represents, or a key should be provided.

Sociograms

The term 'socio' means 'denoting social or society'. A sociogram presents data describing relationships between members of social groups.

Sociograms can depict the social relationships of one person or of a complete group of people. It can be a useful way of identifying popular children and also those who may need some help settling into the group.

However, it can be misleading, and should be treated with some caution

The sociogram below shows the inter-relationships of a group of children.

Fig 8.14 A sociogram

Number of times each child in a class was quoted as being the best friend of another child in the class

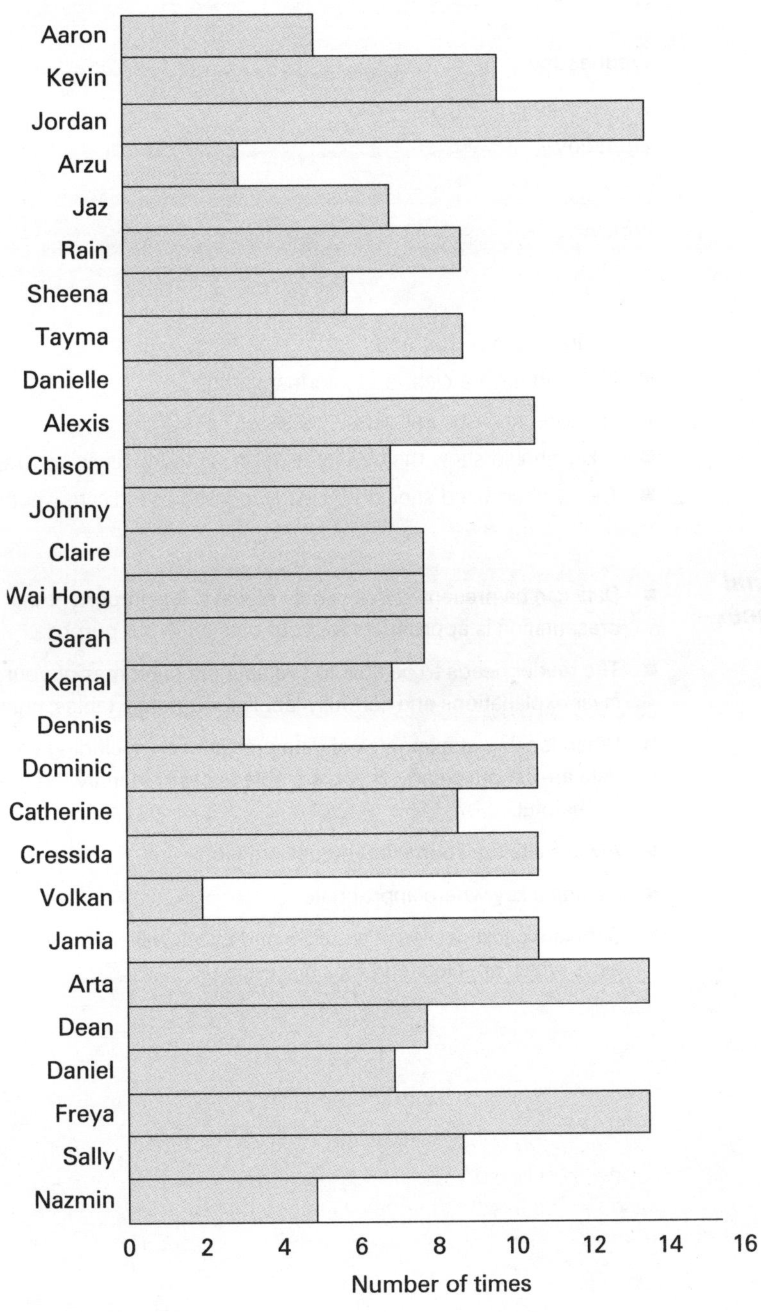

> **remember** A sociogram is an excellent way of depicting the social structure of a group.

When drawing a sociogram:

- It should have a clear and meaningful title.
- The different group members should be clearly identified.
- The axis depicting frequency of contact should be clearly labelled.

Pictographs

A **pictograph** works in the same way as a bar chart, but pictures are used instead of bars to represent the data. This is a very visual graph and may have a greater impact on the reader than a bar chart.

Fig 8.15 A pictograph

The average number of nappy changes in a typical week in the baby room of Bathtown Day Nursery

> **remember** It will be helpful to refer back to this section as you plan your project.

When drawing a pictograph:

- It should have a clear and informative title.
- The symbols used should be consistent.
- A key should show the quantities represented by each picture.
- The symbols used should be clearly labelled to indicate what they represent.

Professional Practice

- **Data can be presented in a variety of ways. It is important that the chosen method of presentation is appropriate for your data and your purpose.**
- **The reader needs to be able to evaluate the outcomes of your research easily, so provide clear explanations and carefully label all diagrams, tables, charts and graphs.**
- **When looking at examples of data presentation, including your own, consider if the data are set out clearly, if you are able to easily identify the main outcomes, if the labels are helpful.**
- **Always cite the source of your information.**
- **Include a key where appropriate.**
- **Software packages, such as SPSS and Excel, will enable you to present your data in ways which are clear and look professional.**

P4

In conjunction with the specific guidance given to you by your tutors, carry out the information-gathering stage of your research project, taking into account the following:

- Keep to the guidelines or parameters agreed with your tutors
- Be constantly aware of the timeframe you have been given
- Keep in mind your hypothesis for the research
- Ensure that you use a range of primary and secondary sources
- Regularly re-read your aims and objectives to ensure that you keep 'on task'
- Remind yourself of your parameters, and stick to them
- Work ethically in all that you do
- Write a time plan, and keep to it
- Set up a clear system for keeping any notes and records
- Use the tutorial support that is available.

Refer to the relevant sections of this unit for guidance on using research methods.

Be able to evaluate the research project

Factors to consider

Validity

Validity refers to how accurately a subject has been researched. Ask yourself, can the research be said to be both genuine and soundly based? A research tool is valid if it measures what it claims to measure. In research terms, validity is giving a true representation of what has been researched; a piece of research that is valid addresses what it says it addresses, and its findings are less likely to be disputed. It is important that researchers are as sure as they can be that their participants have told them the truth.

Reliability

A research finding that can be repeated is reliable. **Reliability** refers to the consistency of the outcome. Any identified change to practice needs to be supported by evidence that is consistent – it has to be reliable. This applies equally to the field of early years; an outcome will not be considered as reliable evidence if it is only applicable to one research project or to one sample group of participants. It is important to establish that another similar research enquiry would achieve the same results.

Unfortunately, an outcome can be reliable, yet not be valid. You might receive the same answers from your participants if you ask them the same set of questions more than once but, if those questions were not properly formulated for investigating your aim, the results, although consistent, would not be valid.

Re-testability

remember

Successful replication of research is the only way to demonstrate reliability.

Re-testability is directly linked to reliability. In research, re-testing is one way of assessing reliability.

Researchers should ask themselves: Would the same results be achieved if the enquiry was replicated (carried out again)?

For most research on a level 3 early years course, replication will not be practicable. It is, therefore, important to be able to justify your choice of research method and make the best of it by careful selection of participants and careful preparation of questions, observations, and so on.

Professional Practice

Important questions are:

- Was the method reliable? Would replication achieve the same results?
- Was it the best method for the subject being studied?
- What were the alternatives?
- Would the outcomes have been different if another method had been used?

Representative groups

Valid results can only be achieved if participants (the target group) are genuinely representative. Therefore, targeting research appropriately is vital.

For example, it would be of limited value to ask a retired nursery nurse how successful they consider the introduction of the Foundation Stage Curriculum to be from a practitioner's point of view. To obtain a genuinely useful response, the researcher would need to ask a practitioner who has worked both prior to and with the Foundation Stage guidelines.

Triangulation

Validity can be augmented through triangulation (supporting your findings from research in more than one way).

For example, both questionnaires and interviews could be used to obtain parents' views regarding safety aspects of the local park. These responses could then be supported by observations made by the researcher after spending time at the park in question. If results from the three methods support each other, it will enhance the validity of the overall research project.

Bias, error and the misuse of statistics

Bias can be either intentional or unintentional. The person collecting statistics, asking questions, etc. may have a strong personal view on the subject; they may skew outcomes by subjectively recording what is said during an interview; or they could manipulate the results to give the answer they were predicting or hoping for. Statistics in secondary data should always be treated cautiously, and whenever possible the findings should be backed up by other research.

Error can occur when data are incorrectly dealt with or misinterpreted, and it can also occur when questions are misleading or carelessly worded. Again, backing up statistics from questionnaire data with those from another form of research can help ensure a more accurate overall outcome.

Refer to page 393 for validity and reliability.

At times, statistics can be misleading. They can be manipulated to show one thing, when the raw data really suggest something else. School achievement tables are a good example of this.

Table 8.9 A-level results, showing pupils with three grades A–C

School	1998	1999	2000
School A	80%	82%	80%
School B	61%	63%	63%
School C	35%	38%	42%
School D	58%	63%	62%
School E	49%	51%	48%

To someone who is not familiar with the schools included in this table, it would seem clear that School A is the better school because the results are far better at A level (80% gain at least three passes at A–C) than those of any other school. This figure is a consistent achievement by the school, and they should be commended for it accordingly. However, to someone who is familiar with the school's policy of selective entry at Year 7 and for the sixth form (where only pupils with five GCSEs at A–C are admitted), it would seem logical that its results are the best.

No other school in the table has selective entry at any stage, and School C (with 42% of pupils gaining at least three passes at A–C) has increased its achievement levels consistently over the past three years (35% to 38% to 42%). This clearly indicates an improving academic record.

Statistics such as these can therefore mislead prospective parents who are looking to select a school for their child. The improving school (School C) may well be the better choice for the child concerned, as it is clearly improving the overall standard of results of pupils 'across the board' of academic ability.

Professional Practice

- **Careful selection of participants is needed. They must always be representative.**
- **Mutually supportive research methods (triangulation) enhance the validity of research.**
- **Replication confirms the reliability of findings.**
- **Methods of analysing and presenting data should not produce a misleading picture of the results.**

Evaluation and conclusion

remember You should use the results of your research appropriately, i.e. ethically.

Once the finding-out and presentation stages of your research project have been completed, you will need to evaluate what you have learned and what you have achieved, and reach a conclusion. This will involve:

- making a comparison of your findings with your hypothesis
- writing a discussion of your findings
- linking your results to current research
- identifying the limitations of your project
- identifying potential areas for further development
- noting how you have taken into consideration issues of bias and error
- noting how you have taken into consideration ethical issues such as confidentiality and data protection, and human rights
- explaining the use and misuse of research and how you have worked to maintain valid and reliable outcomes.

Making recommendations

From the research you have carried out, you will need to explain and justify any recommendations that you are able to make to support practitioners in their work. For example, that:

- children at your placement are not using the small-scale construction sets because …
- the children's apparent lack of interest in selecting books to look at by themselves is due to …

In both these cases, the practitioners involved may be able to take into account the outcomes of your research and make appropriate changes to the way they work or present resources, thereby improving the experience for the children. A great outcome!

You may also be able to explain and justify a recommendation to support the work of policy makers. For example, that:

- the input of time from parents in the local preschool has increased due to …
- greater involvement of non-English speaking parents within the school has been seen since … .

In these cases, what you have identified through your research may demonstrate how a change to policy or procedure has helped build on the setting's partnership with parents. Again, this would be a great outcome.

activity
INDIVIDUAL WORK 8.5

P5

M2

In conjunction with the specific guidance given to you by your tutors, present and report your findings in a format relevant to the research methods that you have chosen to use for your research project. Include the following:

- Explain the outcomes of each primary research source used.
- Explain the outcomes of each secondary research source used.
- Refer back to your aims and objectives and explain how they were met.
- Refer to your parameters, linking them to your outcomes.
- Note any bias, or potential for bias.
- Note any known errors that have occurred.
- Explain the ethical considerations that you have taken into account.

Refer to the relevant sections of this unit for guidance on using research methods, presenting information and issues of bias, error and ethics.

activity
INDIVIDUAL WORK 8.6

D1

Expanding upon the activity above, write an analysis of the research methods that you have used during your project, noting how any issues of bias or error, or identified potential for bias or error, could have been reduced by altering the approach taken or the research methods chosen by you for the project.

Refer to the relevant sections of this unit for guidance on bias and error.

activity
INDIVIDUAL WORK 8.7

P6

M3

In conjunction with the specific guidance given to you by your tutors, discuss the findings of your research, taking into account the following:

1. How your findings relate directly to your original hypothesis, i.e. whether your hypothesis was supported or not, and how you are able to support your findings.
2. To what extent your hypothesis was supported or not?
3. What you have learned generally about setting a hypothesis.

Refer to the relevant section of this unit to remind you about setting a hypothesis.

Understand the implications of and ethical issues related to using research in children's care, learning and development

Costs vs. benefits

As you are a student carrying out a small-scale project, it is unlikely that the outcomes of your research will benefit anyone other than yourself. Any risks that might be taken during the research process need to be balanced against the benefits that the outcomes of the research will bring (this is sometimes known as the costs:benefits ratio). When this is a personal piece of work undertaken as part of a course, you need to be absolutely sure that the benefits (primarily to yourself) justify the costs (primarily borne by others).

In a larger-scale piece of research, any potential risks should be identified at the onset, and the benefits of the research should be clearly set out by the researcher.

Who commissions the research?

It is worth considering who might commission a piece of research and their reasons for doing so. It is important that society knows who is behind research studies that affect people and society in general. If the organisation or individual who has commissioned the research has a vested interest in its outcome, this might suggest that there is an element of subjectivity.

Ethical issues

Ethics are the principles or moral codes used as guidelines for the behaviour standards common to all people within a group or profession. Ethics determine what is right and wrong; they help to maintain standards.

Individual definitions of the term 'ethics' may vary slightly, but most people will agree that, in general, ethics act as guidelines for the decisions we each have to make and the consequences that may arise from any course of action we take. They are directly linked to the values and morals of both individuals and society as a whole. Ethics, therefore, are about doing what is right according to the majority, linking personal values, standards of behaviour and conscience to actions.

Research ethics are the rules governing good and bad practice in the field of research. To behave unethically during the research process is to behave badly when dealing with the views and contributions of any of your participants. In research, ethics include consideration of the participants' rights, the importance of confidentiality and issues concerned with preserving anonymity.

Human rights

Every individual who agrees to take part in research has rights. This also applies to children and vulnerable adults when permission is given on their behalf for them to take part in research. It is expected that the researcher is courteous, respectful and ensures confidentiality at all times.

Ref to Unit 6, page 292, to remind yourself about human rights legislation.

Obtaining consent

Full permission from participants, and from any organisation they may be considered to represent, is needed prior to the commencement of any research. This applies equally to research carried out internally in your own placement or work setting.

It is important that you obtain all appropriate permissions before carrying out your research. If participants are young (school age or younger), you must obtain the permission of their parents or guardians. The research may be considered to be completely non-threatening and non-intrusive (e.g. asking children questions about favourite toys or television programmes), but the general principle of obtaining permission from the adult with responsibility for the children concerned is still important.

In a school or early years setting, the head teacher or manager will need to give their written consent, as they are *in loco parentis* while children are in their care.

This permission must be arranged well in advance, so time management and planning should take this into account. A letter of support from a course tutor will usually be sufficient proof of the authenticity of the project.

The following details may also be required:

- your name
  - a contact telephone number
  - your college's telephone number (plus your tutor's name)
- dates of planned involvement by the setting, for example:
  - letters to parents (if needed)
  - interviews (How many? Who will be interviewed?)

- distribution plans for any surveys
- collection arrangements for surveys
- the time plan for your research
- the availability of the research findings to the participants, or their parents/guardians
- details of who else will have access to the research findings
- issues of identification or confidentiality within the research:
  - What guarantees have been given?
  - If guaranteed, how will anonymity be assured?

Vulnerability of client groups

People who are unable to understand fully the possible consequences of being involved in research and cannot therefore give informed consent can be described as being vulnerable. In these situations, those responsible for them, or for guiding and/or supporting them in their decision-making, must be fully informed and consulted by the researcher.

> **remember**
> Every participant in a research project has rights. These include:
> - guaranteed privacy
> - observation of their right to withdraw at any point
> - anonymity
> - confidentiality
> - respect at all times
> - trust that their contribution will be portrayed fairly and accurately.

Confidentiality and access to information

Confidentiality issues apply when a piece of research is to be published, i.e. Who will read it? Who will have access to it? Always ask yourself: Was permission given by all those involved?

Participants who agree to help in the research process are putting their trust in the researcher, i.e. in you. You therefore have a responsibility to set clear guidelines as to how, when and where the outcomes of research are to be published. An individual participant will also need to know if they will be identified within the findings. If it is agreed that they will not, then it is imperative that this agreement is adhered to.

You need to clarify the different ways in which a participant can be identified in research, other than by name. If, for example, in a piece of research about changes facing primary school teachers, reference is made to the written planning required of teachers during their probationary teaching year, it will be very obvious whose responses are being referred to if one teacher in the participating school has been teaching for 20 years and the others are newly qualified. Therefore, the individual participants will be identified quite easily. Similarly, initials will easily identify participants with more unusual names.

Data protection

The privacy of, and rights of access to material relating to, any individual are covered by legislation.

Refer to Unit 6, page 299, to remind yourself about the Data Protection Act 1998.

Responsibilities

> **remember**
> You will find it helpful to locate copies of all relevant legislation, read through the main aspects of each, and note which elements could be relevant to your own project.

Ethical research involves responsibility. As a researcher you will have a responsibility to all your participants to ensure that their privacy is not invaded unnecessarily, or without their permission. Participants are doing you a favour by participating in your research. At times, you may ask for responses on topics that may be sensitive to them. Their sensitivity should be respected and treated accordingly.

It is unethical to carry out research without the participants knowing that it is taking place (i.e. covert observation or casual conversations). This is particularly important if you are carrying out research in your workplace. Covert research breaks the trust of colleagues if, for example, information given in conversation is used in a subsequent piece of research. This also applies to observing and recording the actions and/or conversations of colleagues without their knowledge.

There are occasions when ethical considerations may not be as necessary, for example if you were carrying out observations in a public place (e.g. watching students socialise around the college campus or children playing in a park).

The research methods chosen for any project will have an impact on the way the findings of research are presented. At the outset of a piece of research, the proposed methods should be fully considered, to ensure that they will convey a true representation of participants' contributions.

Policy and procedures

Before starting any research project, you need to have consulted your supervisor. In many cases, this will be your tutor. Some establishments may have a policy for research projects that are undertaken as part of course requirements, and this is common in medical, nursing and health and social care settings. This acts as a check with regard to the ethical implications of research proposals and the viability of the project. Check this out in your college or setting, but make sure that your tutor is aware of your research proposal, so that guidance and supervision can be given during the research process.

Professional Practice

- **You need to be aware that sensitive subjects may also affect you, the researcher. The responses you receive and the material you read in the literature may at times be distressing.**
- **It is important for all researchers to have supervision. Supervision helps you with the process and practical application of your project. It also helps you deal with stress and concerns. Professional researchers are supervised, as well as student researchers. Your tutor will usually supervise your research project.**

Codes of practice

remember

Ethics are linked to standards of behaviour, to values and to your conscience. Reading examples of ethical codes of practice will help you to consolidate your understanding of the codes and charters that many professionals adhere to in their practice.

Various professions produce their own codes of ethics. Examples include:

- health districts – each has an ethics committee
- doctors – the British Medical Association
- psychologists – the British Psychological Society
- social workers.

To build on your understanding of ethics, try accessing an overview of a code of ethics for a relevant profession. Read its main points and consider how the ethical principles for that profession might apply to your role in early years.

Certain bodies have issued guidance or codes of practice specifically for research and, although these have been written for 'professional' researchers, you should attempt to adhere closely to the guidance that they give. Codes of research practice or research ethics are common in many professional bodies and higher education institutions and can be accessed on line. Useful sites to investigate are those belonging to the British Psychological Society and the British Sociological Association.

British Psychological Society
www.bps.org.uk
British Sociological Association
www.britsoc.co.uk

The ethical issues related to different research methods

Ethical issues occur in all forms of primary research. Below are brief summaries of the most pertinent aspects in relation to the most commonly used primary research methods.

Interviews

- Interviews put the researcher (you) in a position of power. You should not use your control of the situation to your own advantage.
- Leading questions can be a problem, with personal bias making the approach subjective rather than objective.
- Sensitivity is needed, as is awareness of how the outcomes of interviews are to be used.
- It is important that you take into consideration how the interview may affect the participants.
- There are issues in relation to confidentiality, anonymity and the sensitivity of the subject matter.

Surveys

- Using a survey (or questionnaire) approach also raises issues of confidentiality, anonymity and the sensitivity of the subject matter.
- Leading questions can be a problem here too.

Case studies

- Case studies involve discussion of a real situation, and respect for the people portrayed in the case study is needed.
- It would not usually be appropriate to identify the individuals involved.
- It is important to consider how the outcomes of the research will be used and who will have access to it.
- Awareness of personal bias is important.

Observations

- Appropriate permission is particularly important if observing informally, or when observing individuals who are unable to give permission for themselves.

Effects on policy and practice

It can be useful to consider the impact of key reports and organisations, for example the Social Care Institute for Excellence (SCIE). The aim of this independent charitable organisation, which was launched in October 2001, is to improve social care within society. SCIE's role is to develop and promote knowledge and understanding of good social care practice. Within the ethos of research, it can:

- help with the review of policy
- help demonstrate how knowledge underpins policy or development
- help make clear the views of people within society, through the outcomes of research
- help build on diversity within an organisation.

As part of the BTEC National CCLD Course, you will be required to evaluate pieces of published research and will be asked to comment on various aspects, including the ethical issues.

Contemporary research

There is a wealth of contemporary research into the lives and care of young children and their families; two of the many examples of the work that is being done include:

- an overview of children in public care and
- a report on the early impacts of Sure Start local programmes on children and their families.

Children in public care

This overview of the experiences of children in public care was undertaken by renewal.net on behalf of the Office of the Deputy Prime Minister in October 2005. It identifies the reasons why this group has poor experiences of education and schooling and why this may be implicated in social exclusion later in their lives. It outlines the problem and the causes; interventions that have been put in place and checklists for good practice.

Early impacts of Sure Start

Cross-sectional Study of 9- and 36-Month Old Children and their Families (HMSO, 2005) is a report from November 2005. One of the main goals of Sure Start programmes is to improve the functioning of children and families in the areas served by the local programmes. Preliminary findings suggest that there appears to be a difference in the improvements noted depending on the amount of deprivation and lack of available resources in families. For example, teenage parents, lone parents and workless households were found to be less likely to benefit as much as less disadvantaged families.

Think how the organisation SCIE might be helpful here.

Professional Practice

- Researchers need to keep abreast of any relevant issues in their subject area.
- Researchers should never ignore the ethical issues bound up in the research process. They should always think about how they would want to be treated if they were participants and should always show respect to those who agree to participate. Don't forget that this applies to you, as a researcher.
- Participants in research have rights. These must be acknowledged and respected.

activity
INDIVIDUAL WORK 8.8

P7

M4

1 In conjunction with the specific guidance given to you by your tutors, draw up a list of improvements that you could make to the research you have carried out, making sure that you refer to the following:
   (a) how you chose your topic
   (b) why you elected to work within your identified parameters (if applicable)
   (c) the way you planned your research
   (d) the way you conducted the research
   (e) your time management, i.e. your planning and progress throughout the research project
   (f) your choice of primary and secondary research methods
   (g) your presentation of the findings of the research
   (h) your analysis of the findings of the research
   (i) your ability to identify bias or error
   (j) the discussion of your findings in relation to your hypothesis
   (k) the ethical considerations that you have taken into account
   (l) your evaluation and conclusion.
2 Comment generally on your own ability as a researcher and how your research skills could be further developed.
3 Make clear any developments in knowledge and understanding gained from the research.
4 Make clear any possible implications that the research results could have for your personal practice.
5 Make clear any possible implications that the research results could have for current practice in the sector.

activity
INDIVIDUAL WORK 8.9

D2

1 Having completed your research project, prepare a short presentation on the purpose and role of research in the early years sector. Ideally you would:
   (a) Provide examples from the recent past, indicating their value to the sector.
   (b) Provide examples from the more distant past, noting the effect they have had on contemporary practice.
   (c) Refer to the relevance of your own research topic and the value that you see in your outcomes.
2 Be ready to answer questions on your research project.
3 Prepare a handout to give to others, outlining the main points from your presentation.

Progress Check

1. Why is research important?
2. What is the difference between primary and secondary research?
3. Define the terms 'qualitative' and 'quantitative'.
4. What is meant by objectivity?
5. What is a hypothesis?
6. What are the advantages and disadvantages of interviews?
7. List at least five important points to remember when planning a questionnaire.
8. What is the purpose of the control group in an experiment?
9. What is action research?
10. Give an example of how case studies can be used.
11. List as many secondary sources of information as you can.
12. List as many ways as can you think of to present statistical data.
13. Explain validity and reliability.
14. Give an example of research affecting practice.
15. What do research ethics involve?

Promoting Healthy Development and Living for Children and their Families

This unit covers the following objectives:

- Understand factors affecting the health and physical development of children
- Understand nutritional needs
- Know how to maximise opportunities for the promotion of healthy living to children and their families

This unit will help you develop an understanding of what affects the health and physical development of children and how you as a practitioner can support this, by maximising opportunities for promoting health and well-being within daily practice and through planned activities and learning. It will introduce to you some of the factors that can impact on health, with an emphasis on the aspects that you can do something about, for example hygiene practice, food and nutrition, exercise, prevention and management of illness, and attitude. It should be remembered that children's understanding of their own health will be linked to their age and stage of development, and this must be taken into account when introducing health topics within your placement or work setting.

grading criteria

To achieve a **Pass** grade the evidence must show that the learner is able to:	To achieve a **Merit** grade the evidence musty show that, in addition to the pass criteria, the learner is able to:	To achieve a **Distinction** grade the evidence must show that, in addition to the pass and merit criteria, the learner is able to:
P1 outline factors that affect the health and physical development of children page 413	**M1** explain factors that affect the health and physical development of children page 413	**D1** evaluate the potential effects of two factors that affect the health and physical development of children and their families. page 414
P2 describe types of macronutrients and micronutrients and their roles in the diet page 439	**M2** explain the roles of the various components of a balanced diet page 441	**D2** use two examples from work placements to evaluate the promotion of healthy living to children and their families. page 447
P3 describe the requirements of a balanced diet page 441	**M3** use two examples from work placements to explain the role of the promotion of healthy living to children and their families. page 447	

To achieve a **Pass** grade the evidence must show that the learner is able to:	To achieve a **Merit** grade the evidence musty show that, in addition to the pass criteria, the learner is able to:	To achieve a **Distinction** grade the evidence must show that, in addition to the pass and merit criteria, the learner is able to:
P4 use examples from work placements to describe how opportunities for the promotion of healthy living to children and their families can be maximised. page 445		

Understand factors affecting the health and physical development of children

Healthy development

Models of health

Health can be described in terms of three different models:

- the medical model of health
- the **social model** of health
- the **holistic model** of health.

The medical model of health

The medical model (or biological model) looks at a person's health in terms of the body's natural defences and immunity, genetically inherited conditions, individual levels of exercise, diet and lifestyle. It sees the body as a machine that can be restored to health by medical intervention. The responsibility for health lies with the medical profession whose role is to understand disease and find cures.

The social model of health

The social model sees health as being not just about biology and medical intervention but also as being influenced by the wider natural, social, economic and political environment. This includes, for example, housing, social class, affluence and poverty. This model places emphasis on health promotion/education.

The holistic model of health

The holistic model looks at the individual person as a whole. It can be broadly described as being concerned with 'mind, body and soul'.

The World Health Organization (WHO) is concerned with health in its holistic sense. In 1946, the WHO defined health as being: 'a state of complete physical, mental and social well-being, not merely the absence of disease and infirmity'.

In 1984, the WHO stated that health is: 'a resource for everyday life, not the objective of living; it is a positive concept emphasising social and personal resources as well as physical capabilities'.

In 1986, it defined health promotion as: 'The process of enabling people to increase control over, and improve their health ... Health is a positive concept emphasising social and personal resources, as well as physical capacities. Therefore, health promotion is not just the responsibility of the health sector but goes beyond lifestyles to well-being.'

Gaining skills and competence

Understanding how to take care of our health develops gradually through the encouragement and example of those who care for and influence us, and the skills involved require much practice. As adults, we teach children to wash their hands before meals and after using the toilet; we encourage them to clean their teeth after meals and before bed; we promote covering mouth and nose when sneezing and coughing, discarding rubbish carefully and avoiding obvious potential sources of infection, such as animal faeces. Giving clear explanations appropriate to a child's level of understanding is important if children are to learn the reasons why something is good, or not good, for their health. If the reason why something should or should not be done is not fully understood, then the child is less likely to follow good health and hygiene practice.

case study 9.1

Millie

Millie is four years old and has a nasty cough and cold virus. She sneezes frequently, and her nose is very drippy. The coughing comes on suddenly, causing her to cough quite violently on and off for several minutes at a time.

activity
INDIVIDUAL WORK

1 What would you expect Millie to do to help contain the viral infection as much as possible?
2 What would you expect to do for her?
3 How would you explain the importance of containing the infection to Millie?
4 How could you model good hygienic practice for Millie and any other children present?

Meeting potential

An individual's potential for healthy development will be dependent upon many factors:

- genetic
- social and economic
- environmental
- lifestyle
- access to services.

Refer to page 412, where these are set out as a table, followed by discussion.

For a child to meet their health potential all negative factors should be addressed and compensated for wherever practical. Parents are not always able or willing to make changes for their family so education will play a vital part, helping children to make informed choices when they are in a position to do so, for example in relation to smoking, diet and exercise.

Approaches to preventing illness

The three main approaches are:

- environmental approaches
- public health approaches
  - immunisation
  - screening
- educational approaches.

Environmental approaches

Globally, environmentalists strive to improve both health and the quality of the planet by highlighting the effects of adverse factors, such as pollution.

Fig 9.1 Pollution

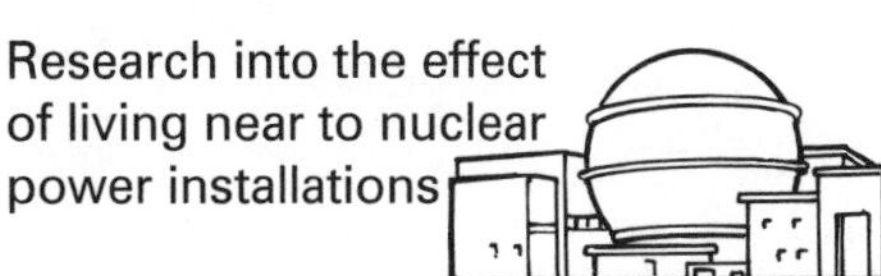

However, it is not just environmentalists who are responsible for monitoring environmental hazards to health, as emerging concerns from local communities and pressure groups demonstrate. Health Action Zones (HAZs) were set up from 1999 in underprivileged areas, with the aim of bringing together different sectors of local government such as housing, social services and health. HAZs are able to tackle the wider environmental issues that have an impact on health and, therefore, reduce health inequalities. Individuals can also have an impact on environmental approaches by such measures as reporting hazards in the environment, responsible recycling, and maintaining satisfactory standards of hygiene in their personal environments.

Public health approaches

Traditional public health approaches have tended to focus on concerns about sanitation and nutrition, as well as on the eradication of disease and control of infection. Penn and Thurtle (2005) describe public health as being concerned with the overall health and well-being of the community, and there are clear links to environmental approaches, as well as to issues of inequality and poverty. The interventions and individuals identified in the following figure will continue to be essential to the health of the community, but wider issues such as child poverty and socioeconomic deprivation also need to be tackled.

Fig 9.2 Public health resources to prevent illness

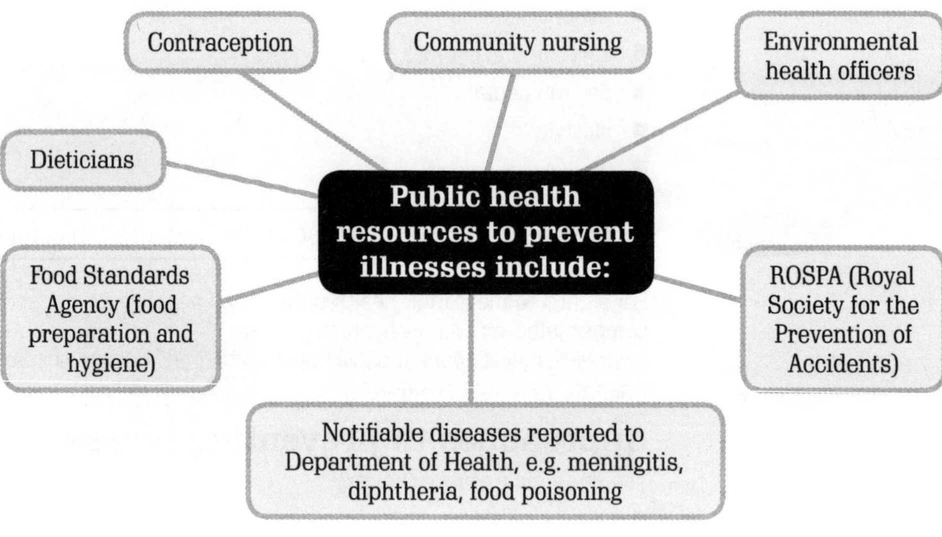

Fig 9.3 Effective health education is rooted in information

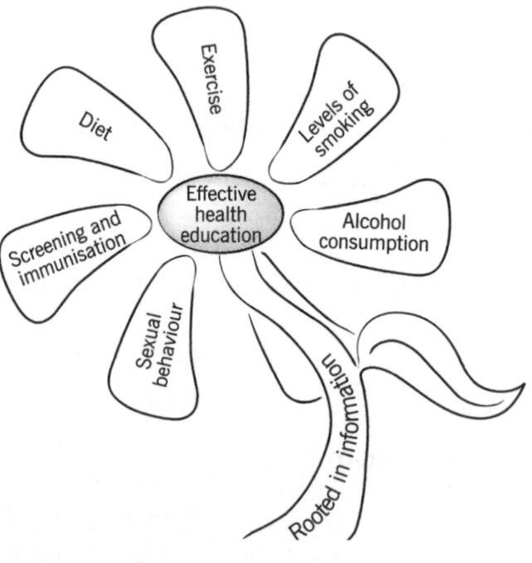

Immunisation

Refer to page 434 for a detailed discussion of immunisation.

Screening

Screening is the process of examining a whole population to determine who is showing signs of having a particular condition or disease and who may develop or be predisposed to a condition or disease. Screening in the UK is available for every child, with the consent of their parents.

Screening is important because it:

- enables early intervention where a problem is confirmed
- keeps parents informed about their child's progress or likely progress
- highlights the need for specific areas of stimulation for a child to meet their potential
- raises awareness for the future and allows informed decisions to be made, with or without genetic counselling.

Fig 9.4 Foetal screening

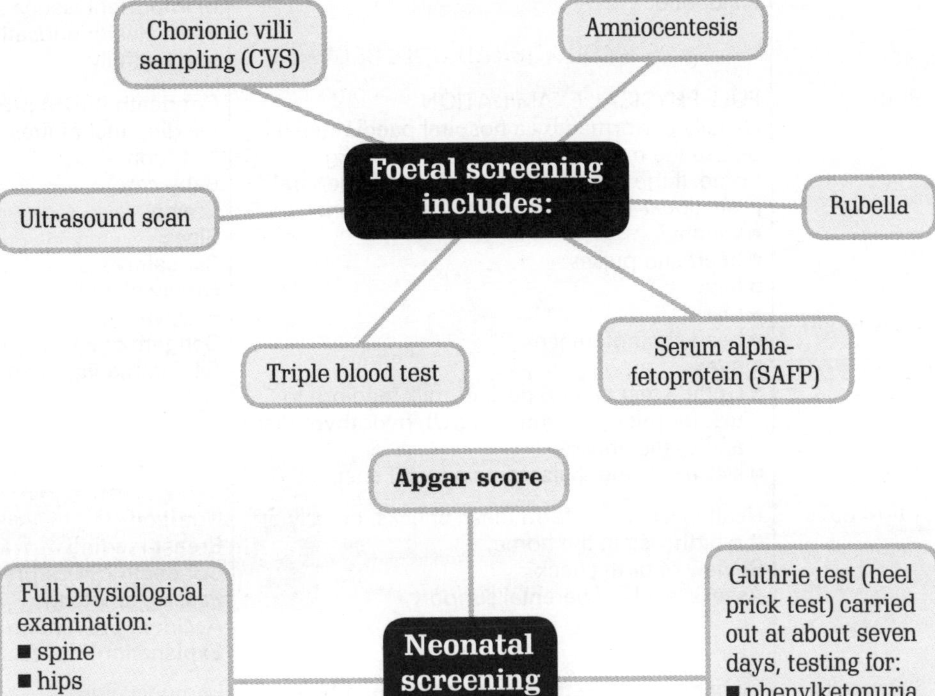

Fig 9.5 Neonatal screening

Neonatal screening includes:

- **Apgar score**
- Guthrie test (heel prick test) carried out at about seven days, testing for:
  - phenylketonuria (PKU)
  - hypothyroidism
  - cystic fibrosis
- **Reflexes**
- Full physiological examination:
  - spine
  - hips
  - organs
  - mouth and palate

Refer back to Unit 3, pages 113 and 118, for further information on the Apgar score and the primitive reflexes present at birth.

Fig 9.6 Infant screening

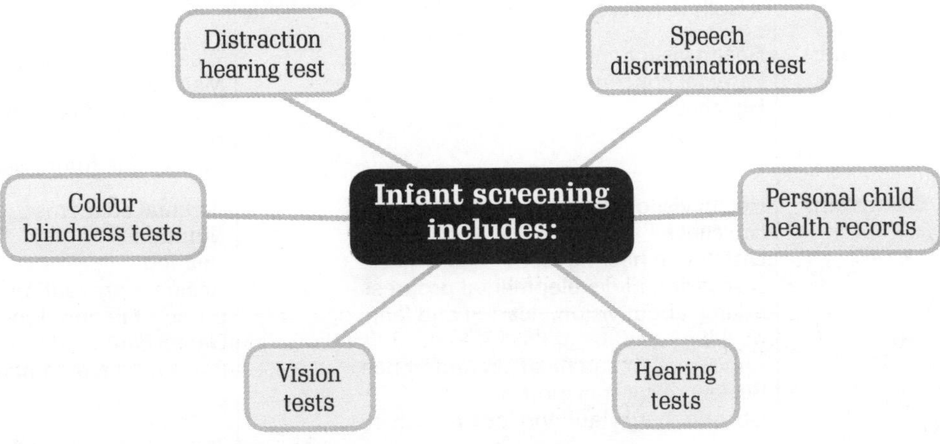

The above tests are carried out on all young infants. Any concerns are followed up with support from appropriate specialists (e.g. speech therapist, paediatrician).

The table below describes a general screening programme following a child through the earliest years.

Table 9.1 The child health screening programme

Age	Screening procedure	Health promotion
	These procedures are performed by midwives, doctors and health visitors throughout childhood.	Health visitors discuss the following issues with parents and carers to heighten their awareness of important issues affecting their child at critical ages. Health education is offered appropriately and tactfully.
Birth	FULL PHYSICAL EXAMINATION Usually performed by a hospital paediatrician before the mother and baby are discharged home. If the baby is born at home the general practitioner will conduct the examination: ■ weight ■ heart and pulses ■ hips ■ testes ■ head circumference ■ eyes ■ Guthrie test (after 6 days of milk feeding) to test for phenylketonuria (PKU), hypothyroidism and cystic fibrosis ■ sickle cell and thalassaemia test if suspected	Cot death (SIDS) prevention Feeding techniques Nutrition Baby care Crying Sleep Car safety Family planning Passive smoking Dangers of shaking baby Sibling management
10–14 days	Health visitors perform these checks, usually at the birth visit in the home. Review of birth check Assess levels of parental support	Nutrition Breast-feeding Cot death (SIDS) prevention Passive smoking Accident prevention: bathing, scalding and fires Explanation of tests and results
6–8 weeks	All babies receive this check performed by the GP and health visitor. REVIEW: Parental concerns, e.g. vision, hearing, activity Risk factors, including family history of abnormalities FULL EXAMINATION INCLUDING: ■ weight ■ head circumference ■ length ■ hip check ■ testes ■ eyes: squint, movement, ■ tone and general development ■ heart and pulses ■ Guthrie test result given to parents	Immunisation Nutrition and dangers of early weaning Accidents: falls, fires, over-heating, scalds Hearing Recognition of illness in babies and what action to take, e.g. fever management Crying Sleeping position Cot death (SIDS) prevention Passive smoking Review of car safety
2–4 months	Health visitor check Parental concerns Hip check	Weighing as appropriate Maintain previous health promotion Promotion of language and social development Hearing Discourage future use of baby walkers
6–9 months	Health visitor check Hip check Distraction hearing test Discussion of developmental progress asking about vision, hearing and language development Check weight and head circumference Review of car transport Observe behaviour and look for squints	Parental concerns Nutrition Hearing Accident prevention: fires, choking, scalding, burns, stair and door gates, fire guards, etc. Dental care Play and development needs

Source: Keene (1999, pp. 90–1)

Educational approaches

Educational approaches are usually underpinned by the idea that giving individuals the knowledge and understanding to improve their health will enable them to make the correct decisions. This can be achieved by the dissemination of information about health and well-being, but effectiveness can be affected by the quality of the information given and the right of the individual to accept or reject the information. Schools and early years settings are likely to take an educational approach to health promotion and will foster the acquisition of skills, as well as knowledge.

Educational approaches include health promotion programmes.

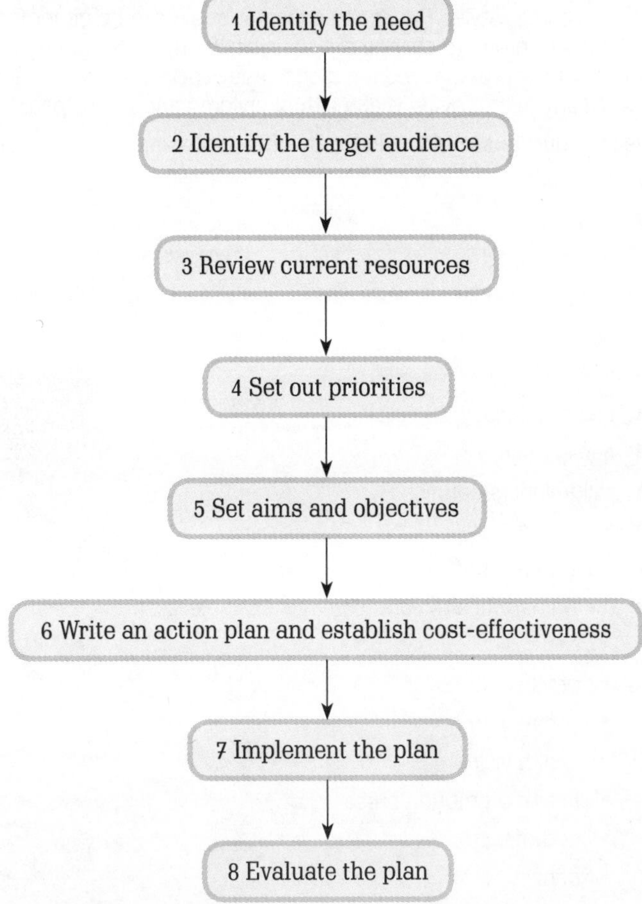

Fig 9.7 Health promotion programmes: planning a health promotion campaign

Most local health authorities have a health promotion office, often situated in a main hospital. This is an excellent source of information. Often there is provision for researching and reading current literature, and the facility to order a vast array of resources, including printed literature, videos and three-dimensional aids. Many resources are available in alternative forms, such as audiotapes and Braille, and translated into a range of languages.

Health promotion staff are often willing to attend functions and provide display materials. Sometimes these are free of charge, or a small charge is made to cover administration costs. Before developing a new health promotion resource, it is worth finding out if there is already sufficient material on the market. There is no point in re-inventing the wheel – your efforts would be better placed in developing something that is really needed.

Health-related charities produce their own **health education** materials.

The Health Education Authority has now been amalgamated into the Health Development Agency. It has a useful website for further information on health education.
www.hda.nhs.uk

The government site 'Wired for Health' is also a useful source of information on health education topics and activities.
www.wiredforhealth.gov.uk

Ways of living to bring about good health

Living a healthy life is often influenced by circumstances, but it is also influenced by the people around us, family and friends as well as professionals. These can be termed our 'health educators'.

A health educator is anyone who has influence over someone else with regard to their health choices and lifestyle. The health educator's role can be either formal or informal; some attempts to promote change are clear, while others are more covert (disguised). The high levels of peer pressure seen in modern-day society increase the need for a sensitive approach particularly in improving the health of children and young people.

Health educators could include any of the following:

- parents
- siblings
- grandparents
- extended family
- peer group
- teachers
- preschool/playgroup staff
- nursery staff
- childminders/nannies
- after-school staff
- playscheme staff
- the primary health care team, for example:
  - GP
  - practice nurse
  - community nurse
  - health visitor
  - health promotion nurse
  - midwife
  - dentist
  - orthodontist
  - dental hygienist
  - pharmacist
  - optician
  - chiropodist
  - counsellor
- the media, for example:
  - television
  - newspapers
  - journals
  - magazines
  - radio.

Health education allows people to make informed choices. Society cannot dictate; it can only advise. **Health promotion campaigns** aim to raise understanding of the consequences of the choices that each individual makes for themselves and, if parents, for their children. Those of us living in the West have come to expect our choices to be informed. The vaccination programmes carried out in the developing world with the object of achieving

herd immunity are clearly well meaning and contribute to the health and well-being of many children and their families. They do not, however, allow for informed choice.

Government-led health promotion

National targets to improve the health of the UK population are set out by the government. The White Paper *Our Healthier Nation* (Department of Health, 1998) cites the two main aims of the government as being to improve the health of:

- the population as a whole by increasing the length of people's lives and the number of years people spend free from illness
- the worst off in society and to narrow the health divide.

Current targets

The National Service Framework for Children, Young People and Maternity Services (Department of Health, 2004) is a 10-year programme that sets out clear standards for promoting the health and well-being of children and young people and extends the aims of *Our Healthier Nation*. Key priorities include:

- early identification of illnesses, environmental factors or activities that may lead to ill health
- the promotion of healthy diets and physical exercise for children
- ensuring that children's emotional and social well-being is maximised
- keeping children and young people safe
- advice on avoiding alcohol, smoking, drug-taking and substance abuse
- reducing the risks of teenage pregnancy.

Factors affecting health

Lalonde (1974), who is considered to be the founder of modern health practice, identified four 'fields' of health as shown in the diagram below.

Table 9.2 Factor effecting health

Environmental influences
Extent and nature of health services
Genetic and biological influences
Individual lifestyle

Environmental influences

Environment and health status are inextricably linked and the type of environment or geographical location in which a child lives can exert powerful effects on their health.

Apart from the obvious environmental dangers of heavily industrialised areas, traffic fumes and pollution, a child's health will be influenced by the type and quality of housing in which they live and the amount of access to clean air and open spaces; it is known that there are links between living in socioeconomically deprived areas and having lower quality of life and poorer health. Rates of accidental injuries are also known to be significantly higher in deprived areas with poorly maintained housing stock and high volumes of traffic.

Extent and nature of health services

Although the health of the general population has increased in recent years, there are still significant differences in health between social classes and ethnic groups. Moore (2002) suggests that the minority groups that are most in need of health interventions are less likely to gain access to them, owing to the social and economic barriers that prevent take-up of services. The National Service Framework for Children, Young People and Maternity Services is part of the Every Child Matters Agenda for Change and represents an opportunity to redress health inequalities for children and their families.

Every Child Matters Agenda for Change
www.everychildmatters.gov.uk/health/nhs

Genetic and biological influences

Genetic and biological factors influence our health, but we have only limited influence over them; we can only modify some of the known outcomes. Identification of the specific genes responsible for some conditions include the identification of Down's syndrome as a trisomy of chromosome 21 and, more recently, the advances in identifying ovarian cancer as C125.

Clearly, early identification through gene technology can be extremely helpful in alleviating some of the long-term problems of various conditions, but the manipulation of genes also raises a range of ethical issues.

The UK government recognises that many factors affect health and has categorised these factors as shown in the table below, based on Lalonde's 'health field' concept.

Table 9.3 Factors affecting health

Fixed	Social and economic	Environmental	Lifestyle	Access to services
Genes	Poverty	Air quality	Diet	Education
Sex	Employment	Housing	Physical activity	NHS
Ageing	Social exclusion	Water quality	Smoking	Social services
		Social environment	Alcohol	Transport
			Sexual behaviour	Leisure
			Drugs	

Refer back to Unit 3, page 110, for information on genetic inheritance.

Causes of ill health

The **causes of ill health** are many and varied. The following summaries are based on *Our Healthier Nation* (Department of Health, 1998).

Social and economic factors affecting health

Social and economic factors affecting health include poverty, unemployment and social exclusion; these can make it hard for some people to focus on their health and, for example, give up smoking. Smoking may be something that they feel gives them pleasure and keeps them going. Having limited access to shops can often mean buying from smaller (more expensive) local stores and therefore using limited resources in uneconomic ways. It is recognised that, although people often acknowledge what steps they need to take to improve their health, the level of hardship and social exclusion that they face makes it difficult for them to act upon it. Common conditions prevalent in the lower social classes include a higher rate of infection, respiratory disease and depression.

In 1980, the Black Report noted the significance of social, economic and environmental influences on health. It referred to the issues that were at the heart of the welfare state:

- health care
- social care
- welfare benefits

and how these had been seen as a means to reduce the differences between the social classes. However, as the report pointed out, even after 40 years of the NHS, appropriate provision was still not being made.

Environmental factors affecting health

Some of the environmental factors affecting health are pollution, inadequate housing and lack of sufficient heating and lighting. Living in an atmosphere of fear or mistrust can also affect health. Crime and racial tension in communities has a direct impact on health and mental well-being, and workplace stress also takes its toll on many people in the employment sector owing to heavier workloads, increased targets and greater pressures to meet deadlines.

Lifestyle factors affecting health

The **lifestyle factors affecting health** are largely choices that we make about how we live, perhaps in response to outside influences over which we have little control. For example, longer working days and the accompanying mental exhaustion have, for some people, led to a decrease in the level of their physical activity.

Longer working hours lead many people to rely on fast foods and freezer meals, in place of the home cooking that was usual in past generations.

Dependence on smoking, alcohol and recreational drugs has increased, particularly in young people.

'In 1996 28% of boys aged 15 and 33% of girls aged 15 smoked regularly and these figures are rising' (Department of Health, 1998, 2.21).

Lopez *et al*. (1994) estimate that: 'for every 1,000 young smokers, one will be murdered, six will be killed in a road accident and 250 will die before their time because they smoke' (cited in Department of Health, 1998).

Teenage pregnancy rates continue to rise, reducing the opportunities for education, training and employment for these young people, and continuing the cycle of disadvantage.

You may find it helpful to refer back to the cycle of disadvantage in Unit 6, page 287.

Fig 9.8 Teenage pregnancy rates continue to rise

remember If you are able to explain the meaning of something to another person, it is likely that you have a clear understanding of it yourself.

Access to services

The government summarises the impact of having access to high-quality services as follows:

> 'A decent education gives children the confidence and capacity to make healthier choices.
>
> Leisure services have a real influence on health.
>
> Ill health is not spread evenly across our society.
>
> The link between poverty and ill health is clear. In nearly every case the highest incidence of illness is experienced by the worst off social classes.'

(Department of Health, 1998)

activity
INDIVIDUAL WORK 9.1

P1

M1

1 Make a list of factors that affect the health and physical development of children. Use the statement above to start you off.
2 Give a written explanation of what each factor can mean to a child's health and general well-being.
3 Try voicing your explanations to a friend.

Government plans for improving health

The main ethos (distinctive feature) of central government plans for improving health is to work in co-operation with local health authorities. This involves setting out overall health targets for the nation but encouraging interpretation of the targets by local health authorities, according to the needs of the local population, in consultation with health professionals and community representatives. These are known as health improvement plans (**HImPs**) and are three-year programmes.

The development of this government-led approach fits in with the recommendations of the World Health Organization's programme *Health for All 2000*, in which the WHO states that:

> 'The focus of the health care system should be on primary health care – meeting the basic needs of each community through services provided as close as possible to where people live and work, readily accessible to all, and based on full participation.'
>
> (WHO, 1985, page 5)

Extending life expectancy

As already discussed, as individuals we can make lifestyle choices that help maintain good health. These choices will hopefully also help to prolong our lives. At government level there are also targets to support us. Currently there are four priority health areas cited in government targets:

- heart disease and stroke
- accidents
- cancer
- mental health.

The government targets for each priority health area are set out below and on the Nelson Thornes website together with a table indicating the proposed contract for how the targets can be met, nationally, locally and individually. Each table includes social and economic, environmental, lifestyle and service issues that can be addressed.

Heart disease and stroke

By 2010, the government target is 'to reduce the death rate from heart disease and stroke and related illnesses amongst people under 65 years by at least a further third'.

Accidents

The government target for accidents is 'to reduce accidents by at least a fifth'.

Cancer

The government target for cancer is 'to reduce the death rate from cancer amongst people under 65 years by at least a further fifth'.

Mental health

The government target with regard to mental health is 'to reduce the death rate from suicide and undetermined injury by at least a further sixth'.

Look on the Nelson Thornes website for tables relating to the national contracts for heart disease and stroke; accidents; cancer; and mental health. www.nelsonthornes.com/btec

activity
INDIVIDUAL WORK 9.2

D1

1 Make a copy of the table below and list on it the ways in which you think each of these priority health areas could have an impact on the health and physical development of children. Consider both the short-term and long-term impacts.

2 Give a detailed explanation of the potential effects of two of the factors on your list.

Table 9.4

Heart disease and stroke		Accidents	
Short-term impact	Long-term impact	Short-term impact	Long-term impact

Factors affecting children's health and physical development

Other factors that affect the health and physical development of children are shown in Fig 9.9:

Fig 9.9 Factors that affect the health and physical development of children

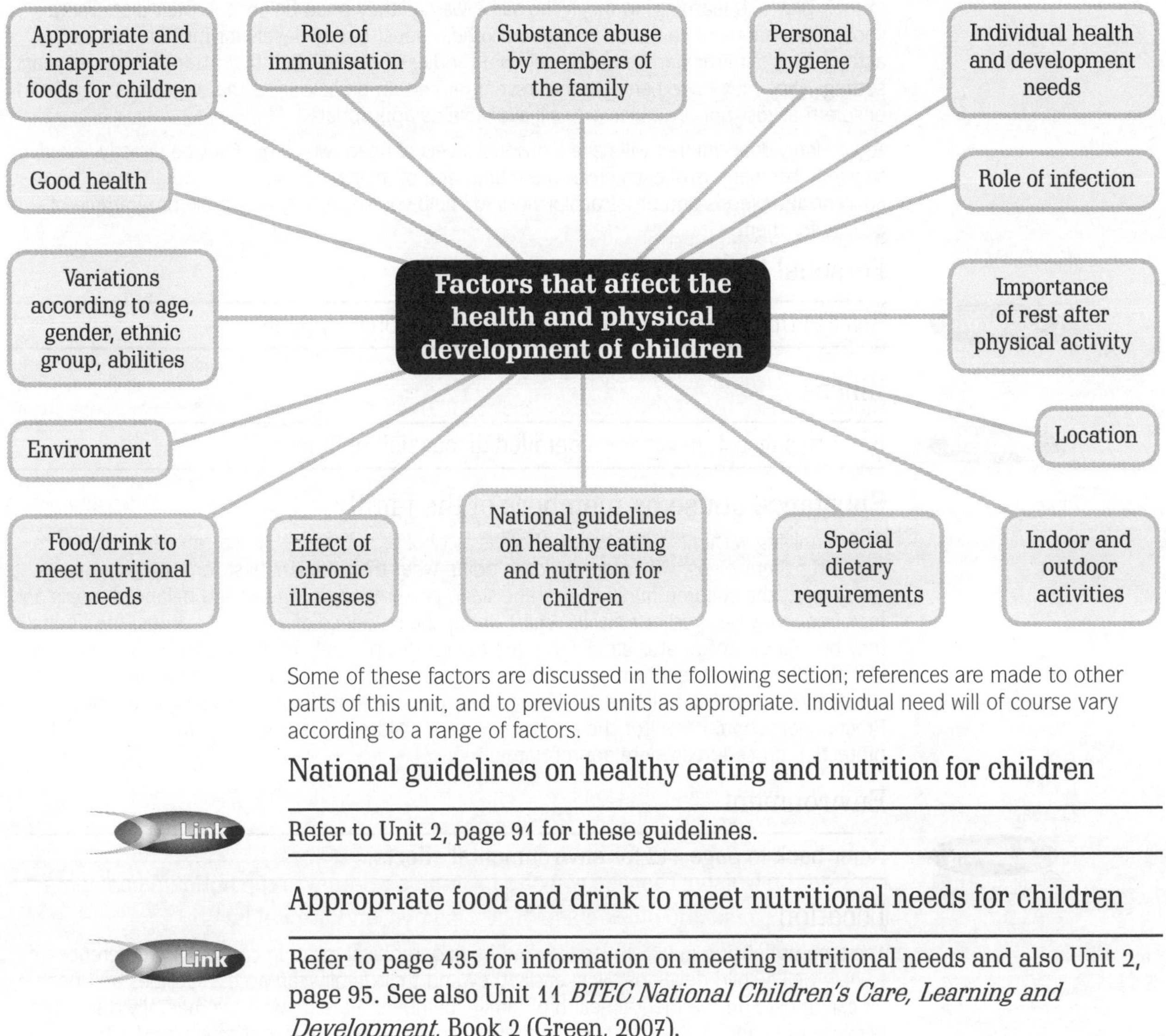

Some of these factors are discussed in the following section; references are made to other parts of this unit, and to previous units as appropriate. Individual need will of course vary according to a range of factors.

National guidelines on healthy eating and nutrition for children

Link

Refer to Unit 2, page 91 for these guidelines.

Appropriate food and drink to meet nutritional needs for children

Link

Refer to page 435 for information on meeting nutritional needs and also Unit 2, page 95. See also Unit 11 *BTEC National Children's Care, Learning and Development*, Book 2 (Green, 2007).

Special dietary requirements

Link

Refer to Unit 2, page 95 and pages 428–431 for information on special diets.

Indoor and outdoor activities

To support and encourage healthy development, practitioners should plan and set up a range of indoor and outdoor activities to encourage:

- balance
- co-ordination
- development of gross and fine motor skills
- manipulation skills
- hand–eye co-ordination
- extension of skills.

A useful source of information would be Unit 12, Physical Activities for Children, in *BTEC National CCLD*, Book 2 (Green, 2007).

Rest after physical activity

At times, children seem to have endless energy, but it is important that there is balance in their play and learning, in much the same way as they need balance in their diet. There should be periods of calm and relaxation to help boost energy levels for further physical activity. This is particularly essential when a toddler or young child first attends an early years setting. They may have been used to resting at certain times during the day, and staff should ensure that rest opportunities are still available as appropriate.

Again, individual children will have individual levels of need, which may not be directly linked to age. Observations of each child, the monitoring of their progress, including attitude, concentration levels and physical alertness will help you to identify a suitable programme of activity for them.

Personal hygiene

Refer to Unit 2, page 471, for guidance on personal hygiene.

Illness

Refer to pages 418–433 for a detailed discussion of illness.

Substance abuse by members of the family

Children living within families where there is alcohol or substance abuse can easily be left to look after themselves, with older children doing what they think is best for younger siblings. As a result, the children may have erratic sleep patterns, lack regular and balanced meals and may frequently be tired or unwell. Whilst under the influence of alcohol or drugs, the adults may be unaware of what their children are doing; this not only puts the children at increased risk of suffering accidents within the home but also means that they live in an environment where there is less stimulation, praise and awareness of how their needs should be met. Practitioners should monitor the progress of such children carefully, being mindful of child protection procedures where appropriate.

Environment

Refer back to page 412 for environmental effects.

Location

The type of housing in which you live and its geographical location can make a difference to how well a child develops. How easily they and their family can access facilities and fresh air can impact on the mental health of family members. Parents who are mentally distracted because of financial, housing or any other concern are likely to find it much harder to remain focused on identifying what is best for their children and meeting their needs.

The table below summarises the main effects on health of the three socioeconomic factors: poverty, housing and unemployment. Use the case studies that follow it to explore socioeconomic issues further.

Table 9.5 Socioeconomic factors affecting health

Poverty	Housing	Unemployment
Money problems	High-rise flats/isolation	Lowest income group
Unpaid bills	Lack of stimulus	Low self-esteem
Debts	Insufficient heat	Stigma
Lack of leisure activities	Overcrowding	Social exclusion
Poor diet	Lack of labour-saving equipment	Boredom
	Disordered communities	Depression
	Communities in fear	

case study 9.2

Wilson, Marlow and Maisie

The Johnston family lives in a two-bedroom flat on the sixth floor of a high-rise flat in north London. Mr Johnston is a builder who is currently unemployed; Mrs Johnston was a cashier in a supermarket but has not worked since her children were born. Wilson is 10, Marlow is eight and Maisie is two.

The family have been asking to be rehoused since before Maisie was born as they have very limited space, and Maisie still shares a bedroom with her parents out of necessity, not choice.

Mr Johnston takes the boys to school each morning, but then returns to the flat. He spends long hours staring out of the window. His (initially) weekly visits to the Job Centre have ceased, as he has lost faith that he will regain employment. Mrs Johnston rarely goes out because the lift in the block of flats is unreliable and Maisie is only just walking. Maisie is quite a sickly child; she sleeps a great deal during the day and is unsettled at night. The estate is a place of tension, and the boys do not play out after school. None of the family goes out after dark and friends are not encouraged to visit.

activity
INDIVIDUAL WORK

1 What socioeconomic issues can you identify?
2 What do you consider will be the likely impact on the health of the children?
3 What do you consider will be the likely impact on the health of the parents?
4 Is there likely to be any long-term impact on Maisie's development if the family's situation does not change?
5 Could the Johnston family do anything else to improve their situation, do you think?

case study 9.3

Arabella, Chloe and Josh

The Stenner family lives in a four-bedroom house in north London. Mr Stenner was an office manager in a company which has just gone into liquidation. He is now unemployed. Mrs Stenner is a qualified book-keeper but has not worked since her children were born. Arabella is 10, Chloe is 8 and Josh is 2. Mr and Mrs Stenner have owned their home for 12 years, and each child has their own bedroom.

Mrs Stenner and Josh take the girls to school each morning, returning home after coffee with friends. Mr Stenner spends long hours in the garden. He surfs the Internet to see what employment opportunities are available locally and is grateful that he does not have to stand and read the notice board at the local Job Centre. He is unsure whether he will find similar employment. Mrs Johnston is enjoying having her husband around more and Josh, who is an active little boy, loves helping him in the garden. The children have had to give up some of their out-of-school activities because of the family's reduced finances but are able to have friends to play instead.

activity
INDIVIDUAL WORK

1 What socioeconomic issues can you identify for this family?
2 Do you consider that there will be any likely impact on the health of the children?
3 Do you consider that there will be any likely impact on the health of the parents?
4 Is there likely to be any long-term impact on Josh's development if the situation for the family does not change?
5 Could the Stenner family do anything else to improve their situation, do you think?

Fig 9.10 What effect does housing have on the lifestyle of the people in it?

In many ways the situations for the Johnstons and the Stenners are similar, but think how the two case studies compare in real terms? Remember these examples for future reference. You may also find it helpful to refer back to the socioeconomic issues listed in the table on page 416.

Illness

The medical needs of a child clearly take precedence when they are ill, but their social, emotional and cognitive needs should also be taken into account. The **impact of ill health** can be wide reaching because illness can affect children in a number of ways, particularly emotionally, as they may feel confused or scared about what is happening to them. During periods of short-term illness a slight change in routine or diet does not normally have any significant impact, but with long-term conditions there can be considerable changes in behaviour, diet and habit that can be difficult to cope with.

Refer to pages 424–431 for details about some common chronic conditions.

Needs of children who are ill

Children's reaction to illness and its subsequent impact on them is directly linked to their age and stage of development. They need to have their questions answered honestly and be kept informed as to what will happen next, without alarming them unduly. As with adults, children are more likely to be able to cope with whatever treatment or investigation they need if they have some idea of what to expect.

It is important that children are not told that 'it won't hurt', if it clearly will, as this will be likely to affect their security even further and may cause them to lose their trust in the adults caring for them. In recent years, parents have been able to stay with their child in hospital for much of the time. This is partly due to the work of the organisation Action for Sick Children.

Action for Sick Children
www.actionforsickchildren.org

A child who is in full health is usually able to benefit from any of the opportunities that are offered to them, building on previous learning, practising their developing skills and enjoying the challenge of new experiences. However, when children are unwell, particularly if they have a chronic condition, there will be times when they are unable to take up an opportunity, or join in with a new experience, because they are simply not feeling well enough. Early years practitioners should consider how these children can best be supported in their activities and new learning, ensuring that they receive as much help as possible to maximise their ability to learn.

Factors to consider in relation to a child who is ill or has a chronic condition include the following:

- appetite
- behaviour
- social interaction
- learning.

Fig 9.11 Impact of ill health on children

The impact of ill health on children

Apetite
- Appetite may become poor or fussy.
- Nutritional intake may become unbalanced.
- Snacks may be eaten rather than full meals, changing food intake routines.
- Extra treats may beome an expectation from which a child is not easily 'weaned'.

Emotional behaviour
- Behaviour often regresses, being less tolerant and more demanding.
- A child often needs more direct comforting.
- A child's trust can be easily lost.
- A child may display attention-seeking behaviour.
- Clinging is common, as children are often feeling frightened and uncertain.
- Unpredictable behaviour swinging from excitement to tantrums quite easily.

Social interaction
- An ill child may be less interested in interacting with others.
- Children may become withdrawn and isolated through their illness.
- There may be a greater emphasis on interacting with adults, losing the skills needed to interact and negotiate in play situations.

Cognitive skills
- Formal learning may cease or be restricted by on-going or debilitating treatment.
- Children may begin to lapse behind their peers if treatment is long term.
- Passive stimulation may be all a child can cope with.

Professional Practice

- Children need a great deal of emotional support during periods of illness.
- Patience and understanding are vital.
- Children need clear explanations as to what will be happening to them, including routine procedures such as temperature taking and blood pressure checks.
- All explanations should be appropriate for the child's age and level of understanding.

Life-limiting illness

When a child has a life-limiting or terminal illness, the family will benefit from support. As well as the needs of the child, those of their parents and other family members should be taken into account. Supporting the family gives indirect support to the child.

Families face a range of difficulties when a child is ill. There are changes to the usual routine, particularly if the child is in hospital or a **hospice**, and there may be times when family members feel isolated because they are unable to leave the family home, or because they need to stay with their child in hospital for prolonged periods.

Meeting other families in similar circumstances is an important source of support; they may perhaps link up via support groups for the condition or via parent networks set up locally or within the hospital itself. These groups enable parents to share experiences and discuss and explore issues of mutual concern. They are able to meet others whose child has reached a different stage in their condition.

Families need support from many different people, for many different reasons.

Health professionals will:

- reassure parents that they are experienced and knowledgeable about their child's condition
- reassure parents about their child's condition and any prognosis
- keep parents informed about day-to-day changes in their child's condition and what procedures are planned or being considered
- provide information about the treatment options about which they may need to make decisions
- link parents with support groups for families with a child with the same condition
- occupy siblings while parents speak with specialists, enabling the parents to concentrate on the information they are being given without distraction.

Employers, schools and others will:

- support the parents' need to be with their ill child
- support the daily running of households when a child is in hospital
- offer educational support if home tutoring is needed
- support families on low incomes to help finance hospital visits
- support siblings by understanding that they too have needs and feelings during the illness or hospitalisation of another child in the family
- give appropriate levels of information to siblings in accordance with parents' wishes.

Role and responsibilities of early years workers

When supporting the relatives of a terminally ill child, early years practitioners need to provide practical non-specific support, for example, making them feel welcome and having time for them, as well as more specific support, such as keeping the parents informed of a child's progress and of changes in routine or to type or dosage of medication.

Support from early years practitioners should be flexible to enable the parents to continue some degree of normality with the other children in their family.

Professional Practice

- **Sensitivity is needed at all times when supporting terminally ill children and their families.**
- **It is important to remember that parents will often forget, or not take in, what they have heard, because they are distressed at the time.**
- **Siblings need support too.**

Financial implications for families

Extra financial needs can be incurred when a child is ill. One parent may have to give up working temporarily to take on the caring role. Additional resources may be needed to cope with, for example increased heating costs, additional wash loads, and so on. Support can often be obtained from a medical social worker, who can help with such issues as the cost of transport or childcare facilities. They may also be involved in arranging for interpreters or an advocate for families where English is not the first language or the parents have difficulty in understanding or expressing information.

Parents in financial difficulties can apply for support to organisations such as the Benefits Agency, the Citizens Advice Bureau and other groups dealing with welfare issues. These provide both financial and practical help.

Refer back to Unit 1, page 23, for information on advocates.

Professional Practice

- **It can be helpful to use published materials, locally displayed posters and fliers, and the Internet, to put together a range of contact details for support groups that could help the parents in your area, or at your setting.**
- **Giving out contact details can be a very helpful and supportive thing to do, but the action is only of help if the information is up to date. Re-check details from time to time, and update and discard as appropriate.**

Care settings for children with illnesses

Treatment can take place in the home or in hospital and, when children are terminally ill, a hospice. The need for medical treatment or intervention is of course a priority, but it should not overshadow the child's need to play. Play is invaluable in reducing stress and uncertainty and can offer a positive focus for the whole family. The age and stage of a child's development and understanding will determine how much they are told about their illness and treatment and which approaches are taken.

In early years settings, practitioners should be flexible to incorporate a child's needs. They must ensure that reporting procedures with regard to illness whilst at the setting are clear and known to all staff. The procedure for administering medicines should also be fully understood by all those involved.

Refer to Unit 2, page 37, for details on administering medicines.

Treatment in the home

Common childhood illnesses will always be treated at home, unless there are complications. The parents' role will expand to include nursing skills and play provision, taking into account the child's age and general interests. Children may have less energy than usual and may spend much of the day resting; therefore activities will need to be easily managed, offering satisfying play without too much effort.

Suitable activities include colouring and drawing, dot-to-dot books and simple puzzles. Construction materials that are easily handled and not too fiddly are better than those that require a great deal of concentration and dexterity. Activities involving small pieces should be placed on deep-sided trays if the child is in bed, to avoid knocking off vital parts which may affect the child's satisfaction with the activity as a whole.

Children like to read and hear familiar books and stories, often asking to have them repeated many times. This is a common practice with young children generally, and, when unwell, slightly older children may find it reassuring too.

case study 9.4

Lucy

Lucy is three and a half years old and currently has chickenpox. She is absolutely covered in spots and also has them internally. She has been in great discomfort and very distressed at times but is beginning to feel a little better. Lucy's mother has asked you for advice concerning the best way to occupy Lucy.

activity
INDIVIDUAL WORK

1 What toys and activities would you suggest for Lucy, bearing in mind how she is feeling?
2 Would you recommend that her mother plays with Lucy, or for Lucy to play alone?
3 What would you have suggested for an older child to do in similar circumstances?
4 How would you occupy a young toddler in this situation?

Treatment in hospital

For some children, a stay in hospital becomes a necessity either because of illness or an accident. **Preparing children for hospital** is an important part of the practitioner's role. Clearly, it is easier to prepare a child for a planned admission to hospital, as there is time to talk about it in advance at a pace suitable to the child's age and understanding, whereas when a child is admitted as an emergency there is little time to talk about what they will see, hear or experience. Children are only admitted to hospital when it is absolutely necessary. Whenever possible they are treated at home.

A week or so before the due admission date, discussion about the hospital can be introduced; opportunities to role play hospital 'scenes' may be very helpful to a child. If the hospital offers a pre-admission tour of the ward, this can be very useful in acclimatising a child to what to expect when they arrive, thereby helping to reduce their anxiety and consequently their parents' too.

Preparation a few days before the child is admitted

During the few days prior to the child's admission to the ward, it is useful to talk through the information sent from the hospital. This will usually give details of what is on offer in the playroom and details of the hospital school, together with what the child needs to take into hospital. It can be helpful to let the child buy something new to take into hospital, such as pyjamas, or a flannel and toothbrush.

Hospital staff recognise the need for children to take with them whatever comforts them. Older children may at times feel embarrassed to take in their teddy or comforter (in case their friends visit them). Parents could take a teddy along without the child knowing; teddy will then be there to comfort the child when they need it without the child feeling foolish.

During this time, children should be reassured if they are anxious and have their questions answered clearly and as honestly as possible.

Once the child is on the ward

It is important for all children to become familiar with the layout of the hospital ward, particularly older children, as this will allow them more autonomy and enable them to feel more in control.

Children will need to be introduced to the hospital play staff, usually a nursery nurse, who will often be trained in hospital play. Encouraging children to select play materials as soon as possible after arrival will occupy them both physically and mentally and help to ease some (understandable) nerves.

On hospital wards, there are various staff especially trained to work with children. These include:

- play specialists, who are often nursery nurses who have qualified initially through level 3 courses and then taken a specialist course in hospital play
- teachers, who work with the children who are well enough, linking activities to the appropriate stage of the National Curriculum or, for younger children, the Foundation Stage Curriculum
- nursery nurses, who support the work of the teachers and play specialists. They are often on duty outside of 'school hours' and encourage and arrange a variety of play activities for children of all ages. Nursery nurses are often happy to involve the siblings of the children who are currently having treatment.

Play on the ward often includes medical props to help familiarise children with what they may see, for example medical kits, involving stethoscope, eye patch, and so on. Activities may include syringe painting (without the needles, of course) or making plaster casts of children's hands. A range of books giving positive images of hospital routines and treatments are usually to be found on hospital wards. Teddies and dolls can be bandaged, injected or given other treatments that it is felt appropriate to simulate.

Treatment in hospices

Many terminally ill children are cared for in hospitals or at home. Others benefit from time in a children's hospice, which is a place of care and treatment specifically for terminally ill children. Although there are not huge numbers of hospices for children, these play an important role.

Some hospices have a community team who will help to care for the child in the family home. Hospices offer support for parents and families, as well as the ill child, and they discuss with the family what will meet the needs of the child and the whole family and do what they can to meet those needs.

Hospices also offer training in bereavement skills to other professionals who may become involved with families who have lost a child, or will shortly face such a loss.

The support offered to families of a terminally ill child involves:

- respite care
- care of siblings
- emotional support
- practical help and advice
- opportunities to grieve
- opportunities to share experiences with others.

In supporting the child, hospices offer:

- 'normal' routines whenever possible
- opportunities to discuss their futures

- opportunities to talk about their families and what will happen when they die (where this is applicable).

Staff who work in terminal care need to be sensitive to the parents' emotionally fragile state. They try where they can to build up a rapport with them, which can help the staff to support the parents after they have been bereaved. Becoming aware of a family's cultural practice is important, to ensure that cultural traditions are both valued and maintained.

Families will go through different stages of grieving. There will usually be shock, even if the death was known to be imminent, followed by confusion, fear, anger and guilt. Parents may feel that they will never be able to cope again and that they no longer have a role in life. These feelings can be particular acute if they have cared for their child intensively over a long period of time. Anger and guilt arise, as the unfairness of the situation takes hold. Why their child? What had the child done to deserve such a death? They may also start to question whether they did all they could have done for the child.

This is a difficult time for families and also for those who work to support them.

Conditions

The following section provides an outline of a range of conditions that you may come across. Apart from gastroenteritis, which is more likely to be acute, they are chronic conditions.

Gastroenteritis

What is gastroenteritis?
Gastroenteritis is the most common irritant of the stomach and intestinal lining.

What causes gastroenteritis and how is it spread?

- It is caused by bacteria and viruses.
- It can be spread in food due to poor hygiene during food handling.
- It can be spread by direct or indirect contact.

Recognising gastroenteritis
Children appear unwell, lethargic and miserable before the onset of the main symptoms, which include:

- vomiting
- diarrhoea
- raised temperature
- loss of appetite.

Initial actions

- Only clear fluids (cooled boiled water) should be given for 24 hours.
- Dehydration drinks may be used for children over the age of one year, particularly if symptoms are severe.

Ongoing care

- Breastfed babies should continue to breastfeed as usual.
- If there is no improvement after 24 hours, medical advice should be sought, particularly in very young children.
- Continue with clear fluids, together with 'ice-pops' to give the child some sugar.
- Light foods should be offered when the child's appetite returns.
- Diet drinks are not considered to be suitable.

Possible complications

- Dehydration can easily occur in very young children and babies.
- If children cease to pass urine frequently, medical advice should be sought.
- Intravenous fluids may need to be given in severe cases.

Immunisation?
There is no immunisation available.

Incubation period and potential to infect others?

- There is no known incubation period.
- Strict hygiene is needed to try and minimise the spread of infection.
- Gastroenteritis often 'sweeps' through families, nurseries and schools.

Eczema

What is eczema?

Eczema is due to an allergic reaction and is common amongst young children. It dries the skin, forming itchy inflamed areas which crack open and often weep. It is extremely unpleasant and causes great misery to many children. Fortunately, the majority of children cease to be affected by eczema by the time they reach puberty. Some, however, continue to suffer from eczema, along with asthma (another allergic reaction).

What causes eczema?

Eczema is a reaction to a 'trigger factor'. These triggers vary between individuals, with common causes being dairy produce, washing powders and soaps. It can also be triggered or exacerbated by stress or excitement.

Recognising eczema

The initial signs of eczema usually appear between 3 and 18 months. It occurs initially on the face and scalp, the shins and forearms; later it affects the backs of knees, inside of the elbow joints and the ankles. Symptoms include:

- dry scaly skin which cracks and itches
- the itchy rash often weeps
- the sore areas crust over
- in the long term, the skin becomes thickened and leathery. Young children find it difficult to sleep due to the itching.

Initial actions

- If a child develops itchy or sore areas of skin, they should be seen by a health professional to confirm or discount a diagnosis of eczema.
- Childcare staff need to be aware that a child's condition may become more acute in extremes of weather. Children with eczema become very sensitive to changes in temperature.

Ongoing care

- It is important to keep the skin softened, using an emollient cream.
- Emollients should be applied regularly throughout the day, and this is particularly important after a bath. It can often be helpful to cover the affected area with cotton tubular sleeves (bandages).
- Special bath oils can be used to help remoisten the skin, which naturally loses its oils through bathing.
- Affected children should not use normal soaps; special preparations are available.
- Children should be taught to avoid any known trigger factors.
- Keeping fingernails cut short helps minimise scratching.
- Very young children may benefit from wearing cotton mittens at night.
- Loose cotton clothing helps the skin breathe and reduces chaffing of the skin.
- Some children need prescribed products to help control the effects of eczema.
  - Corticosteroids can be prescribed as creams or ointments for very intense phases.
  - Antihistamines are also used to reduce the itching, helping children to sleep better.
  - For some children, forms of Chinese medicine have been helpful in treating both eczema and psoriasis (under the guidance of a recognised and qualified practitioner).

> **remember**
> Any referral to an 'alternative' practitioner should always be with the full knowledge of the child's GP, as there could be contraindicative effects if treatment is used in conjunction with their current medication.

Possible complications

- Antibiotics, taken orally or as creams, may become necessary to counter the effects of secondary infections caused by excessive scratching.
- Children with severe eczema can become the victims of teasing. Early years staff should be ready to deal with this.

Familial?

- Many children with eczema are born into families where there are others with a range of allergic conditions.
- Many will have parents or older siblings who had eczema as a child.

Professional Practice

- Consideration is needed to ensure that children with eczema are not excluded from activities because of their condition.
- Applying creams to the affected areas during the day should be done without fuss and with some privacy.
- It is important to wear disposable gloves when applying the creams, to avoid any risk of introducing infection to the child and to prevent the absorption of corticosteroids into your own skin.

case study 9.5

Christopher

Christopher is four years old and is severely affected by eczema. His hands are leathery and regularly encrusted with scabs from the weeping sores. He is pale and lethargic most of the time due to lack of sleep and constant discomfort.

activity
INDIVIDUAL WORK

1 The other children in the nursery are reluctant to hold Christopher's hands; they say that his hands feel strange and rather unpleasant. How will you deal with this during circle games, such as 'Farmer's in the den', without making Christopher feel isolated or different?

2 Christopher loves finger-painting and playing in the sand and water. How will you ensure that his skin is protected while he plays? What precautions should you take?

Psoriasis

What is psoriasis?

Psoriasis is a severe skin condition, which most commonly appears from the age of 10 onwards but is occasionally seen in younger children where there is a strong family history of the condition.

What causes psoriasis?

- It is considered to be an inherited condition, but its cause is unknown.
- The first incidence of psoriasis often follows a period of stress or an infection involving damage to the skin.
- The most common form of psoriasis in young children is guttate psoriasis which causes small patches of the skin rash, often as a result of a severe sore throat.
- The skin cells form at a rate 10 times faster than the body discards cells, resulting in the thickened patches that appear on the skin.

remember

Any referral to an 'alternative' practitioner should always be with the full knowledge of the child's GP.

Recognising psoriasis

- A thickened red rash appears on the scalp, arms, legs and body; the rash is often covered with silvery scales.
- The rash is not usually itchy but may irritate through tightening the skin, and there is a general feeling of discomfort.

Initial actions

Referral to a dermatologist (skin specialist) is needed; the dermatologist will consider the severity of the condition and treat as appropriate, usually with medications similar to those used for eczema.

Ongoing care

- Treatment is with emollient creams, coal tar products and corticosteroids, both through direct application and used as bath oil.
- As with eczema, treatment with Chinese medicines may benefit some people with psoriasis.

Possible complications

- Secondary infections can occur.
- Social isolation is possible if the condition is very noticeable.
- Familial?
- Psoriasis is considered to be an inherited condition.
- It is also a condition for life, although for many people it can be managed quite well with medication.

Asthma

What is asthma?

Asthma is a condition of the lungs. It is a narrowing of the airways, which is reversible with the right treatment. The narrowing of the airways reduces the child's ability to breathe freely. The walls of the airways (bronchioles) swell and become inflamed. The inflamed airways secrete a sticky mass.

What causes asthma?

An asthma attack can be caused by a variety of 'triggers':

- infections
- going out into the cold air
- cigarette smoke
- exercise
- excitement or stress
- fumes (e.g. from cars)
- allergies to animals, pollen or dust
- food allergies.

Many children with asthma belong to families where allergies are common.

Fig 9.12 Triggers for asthma

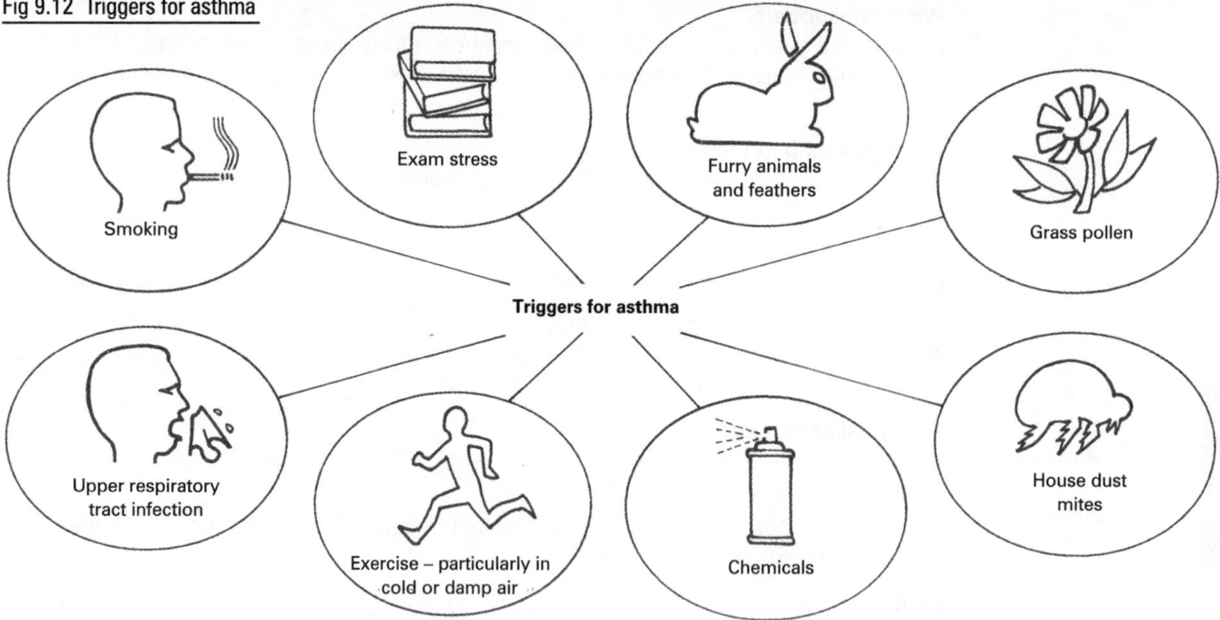

Recognising an asthma attack

Symptoms are:

- coughing
- shortness of breath
- wheezing
- a tightness in the chest area.

Initial actions

- You will need to keep calm in order to encourage calm in the child.
- If this is a child's first attack, seek medical help.

Managing an attack

Keene (1999) sets out a 10-point plan for managing an asthma attack:

1. Reassure the child.
2. Encourage relaxed breathing – slowly and deeply.
3. Loosen tight clothing around the neck.
4. Sit the child upright and leaning forward, supporting themselves with their hands in any comfortable position.
5. Stay with the child.
6. Give the child their bronchodilator to inhale if they are known to be asthmatic – dosage according to the GP's instructions.
7. Offer a warm drink to relieve dryness of the mouth.
8. Continue to comfort and reassure. Do not panic, as this would increase the child's anxiety which will impair their breathing.
9. When the child has recovered from a minor attack they can resume quiet activities.
10. Report the attack to the parents when the child is collected. If the child is upset by the episode, the parents should be contacted immediately.

An ambulance should be called if:

- It is the child's first known attack.
- After 5–10 minutes, there is no improvement in the child.
- The child becomes increasingly distressed and exhausted.
- Lips, mouth or face begin to go blue.

Ongoing care

There are two different types of inhalers:

- Preventers – these contain medicines to reduce the swelling and mucus in the airways; they are usually in brown/orange inhalers and are used on a regular basis to prevent asthma attacks.
- Relievers – these contain medication that dilates the airways; they are usually in blue inhalers and are used to relieve symptoms of wheezing and coughing when an attack occurs or are used prior to exercise to prevent an attack.

Possible complications

- Each year a small number of children die during an asthma attack.

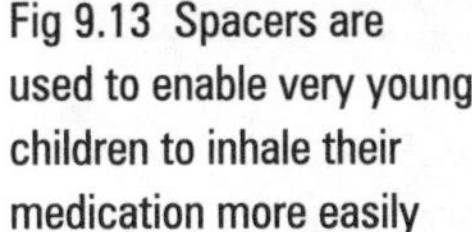
Fig 9.13 Spacers are used to enable very young children to inhale their medication more easily

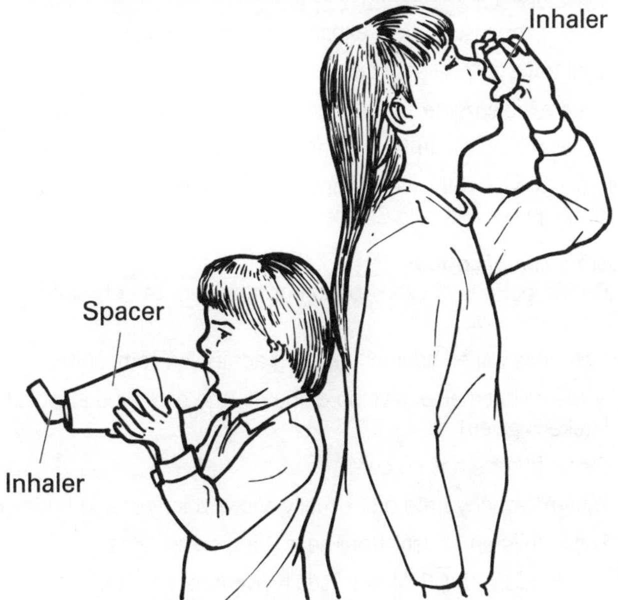

Professional Practice

- Each setting should have a written plan for each known asthmatic child, issued by the asthma nurse at the child's GP practice.

Cystic fibrosis (CF)

What is CF?

Cystic fibrosis is a serious genetic condition of the respiratory and digestive systems. It is a life-limiting condition in which the secretions produced by the lungs are unable to flow away in the normal manner. The secretions build up in the airways, subsequently restricting breathing. Risk of infection of the airways is high. The digestive tract is affected as the pancreas is not able to produce the appropriate enzymes needed to break down food and absorb it into the body's system.

What causes CF?

- Cystic fibrosis is inherited as an autosomal recessive condition.
- Approximately 1 in 1500 children has CF.
- It is more prevalent in some ethnic groups than in others. The highest incidence is seen in Caucasians (light-skinned people of European, North African, SW Asian and Indian origin). It is rare in families of African-Caribbean origin and almost non-existent in people of Far Eastern origin.

Recognising CF

- CF is present in some infants from birth. It is detected by the presence of a blockage (called meconium ileus) at the opening of the intestine.
- The Guthrie test at seven days after birth includes a test for CF.
- Infants not diagnosed at birth may fail to thrive during the first few months of life due to malabsorption of food.
- Chest infections and coughs can indicate chest problems associated with CF.
- Diarrhoea and fatty, offensive stools can indicate digestive problems associated with CF.

Initial actions

- Any suspicion of CF must be referred immediately to the GP.
- A 'sweat' test is occasionally the initial action, if parents have noticed a salty taste to their child's skin, but this form of testing can be quite distressing for a child.
- Genetic testing will confirm whether the suspected diagnosis is correct.

Ongoing care

The ongoing care of a child with cystic fibrosis involves:

- physiotherapy of the chest at regular intervals throughout the day to loosen secretions (known as percussion physiotherapy)
- regular exercise to help expand the lungs regularly
- antibiotics to prevent chest infections
- pancreatic enzyme supplements, taken at each mealtime to help absorb food
- a diet that is low in fat, but high in protein and carbohydrates.

Children with CF will have continuous care and support from a dietician, a community children's nurse and/or a CF specialist.

Possible complications

- During periods of exacerbation or infection, the physiotherapy sessions may need to be more intensive.
- Infections will sometimes result in admission to hospital.
- Some children also develop diabetes (the only type in which a high-carbohydrate/sugar intake is given).
- Cystic fibrosis has no cure.
- A high-carbohydrate diet usually allows a longer and better quality of life.
- Some children benefit from heart-lung transplants.
- Individuals with CF do not usually live into old age.

Diabetes mellitus (type 1 diabetes)

What is diabetes mellitus?

Diabetes mellitus is an endocrine disorder in which the pancreas does not make enough insulin. Insulin helps the body to use and store sugar. When it is not used efficiently the sugar overflows into the urine.

What causes diabetes mellitus?

- It is often triggered following a severe viral infection.
- It is not an inherited condition, but there is a familial trait to diabetes.

Recognising diabetes mellitus

- Most children are diagnosed following a sudden onset of the two most common symptoms:
  - extreme thirst
  - frequently passing urine.
- Also, the breath may smell of pear drops.
- Less obvious onset includes:
  - tiredness
  - constant lethargy
  - weight loss
  - loss of appetite
  - urinary tract infection due to excessive sugar in the urine.

Initial actions

- Medical diagnosis involves testing urine and blood for excessive sugar levels.
- A short stay in hospital is usual in order for the child's blood sugar levels to be stabilised and their dietary needs agreed and understood by parents.

Ongoing care

- Insulin injections and a carefully controlled diet will be necessary for life.
- Checks on blood sugar levels are taken (at least) daily.
- Diet will be monitored by a dietician.
- A 'healthy heart' diet is needed (high-fibre, low-sugar, low-fat).
- A return to hospital is unlikely, unless illness causes dehydration.

Possible complications

- Dehydration may occur.
- An imbalance of blood sugar levels can lead either to hypoglycaemia (sweating and clammy skin – child needs to be given extra sugar or a boost of sugar) or hyperglycaemia (sugar levels are too high, so extra insulin is needed).
- Signs of a hypoglycaemic attack include sweating, dizziness, confusion and rapid breathing. A snack or a glucose drink or similar should be given to the child. It is important that someone remains with the child until they have stabilised.
- Illness, under-dosing on insulin and sudden growth spurts can all affect the blood sugar level.
- Common reasons for hypoglycaemia are:
  - unusual exercise (e.g. extra games)
  - not enough carbohydrate (e.g. missed snack)
  - too much insulin (e.g. mistaken dose).
- Common reasons for hyperglycaemia are:
  - less exercise than usual (e.g. missed games)
  - not enough insulin (e.g. growing out of dose)
  - too much carbohydrate (e.g. extra snacks)
  - sudden excitement or strain (e.g. exams)
  - infection (e.g. a cold).

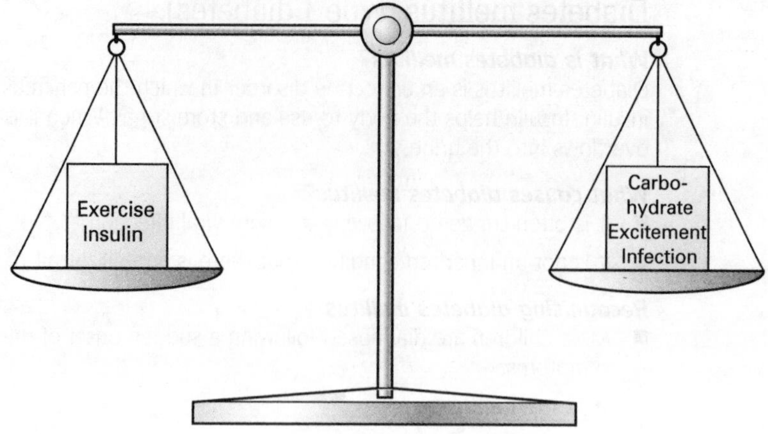

Fig 9.14 Blood glucose is kept steady by a balance between exercise and insulin on one side and carbohydrate, excitement and infection on the other

See *Child Health: Care of the Child in Health and Illness* by Keene (1999, page 259).

Professional Practice

- Supplies of glucose tablets should be taken with you when you accompany a child with diabetes on any outing.
- Supplies should be readily available in the school or early years setting.
- Children with diabetes should be closely observed during exercise, particularly if they are trying something new.
- Contact numbers for parents should always be readily available.
- Staff working with a child with diabetes should be taught how to cope with their needs and any attacks.
- Privacy should be allowed when children have to test their blood sugar levels during the day.
- Catering staff should be informed and be able to deal with special dietary needs.
- Good long-term dietary care will help prevent other ill health, such as heart, liver and vascular disease and eye disease.

case study 9.6

William

William is five years old and is diabetic. He is on his first school trip to the zoo. He is very excited and has rushed around from enclosure to enclosure during the morning. At lunch time, William was so busy talking to his friends about their favourite animals that he did not eat very much of his packed lunch. As the afternoon wore on, William became lethargic and by the time he got onto the coach he was sweating a great deal and stumbled getting into his seat. Other children were also tired and stumbling.

activity
INDIVIDUAL WORK

1 Would you be concerned about William?
2 What signs of hypoglycaemia is William possibly displaying?
3 What would you do initially?
4 With hindsight, what else should staff have done?
5 What have you learned from this case study?

Fig 9.15 The 'gluten-free' symbol

Coeliac disease

What is coeliac disease?

Coeliac disease is a condition affecting the lining of the small intestine. It is an immunological reaction to gluten, a protein found in wheat, rye and barley; some people have a reaction to oats, too. Children are usually diagnosed when they start to have solid food from about six months onwards. In adults, coeliac disease can occur at any time, often triggered by an unknown cause.

What causes coeliac disease?

- The reaction to gluten causes the villi protrusions along the intestine to become flattened and therefore reduces the surface for absorption of food.

Recognising coeliac disease

- Babies fail to thrive in the usual way; they do not put on weight and are low on the centile charts.
- Young children become very unwell, lethargic and miserable, with abdominal bloating.
- Stools are pale, fatty, smell unpleasant and are difficult to flush away.

Initial actions

- There has usually been some concern shown for the child (or adult) prior to diagnosis.
- Blood tests and faecal samples are taken initially.
- A biopsy of the jejunum usually follows if concerns are raised by the results of tests on blood and faeces.
- A dietary 'challenge' would be carried out in early puberty.

Ongoing care

- A gluten-free diet is necessary throughout life.
- Gluten is found in many everyday foods and it takes time to identify all foods that need to be avoided.
- Guidance is given from a dietician to help establish a balanced diet.
- Coeliac UK gives helpful advice and a regularly updated food list.
- Many supermarkets now display a gluten-free symbol on suitable foods.
- Since November 2005, new food laws require all forms of gluten to be indicated on packaging.

Possible complications

- Iron-deficiency anaemia is a possibility due to malabsorption of food.
- Calcium deficiency can also be present, again due to malabsorption.
- In the long term, there is a higher incidence of intestinal cancer in people with untreated coeliac disease.
- For individuals diagnosed at later ages, further problems can occur:
  - osteoporosis, which is a calcium-deficient condition resulting in repeated fractures
  - osteopaenia, which indicates borderline osteoporosis, and is often picked up during bone density scanning for osteoporosis.
- Bone density scans are offered for individuals where either condition is suspected or calcium supplements (with vitamin D) are then recommended for life.

Familial?

- There is a familial tendency to coeliac disease, but it is not considered hereditary.
- Babies born into a family where coeliac disease has previously been diagnosed should be observed closely for early signs and some health practitioners recommend that gluten should ideally be withheld from their diet until their first birthday. In some cases, early exposure to gluten has been thought to have triggered the condition.

Infection

The human body's natural state is to be healthy and be able to fight off illness. What we put into our bodies and what our bodies are exposed to have an impact on how well our bodies manage to maintain their healthy state, illustrating how important health education programmes can be. It is worth revisiting the definitions of health to consolidate your understanding of what 'health' actually is. Think also about how the body automatically defends itself, through:

- the eyes
  - the blinking mechanism helps prevent particles entering the eyes
  - tears contain a mild antiseptic which cleanses the eyes
- the blood – leucocytes (white blood cells) fight infected tissue and destroy germs
- the skin – sebum is an oily substance that is secreted through the surface of the skin and acts as a protective layer
- mucus
  - each opening into the body (for example, the nose) has a lining of mucus membrane at the entrance to help prevent infections from entering
  - ciliated epithelia (small hairs) trap and collect foreign bodies, such as earwax and mucus from the nose
- the spleen – this is a vascular organ with a large number of blood vessels, which filters out foreign bodies from the blood and produces antibodies
- the gut – good bacteria in the gut kills both good and bad bacteria when fighting infection, causing diarrhoea.

Fig 9.16 Causes of illness

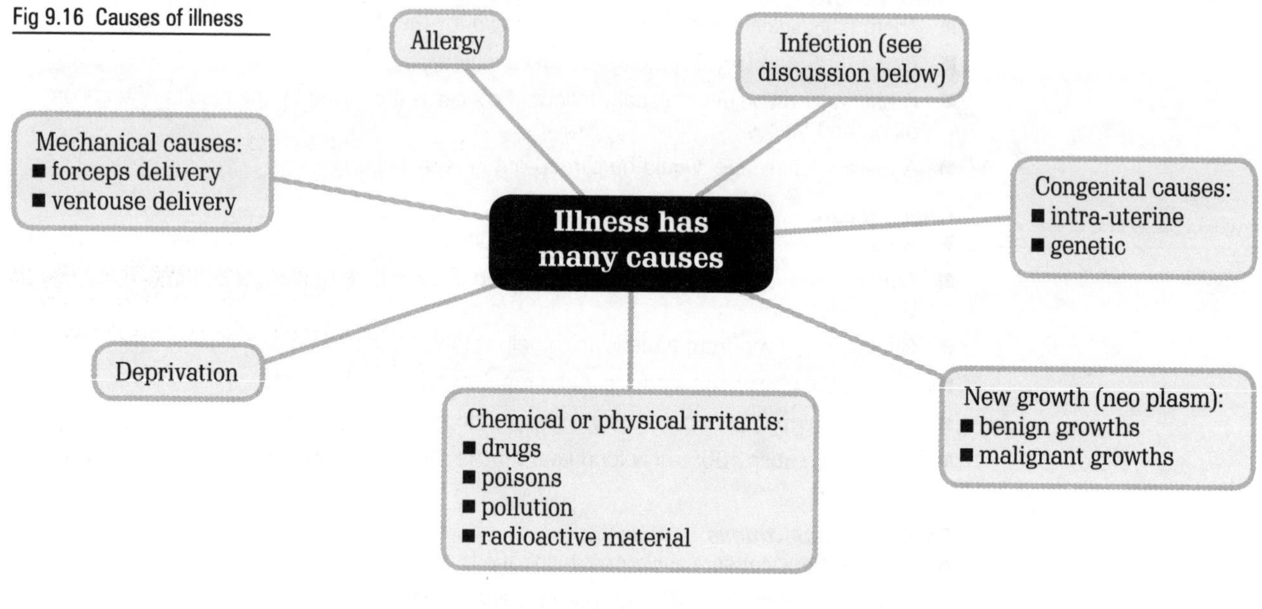

Refer back to page 404 for the definitions of health and to Unit 3, page 110, for genetic factors resulting in congenital or genetically inherited conditions.

Causes of infection

The microbiological (infectious) causes of illness are varied, and this is the area that you will most often deal with as an early years worker. These germs (pathogens) can be roughly divided into five groups:

- bacteria – tough cells which rapidly multiply and thrive in the body's warm, moist conditions; treatable with antibiotics; bacterial infections include ear infections and conjunctivitis
- viruses – parasites which invade other cells and then reproduce themselves; cannot be treated with antibiotics; can be relatively harmless or significantly serious; viral infections include the common cold, influenza and chickenpox
- fungi – spread by contact with the spores of fungi; do no serious harm to humans but cause much irritation and discomfort; some harmless fungi are permanently with us; treatment is with an antifungal product as necessary, for example for athlete's foot
- parasites – organisms spread by cross-infection; can be seen with the naked eye; many different varieties and difficult to eradicate once they have taken hold in a nursery or school class, due to cases of re-infection; examples are scabies, head lice and threadworms

- protozoa – single-cell organisms; many cause human distress through illnesses such as severe stomach upsets, toxoplasmosis (often caught through handling cats or cat litter) and amoebiasis (causing diarrhoea).

Pathogens can enter the body in different ways. They can be:

- ingested – taken in through the mouth
- inhaled – breathed in through either the mouth or the nose
- inoculated – taken in through a break in the surface of the skin.

They can be spread by:

- direct contact – germs transmitted by touch, for example contact with broken skin, kissing and sexual activity
- indirect contact – germs left on surfaces subsequently in contact with another person
- droplet infection – air-borne germs spread through sneezing, coughing, and so on, as microscopic droplets are released into the atmosphere.

Role of immunisation

What is immunity?

Immunity is the body's ability to resist disease. Each individual builds up an immunity to various illnesses during life. Infants are born with a degree of natural immunity to some illnesses and diseases, based on the immunity of their mothers. Breastfeeding for up to four months extends the baby's immunity.

There are different types of immunity. The table below gives examples of how immunity can occur either naturally or be acquired through **immunisation programmes**, and also how immunity can be active, passive or achieved by the herd immunity process.

Table 9.6 Types of immunity

Types of immunity	Description	Example
Active natural immunity	An immune response to a naturally occurring infection that the child has contracted	Antibodies formed following chickenpox or rubella
Active acquired immunity	An immune response to an antigen (a toxin produced by bacteria to make antibodies)	Via the (live) polio vaccine which is given as part of the childhood immunisation programme
Passive natural immunity	Naturally occurring immunity passed across the placenta, and in breast milk	Infants are born with a degree of natural immunity based on their mothers' immunity
Passive acquired immunity	Antibodies are transferred via an injection (immunisation programme)	Ready-made antibodies, such as diphtheria and tetanus given as part of the immunisation programme
Herd immunity	If a high enough proportion of the whole population is immunised it will keep the rest free from the disease (usually needs 90+ per cent)	The HiB vaccine campaign has successfully reduced the incidence of HiB

Immunisation of children

There are **live vaccines** and **non-live vaccines**. As children are particularly vulnerable to contracting disease, a programme of immunisation is recommended by health experts. Immunisation not only protects the immunised child from falling ill, it also helps to protect children with suppressed immune systems who may not be able to have all vaccinations in the programme.

Immunisation is only given with parental consent, and although technically there is no contraindication for a child with a minor cough or cold receiving an immunisation, most people prefer their children to be free from illness at the time when the immunisation is administered. The recommended programme is set out in the table below.

Table 9.7 The immunisation programme

Age	Immunisation	Method
Two months old	Diphtheria, tetanus, pertussis (Whooping cough), polio and *Haemophilus influenzae* type b (Hib) Pneumococcal infection	DTaP/IPV/ Hib and Pneumococcal conjugate vaccine (PCV)
Three months old	Diphtheria, tetanus, pertussis, polio and *Haemophilus influenzae* type b (Hib) Meningitis C (meningococcal group C)	DTaP/IPV/Hib and MenC
Four months old	Diphtheria, tetanus, pertussis, polio and *Haemophilus influenzae* type b (Hib) Meningitis C Pneumococcal infection	DTaP/IPV/Hib MenC and PCV
Around 12 months	Haemphilus influenza type b (Hib) and meningitis C	Hib/MenC
Around 13 months	Measles, mumps and rubella (German measles) Pneumococcal infection	MMR and PCV
Three years four months to five years old	Diphtheria, tetanus, pertussis and polio Measles, mumps and rubella	DTaP/IPV or dTaP/IPV and MMR
Thirteen to eighteen years old	Tetanus, diphtheria and polio	Td/IPV

Source: Department of Health, Crown Copyright 2006

Professional Practice

- Children sometimes have a slight reaction to immunisations, such as having a raised temperature and feeling miserable. If this occurs, plenty of fluids should be given, along with paracetamol.
- A careful eye should be kept on the child, particularly a young baby.
- If a raised temperature does not come down within 24 hours, or it continues to rise, medical advice should be sought.
- Some health professionals recommend that paracetamol is automatically given after an immunisation. However, other health professionals support the idea of giving it just beforehand, to minimise the risk of a rise in temperature.
- Paracetamol is not registered to be given to babies under the age of three months. Infant ibuprofen suspension is as effective as paracetamol and is an alternative, but should not be given to children with moderate or severe asthma.
- As with all medication, paracetamol and infant ibuprofen suspension should be given in the doses appropriate for the age of the child.
- Children under 12 should never be given aspirin, because there is a slight risk that it might cause Reye's syndrome.

remember

Children who are HIV positive will not necessarily develop AIDS.

Children with suppressed immunity

Children with certain illnesses or conditions (e.g. leukaemia, HIV and AIDS) may have **suppressed immunity**. It is not appropriate to give these children live vaccines, as a live vaccine is a weakened version of the condition itself. Artificial vaccines can sometimes be offered to these children and to those in close contact with them, such as siblings.

Homoeopathic immunisations

Some parents choose not to have their children immunised through the mainstream programme but may choose to use homoeopathic alternatives instead. There is little evidence to support the efficacy of the homoeopathic alternatives, but they do offer a degree of protection for some children. Although immunisation is recommended for most healthy children, as an early years professional you should respect parents' right to choose not to have their child immunised and make no value judgements about them.

Understand nutritional needs

Diet and lifestyle

Diet and lifestyle are important factors in children's health and can have a considerable impact on their well-being during childhood and later as adults. Children rarely have the choice of avoiding any adverse aspects of their family's lifestyle that may affect their health; such aspects may include:

- inadequate or unbalanced diet
- exposure to cigarette smoke
- lack of fresh air and exercise
- failure to protect child from effects of alcohol or other forms of substance misuse.

The government is keen to address all of the factors that can affect a child's future health, and interventions have been planned to improve dietary intake and participation in sport and exercise. However, interventions should be planned in tandem with education programmes in order for the root causes of the problems to be tackled. Again, there appear to be links between the factors outlined above and social class.

- Poor standards of nutrition are more likely to occur in the lower social classes, and it is reported that children in working class families are less likely to eat sufficient fruit and vegetables and more likely to eat processed foods and foods high in sugars and fat. Poor diet can lead to malnutrition, vitamin and mineral deficiencies, obesity, dental decay, constipation, and cardiovascular disease.
- Smoking is also reported to be more prevalent in Social Classes IV and V. Babies and children in homes where people smoke have no choice but to be passive smokers and this can result in a higher incidence of sudden infant death syndrome, respiratory infections, asthma, heart disease, and lung cancer.
- Middle class people are more likely to take regular exercise and other associated social activities (Moore, 2002). Regular exercise can improve cardiovascular health and reduce stress, and there are implications for children whose parents have insufficient money or awareness of the benefits of exercise.

Nutritional needs

A good, balanced diet is one which includes all the nutritional requirements for the growth, maintenance and development of the body. The food that we eat helps us to maintain and repair our body tissues, keeping muscles and organs functioning. It also helps to prevent infection and supplies us with our energy needs. A balanced diet should abide by the principles of diet and nutrition and include elements from the four main food groups:

- proteins, which help growth, development and tissue repair
- carbohydrates, which provide energy
- vitamins, minerals and fibre, for general good health and the prevention of illness
- dairy products, which are high in calcium, enhancing and maintaining bones and teeth.

A fifth food group – fats and oils – comprises higher-level energy-giving foods which should be consumed sparingly by adults.

Fig 9.17 The food groups

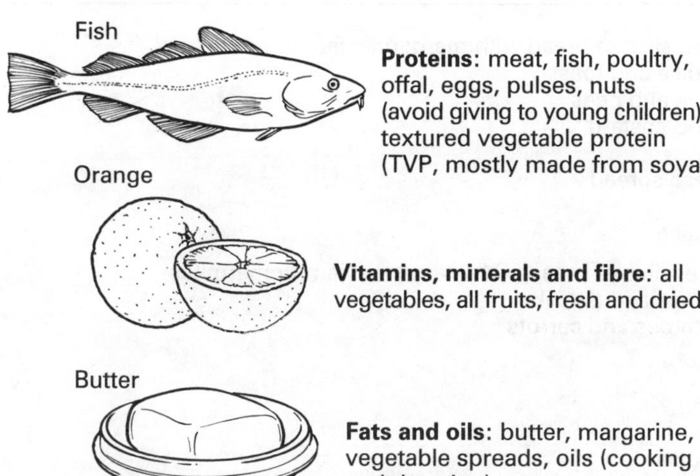

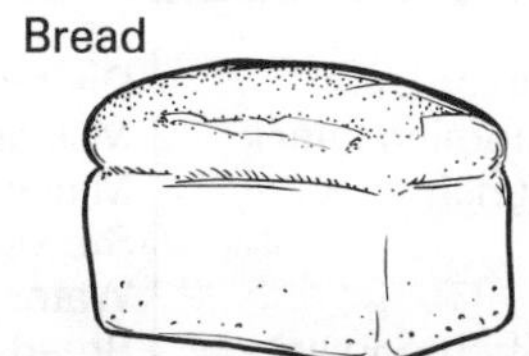

Many foods contribute to more than one food group: for example, meat is a good source of iron, and pulses are a good source of fibre, but Figure 9.17 indicates where the main benefits of each food lie.

Levels of nutritional need vary according to a range of factors. These include:

- age
- gender
- level of regular exercise
- pregnancy (there are additional needs).

Our diets and nutritional intake will be influenced by:

- any special dietary requirement (e.g. intolerance or allergy)
- cultural guidelines and taboos
- personal or family dietary choices (e.g. vegetarian or vegan diets)
- personal preferences and taste.

In the home, nutrition and diet will be influenced by:

- knowledge of ingredients and cooking and what makes up a well-balanced diet
- finances
- accessibility of shops and markets
- time available to whoever prepares and cooks
- family eating habits.

In schools and early years settings, nutrition and diet should be influenced by:

- knowledge of nutrition and diet
- government guidelines
- financial budgets
- promotion of a broad range of foods from around the globe.

A balance of appropriate nutrition is required both to support healthy development during childhood and adolescence and to maintain our bodies throughout life, ensuring that we look and feel healthy, have the energy that we need to live a fulfilling life and are able to fight off infection. Diet plays a significant part in helping us to avoid a range of serious health conditions, such as heart disease, type 2 diabetes and some cancers.

Children have their own preferences with regard to food, and these should be accommodated up to a point. There should be a balance between allowing a child to select what they eat or do not eat and encouraging them to try a range of new and familiar foods.

When preparing meals for children, their dietary needs should be considered. Some children have food intolerances or an allergy; others may come from families which follow vegetarian or vegan diets; or cultural practice may govern what the child may eat.

Refer back to pages 428–431 for descriptions of cystic fibrosis, coeliac disease and diabetes mellitus, each of which has specific dietary needs, and to Unit 2, page 95, for a table showing the food-related customs of a range of cultures.

Table 9.8 Sample menu

Monday	On arrival	Diluted fruit juice, slice of bread with margarine, jam or marmite
	Morning snack	Milk or diluted juice and toast
	Lunch	Minced lamb, rice and peas Stewed apple and custard Water
	Afternoon snack	Bread with cheese spread Apple slices Milk or diluted juice
Tuesday	On arrival	Diluted fruit juice, slice of bread with margarine, jam or marmite
	Morning snack	Milk or diluted juice and oatcake
	Lunch	Pork hotpot, potatoes and carrots Custard tart Water
	Afternoon snack	Egg sandwiches Banana Milk or diluted juice

Wednesday	On arrival	Diluted fruit juice, slice of bread with margarine, jam or marmite
	Morning snack	Milk or diluted juice and toast
	Lunch	Bean and vegetable pastabake Milk pudding Water
	Afternoon snack	Toast and marmite Yoghurt Milk or diluted juice
Thursday	On arrival	Diluted fruit juice, slice of bread with margarine, jam or marmite
	Morning snack	Milk or diluted juice and rice cake
	Lunch	Pork curry and rice Fruit fool Water
	Afternoon snack	Fruitbread Apple slices Milk or diluted juice
Friday	On arrival	Diluted fruit juice, slice of bread with margarine, jam or marmite
	Morning snack	Milk or diluted juice and toast
	Lunch	Fish cakes, mashed potato and baked beans Cake and custard Water
	Afternoon snack	Bread with cheese spread Banana Milk or diluted juice

case study 9.7

Dillon and Ramjit

The menus for young children shown in the above table do not take into account any special dietary requirements. You have been asked to suggest alternatives for Monday and Wednesday, to accommodate Dillon who has coeliac disease, and for Thursday and Friday, to accommodate Ramjit who is from a practising Buddhist family.

1 What will you change?
2 What difference will this make to the nutritional balance?
3 How will you ensure that Dillon and Ramjit are not made to feel different from anyone else?

Macronutrients

Carbohydrates

Carbohydrates can be classified under three main headings:

- sugars
- starches
- fibre, soluble and insoluble.

Carbohydrates are needed for:

- energy and activity
- the maintenance of body temperature
- keeping the body's normal functions running smoothly.

Children need a good intake of energy-rich foods to enable them to play, explore and learn freely.

The different types of carbohydrate are ranked according to their effect on blood sugar levels; this is known as the glycemic index. Foods with a low glycemic index provide us with energy that is absorbed and used slowly within the body, so these provide energy over a long period of time. Foods with a high glycemic index give us a 'rush' of energy that will soon fade.

Low-glycemic foods are therefore of greater value to children and adults, especially at the start of the day. A breakfast of porridge (low GI) will give longer-lasting energy levels than a bowl of rice crispies (high GI). It will also lessen the need for a mid-morning boost of energy from chocolate or similar.

Most sugary foods are high GI and should therefore be eaten sparingly. Snacks of bananas, dried apricots or grapes, which are low GI, are preferable.

Examples of starchy foods are breads, cereals, rice and pasta. Whole grains are higher in fibre than refined grains are. Fibre is needed to aid digestion and avoid problems such as constipation.

remember

Finding out which foods are low on the GI table will help you provide an energy-rich diet for the children in your care.

Fibre can be either soluble (e.g. oatmeal; legumes such as beans, peas and lentils; bananas; apples and oranges), or insoluble (e.g. wheat, rice, legumes, plus many vegetables and fruits). Too much insoluble fibre can fill children up too quickly and can also cause diarrhoea, flatulence and general tummy upsets.

Proteins

As the diagram on page 435 shows, protein is mainly found in foods such as meat, fish, poultry, eggs, pulses and nuts. It is also found in textured vegetable protein which is mostly made from soya. Protein is needed to support the healthy growth and development of:

- muscles and connective tissues
- skin and hair
- the immune system.

It also plays an important role in blood, helping to maintain good levels of haemoglobin, and helps control the metabolism.

remember

Nuts should not be given to very young children.

Although protein is found in plant sources, most meat-eating people will gain the greatest amount of the protein from animal sources. Vegetarians and vegans need to ensure that they have sufficient intake of protein-rich foods to avoid the occurrence of deficiencies such as anaemia. Soya, pulses, grains, seeds and nuts form an important part of the vegan diet, with eggs also contributing to a vegetarian diet.

Fats

Fats can be saturated, unsaturated or polyunsaturated.

- When at room temperature, saturated fat tends to be found in a solid form, for example in butter and some margarines.
- Unsaturated and polyunsaturated fat is found in oils and oily fish such as sardines, salmon, etc.

Fat is needed to help provide energy, but care should be taken not to eat too much fat as this can cause weight increase and may contribute to health problems, such as heart disease, later on. Foods containing unsaturated fats are thought to help lower cholesterol levels and help to maintain general health and well-being.

Micronutrients

Vitamins

Each vitamin plays a role in the health and development of the body.

Refer back to Unit 2, page 91, for a table showing a range of everyday foods from which vitamins can be obtained, the function of each vitamin, and potential problems if intake is insufficient.

Minerals

The body requires a range of minerals, the essential minerals and the trace minerals, in order to function fully.

Refer back to Unit 2, page 92, for a table showing a range of everyday foods from which minerals can be obtained, the function of each mineral, and potential problems if intake is insufficient.

A useful reference would also be Unit 11 in *BTEC National Children's Care, Learning and Development*, Book 2 (Green, 2007).

1 Design a two-course meal suitable for a five-year-old child's main meal of the day; it is to be served at lunchtime.

2 Identify clearly where both the macro- and micronutrients will be found in the meal and the role that each plays in supporting the child's health and general well-being.

Water

Water plays an important part in our diet: it keeps us hydrated; it dilutes toxins and helps prevent constipation. Children should be encouraged to adopt the habit of drinking water, rather than fruit juices or other flavoured drinks. The amount of water needed daily will vary from person to person and will also be affected by the time of year and overall temperature, and the level of activity being undertaken.

Water should be readily available to children throughout the day. Adults should be aware of any child who does not seem to drink regularly and encourage them to do so, especially during warmer weather and during or after physical activity and sport.

Concept of a balanced diet

A healthy diet offers a range of foods from each food group, ensuring that the diet is well balanced, and is not deficient in any area. Encouraging children to try seasonal fruits and vegetables and foods from different cultures will promote a healthy and diverse approach to diet throughout life.

Fig 9.18 How a balanced diet promotes health and development

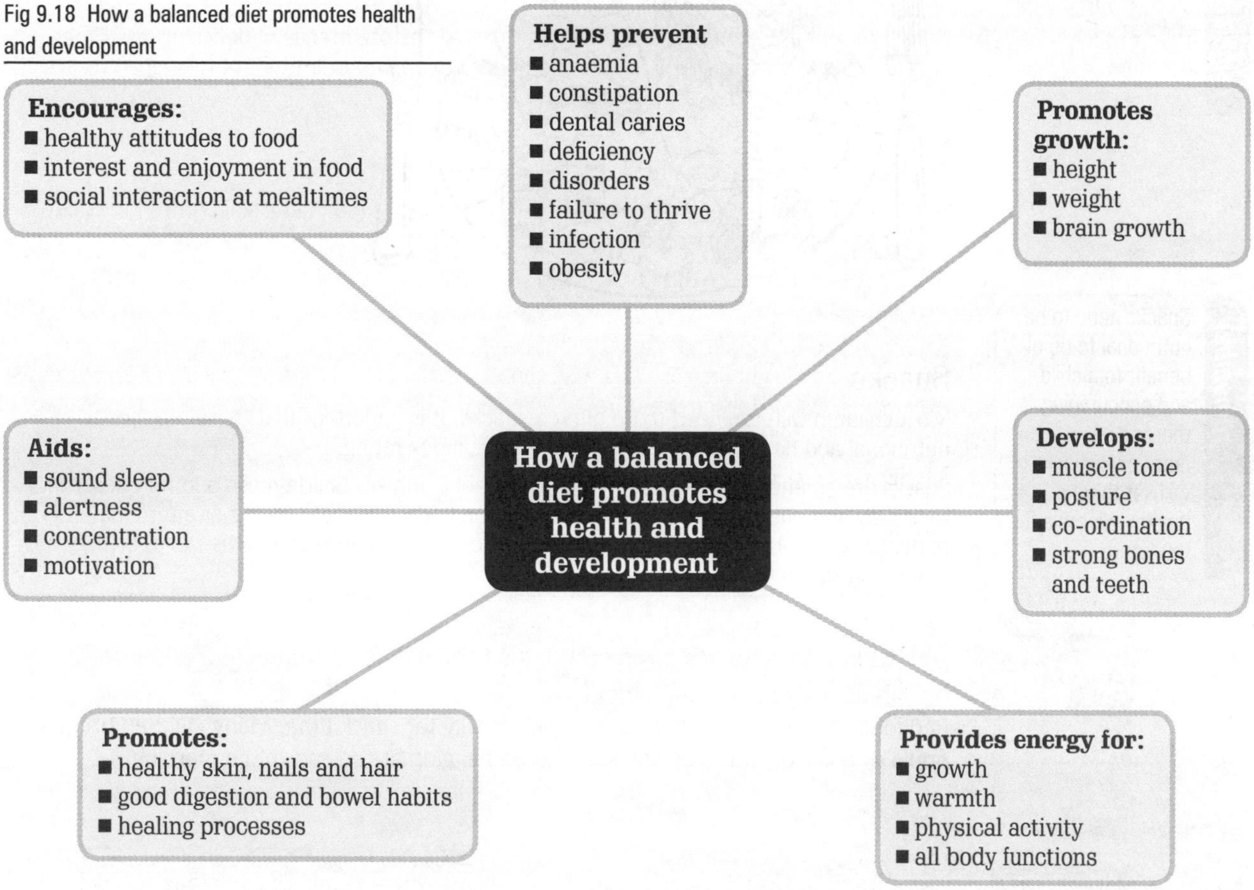

How a balanced diet promotes health and development

Encourages:
- healthy attitudes to food
- interest and enjoyment in food
- social interaction at mealtimes

Helps prevent
- anaemia
- constipation
- dental caries
- deficiency
- disorders
- failure to thrive
- infection
- obesity

Promotes growth:
- height
- weight
- brain growth

Aids:
- sound sleep
- alertness
- concentration
- motivation

Develops:
- muscle tone
- posture
- co-ordination
- strong bones and teeth

Promotes:
- healthy skin, nails and hair
- good digestion and bowel habits
- healing processes

Provides energy for:
- growth
- warmth
- physical activity
- all body functions

Refer back to Unit 2, page 94, for a table showing the estimated average requirements (EARs).

Planning a diet for children

- Children need a diet that is high in protein and carbohydrates to meet their high energy needs. The carbohydrates should ideally come from starchy foods such as potatoes, breads and cereals.
- Think about both colour and texture when planning meals, as an attractive meal will be more appealing, especially to a fussy or reluctant eater.
- Vary the meals that are offered to children, but do not offer more than one new food at a time.
- Large portions can be off-putting. It is better for a child to eat all of a small meal than half of a larger one, as it encourages good habits.

Daily portions for children

remember Children have preferences too.

As a guideline for meeting the dietary needs of young children, a good daily balance would include:

- five portions of fruit or vegetables
- two portions of protein foods
- two portions of dairy foods plus one pint of milk
- four portions of carbohydrates.

At each meal you should be aiming to provide a balance of foods in the proportions shown in the diagram.

Fig 9.19 A balanced meal

remember Snacks need to be nutritional to be of benefit to a child, and encouraging them to eat nutritional snacks will set them a healthy example for the future.

Snacks

Most children will also need to be offered snacks. It is important that these are mostly nutritional and healthy and have a low glycemic index rating.

Snacks are an important part of a child's nutritional intake. Children use a lot of energy in their play and often need an energy boost in the middle of the morning or afternoon. This is particularly important if they are at a stage when physical development is rapid, or they are more active than usual.

case study 9.8 Redhouse Nursery School

Redhouse Nursery School has a fruit-only policy for snack time. Many children bring an apple or a carrot, but they still seem to be flagging at the end of the morning.

activity INDIVIDUAL WORK

1 Why is this do you think?
2 What fruit would offer them a greater energy boost?
3 Is a fruit-only policy a good idea?
4 What other healthy options could be included?

Refer back to Unit 2, page 94, for a table listing healthy snacks.

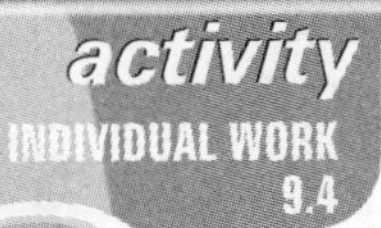

activity
INDIVIDUAL WORK 9.4

P3

M2

1 Imagine you are working as a live-in nanny to a two-year-old girl and a six-year-old boy.
   (a) Explain the requirements of a balanced diet for the children.
   (b) Produce a chart of meals for a period of five days that you could provide for them. This should include breakfast, lunch and tea, with snacks and drinks as you feel are appropriate.
   (c) Annotate your chart to show clearly how the various foods support the concept of a healthy diet for the children. Expand on this further by providing a detailed written explanation.

2 Plan a midday meal for a group of four-year-olds, ensuring that there are three colours and three textures within the meal. You can plan a meal from any culture you wish.
   (a) What have you included for colour?
   (b) What textures have you provided?
   (c) What food groups have you incorporated into your meal?
   (d) Are any food groups not represented? Is this a problem, do you think?

Further information on nutritional sources can be found in *A Practical Guide to Child Nutrition* by Dare and O'Donovan (1996), *Feeding the Under-5s* by Dyson and Meredith (2006) or *Eating Well for the Under-5s in Child Care* by Walker (1998), which includes a CD-ROM, the CHOMP menu planner, to help with menu planning, and nutritional advice for young children in all early years settings.

Malnutrition

Malnutrition, which is still seen in the UK today, is clinically defined by a low body mass index. Malnutrition, or undernourishment as it is often called, can be caused by lack of nutrition or can be due to medical conditions such as coeliac disease, cystic fibrosis and diabetes. The percentile charts that monitor a child's growth, particularly weight in babies and toddlers, are often the first indication that a child is not getting enough nutrition, but it should always be remembered that some children are simply of a light build.

When children are ravenously hungry, constantly thin and/or tired and often in poor health, practitioners should monitor the child carefully, noting their concerns and discussing them with superiors. Malnutrition can be a sign of neglect.

Refer back to Unit 5, page 243, for signs and symptoms of abuse.

Professional Practice

- There are many hidden extras in processed foods, particularly sugar and salt. Whenever possible, offer fresh foods to children and do not provide salt or sugar on the table for them to add to their foods.
- No child should ever be forced to eat, nor should they be forced to eat any particular food.
- Parents should be kept fully informed if their child refuses food, particularly whole meals.
- Some children will benefit if food is made more appealing visually, for example by emphasising colour.

For ideas on raising children's interest in food and making food fun refer to *Food and Cooking* by Green (2004).

Fig 9.20 Making food fun

Know how to maximise opportunities for the promotion of healthy living to children and their families

Opportunities

When working with children and young people, it will be possible to introduce topics of study and discussion to help them build up an understanding of how their bodies function, what influences good bodily health and how they can help to maintain good health for themselves. It will be important to plan activities, provide resources and use language appropriate to the children's level of understanding. The same topics can be covered several times, each time building on previous learning and consolidating understanding.

Health care teams

Health care teams support both the promotion of health and the care to maintain it and are made up of a range of health professionals. These include those who focus on health care and health education at each of the three different levels of health care:

- primary health care – health care in the community, involving GP practices, dentists, opticians, and so on
- **secondary health care** – all referrals for health care, for example to hospital departments for further treatment or investigation
- **tertiary health care** – ongoing care for chronic conditions such as cystic fibrosis. It also includes the involvement of individual health professionals such as the community diabetic nurse.

Primary health education/promotion

Health education is concerned with providing well-rounded information that enables individuals to make informed choices regarding their health.

The aim of primary health education/promotion is to prevent ill health by eliminating the likelihood of contracting a disease in the first place. An example of this is the childhood immunisation programme. Nationwide immunisation can have a significant impact on the incidence of some illnesses, such as the immunisation programmes for haemophilus influenzae type B (HiB) and measles, mumps and rubella (MMR), which have dramatically reduced the incidence of these childhood diseases in the UK. Worldwide eradication of smallpox was also due to immunisation.

In the UK, parents are presented with an explanation of the MMR vaccination and its merits and are actively encouraged to have their children vaccinated. In developing countries, however, vaccination decisions are largely made on behalf of the population, and parents are simply told that their child 'needs' whatever vaccination is being given.

Refer back to page 434 for the current guidelines on immunisation.

Secondary health education/promotion

Secondary approaches to health education/promotion include screening procedures. Examples are the PKU (phenylketonuria) test on blood taken from seven-day-old infants via a heel prick (the Guthrie test) and cervical screening in women, where a presymptomatic change may be detected, allowing early intervention.

Tertiary health education/promotion

The tertiary approach to health education/promotion is aimed at the control and reduction of illness and is concerned with helping individuals to achieve their full health potential. An example of this is supporting the control of chronic asthma and diabetes. Tertiary health education/promotion often involves the use of leaflets and other printed resources. It also includes the involvement of support groups.

You may find it helpful to refer to *Health Promotion: Foundations for Practice* by Naidoo and Wills (2000) for further reading on the different levels of health care, education and promotion.

case study 9.9 Klaus

Klaus is six years old. He has recently been diagnosed as having type 1 diabetes (insulin dependent), as opposed to type 2, which is non-insulin dependent. Klaus spent three days in hospital while his condition was stabilised and he and his parents acclimatised to planning for his diabetic dietary needs. Klaus and his parents are now at home being supported by the primary health care team through the diabetic specialist nurse, who oversees most of his care. The diabetic nurse supervises the administration of his injections and checks his blood sugar levels. This responsibility will soon transfer to Klaus's parents, who will be able to get support via a telephone link. Klaus is also having regular appointments with a dietician at the local hospital, to monitor his food intake and balance.

activity INDIVIDUAL WORK

1 Which members of the primary health care team have been involved in the care of Klaus to date?
2 Who would be involved in his long-term care?
3 Why is this important?

case study 9.10 Mollie

Mollie is two years old and has cystic fibrosis (CF). She is the first member of her generation in her family to have the condition although it has occurred twice before in the family (an uncle and an aunt are currently affected). Mollie's mother had been (positively) carrier-tested prior to her pregnancy and, although foetal screening for the condition is now available, she opted not to have her unborn infant screened, because of the risk of miscarriage. As there was a definite possibility of Mollie's having CF, health professionals monitored her from birth, watching for the earliest signs and offering appropriate advice regarding specialised dietary needs.

activity
INDIVIDUAL WORK

1 Which members of the health care profession have been involved to date?
2 What role did the primary health care professionals play in the pregnancy?
3 Will any other form of health care be needed for the future?

remember
That includes you!

Role of health educators

The **role of health educators** is to educate individuals about issues that affect their health and well-being so that they can change their beliefs and behaviour. (Giving people information so that they can choose to make changes empowers them.) In early years settings, the aim should be to involve both children and their families.

Refer back to page 410 for a list of people who are health educators.

Planning activities to help children and young people learn about their body, how it works and how they can keep healthy.

Topic work could be based on any of the following:

- the heart and blood
- breathing
- digestion and excretion
- the senses
- the skeleton and muscles
- food and nutrition
- genetics
- body words
- exercise and movement.

These are just suggestions, there are many more. What other ideas can you think of?

Activities could include:

- finding information from reference books
- finding information using Internet search engines
- reading stories about going into hospital, having an illness, breaking bones, etc.
- singing songs and rhymes linked to health
- setting up displays and interest tables of relevant artefacts, books, pictures and photos
- model-making with a range of media (e.g. straws for bones, balloons for lungs)
- science activities using pumps, rubber tubing and coloured water for blood
- drawing round individuals and making a life-sized person
- using blindfolds to simulate lack of vision
- using ear plugs to simulate lack of hearing
- making creative food plates using advertising material or food labels
- feeding teddy for a week, planning his diet and deciding if he is keeping well, or not
- turning the role play area into a surgery, hospital, ambulance, etc.
- setting up an immunisation clinic for dolls and teddies
- painting with syringes (needles removed), printing with stethoscopes
- bandaging dolls and teddies
- visits from health professionals such as dentist, doctor, nurse, health visitor, ambulance paramedics
- watching age-appropriate DVDs on health professionals and how they work
- visits to a hospital, dental surgery
- looking over an ambulance

- carrying out research on health issues
- designing posters to promote health care
- designing a pamphlet to raise awareness of a health issue.

Again, these are just suggestions, there are many more. What other ideas can you think of?

Taking time to discuss and promote health issues with children within context is also important. For example:

- demonstrating careful hand washing and explaining why it is important in preventing cross-infection
- even on cold days, giving enthusiastic encouragement to children reluctant to play outside, explaining why exercise is good for the body and how fresh air helps us
- making mealtimes relaxed and sociable, eating with the children if possible, 'trying' new foods together
- using positive language at all times to encourage exercise and enjoyment of food.

Involving families

Families can easily be included in health promotion activities. For example:

- Introduce a 'new fruit' day and ask parents to provide something different for everyone to try.
- Invite parents to attend when you have a visit from a health professional.
- Ask children to keep a diary of what they eat and help them highlight 'good' foods and identify where the best nutrition is found (it is not appropriate to simply point out 'bad' foods).
- Ensure that menus for children's meals are healthy and are displayed well.

1 Explain in what ways you have seen healthy living promoted to children and their families either at your current placement or a previous one.

2 List other activities that you consider have contributed towards supporting children's health.

3 How could these activities have been used to promote healthy living to the whole family too?

Facilitating change

Any campaign to pass on information should be accessible to its target audience; it needs to appeal, be visually interesting, and the information should be readily available and free from patronising or moralistic tones. Presentation, language and content are all important.

When designing a leaflet on a health issue, it is important to remember a few key points:

- Choose an issue that particularly interests you or is relevant to your target audience (e.g. parents, young children, teenagers).
- Aim to inform or educate people about the issue.
- Your leaflet will benefit from being as visual as possible.
- Remember to consider a range of languages and ethnic groups wherever practical.

The following will also need to be taken into account:

- visual presentation
- language style
- promotional content.

Visual presentation

- Visual presentation is important to gain initial attention.
- Photographs, cartoons and illustrations can all be used successfully.
- The visual approach selected should be relevant to the main target group but not exclude others who may also find it useful.
- Illustrations should be bolder and clearer in information aimed at young children than in information aimed at teenagers, where a cartoon or graphic design would be more likely to appeal.

Language style

- The language used should be relevant to the targeted group.
- Teenagers will appreciate language that is more contemporary.
- Children need a greater ratio of visual to written information.
- Translations into languages other than English should be made where possible.
- Written text aimed at young children should be easy to read and set in large, bold type. It should be presented using upper- and lower-case lettering and punctuated correctly:
  - Use capitals only at the start of sentences and for proper names.
  - Write in short sentences and do not forget to use full stops at the ends of sentences.

Promotional content

- The content should start with the main emphasis of the health promotion programme.
- Positive messages should be made very clear.
- Judgemental statements that could annoy or alienate the reader should be avoided. For example, avoid statements such as 'Only a fool continues to ...'.
- Getting the balance of information right is crucial to ensure that the message is taken in.
- Too much information can put people off reading any further.
- Too little information can leave the reader both unimpressed and uninformed.

remember It is always important to consider how the message is put over to people who have limited vision or literacy.

Working with older children and teenagers

If you were encouraging older children and teenagers to find out what current government health promotion campaigns there are in the local area, you could suggest that they work together in a group and:

1. Research and gather information on each campaign for different target groups, ensuring that they include young children in this.
2. Consider what elements of each campaign appeal to them personally, using the points raised above as a guideline to help get them started.
3. Select three pieces of promotional material they have found and ask a range of people questions about them. For example:
   (a) What do they think of them?
   (b) Would they be likely to pick them up?
   (c) Would they be likely to read them?
4. Collate the outcomes of their group's findings.
5. Come to conclusions about the potential success of the promotional materials they selected.
6. Reflect on what they have learned from this activity about preparing information materials for other people.
7. Consider how accessible the resources they found in the above activity would have been for people who have limited vision or literacy.
8. Consider how the resources could have been made more accessible to them.

Suitable topics

Suitable topics for a health promotion campaign for older children and teenagers would be:

- tackling cross-infection in schools ('tummy bugs', threadworms, and so on)
- exercising during everyday activities
- understanding food values.

What other suggestions would you give them?

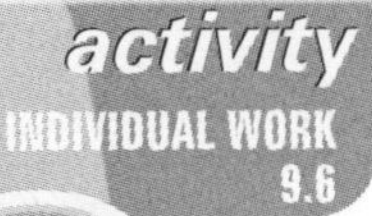

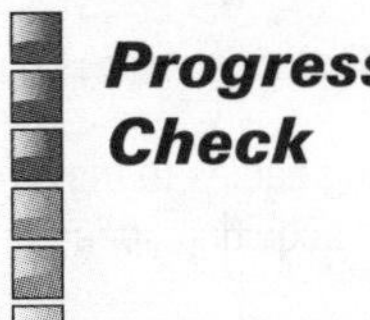

D2

1 Choose two examples of health promotion carried out in your placement.
2 Provide the planning, aims and resources used for each activity.
3 Explain how staff considered their overall aims to be relevant to the promotion of healthy living for the children and their families.
4 Provide an evaluation of the success of each health promotion activity.
5 Make clear what you have learned from these examples and how this learning will influence your planning for the future.

Progress Check

1 What are the benefits of screening?
2 List at least 10 people who could be considered to be health educators.
3 Give an example of a fixed factor influencing the health of an individual.
4 What are the four priority health areas being targeted by the UK government?
5 Give at least three examples of socioeconomic factors that affect health, linked to poverty.
6 Give at least three examples of socioeconomic factors that affect health, linked to housing.
7 Give at least three examples of socioeconomic factors that affect health, linked to unemployment.
8 List at least 10 of the effects that ill health can have on a child.
9 Give three examples of chronic conditions that can affect children.
10 What are the five groups of pathogens (germs) called?
11 Define the terms 'ingested', 'inhaled' and 'inoculated'.
12 What are the body's natural defences?
13 What is meant by the term 'herd immunity'?
14 What is the difference between active natural immunity and active acquired immunity?
15 Which level of health care looks after the long-term care of chronic conditions?

Glossary

ABC behaviour strategy
A strategy for handling situations that considers the antecedent, the behaviour and the outcome of the behaviour

ABC procedure
A sequential emergency first aid process

Accommodation
Jean Piaget's term for the process by which a child modifies their understanding to acquire a new concept

Accurate records
Factual records kept by the setting following an accident or concern

Active listening
Ensuring that you are focusing on what you are listening to

Advocacy
Representing another individual or speaking on their behalf

Aggressive
Taking a forceful approach

Alternative forms of care
The range of care options available to children

Anonymity
Ensuring that an individual's identity remains unknown

Apgar score
Health score given to a baby at birth, recorded on a chart

Aphasia
Inability to express thoughts in words

Artificial ventilation
Breathing for another person, when that person is unable to do so

Assertive
Being able to put your ideas or viewpoint across without aggression

Assessment
An evaluation of, for example, someone's needs, the quality of a learner's work, or potential risks

Assimilation
Jean Piaget's term for a child trying to understand a new concept by fitting it into their present understanding

Associative play
The stage of play when children play with the same activity but are not yet playing co-operatively

Attitudes and values
Attitudes are ways of thinking or behaving; values are moral standards

Audit
An inspection

Aural stimulation
Stimulation through sound

Baby massage
A pleasurable form of physical contact, which aids relaxation and can help the bonding of parent and child

Baby signing
A scheme to enable hearing babies to make their needs known prior to acquiring speech

Bar chart
A method of presenting data that is particularly useful for showing descriptive categories

Barrier to communication
Any obstruction to understanding between more than one individual

Behaviour management
Strategies for setting children boundaries

Behaviour policies
Written agreements setting out the behaviour management (of an early years setting)

Bias
An inclination to favour one view over another, prejudice, lack of objectivity

Body language
Non-verbal signals, including gestures and facial expressions

Bonding
The close relationship formed between a child and one or more of the main carers

Burn-out
Suffering from exhaustion due to overstimulation

Care of the environment
Considering the safety needs of the early years setting

Care order
A legal order in which a child is placed in the care of the local authority

Caudal
Referring to the lower parts of the body

Causes of ill health
The range of reasons why individuals become ill

Centile chart
A chart used to record the growth in infants and young children

Cephalo
Referring to the head

Checklist
In a questionnaire, a list of optional answers; the respondent is asked to tick those that apply. In observation, a prepared list of behaviours; the observer ticks those that they see

Chest compression
An emergency first aid procedure

Child assessment order
A legal order applied for in court when a child is considered to be at risk or already suffering significant harm

Child protection register
A computerised list, kept by the local authority of children who are considered to be 'at risk'

Chromosome
Part of the human genetic make-up

Classical conditioning
Learning as the result of conditioned responses; the term is often associated with Ivan Pavlov

Closed questions
Questions where the respondent is offered a choice of replies or the answer is limited (e.g. to yes or no)

Codes of practice
The procedures (usually written down) by which a setting or profession operates

Cognitive development
The development of knowledge through thinking and problem-solving

Colic
Acute spasmodic abdominal pain common in young babies

Communication
The means of passing and receiving information

Communication cycle
A reciprocal form of passing and receiving information

Confidentiality
Keeping information to yourself; not passing on information inappropriately, thereby respecting the privacy of others

Conservation
Being able to understand change in quantity, size and number; the term is often associated with Jean Piaget

Containment
Helping a child to express his or her emotions safely

Continuity of care
Routine and familiarity which helps children feel secure

Cooled boiled water
Used to prepare formula feeds and to clean the eyes of newborn babies

Co-operative play
The stage of play when children play with each other, sometimes taking on simple roles or making simple rules for their games

COSHH
Control of Substances Hazardous to Health Regulations 2002

Cross-infection
The passing of infection from one person to another

Culture
The customs, values, beliefs, etc. of a particular social group or society

Cycle of disadvantage
The process whereby the experiences of one generation of a family have an impact on the next, continuing some or all of the problems they face

Development
The changes that take place as an individual grows and ages

Developmental delay
The term often used when a child's development is not following the pattern of averages (or norms)

Developmentally appropriate
What is expected of a child at a given stage of development

Developmental norms
Typical patterns of growth and development

Direct contact
Cross-infection through contact with an infected individual

Disclosure
Telling someone about the abuse suffered, either currently or in the past

Discrimination
The unfair treatment of an individual, group or minority, based on prejudice

Disequilibrium
A term used by Jean Piaget to describe the state where a child does not fully understand new concepts

Distal
A distance away from the central point (of the body)

Diversity
Being different or varied

Droplet infection
A common cause of cross-infection

Dysfluency
Being unable to speak words fluently, stammering; a common (temporary) occurrence in young children

Dysphasia
Difficulty in expressing thoughts in words

Egocentricity
Placing self at the centre of everything; young children do not understand the necessity for their needs to be deferred or for anyone else's needs to be considered

Emergency protection order
An order of law, applied for through the courts to help protect children from harm

Emotional abuse
The continual rejection, terrorising or criticism of an individual

Emotional disturbance
Evidenced by behaviour which causes concern and needs professional intervention (when serious or long term) or sensitive handling by parents and carers (for temporary or common problems such as tantrums)

Empiricists
Those who uphold the theory that knowledge is gained from experience (the nurture side of the nature–nurture debate)

Enactive mode of representation
Thinking based on memory of actions (the term is associated with Jerome Bruner)

Environmental factors
Any influences from outside an individual that could have an impact on the individual in any way

EPOCH
The organisation End Physical Punishment of Children

Equality
The state of being equal, of having an equal opportunity

Equity
Fairness combined with equal opportunity

Ethos
The characteristic attitudes and character of, for example, a group

Evacuation procedures
The planned process of removing children from an unsafe situation to a safe environment

Evaluation
Reflecting on and giving consideration to a past event, action or project

Event sample
In observation, a record of the frequency, duration or other aspects of pre-selected behaviour(s)

Evidence
Supportive material or information

Exploratory play
Play in which a child is able to find out by experimentation and discovery

Eye contact
Looking directly at an individual when conversing or explaining something to them

Feminist model
An approach taken (specifically) from the perspective of women

First aid
The emergency actions taken following an accident or sudden illness

Foetal alcohol syndrome (FAS)
Physical and cognitive abnormalities often found in children born to alcoholic mothers

Food-related customs
Acceptable and unacceptable foods linked to culture

Foundation Stage Curriculum
A government-led curriculum for children from age three years

Free play
Play which is undirected

Genotype
The complete genetic inheritance of an individual

Gillick competence
The principle that the child is able to make their own decisions and give informed consent (now known as the Fraser ruling)

Good-enough parenting
A term used to refer to parenting that is adequate, although it may not be considered to be ideal by many people

Growth
Increasing in size, height, weight, and so on

HASAWA
The Health and Safety at Work etc. Act 1974, 1999

Health
The state of well-being

Health education
Learning about health, either formally or informally

Health promotion
Proactive encouragement on health issues

Health promotion campaigns
Information on specific health issues being actively distributed or advertised through the media or other means

Herd immunity
The immunity of a high enough proportion of society to dramatically reduce the likelihood of becoming infected with the condition; it is maintained by vaccination programmes

High/Scope
A specific programme of learning, in which children take responsibility for their own learning; the programme encourages the process of 'plan, do and review'

HImPs
Health Improvement Programmes, initiated by the government

Historical perspective
Considering what has happened in the past and its relevance to the present

Holistic model
An approach that takes account of the whole person

Hospice
Care setting for individuals who are terminally ill

Hot-housing
Overstimulating (children) to achieve more at an early age

Human resources
The personnel (staff, parents, professionals, and so on) of a setting

IAPS
Abbreviation for impact-absorbing playground surfaces

Iconic mode of representation
Thinking using mental images (the term is associated with Jerome Bruner)

Identifying needs
Being able to recognise a need using professional judgement, knowledge and understanding

Immunisation programme
A process of giving vaccinations (usually to children) to prevent illness and to help eradicate certain medical conditions from society

Impact of ill health
Any outcome that occurs due to the ill health of an individual or their family

Incest
Sexual intercourse between two relatives who are too closely linked to be able legally to marry

Indicators of abuse
Signs and symptoms that may be seen in children, which could suggest that abuse has taken place

Indirect contact
Cross-infection where there is no specific contact with an infected individual

Institutional discrimination
The policies or practices of an organisation which systematically discriminate against a minority group or groups

Interpersonal skills
Communicating with others in a positive (good skills) or negative (bad skills) manner

Intersubjectivity
An innate predisposition to relate to other people

Laissez-faire model
Taking an approach involving unrestricted freedom or indifference

Language acquisition device
In the theory of language development associated with Noam Chomsky, the term for a hypothetical inborn mechanism in the brain that predisposes children to acquire language

Lifestyle factors affecting health
Lifestyle choices, such as smoking, that have an impact on health

Line graph
A method of presenting data, particularly useful for showing trends or changes in quantity

Live vaccines
A vaccine which uses a small amount of the 'live' condition; live vaccines are not given to individuals with suppressed immunity

Local Safeguarding Children Boards (LSCBs)
A group of professionals who meet to discuss individual child abuse or protection cases

Longitudinal study
A study in which a single individual or a group of individuals is studied at intervals over a period of time

Long-term consequences of abuse
The ongoing effects suffered by an individual following abuse

Managing unacceptable behaviour
Methods of lessening undesirable behaviour in children

Marginalise
Treating someone or something as insignificant or unimportant; to place at the edge (of importance)

Maturational
To do with the biological process of development

Mean
The average that is most widely understood. It is calculated by adding together a set of numerical scores and dividing by the total number of scores in the set

Median
The middle number in a ranked set of numerical scores

Medical model
An approach taken (specifically) from a medical perspective

Minority ethnic group
A group of people with a common race or culture who are different from most of the people in a country or society

Mode
The score that is the most common in a set of data

Monotropy
A term associated with John Bowlby, referring to the attachment of an infant to only one carer

Montessori philosophy
A specific programme of learning, with its own range of resources

Movement and flow chart
A method of observation that looks at how a child spends their time

National Curriculum
The curriculum followed by children in all state schools

Nativists
Those who uphold the theory that knowledge is innate (the nature side of the nature–nurture debate)

Natural immunity
A degree of immunity present in the body without the use of vaccination

Nature–nurture debate
The question of whether individuals acquire knowledge through their genetic inheritance or through what they experience from birth onwards

Negative images
Illustrations or descriptions that portray prejudiced attitudes towards certain people, including their supposed limitations

Neglect
A form of abuse where the care of a child is insufficient or inappropriate

Neonatal jaundice
A problem with the function of the liver during the first weeks of life

Neonate
An infant in the first month of life

Non-live vaccines
Artificially made vaccinations, often given to individuals with suppressed immune systems caused by conditions such as leukaemia, HIV or AIDS

Non-participant observation
A method of studying behaviour in which the researcher remains separate from the group being observed

Non-verbal communication
The messages that are given through body language and facial expression

Normative development
The expected rate of development, according to averages

Objectivity
Being without any prejudgement or bias

Observation
A method of studying behaviour by watching and recording what the people being studied do

Open adoption
Adoption where an element of contact remains between the child and their birth mother/family

Open questions
Questions which encourage the respondent to answer freely and give detailed answers

Operant conditioning
Methods of reinforcing voluntary behaviour (e.g. positive reinforcement), often associated with B. F. Skinner

Paedophile
An individual who is sexually interested in children; the term is commonly used to describe anyone who sexually molests children

Parallel play
The stage of play when children play alongside other children

Paramountcy principle
A main principle of the Children Act 1989 and 2004 where the welfare of the child must be the paramount consideration

Paraphrasing
To restate what you have heard; used to clarify understanding

Parents' expectations
What parents expect (of an early years setting) when they leave their child in the setting's care

Participant observation
A method of studying behaviour in which the researcher acts as a member of the group being observed

Pathogen
A micro-organism, such as a bacterium or virus, that causes disease

Perception
The process by which the brain makes sense of information received from the senses; insight or awareness

Persona dolls
Dolls designed to represent children from various cultures and/or with a range of disabilities

Personal presentation
The manner in which someone presents themselves to others, for example the way the person dresses, speaks and acts

Personal safety
Being responsible for own safe working practice

Phenotype
The physical and behavioural characteristics of a person that are visible and are the result of the interaction between genetic inheritance and environment

Physical abuse
Action directed against a child that is physically harmful and inflicts injury

Physical environment
The surroundings (building, room layout, lighting, ventilation, etc.)

Physical resources
The range of equipment available

Pictograph
A method of presenting data in a pictorial form, using symbols; it has similar uses to a bar chart

Pie chart
A method of presenting data using a circular chart, which resembles a pie; the 'pie' can be 'sliced' into portions to represent the quantities or percentages in categories

Plan, do and review
A process of planning and evaluation associated with the High/Scope programme of learning

Play therapy
The use of play to help alleviate some of the effects of abuse or other traumas experienced in childhood

Police protection
Legal protection of a child from harm

Policies
A set of principles used as the basis for decisions or actions

Portage
A daily home-teaching programme specified for the individual child

Positive images
Illustrations or descriptions that portray all the individuals depicted in a positive way

Positive reinforcement
Rewarding good behaviour (rather than responding to undesirable behaviour); a principle of operant conditioning

Potential hazard
Any situation which has the potential to cause harm

Predisposing factors
Any known cause that could indicate a specific outcome

Prejudice
An opinion formed in advance, a prejudgement

Preparing children for hospital
Considering children's physical, emotional and cognitive needs prior to planned hospitalisation

Primary health care
The care of health within the community, includes doctors, nurses, dentists, opticians, and so on

Primary research
Research you have carried out yourself

Primary socialisation
The process whereby a child learns about society from their immediate family and others close to them

Principles of diet and nutrition
The basis of healthy eating

Professional
A person who is qualified, competent and experienced at what they do

Professional practice log
An individual student's folder containing plans, reports and observations, together with general placement information, usually assessed by tutors or placement supervisor

Proximal
Close to the central point (of the body)

Psychological model
An approach taken (specifically) from a psychological perspective

Pyrexia
A high temperature, fever

Qualitative research
Research which obtains the viewpoints and personal feelings of individual participants; data produced are descriptive, not numerical

Quality assurance
The maintenance of set standards, achieved when specified criteria have been met

Quantitative research
Research which produces results that can be expressed numerically, using charts, tables, and so on

Racism
The belief that some races have cultural characteristics that make them superior (or inferior) to others

Range
In statistics, the difference between the lowest and highest result found in numerical data

Raw data
The information gathered during the research process before it has been collated, for example information taken from questionnaires

Recovery order
A legal order enabling the police to take into their possession a child who is the subject of police protection or an emergency protection order, if they are missing, have run away or been abducted from the person responsible for their care

Recovery position
The position individuals are placed in following an accident or sudden illness, after their situation has been stabilised, whilst they await further medical treatment (e.g. following an accident), or rest (e.g. following an epileptic fit)

Referral procedures
The process of reporting concerns about a child's safety

Reflection
The process of giving something thoughtful consideration

Reflective listening
Where the listener echoes the last (or most significant) words spoken by the speaker

Reflex
An involuntary response to a stimulus, for example blinking

Reliability
In research, the consistency of findings or of the instrument, such as a questionnaire, used to collect data

Replication
Being able to repeat something and get the same outcomes. In research, replication is used to test reliability

RIDDOR
Reporting of Injuries, Diseases and Dangerous Occurrences Regulations 1995

Rights
Our entitlements as individuals

Role of health educators
To raise awareness of health issues relevant to the target audience

Routines
A set procedure that should meet the needs of all concerned

Safety marks
National standards regarding safety, printed on the packaging of objects to guide consumers as to their suitability for the intended use or recipient; found, for example, on toys, baby equipment, electrical appliances

Scaffolding
A term usually associated with Jerome Bruner; the adult supports and extends a child's learning

Schema
An internal representation of knowledge, which is adapted through assimilation and accommodation

Screening
Tests carried out to identify if an individual is showing signs of a disease or may be predisposed to develop it. Screening of the foetus/embryo is carried out during pregnancy; screening is also done during childhood. Sometimes, whole populations are screened as a public health measure

Secondary health care
Involves early intervention on health issues, often linked to the outcomes of screening

Secondary research
Use of material from research which has not been directly carried out by you

Secondary socialisation
The process whereby a child learns about society from social contacts outside the immediate family and social group, including teachers, early years professionals, and so on

Self-awareness
Being able to understand how you are perceived by others and the impact that you have on other individuals

Self-concept
An understanding of our own identity that includes how we are seen by others

Self-protection strategies
Ways in which to keep ourselves safe and to be able to reject involvement in situations or unwanted advances

Sequential
Occurring in a particular order

Setting boundaries
Stating acceptable limitations

Sexual abuse
Subjecting someone to sexual activities that are likely to cause psychological or physical harm and to which they have not given, or are unable to give, informed consent

Sharing information
Passing on knowledge to others

Short-term consequences of abuse
Effects that take place immediately, for example physical pain, injuries or infection

Signed language
Communication without the necessity for speech

Skin care
Appropriate care of different types of skin

Snapshots
Brief observations of a child's behaviour

Social and economic factors affecting health
Issues such as poverty that are linked to health problems

Social constructivist theory
The theory that children learn by exploring a range of experiences and objects from everyday life, for example in play

Social learning theory
The theory that children learn by observing and copying others; supported by the results of Albert Bandura's Bobo doll experiments

Social model
An approach taken (specifically) from the perspective of society

Sociogram
A way of studying and depicting the relationships in a group

Sociological model
A model that explains behaviour by looking at how society is structured and works

Solitary play
Playing alone, a normal stage of development in young children

Spontaneous play
Play that is unplanned, undirected and allows freedom

Stages of play
The changes in how children's play develops, usually linked to age

Standard Attainment Tasks (SATs)
Tests carried out at regular intervals during formal schooling

Standard deviation
A statistical measurement of the spread of scores, which assesses the average distance of all the scores from the mean

Steiner philosophy
A specific learning process with its own ethos

Stereotyping
Categorising people according to their group, not seeing their individuality

Sterilising techniques
Methods of ensuring that utensils (bottles, teats, etc.) used for babies are free from bacteria

Stimulate
To arouse curiosity, interest and development

Stimulating play
Activities or objects which stimulate

Structured play
Play which is predetermined or has specific constraints

Subjective
Based on personal opinion or belief, biased

Submissive
Avoiding conflict or confrontation

Supervision order
A legal order in which a child is under the supervision of the local authority, but where the authority does not have parental responsibility

Suppressed immunity
Where the immune system is impaired in some way, leaving an individual susceptible to infection

Symbolic play
The use of objects to represent other objects in play

Symbolic mode of representation
Being able to use symbols such as language or number to represent the world (the term is associated with Jerome Bruner)

Table
The most basic method of presenting numerical or written information

Target child
The child who is the focus of an observation

Teamwork
Working co-operatively with a group of colleagues

Tertiary health care
Ongoing care of chronic conditions, often by specialist community-based health professionals

Theories
Explanations involving abstract ideas and philosophies

Therapeutic play
Play which is provided in order to alleviate, restore or heal

Time sample
In observation, a record of behaviour taken at pre-decided intervals

Tokenism
Making only a small effort, or providing no more than the minimum, in order to comply with criteria or guidelines

Topping and tailing
Washing a baby's facial area and changing its nappy

Tourist approach
Focusing on the diversity of other cultures in the way that a tourist would without having equality fully embedded in the setting's practices

Transmission model
An approach in which the adult controls the learning process, often suppressing the child's own initiative

Treasure basket
A small basket of natural objects; ideal for babies from about six months of age, it enables exploration of a range of natural materials, smells and shapes

Turn-taking
Responses made by young babies to adults when they make 'conversation' with them. This can be an expression, a movement, a smile or a sound

UN Convention on the Rights of the Child
This international constitution was adopted by the United Nations Assembly in 1989 to uphold agreed rights for children whenever possible

Underpinned
Supported and strengthened (by knowledge and understanding)

Validity
In research terms, a method, such as a questionnaire, has validity if it measures what it claims to do

Visual stimulation
Stimulation through sight

Vocational
Learning through practical experience as well as theory

Weaning
The introduction of solid food to young babies

World Health Organization (WHO)
An agency of the United Nations that aims to help all peoples of the world to achieve the best possible level of health

Written record
In observation, a record of what the participant is doing

Zone of proximal development (ZPD)
The term used by Lev Vygotsky for the area between the child's actual development and the potential level that they could achieve with additional support from the adult

Bibliography and Suggested Further Reading

Abbott, L. and Moylett, H. (1997) *Working with the Under-3s: Responding to Children's Needs*. Open University Press, Milton Keynes.

Acheson, D. (1998) *Independent inquiry into inequalities in health: Report of the independent inquiry into inequalities in health*. The Stationery Office, London.

Allen, N. (1996) *Making Sense of the Children Act*. John Wiley & Sons, Chichester.

Ashman, C. and Green, S. (2005) *Managing Environment and Resources*. David Fulton Publishers, London.

Axline, V. (1964) *Dibs: In Search of Self*. Penguin, London.

Bandura, A. (1965) Influence of model's reinforcement contingencies on the acquisition of imitative responses. *Journal of Personality and Social Psychology*, **1**, 589–95.

Barnes, P. (1998) *Personal, Social and Emotional Development of Children*. Blackwell, Oxford.

Baston, H. and Durward, H. (2001) *Examination of the Newborn: A Practical Guide*. Routledge, London.

Beattie, A. (1993) The changing boundaries of health. In: *Health and Well-being: A Reader* (eds. Beattie, A., Gott, M., Jones, L. and Sidell, M.). Macmillan/Open University, Basingstoke.

Beaver, M., Brewster, J., Jones, P., Keene, A., Neaum, S. and Tallack, J. (2001) *Babies and Young Children*, 2nd edn. Nelson Thornes, Cheltenham.

Bee, H. (1992) *The Developing Child*, 6th edn. Allyn and Bacon, Boston, MA.

Bee, H. (2004) *The Developing Child,* 10th edn. Allyn and Bacon, Boston, MA.

Bell, J. (1998) *Doing Your Research Project*, 2nd edn. Open University Press, Buckingham.

Bentzen W. R. (2000) *Seeing Young Children: A Guide to Observing and Recording Behaviour*, 4th edn. Delmar, Albany, NY.

Bichard Report (2004) Criminal Records Bureau, London.

Black, D., Morris, J., Smith., C. and Townsend, P. (1980) Inequalities in Health: Report of a research working group. Department of Health and Social Security, London.

Blaxter, M. (1990) *Health and Lifestyles*. Tavistock/Routledge, London.

Bowlby, J. (1953) *Child Care and the Growth of Love*. Penguin, London.

Brain, C. and Mukherji, P. (2005) *Understanding Child Psychology*. Nelson Thornes, Cheltenham.

Bray, M. (1991) *Poppies on the Rubbish Heap: Sexual Abuse – The Child's Voice*. Canongate Press, Edinburgh.

Breuilly, E. and Palmer, M. (1993) *Religions of the World*. Harper Collins, London.

Brown, B. (1998) *Unlearning Discrimination in the Early Years*. Trentham Books, Stoke-on-Trent.

Brown, B. (2001) *Persona Dolls in Action: Combating Discrimination*. Trentham Books, Stoke-on-Trent.

Bruce, T. (1991) *Time to Play in Early Childhood Education*. Hodder & Stoughton, London.

Bruce, T. (2004) *Early Childhood Education*, 2nd edn. Hodder & Stoughton, London.

Bruce, T. and Meggitt, C. (1996) *Childcare and Education*. Hodder & Stoughton, London.

Brumfitt, K., Barnes, S., Norris, L. and Jones, J. (2001) *Human Resources*, Vocational Business series 4. Nelson Thornes, Cheltenham.

Burnard, P. (1992) *Communicate! A Communication Skills Guide for Health Care Workers*, Edward Arnold.

Burnard, P. (1995) *Learning Human Skills: An Experiential and Reflective Guide for Nurses*, 3rd edn. Butterworth and Heinemann, London.

Carroll, J. (1998) *Introduction to Therapeutic Play*. Blackwell, Oxford.

Cattanach, A. (1992) *Play Therapy with Abused Children*. Jessica Kingsley Publishers, London.

Carver, V. (1980) *Child Abuse: A Study Text*. Open University Press, Milton Keynes.

Clements, P. and Spinks, T. (2000) *The Equal Opportunities Handbook*, 3rd edn. Kogan Page, London.

Cullis, T., Dolan, L. and Groves, D. (1999) *Psychology for You*. Nelson Thornes, Cheltenham.

Dare, A. and O'Donovan, M. (1996) *A Practical Guide to Child Nutrition*. Nelson Thornes, Cheltenham.

Dare, A. and O'Donovan, M. (1998) *A Practical Guide to Working with Babies*, 2nd edn. Nelson Thornes, Cheltenham.

Dare, A. and O'Donovan, M. (2000) *Good Practice in Child Safety*. Nelson Thornes, Cheltenham

Dare, A. and O'Donovan. M. (2002) *Good Practice in Caring for Young Children with Special Needs*, 2nd edn. Nelson Thornes, Cheltenham.

David, T. (1993) *Child Protection and Early Years Teachers*. Open University Press, Milton Keynes.

Department for Education and Employment (DfEE) (1994) *Code of Practice on the Identification and Assessment of Special Educational Needs*. HMSO, London.

DfEE (1995) *Key Stages 1 and 2 of the National Curriculum*. HMSO, London.

Department for Education and Skills (DfES) (2001) *Special Educational Needs Code of Practice*. DfES, London.

DfES (2003) *Birth to Three Matters*. DfES, London.

DfES (2004) *Every Child Matters*. DfES, London.

DfES (2005) *Cross-sectional Study of 9-and 36-Month Old Children and their Families*. HMSO, London.

Department of Health (1991a) *Child Abuse: A Study of Inquiry Reports 1980–1989*. HMSO, London.

Department of Health (1991b) *Working Together under the Children Act 1989*, HMSO, London.

Department of Health (1995) *Child Protection: Messages from Research*. HMSO, London.

Department of Health (1998) *Our Healthier Nation*. HMSO, London.

Department of Health (2000) *Framework for the Assessment of Children in Need and their Families*. HMSO, London.

Department of Health (2004) *The National Service Framework for Children, Young People and Maternity Services*. HMSO, London.

Donaldson, M. and McGarrigle, J. (1974) Some clues to the nature of semantic development. *Journal of Child Language*, **1**, 185–94.

Dowling, M. (2000) *Young Children's Personal, Social and Emotional Development*. Paul Chapman Publishers, London.

Doyle, C. (1990) *Working with Abused Children*. Macmillan, London.

Drake, J (2001) *Planning Children's Play and Learning in the Foundation Stage*. David Fulton Publishers, London.

Dryden, L., Forbes, R., Mukherji, P. and Pound, L. (2005) *Essential Early Years*. Hodder Arnold, London.

Duffy, B. (1998) *Supporting Creativity and Imagination in the Early Years*. Open University Press, Milton Keynes.

Dyson, A. and Meredith, L. (2006) *Feeding the Under 5s*. David Fulton Publishers, London.

Elliott, M. (ed.) (1992) *Protecting Children Training Pack*. HMSO, London.

Elliott, M. (ed.) (1993) *Female Sexual Abuse of Children: The Ultimate Taboo*. Longman, Harlow.

Every Child Matters. http://www.everychildmatters.gov.uk

Fantz, R. L. (1961) The origin of form perception. *Scientific American*, **204**(5), 66–72.

Fawcett, M. (1996) *Learning Through Child Observation*. Jessica Kingsley Publishers, London.

Flekkøy, M. G. and Kaufman, N. H. (1997) *The Participation Rights of the Child*. Jessica Kingsley Publishers, London.

Flekkøy, M. G. and Kaufman, N. H. (1997) *Rights and Responsibilities in Family and Society*. Jessica Kingsley Publishers, London.

Flynn, H. and Starns, B. (2004) *Protecting Children: Working Together to Keep Children Safe*. Heinemann, London.

Ganeri, A. (2005) *The Atlas of World Religions*. Franklin Watts, London.

Garcia, J. (2000) *Sign with Your Baby*. Northlight Communications, USA.

Gibson, E. J. and Walk, R. D. (1960) The visual cliff. In *Psychology in Progress, Readings from Scientific American*. Freeman, San Francisco, 51–8.

Gilbert, P. (2000) *A–Z of Syndromes and Inherited Disorders*, 3rd edn. Nelson Thornes, Cheltenham.

Green, S. (2000) *Research Methods in Health, Social and Early Years Care*. Nelson Thornes, Cheltenham.

Green, S. (2004) *Baby and Toddler Development Made Real*. David Fulton Publishers, London.

Green S. (2004) *Food and Cooking*. David Fulton Publishers, London.

Green, S. (2004/5) (Series ed.), *Ready, Steady, Play!* David Fulton Publishers, London.

Green, S. (2006/7) (Series ed.) *From Birth to 3*. Routledge Publishers, London.

Green, S (2007) BTEC National Children's Care, Learning and Development Book 2. Nelson Thornes, Cheltenham

Green, S. (2007) (Series ed.) *Bringing Educational Philosophies to your Early Years Practice*. David Fulton Publishers, London.

Gregory, J. (2003) *Sickened*. Century, London.

Guidance to the National Standards for Under Eights Care 3rd edn. (2005). OFSTED, London.

Haralambos, M. and Holborn, M. (2000) *Sociology: Themes and Perspectives*. Collins, London.

Hobart, C. and Frankel, J. (1999) *A Practical Guide to Child Observation and Assessment*, 2nd edn. Nelson Thornes, Cheltenham.

Hobart, C. and Frankel, J. (2004) *A Practical Guide to Child Observation and Assessment*, 3rd edn. Nelson Thornes, Cheltenham.

Hobart, C. and Frankel, J. (2005) *Good Practice in Child Protection*. Nelson Thornes, Cheltenham.

Hobart, C. and Frankel, J. (2006) *A Practical Guide to Activities for Young Children*, 3rd edn. Nelson Thornes, Cheltenham.

Hodge, M. (2000) *Curriculum Guidance for the Foundation Stage*. QCA/DfES, London.

Holt, N. (2007) Green, S. (Series ed.) *Bringing The High/Scope Approach to your Early Years Practice*. David Fulton Publishers, London.

Hucker, K. (2001) *Research Methods in Health, Care and Early Years*. Heinemann, London.

Hurst, V. and Joseph, J. (1998) *Supporting Early Learning: The Way Forward*. Open University Press, Milton Keynes.

Hutchin, V. (2003) *Observing & Assessing for the Foundation Stage Profile*. Hodder Murray, London.

Isaacs, B. (2007) Green, S. (Series ed.) *Bringing The Montessori Approach to your Early Years Practice*. David Fulton Publishers, London.

Isaacs, S. (1933) *Social Development in Young Children*. Routledge and Kogan Paul, London.

Jackson, V. (1996) *Racism and Child Protection*. Cassell, London.

Jameson, H. and Watson, M. (1998) *Starting and Running a Nursery*. Nelson Thornes, Cheltenham.

Jarvis, M. (2001) *Angles on Child Psychology*. Nelson Thornes, Cheltenham.

Karp, C. and Butler, T. (1996) *Treatment Strategies for Abused Children*. Sage, London.

Kay, J. (2004) *Good Practice in the Early Years*, 2nd edn. Continuum Press, London.

Keene, A. (1999) *Child Health: Care of the Child in Health and Illness*. Nelson Thornes, Cheltenham.

Kempe, C. H. (1992) in *Protecting Children Training Pack* (ed. Elliott, M.). HMSO, London.

Kindersley, B. and Kindersley, A. (1997) *Celebration, Children Just Like Me*. Dorling Kindersley, London.

Lalonde, M. (1974) *A New Perspective on the Health of Canadians*. Ministry of Supply and Services, Ottowa.

Lay, M. Z. and Dopeyra, J. E. (1977) *Becoming a Teacher of Young Children*, 2nd edn. Heath & Co, Washington DC.

Lindon, J. (1999) *Understanding World Religions in Early Years Practice*. Hodder & Stoughton, London.

Lindon, J. (2001) *Understanding Children's Play*. Nelson Thornes, Cheltenham.

Lindon, J. (2005) *Understanding Child Development*. Hodder Arnold, London.

Malik, H. (2003) *A Practical Guide to Equal Opportunities*, 2nd edn. Nelson Thornes, Cheltenham.

Makins, V. (1997) *Not Just a Nursery: Multi-agency Early Years Centres in Action*, National Children's Bureau, London.

McNeill, P. (1990) *Research Methods*. 2nd edn. Routledge, London.

Meadows, R. (1993) *ABC of Child Abuse*, 2nd edn. BMJ Publishing, London.

Miller, L. (1997) *Closely Observed Infants*. Duckworth, London.

Minett, P., Wayne, D. and Rubenstein, D. (1994) *Human Form and Function*. Collins Educational, London.

Moore, S. (2002) *Social Welfare Alive!* 3rd edn. Nelson Thornes, Cheltenham.

Mosely, J. (1998) *Quality Circle Time in the Primary Classroom: Your Essential Guide to Enhancing Self-esteem, Self-discipline and Positive Relationships*. LDA Publishers, Wiltshire.

Moyles, J. (1989) *Just Playing? The Role and Status of Play in Early Childhood Education*. Open University Press, Milton Keynes.

Moyles, J. (ed.) (1994) *The Excellence of Play*. Open University Press, Milton Keynes.

Mukherji, P. (2001) *Understanding Children's Challenging Behaviour*. Nelson Thornes, Cheltenham.

Mukherji, P. and O'Dea, T. (2000) *Understanding Children's Language and Literacy*. Nelson Thornes, Cheltenham.

Murphy, M. (1995) *Working Together in Child Protection*. Arena, Hants.

Naidoo, J. and Wills, J. (2000) *Health Promotion: Foundations for Practice*, 2nd edn. Baillière Tindall, London.

Neaum, S. and Tallack, J. (2000) *Good Practice in Implementing the Pre-School Curriculum*, 2nd edn. Nelson Thornes, Cheltenham.

Nicol, J. (2007) Green, S. (Series ed.) *Bringing The Steiner Waldorf Approach to your Early Years Practice*. David Fulton Publishers, London.

Nilsson, L. and Hamberger, L. (2003) *A Child is Born*. Doubleday, London.

Nursery World (1999) *All About Celebration: Activity Handbook*. TES, London.

Oaklander, V. (1988) *Windows to Our Children*. The Gestalt Journal Press, USA.

Oates, J. (1999) *The Foundations of Child Development*. Blackwell, Oxford.

Ogier, M. (1998) *Reading Research: How to Make Research More Approachable*. 2nd edn. Baillière-Tindall, London.

Penn, H. and Thurtle, V. (2005) Hoping for Health. In *Understanding Early Childhood: Issues & Controversies* (ed. Penn, H.). Open University Press, Maidenhead.

Polit, D. F. and Hungler, B. P. (1991) *Nursing Research: Principles and Methods,* 4th edn. J.P. Lipincott, Philadelphia.

Porritt, L. (1990) *Interaction Strategies: An Introduction for Health Professionals*, 2nd edn. Churchill Livingstone, London.

Pound, L. (1999) *Supporting Mathematical Development in the Early Years*. Open University Press, Milton Keynes.

Pound, L. (2005) *How Children Learn*. Step Forward Publishing, Leamington Spa.

Pre-School Learning Alliance (1996) *Equal Chances: Eliminating Discrimination and Ensuring Equality in Pre-schools*, Revised edn. PLA, London.

Qualifications and Curriculum Authority (QCA) (2000) *Curriculum Guidance for the Foundation Stage*. DfEE, London.

Qualifications and Curriculum Authority (QCA) (2000) *Early Learning Goals*. DfES, London.

Reder, P., Duncan, S. and Gray, M. (1993) *Beyond Blame: Child Abuse Tragedies Revisited*. Routledge, London.

Riddall-Leech, S. (2005) *How to Observe Children*. Heinemann, Oxford.

Roberts, A. and Harpley, A. (2006) *Helping Children to be Skilful Communicators, Birth to Three* series. Routledge Publishers, London.

Roberts, A. and Harpley, A. (2006) *Helping Children to Stay Healthy, Birth to Three series*. David Fulton Publishers, London.

Roberts, A. and Harpley, A. (2007) *Helping Children to be Strong, Birth to Three series*. David Fulton Publishers, London.

Roberts, A. and Harpley, A. (2007) *Helping Children to be Competent Learners, Birth to Three series*. David Fulton Publishers, London.

Robinson, M. (2003). *From Birth to One, the Year of Opportunity*. Open University Press, Buckingham.

Rodger, R. (2003) *Planning an Appropriate Curriculum for the Under Fives*, 2nd edn. David Fulton Publishers, London.

Roth, I. (1990) *Introduction to Psychology*, Vol.1. The Psychology Press and The Open University, Hove.

Sadek, S. and Sadek, J. (1996) *Good Practice in Nursery Management*. Nelson Thornes, Cheltenham.

Schaffer, R. (1977) *Mothering*. Fontana, London.

Sereny, G. (1999) *Cries Unheard: The Story of Mary Bell*, Macmillan, London.

Sharman, C., Cross, W. and Vennis, D. (2004) *Observing Children: A Practical Guide*, 3rd edn. Continuum, London.

Sheridan, M. (1997) From Birth to Five Years: Children's Developmental Progress, 7th impression (revised and updated by Marion Frost and Dr Ajay Sharma). Routledge, Abingdon.

Siraj-Blatchford, I. and Macleod-Brudenell, L. (1999) *Supporting Science, Design and Technology in the Early Years*. Open University Press, Milton Keynes.

Siraj-Blatchford, I. and Clarke, P. (2000) *Supporting Identity, Diversity and Language in Early Years*. Open University Press, Milton Keynes.

Smidt, S. (2005) *Observing, Assessing & Planning for Children in the Early Years*. RoutledgeFalmer, London.

Tassoni, P. and Hucker, K. (2000) *Planning Play and the Early Years*. Heinemann, Oxford.

Tassoni, P., Beith, K., Eldridge, H. and Gough, A. (2002) *Diploma in Child Care and Education*, Heinemann, London.

Thornton, L. and Brunton, B. (2007) Green, S. (Series ed.) *Bringing The Reggio Approach to your Early Years Practice*. David Fulton Publishers, London.

Walker, C. (1998) *Eating Well for the Under-5s in Child Care*. The Caroline Walker Trust, St Austell.

Walker, M. (2006) *Children's Care, Learning and Development, NVQ Handbook*. Nelson Thornes, Cheltenham.

Walker, M. (2007) *Activities for Older Children*. Nelson Thornes, Cheltenham.

Walsh, M., Stephens, P. and Moore, S. (2000) *Social Policy and Welfare*. Nelson Thornes, Cheltenham.

Waterhouse, L. (ed.) (1993) *Child Abuse and Child Abusers*. Jessica Kingsley Publishers, London.

Whitehead, M. (1999) *Supporting Language and Literacy in the Early Years*. Open University Press, Milton Keynes.

Index

Page numbers in italics indicate figures or tables